Interchange in Pre- and Protohistory

Case Studies in Iberia, Romania, Turkey and Israel

Edited by

Ana Cruz and Juan F. Gibaja

BAR International Series 2891

2018

Published in 2018 by
BAR Publishing, Oxford

BAR International Series 2891

Interchange in Pre- and Protohistory

ISBN 978 1 4073 1636 9

COVER IMAGE *Drawing by Luís Pascual Repiso. Originally published in Rojo Guerra et al. (2005):* Un desafío a la Eternidad: Tumbas monumentales del Valle de Ambrona. Arqueología en Castilla y León, Memorias Arqueología en Castilla y León *14. Junta de Castilla y León, Consejería de Cultura y Turismo.*

Printed in England

BAR
PUBLISHING

BAR titles are available from:

BAR Publishing
122 Banbury Rd, Oxford, OX2 7BP, UK
EMAIL info@barpublishing.com
PHONE +44 (0)1865 310431
FAX +44 (0)1865 316916
www.barpublishing.com

Acknowledgements

The diverse complexity of archeology as a science invites a myriad of approaches, from the purely scientific to the philosophical and even romanticized, all of which have contributed to a considerable body of knowledge, for which we are grateful.

This work covers a wide geographical scope within a scientific field where cultural practices and material cultures converge, to provide us with knowledge of how people lived their daily lives. However, archaeological resources are perpetually at risk, and for this reason the archaeological sites and monuments presented here are preserved in text as part of our international heritage.

First and foremost, we offer our sincerest gratitude to the various authors for their generous contributions which constitute this book, highlighting their achievements in the formulation of knowledge.

We greatly thank our English language reviser Luis Santos and our colleague and friend José Martinho Lourenço for the maps used in the presentation of each chapter.

Thanks are due to the institutions that have supported this endeavors: the Polytechnic Institute of Tomar (Portugal), through the Transdisciplinary Center for Archeology and the Communication and Image Office, and Barcelona's Superior Council of Scientific Investigations (Spain), through the projects: "Aproximación a las primeras comunidades neolíticas del NE peninsular a través de sus prácticas funerarias (HAR2011-23149)", "Aproximación a las primeras comunidades neolíticas del Mediterráneo noroccidental: construyendo respuesta desde los análisis paleoantropológicos y genéticos" Ministerio de Economía y Competitividad (HAR2015-67323-C2-1-P y HAR2015-67323-C2-2-P), "La difusión del neolítico en el Mediterráneo centro-occidental: agricultura, innovaciones tecnológicas y carbono 14" (HAR2016-75201-P) and "Los caminos de la expansión neolítica en el Mediterráneo y Centro Europa" (201710I040).

Our special thanks are extended to the Editorial Team at BAR Publishing, for their patience and overall professionalism.

Ana Cruz & Juan F. Gibaja

Table of Contents

Lists of Illustrations, Figures, Maps and Tables

Chapter 1

Cătălin Lazăr, Monica Mărgărit, Valentin Radu: **Between Dominant Ideologies and Techno-economical Constraints: *Spondylus* Ornaments from the Balkans in the 5th Millennium BC**

Chapter 2

Bahattin Çelik: **A Cult Tradition of the Pre-Pottery Neolithic Period in the Southeastern Region of Turkey**

List of Contributors

Rodrigo Banha da Silva

Is a PhD Assistant Professor at Humanities and Social Sciences Faculty of Nova University (Lisbon), and Investigator at CHAM-Portuguese Centre for Global History. Specialized in Urban Archaeology, he works specially in Lisbon's Region sites from Iron Age and Roman Republican and Imperial periods.

Cristina Barrocas Dias

Professor at the Department of Chemistry. Évora University (Portugal). HERCULES Lab - Cultural Heritage, Studies and Safeguard. Analytical Chemistry of organic materials used in cultural heritage objects.

ORCID: 0000-0002-1707-2209

David Ben-Shlomo

Is an Associate Professor at the Department of the Archaeology and Land of Israel Studies at Ariel University. His main research interests are South Levantine archaeology of the Bronze and Iron Ages, ancient iconography, and the analytical study of pottery and ceramic materials employing petrographic analysis.

Pilar Bravo

Is an Archaeologist of the company Codex Arqueologia i Patrimoni.

António Faustino Carvalho

Before joining the University of Algarve in 2001, the author was part of the team that created the Côa Valley Archaeological Park. To date, he has led multidisciplinary research projects (from lithic technology to genetic and multi-isotope approaches) on the study of Iberian early farming communities.

Deborah Cassuto

Has been a staff member at Tel Burna since 2010. Debi's PhD dissertation, at Bar Ilan University, is on the Iron Age textile production at Tell eṣ-Ṣâfī/Gath. An AIAR fellow, her previous publications deal with the excavations at Tel Burna and textile production in the southern Levant.

Nuria Castañeda

Post-doctoral researcher at the Université Paris I-Panthéon Sorbonne, Research in Paris during 2016. Specialist in lithic technology, her main research interests are the transmission of technical knowledge in Prehistory, socio-economic changes through lithic industries, flint mining in Prehistoric Europe, and lithic analysis by means of experimentation and statistics.

Bahattin Çelik

Is a Professor, Head of the Department of Archaeology at Ardahan University-Turkey. His publications deal with Epi-paleolithic and Neolithic Periods in the Anatolian and Mesopotamian. Since 2015, he has directed the PPN Period in Urfa Region Project.

Ana Cruz

Is the Head of the Center of Transdisciplinary Archaeologies of the Institute Polytechinc of Tomar. Is a Post-Doctoral student at the Geology Department of the School of Sciences of Life and Environment from the Univeristy of Trás-os-Montes and Alto Douro. Is a member of the Arcaheology Unit of the Geology Department (SSLE).

Miriam Cubas

Is a postdoctoral researcher associated to the BioArch-Department of Archaeology, University in York, and the Aranzadi Society of Sciences. Her research is focused on biomolecular and mineralogical analysis of prehistoric pottery, especially related to the introduction and dispersal of the earliest pottery in Atlantic Europe.

Ana Curto

PhD candidate at the University of Kent, studying diet and health of past populations. She earned her Biology BSc at the University of Évora and her Human Biology and Evolution MSc at the University of Coimbra. She participated in various archaeological excavations, including at Morgado shelter.

Antonio de Freitas

Is a Researcher at the University of Minho and a Scientific Adviser to the Gulbenkian Museum and member of the Tel Burna project. He studied at SOAS and Cambridge (UK) and taught at Universities in Portugal, UK, USA and Chile. He is a specialist in ancient languages and an epigraphist.

Arturo de Lombera-Hermida

Archaeologist at the University of Santiago of Compostela. His research is focused on the lithic technology of the Paleolithic societies, specially on quartz-based assemblages, and the first human settlement of Western Europe.

Jorge de Oliveira

Is a Professor of Prehistory at the Departament of History and Évora University (Portugal) and Investigator at CHAIA – Centre for Art History and Artistic Research/ UÉ.

ORCID: 0000-0001-6297-1273.

João Carlos de Senna-Martinez

Is Professor of Archaeology (Retired), Faculty of Arts, Lisbon University and Senior Researcher, Centre for Archaeology (Uniarq). Coordinates research on Primitive Society and Metallurgy from the Centre and Northern Portugal.

Author of extensive scientific production he is responsible for several exhibitions in National and Regional Museums.

Luís Dias

Biochemistry PhD student. Department of Chemistry. Évora University (Portugal). HERCULES Lab - Cultural Heritage, Studies and Safeguard.

ORCID: 0000-0001-8536-3131

Stephanie Duboscq

Her main areas of research lie in the field of the Catalan Neolithic. In her PhD thesis she looked for possible social asymmetries by gender and age of the individuals and from data derived from the funerary remains within the culture "Sepulcres de Fossa" (Middle Neolithic).

Ramón Fábregas Valcarce

PhD, Professor of Prehistory at the University of Santiago de Compostela. His research is centered in the material culture and settlement patterns by the Neolithic and Bronze Age societies of NW Iberia. Related to this research line are books and papers published on lithics, rock art and exchange among the Late Prehistoric groups of that region.

Teresa Fernandes

PhD in Biology, researcher in Biological Anthropology at CIAS (Research Center for Anthropology and Health, in the unit Past Cultures and Populations, University of Coimbra, Portugal), professor of Biological Anthropology at the University of Évora (Portugal). She has been working on skeletal human remains from archaeological context, focused in paleopathology, diet and funerary behaviour.

Juan F. Gibaja

PhD in Prehistory from the Universitat Autònoma de Barcelona in 2002. In 2016 he obtained a permanent contract as CSIC (Spanish Research Council) as researcher. Specialist in use-wear analysis, his research has focused in recent years on the transition and funerary practices from Mesolithic to Neolithic in the Central and Western Mediterranean.

Paloma González

Universitat Autònoma de Barcelona, Prehistory, Faculty Member.

Emiliano Hinojo

Is an Archaeologist of the company Codex Arqueologia i Patrimoni.

Cătălin Lazăr

Is an archaeologist at National History Museum of Romania and associate researcher at the University of Bucharest (Romania). His research interests include survey and excavation of Neolithic and Eneolithic sites in South-Eastern Europe, tell settlements, chronology, funerary behaviors, paleodemography and mortuary practices in South-Eastern Europe.

Joan Manel Coll

Is an Archaeologist of the Arrago, S.L.

Ana Manhita

PhD in Chemistry. Évora University (Portugal). HERCULES Lab - Cultural Heritage, Studies and Safeguard. Working in Analytical Chemistry of organic and inorganic materials used in cultural heritage objects.

ORCID: 0000-0002-6350-9408

Monica Mărgărit

Is Reader at 'Valahia' University of Targoviste (Romania) that studies prehistoric hard animal materials industry in archaeology. Her research interests include the ornaments, tools, and other items discovered in Mesolithic, Neolithic and Eneolithic sites from South-Eastern Europe, in terms of traseology, typology, technology, and functionality.

Araceli Martín

Has worked in the SAP (1981-2016) as a territorial archaeologist and is a specialist from the Neolithic periods to the Bronze Age. She has intervened in Bòbila Madurell as co-director in 1987-1988 and as coordinator with Dr. Rafael Mora between 1991-1992.

Alba Masclans

My PhD research is focused on studying the NE Iberian Peninsula Neolithic axes and adzes using traceological/ use wear analysis and 3D methods. An experimental program is being developed headed to systematize a methodology in order to study hornfels, eclogite and jadeite polished axe and adzes use wear.

Chris McKinny

Has a PhD from Bar Ilan University (Israel). His dissertation focused on the historical geography and archaeology of the town lists of Judah and Benjamin in the book of Joshua. Chris is also a core staff member of the Tel Burna Archaeological Project and currently involved in several other writing and research projects. He is the author of "My People as Your People: A Textual and Archaeological Analysis of the Reign of Jehoshaphat" (Peter Lang, 2016). Chris currently serves as an adjunct faculty member at Texas A&M University Corpus Christi, The Master's University (IBEX), and William Jessup University.

José Mirão

Professor at the Department of Geosciences. Évora University (Portugal). HERCULES Lab - Cultural Heritage, Studies and Safeguard. Physical and material sciences methodologies and tools for the study and valorisation of cultural heritage.

ORCID: 0000-0003-0103-3448

Berta Morell

Is a PhD candidate in Prehistory at the Autonomous University of Barcelona. Her research focuses on the statistical analysis and bayesian modeling of radiocarbon dating. Specifically her thesis deals with the temporality of the raw material exchanges and the funerary pattern changes during the Middle Neolithic in the NE of the Iberian Peninsula.

Millán Mozota

As a technician of the Department of Archeology and Anthropology of CSIC. Her PhD deals with the society and economy of the Neanderthal populations in the Upper Pleistocene and focuses on the study of bone tools, and on the anthropic use of hard animal materials such as antler, bone and tooth. More recently, He has been working in neolithic times bone tools.

Xavier Oms

Universitat de Barcelona, Departament de Prehistòria, Història Antiga i Arqueologia.

Antoni Palomo

He is curator of the Museum of Archeology of Catalonia.

Pierre Petrequin

Is director of research emeritus at the National Center of Scientific Research, France. His research is now focused on the exploitation and circulation of Neolithic alpine jade axeheads in Europe (JADE project, National Research Agency, France) and the ethnoarchaeological approach of stone axes in New Guinea.

Jesús V. Picazo Millán

Is an Associate Professor of Prehistory in the Department of Sciences of the Antiquity of the University of Zaragoza and member of the research group Primeros Pobladores del Valle del Ebro. He has developed his research in the final stages of Prehistory in the NE of the Iberian Peninsula, especially Bronze Age and Early Iron Age.

Javier Plasencia

Is an archaeologist and his PhD is focused in Dynamic changes in the Middle and Final Neolithic in western Mediterranean and Bòbila Madurell site. He is member of CEPAP-UAB since 2005, a research team located at Universitat Autònoma de Barcelona (Barcelona, Spain). His responsibilities in the researcher group includes different areas of knowledge; landscape, settlement pattern and study of lithic artefacts and ceramic materials.

Eduardo Porfírio

Is an archaeologist with a degree in History, variant of Archaeology, University of Coimbra, Portugal (1999), frequency of the Master degree "Archaeology and territory", University of Coimbra, Portugal. Project manager and archaeologist at Palimpsesto, Estudo e Preservação do Património Cultural, Lda. Researcher at Centro de Estudos de Arqueologia, Artes e Ciências do Património, University of Coimbra, Portugal.

Valentin Radu

Is an archaeoichthyologist and malacologist at National History Museum of Romania (Romania). His research interests include the study of the shells, snails, reptiles, and fish from the archaeological sites in South-Eastern Europe, but also all aspects of aquatic food sources, seasonality, and marine/freshwater paleoenvironmental conditions.

Cláudia Relvado

Currently a researcher at the Research Centre for Anthropology and Health, studying diet, weaning and health in past populations. She earned her MSc in Human Biology and Evolution at the University of Coimbra. She has been participated in various archaeological excavations.

Gerard Remolins

Bachelor in History from University of Barcelona. Master in Cartography and Geographic Information Systems from and Master in Archeology of the Quaternary. Specialized in Space Archeology and Geostatistics. CEO at ReGiraRocs SL and currently PhD in spatiotemporal variability of funerary structures in the Pyrenees from the Middle Neolithic to the final bronze.

Cheila Ribeiro

Currently working on her master thesis about the medieval diet and health. With a BSc in Human Biology, by Évora University. She has been participated in various archaeological excavations, including at Morgado shelter.

Leonor Rocha

Is a Professor of Archaeology at the Departament of History and Évora University (Portugal), and Investigator at CEAACP - Center for the Study of Archeology, Arts and Heritage Sciences/UALg. Vice director of the School of Social Sciences of the University of Évora.

ORCID: 0000-0003-0555-0960.

José Mª Rodanés Vicente

Is a Professor of Prehistory at the University of Zaragoza (Department of Sciences of Antiquity) Research of the group Primeros Pobladores del Valle del Ebro. Specialist in Recent Prehistory of the Ebro Valley.

Carlos Rodríguez-Rellán

PhD in Prehistory at the Universidade de Santiago de Compostela. He is specialist in lithic industry and prehistoric rock art, having published more than 70 papers, book chapters and books dealing with these topics.

Jordi Roig

Is an Archaeologist of the Arrago, S.L.

Luis Santos

PhD.; MSc; BSc.Hons Environmental Biology. Landscape Management Course Leader, Researcher of the Geosciences Quaternary Group and Natural Hazards Research Center. Polytechnic Institute of Tomar, Estrada da Serra, Quinta do Contador, 2300-313 Tomar - Office L214.

Miguel Serra

Is an archaeologist with a degree in History, variant of Archaeology, University of Coimbra, Portugal (1999), frequency of the Master degree "Archaeology and territory", University of Coimbra, Portugal. Technician at Heritage and Tourism office, Municipality of Serpa, Portugal. Researcher at Centro de Estudos de Arqueologia, Artes e Ciências do Património, University of Coimbra, Portugal.

Itzhaq Shai

Is a Senior Lecturer and Director of the Institute of Archaeology and the Head of the Department of Land of Israel Studies and Archaeology at Ariel University. His publications deal with Bronze and Iron Ages in the southern Levant. Since 2009, he has directed the Tel Burna Archaeological Project.

Casey Sharp

Completed his first MA in religion at the University of Georgia specializing in the sources of the Hebrew Bible. He received his second MA in archaeology at the University of Haifa, where he focused on the Middle Bronze Age in the southern Levant and the ancient Mediterranean world.

Maria Eulàlia Subirà

PhD in Biology (Anthropology). UAB (Spain).Permanent full-time lecturer. Anthropology Unit, Department of Biology and Ecology. UAB. Research investigation on paleodiet, isotope analysisi, paleopathology, reconstruction on past population.

Rodrigo Villalobos García

Is a PhD – University of Valladolid, 2015. Research is primarily focused on the social archaeology of the Iberian Peninsula Neolithic and Copper Age. Aspects such as mining, crafting and distribution of socio-technic artefacts (such as variscite and other greenstone ornaments), megalithic.

Abstract

This book initiated with the desire to be a knowledge diffusion tool, for experienced researchers, students, and even enthusiast amateur archaeologists. The chronological, geographical and thematic framework in which the different chapters are framed are so broad that, without a doubt this is a "broad spectrum" monograph. The addressed themes, however interrelated allow the reader to have a broad, yet synthetic vision of the various subjects exploited, produced and exchanged throughout much of the recent prehistory at the two extremes. of the Mediterranean. However, this is an entangled geographical framework, throughout the texts references are made to the contacts that communities living in those periods had with other groups settled in other parts of Europe, Asia and Africa.

Although this variability of periods and geographical contexts can lead the reader to miss details of historical moments or sites recorded in each of the chapters, such information can be obtained through the extensive bibliography quoted by each of the authors.

The reader will certainly revel in a diachronic perspective of the importance that certain raw materials and items have had for the prehistorical societies, how they were studied and analysed by the different authors, what type of techniques can be applied, and above all, the proposed interpretative implications.

This last aspect, the interpretative, we believe is one of the most important milestones that emerge from this work. For the authors, the relevant is not to analyze such raw materials or items themselves, but the information they have provided to build and raise multiple interpretations of social, economic and technical behaviours. This is a merit of the researchers who have written the texts, because often the conclusions of many of these studies end up focusing on the more technical and methodological aspects, forgetting the people who in the past elaborated and used them. We understand as archaeologists that the ultimate objective of our research is to make historical interpretations.

In short, the editors, the coordinators and the authors of this book hope that this work can attract the interest of all those dedicated people and lovers of archaeology, increasing the knowledge of our most remote ancestors. As coordinators, we take these words to thank them for all the effort they have made so that today this book is a reality.

Introduction

On April of 2015, in the Polytechnic Institute of Tomar (Portugal), Dr. Ana R. Cruz organized the 2nd Peninsular Roundtable dedicated to the thematic "Tráfego de Objetos: Sintomas das ideologías dominantes na Iberia" in translation "Objects routing: Symptoms of the Dominant ideologies in Iberia". Shortly after the symposium, and due to the discussions and generated opinions, the initiative to edit a volume focused on this topic was put forward, converging examples, not only of the prehistory of the Iberian Peninsula, but also other Mediterranean regions and Central European areas.

Questions on the origin, supply and exchange of raw materials were intensely discussed in recent decades. If one is to revise the European bibliography on the Iberian Peninsula, it will perceive the importance of these themes and the associated large number of publications. However, in such literature, there are not many occasions where the main objective is to present an interpretative discourse of the handled information, that is to say, to make the connection between the object per se to the societies that generated them.

This book is not intended to build a report around a common theme, about a specific period or a particular material. Our idea is to explain how different researchers working on different topics address the issues of intergroup relationships through the analysis of certain raw materials. This more diachronic view allows the reader to obtain a broader view on some of the research lines that are being dealt with in different areas of the Mediterranean. We understand that this monographic book opens its doors to researchers who work over a large chronological period, and not so much about a specific moment for which there are usually Congresses and published monographic works. Some research routes that can help other researchers to know some of the lines of work that are currently being carried out and the methodologies used to know the origin of the raw materials used and analysed in the preparation of Ornaments, ceramic vessels, lithic instruments, etc.

The interest of the scientific community to discover the origin of the archaeological objects as means of approximation to multiple aspects of social, economic and ideological character, is the DNA of research since the inception of Archaeology. However, in recent years, such aspects gained enormous relevance as a result of the multiple radiometric techniques that are applied, offering better resolution, in determining the sources of raw material. Such techniques, in any case, are available to researchers and investigators who have very different theoretical approaches, implying distinct hypothesis and equally diverse interpretations. Looking through the different chapters this book, the reader will be aware of the multitude of hypothesis and interpretations that keep this science alive.

The studies put forward in this volume reflect the theoretical proposals and new radiometric technologies applied to multiple materials, from ceramics, lithic tools, shell ornaments, amber to the use of dyes. All papers presented, without exception, hold as a common link the use of radiometric techniques, especially in relation to the recognition of the origin of such artefacts, giving us a broad geographical coverage of such past societies. Information that refers to the existence, during the Neolithic period and in some cases earlier, of consolidated contact networks between communities geographically remote from each other. Sporadic contacts and intergroup relations allowed them to supply themselves with certain items used in artisan activities or due to their importance used in funerary practices. Be that as it may, in all certainty, these relationships between populations did not simply remain in the exchange of objects or raw materials, but they served to maintain other types of linkages at a much higher level to ensure the proliferation of the groups and their socio-economic organization.

It is precisely the action of obtaining, treating and producing goods made with exogenous materials that led many authors, as can be seen in the various articles of this book, to talk about issues as relevant as the origins of the Neolithic. The role that these assets had in the socio-economic structure of human groups studied, their linkage with the symbolic, the information they provide in relation to the existence or not of social dissymmetry – as materials used by certain persons or documented in their burials-, or the data they offer us about the complex networks and interactions that existed in the prehistory between communities settled in different areas of the Mediterranean. In short, the works presented in this volume refer to us and talk about ourselves, our history and our present.

Although the initial idea was to coordinate a book in which there were articles referring to contexts from different parts of the Mediterranean, several factors have prevented it: the time requested of the authors to send their texts (avoiding that the book ended up taking Several years); the number of researchers whose studies focus on the theme of the book; the researchers who participated in the proceedings of the Congress where this work initiated; and those researchers personally invited by the editors, from recognised merit or innovation. In any case, the achieved results present chapters referring to periods, deposits and materials found in archaeological contexts located at both ends of the Mediterranean.

Making a brief comment on each one of the presented papers:

1. Catalin Lazar, Monica Maragarit and Valentin Radu present a detailed study around the *Spondylus* ornaments in the Balkan area, South-eastern Romania, towards the 5th Millennium BC. The way they were obtained and treated was not only related to economic activities, being an element of exchange widely used in that period, and whose origin should be sought in the Mediterranean or the Atlantic, but has a social and symbolic value to the usually documented use in funerary contexts. So much so, that the authors claims: "The Spondylus ornaments used by past communities in domestic activities or in funeral contexts as part of construction, affirmation and maintenance of ideologies, identity process". Interpretations referring to the scope of the ritual, social identity, status, after death, among others, are continuously present in this work.

2. Bahattin Çelik presents us with an interesting work on the first Neolithic settlements of the South-eastern Turkey in which cult structures built with pillars are documented. This type of settlement forms part of the Neolithic genesis and the social, economic and ideological changes that occurred in the east of the Mediterranean during the Pre-pottery Neolithic period A and part of the period B (PPNA and PPNB). Its importance is essential to address the study of those societies in which this constructive tradition is found not only in Turkey but also in Syria or Iraq.

3. The work of Miriam Cubas brings us back to the down of the Neolithic period in the Iberian Peninsula through her studies on the provenance, technology and morphology of ceramic production. After carrying out a thorough and detailed presentation of the published state of the art, the author lays out the possibilities offered by the study of determination of different materials used in the ceramics as a means of approximation to the source areas controlled by those first communities of farmers and pastoralists. It also addresses the contacts that they could maintain between different Neolithic societies and their relationship with the origin of certain technical and decorative traditions.

4. The work of Antonio F. Carvalho introduces a new and revolutionary variable that combines with the various radiometric studies carried out in different documented materials from ancient middle Neolithic contexts of Portuguese Extremadura: The Isotopic analyses on human bone remains. The author combines this information in a brilliant way, not only to evaluate the contacts between groups, but also the degree of mobility of the studied populations. Furthermore, the author seeks to deepen the knowledge of the social organization of Neolithic communities allegedly considered egalitarian.

5. Ramón Fábregas, Arturo de Lombera, Carlos Rodríguez-Rellán and Pierre Petrequin show us the importance of alpine origin axe production, not only in much of central and Western Europe, but particularly in the Iberian Peninsula. Its distribution from Catalonia to Galicia has led them to consider the importance that in the Neolithic period, as well as in more recent periods, exchange networks represented. Contacts between groups hundreds of kilometres apart is demonstrated using such axes. Their presence, often in funerary contexts, confers to these instruments an importance that exceeds the purely functional aspects.

6. The work of Juan F. Gibaja and collaborators addresses the study of the origin and production of a set of instruments and ornaments that are usually documented in the Neolithic sepulchres from the northeast Iberian Peninsula, which is known as the "culture of Fosa graves". For this it takes as reference the most important deposit, the site holding the largest number of graves and known by the richness of its archaeological material: the Bòbila Madurell-Can Gambús. The differences in the contents of graves and funerary structures have been the elements to propose interpretations referring to social dissymmetry within these societies.

7. Also on this thematic, Lusa analyses the work of Leonor Rocha, Jorge de Oliveira, Cristina Barrocas Dias, José Mirão, Luís Dias and Ana Manhita, centred their study on the determination and Origin of cinnabar and Amber. These materials, documented in many megalithic monuments of the Portuguese Alentejo, have their source areas located hundreds of kilometres from the analysed sites. However, this work does not only stop at that interpretative level, which explains the consolidated contacts and commercial networks that existed at that time, but goes beyond. The fact that such materials are associated with certain burials and individuals allows them to propose explanations of a social nature. In other words, they had a symbolic value that also reflected the social status of the individual who possessed them.

8. The work of Ana Cruz focuses on the analysis of the different funerary strategies documented in the shelter of Morgado Superior, along different moments of prehistory, from the Neolithic to the Bronze Age. The archaeological material from the Bronze Age refers to relations and exchanges between communities settled in different parts of the Portuguese geography, and even with the Spanish region of Almería. The contemporaneousness between the sepulchral dolmen contexts and those made in caves is an interesting problem that the author approaches. Finally, both the type of deposit and the documented materials are compared with other Portuguese archaeological contexts, which facilitates its synchronous reading.

9. Rodrigo Villalobos' contribution is extremely suggestive. The quantitative evaluation carried out by a series of variables in relation to certain artefacts and ornaments elaborated from the Neolithic to the copper age in the north Spanish plateau context, allows him to make certain interpretative inferences of Social, economic and of symbolic character. For this, it quantifies in each of the periods the amount of energy invested in the production of such objects/ instruments, the number of colours employed and the proportion of people involved in such production.

10. Nuria Castañeda studies the importance of lithic tools in archaeological contexts of the Chalcolithic-bronze age in the Iberian Peninsula. Comparatively, in such contexts the metal objects and instruments, are those that have acquired significant relevance in making interpretative constructions. In this sense, it is surprising the little attention that the lithic studies have received in deposits of such periods with respect to previous moments. However, as the author demonstrates, the information they provide with regards to the economic, social and symbolic activities in which their production and use are framed are fundamental to understanding the societies in analysis.

11. Rodrigo Banha da Silva presents a rigorous and detailed view of Late Bronze Age contexts in the territories surrounding the Tagus estuary (Portugal). By assessing the existing information, not only of the treated period, but also of previous moments. The author makes a significant effort to raise interpretations of socio-economic character. This work refers to issues as relevant as the presence of central settlements that manage certain resources, the production and control of exchanges, etc. As Rodrigo Villalobos, does for the north of the Spanish plateau, he also quantifies in each of the treated periods: the amount of energy invested in the production of such objects/instruments, the number of colours employed and the number of individuals involved in such production.

12. Eduardo Porfírio and Miguel Sierra. Once again with an interesting article that deals with the analysis of the raw materials of exogenous origin documented in Portuguese deposits. Its origin coming from different points of the peninsula, as well as influences from other areas of the Mediterranean, the Atlantic or North Africa. This paper reflects the broad and consolidated networks of interchange in the recent prehistory, from the Chalcolithic until the end of the Bronze Age. To discuss this diversity of contacts and relationships, they present as an example the study they have developed around a hypogeum, that of Torre Velha 3, located in the Alentejo region.

13. José M. Rodanés and Jesús V. Picazo through the analysis of certain assets and their chronological correlation evaluate the genesis of Late Bronze age and Early Iron Age societies through the contacts that could exist between different communities. External influences from different points and the roles played by indigenous communities in the development of this historical process is addressed in a brilliant way. Without a doubt, this work opens new ways of thinking and discussing these periods.

14. Itzhaq Shai, Casey Sharp, Antonio de Freitas, Deborah Cassuto and Chris McKinny present us a tremendously interesting contribution. It addresses the study of contacts and Intergroup relations during the Bronze Age of communities located in the southern Levant with others located in different parts of the Mediterranean such as: Egypt, Cyprus, northern Syria and the Aegean. In this respect, different materials analysed, with special attention to ceramics, are the guiding thread that leads the authors to propose the existence of a complex network of contacts during that historical moment.

15. The interesting article by David Ben-Shlomo on the Philistine communities of the southern coastal plains of Israel during the beginning of the Iron Age reiterates the information that certain elements of the archaeological record, especially the Ceramics contribute to the knowledge of the origin of some populations and the influences and contacts they have had with other groups settled in various areas of the eastern Mediterranean. It is certainly another valuable contribution to this book in which ceramics play an important role as means of historical interpretation.

In short, the book can be read from two different perspectives. On the one hand, the information that each author offer from the studies developed in relation to the studied period, the analysed deposits and the treated materials. This information has an individual character and can only be related to chapters focused on periods and similar geographical areas. On the other hand, a general reading can be made in relation to the different techniques that are being used for the study of the materials and the interpretative proposals based on the obtained results. This last vision can offer the reader an image of the methodologies used and the possibilities that they offer.

When all is said and done, we want to finalise by thanking all the authors who have contributed towards this book, to those who participated in that second Peninsular Roundtable held in Tomar, to the institutions involved (Institute Polytechnic of Tomar, Intitución Milá and Fontanals – CSIC-, ANA. And to the editorial itself British Archaeological reports (BAR) and its editors, for all the efforts made, and of course, to Thomas Perrin, Laure Salanova, Rafael Garrido and Leonardo Garcia Sanjuán for the book review. Their analysis, valuation and opinions which have most certainly contributed to improve this new step in the knowledge of Peninsular Archaeology.

Ana Cruz & Juan F. Gibaja

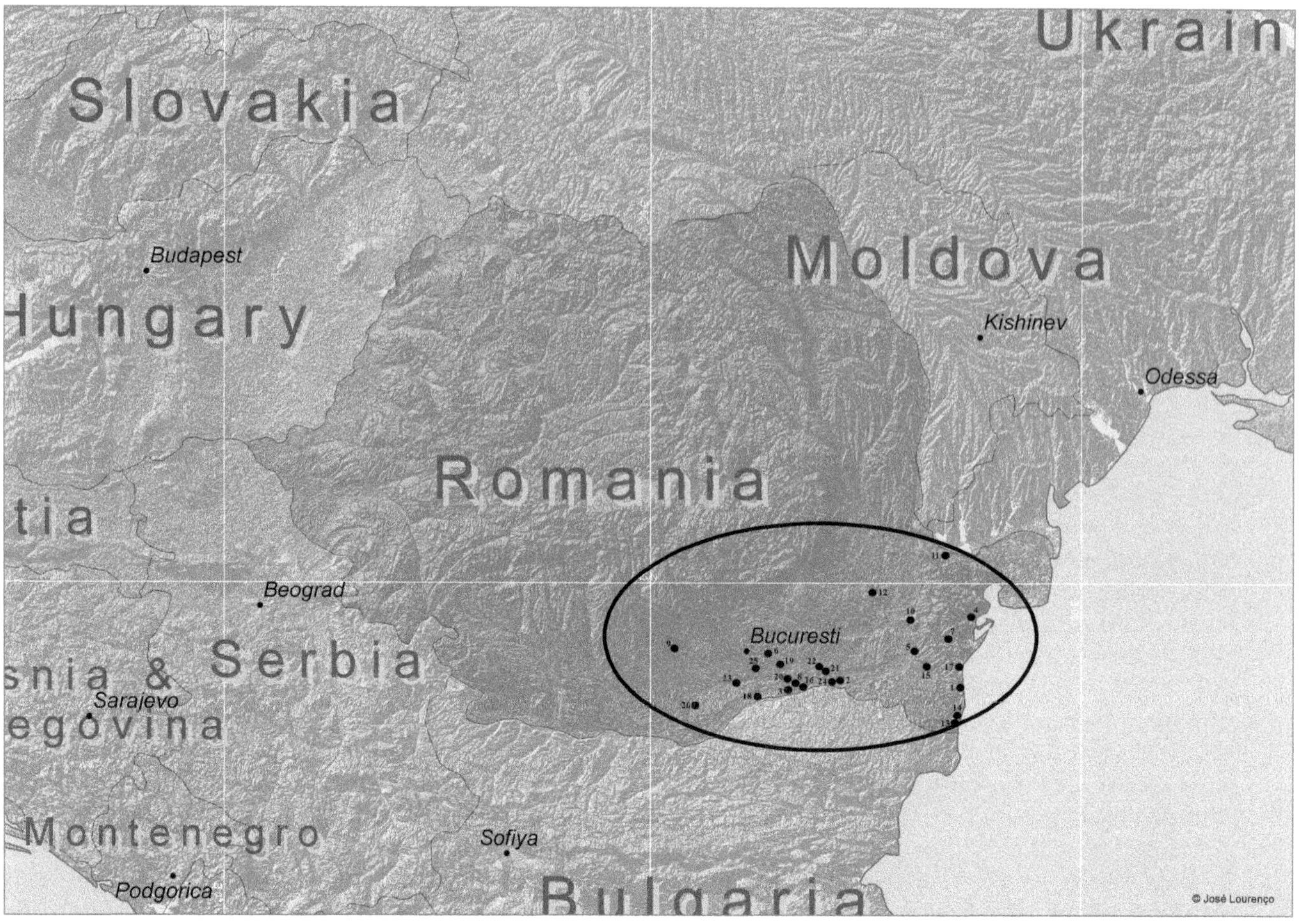

Romania - Map of the target area and the archaeological sites.
Source: José Martinho Lourenço.

Chapter 1

Between Dominant Ideologies and Techno-economical Constraints: *Spondylus* Ornaments from the Balkans in the 5th Millennium BC

Cătălin Lazăr[1], Monica Mărgărit[2], Valentin Radu[1]

[1] National History Museum of Romania, Calea Victoriei, no. 12, sector 3, 030026, Bucharest, Romania, lazarc@arheologie.ro, raduvalentin@hotmail.com

[2] Valahia University of Târgovişte, Bd. Carol I, Nr. 2, 130024, Târgovişte, Dâmboviţa County, Romania, monicamargarit@yahoo.com

Abstract: The ornaments made by *Spondylus* shells play a significant role in evolution and development of human communities from the 5th millennium BC in the Balkans. This paper focuses on the *Spondylus* ornaments discovered in Southeastern Romania dated to the Eneolithic (c. 5000-3900 cal. BC). These items enabled identification of the same technological elements (manufacturing process), economic activities (exchange networks), but also the social expression and symbolism of the *Spondylus* ornaments used by past communities in domestic activities or in funeral contexts as part of construction, affirmation and maintenance of ideologies, identity and personhood. Our approach will include a malacological study, a techno-typological examination, and use-wear analysis. Another issue targeted is the evaluation of the relationship and ratio of *Spondylus* with other species of shells (e.g. *Glycymeris*, *Dentalium, Cardium* and *Unio*) used by local communities, in order to understand Eneolithic people's preferences for these exotic raw materials and to determine the differential use of these artefacts in various activities or rituals.

Keywords: Eneolithic, Balkans, Romania, *Spondylus*, settlements, cemeteries.

Introduction

Since early times, ornaments play a primordial role in the inter-human symbolic communication of social, gender, economic or cultural information, thus being a multivalent element in human past societies. It is true that, in traditional societies, the possession and display of a certain type of ornament is submitted to strict rules, in which the aesthetic role is secondary, because the ornament becomes in this case a means of transmitting information regarding the ethnical, social, age class or gender affiliation (e.g. Preston-Whyte 1994; Sciama and Eicher 1998). Moreover, long-distance trade of ornaments allowed tracing of ethno-linguistic diversity during the Early Upper Paleolithic (Vanhaeren and d'Errico 2006); the geography of Mesolithic social, ethnic and linguistic groups (Newell *et al.* 1990), or the changes in cultural geography during the Mesolithic-Neolithic transition (Rigaud 2011; Rigaud *et al.* 2015). It is also the case of ornaments made of *Spondylus* shells, which probably represented for the communities far away from the Mediterranean "an ensemble of beliefs and myths aimed mainly at providing an account of the supernatural origins of the shells" (Seferiades 2010, 186).

In the world "of the living", decoration has innumerable functions however, in "the other world" was its function the same? As an answer to this question, we invoke the simplest hypothesis, that of an ornament accompanying the deceased. Thus, it could be an element that belonged to the deceased and was worn by him/her throughout his/her life. In the second case, the ornament may have been deposited following a ritual, signifying the status (the social identity of the individual during his life) or protecting the individual in his new status, after death. The strong spiritual charge accompanying these items is demonstrated, for instance, by the presence in the Varna I Eneolithic cemetery of a large number of bracelet fragments, which cannot be assembled to obtain complete pieces. This may mean that a part of the object was kept to circulate in the world of the living (or was deposited elsewhere), while the other part was deposited in the world of the dead (Chapman *et al.* 2008).

The importance and significance of *Spondylus* artefacts in European prehistory is proven by their circulation on wide area, from the region of their provenience (Mediterranean basin) to the Caucasus mountains, North to the Baltic region and Atlantic Ocean (Seferiades 2010).

Throughout Europe, the use of the *Spondylus* coincides with the arrival of the first modern humans. In the Lezetxiki cave, from Spain, we have the oldest testimony of this kind in the Aurignacian level (Arrizabalaga *et al.* 2011). Starting with the Neolithic, the colonizing farmers brought a new way of life based on specific elements (e.g. domesticated sheep and cattle, wheat and barley, female-centered domestic rituals, etc.), but also now *Spondylus* artefacts into the colder, damper climate of temperate Europe for the first time (Anthony 2010, 33). Thus, its distribution became pan-European, and the shell trade network that extended from Greece to northern France and Germany between 5500 and 5000 BC (Anthony 2010; Seferiades 2010), some specimens of this bivalve have been found at sites up to the English Channel (Taborin 1974; Seferiades 1995; 2010; Kalicz and Szénászky 2001). In the Southeastern Europe, the number of the sites containing in their inventory objects made of *Spondylus* is estimated at about 200, ranging from the Early Neolithic to around 4300 BC (Dimitrijević and Tripković 2006). It is also interesting to note that, according to the distribution map of the *Spondylus* pieces published by Todorova (2000), they are grouped in the Black Sea Region and the Carpathian Basin and not in the areas in proximity to their natural habitat.

This paper focuses on the Eneolithic *Spondylus* ornaments discovered in the Southeastern Romania (c. 5000-3900 cal. BC). The target area selected and the proposed key period are not accidental, because it reflected in an optimal manner archaeological realities from the 'golden 5th millennium'. The Southeastern Romania is a geographic area ranging between Olt River to the west, and the Black Sea to the east. In south the target area is bordered by the Danube and in the north by the hilly region of the Carpathian Mountains (Figure 1).

This region has been very populated in prehistory, with the documentation of more than 200 settlements and cemeteries in the 5th millennium BC alone.

The ornaments made by *Spondylus* shells play a significant role in the evolution and development of human communities from the Balkans. These items enabled identification of the same technological elements (manufacturing process), economic activities (exchange networks), but also the social expression and symbolism of the *Spondylus* ornaments used by past communities in domestic activities or in funeral contexts as part of construction, affirmation and maintenance of ideologies, identity and personhood process. Our approach will include a malacological study, a techno-typological examination, and use-wear analysis. Another issue targeted is the evaluation of the relationship and ratio of *Spondylus* with other species of shells (e.g. *Glycymeris*, *Dentalium*, *Cardium* and *Unio*) used by local communities, in order to understand Eneolithic people's preferences for these exotic raw materials and to determine the differential use of these artefacts in various activities or rituals.

2. The chrono-cultural background

The 5th millennium BC was a flourishing development period for the Eneolithic civilization of Southeastern Europe, and it is known as the 'golden 5th millennium' because of the substantial progress made by human communities (Bailey 2000; Anthony 2010).

Starting from 5000 BC in Northeast Bulgaria and Southeastern Romania (Figure 1) are visible some major socio-economic changes in human communities, reflected both in ideology and religion. Thus, it consists in the creation of tell settlements, that arise as a form of the space utilization, but also new architectural solutions (e.g. bigger and multi-roomed houses sometimes with two stories or stone foundations), and a symmetrical organisation of the buildings in the settlement area. Concomitantly, there is an evident development of the settlement defense systems (ditches, banks and palisades), the emergence of extramural cemeteries, and the adoption of new raw materials (e.g. copper, gold, graphite), that led to technological evolution (e.g. pottery, lithic industry, etc.) and metallurgical innovation (Todorova 1986; Bailey 2000; Petrescu-Dâmbovița 2001a; 2001b; Anthony 2010; Popovici 2010; Hansen 2013). This evolution of human communities, which consisted in adopting of a new lifestyle, economic development and a new way of environmental exploitation and control, the development of complex and stratified societies, is well reflected in the funerary practices, particularly in cemeteries where the emergence of elites and socio-economic differences are visible, as demonstrated by the wealthy graves from Varna I cemetery or other contemporary funerary areas (Bailey 2000; Slavchev 2010; Borić 2015).

This time span (c. 5000-3900 BC) is known as the Eneolithic (Copper Age or Chalcolithic), and it is characterised by some human communities (so-called archaeological cultures) with specific material cultural elements (especially pottery) that have a limited spatial distribution (Lazăr 2012a).

In the study area, the analysed time-span corresponds to the Early and Middle Eneolithic, covering three cultures known as Hamangia, Boian, and Gumelnița (Petrescu-Dâmbovița 2001a; 2001b), which corresponded to some cultures from Northeast Bulgaria, in fact the same populations, but with different terminology (except for the Hamangia culture) (Todorova 1986). The Hamangia and Boian began their evolution in the 6th millennium BC (first two phases of both cultures), and ends in the mid-5th millennium BC (c. 5200-4500 BC), while the Gumelnița covered the second half of the 5th millennium BC and beginning of the 4th millennium BC (c. 4500-3900 BC) (Petrescu-Dâmbovița 2001a; 2001b). Nevertheless, available radiocarbon data for different sites proves that the strict boundaries defined for those cultures (based on ceramic typology and their stratigraphic distribution) are not so clear (Table 1).

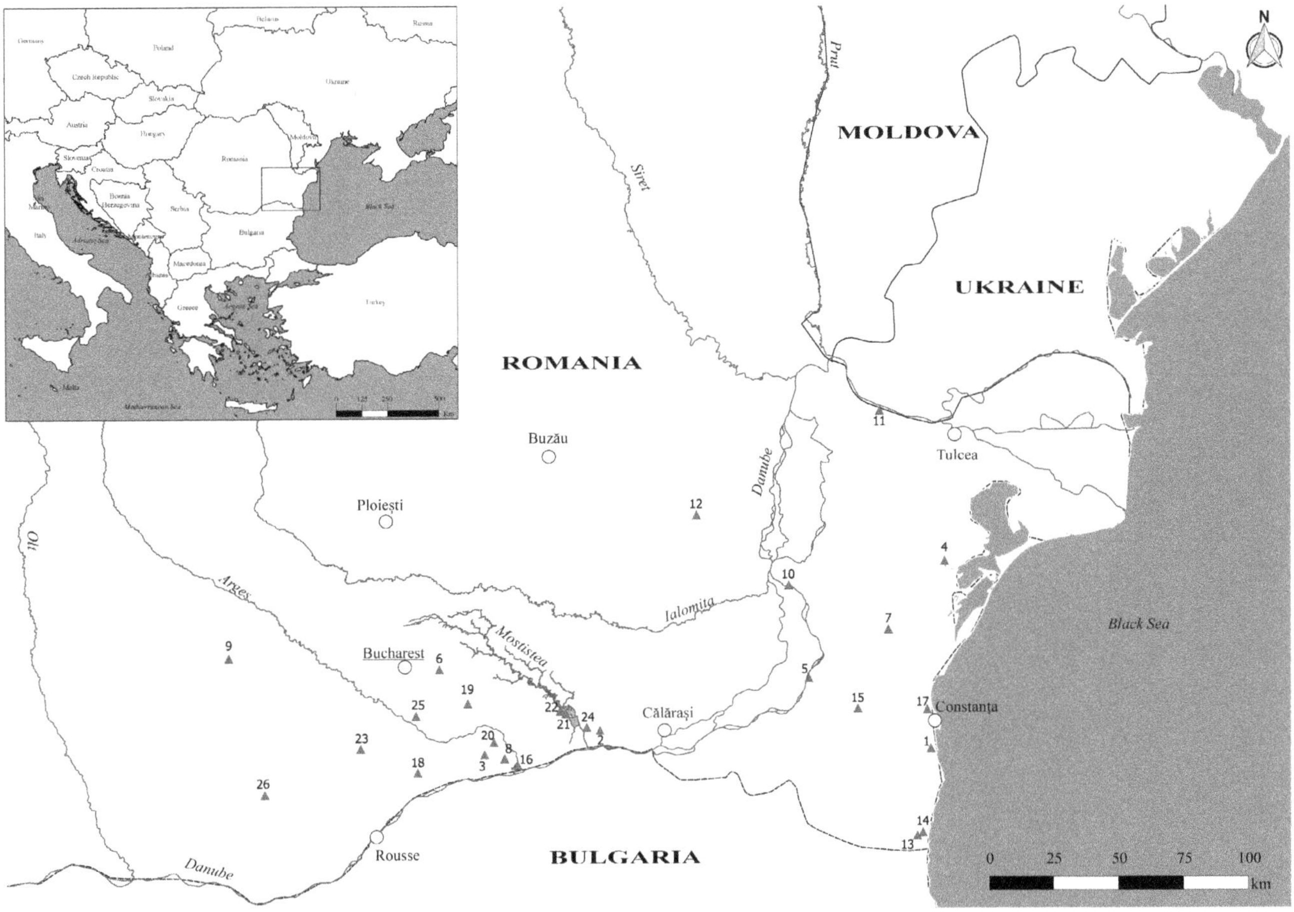

Figure 1. Map of the target area and the archaeological sites mentioned in the text: 1 - Andolina, 2 - Agigea, 3 - Căscioarele (Ostrovel and D'aia Parte), 4 - Ceamurlia de Jos, 5 - Cernavoda, 6 - Cernica, 7 - Cheia, 8 - Chirnogi (I and II), 9 - Glavacioc, 10 - Hârşova, 11 - Isaccea-Suhat, 12 - Însurăţei, 13 - Limanu, 14 - Mangalia, 15 - Medgidia, 16 - Olteniţa, 17 - Palazu Mare, 18 - Pietrele, 19 - Popeşti-Vasilaţi, 20 - Radovanu, 21 - Sultana-Malu Roşu, 22 - Sultana-Valea Orbului, 23 - Tangîru, 24 - Vărăşti-Grădiştea Ulmilor, 25 - Vidra, 26 - Vităneşti. | Source: By the Authors.

According to Romanian archaeologists, the Hamangia and Boian communities influenced and contributed to the emergence of the Gumelniţa culture (Petrescu-Dâmboviţa 2001a; 2001b). However, this assertion is only a conventional approach; recent aDNA analysis has demonstrated that the Boian and Gumelniţa populations have similar genetic features, due to a common origin in Southwestern Anatolia from where they arrived in the Balkans after a slow migration process (Hervella *et al.* 2015). Moreover, other archaeological data seems to indicate the same thing (e.g. pottery evolution or some tell settlements that started during the late phases of the Boian culture and continuously develops until the end of the Gumelniţa culture) (Bailey 2000; Popovici 2010).

3. The finds context

The *Spondylus* ornaments that are the subject of the current paper were discovered in domestic and funerary contexts from 22 Eneolithic sites Southeastern Romania (Figure 1). Hamangia and Boian communities specifically comprise flat settlements (Table 2), but there some tell settlements that started during the Boian culture and continued during Gumelniţa (e.g. Căscioarele-Ostrovel, Căscioarele-D'aia Parte, Hârşova, and Radovanu). In case of the Gumelniţa communities, tell settlements are the characteristic habitation type (Table 2).

Some of them represent an ideal archaeological situation, because they are derived from settlements associated with extramural cemeteries (e.g. Pietrele, Radovanu, Sultana-Malu Roşu, etc.). There are some exceptional situations, as at Căscioarele where two tell settlements (Căscioarele-D'aia parte and Căscioarele-Ostrovel) used a single cemetery, or cases of one tell settlement using two cemeteries (e.g. Chirnogi) (Lazăr 2011). Other times, as in case of Sultana-Malu Roşu, the people from a flat settlement (Boian) and a tell settlement (Gumelniţa) used the same cemetery (Lazăr *et al.* 2012; Lazăr 2014). For the Hamangia culture, there are some funerary areas (e.g. Cernavoda) that are used by several flat settlements (Lazăr 2012b), and in other cases only the cemeteries (e.g. Agigea, Limanu, and Mangalia) are found without paired settlements (Slobozianu 1959; Volschi and Irimia 1968; Voinea *et al.* 2009). The last situation is attested also in Boian communities (e.g. Popeşti-Vasilaţi and Sultana-Valea Orbului) (Şerbănescu 1999; 2002).

Therefore, there was much variation, allowing a wide contextual analysis. Unfortunately, the data regarding the

Spondylus ornaments is incomplete, and in some situation there is information available only for the cemeteries (e.g. Cernavoda, Cernica, Chirnogi, Vărăşti, etc.) without those from their related settlements. In other cases, the cemeteries did not contain *Spondylus* ornaments (e.g. the second cemetery from Sultana-Malu Roşu).

There are over 100 radiocarbon datings available for 12 sites of those analysed in this paper (n=22) that secure the sites within the regional chronology. According to the AMS radiocarbon data obtained so far, the analysed sites ranges between 5466 - 3961 cal. BC with a 95.4% probability (Table 1).

The items discovered in the settlements were identified in association with buildings, foundation trenches, pits, or waste dumping areas (Galbenu 1963; Comşa 1973; Micu 2004; Toderaş *et al.* 2009; Voinea *et al.* 2009; 2014; Mărgărit and Popovici 2012; Mărgărit *et al.* 2014), while in the cemeteries the *Spondylus* artefacts appeared in graves (in association with the deceased bodies), and rarely in some ritual pits (Comşa 1973; Şerbănescu 1999; 2002; Voinea *et al.* 2009; Lazăr 2014; Lazăr and Voicu 2015; Mărgărit and Vintilă 2015). The pieces from graves represent personal ornaments (jewellery) and clothing accessories.

4. *Spondylus* shell origins and acquisition

Around the world, there are documented over 60 species of *Spondylus* (Huber 2010), but only the genus *Spondylus gaederopus* was used as main source of raw material for various ornaments in different parts of Europe during prehistory (Seferiades 2010; 2013).

The *Spondylus gaederopus* (Linnaeus 1758) is a mollusc (phylum *Mollusca*) of the class Bivalvia (bivalves), and it consists of two unequal valves that are connected with a ball-and-socket type hinge (Seferiades 2010). The upper valve (left) is less concave, with a thickness of up to approximately 2 cm, and it shows the outer scaly or spiny pronounced blades.

This species can grow to a height of 15 cm, and lives in warm seas, at depths from 2 to 30 m, relatively isolated and strongly attached to rock (Borello and Michelli 2005; Seferiades 2010).

The lower valve (right) is thicker (up to 5.5 cm) with concave but not such highly colored blades (Titschack *et al.* 2009; Seferiades 2010). On the outside, the shell is highly colored, varying from violet to crimson or red-violet, and their flesh is edible, with a taste similar to that of oysters (Fischer *et al.* 1987; Seferiades 1995; 2010).

The issue of the origin of the species, for the specimens identified in European prehistory, has long been disputed. Most authors (Halstead 1993; Seferiades 1996; 2000; 2010; 2013; Müller 1997; Anthony 2010) agree that the *Spondylus* shells grew in the Aegean and the Adriatic Seas, and in other parts of the Mediterranean Sea, but not in the Black Sea, due to the water temperature and the salinity (Seferiades 2010). Only some authors from South-eastern Europe (Berciu 1940; Comşa 1973; Todorova 2000; 2002) argued for a local, viz. Black Sea, origin of the species. However, the oxygen and strontium isotopes analysis made on some *Spondylus* shells from Central and Southeaster European Neolithic have shown they were of Mediterranean origin, and not from old fossil deposits on land or from the Black Sea (Shackleton and Elderfield 1990; Seferiades 2010). Moreover, other recent studies (Miller 2003; Bajnoczi *et al.* 2012; Gardelková-Vrtelová and Golej 2013) have introduced new argument to support the use of fresh valves of *Spondylus* by prehistoric humans, and shows that those shells are gathered from the beach are more fragile during processing, and tend to break, unlike those gathered while alive. Other authors (Seferiades 2010) have argued that, if exposed for a long time to the sunlight on the beach, the shells lose their colour, and probably the specimens used by prehistoric communities for ornaments must be obtained by diving. Consequently, the *Spondylus* specimens used by Eneolithic communities from South-eastern Romania were acquired by importing them from the Mediterranean area as raw material (valves) or as finished pieces (artefacts).

5. The use and production of *Spondylus* ornaments

The *Spondylus* shell shape, thickness, and dimension provide enough raw materials for different kinds of ornaments (Seferiades 2010; Gardelková-Vrtelová and Golej 2013). On the other hand, the different morphological aspects of the shell have generated constraints for prehistoric craftsmen, which determined their selection in order to create a certain type of object.

However, most of ornaments used by human communities from the study area were made from the *Spondylus* valve. An array of *Spondylus* adornments, from beads of different shapes and sizes, to belt elements, pendants, anthropomorphic figurines and massive bracelets, were documented in the Romanian Eneolithic (Table 2).

The first typological category is represented by beads with several subtypes. The bilobate or trilobate beads, with triangular section, convex extremities and convex-concave sides comprised a very interesting category. The pieces are endowed with two/three perforations, asymmetrically disposed. For the processing of these pieces, in a first stage, out of the valve was extracted a rectangular splinter. Yet we cannot reconstruct the proceedings which accompanied the debitage operation, due to subsequent technological interventions. The bilobate/trilobate morphology was obtained by oblique cuts, progressively deepened (Figure 3.2).

The lack of characteristic marks of these cuts seems to demonstrate that the piece's shaping was made in a subsequent stage. The perforation was made by alternative rotation (the specific marks are still visible), bilateral, holding the tool oblique compared to the piece surface,

Table 1. Summary of AMS ^{14}C radiocarbon dates related to archaeological sites that contain the *Spondylus* ornaments from South-eastern Romania. The calibration of the radiocarbon dates was made with OxCal v4.2 (Bronk Ramsey 2009). Calibration with 2σ confidence is based on the IntCal13 dataset (Reimer *et al.* 2013).

Site	Type*	^{14}C date (BP)	2 σ calibrated (cal.BC)	References
Cheia	FS	6141 ± 29	5208-5003	Balasse *et al.* 2014
Cheia	FS	6138 ± 44	5215-4962	Balasse *et al.* 2014
Cheia	FS	6064 ± 26	5047-4856	Balasse *et al.* 2014
Cheia	FS	6020 ± 43	5022-4798	Brehard and Bălăşescu 2012
Cernavoda	C	5975 ± 35	4959-4749	Unpublished
Cernavoda	C	6350 ± 35	5466-5226	Unpublished
Cernavoda	C	6310 ± 40	5367-5215	Unpublished
Căscioarele-D'aia Parte	C	5795 ± 35	4722-4548	Unpublished
Căscioarele-Ostrovel	TS	6100 ± 50	5210-4856	Lazăr *et al.* 2013
Căscioarele-Ostrovel	TS	5780 ± 65	4786-4488	Brehard and Bălăşescu 2012
Cernica	C	6095 ± 35	5207-4909	Mărgărit and Vintilă 2015
Radovanu	TS	5850 ± 70	4897-4540	Brehard and Bălăşescu 2012
Radovanu	TS	5855 ± 35	4823-4613	Lazăr *et al.* 2013
Sultana-Malu Roşu	C	6020 ± 40	5011-4799	Lazăr *et al.* 2012
Sultana-Malu Roşu	C	5936 ± 50	4943-4712	Hervella *et al.* 2015
Sultana-Valea Orbului	C	5790 ± 40	4763-4536	Unpublished
Sultana-Valea Orbului	C	6225 ± 35	5303-5063	Unpublished
Căscioarele-Ostrovel	TS	5500 ± 40	4450-4264	Unpublished
Căscioarele-Ostrovel	TS	5450 ± 35	4353-4246	Unpublished
Hârşova	TS	5575 ± 65	4546-4274	Brehard and Bălăşescu 2012
Hârşova	TS	5425 ± 40	4353-4173	Brehard and Bălăşescu 2012
Hârşova	TS	5304 ± 51	4315-3992	Brehard and Bălăşescu 2012
Pietrele	TS	5602 ± 47	4523-4350	Reingruber and Thissen 2009
Pietrele	TS	5539 ± 43	4460-4330	Reingruber and Thissen 2009
Pietrele	TS	5424 ± 33	4344-4235	Reingruber and Thissen 2009
Pietrele	TS	5366 ± 34	4329-4058	Reingruber and Thissen 2009
Sultana-Malu Roşu	TS	5250 ± 40	4230-3973	Lazăr *et al.* 2016
Sultana-Malu Roşu	TS	5230 ± 50	4174-3961	Lazăr *et al.* 2016
Sultana-Malu Roşu	TS	5630 ± 40	4538-4365	Lazăr *et al.* 2016
Sultana-Malu Roşu	TS	5570 ± 40	4486-4342	Lazăr *et al.* 2016
Sultana-Malu Roşu	C	5507 ± 55	4458-4258	Hervella *et al.* 2015
Sultana-Malu Roşu	C	5680 ± 35	4614-4406	Unpublished
Vărăşti	C	5525 ± 35	4451-4331	Unpublished
Vităneşti	TS	5379 ± 27	4331-4075	Brehard and Bălăşescu 2012
Vităneşti	TS	5430 ± 40	4354-4177	Brehard and Bălăşescu 2012
Vităneşti	TS	5400 ± 40	4344-4072	Brehard and Bălăşescu 2012

** C = cemetery; FS = flat settlement; TS = tell settlement.*
Light grey = Hamangia culture; Medium grey = Boian culture; Dark grey = Gumelniţa culture.

which determined the flared morphology of the perforation walls. The deformation of the perforations, towards the inner wall, demonstrates the attaching modality of the piece. In the case of bilobate/trilobate beads, the usage is demonstrated by deforming the wall between the perforations (Figure 3.3), almost until fracture, and by a pronounced facet, developed parallel to the piece's axe, in the area between perforations, which generated, in some cases, the evolution from a triangular section of the pieces, towards a trapezoidal section. The inner side presents a strong polish and, moreover, the area is very flattened and smooth when touched. We may assume that there was a catching system, by sawing the piece.

Another important bead category is that of the tubular beads, with straight profile, parallel rectilinear edges and circular section (Figures 2.1, 4.9, 5.1, 5.4).

Even in this case we cannot identify with certitude, the debitage proceedings. Nevertheless, we personally believe in using sawing at least in a final stage of the debitage. By simple percussion (even though we cannot exclude it), cannot be controlled the fracture manner and, in this case, we observe the need of a quite standardized blank. The surface pieces were entirely shaped, by an extremely fine abrasion (Figures 4.8, 4.10). The perforation was performed by bifacial rotation from which resulted the slightly flared walls at both extremities, but the specific marks of this proceeding are rarely visible (Figure 4.7). The extremities were generally strongly rounded, with the appearance of a small concave facet (Figures 2.2-4, 4.11, 5.2, 5.3, 5.6).

Moreover, it seems to correspond, in length, to a flattened and fine surface. We may assume that this is the area affected by the utilization of the pieces. The same technical data are actual also for the fusiform (Figure 5.1), and biconvex beads (Figures 4.6, 5.1), the morphological difference being created by the abrasion procedure. The cylindrical beads (Figures 5.4-5) seem to have been segmented out of the tubular beads (perhaps after fracturing), because their extremities are irregularly cut and the perforations are asymmetrical, relative to the piece's axis - hence the conclusion that they derive from already finished pieces.

The pieces of button type (Figure 2.5) were rigorously finished, so that we do not know the technique used to remove it from the valve. The perforation was carried out

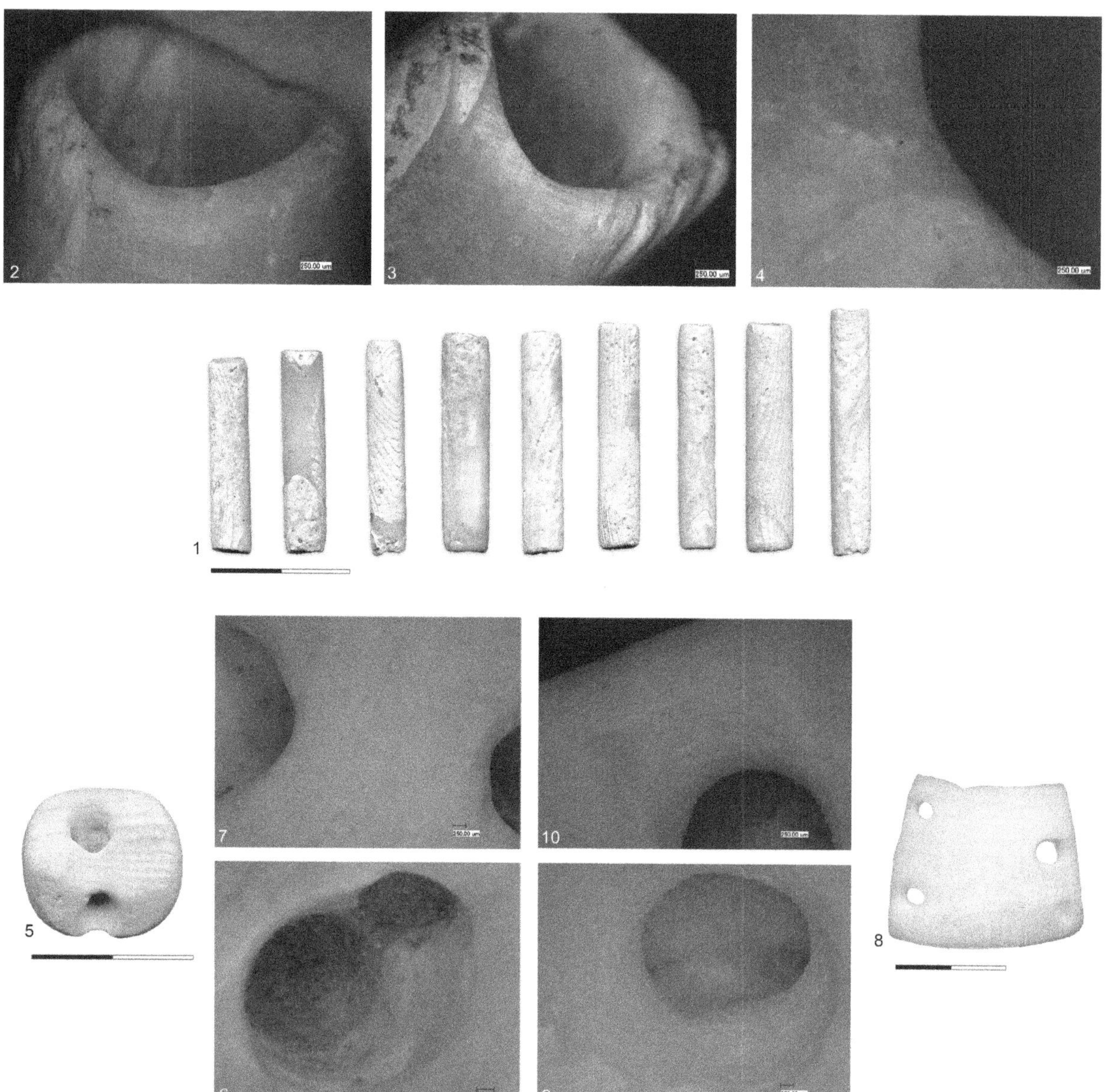

Figure 2. ***Spondylus*** **adornments from Hamangia culture (funeral context - Cernavoda cemetery): 1: tubular beads; 2-3: extremities with a concave facet; 4: smooth aspect of the extremity, on the level of the concavity; 5: button; 6: button perforation detail; 7: perforation wear detail; 8: perforated platelet; 9: perforation detail; 10: wear of the perforation wall. | Source: By the Authors.**

through bilateral rotation (Figure 2.6). The inner wall of the perforation is deformed, and the surface situated in between the two facets of the perforation coming from both sides is smooth and strongly polished (Figure 2.7). Also, there are biconvex pieces of *Spondylus*, presenting a flat facet with polish and a concavity marked off by the facet. The perforation is cylindrical, without rotation marks in the inside, but with a strong deformation, which corresponds exactly to the flat usage facet. Obviously the pieces were sawn, the friction generating the appearance of the facet. For that matter, their dimensions suggest their use as buttons which were attached to clothing (Table 2). The pendants with different shapes represent another interesting category documented in several Eneolithic sites (Table 2). In most cases, they were geometrical, but other shapes are attested. Thus, in the Cernavoda cemetery (Hamangia culture) is documented an arc-shaped pendant (Figure 6.4) that imitated a boar canine (Kogălniceanu 2012; Mărgărit 2012). A similar item was discovered in the Radovanu site (Figure 6.1) from the Boian culture (Mărgărit *et al.* 2014).

Table 2. Presence of the different types of *Spondylus* ornaments in Eneolithic sites from Romania.

Site	Type*	Beads**					Bracelet	Other items***					Reference
		T	C	Bi	B/T	F		P	R	B	Pl	I	
Agigea	C						•	•					Slobozianu 1959
Andolina	C				•								Comşa 1973
Căscioarele-D'aia Parte	C	?	?				•						Lichter 2001
Căscioarele-Ostrovel	TS	?						?					Schuster 2002
Ceamurlia de Jos	FS						•						Voinea *et al.* 2009
Cernavoda	C	•	•	•	•		•	•		•	•	•	Kogălniceanu 2012; Mărgărit 2012
Cernica	C	•	•	•	•	•	•			•	•		Mărgărit and Vintilă 2015
Chcia	FS	•		•				•				•	Voinea *et al.* 2014
Chirnogi I	C						•						Lazăr 2012a
Chirnogi II	C	•					•						Lazăr 2012a
Glavacioc	TS						•						Mirea and Frânculeasa 2005
Hârşova	TS	•	•	•			•						Galbenu 1963; Mărgărit and Popovici 2012
Isaccea-Suhat	FS				•		•	•					Micu, 2004
Însurăţei	TS							•					Beldiman and Sztancs 2006
Limanu	C	•	•				•		•				Voinea *et al.* 2009
Mangalia	C						•						Volschi and Irimia 1968
Medgidia	FS						•						Comşa 1973
Olteniţa	C				•								Lazăr 2012a
Palazu Mare	C	•					•						Voinea *et al.* 2009
Pietrele	TS	•	•	•			•	•					Berciu 1956; Toderaş *et al.* 2009; Hansen *et al.* 2011
Popeşti-Vasilaţi	C			•	•								Şerbănescu 1999
Radovanu	TS							•					Mărgărit *et al.* 2014
Sultana-Malu Roşu	TS						•						Unpublished
Sultana-Malu Roşu	C	•	•	•	•	•							Beldiman *et al.* 2008; Lazăr and Voicu 2015
Sultana-Valea Orbului	C	•	•	•	•		•			•			Schuster 2002; Şerbănescu 2002; Şerbănescu *et al.* 2007
Tangîru	TS						•				•		Comşa 1973
Vărăşti	C				•								Comşa1973
Vidra	TS	•						•					Müller 1997; Schuster 2002
Vităneşti	TS						•						Unpublished

* *C = cemetery; FS = flat settlement; TS = tell settlement.*
** *B/T = bilobate / trilobate bead; Bi = biconvex bead; C = cylindrical bead; F = fusiform bead; T= tubular bead.*
*** *B = button; I = idol; P = pendant; Pl = platelet; R = ring.*

This situation reflects recycling of some broken parts from bracelets. Probably, also the perforated plates documented in few sites (Table 2) were related to recycling of broken bracelets.

The most spectacular category is represented by the *Spondylus* anthropomorphic figurines (Figure 6.3). Currently, there are documented only two pieces of this type (Table 2), both belonging to Hamangia communities (Kogălniceanu 2012; Voinea *et al.* 2014). Taking into account the fact that items are perforated, they were probably used as pendants.

Extremely interesting are the massive pieces of *Spondylus* valve (Figures 2.8, 3.5).

Their form was also created by a method of direct shaping, by abrasion. They present perforations, accomplished by rotation (Figure 2.9). The usage is characterized by a strong deformation of the two perforations symmetrically placed - deformations accompanied by the appearance of a depression developed on the upper side (Figure 3.7), between perforations and on the lower side, starting from perforation, towards the extremity (Figures 2.10, 3.6).

The well-defined depression could not be created, but after a prolonged pressure, the piece being strongly used before its deposal in the grave. The specialist literature considers these pieces belt elements (Bonnardin 2009).

Bracelets made of *Spondylus* are of two types. The first type is the massive bracelet. For the processing of the bracelet was used the natural form of the valve, preserving an area from the main plateau, with the principal teeth and pits, in order to confer a special aesthetic aspect. The edges of the pieces seem to have been shaped by percussion, after which the surfaces were thoroughly smoothed. On the lower side, it presents a strong polish, with scratches perpendicular to the extremity, which may have developed subsequently to the utilization. In one case from the Cernica cemetery (Figure 3.4), there is an interesting recycling procedure, namely the appearance of cracks, developed perpendicular to the two openings, since on both sides perforations were made by rotation, applied from the upper side. In this manner, the extension

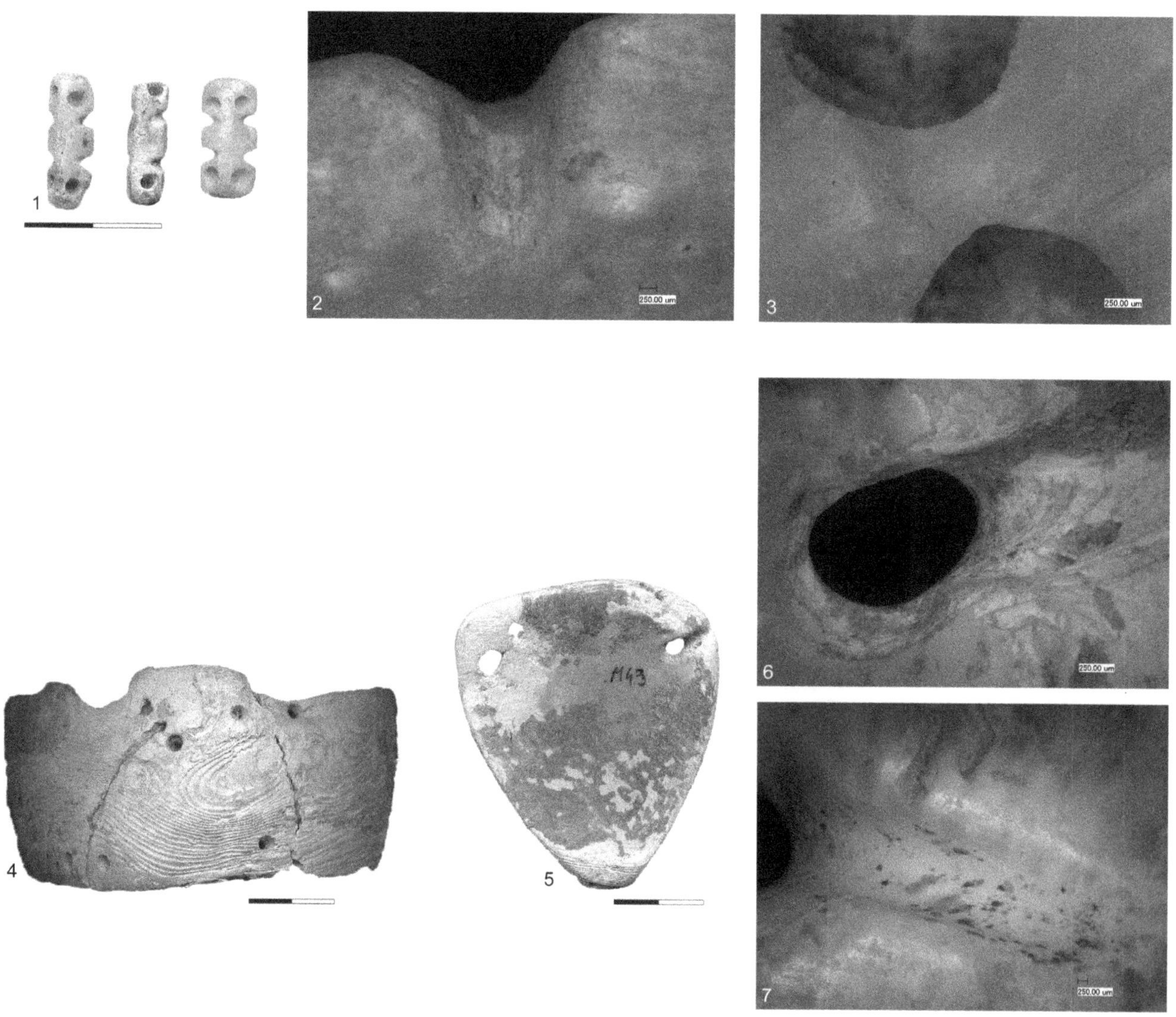

Figure 3. ***Spondylus*** **adornments from Boian culture (funeral context: 1 – Sultana-Malu Roșu cemetery; 4, 5 – Cernica cemetery): 1: trilobate beads; 2: morphology obtained by cutting; 3: deformation of the perforations; 4: massive bracelet; 5: perforated platelet; 6: deformation of the perforation; 7: depression developed on the upper side. | Source: By the Authors.**

of the cracks was stopped, by introducing a thread through the perforations and fixing the cracked parts (Mărgărit and Vintilă 2015). The second type refers to the bracelets whose sides were thinned, finished by a smooth shaping, which destroyed the technological traces of the previous stages. In the case of the thin bracelets, we could also identify cases of recycling. For instance, previously we mentioned the case of boar canine shape pendants from Radovanu and Cernavoda (Kogălniceanu 2012; Mărgărit *et al.* 2014), processed from a broken *Spondylus* bracelet, and in order not to lose it, the fragments were perforated (Figure 4.2) and cut/polished (Figures 4.3, 4.5), allowing the objects to be used as a pendants. The same recycling procedure is also confirmed in the settlement of Isaccea (Boian culture) (Micu 2004) or in the Boian level of Hârşova (Galbenu 1963), but also in the Gumelniţa tell-settlements of Sultana-Malu Roşu (Figure 4.4) and Vitănești (Figure 4.1).

6. Sultana-Malu Roşu site: a case study

Our research from Sultana-Malu Roşu site in the last 15 years revealed new data about the use of the *Spondylus*

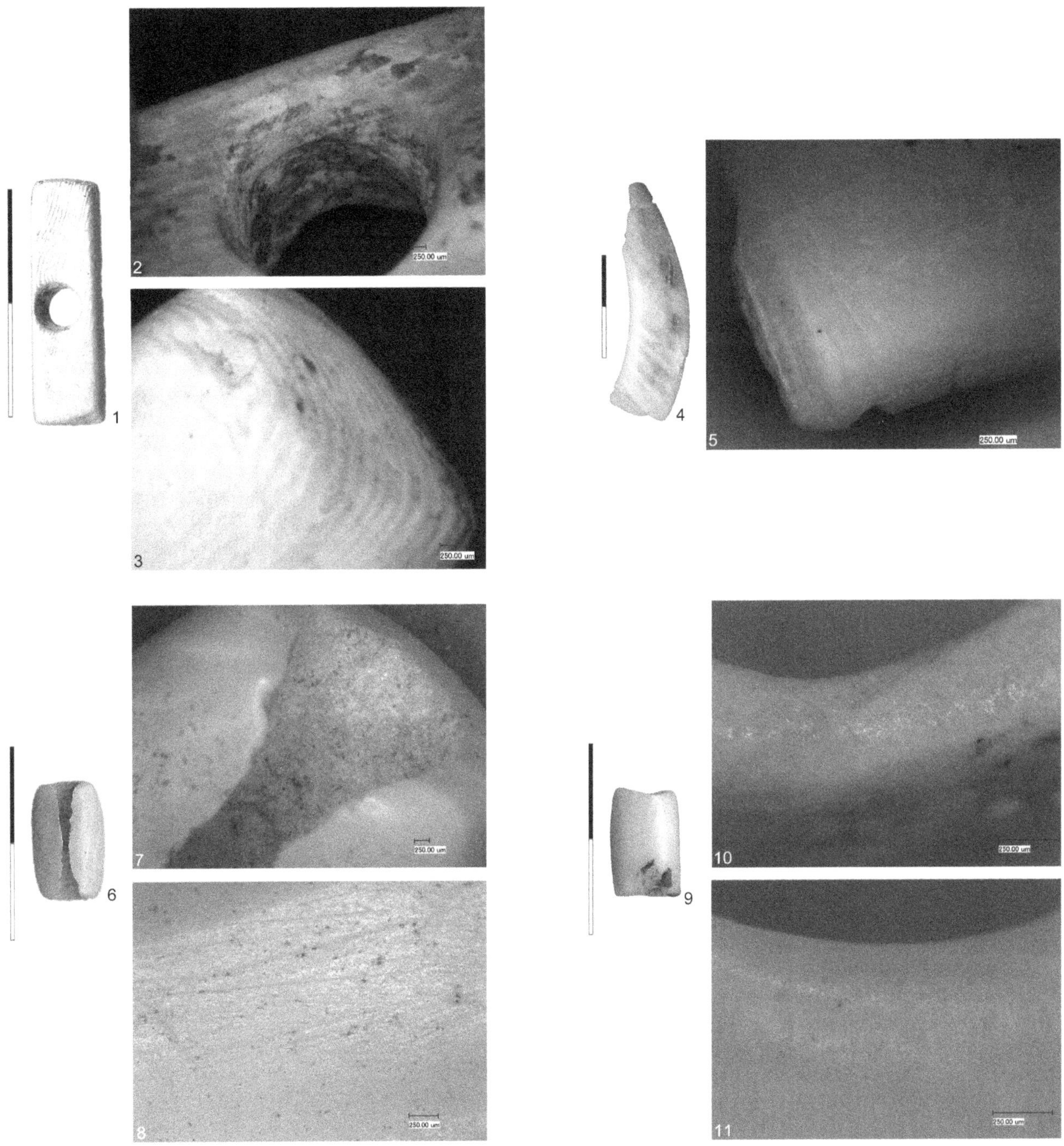

Figure 4. ***Spondylus*** **adornments from Gumelniţa tell dwellings (domestic context: 1 – Vitănești; 4 – Sultana-Malu Roşu; 6, 9 – Hârşova): 1: pendant; 2: perforation detail; 3: abrasion of the extremity; 4: bracelet; 5: recycling of a fractured bracelet by sawing; 6: biconvex bead; 7: perforation detail; 8: abrasion of the surface; 9: tubular bead; 10: abrasion of the extremity; 11: concave extremity. | Source: By the Authors.**

shells by human communities in the 5th millennium BC. Benefiting from an ideal archaeological situation that consisted in a flat settlement (Boian culture), tell settlement (Gumelniţa culture) and common cemetery used by the both communities, but also the clear finds context of the artefacts, it was possible to track the use pattern of *Spondylus* artifacts over a period of about 1,000 years (Lazăr *et al.* 2012).

The first observation is that no *Spondylus* pieces were found in the flat settlement of the Boian communities (c. 5000-4500 cal. BC). Instead, in the Boian graves contemporary with the flat settlement there are attested many ornaments made of this marine shell. In the tell settlement were identified several *Spondylus* artefacts, but not as many as in the Gumelniţa graves from the common cemetery. A total of 84 graves have been excavated in the cemetery between 2006 and 2014, but only 24 graves contained grave goods (Lazăr *et al.* 2008; 2009; 2012; Lazăr and Voicu 2015). *Spondylus* ornaments were found in 10 graves, representing the second most common raw material used for ornaments.

From the typological perspective, in the tell settlement from Sultana-Malu Roşu were identified three fragments of thin *Spondylus* bracelets, at which we cannot longer identify the succession of procedures from the debitage stage (as we have previously detailed). Their surface was smoothly shaped. It is worthy of notice that the recycling procedure of two of the pieces was incomplete. In the first sample, the fracture plan was shaped, while in the second, a segmentation procedure was initiated, by sawing, at both extremities. Such bracelets (fractured or whole) do not appear in the graves from the cemetery. We wonder if they were meant to be worn only during lifetime, without having a symbolic meaning connected to the funerary cult. At the same time, it is true that we are talking about fragments of pieces, which didn't get to be repaired, so in that moment they didn't fulfill the function of ornaments, being probably abandoned.

The typological picture for the pieces of *Spondylus* valves identified in the graves from the common cemetery is different from the one in the tell-settlement. *Spondylus* ornaments were present in 9 graves (Table 3) (Lazăr *et al.* 2012; Lazăr 2014; Lazăr and Voicu 2015). Between them there are differences in the funerary inventory, which might offer us clues regarding their belonging to one of the two communities which used the same cemetery. The type of beads that is best represented is the cylindrical one. In grave no. 1, they are associated with tubular, biconvex and fusiform beads. We are nevertheless referring to the most diversified grave in terms of ornament typology. On the contrary, in another grave with an important group of the cylindrical beads (grave no. 73), they are associated exclusively with the perforated shells of *Lithoglyphus naticoides*. Another type of bead which draws out attention is that of the bilobate /trilobate beads. They are present in a single grave (grave no. 69), representing the entire *Spondylus* inventory in this grave with the exception of a tubular bead. From the data available for other Eneolithic settlements and cemeteries (Table 2), such beads appear in Hamangia and Boian contexts. They are no longer attested within Gumelniţa culture. We may assert, at least for grave no. 69, its belonging to the Boian community. These bilobate and trilobate beads seem to represent the only distinct element between the two entities, at the level of *Spondylus* ornaments.

The pieces present different wear degrees, from the appearance of the wear concavities at the tubular and fusiform beads and deformations of the perforation sides, at the trilobate beads, as a consequence of the thread pressure, to profound changes in surface, with the destruction of the piece and the fracture of the perforation wall. The fact that most of the pieces from the Sultana-Malu Roşu cemetery present traces of wear can prove that they were worn during lifetime as well. So, it can be supposed that they were not created exclusively for the

Table 3. Distribution of *Spondylus* ornaments in the graves from the Sultana-Malu Roşu cemetery.

Grave no.	Beads					Total
	Tubular	*Cylindrical*	*Biconvex*	*Bilobate / Trilobate*	*Fusiform*	
1	8	49	7		3	67
13	7	1				8
14	2					2
36		1				1
44	1					1
62		2	2			4
68		6				6
69	1			32		33
72		5				5
73		164				164
Total	**19**	**228**	**9**	**32**	**3**	**291**

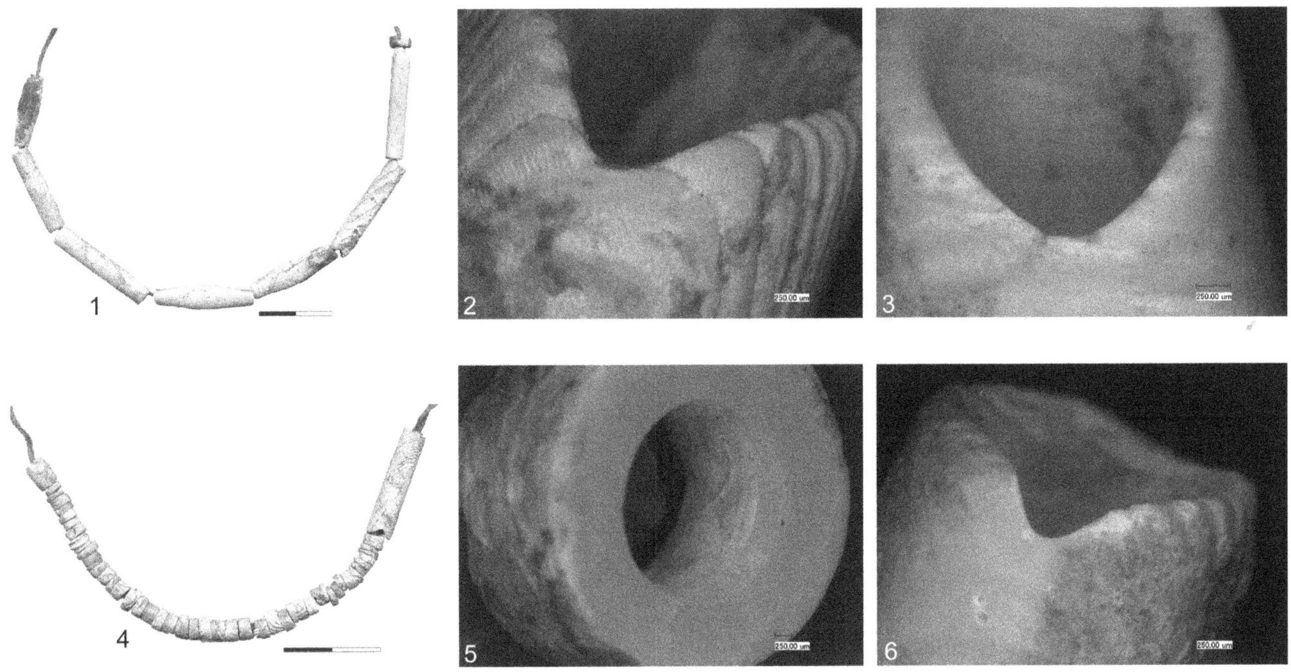

Figure 5. *Spondylus* adornments from Gumelniţa culture (funeral context – Sultana-Malu Roşu cemetery): 1: tubular, biconvex and cylindrical beads; 2-3, 6: concave extremities; 4: tubular and cylindrical beads; 5: perforation detail of a cylindrical bead. Source: By the Authors.

funerary domain. It is obvious that these ornaments had a special significance in the context of the treatment of dead people, but we cannot grasp these significances. Also, from distribution point of view, *Spondylus* ornaments seem to be common for male, female and child graves, a fact that does not support distinctions based on age-gender classes (Lazăr and Voicu 2015).

In sum, the situation from Sultana-Malu Roşu site reflects the evolution of *Spondylus* artefacts using by two cognate communities (according to aDNA data - Hervella *et al.* 2015). Thus, the first communities (Boian) apparently were not using the *Spondylus* shells in domestic contexts, but only in funeral rituals. Subsequently the Gumelniţa communities used these pieces in both domestic and funerary contexts. It is interesting that these communities have differentiated choices at typological level regarding the use of *Spondylus* artefacts.

7. Discussions and conclusions

As we previously mentioned, most of the shell ornaments from Southeastern Romania were made from *Spondylus*, which demonstrates the importance and value of these ornaments for the Eneolithic communities. It is interesting that, at the beginning of 5th millennium BC (Boian and Hamangia communities), this kind of item could be found mainly in cemeteries and rarely in the settlements; after 4500 BC (Gumelniţa communities), their quantity increases and it can be found frequently both in settlements and in cemeteries.

The comparison of *Spondylus* ornaments from the study region with those made from other shells species (Table 4) shows us that it ranks second in the preferences of Eneolithic communities (Figure 6.4).

Preferences for this exotic raw material (e.g. *Dentalium* and *Spondylus*) of non-local origin indicated probably a kind of dominant ideology certainly related of economy, society, identities, religious beliefs, or mythology.

As previously mentioned, the origin of the *Spondylus* shells used as raw material by Neolithic and Eneolithic communities from Balkans was in the Mediterranean area. The development of a *Spondylus* network that connect the source location from the Aegean and the Adriatic Seas with Southeastern and Central Europe is know since Early Neolithic, but it maximum evolution point was in the 5th millennium (Seferiades 1995; Chapman and Gaydarska 2007; 2015). Currently it is well documented the existence of some *Spondylus* production sites in Grecee (e.g. Dimitra, Dikili Tash, Dispilio, Sitagroi, etc.) (Infantidis 2011; Chapman and Gaydarska 2015). Probably most of the Eneolithic *Spondylus* ornaments discovered in the Southeastern Romania are related to these production centres, located at a minimum distance of 450-800 km, and the long-distance exchange networks.

However, in the Balkan area are confirmed as belonguing to workshops of *Spondylus* ornaments at Orlovo (Bulgaria) and Hârşova (Romania) (Galbenu 1963; Chapman and Gaydarska 2015). Thus, in burnt house from Hârşova tell

Table 4. The *Spondylus* artefacts distribution compared with other Molluscan species used by Eneolithic communities.

Site	Type*	Molluscs						Reference
		Spondylus	*Glycymeris*	*Dentalium*	*Cardium*	*Unio*	*Lithoglyphus*	
Agigea	C	2						Slobozianu 1959
Andolina	C	28		65				Comşa 1973
Cernavoda	C	71	4					Mărgărit 2012
Cernica	C	242	13	47				Mărgărit and Vintilă 2015
Cheia	FS	6			3			Voinea *et al.* 2014
Hârşova	TS	6		45		18		Galbenu 1963; Mărgărit and Popovici 2012
Limanu	C	44		703				Hartuche 1966; Galbenu 1970; Haşotti 1997
Mangalia	C	4						Volschi and Irimia 1968
Palazu Mare	C	1						Voinea *et al.* 2009
Popeşti-Vasilaţi	C	14						Şerbănescu 1999
Radovanu	TS	1						Mărgărit *et al.* 2014
Sultana-Malu Roşu	TS	5			1	8	108	Unpublished
Sultana-Malu Roşu	C	286		19			322	Lazăr and Voicu 2015
Vărăşti	C	16		1				Comşa 1973
Vităneşti	TS	1				3		Unpublished
Total		**727**	**17**	**880**	**4**	**29**	**430**	

* *C = cemetery; FS = flat settlement; TS = tell settlement.*

settlement were discovered more than 40 *Spondylus* items in association with tools (e.g. copper chisel, awls, etc.) used for shell processing (Galbenu 1963). In settlement from Orlovo were identified several *Spondylus* artefacts from all production phases that indicate a local production (Chapman and Gaydarska 2015). Both cases proving the existence of some local processing centres, but also the fact that the *Spondylus* not arrive in the Balkans only as finished artefacts. Moreover, the situation indicate the presence that settlements of some specialised individuals with necessary knowledge and skills to produce, repair and recycle the *Spondylus* items.

Over time, many authors have written about the social expression and symbolism of the *Spondylus* ornaments used by past communities in domestic activities or in funeral contexts both for aesthetic and cultural reasons, but also as part of construction, affirmation and maintenance of ideologies, identity and personhood process (e.g. Halstead 1993; Müller 1997; Borrello and Micheli 2005; Dimitrijević and Tripković 2006; Chapman *et al.* 2008; Seferaides 2010; Ifantidis 2011; Rigaud 2011; Chapman and Gaydarska 2015, etc.).

Nevertheless, the analysis of the *Spondylus* artefacts from Southeastern Romania in the Eneolithic sequence has given us a series of interesting evidences concerning these assertions, based on the individual and collective choices of human communities. Thus, at beginning of the 5th millennium BC (c. 5000-4500 BC) in the Hamangia and Boian societies there are some particular artefacts that were no longer encountered at the end of the period. For instance, the wide massive bracelets made of the right valve of the shell (Chapman *et al.* 2008) are documented only for these communities (e.g. Cernavoda, Sultana-Valea Orbului, etc.). Also, the bilobate and trilobate beads seem to represent an exclusive element used only by Boian communities. Considering that the Boian population arrived in the Balkans around 5000 BC (Hervella *et al.* 2015), and similar items were found from European Turkey (near to the origin place of these populations) and also in north-eastern Bulgaria, shows that it probably marks an element linked to the origin of these people, but also reflecting their migration route from south-western Anatolia to south-eastern Europe. Another original artefact type used exclusive by the Hamangia communities consists in anthropomorphic figurine-pendants (or as accessories attached on clothing discovered especially in cemeteries (e.g. Cernavoda and Durankulak) (Todorova 2002; Kogălniceanu 2012) or settlements (e.g. Cheia) (Voinea *et al.* 2009). It is interesting that besides these *Spondylu*s idols in Hamanagia communities are documented similar

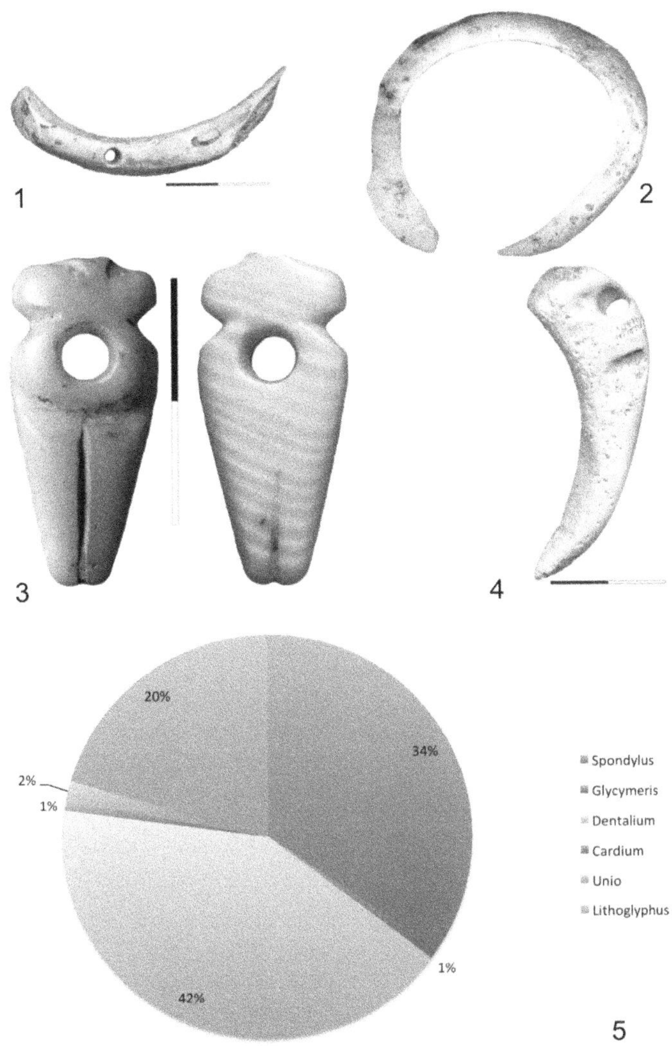

Figure 6. *Spondylus* items from domestic contexts – 1: Radovanu (Boian), 2: Glavacioc (Gumelniţa), without scale (after Mirea and Frânculeasa 2005), 3: Cheia (Hamangia), 4: Cernavoda (Hamangia) (after Voinea *et al.* 2014). *Spondylus* artefact distribution compared with other molluscan species used by Eneolithic communities (5). | Source: By the Authors.

pieces made of marble (e.g. Cernavoda, Peştera Liliecilor) (Kogălniceanu 2012; Voinea 2014). Undoubtedly, these pieces reflect a form of symbolic expression of those communities, related to construction of identities and personhood.

Another important observation for the communities from the first half of the 5th millennium BC (Boian and Hamangia) is the total absence of complete *Spondylus* bracelets from the settlements, and in the case of bracelet fragments they are very rare (only 3 site - Ceamurlia de Jos, Medgidia, and Radovanu) (Haşotti 1997; Mărgărit *et al.* 2014). Otherwise, from the quantitative point of view, no other *Spondylus* artefacts are frequent in the Boian and Hamangia settlements. Probably, this situation reflects a kind of restriction in use of *Spondylus* items in domestic contexts, and their exclusive destination for funerary use.

Instead, in the second half of the 5th millennium BC, things are changing. Thus, in the settlements of Gumelniţa communities are documented many *Spondylus* items, including complete bracelets. From the typological point of view can be observed the disappearance of wide massive bracelets made from the right valve of the shell, and their replacement by thin bracelets manufactured from the left shell (Chapman *et al.* 2008). Although the number of artefacts increased considerably after 4500 BC compared to the previous period, the diversity of types decreased significantly. Therefore, alongside with wide massive bracelets, some items as rings, anthropomorphic pendants, buttons, bilobate and trilobate beads are no longer documented in Gumelniţa settlements and cemeteries. Moreover, our research at the Sultana-Malu Roşu complex documented the differentiated use of *Spondylus* items in settlement and cemetery, which reflects an evolution of symbolic and ideological concepts of those communities, but also a different way of constructing identities of the living and dead. Thus, in the second half of the 5th millennium BC, the recycling, repair and reuse of broken items was more extensive, which demonstrates that the *Spondylus* pieces kept their ancestral value. Probably most obvious example in this direction is the *Spondylus* bracelet from grave no. 43 in the Varna I cemetery that was repaired with two gold fasteners (Seferiades 1995), which indicates that the emergence of new raw materials (as gold and copper) does not alter the importance of these pieces. Finally, the use-wear analysis performed on the *Spondylus* artefacts indicates that past humans intensively wore these ornaments. In the case of items from the graves, this observation shows that the pieces were not created exclusively to be deposited as grave goods. Thus, the objects made of *Spondylus* were transmitted from generation to generation as was previously noted by other authors (Seferiades 2010, Chapman and Gaydarska 2007), being an active reflection of concepts of wealth, power, and prestige in Eneolithic society. Moreover, their use mostly in graves (funerary domain) implies an enchained relation with the person(s) keeping, using or exchanging the *Spondylus* pieces in the world of the living. The widespread of this practice in the Balkans during the 5th millennium BC would be an important support for the notion of ancestral relations (Chapman and Gaydarska 2007), but also a strong indicator of the process by which individual and collective identities or personhood were built by the past communities.

In summary, our survey of *Spondylus* artefacts in the 5th millennium BC from Southeastern Romania indicates the importance of that raw material in the Eneolithic period, and demonstrates complex interfaces between this marine shell and past communities. They also reflects the relation between the people who manufactured, transported, traded, used, inherited, sacrificed and abandoned them. Furthermore, the items manufactured of spiny oyster depicted a kind of shared identity between distant geographic areas, but also a form of connecting people from these regions. Without doubt, the *Spondylus* items can be considered as active agents of social structures, mentalities, ideologies, ideas, beliefs, and the organizing principles of the peoples who manipulated, used and desired them. On the other hand, the process of transformation of the shells into ornaments changed their meaning from natural elements in material culture associated with people and their identities.

The *Spondylus* shells reflect the existence of a dominant ideology in 5th millennium BC that probably began in the Early Neolithic, when for the first time the networks for the exchange and distribution of this shell were developed, and in which artefacts made of this raw material had a key role with multiple connotations and meanings.

Acknowledgements

The authors thank Professor John Chapman for improving the English translation of this paper, and Pavel Mirea for the unpublished photo of *Spondylus* bracelet from Glavacioc.

This work was performed as part of the Partnerships in Priority Areas Program - PN II, developed with the support of MEN - UEFISCDI, project no. PN-II-PT-PCCA-2013-4-2302.

References

Anthony, David W. "The Rise and Fall of Old Europe." In *The Lost World of Old Europe. The Danube Valley, 5000-3500 BC*, edited by David W. Anthony, and Jennifer Y. Chi, 29–57. New York: Princeton University Press, 2010.

Arrizabalaga, Alvaro, Álvarez-Fernández, Esteban, and Iriarte, Maria-José. "*Spondylus* sp. at Lezetxiki Cave (Basque Country, Spain): First Evidence of its use in Symbolic Behaviour during the Aurignacian in Europe." In *Spondylus in Prehistory: New Data & Approaches - Contributions to the Archaeology of Shell Technologies*, edited by Fotis Ifantidis, and Marianna Nikolaidou, 11–16. Oxford: British Archaeological Reports, 2011.

Bailey, Douglass W. *Balkan Prehistory. Exclusion, Incorporation and Identity*. London: Routledge, 2000.

Bajnóczi, Bernadett, Schöll-Barna, Gabriella, Kalicz, Zsuzsanna Siklósi, Hourmouziadis George H., Ifantidis, Fotis, Kyparissi-Apostolika, Aikaterini, Pappa, Maria, Veropoulidou, Rena, and Ziota, Christina. "Tracing the source of Late Neolithic *Spondylus* shell ornaments by stable isotope geochemistry and cathodoluminescence microscopy." *Journal of Archaeological Science* 40, no. 2 (2013): 874–882.

Balasse, Marie, Tornero, Carlos, Bréhard, Stéphanie, Ughetto-Monfrin, Joël, Voinea, Valentina, and Bălăşescu, Adrian. "Cattle and Sheep Herding at Cheia, Romania, at the Turn of the Fifth Millennium cal BC. A View from Stable Isotope Analysis." In *Early farmers: the view from archaeology and science*, edited by Alasdair Whittle, and Penny Bickle, 115–142. Oxford: Oxford University Press, 2014.

Beldiman, Corneliu, and Sztancs, Diana-Maria. "Industria preistorică a materiilor dure animale." In *Cronica Cercetărilor Arheologice din România, Campania 2005*, edited by Mircea Angelescu, and Florela Vasilescu, 201–204. Bucuresti: cIMeC – INP, 2006.

Beldiman, Corneliu, Lazăr, Cătălin, and Sztancs, Diana-Maria. "Necropola eneolitică de la Sultana-*Malu-Roşu*, com. Mânăstirea, jud. Călăraşi. Piese de podoabă din inventarul M1." *Buletinul Muzeului Judeţean Teohari Antonescu Giurgiu* 11 (2008): 59–72.

Berciu, Dumitru. "Însemnări pentru preistoria Peninsulei Balcanice. Podoabe mediteraneene în regiunea „Porţilor de Fier"". *Balcanica* 2-3 (1939-1940): 446-452.

Berciu, Dumitru. "Cercetări şi descoperiri arheologice în regiunea Bucureşti." *Materiale şi Cercetări Arheologice* II (1956): 491–562.

Bréhard, Stéphanie, and Bălăşescu, Adrian. "What's Behind the Tell Phenomenon? An Archaeozoological Approach to Eneolithic Sites in Romania." *Journal of Archaeological Science* 39, no. 10 (2012): 3167–3183.

Bonnardin, Sandrine. *La parure funéraire au Néolithique ancien dans les Bassins parisien et rhénan Rubané, Hinkelstein et Villeneuve-Saint-Germain*. Mémoire de la Societé Préhistorique Française XLIX. Paris: Societé Préhistorique Française, 2009.

Borić, Dusan. "Mortuary Practices, Bodies, and Persons in the Neolithic and Early–Middle Copper Age of South-East Europe." In *The Oxford Handbook of Neolithic Europe*, edited by Chris Fowler, Jan Harding, and Daniela Hofmann, 927–958. Oxford: Oxford University Press, 2015.

Borrello, Maria A., and Micheli, Roberto. "*Spondylus gaederopus*, gioiello dell'Europa preistorica." *Preistoria Alpina* 40, no. 1 (2005): 71–82.

Bronk Ramsey, Christopher. "Bayesian Analysis of Radiocarbon Dates." *Radiocarbon* 51 (2009): 337–360.

Chapman, J. and Gaydarska, B. 2007. *Parts and Wholes: Fragmentation in Prehistoric Context*. Oxford: Oxbow Books.

Chapman, John, and Gaydarska, Bisserka. "*Spondylus Gaederopus/Glycymeris* Exchange Networks in the European Neolithic and Chalcolithic." In *The Oxford Handbook of Neolithic Europe*, edited by Chris Fowler, Jan Harding, and Daniela Hofmann, 639–655. Oxford: Oxford University Press, 2015.

Chapman, John, Gaydarska, Bisserka, and Slavchev, Vladimir. "The life histories of *Spondylus* shell rings from the Varna I Eneolithic cemetery (Northeast Bulgaria): transformation, revelation, fragmentation and deposition." *Acta Musei Varnaensis* VI (2008): 139–161.

Comşa, Eugen. "Mormântul neolitic descoperit lângă satul Andolina." *Studii şi Cercetări de Istorie Veche* 12 (1961): 359–362.

Comşa, Eugen. «Parures néolithiques en coquillages marins découverts en territoire roumain.» *Dacia* NS 17 (1973): 61–76.

Comşa, Eugen, and Cantacuzino, Gheorghe. *Necropola neolitică de la Cernica*. Bucureşti: Editura Academiei Române, 2001.

Dimitrijević, Vesna, and Tripković, Boban. "*Spondylus* and *Glycymeris* bracelets: trade reflections at Neolithic Vinča-Belo Brdo." *Documenta Praehistorica* XXXIII (2006): 237–252.

Fischer, Wolfgang, Bauchot, Marie-Louise, and Schneider, Marie, (eds.). *Fiches FAO d'Identification des Espèces pour les Besoins de la Pêche-Méditerranée et Mer Noire-Zone de Pêche 37*. Révision 1. Vol. I: Végétaux et Invertébrés. Rome: FAO, 1987.

Galbenu, Doina. «Neolitičeskaja masterskaja dlja obrabotki ukrašenij v Chyršove.» *Dacia* NS 7 (1963): 501–509.

Galbenu, Doina. "Aşezarea şi cimitirul de la Limanu." *Materiale şi Cercetări de Arheologie* IX (1970): 77–86.

Halstead, Paul. "*Spondylus* shell ornaments from late Neolithic Dimini, Greece: specialized manufacture or unequal accumulation?" *Antiquity* 67 (1993): 603–609.

Hansen, Sven, Toderaş, Meda, Reingruber, Agathe, Gatsov, Ivan, Klimscha, Florian, Nedelcheva, Petranka, Neef, Reinder, Prange, Matthias, Price, T. Douglas, Wahl, Joachim, Weninger, Bernhard, Wrobel, Heide, Wunderlich, Jürgen, and Zidarov, Petar. "Der kupferzeitliche Siedlungshügel Magura Gorgana bei Pietrele in der Walachei. Ergebnisse der Ausgrabungen im Sommer 2007." *Eurasia Antiqua* 14 (2008): 17–98.

Hansen, Sven, Toderaş, Meda, Reingruber, Agathe, Nowcki, Dirk, Norgaard, Heide, Spânu, Daniel and Wunderlich, Jürgen. "Die kupferzeitliche Siedlung Pietrele an der Unteren Donau." *Eurasia Antiqua* 17 (2011): 45–120.

Hansen, Sven. "Innovative Metals: Copper, Gold and Silver in the Black Sea Region and the Carpathian Basin During the 5th and 4th Millennium BC." In *Metal Matters; Innovative Technologies and Social Change in Prehistory and Antiquity*, edited by Stefan Burmeister, Sven Hansen, Kunst Michael, and Nils Müller-Scheeßel, 137–167. Rahden: VML, Verlag Marie Leidorf, 2013.

Harţuche, Nicolae. "Un vas de marmură descoperit într-un mormânt de tip Hamangia." *Revista Muzeelor* III, no. 5 (1966): 445–446.

Haşotti, Puiu. *Epoca neolitica in Dobrogea*. Constanţa: Ex Ponto, 1997.

Hervella, Monserrat, Rotea, Mihai, Izagirre, Neskuts, Constantinescu, Mihai, Alonso, Santos, Ioana, Mihai, Lazăr, Cătălin, Ridichie, Florin, Soficaru, Andrei Dorian, Netea, Mihai G., and de-la-Rua, Concepcion. "Ancient DNA from South-East Europe Reveals Different Events during Early and Middle Neolithic Influencing the European Genetic Heritage." *PLoS ONE* 10, no. 6 (2015). e0128810. doi:10.1371/journal.pone.0128810.

Huber, Markus. *Compedium of Bivalves*. Hackenheim: ConchBooks, 2010.

Infantidis, Fotis. "Cosmos in Fragments: *Spondylus* and *Glycymeris* Adornment at Neolithic Dispilio, Greece. " In *Spondylus in Prehistory: New data and approaches. Contributions to the archaeology of shell technologies*, edited by Fotis Infantidis, and Marianna Nikolaidou, 123–137. Oxford: British Archaeological Reports, 2011.

Kalicz, Nandor, and Szénászky, Julia. "Spondylus-Schmuck im Neolithikum des Komitats Békés, Südostungarn." *Praehistorische Zeitschrift* 76 (2001): 24–54.

Lazăr, Cătălin. "Some Observations about Spatial Relation and Location of the Kodjadermen-Gumelniţa- Karanovo VI Extra Muros Necropolis." In *The Lower Danube in Prehistory: Landscape Changes and Human Environment Interactions - Proceedings of the International Conference, Alexandria 3-5 November 2010*, edited by Steve Mills, and Pavel Mirea, 95–115. Bucureşti: Renaissance, 2011.

Lazăr, Cătălin, (ed.). *The Catalogue of the Neolithic and Eneolithic Funerary Findings from Romania*. Bucharest: Cetatea de Scaun, 2012a.

Lazăr, C., and Mărgărit, Monica "Necropola de la Cernavodă: între mit şi realitate." *Pontica* XLV (2012b): 405–436.

Lazăr, Cătălin. "The Eneolithic necropolis from Sultana-Malu Roşu (Romania) – a case study." In *Mobility and Transitions in the Holocene. Proceedings of the XVI World Congress of the International Union of Prehistoric and Protohistoric Sciences, vol. 9*, edited by Luiz Oosterbeek, and Claudia Fidalgo, 67–74. Oxford British Archaeological Reports, 2014.

Lazăr, Cătălin, and Voicu, Mădălina. "The distortion of archaeological realities through objects: a case study. " In *Homines, Funera, Astra 2. The Archaeology of Death in Ancient Times: Life beyond Life? Proceedings of the International Symposium on Funerary Anthropology 23-26 September 2012 '1 Decembrie 1918' University* 2015. *(Alba Iulia, Romania)*, edited by Raluca Kogălniceanu, Mihai Gligor, Roxana-Gabriela Curcă, and Susan Stratton, 59–68. Oxford: Archaeopress, 2015.

Lazăr, Cătălin, Andreescu, Radian, Ignat, Theodor, Florea, Mihai, and Astalos, Ciprian. "The Eneolithic Cemetery from Sultana-Malu Roşu (Călăraşi county, Romania). " *Studii de Preistorie* 5 (2008): 131–152.

Lazăr, Cătălin, Andreescu, Radian, Ignat, Theodor, Mărgărit, Monica, Florea, Mihai, and Bălăşescu, Adrian. "New Data on the Eneolithic Cemetery from Sultana-Malu Roşu (Călăraşi county, Romania*)*." *Studii de Preistorie* 6 (2009): 165–199.

Lazăr, Cătălin, Voicu, Mădălina, and Vasile, Gabriel. "Traditions, Rules and Exceptions in the Eneolithic Cemetery from Sultana-

Malu Roşu (Southeast Romania)." In *Homines, Funera, Astra. Proceedings of the International Symposium on Funerary Anthropology, 5-8 June 2011, 1 Decembrie 1918' University (Alba Iulia, Romania)*, edited by Raluca Kogălniceanu, Mihai Gligor, Roxana-Gabriela Curcă, and Susan Stratton, 107–118. Oxford: British Archaeological Reports, 2012.

Lazăr, Cătălin, Vasile, Gabriel, and Ştefan, Cristian. "Consideraţii privind resturile osteologice umane din cadrul unor aşezări eneolitice din sud-estul României." *Studii de Preistorie* 10 (2013): 67–88.

Lazăr, Cătălin, Mărgărit, Monica, and Bălăşescu, Adrian. "Dogs, jaws, and other stories: Two symbolic objects made of dog mandibles from southeastern Europe." *Journal of Field Archaeology* 41, no. 1 (2016): 101–117.

Lichter, Clemens. *Untersuchungenzu den Baut endes südosteuropäischen Neolithikums Chalkolithikums*. Mainz am Rhein: Verlag Philipp Von Zabern, 2001.

Mărgărit, Monica. "Shell adornments from the Hamangia cemetery excavated at Cernavoda – Columbia D. Techno-typological analysis." In *Homines, Funera, Astra. Proceedings of the International Symposium on Funerary Anthropology, 5-8 June 2011, 1 Decembrie 1918' University (Alba Iulia, Romania)*, edited by Raluca Kogălniceanu, Mihai Gligor, Roxana-Gabriela Curcă, and Susan Stratton, 97-106. Oxford: British Archaeological Reports, 2012.

Mărgărit, Monica, and Popovici, Dragomir Nicolae. "From block to finished object. Function of the personal ornaments in the eneolithic settlement from Hârşova-tell (judeţul Constanţa, Romania)." *Acta Archaeologica Carpathica* XLVII (2012): 91–114.

Mărgărit, Monica, Ştefan, Cristian Eduard, Dumitraşcu, Valentin. "Management of osseous materials for processing artifacts in the Boian settlement of Radovanu - La Muscalu (Romania). " *Archaeologia Bulgarica* 18, no. 3 (2014): 1–34.

Mărgărit, Monica, and Vintilă, Camelia-Mirela. "New information from old collections. Reevaluation of personal adornments made of hard animal materials from the necropolis of Cernica." *Studii de Preistorie* 12 (2015): 81–115.

Micu, Cristian. "Observaţii privind industria materiilor dure animale în aşezarea neolitică de la Isaccea, punctul „Suhat". " In *Prinos lui Petre Diaconu la 80 de ani*, edited by Ionel Cândea, Valeriu Sârbu, and Marian Neagu. Brăila-Călăraşi: Istros, 2004.

Miller, Margaret. "Technical Aspects of Ornament Production at Sitagroi." In *Prehistoric Sitagroi: Excavations in Northeast Greece, 1968-1970, Vol. 2*, edited by Ernestine S Elster, and Colin Renfrew, 369–382. Los Angeles: University of California, Cotsen Institute of Archaeology, 2003.

Mirea, Pavel, and Frânculeasa, Alin. "Locuirea eneolitică gumelniţeană de la mănăstirea Glavacioc, jud. Argeş." *Argesis. Studii si Comunicari* XIV (2005): 55–74.

Müller, Johannes. Neolithische und Chalkolithische Spondylus-Artefakte: Anmerkungen zu Verbietung, Tauschgebiet und sozialer Funktion. In *ΧΡΟΝΟΣ: Beiträge zur prähistorischen Archäologie zwischen Nord- und Südosteuropa. Festschrift für Bernhard Hänsel*, edited by Cornelia Becker, Marie L. Dunkelmann, Carola Metzner-Nebelsick, Heidi Peter-Röcher, Manfred Roeder, and Biba Teržan, 91–106. Espelkamp: Marie Leidorf GmbH, 1997.

Newell, Raymond R., Kielman, David, Constandse-Westermann, Trinette S., van der Sanden, Wijnand Antonius Bernardus, and van Gijn, Annelou. 1. *An Inquiry into the Ethnic Resolution of Mesolithic Regional Groupe. The Study of Their Decorative Ornaments in Time and Space*. Leiden: Brill, 1990.

Petrescu-Dâmboviţa, Mircea. "Eneoliticul timpuriu." In *Istoria Românilor, vol. I. Moştenirea timpurilor îndepărtate*, edited by Mircea Petrescu-Dîmboviţa, and Alexandru Vulpe, 148–154. Bucureşti: Editura Academiei Române, 2001a.

Petrescu-Dâmboviţa, Mircea. "Eneoliticul dezvoltat." In *Istoria Românilor, vol. I. Moştenirea timpurilor îndepărtate*, edited by Mircea Petrescu-Dîmboviţa, and Alexandru Vulpe, 154–168. Bucureşti: Editura Academiei Române, 2001b.

Popovici, Dragomir Nicolae. Copper Age Traditions North of the Danube River. In *The Lost World of Old Europe. The Danube Valley, 5000-3500 BC*, edited by David W. Anthony, and Jennifer Y. Chi, 91-111. New York: Princeton University Press, 2010.

Preston-Whyte, Eleanor. *Speaking with Beads: Zulu Arts from Southern Africa*. New York: Thames and Hudson, 1994.

Reimer, Paula J., Bard, Edouard, Bayliss, Alex, Beck, J.Warren, Blackwell, Paul G., Bronk Ramsey, Christopher, Buck, Caitlin E., Cheng, Hai, Edwards, R. Lawrence, Friedrich, Michael, Grootes, Pieter M., Guilderson, Thomas P., Haflidason, Haflidi, Hajdas, Irka, Hatté, Christine, Heaton, Timothy J., Hoffmann, Dirk L., Hogg, Alan G., Hughen, Konrad A., Kaiser, K. Felix, Kromer, Bernd, Manning, Stuart W., Niu, Mu, Reimer, Ron W., Richards, David A., Scott, E. Marian, Southon, John R., Staff, Richard A., Turney, Christian S. M. and van der Plicht, Johannes. "IntCal13 and Marine13 Radiocarbon Age Calibration Curves 0–50,000 Years cal BP." *Radiocarbon* 55, no. 4 (2013):1869–1887.

Reingruber, Agathe, and Thissen, Laurens. "Depending on ^{14}C Data: Chronological Frameworks in the Neolithic and Chalcolithic of Southeastern Europe." *Radiocarbon* 51, no. 2 (2009): 751–770.

Rigaud, Solange. *La parure: traceur de la géographie culturelle et des dynamiques de peuplement au passage Mésolithique-Néolithique en Europe*. Unpublished Ph.D. Thesis,Université Bordeaux 1, France, 2011.

Rigaud, Solange, d'Errico, Francesco, and Vanhaeren, Marian. "Ornaments Reveal Resistance of North European Cultures to the Spread of Farming." *PLoS ONE* 10, no. 4 (2015). e0121166. doi:10.1371/journal.pone.0121166.

Schuster, Christian. "Zu den Spondylus-Funden in Rumänien." *Thraco-Dacica* 23, no. 1-2 (2002): 37–84.

Sciama, Lidia D., and Eicher, Joanne, (eds.). *Beads and Bead Makers: Gender. Material Culture and Meaning*. Oxford and New York: Berg, 1998.

Seferiades, Michel Louis. "*Spondylus gaederopus*: The Earliest European Long Distance Exchange System. A Symbolic and Structural Archaeological Approach to Neolithic Societies." *Porocilo o raziskovanju paleolitika, neolitika in eneolitika v Slovenia* 22(1995): 233–256.

Seferiades, Michel Louis. "La route néolithique des spondyles de la Méditerranée à la Manche. " In *Nature et culture. Actes du Colloque International de Liège 13-17 decembre 1993*, edited by Marcel Otte, 291–358. Liège: ERAUL, 1996.

Seferiades, Michel Louis. "*Spondylus gaederopus*: the earliest European long distance exchange system." In *Karanovo III. Beiträge zum Neolithikum in Südosteuropa*, edited by Susan Hiller, and Vassil Nikolov, 423–437. Wien: Phoibos Verlag, 2000.

Seferiades, Michel Louis. 2010. "*Spondylus* and Long-Distance Trade in Prehistoric Europe." In *The Lost World of Old Europe.*

The Danube Valley, 5000-3500 BC, edited by David W. Anthony, and Jennifer Y. Chi, 179–190. New York: Princeton University Press, 2010.

Seferiades, Michel Louis. "Spondyles roumains, Spondyles americains." In *Facets of the past: the Challenge of the Balkan Neo-Eneolithic: Proceedings of the international symposium celebrating the 85th birth anniversary of Eugen Comşa*, edited by Alexandra Comşa, Clive Bonsall, and Lolita Nikolova, 247–272. Bucharest: The Publishing House of the Romanian Academy, 2013.

Shakelton, Judith, and Elderfield, Henry. "Strontium isotope dating of the source of Neolithic European *Spondylus* shell artefacts." *Antiquity* 64, no. 243 (1990): 312–315.

Slavchev, Vladimir. 2010. "The Varna Eneolithic Cemetery in the Context of the Late Copper Age in the East Balkans." In *The Lost World of Old Europe. The Danube Valley, 5000-3500 BC*, edited by David W. Anthony, and Jennifer Y. Chi, 192–210. New York: Princeton University Press, 2010.

Slobozianu, Horia. "Consideraţii asupra aşezărilor antice din jurul lacurilor Techirghiol şi Agigea." *Materiale si Cercetari Arheologice* 5 (1959): 737–743.

Şerbănescu, Done. "Necropola neolitică de la Popeşti, com. Vasilaţi, jud. Călăraşi." In *Cultura Boian pe teritoriul României*, edited by Marian Neagu, 28–29. Călăraşi: Ministerul Culturii, 1999.

Şerbănescu, Done. "Observaţii preliminarii asupra necropolei neolitice de la Sultana, jud. Călăraşi." *Cultura si Civilizatiei la Dunarea de Jos* XIX (2002): 69–86.

Şerbănescu, Done, and Soficaru, Andrei Dorian. "Sultana, com. Mănăstirea, jud. Călăraşi, Punct: Valea Orbului." In *Cronica Cercetărilor Arheologice din România. Campania 2005* edited by Mircea V. Angelescu, and Florela Vasilescu, 343–347. Bucureşti: Cimec, 2006.

Şerbănescu, Done, Comşa, Alexandra, and Mecu, Laurenţiu. "Sultana, com. Mănăstirea, jud. Călăraşi, Punct: Valea Orbului." In *Cronica Cercetărilor Arheologice din România. Campania 2006* edited by Mircea V. Angelescu, and Florela Vasilescu, 351–352. Bucureşti: Cimec, 2007.

Taborin, Yvette. "La parure en coquillage de l'Épipaléolithique au Bronze Ancien en France (I)". *Gallia Préhistoire* 17, no. 1 (1974): 101–179.

Titschack, Jürgen, Radtke, Ulrich, and Freiwald, André. "Dating and characterization of polymorphic transformation of aragonite to calcite in Pleistocene bivalves from Rhodes (Greece) by combined shell miscrostructure, stable isotope, and elektron spin resonance study." *Journal of Sedimentary Research* 79 (2009): 332–346.

Toderaş, Meda, Hansen, Sven, Reingruber, Agathe and Wunderlich, Jürgen. "Pietrele-Măgura Gorgana: o aşezare eneolitică la Dunărea de Jos între 4500 şi 4250 î.e.n." *Materiale şi Cercetări Arheologice* NS 5 (2009): 39–90.

Todorova, Henrieta. *Kamenno-mednata Epokha v Bulgariya. Peto Khilyadoletie predi NovataEra*. Sofia: Izdatepstvo Nauka i Izkustvo, 1986.

Todorova, Henrieta. "Die Spondylus – Problematik heute." In *Karanovo, Bd. III. Beiträge zur Neolithikum in Südosteuropa*, edited by Susan Hiller, and Vassil Nikolov, 415–422. Wien: Phoibos Verlag, 2000.

Todorova, Henrieta. "Die Mollusken in den Gräberfeldern von Durankulak." In *Durankulak, Band II. Die Prähistorischen Gräberfelder, teil 1*, edited by Henrieta Todorova, 177–190. Sofia: Publishing House Anubis Ltd., 2002.

Vanhaeren, Marian, d'Errico, Francesco, Billy, Isabelle, and Grousset, Francis. "Tracing the source of Upper Palaeolithic shell beads by strontium isotope dating." *Journal of Archaeological Science* 31, no. 10 (2004): 1481–1488.

Vanhaeren, Marian, and d'Erico, Francesco. "Aurignacian ethno-linguistic geography of Europe revealed by personal ornaments." *Journal of Archaeological Science* 33, no. 8 (2006): 1105–1128.

Voinea, Valentina, Neagu, George, and Radu, Valentin. "*Spondylus* Shell Artefacts in Hamangia Culture." *Pontica* 49 (2009): 9–25.

Voinea, Valentina, Grigoruţă, Oana, and Cărpuş, Cornelia. "Hard animal material adornments discovered in Hamangia settlement from Cheia/ Podoabe din materii dure animale descoperite în aşezarea Hamangia de la Cheia." In *An overview of the exploitation of hard animal materials during the Neolithic and Chalcolithic/O privire asupra exploatării materiilor dure animale de-a lungul neoliticului şi calcoliticului*, edited by Monica Mărgărit, Gaelle Le Dosseur, and Aline Averbouh, 101–136. Târgovişte: Editura Cetatea de Scaun, 2014.

Volschi, Vanda, and Irimia, Mihai. "Descoperiri arheologice de la Mangalia şi Limanu, aparţinând culturii Hamangia." *Pontica* I (1968): 78–87.

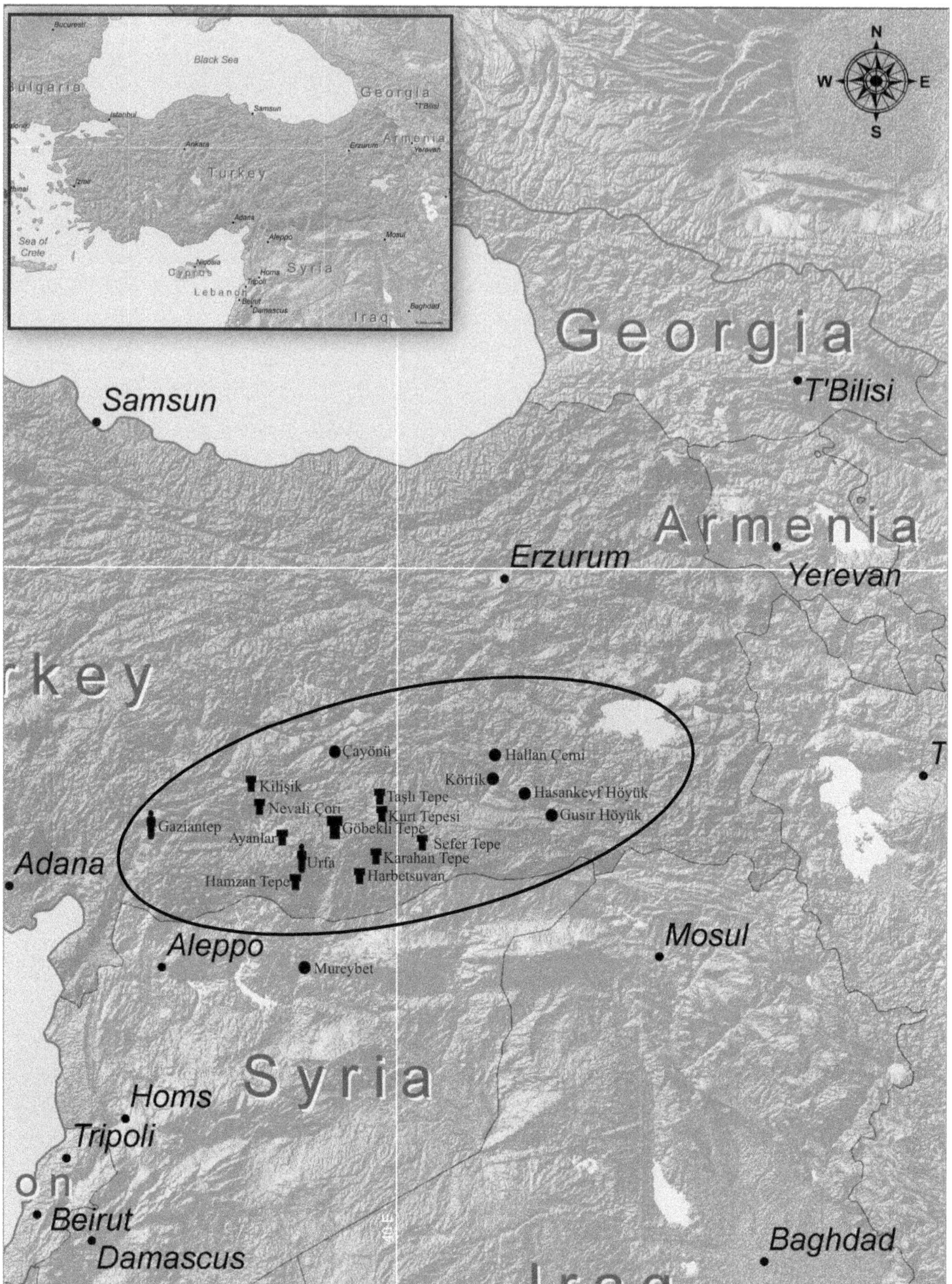

Turkey - Southeastern region.
Source: José Martinho Lourenço.

Chapter 2

A Cult Tradition of the Pre-Pottery Neolithic Period in the Southeastern Region of Turkey

Bahattin Çelik

Associate Professor, Ardahan University, Faculty of Human Sciences and Literature, Department of Archaeology, Yenisey Campus 75000-Ardahan, Turkey
bahattincelik@ardahan.edu.tr

Abstract: Some of the Neolithic period settlements, recently discovered during the surface exploration surveys and excavations conducted in Şanlıurfa province at southeast region of Turkey, brought to evidence cult buildings. Such cult buildings contain pillars apparently similar to pillar cult buildings characteristic of Şanlıurfa, Adıyaman, Siirt, Batman and Gaziantep provinces located in Southeast Anatolia Region. In general, the relationship between the cult buildings and the pillars is widely recognized. However, the proposed theories, as whether the settlements containing pillars are solely in the form of cult centers is still under debate. The fact that the settlements containing cult buildings are very close to each other, co-existence of both civilian and cult buildings as is the case in Çayönü and *Nevali Çori,* or sole existence of cult areas, as is the case in *Göbekli Tepe* settlement remain yet unexplained, regarding the period in question. Based on the analogy of the pillars located in the cult buildings discovered in the settlements recently excavated in Şanlıurfa', it is proposed that such pillar is coetaneous with Layer II of *Göbekli Tepe* and the cult building from *Nevali Çori.* The cult tradition in the region is frequent until the end of Pre-Pottery Neolithic Period A and to the midst of Period B.

Keywords: Şanlıurfa, "T" shaped Pillar, Pre-Pottery Neolithic Period, and the Cult Building.

1. Introduction

Archaeological excavations of settlements such as Çayönü, Hallan Çemi, Körtik Tepe, Gusir Höyük, Hasankeyf Höyük, Nevali Çori, Göbekli Tepe, Şanlıurfa-Yeni Mahalle, Karahan Tepe, Sefer Tepe, Hamzan Tepe, Taşlı Tepe, Kurt Tepesi and Harbetsuvan Tepesi, which reflect the earliest stages of the Pre-Pottery Neolithic Period, in Southeast Anatolia Region (Map 1), is an indicator that the region played a significant role in emergence of the Neolithic lifestyle (Figure 1).

The general perception is that in early stages societies built their economies on the hunter gatherer practices. The "Gazelle Hunt Tradition" originated from the Natufian period in hunting, and corresponding to an increase in the variety of flint tools enabling such lifestyle to persist for approximately 1000 years, leading to the construction of cult buildings. Most probably, such settlements were covered with earth and abandoned, however from the end of 9 thousand B.C., the sites that accommodated the first farming societies started to emerge at the plains and waterfronts.

The recent studies conducted in Şanlıurfa province enabled the discovery of settlements that point out the existence of a distinct era during the Pre-Pottery Neolithic Period. It is accepted that settlements founded at highland terrain with altitudes varying in the range from 600m to 1000m adopted a lifestyle that rather depend on hunter gatherer economy. The sites inhabited by such societies, who did not engage in agricultural activities, but displayed signs indicating that cereals fit for cultivation were part of the culture, are Göbekli Tepe, Nevali Çori, Şanlıurfa-Yeni Mahalle settlements which were either excavated or are currently under excavation. This peculiarity should probably be present in similar settlements such as Hamzan Tepe, Karahan Tepe, Sefer Tepe, Taşlı Tepe, Kurt Tepesi and Harbetsuvan Tepesi, which are not yet excavated. Another characteristic of the settlements in the region is that all settlements feature "T" shaped pillars, such as Göbekli Tepe and Nevali Çori. Furthermore, two artefacts displayed in Adıyaman and Gaziantep Museums cannot be localized with certainty further represent similar finds that match the characteristics, may of this period.

The number of settlements, where "T" shaped pillars were revealed, increased as a consequence of recent studies conducted in Şanlıurfa province. The settlements recently excavated can be listed as Nevali Çori, Göbekli Tepe, Şanlıurfa-Yeni Mahalle, Karahan Tepe, Hamzan Tepe, Sefer Tepe, Taşlı Tepe, Kurt Tepesi, Harbetsuvan Tepesi and Ayanlar Höyük.

2. Recently Discovered Neolithic Settlements

Recently Taşlı Tepe, Kurt Tepesi, Harbetsuvan Tepesi and Ayanlar Höyük settlements were added to settlements list characterized by "T" shaped pillars, which are Şanlıurfa-Yeni Mahalle, Karahan Tepe, Hamzan Tepe and Sefer Tepe settlements. Out of all these settlements, Ayanlar Höyük and Karahan Tepe settlements are major settlements at the scale of Göbekli Tepe as they cover an area larger than 100 decares[1].

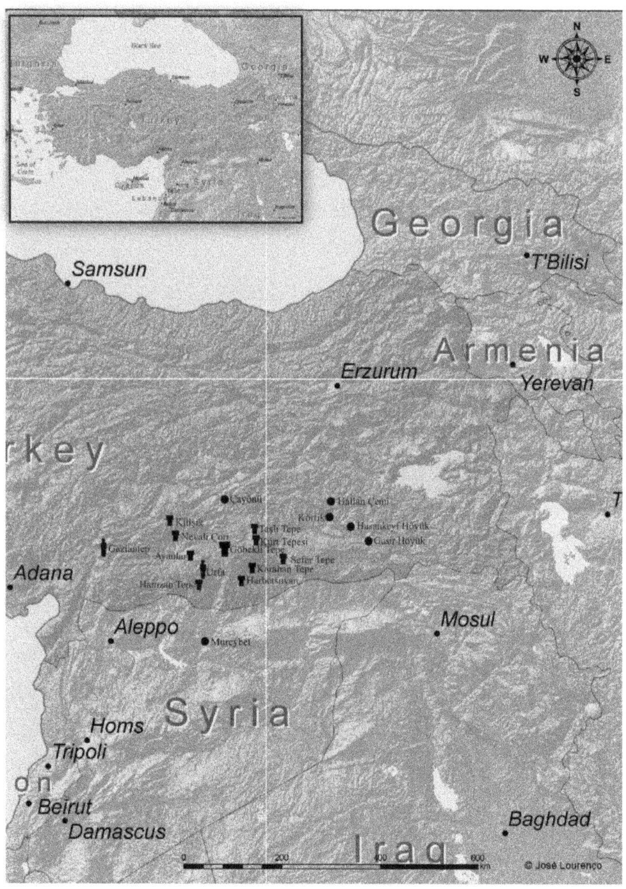

Map 1. Neolithic sites in Southeast Anatolia region. Source: by the Authors.

2.1. Şanlıurfa-Yeni Mahalle (Balıklıgöl Höyüğü)

A salvage excavation was carried out on the revealed portion of the mound in Yeni Mahalle quarter located at sacred Balıklıgöl area within the former Şanlıurfa downtown locality (Çelik 2000a, 4-6; Çelik 2007, 165-178; Çelik 2011a, 139-164). The length of excavated soil profile was approximately 15 meters, with a height varying in the range from 1 meter to 2 meters, and a width varying in the range of 30 cm up to 70 cm. The excavation was carried out only for a brief period of time due to narrowness of the excavation site and the roadside location of the profile. 13 layers were identified in the profile, all from Pre-Pottery Neolithic Period. Some of the base layers observed at the profile were excavated, and four distinct *terrazzo* type floor layers were discovered in separate stratigraphical layers. Traces pertaining to the remnants of round plan buildings were discovered, where it is clearly perceptible that the floors of such buildings were also covered with *terrazzo* floors.

The lithic finds from the Yeni Mahalle profile comprise flint stone and obsidian, although in very scarce quantities. When the arrowheads discovered are studied, their resemblance those encountered in the region from the end of the Pre-Pottery Neolithic Period A until the intermediate stage of Pre-Pottery Neolithic Period B is apparent (Cauvin 1994, 78-95). Similar arrowheads are also characteristic of settlements such as Göbekli Tepe (Schmidt 2001, p. 52, figure 10: 3,4,6), Nevali Çori (Schmidt 1988, 171-174, abb.11:1-6, abb.12:1-3), Çayönü[2], Cheikh Hassan (Abbes 1993, figures 7.13,14, figures. 8.10), Mureybet IVb (Cauvin 1994, p. 79, figure 24:1, 3), Cafer Höyük (Cauvin 1994, figure 26:3) and Karahan Tepe (Çelik 2000b, 6-8).

The radiocarbon analyses carried out on the coal samples collected from the excavations at Yeni Mahalle revealed that the settlement is coetaneous with the other Neolithic centres located in the region. The fact that Urfa statue was by coincidence in the vicinity of the settlement in 1993 during the salvage excavation carried out in the area, was proven to be from a Neolithic settlement (Hauptmann 2003, 622-636). The style of the statue demonstrates that it is a successor of the "T" shaped pillars discovered in Göbekli Tepe and Nevali Çori (Figure 2).

Moreover, the studies conducted in Yeni Mahalle quarter further revealed a piece of pillar, which was picked up and used on the bonded wall of a cave, which was erected *post facto* (Çelik 2014, Figure 21). This particular piece pointed out to the existence of "T" shaped pillar tradition in Yeni Mahalle settlement.

2.2. Hamzan Tepe

Hamzan Tepe settlement is located 10 km south of Şanlıurfa and is a small scale settlement which initially served as an open air station during the Palaeolithic Age and then inhabited during the Neolithic Period (Çelik 2010, 257-268; Çelik 2004, 3-5). Presence of a "T" shaped pillar (Figure 3), as well as cisterns with broad brinks carved into the bedrock, small burrows that appear to be

[1] Göbekli Tepe settlement covers an area of circa 80 decares.

[2] The majority of the arrowheads of this type are from the Channelled Buildings period. See Coşkunsu 1999, p. 223.

constructed by employing pool construction technique, and the remnants of round plan buildings revealed at Hamzan Tepe settlement indicate that the settlement is coetaneous with the other Neolithic settlements in the region (Beile-Bohn *et al.* 1998, 47-50, abb. 20). Hamzan Tepe settlement accommodates both civilian and cult areas simultaneously, as such in Nevali Çori and Çayönü settlements (Çelik 2014, p. 22). Flint finds from Lower Palaeolithic period, Byblos and Nemrik type arrowheads and scarce amount of obsidian blades and flake fragments peculiar to the Pre-Pottery Neolithic period were discovered during the studies (Çelik 2010, 259-262).

Figure 1. Urfa-Yeni Mahalle statue (photo by G. Tan).

2.3. Karahan Tepe

Karahan Tepe is located 63 km southeast of Şanlıurfa, between the limestone plateaus also known as Tektek Mountains (Çelik 2000b, 6-8; Çelik 2011b, 241-253). The most significant feature of the settlement is that the settlement covers an area identical to the scale of Göbekli Tepe settlement, and that there are 266 *in-situ* "T" shaped pillars (Çelik 2000b, p. 6) present at the settlement. Inhabited only during the Pre-Pottery Neolithic Period, some of the "T" shaped pillars revealed at the settlement as a result of illegal excavations featured rounded upper edges (Figure 4), snake reliefs, while other pillars contained triangular headed snake reliefs. Animal figures carved by employing scraping technique are also discovered on portions of some pillars (Çelik 2011b, figure 12a-b). Furthermore, a statue fragment with broken phallus was also discovered as identical to the finds in Göbekli Tepe (Çelik 2011c, 91-95). A stone quarry where 4m long "T" shaped pillar, not yet fully excavated, the pools which are also carved into the bedrock, and small burrows used for construction of pools discovered in Karahan Tepe settlement demonstrate that the settlement presents identical characteristics, comparable to other Neolithic settlements in the region (Beile-Bohn *et al.* 1998, 47-50, abb. 20). The studies conducted at the settlement revealed bipolar and unipolar cores, end scrapers, perforators, burins, sickle blades, Byblos, Nemrik and Aswad type arrowheads peculiar to the Pre-Pottery Neolithic period (Çelik 2011b, 243-246, figures 17-23).

2.4. Sefer Tepe

Sefer Tepe settlement is located approximately 70 km east of Şanlıurfa, within the borders of Viranşehir borough (Çelik 2006, 23-25). The settlement site is a small mound, and was established at the spot where the plateaus end and the plain starts. The plain so-called Viranşehir Plain extends towards the north and east of Sefer Tepe settlement. The south and west of the settlement is surrounded by the calcareous plateaus known as Tektek Mountains.

There are 16 "T" shaped pillars on the surface of the settlement, all of which were erected *in-situ* style (Güler *et al.* 2012, figure 7-9; Çelik 2006, p. 23). With this positioning, the pillars substantially resemble the pillars at Göbekli Tepe Layer II. architecture (Schmidt 2002, p. 8, figure 7 see L10-71, L9-80, L9-55, L9-56 trenches), the pillars at Nevali Çori (Hauptmann 1991/1992, p. 28, abb. 21) and the *in-situ* pillars located on the surface of Karahan Tepe (Çelik 2000b, 6-7). Furthermore, an intact "T" shaped pillar, with 1.98 cm height revealed as a result of illegal excavations, was also discovered (Figure 5). Byblos type arrowheads made of flint and obsidian blade fragments, although in scarce amounts, were discovered in the settlement (Güler *et al.* 2013, figure 22; Çelik 2006, 24-25).

Figure 2. An in-situ pillar from Hamzan Tepe (photo by B. Çelik).

Figure 3. Pillar with snake relief from Karahan Tepe (photo by B. Çelik).

Figure 4. "T" shaped pillar from Sefer Tepe. (Illustrated by B. Çelik).

2.5. Taşlı Tepe

Taşlı Tepe is located approximately 65 km northeast of Şanlıurfa, within the provincial borders of Siverek borough. Characterized as a small-scale mound, the settlement covers a surface area of approximately 12 decares (Çelik *et al.* 2011, 225-236).

Today, the area covered by the settlement is used for agricultural activities. Majority of the small finds observed at Taşlı Tepe settlement are bipolar flint cores, flakes, blades and production wastes. Furthermore, drills and flakes made of obsidian were also discovered. When the tools made of flint were analysed as a whole, it is observed that these tools, such as arrowhead and sickle blades, are characterized as belonging to the Pre-Pottery Neolithic Period in terms of technology and typology.

"T" shaped pillar and pillar fragments are frequently found at the Taşlı Tepe settlement as a result of illegal excavations. The apparent length of a pillar discovered in fragments is 152 cm (Figure 6).

By virtue of these dimensions, the pillars substantially resemble the Göbekli Tepe Layer II pillars (Schmidt 2002, p. 8, figure 7 see L10-71, L9-80, L9-55, L9-56 trenches), pillars of the Nevali Çori temple building (Hauptmann 1991/1992, p. 28, Abb. 21), and those located at the surface of Karahan Tepe (Çelik 2000b, 6-7, figure 1) and Sefer Tepe (Güler *et al.* 2012, figure7-9; Çelik 2006, 23-25, figure 2) settlements. Moreover, a fragment of terrazzo floor was also discovered at Taşlı Tepe (Çelik *et al.* 2011, figure 8). Analogous terrazzo floors revealed the great majority of settlements from the Neolithic period are also encountered at Göbekli Tepe, Nevali Çori (Hauptmann 2007, p. 142, figure 7, figure 8a-b) and Şanlıurfa Yeni Mahalle (Çelik 2007, figure 16; Çelik 2011a, 141-143, figure14-16) mound in the region. In conclusion, the excavated and exposed finds at the settlement indicate that Taşlı Tepe settlement is coetaneous with other Neolithic settlements in the region.

2.6. Kurt Tepesi

Discovered recently, Kurt Tepesi settlement (Güler and Çelik 2015, 78-79, pic. 1-2,21) is located 47 km east of Şanlıurfa province and 3 km south of Sumaklı village. Kurt Tepesi settlement is located on a hill that dominates Çoban Creek Pass, which serves as a passageway between Harran Plain and Viranşehir region (Çelik 2014, p. 11). It is a small mound established on a ridge formed by high calcareous plateaus and covers an area of approximately 7 decares.

Small cavern groups and a pool carved on the bedrock were identified on the calcareous rocks surrounding the mound. Furthermore, the quarries identifyed as the probable extraction site for the "T" shaped pillars are also located northeast of the hill.

"T" shaped pillars revealed as a result of an illegal excavation pit in Kurt Tepesi settlement are identifyed as belonguing to Pre-Pottery Neolithic Period. The pillars are approximately 2.5 m long, with width varying in the range of 50 cm to 70 cm, and their thickness is 25 cm. One of the "T" shaped pillars contains both a broad groove in the form of a necktie and a single-strip chevron pattern on a polished area located at the side of the pillar (Figure 7).

Figure 5. An exemplary pillar from Taşlı Tepe (photo by B. Çelik).

Similar patterns are also recognized from the "T" shaped pillars registered at Nevali Çori (Schmidt 2010, figure 5) and Göbekli Tepe (Schmidt 2010, figure 5; Schmidt 2007, figure 11). The studies conducted at Kurt Tepesi revealed that Flint is extensivly used as raw material, and that the obsidian is present in very scarce quantities. The finds excavated from this site include Byblos type arrowheads made of Flintstone, scrapers, drills, silica sickle blades and obsidian blades. Moreover, stone beads and pestle parts made from basalt stone were also discovered. The dimensions of the pillars here are similar with the Cult Building in Nevali Çori and Layer II of Göbekli Tepe. Consequently, Kurt Tepesi settlement is considered to be coetaneous with other Neolithic settlements in the region.

2.7. Harbetsuvan Tepesi

Discovered recently, Harbetsuvan Tepesi is located 45 km east of Şanlıurfa, between calcareous plateaus named Tektek Mountains. Its altitude above sea level is 714 m. The settlement covers an area of circa 6 decares. The settlement is considered to have been inhabited only during the Pre-Pottery Neolithic Period. The most significant characteristic of the settlement are the existence of *in situ* "T" shaped pillars. Several "T" shaped pillars were deliberately destroyed as a result of illegal excavations. One of the broken pillars with no decoration was re-assembled and identified to be 160 cm long, 70 cm to 50 cm wide with a thickness of 22 cm (Figure 8) (Çelik 2014, 12-14, figure 7).

Another "T" shaped pillar discovered in the settlement contains necktie and finger reliefs (Çelik 2014, figure 8). *Harbetsuvan* settlement is located approximately 7 km southwest of Karahan Tepe settlement. Traces of a circular foundation with circa 15 m diameter are present on the settlement surface. As it stands, the building resembles circular "F Building" discovered at Layer II/III of Göbekli Tepe (Notroff *et al.* 2016, figure 5.1; Schmidt 2010, figure 2). The studies conducted in the settlement revealed that the raw material extensively used is Flintstone, and a small amount of obsidian finds are also present. Bipolar cores made of Flint, shoulder blades and silica sickle blades, Byblos type arrowheads and obsidian blade pieces, which are peculiar to Pre-Pottery Neolithic period, were discovered. The pillars that resemble those with no relief at *Harbetsuvan* settlement, the majority were discovered in *Karahan Tepe* (Çelik 2011b, figure 8, 10). The settlement appears to be a satellite settlement due to its proximity to Karahan Tepe. Harbetsuvan Tepesi is considered to be a settlement of almost identical scale to the Sefer Tepe Hamzan Tepe, Kurt Tepesi and Taşlı Tepe settlements due to its surface area of 5 decares. The dimensions of the pillars here are similar with the cult building in Nevali Çori and Layer II of *Göbekli Tepe*. Based on similarities, Harbetsuvan Tepesi settlement should be dated to the same period as other settlements in the region.

2.8. Ayanlar Höyük

Discovered in 2013 for the first time, Ayanlar Höyük (Çelik 2014, p. 19, figures 18-19) is located partially underneath, and extends towards north of a village located circa 30 km west of Şanlıurfa. The settlement covers an area of circa 140 decares.The height of the mound is approximately 10 m. Its altitude above sea level is 733 m. The village settlement covers the southern part of the mound.

Figure 6. An exemplary patterned pillar from Kurt Tepesi (photo by B. Çelik).

There are total of 6 knolls on the mound. Today, the land is covered with pistachio groves. The studies conducted revealed ceramics from early and middle Byzantium periods as well as finds from Pre-Pottery Neolithic period. Moreover, blade, flake fragments, arrowhead and scraper fragments all made of Flintstone, bipolar and mono-polar cores, core renewal pieces, shoulder blades, hammers and very scarce obsidian flakes and blades were encountered. Stone bowls made of limestone, basalt lower and upper grinding stones and pestles, chlorite stone vessel fragments and stone dish fragments (Ercan and Çelik 2013, 16-20) are amongst the finds excavated from the site.

A stone piece with hollow center (Çelik 2014, figure 19; see Schmidt 2010, figure 21 for similar finds) which we recognize from the cult buildings that accommodate "T" shaped pillars was also discovered at the village cemetery located on one of the knolls on the mound. Although no "T" shaped pillar were discovered at Ayanlar Höyüğü, the stone pieces disclosed here offer important hints that this settlement might be a cult center just like Göbekli Tepe and Karahan Tepe. In particular, a statue fragment identifyed as a lion's head points out to the fact that Ayanlar Höyüğü accommodated cult buildings (Ercan and Çelik 2013, figures 1a-d, 2a-d, 3a-d).

Ayanlar Höyük settlement is coetaneous with other Neolithic settlements in the region due to the similar characteristics to those encountered at Göbekli Tepe and Karahan Tepe.

3. Adıyaman Kilişik Locality

During 1960s, one "T" shaped pillar were discovered in the vicinity of Kilisik village in Adıyaman-Kahta borough. Currently on display at Adıyaman Museum, the height of this pillar is approximately 80 cm. This pillar also bears similar features resembling the pillars discovered in Göbekli Tepe, Nevali Çori, Karahan Tepe, Hamzan Tepe and Sefer Tepe, Harbetsuvan Tepesi and Kurt Tepesi. The settlement site from which this pillar was, is still not yet discovered (Hauptmann 2000, 5-9; Hauptmann 2012, 13-22). However, such pillar was found on the west banks of River Euphrates, this is an extremely important find, as this is the only known record in this particular geographical region. Kilişik pillar can be dated to the same period as other settlements in relative proximity to the region.

3.1. Gaziantep Statue

Though the exact location of its discovery is still unknown its magnificence grants it a place in Gaziantep Museum and considered to be a successor of the "T" shaped pillars, bears similar characteristics with the statues excavated at Göbekli Tepe, Nevali Çori and Karahan Tepe (Çelik 2005, 28-29). This statue is an important and remarkable artefact as it demonstrates the fact that the "T" shaped pillar tradition expanded up to the Gaziantep Region, the west bank of River Euphrates (Bulgan and Çelik 2011, 85-90). The statue is dated as belonguing to the early Pre-Pottery Neolithic Period B.

Figure 7. An exemplary pillar from Harbetsuvan Tepesi (photo by B. Çelik).

Figure 8. A pillar from Harbetsuvan Tepesi (photo by B. Çelik).

4. Evaluation and Conclusion

The conducted studies revealed the fact that Şanlıurfa-Yeni Mahalle, Sefer Tepe, Taşlı Tepe, Hamzan Tepe, Karahan Tepe, Kurt Tepesi, Ayanlar Höyük and Harbetsuvan Tepesi settlements present identical characteristics with Layer II of Göbekli Tepe and Nevali Çori Cult Building (Moetz and Çelik 2012, 695-709). The existence of round plan buildings only encountered in Hamzan Tepe and Şanlıurfa-Yeni Mahalle out of listed settlements are unique characteristic not yet observed in any other location within Şanlıurfa region. Similar structures to the round plan buildings dated to early era of Pre-Pottery Neolithic Period are also identifyed from settlements such as Çayönü, Hallan Çemi (Rosenberg 2007, 1-11), Gusir Höyük (Karul 2011, 1-17), Körtik Tepe (Özkaya and San 2007, 21-36) and Hasankeyf Höyük (Miyake *et al.* 2012, 3-7) in the region, though further studies are required to establish a paralell.

The common trait of settlements such as Göbekli Tepe, Nevali Çori, Karahan Tepe, Sefer Tepe, Taşlı Tepe, Hamzan Tepe, Şanlıurfa-Yeni Mahalle, Kurt Tepesi, Ayanlar Höyük, and Harbetsuvan Tepesi, and the finds such as the pillar from Adıyaman Kilişik Locality and Gaziantep Statue is that pillars or statues that are successors of these pillars are all identifyed as belonging to the same period and therefore contemporaneous in terms of cultural practices. Such pillars are erected as pairs opposing each other at the centre of buildings generally featuring round or square plan. This building tradition is further experienced at Qermez Dere, and Nemrik settlements located in n Iraq, which are dated to early PPNA (Sicher-Akman 2001, 389-394).

Presence of a small "T" shaped pillar discovered at Layer IIIA of Mureybet settlement located in Lower Euphrates valley in Syria (Stordeur and Lebreton 2008, 619-644) demonstrates the fact that the pillar architectural tradition also extended towards southern parts of the region. Moreover, similar pillars are also discovered at Gusir Höyük currently under excavation at areas soon to be flooded by Ilısu Dam (Karul 2011, figure 5).

The tradition of pillar erection experienced during the period that elapse from the end of Pre-Pottery Neolithic Period A[3] until the midst of PPNB[4] was discontinued at the end of Pre-Pottery Neolithic Period B[5]. After this period, even the statues from Neolithic Period, which are considered to be succession of the pillar tradition, are not part of the archaeological finds. This fact might probably arise from lack of research on the Pre-Pottery Neolithic Period. However, it is highly possible that future research and studies may reveal many more settlements in Gaziantep, Mardin and Adıyaman provinces where the Cult Building and pillar tradition of this period is most frequent.

Abbreviations and Bibliography

Abbes, Fredrich., "Méthode d'approce de la variabilité du debitagé laminaire, application à desarmatures perçantes de Cheikh Hassan (Syrie. VIIIe millénaire B.C.)." *Cahiers del'Euphrate 7*, (1993): 119-150.

Beile-Bohn, Manuela., Christopher Gerber, Michael Morsch and Klaus Schmidt. "Neolithische Forschungen in Obermesopotamien. Gürcütepe und Göbekli Tepe." *Istanbuler Mitteilungen 48*, (1998): 5-78.

Bulgan, Fatma. and Çelik, B., "A New Statue From Gaziantep in Southeast Turkey / Türkiye'nin Güneydoğusundaki Gaziantep'ten

[3] End of circa 10 thousand BC.
[4] Midst of circa 9 thousand BC.
[5] End of circa 9 thousand BC.

Yeni Bir Heykel." In *Işın Yalçınkaya'ya Armağan Kitabı, Studies in Honor of Işın Yalçınkaya*, Edited by Harun Taşkıran, Metin Kartal, Kadriye Özçelik, M.Beray Kösem and Gizem Kartal, 85-90, Ankara: Bilgin Kültür Sanat Yayınları, 2011.

Cauvin, Jaques. *Naissance des divinitès, naissance de l'agriculture*. La révolution des symboles au Néolithique, Editions CNRS, Paris: 1994.

Coşkunsu, Güner. *Classification of Çayönü Pre-Pottery Neolithic Period Arrowheads According to Morphological Characteristics and Identification of the Functions via Trace of Use Analysis of the Flintstone Arrowheads / Çayönü Çanak Çömleksiz Neolitik Dönem Okuçlarının Biçimsel Özelliklerine Göre Sınıflandırılması ve Çakmaktaşı Okuçlarının Kullanım İzi Analizi ile İşlevlerinin Belirlenmesi*. Unpublished Post Graduate Thesis / Istanbul University, Institute of Social Sciences, Faulty of Literature, Prehistory Major, Istanbul: 1999.

Çelik, Bahattin, "An Early Neolithic Settlement in the Centre of Sanliurfa, Turkey", *Neo-Lithics 2/3* (2000): 4-6.

Çelik, Bahattin, "A New Early-Neolithic Settlement: Karahan Tepe", *Neo-Lithics 2-3* (2000): 6-8.

Çelik, Bahattin, "A New Early Neolithic Settlement in South-eastern Turkey: Hamzan Tepe", *Neo-Lithics 04-2* (2004): 3-5.

Çelik, Bahattin, "A New Statue of the Early Pre-Pottery Neolithic Period from Gaziantep, South-eastern Turkey", *Neo-Lithics 05-1* (2005): 28-29.

Çelik, Bahattin, "A New Early Neolithic Settlement in South-eastern Turkey: Sefer Tepe", *Neo-Lithics 06-1*, (2006): 23-25.

Çelik, Bahattin, "Şanlıurfa-Yeni Mahalle, Balıklıgöl Höyüğü", In *Anadolu'da Uygarlığın Doğuşu ve Avrupa'ya Yayılımı. Türkiye'de Neolithic Dönem, Yeni Kazılar, Yeni Bulgular / Birth of Civilization in Anatolia and Dissemination to Europe / Neolithic Period in Turkey, New Excavations and New Finds*, edited by. Mehmet Özdoğan and Nezih Başgelen, 165–178. Istanbul: Archaeology and Art Publications, 2007.

Çelik, Bahattin, "Hamzan Tepe in the Light of New Finds", *Documenta Preahistorica XXXVII* (2010): 257-268.

Çelik, Bahattin: "Şanlıurfa-Yeni Mahalle", In *The Neolithic in Turkey. New Excavation and New Research*, edited by Mehmet Özdoğan, Nezih Başgelen and Peter Kuniholm, 139-164. Istanbul: Archaeology and Art Publications, 2011.

Çelik, Bahattin, "Karahan Tepe: A new cultural Centre in the Urfa area in Turkey", *Documenta Praehistorica XXXVIII* (2011): 241-253.

Çelik, Bahattin, "A New Statue From Karahan Tepe." in: *Işın Yalçınkaya'ya Armağan Kitabı, Studies in Honor of Işın Yalçınkaya*, Edited by Harun Taşkıran, Metin Kartal, Kadriye Özçelik, M.Beray Kösem and Gizem Kartal, 91-95, Ankara: Bilgin Kültür Sanat Yayınları, 2011.

Çelik, Bahattin, Güler, Mustafa and Güler, Gül. "A New Pre-Pottery Neolithic Settlement in Southeast Turkey: Taşlı Tepe", *Anatolia / Anadolu 37* (2011): 225-236.

Çelik, Bahattin, "Differences and Similarities between the Settlements in Şanlıurfa Region where "T" Shaped Pillars are Discovered." *TÜBA-AR 17* (2014): 9-23.

Ercan, Müslüm. and Çelik, Bahattin. "Şanlıurfa Müzesi'nden Neolitik Döneme Ait Bir Grup Eser / A Group of Artefacts From Neolithic Period in Şanlıurfa Museum", *Anadolu/Anatolia 39* (2013): 13-54.

Güler, Mustafa and Çelik, Bahattin. "Şanlıurfa Region Neolithic Period Research.", *Belgü 1/1* (2015): 75-102.

Güler, Mustafa, Çelik, Bahattin and Güler, Gül. "Viranşehir İlçesinden Yeni Çanak Çömleksiz Neolitik Dönem Yerleşimler / New Pre-Pottery Neolithic Settlements from Viranşehir District", *Anadolu / Anatolia 38* (2012): 157-191.

Güler, Gül, Çelik, Bahattin and Güler, Mustafa. "New Pre-Pottery Neolithic sites and cult centres in the Urfa Region", *Documenta Peahistorica XL* (2013): 291-304.

Hauptmann, Harald. "Eine Siedlung des akeramischen Neolithikums am mittleren Euphrat", *Nürnberger Blaetter zur Archaeologie 8/9* (1991/92): 15-33.

Hauptmann, Harald. "Ein frühneolithisches Kultbild aus Kommogene", In *Gottkönige am Euphrat, Zaberns Bildbände zur Archaeologie*, Edited by J. Wagner, 5-9, Munchen: 2000.

Hauptmann, Harald. "Eine frühneolitische Kultfigur aus Urfa", In *From Village to Cities. Early Villages in the Near East*, Edited by M. Özdogan, H. Hauptmann and N. Başgelen, Vol. 1, 622-636. Istanbul: Archaeology and Art Publications, 2003.

Hauptmann, Harald. "Neolithic Period at Nevali Çori and Urfa Region", In *Birth of Civilization in Anatolia and Dissemination to Europe / Neolithic Period in Turkey, New Excavations and New Finds / Anadolu'da Uygarlığın Doğuşu ve Avrupa'ya Yayılımı. Türkiye'de Neolithic Dönem, Yeni Kazılar, Yeni Bulgular,* Edited by M. Özdoğan and N. Başgelen, 131-164. Istanbul: Archaeology and Art Publications, 2007.

Hauptmann, Harald. „Ein fruhneolithisches Kultbild aus Kommagene", In *Gottkönige am Euphrat: Neue Ausgrabungen und Forschungen in Kommagene*, Edited by J. Wagner, 13-22. Darmstadt / Mainz: 2012.

Karul, Necmi. "Gusir Höyük", In *The Neolithic in Turkey, New Excavation and New Research, The Tigris Basin*, Edited by M. Özdoğan, N. Başgelen and P. Kuniholm, 1-17. Istanbul: Archaeology and Arts Publications, 2011.

Miyake, Yuyaka, Maeda, O., Tanno, K., Hongo, Hitomi and Gündem, C.Y., "New Excavations at Hasankeyf Höyük: A 10th millennium cal. BC site on the Upper Tigris, Southeast Anatolia", *Neo-Lithics 1/12* (2012): 3-7.

Moetz, Kemal and Çelik, Bahattin. "T Shaped Pillar Sites in the Landscape around Urfa." in: *Proceedings of the 7th International Congress on the Archaeology of the Ancient Near East. Vol. 1: Mega-cities & Mega-sites*, Edited by R. Matthews and J. Curtis, 695-709. Wiesbaden, Harrassowitz Verlag: 2012.

Notroff, Jens., Dietrich, Oliver. and Schmidt, Klaus., "Gathering of the Dead? The Early Neolithic Sanctuaries of Göbekli Tepe, South-eastern Turkey." In *Death Rituals, Social Order and the Archaeology of Immortality in the Ancient World "Death Shall Have No Dominion"*, Edited by C. Refrew, M.J. Boyd, and I. Morley, 65-81, Cambridge: Cambridge University Press, 2016.

Özkaya, Vecihi. and San, Oya. "Körtik Tepe, Initial Observations on Cultural texture in the light of Finds / Bulgular Işığında Kültürel Doku Üzerine İlk Gözlemler." In *Birth of Civilization in Anatolia and Dissemination to Europe, Neolithic Period in Turkey, New Excavations and New Finds / Anadolu'da Uygarlığın Doğuşu ve Avrupa'ya Yayılımı. Türkiye'de Neolitik Dönem, Yeni*

Kazılar, Yeni Bulgular, 21-36. Istanbul: Archaeology and Art Publications, 2007.

Rosenberg, Michael., "Hallan Çemi", In *Birth of Civilization in Anatolia and Dissemination to Europe, Neolithic Period in Turkey, New Excavations and New Finds / Anadolu'da Uygarlığın Doğuşu ve Avrupa'ya Yayılımı. Türkiye'de Neolitik Dönem, Yeni Kazılar, Yeni Bulgular,* Edited by M. Özdoğan and N. Başgelen, 1-11. Istanbul: Archaeology and Art Publications, 2007.

Schmidt, Klaus, "Nevali Çori: Zum Typenspectrum der Silexindustrie und der Übrigen Kleinfunde", *Anatolica 15* (1988): 161-201.

Schmidt, Klaus, "Göbekli Tepe, Southeastern Turkey. A preliminary report on the 1995-1999 excavations" *Paléorient 26/1* (2001): 45-54.

Schmidt, Klaus, "The 2002 Excavations at Göbekli Tepe (Southeastern Turkey), Impressions from an Enigmatic Site", *Neo-Lithics 2/2* (2002): 8-13.

Schmidt, Klaus, "Göbekli Tepe", In *Birth of Civilization in Anatolia and Dissemination to Europe, Neolithic Period in Turkey, New Excavations and New Finds / Anadolu'da Uygarlığın Doğuşu ve Avrupa'ya Yayılımı. Türkiye'de Neolitik Dönem, Yeni Kazılar, Yeni Bulgular,* Edited by M. Özdoğan and N. Başgelen, 115-129. Istanbul: Archaeology and Art Publications, 2007.

Schmidt, Klaus, "Göbekli Tepe - the Stone Age Sanctuaries. New results of ongoing excavations with a special focus on sculptures and high reliefs" *Documenta Praehistorica XXXVII* (2010): 239-255.

Sicher-Akman, Martina. "Die Rundhütte als Ursprung Zur Entwicklung erster runder Hütten zum geregelten Rechteckbau." Lux orientis In *Archaeologie zwischen Asien und Europa, Festschrift für Harald Hauptmann zum 65.* Edited by R. M. Boehmer and Joseph Maran, 389-394. Geburtstag. Rahden: 2001.

Stordeur, Daniela. and Lebreton, M. "Figurines pierres à rainures, «petits objets divers » et manches de Mureybet." In *Le site néolithique de Tell Mureybet (Syrie du Nord), En homage à Jacques Cauvin,* BAR International Series 1843, Vol. II, Edited by J. J. Ibáñez, 619-644. Oxford: British Archaeological Reports, 2008.

Spain - Cantabrian region.
Source: José Martinho Lourenço.

Chapter 3

Circulation of Products or Ideas? Earliest Pottery Evidence in the Cantabrian Region (North Spain)

Miriam Cubas

BioArCh-University of York, Sociedad de Ciencias Aranzadi, Wentworth Way, YO10 5DD
mcubas.morera@gmail.com

Abstract: Pottery is one of the main elements that have been repeatedly used to determine the cultural filiation of human groups and their possible medium or long distance contacts, through patterns of morphological and decorative similarity of the vessels. Mineralogical and chemical analytical techniques allow new hypothesis to be proposed about the local or distant provenance of the raw materials. In this contribution, the technological features from the first evidences of pottery in the Iberian Peninsula are reappraised, followed by a case study focusing on the Cantabrian region. In this region, the late use of pottery technology has been recorded enabling us to correlate these products with those documented in neighbouring areas.

Keywords: pottery; analytical techniques; raw material procurement; cultural transmission; Neolithic.

1. Introduction

The processes of pottery technology usage in Europe has traditionally been associated with the spread and consolidation of farming. However, an increasing number of studies focused on the first evidence of pottery in diverse geographic areas reveals that such processes were characterised by their own dynamics, independently of the development of farming economies. In this way, the well-known example of Jomon pottery (e.g. Budja 2011; Sakaguchi 2009) has been associated with pottery from the Amur valley in Russia (Kuzmin 2010, 2013a, b, c) and other cases in the far south-east of China (Chi 2002). Further examples are known in other continents in which the connection between a farming economy and the introduction of ceramic technology is absent (Farrell *et al.* 2014; Huysecom *et al.* 2009). In Europe, this absence of a link between ceramics and farming has been cited for sites attributed to the Ertebølle culture in the Baltic (Hallgren 2004) and other possible late hunter-gather societies, such as La Hoguette, Limburg and Swifterbant (Crombé 2009).

Nonetheless, in general terms, the introduction of pottery technology in Western Europe is related to the expansion of *Linearbandkeramik* in central Europe and *impressa* ware in the Mediterranean. Within these general trends, the appearance of pottery technology in the Iberian Peninsula is normally associated with the spread of the Neolithic, although in a few cases it has been cited in hunter-gatherers contexts (see, among others, Rojo *et al.* 2015; Utrilla and Mazo 2014).

Pottery is one of the main elements that have been repeatedly used to determine the cultural filiation of human groups and their possible medium or long distance contacts, through patterns of morphological and decorative similarity. Aspects related to these traits have frequently been used to establish possible influences on pottery production among human groups in different areas. With this background, the situation in north Spain is paradigmatic, as the late appearance of ceramics in the region is associated with the total lack of traits, particularly decoration, that would allow the establishment of links with other parts of the Iberian Peninsula. This paper aims to present an overview of the earliest pottery, raw materials, products and technological choices at a peninsular scale before concentrating on a case study focused on the Cantabrian region. This will enable a perspective on its technology and the proposal of a series of hypotheses on the role of the first ceramics in this region.

2. The study of the distribution and production of archaeological pottery

The first studies on the production and distribution of archaeological pottery in the 1960s were motivated by the paradigm of *ceramic ecology* (Matson 1965), clearly connected with New Archaeology. This encouraged studies of ceramic technology through the application of different analytical methods (Matson 1981; Shepard 1980; Rice 1981, 1982, 1987; Rye 1994). Thus, within the framework of ceramic ecology, such methods as petrography and X-ray diffraction were applied to archaeological pottery

(Rice 1987) and the concepts of *production* and *distribution* began to form part of the main studies within this tendency. In the 1980s, ethno-archaeological studies were introduced (Arnold 1985, 2000, 2005, 2006) to document different behaviours and contexts of production and used to explain archaeological reality. By the end of the last century, archaeological ceramic studies were enhanced by the introduction of the *chaîne opératoire* framework (Lemonnier 2002).

These approaches have rarely been applied to the earliest pottery despite their potential. Instead, the study of the processes of the spread of this technology has been based on the stratigraphic record of the assemblages and the chronology of the sites where they were found (Jordan *et al.* 2016). Studies focusing on the first pottery vessels are scarce despite displaying great value for the interpretation of a technology with its beginnings in nomadic societies in eastern Eurasia (Hommel *et al.* 2016).

In addition, the study of exchange networks through archaeological pottery is harder than in the case of other abiotic materials such as flint and variscite. This is basically due to the characteristics of pottery. In the first place, pottery is a completely artificial material that previously did not exist in nature and may be made with a mixture of raw materials (clay and temper) that might not have come from the same geographic source. Indeed, clay deposits are usually large in size with a degree of internal variability. This clearly contrasts with provenance studies of artefacts made from flint and variscite as their manufacture only involves a transformation of the morphology from the original material without altering its initial properties. Furthermore, pottery may not reflect the same composition as the original source, since technological and cultural processes, such as the addition of temper, can alter the composition substantially. It is equally important to determine the production context (Tite 2008) as this may not be the place where the remains have been documented. Despite these impediments, ceramic studies are able to propose an hypothetical raw procurement area and follow other approaches, such as the characterisation of the pottery manufacturing processes and the identification of the different technical solutions employed during production, however these still remain underdeveloped.

Figure 1. Pottery from El Barranquet (by Bernabeu and Martí 2014).

3. Chronology of the appearance of pottery in the Iberian Peninsula

The first evidence of pottery in the Iberian Peninsula is recorded around 5650-5550 cal BC (Bernabeu and Martí 2014) in the Mediterranean region (El Barranquet, Mas d'Is and Cova d'En Pardo) (Figure 1), Atlantic Iberia (Cabranosa and Padrão), the inner Iberian Peninsula (La Paleta), Ebro valley (Peña Larga) and Huesca (Chaves and Forcas II) (Bernabeu and Martí 2014). Most of these sites have recently been related to the so-called impressed horizon (Bernabeu *et al.* 2009) in which pottery assemblages are dominated by impressions made with different kinds of objects, and which are generally similar to the impressed pottery in Liguria, although in some cases, like Nerja, this similarity is less clear (García Borja *et al.* 2014).

Today, the available chronology for pottery technology in the Northern Plateau (Meseta norte) shows it appeared at a similar time to the first pottery on the Mediterranean coast. The earliest evidence in this area comes from Levels III-sup and II at the archaeological site of Mendandia, which situates the appearance of this technology in the middle of the 6th millennium cal BC (Alday 2006). While this is the only site with this chronology in the whole of the Ebro valley, by the second half of the 6th millennium, the technology is clearly documented at the sites of La Vaquera, La Lámpara, La Revilla, Atxoste and Los Cascajos (García Martínez de Lagrán *et al.* 2011). The earliest sites where ceramic technology has been documented in north-east Iberia display a similar chronology of about 5500-5100 cal BC (Oms *et al.* 2016). These pottery vessels exhibit impressed decoration made with shells of *Cerastoderma edule* and *Cerastoderma glacum* or other kinds of objects (Oms *et al.* 2016).

The available information for the southern Iberian Peninsula indicates that pottery was adopted in the second half of the 6th or early 5th millennia cal BC, with evidence at such sites as Cabecicos Negros and Cueva del Toro (Camalich and Martín Socas 2013). In the same way, the first pottery products appear in Portugal in about the mid 6th millennium (Carvalho 2011).

In contrast, pottery appeared at a later date in other parts of Iberia: in the north-west and on the northern coast, where the first products are attributed to the mid-5th millennium cal BC (Prieto-Martínez 2009; Cubas *et al.* 2016).

Therefore, the chronology of the first appearance of pottery in the Iberian Peninsula appears to follow, *grosso modo*, the dynamics of the introduction and spread of domestic species (Balsera *et al.* 2015; Isern *et al.* 2013). However, as noted above, some contexts are associated with an eminently hunter-gatherer economy in which the existence of pottery has been cited (e.g. Rojo *et al.* 2015).

4. The first pottery in Iberia: different production traditions?

4.1. The available information

The appearance of the first pottery in the Iberian Peninsula therefore corresponds to the transmission of technological know-how, and this may occur through different mechanisms of social interaction. Numerous projects and lines of research in the late 20th century, focusing on a fuller interpretation of decorative techniques and compositions as well as analysing the technological traits of pottery, were able to determine several influences in the earliest ceramics and their main technological characteristics. As a result, a full corpus of data about the characteristics of manufacture and production is now available. Decorative and morphological similarity has been the main criterion employed to establish the gradual expansion and cultural filiation between the different areas. Pottery products have traditionally been regarded as indicators to interpret not only the chronology but also the origins and relationships between societies in the early Neolithic. Although a relatively high volume of studies about pottery manufacture technology is now available, true integration between technological, morphological and decorative studies has not taken place.

Andalusia is a pioneering region in characterising Neolithic ceramics, mainly in connection with the importance of *almagra* and the determination of its composition (Navarrete and Capel 1980; Capel *et al.* 1984; Capel *et al.* 2006). Together with this region, the Spanish Levant has also pioneered the application of this type of analytical technique (Gallart 1980a, b) as materials from such emblematic sites as Cova de l'Or, Cova Bernarda, Cova del Barranc Fondo, Cova de la Sarsa and Les Cendres have been analysed. An intensive sampling programme has recently been carried out at Valencian sites (McClure 2004; McClure and Bernabeu 2011). Finally, the third region where most ceramic studies have been performed is Catalonia, where a line of research focused on the management of raw materials used to make pottery began in the 1990s (Aliaga *et al.* 1992; Aliaga *et al.* 1998; Clop-García 2007, 2011). Intensive sampling has recently been undertaken in the Mediterranean area and Ebro valley (Clop-García 2011).

These approaches have been less systematic in other parts of the Iberian Peninsula. Some of the main studies have been carried out in Cueva de La Vaquera (Segovia) (Rubio and Blasco 1988-89), Chaves (Huesca) (Gallart and López 1988), Cueva del Moro (Gallart and Mata 1995a), Cueva Lóbrega, Collado Palomero and Peña Guerra I, II and III (Gallart and Mata 1995b, 1999), El Retamar (Feliú *et al.* 2002; Lazarich *et al.* 2002), Embarcadero del Río Palmones (Domínguez-Bella *et al.* 2004), Mendandia (Ortega *et al.* 2010) and Casa Montero and other sites in its proximity (Díaz-del-Río *et al.* 2011).

Information for the Atlantic coast comes mostly from Portugal (Masucci and Carvalho 2015; Jorge *et al.* 2005; Jorge *et al.* 2013), Galicia (De Andrés and Menéndez 1993) and northern Spain (Vega Maeso 2012; Cubas *et al.* 2013; Cubas *et al.* 2014a; Cubas *et al.* 2014b).

As can be verified, the number of studies has increased considerably in recent years and these have covered not only a larger number of sites but also a greater number of samples, which allow for further representative interpretations to be proposed.

4.2.Appraisal of manufacturing techniques used in the earliest pottery in the Iberian Peninsula

Ceramic technology studies aim to determine the raw materials used in order to establish the different technological choices considered in ceramic production. The addition of different types of temper can also provide useful information. In general, these studies show that the first pottery in the Iberian Peninsula was made with raw materials available in the surroundings of the archaeological sites, although deposits from different sources were used (Clop-García 2011; Cubas 2013; Masucci and Carvalho 2015). This has generally been taken to highlight the local manufacture of the pottery. The existence of allochthonous materials has rarely been cited, apart from, for example, the case of cardial ware at Balma Margineda (Barnett 1995), and a sample from Barranquet (Clop-García 2011: 38), some samples from the Ambrona valley (Clop-García 2011: 42) and cardial fragments in the centre-south of Portugal (Masucci and Carvalho 2015).

Regarding technological characteristics, the use of temper has been documented in the oldest pottery samples analysed in Iberia. The inclusions are mainly grog and crushed calcite (Binder *et al.* 2010; Convertini 2010; Clop-García 2011) although other kinds have been seen in some geographic areas, such as the plant elements identified in the Ambrona valley (Clop-García 2011), bone fragments in central Iberia (Díaz-del-Río *et al.* 2011) and shell fragments at Fuente de Isso (McClure 2010).

The use of temper indicates an intention of modifying the properties of the clay used to make the pottery and therefore reveals a degree of technological knowledge. In this way, the available studies appear to indicate cultural transmission of pottery technology, in which the recipients were made with raw materials obtained in the vicinity of the sites and different types of inclusions were added. Thus, the different technological choices adapted to the local environment.

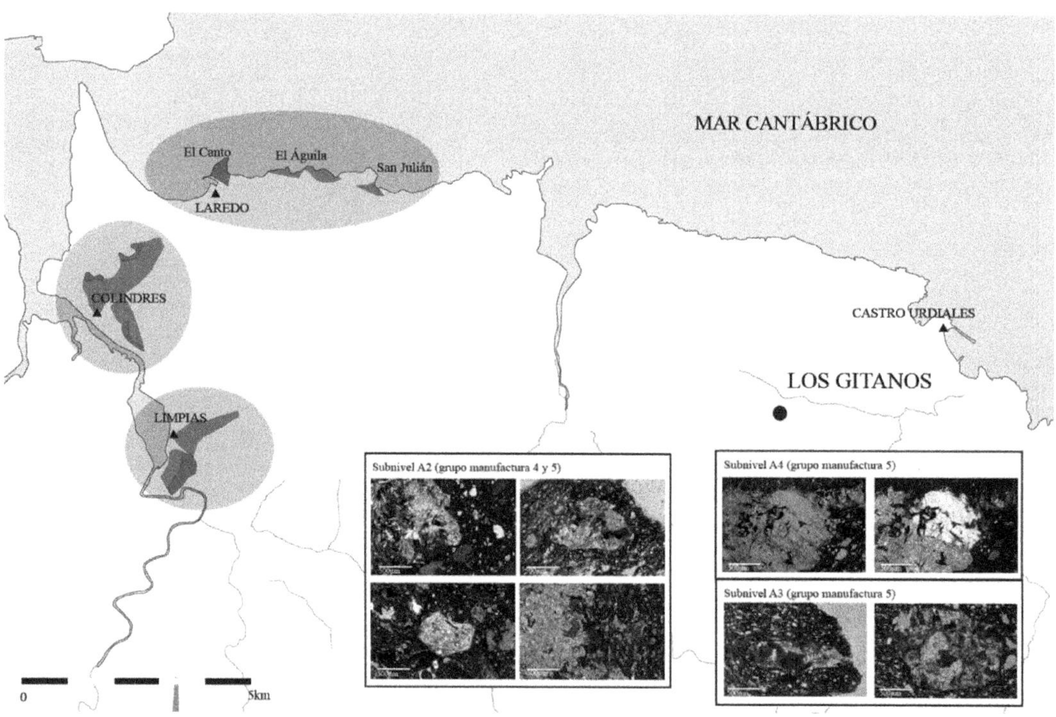

Figure 2. Deposits of Triassic clays available in the area around the site of Los Gitanos, with the samples identified in each of the sub-levels. | Source: By the Author.

5. The first pottery in northern Spain: exchange of products or technological transmission?

Recent studies of the first pottery in northern Spain (Vega Maeso 2012; Cubas *et al.* 2012; Cubas 2013; Cubas *et al.* 2013; Cubas *et al.* 2014) equally attest the use of different clay deposits, usually located in the surroundings of the sites where the potsherds were found. These clay deposits correspond to different geological contexts accessible near the sites. Coherence observed in the mineralogy of the samples and the geology around the sites allows a series of catchment areas to be proposed. This assumes that all the samples suggest a *local* manufacture, owing to their correlation with the geology in the proximity. However, various types of sediment were used to make the pottery recipients as different clay types have been observed. One especially interesting case is the sequence at the site of Los Gitanos, where ceramic assemblages from three archaeological sub-levels have been studied (Cubas *et al.* 2014). In the lower layers (Sub-levels A4 and A3), the clay types came from three different geological environments: Cretaceous limestone and detrital rock, and materials from Keuper outcrops. The first two types are found in the immediate surroundings of the site, whereas the third is located a little further away, at distances of from 7 to 15km (IGME 1976a; IGME 1978b) (Figure 2).

This latter type of raw material has been identified in a small number of samples from the lower sub-levels, whereas a large part of the samples from the upper Sub-level A2 indicate a more frequent use of that type of resource (Cubas 2013; Cubas *et al.* 2014b). The use of ophite-like rock fragments as temper also increases (Figure 3).

Therefore, territorial management varied in the course of the sequence at Los Gitanos, and this has been related to a change in the functionality of the occupation. According to models proposed by ethno-archaeology, raw materials obtained in a radius of 1 to 7km around a site can be regarded as local, whereas those further away would be allochthonous (Arnold 2005). In the case of Los Gitanos, it is thought that the products made with distant raw materials might be indicative of an economic system based on greater mobility of the group rather than of exchanges of products, as recently proposed for other geographic areas (Manen and Convertini 2012). The characteristics of the deposit suggest that Sub-level A2 consists of an accumulation of the waste from successive occupations (Ontañón-Peredo 2005). The most plausible hypothesis envisages socioeconomic activity involving a greater degree of mobility, rather than the exchange of products between different groups. It should also be beared in mind that no evidence has been found supporting the production of pottery in the cave itself. However, other archaeological evidence seems to reflect a change in the functionality of the site, probably associated with the gradual introduction of domestic livestock, which reaches 50% of the faunal assemblage in Sub-level A2 (Ontañón-Peredo *et al.* 2013). In Languedoc, the existence of "imported" recipients at such sites as Jean Cros, has also been associated with functional specialisation (Manen and Guilaine 2010).

As in other parts of the Iberian Peninsula, the earliest ware in northern Spain contains different kinds of inclusions that vary from site to site, although calcite is the most frequent type of temper (Figure 4). Other types found are flint and possibly fragments of such rocks as limestone, sandstone

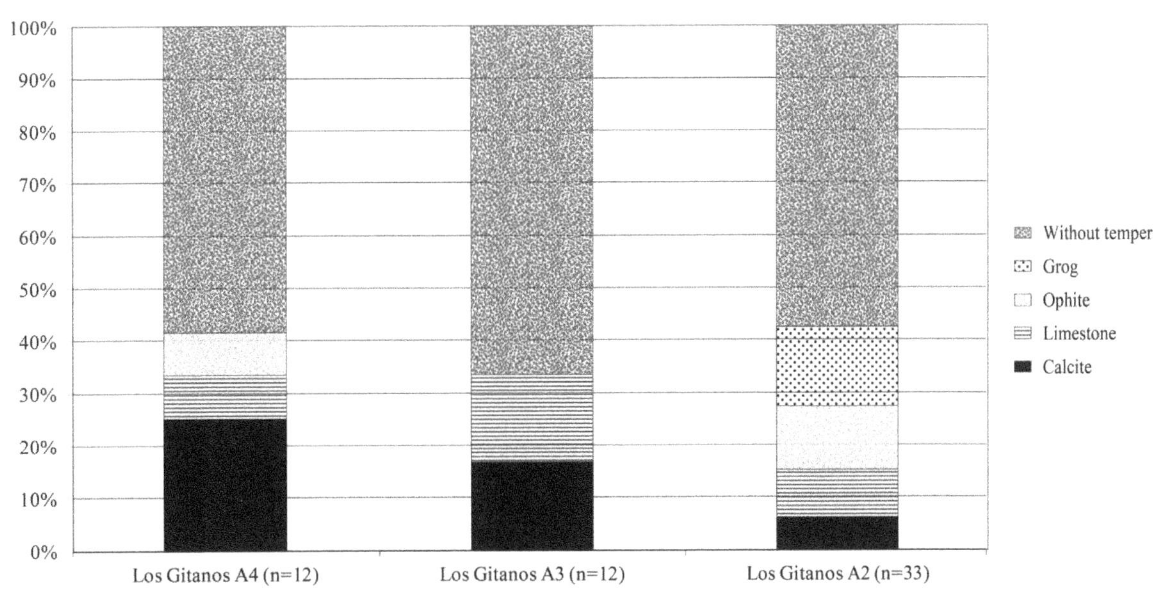

Figure 3. Percentage of potsherds without inclusions and the different types of temper identified in each of the sub-levels at the site of Los Gitanos. | Source: By the Author.

and ophite. Grog has also been documented in the earliest ceramic products, but only in Levels IV and III at the site of Kobaederra and the most recent level in the Los Gitanos sequence (Sub-level A2) (Figure 4).

boquique and cardial, have only been claimed for the site of Arenaza (Apellániz and Altuna 1975). Unfortunately, a recent re-examination of the pottery assemblage from this cave failed to document those sherds.

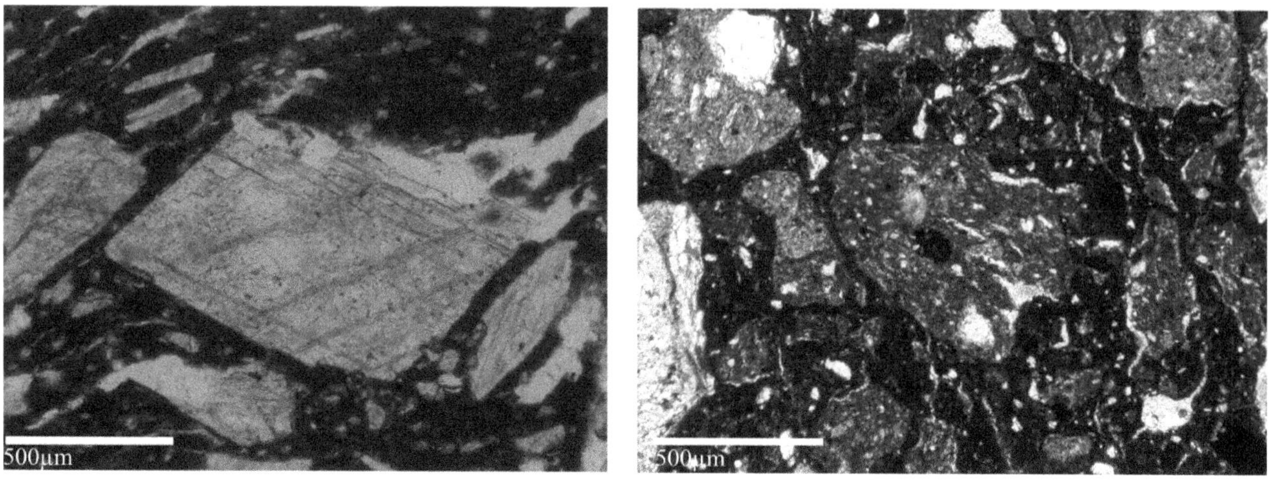

Figure 4. Microphotograph of calcite (left) and grog (right) inclusions. | Source: By the Author.

The repeated use of local clay deposits and the addition of temper are indicative of the technological knowledge displayed in the production of the first pottery recipients documented in northern Spain. This knowledge and the use of local raw materials suggests that the recipients were made by the communities living in the region, and therefore the situation was one of transmission of technological know-how rather than the exchange of products.

6. Other evidence of exchange in northern Spain in the Neolithic

The existence of exchanges and contacts between human populations living to the north and south of the Cantabria Mountains has clearly been documented for the Upper Palaeolithic (Tarriño 2006) and the Mesolithic (Álvarez-Fernández 2006). These were maintained during the 5th millennium cal BC, at least in the eastern part of the region, where sites on the northern side of the mountains have yielded flint types from both sides of the range (Fernández Eraso *et al.* 2005). This has led several authors to propose that the Ebro valley was a possible area of influence in the neolithisation process in the north (Arias 2007; Cubas *et al.* 2016). Pottery technology became widespread in the Ebro valley in the mid-6th millennium, clearly earlier than in the north. Comparison with pottery manufacture studies for sites in the middle-upper Ebro valley and Huesca shows that on both sides of the mountains, local raw materials were used, together with inclusions of calcite and grog. However, this *technological choice* is not exclusive to the first pottery products and is documented in other periods. Therefore another aspect that needs to be considered is the similarity of assemblages in morphological and decorative terms. In general, in the north the morphologies are not representative and decorative patterns traditionally regarded as characteristic of the Early Neolithic, such as

Consequently, no clear correlation exists between the technological, morphological and decorative characteristics of the first ceramic products on the two sides of the Cantabrian Mountains despite the evidence of contacts from at least the Upper Palaeolithic to the early 5th millennium cal BC. However, contacts also existed with Europe across the Bay of Biscay, at least by the 4th millennium, as ground stone axes from the Alps have been documented in northern Spain (Pétrequin *et al.* 2012) (Figure 5).

7. Discussion

The expansion of ceramic technology is undoubtedly evidence of contacts and circulation of technological information. Studies on the raw materials indicate that, in general terms, these are products made with raw materials found in the surroundings of the site and therefore the technology would spread through a process of the transmission of knowledge by various means (Dietler and Herbich 1995). The studies do not reveal a system of exchange of products, as observed in the case of other types of materials, such as beads and adornments, Alpine axes and other lithic artefacts.

However, in several places of the Iberian Peninsula, it is not uncommon to find pottery produced with raw materials from distant geographic origin. Examples are a cardial recipient at Balma Margineda (Barnett 1995), a sample at Barranquet (Clop-García 2011: 38), samples in Ambrona valley (Clop-García 2011: 42) and some cardial fragments in the centre-south of Portugal (Masucci and Carvalho 2015). In the latter case, at least some of the analyses point to the use of raw materials from southern areas, which supports the hypothesis of maritime colonisation of coastal regions (Padrão and Almonda) (Masucci and Carvalho 2015).

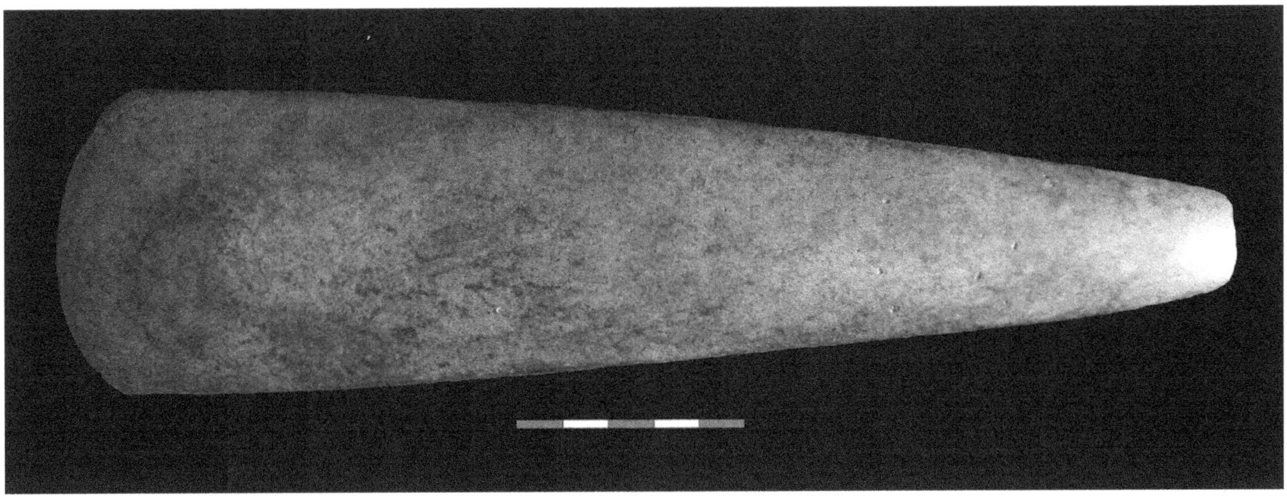

Figure 5. Ground stone axe from the site of Baltzola (Dima, Biscay) (Arkeologi Museoa)

In general, pottery studies show that, in Iberia as a whole and in the Cantabrian region in particular, the technological tradition was specific to each region, raw materials available in the relative proximity of sites were used, and decorative traits were recurrent. The most interesting aspect may be the identification of social actors who manufactured the pottery, especially in areas where the introduction of technology does not represent a clear hiatus in the archaeological record. In this sense, the study of ceramic technology and its relationship with the population is one of the fundamental pillars for understanding the cultural expansion and transmission phenomena. In this way, situations where transference processes are based essentially on the diffusion of knowledge denote biological continuity in the population, which in turn implies the acquisition of technological knowledge by human groups who were already living in an area. This contrasts with transference processes through demic diffusion involving small groups of people who introduce new technology into a region, which would entail a clear hiatus with the prior population substrate at both genetic and cultural level.

Archaeology has succeeded in identifying a series of contacts between different geographic areas through the study of exogenic products. However, our interest should focus on proposing hypotheses and analytical tools to be able to approach processes of cultural interaction and thus analyse the social reality of the groups under study. Pottery technology and, to be more precise, the analysis of pottery technology applied to the first ceramics in Europe would undoubtedly constitute a solid basis on which to propose hypotheses of this kind.

Acknowledgements

I would like to thank the coordinator of this volume, Dr Juan Gibaja, for the trust shown in my research, not only by offering me the opportunity to write this chapter but also by allowing me the chance to study some of the most interesting ceramic assemblages in Catalonia. Miriam Cubas is working within the framework of the European Commission-funded Marie Sklodowska Curie research project *First ceramics of Atlantic Europe: Manufacture and function* (CerAM -IF 653354-).

References

Alday, A., (ed.) *El legado arqueológico de Mendandia: Los modos de vida de los últimos cazadores en la Prehistoria de Treviño.* Valladolid: Junta de Castilla y León. Consejería de Cultura y Turismo (Memorias 15), 2006.

Aliaga, S., M. García-Vallés, T. Pradell, and Vendrell-Saz, M., "Anàlisis mineralògiques de ceràmiques del Neolític Antic de NE de Catalunya." In *9è. Col·loqui Internacional d'Arqueologia de Puigcerdà. Estat de la Investigació sobre el Neolític a Catalunya (Centenari del naixement de P. Bosch Gimpera).* (Andorra: Institut d'estudis Ceretans. Servei d'Arqueologia d'Andorra. Union Internationale des Sciencies Préhistoriques et Protohistoriques, (1992), 144-149.

Aliaga, S., M. Vendrell-Saz, T. Pradell, and M. García-Vallés, «Estudi de les pastes ceràmiques.» In *El poblat neolític de Plansallosa. L'explotació del territori dels primers agricultors-rameders de l'Alta Garrotxa.*, ed. A. Bosch i Lloret, R. Buxó, A. Palomo, M. Buch, J. Mateu, E. Tabernero and J. Casadevall. (La Garrotxa: Museu Comarcal de la Garrtoxa Publicacions eventuals d'Arqueologia de La Garrotxa, 5, (1998.), 77-82.

Álvarez-Fernández, E. *Los objetos de adorno-colgantes del Paleolítico superior y Mesolítico en la Cornisa Cantábrica y en el Valle del Ebro. Una visión europea.* Salamanca: Vítor, 2006.

Apellániz, J. M., and Altuna, J. "Memoria de la III campaña de excavaciones arqueológicas en la cueva de Arenaza I (San Pedro de Galdames, Vizcaya)." *Noticiario Arqueológico Hispánico. Prehistoria* 4 (1975): 183-197.

Arias, P. "Neighbours but diverse: social change in north-west Iberia during the transition from the Mesolithic to the Neolithic (5500-4000 cal BC)." In *Going over: the Mesolithic-Neolithic transition in North-West Europe*, ed. A. Whittle and V. Cummings (Oxford: Oxford University Press Proceedings of the British Academy 144, (2007), 53-72.

Arnold, D. E. *Ceramic theory and cultural process.* Cambridge: Cambridge University Press (New studies in Archaeology), 1985.

Arnold, D. E. "Does the standardization of ceramic pastes really mean specialization?" *Journal of Archaeological Method and Theory* 7, 4 (2000): 333-375.

Arnold, D. E. "Linking society with the compositional analysis of pottery: a model from comparative ethnography." In *Pottery manufacturing processes: reconstitution and interpretation (Actes du XIVème Congrès UISPP)*, ed. A. Livingstone Smith, D. Bosquet and Rémi Martineau, 15-21. Oxford: British Archaeological Reports, 2005.

Arnold, D. E. "The threshold model for ceramics resources: a refinement." In *Ceramic studies. Papers on the social and cultural significance of ceramics in Europe and Eurasia from prehistoric to historic times*, ed. D. Gheorghiu, 3-9. Oxford: British Archaeological Reports, 2006.

Balsera, V, Díaz-del-Río, P. Gilman, A. Uriarte, A. and Vicent. J. M. "Approaching the demography of the prehistoric Iberia through summed calibrated date probability distributions (7000-2000 cal BC)." *Quaternary International* 386 (2015): 208-211.

Barnett, W. K. "Anàlisis petrogràfiques de la ceràmica del neolític recent de la Balma de la Margineda." In *Les excavacions a la Balma de la Margineda (1979-1991)*, edited by J. Guilaine and M. Martzluff, 185-207. Andorra: Govern d'Andorra, 1995.

Bernabeu, J., and Martí, B. «Les premiers groups agropastoraux de la Péninsule Ibérique.» In *La transition néolithique en Méditerranée. The Neolithic transition in the Mediterranean*, ed. C. Manen, T. Perrin and J. Guilaine, 419-438. Paris: Errance, 2014.

Bernabeu, J., Molina, L. Esquembre, M. A. Ortega, J. R. and Boronat Soler J. D. "La cerámica impresa mediterránea en el origen del Neolítico de la Península Ibérica?". In *De Méditerranée et d'ailleurs...(Mélanges offerts à Jean Guilaine)*, 83-95. Toulouse: Centre de la Recherche sur la Préhistoire et la Protohistoire de la Méditerranée (Archives d'Écologie Préhistorique), 2009.

Binder, D., Convertini, F. Manen, C. and Sénépart, I. «Les productions céramiques du Néolithique ancien: proposition d'un protocole d'analyse.» In *Premières sociétés paysannes de Méditerranée occidentale. Structuras des productions céramiques (Séance de la Société Préhistorique Française)*, ed. Manen, C. Convertini, F. Binder D. and Sénépart, I. 29- 42. Paris: Société Préhistorique Française (Mémoire LI), 2010.

Budja, M. "Early neolithic pots and potters in Western Eurasia." *Institut za arheologiju* (2011): 31-67.

Camalich, Mª. D., and Martín Socas, D. "Los inicios del Neolítico en Andalucía. Entre la tradición y la innovación." *Menga* 3 (2013): 103-132.

Capel, J., Huertas, F. Pozzuoli, A. and Linares, J. "Red ochre decorations in Spanish neolithic ceramics: a mineralogical and technological study." *Journal of Archaeological Science* 33, no. 8 (2006): 1157-1166.

Capel, J., Linares, J. Huertas F., and Navarrete Mª. S. "Cerámicas con decoración a la almagra: identificación y caracterización de los términos almagra, aguada y engobe. Proceso decorativo." *Cuadernos de Prehistoria de la Universidad de Granada* 11 (1984): 97-114.

Carvalho, A. F. "Produçao cerâmica no inicio do Neolítico de Portugal." In *Las primas producciones cerámicas: el IV milenio cal AC en la Península Ibérica*, ed. J. Bernabeu, M. A. Rojo and L. Molina, 237-250. Valencia: Universidad de Valencia (Papeles del Laboratorio de Arqueología de Valencia. Extra 12), 2011.

Clop-García, X. *Materia prima, cerámica y sociedad. La gestión de los recursos minerales para manufacturas cerámicas del 3100 al 1500 ANE en el noreste de la Península Ibérica.* Oxford: British Archaeological Reports, 2007.

Clop-García, X. "Caracterización petroarqueológica de cerámicas decoradas del Neolítico antiguo de la Península Ibérica." In *Las primeras producciones cerámicas: el VI milenio cal AC en la Península Ibérica*, ed. Bernabeu J., Rojo M. A. and Molina L., 35-52. Valencia: Saguntum. Papeles del Laboratorio de Arqueología de Valencia. Extra-12, 2011.

Clop-García, X. "Las primeras producciones cerámicas del nordeste de la Península Ibérica: estudios de caracterización." In *III Congreso del Neolítico en la Península Ibérica*, ed. P. Arias, R. Ontañón and C. García-Moncó, 297-303. Santander: Servicio de Publicaciones de la Universidad de Cantabria (Monografías del Instituto Internacional de Investigaciones Prehistóricas de Cantabria, I), 2005.

Convertini, F. «Bilan des études réalisées sur la provenance de la céramique du Néolithique ancien en Méditerranée nordoccidentale. Mise au point d'un protocole analytique.» In *Premières sociétés paysannes de Méditerranée occidentale. Structuras des productions céramiques (Séance de la Société Préhistorique Française)*, ed. Manen C., Convertini F., Binder D. and Sénépart I., 13-27. Paris: Société Préhistorique Française (Mémoire LI), 2010.

Crombé, P. "Early pottery in hunter-gatherers societies of Western Europe." In *Ceramics before farming. The dispersal of pottery among prehistoric Eurasian hunter-gatherers*, ed. Jordan P. and Zvelebil M., 477-498. California: Left Coast Press (Publications of the Institute of Archaeology. University College of London), 2009.

Cubas, M. *La aparición de la tecnología cerámica en la región cantábrica.* Oxford: British Archaeological Reports, 2013.

Cubas, M., Bolado del Castillo R., Pereda Rosales E. M., and Fernández Vega P. A. "La cerámica en Cantabria desde su aparición (5000 cal BC) hasta el final de la Prehistoria: técnicas de manufactura y características morfo-decorativas." *Munibe (Antropologia- Arkeologia)* 64 (2013): 69-88.

Cubas, M., de Pedro I., and Arias P. "La aparición de la tecnología cerámica en Asturias: la aportación de la cueva de Los Canes (Arangas, Cabrales)." *Nailos. Estudios interdisciplinares de Arqueología* 1 (2014): 23-48.

Cubas, M., Doherty, C. García-Heras, M. de Pedro, I. Méndez, D. and Ontañón-Peredo R. "Pottery manufacturing during the Neolithic in the North of Spain: raw material procurement and modification in the cave of Los Gitanos (Castro Urdiales, Spain)." *Archaeometry* 56, no. S1 (2014): 19-35.

Cubas, M., García-Heras, M. Méndez, D. de Pedro, I. Zapata, L. Ibáñez J. J., and González Urquijo J. E. "La tecnología cerámica de los niveles IV y III en el yacimiento de Kobaederra (Cortézubi, Bizkaia). Aprovisionamiento y modificación de las materias primas." *Trabajos de Prehistoria* 69, no. 1 (2012): 51-64.

Cubas, M., Altuna, J. Álvarez-Fernández, E. Armendariz A., Fano, M. Á. López-Dóriga, I. L. Mariezkurrena K., Tapia, J. Teira, L. C. and Arias P. 2016. "Re-evaluating the Neolithic: The Impact and the Consolidation of Farming Practices in the Cantabrian Region (Northern Spain)." *Journal of World Prehistory* 29 (2016): 79-116.

Chi, Z. "The discovery of early pottery in China." *Documenta Praehistorica* XXIX (2002): 29-35.

De Andrés, A. M., Menéndez, P. and Muñoz, I. "Estudio arqueométrico de cerámicas prehistóricas gallegas." In *El Cuaternario en España y Portugal (Actas de la 2ª Reunión del Cuaternario Ibérico)*, 357-367. Madrid: Instituto Tecnológico Geominero de España, 1993.

Díaz-del-Río, P., Consuegra, S. Domínguez, R. Martín-Bañón, A. Virseda, L. Agua, F. Villegas, Mª. A. and García-Heras M. "Identificación de una tradición tecnológica cerámica con desgrasante óseo en el Neolítico peninsular. Estudio arqueométrico de materiales cerámicos de Madrid (5300-3400 cal AC)." *Trabajos de Prehistoria* 68, no. 1 (2011): 99-122.

Dietler, M., and Herbich I. "Ceramics and Ethnic identity: Ethnoarchaeological observations on the distributions of pottery styles and the relationship between the social contexts of production and consumption." In *Terre cuite et société. La céramique, document technique, économique, culturel (XIVe Rencontres Internationales d'Archéologie et d'Historie d'Antibes)*, 459-472. Juan-les-Pins: APDCA, 1995.

Domínguez-Bella, S., Mata, M. P. Ramos Múñoz, J. Castañeda, V. and Sánchez M. Análisis arqueométrico de las cerámicas prehistóricas del embarcadero del río Palmones (Algeciras, Cádiz). In *Avances en arqueometría*, ed. Feliú, M. J. Martín, J. Edreira, M. C. Fernández, M. C. Martínez, M. P. Gil A. and Alcántara R., 138-144 Cádiz: Servicio de Publicaciones de la Universidad de Cádiz, 2004.

Farrell, T. F. G., Jordan, P. Taché, K. Lucquin, A. Gibbs, K., Jorge, A., Britton K., Craig, O. E. and Knecht. R. "Specialized Processing of Aquatic Resources in Prehistoric Alaskan Pottery? A Lipid-Residue Analysis of Ceramic Sherds from the Thule-Period Site of Nunalleq, Alaska." *Arctic Anthropology* 51, no. 1 (2014): 86-100.

Feliú Ortega, M. J., Edreira Sánchez, M. C. and Calleja Gonzalo S. "Informe sobre el estudio de muestras de fragmentos de cerámicas de la excavación El Retamar." In *El asentamiento de "El Retamar" (Puerto Real, Cádiz). Contribución al estudio de la formación social tribal y a los inicios de la economía de producción de la Bahía de Cádiz*, edited by Ramos J. and Lazarich M., 377-390. Cádiz: Servicio de Publicaciones de la Universidad de Cádiz, 2002.

Fernández Eraso, J., Mujika J. A., and Tarriño A. Relaciones entre la Cornisa Cantábrica y el valle del Ebro durante los inicios del Neolítico en el País Vasco. In *III Congreso del Neolítico en la Península Ibérica*, ed. Arias P., Ontañón R. and García-Moncó C., 201-209 Santander: Servicio de Publicaciones de la Universidad de Cantabria (Monografías del Instituto Internacional de Investigaciones Prehistóricas de Cantabria I), 2005.

Gallart, M. D. "La tecnología cerámica." In *Cova de l'Or*, ed. Martí, B. Pascual, V. Gallart, M. D. López, P. Pérez, M. Acuña J. D. and Robles, F., 165-173. Valencia: Servicio de Investigación Prehistórica. Diputación Provincial de Valencia (Serie de Trabajos Varios, núm. 65), 1980a.

Gallart, M. D. "La tecnología de la cerámica neolítica valenciana. Metodología y resultados del estudio ceramológico por medio de microscopía binocular, difractometría de rayos X y microscopía electrónica." *Saguntum* 15 (1980b): 57-91.

Gallart, M. D., and López, F. "Análisis mineralógico de las cerámicas neolíticas de la cueva de Chaves (Casbas, Huesca)." *Bolskam* 5 (1988): 5-26.

Gallart, M. D., and Mata M. P.. "Análisis mineralógico de las cerámicas." *Bolskam* 12 (1995a): 171-180.

Gallart, M. D., and Mata, M. P. Prehistoric pottery from La Rioja (Spain): a textural and mineralogical analysis. In *Estudis sobre ceràmica antiga*, ed. M. Vendrell-Saz, Pradell T., Molera J. and García M., 61-66. Barcelona: Generalitat de Catalunya. Departamento de Cultura, 1995b.

Gallart, M. D., and Mata M. P. El análisis mineralógico y textural de dos cerámicas tipológicamente características del Neolítico, procedentes de La Rioja. In *Arqueometría y arqueología*, ed. Capel J., 57-68. Granada: Universidad de Granada (Monográfica de Arte y Arqueología), 1999.

García Borja, P., Aura Tortosa, J.E., Jordá Pardo, J., Salazar-García DC "La cerámica neolítica de la Cueva de Nerja (Málaga, España): salas del Vestíbulo y la Mina". *Archivo de Prehistoria Levantina* XXX (2014): 81-131.

García Martínez de Lagrán, I., Garrido R., Rojo M. A., Alday A., García Gazolaz J., and Sesma Sesma J. "Cerámicas, estilo y Neolitización: estudio comparativa de algunos ejemplos de la Meseta Norte y Alto Valle del Ebro." In *Las primeras producciones cerámicas: el VI milenio cal AC en la Península Ibérica*, ed. Bernabeu J., Rojo M. A. and Molina L., 83-104. Valencia: Universitat de Valencia (Saguntum. Papeles del Laboratorio de Arqueología de Valencia), 2011.

Hallgren, F. "The introduction of ceramic technology around the Baltic Sea basin in the 6th millennium". In: Knutsson, K. (ed) *Coast to coast- arrival*, 123-143. Wikstroms: Uppsala, 2004.

Hommel, P., Day P. M., Jordan P., and Vetrov V. M. "Early pottery, hunter-gatherers and its interpretation of technological choices in Eastern Siberia." In *Insight from innovation: new light on Archaeological ceramics (Papers presented in honour of Professor David Peeacock's contributions to archaeological ceramic studies)*, ed. Sibbeson E., Jervis B. and Coxon S., 1-18. Southampton: Highfield Press, 2016.

Huysecom, E., Rasse, M. Lespez, L. Neumann, K. Fahmy, A. Ballouche, A. Ozainne, S. Maggetti, M. Tribolo, Ch. and Soriano, S. "The emergence of the pottery in Africa during the tenth millennium cal BC: new evidence from Ounjougou (Mali)." *Antiquity* 83 (2009): 905-917.

IGME. *Castro Urdiales: mapa geológico de España. Escala 1:50.000 (Hoja 36)*. Madrid: Servicio de Publicaciones. Ministerio de Industria y Energía, D. L, 1976a.

IGME. *Valmaseda: mapa geológico de España. Escala 1:50.000 (Hoja 60)*. Madrid: Servicio de Publicaciones. Ministerio de Industria y Energía, D. L, 1978b.

Isern, N., Fort, J..Carvalho, A. F, Gibaja J. F., and Ibáñez J. J. "The Neolithic transition in the Iberian peninsula: data analysis and modelling." *Journal of Archaeological Method and Theory* 21, no. 2 (2013): 447-460.

Jordan, P., Gibbs K, Hommel P., Piezonka, H. Silva, F. and Steele, J. "Modelling the diffusion of pottery technologies across Afro-Eurasia: emerging insights and future research." *Antiquity* 90, no. 351 (2016): 590-603.

Jorge, A., Day, P. M. Valera, A. C. Dias, M. I. and Prudêncio, M. I. "Ceramics, style and exchange in the Early Neolithic Upper Mondego Basin: a technological approach." In *Understanding people through their pottery (Proceedings of the 7th European Meeting on Ancient Ceramics. EMAC '03)*, ed. Dias M. I., Prudêncio M. I. and Waerenborg J. C., 121-128. Lisboa: IPA, 2005.

Jorge, A., Dias M. I., and Day. P. M. "Plain pottery and social landscapes: reinterpreting the significance of ceramic provenance in the Neolithic." *Archaeometry* 55, no. 5 (2013): 825-851.

Kuzmin, Y. V. "The Neolithic of Russian Far East and neighbouring East Asia: definition, chronology and origins." *Bulletin of the indo-Pacific Prehistory Association* 30 (2010): 157-162.

Kuzmin, Y. V. "The beginnings of prehistoric agriculture in the Russian Far East: current evidence and concepts." *Documenta Praehistorica* 40 (2013a): 1-12.

Kuzmin, Y. V. 2013b. "Origin of old world pottery as viewed from the early 2010s: when, where and why?." *World Archaeology* 45 no. 4 (2013b): 539-556.

Kuzmin, Y. V. 2013c. "Two trajectories in the Neolithization of Eurasia: pottery *versus* agriculture (Spationtemporal patters)." *Radiocarbon* 56 (2013c): 1304-1313.

Lazarich, M., Feliú, M. J. Edreira M. C., and Calleja S. "Los productos cerámicos de "El Retamar". Análisis tecnológico, morfológico y funcional." In *Memoria de la excavación arqueológica en el asentamiento VI° milenio a. N. E. de "El Retamar"(Puerto Real, Cádiz)*, ed. Ramos J. and Lazarich M., 157-164. Sevilla: Junta de Andalucía. Conserjería de Cultura (Arqueología Monografías), 2002.

Lemonnier, P. *Technological choices. Transformation in material cultures since the Neolithic*. London: Routledge, 2002.

Manen, C., and Convertini F. "Neolithization of the Western Mediterranean: pottery productions, circulation and recombination." *Rubricatum (Actes Xarxes al Neolític. Circulació i intercanvi de matèries, productes i idees a la Mediterrània occidental (VII-III mil·lenni aC)* 5 (2012): 363-368.

Manen, C., and Guilaine J. Aspects géographiques et chronolculturels du Néolithique ancien languedocien. In *Premières sociétés paysannes du Méditerranée occidentale. Structures des productions céramiques*, ed. Manen C., Convertini F., Binder D. and Sénépart I., 179-189 Paris: Mémoire de la Société Préhistorique Française, 2010.

Masucci, M., and Carvalho A. F. 2015. "Ceramic Technology And Resource Use During The Early Neolithic In Central-Southern Portugal." *Archaeometry* 58, no. 2 (2015): 201-221.

Matson, F. R. "Ceramic ecology: an approach to the study of the Early cultures of the Near East." In *Ceramics and man*, ed. Matson F. R., 202-217. Chicago: Aldine Publishing Company, 1965.

Matson, F. R. "Archaeological ceramics and the physical sciences: problem definition and results." *Journal of Field Archaeology* 8, no. 4 (1981): 447-456.

McClure, S. D. *Cultural transmission of ceramic technology during the consolidation of agriculture in Valencia, Spain*: Unpublished, 2004.

McClure, S. "Ceramic technology at Fuente de Isso." In *El yacimiento de Fuente de Isso (Hellín) y el poblamiento neolítico en la provincia de Albacete*, ed. García Atiénzar, G., 67-75. Albacete: Instituto de Estudios Albacetenses "Don Juan Manuel" de la Excma. Diputación de Albacete (serie I. número 193), 2010.

McClure, S., and Bernabeu, J. "Technological style, *chaîne opératoire*, and labor investment of Early Neolithic Pottery." In *Las primeras producciones cerámicas: el VI milenio cal AC en la Península Ibérica*, ed. Bernabeu J., Rojo M. A. and Molina, L., 53-60. Valencia: Saguntum. Papeles del Laboratorio de Arqueología de Valencia. Extra-12, 2011.

Navarrete, Mª. S., and Capel J. "Algunas consideraciones sobre la cerámica a la almagra del Neolítico andaluz." *Cuadernos de Prehistoria de la Universidad de Granada* 5 (1980): 15-34.

Oms, F. X., Martín, A., Esteve X., Mestres J., Morell B., Subirà E., and J. B. Gibaja. "The Neolithic in Northeast Iberia: chronocultural phases and ^{14}C." *Radiocarbon* 58, no. 2 (2016): 291-309.

Ontañón-Peredo, R., Altuna J., Álvarez-Fernández E., Chauvin, A., Cubas, M., Fernández, R. Gruet, Y. Iriarte, M. J., López-Dóriga, I. L., Mariezkurrena, K., and Zapata, L. «Contribution a l'ètude de la Neolithisation dans la région Cantabrique. La grotte de Los Gitanos (Cantabrie, Espagne).» In *Anciens peuplements littoraux et relations Homme/Milieu sur les côtes de l'Europe atlantique*, ed. M-Y. Daire, Dupont, A., Baudry C., Billard, C. Large J. M., Lespez, L., Normand, E. and Scarre, C., 383-390. Oxford: British Archaeological Report, 2013.

Ontañón-Peredo, R. "La secuencia de la Cueva de Los Gitanos (Castro Urdiales, Cantabria) y el Neolítico cantábrico." In *III Congreso del Neolítico en la Península Ibérica*, ed. Arias, P., Ontañón, R. and García-Moncó C. P, 1035-1043. Santander: Universidad de Cantabria (Monografías del IIIPC, 1), 2005.

Ortega, L. A., Zuluaga, M. C. Alonso-Olazabal, A. Murelaga, X. and Alday A. "Petrographic and geochemical evidence for long-standing supply of raw materials in Neolithic pottery (Mendandia site, Spain)." *Archaeometry* 52, no. 6 (2010): 987-1001.

Pétrequin, P., Errera, M., Martín, A., Fábregas R., and Vaquer, J. «Les haches en jades alpins pendant les Ve et IVe millénaires: l'example de l'Espagne et Portugal dans une perspective européene.» *Rubricatum (Actes Xarxes al Neolític. Circulació i intercanvi de matèries, productes i idees a la Mediterrània occidental (VII-III mil·lenni aC)* 5 (2012): 213-222.

Prieto-Martínez, M. P. "From Galicia to the Iberian Peninsula: Neolithic ceramics and traditions." In *Early farmers, late foragers, and ceramic traditions: on the beginning of pottery in the Near East of pottery in the Near East and Europe*, ed. Gheorghiu, D., 116-149. Cambridge: Cambridge University Press, 2009.

Rice, P. "Evolution of specialized pottery production: a trial model." *Current Anthropology* 22, no. 3 (1981): 219-240.

Rice, P. "Pottery production, pottery classification, and the role of physicochemical analysis." In *Archaeological ceramics*, ed. Olin, J. and Franklin, A., 47-56. Washington: Smithsonian Institution Press, 1982.

Rice, P. M. *Pottery analysis. A sourcebook*. Chicago: University of Chicago Press, 1987.

Rojo, M. A., Tejedor, C., Peña-Chocarro, L., Royo, J. I. Guillén, García Martínez de Lagrán, Í., Arcusa H., San Millán, M., Garrido Pena R., Gibaja. J. F., Mazzuco N., Clemente, I., Mozota, M., Terradas, X., Moreno M. García, J., Pérez, G. Álvarez-Fernández, E. Jiménez, I. and Gómez F. "Releyendo el fenómeno de la neolitización en el Bajo Aragón a la luz de la excavación del Abrigo de Valmayor XI (Mequinenza, Zaragoza)." *Zephyrus* LXXV (2015): 41-71.

Rubio, I. L., and Blasco, Mª. C. "Análisis cerámicos de la cueva de La Vaquera (Torreiglesias, Segovia)." *Zephyrus* 41-42 (1988-89): 149-160.

Rye, O. S. *Pottery technology: Principles and reconstruction.* Washington D. C.: Taxacum (Manuals on archaeology, 4), 1994.

Sakaguchi, T. "Storage adaptations among hunter-gatherers: a quantitative approach to the Jomon pottery." *Journal of Anthropological Archaeology* 28 (2009): 290-303.

Shepard, A. O. *Ceramics for the archaeologist*. Washington D. C.: Carnegie Institution of Washington, 1980.

Tarriño, A. *El sílex en la cuenca vasco-cantábrica y el Pirineo navarro*. Madrid: Ministerio de Cultura (Monografías Centro de Investigación y Museo de Altamira), 2006.

Tite, M. S. 2008. "Ceramic production, provenance and use-a review." *Archaeometry* 50, no. 2 (2008): 216-231.

Utrilla, Pilar, and Mazo, C. *La Peña de las Forcas (Graus, Huesca). Un asentamiento estratégico en la confluencia del Ésera y el Isábena*. Zaragoza: Universidad de Zaragoza (Monografías Arqueológicas. Prehistoria 46), 2014.

Vega Maeso, C. "The ceramics of El Mirón cave: production, morphology and discard." In *El Mirón Cave, Cantabria Spain. The Site and Its Holocene Archaeological Record*, edited by L.G. Straus and R. González Morales, M. R., 372-425. Alburquerque: Univeristy of New Mexico Press 51, 2012.

Portugal - Portuguese Estremadura.
Source: José Martinho Lourenço

Chapter 4

Before Metal. Circulation of Goods and Human Mobility in the Early and Middle Neolithic in Portuguese Estremadura

António Faustino Carvalho

University of Algarve, F.C.H.S., Campus de Gambelas, 8000-117 Faro, Portugal, afcarva@ualg.pt

To Alfredo Bensaúde (1856–1941),
a pioneer in Portugal on mineralogy applied
to the characterisation of archaeological artefacts.

Abstract: This chapter outlines a brief overview of the circulation of goods and human mobility among Early and Middle Neolithic communities in the Estremadura region of central-southern Portugal. It focuses on raw materials of geological origin characteristic of the periods in question (flint, fibrolite, amphibolite, pottery recipes and variscite) together with isotope studies on human mobility that have been published for the whole South-West Iberia. Different models of human mobility and raw material acquirement are proposed for the Early and Middle Neolithic according to the distances between the sources of the materials and the places where they were consumed. There is also little evidence, however significant, for long-distance circulation of exotic / prestige goods, a fact that nuances and ideas on the presumed egalitarian status of these societies "before metal".

Keywords: Neolithic; Portuguese Estremadura; geologic raw materials; human mobility.

1. Introduction

Around the end of the twentieth century, human mobility in the Neolithic and Chalcolithic periods in Portugal was commonly viewed in a two-phase periodization, with a clear division—more conventional than real—set in about the year 3000 BC. Neolithic societies were understood as more mobile, given the archaeological invisibility of their settlement sites. In this earliest stage, the most notable human feature in the landscape was the so-called 'megalithic phenomenon'. Only later, during a second phase of development of these early farming societies, would populations become truly sedentary. This conclusion derived from the recognition of the first 'fortified settlements', dating back to the beginning of the third millennium BC, whose buildings would coincide with the onset of stable agricultural regimes along with more complex stock-keeping practices, i.e. incorporating the exploitation of 'secondary animal products'.

This view goes back, at least, to the works by the Leisner couple, who claimed that 'though solid proof is lacking on the economic state of the megalithic people in the first cultural phase [the Neolithic], the *habitat* itself allows a pastoralism lifestyle and the fact that adzes have been found, right in this phase, leads us to believe that the tilling of the land had already begun. The scarcity of pottery in the small dolmens supports this hypothesis' (Leisner and Leisner 1951, 15; Portuguese original). A greater fixation to the land would take place in the later, Chalcolithic phases of megalithism. Indeed, a few lines ahead, still in the same page, these authors claim that 'agricultural activity intensifies in the dolmen's Eneolithic period, as proven by grinding-stones, sickle flints and the abundant ceramics.'

These ideas were followed by the majority of Portuguese scholars, despite their variable opinions on particular aspects of such changes. As we will see in the following pages, relatively high levels of human mobility seem indeed to have been reached in the Neolithic and Chalcolithic, however we are now, for the first time, obtaining glimpses of its real geographical scale, demographic significance and, perhaps more importantly, under what economic, social and ideological conditions it took place.

Following a preliminary outline on the subject (Carvalho 2015), the aim of this chapter is thus twofold: to present the state of the art regarding provenance of objects and raw materials of geologic origin in the Early and Middle Neolithic of the Estremadura region of central-southern Portugal (Figure 1); and to compile and discuss available isotopic evidence on mobility that has recently been retrieved from the human remains themselves.

However, the available evidence, either archaeological or isotopic, is still very fragmentary and complete depictions of past realities are far from being clearly established:

- An early beginning of cave research in the region, going back to the mid-nineteenth century, and the widely acknowledged decreasing quality of field records during most of the following century, resulted in an impressive *corpus* of artefactual evidence but the corresponding original stratigraphic contexts are generally unknown. Sound chronostratigraphic references are scarce, thus preventing the construction of reliable dating frameworks for the abundant collections housed in museums.

- Secondly, characterization of geologic raw materials from archaeological contexts based on petrographic or chemical analyses has seldom been carried out on a systematic basis, despite its early beginning in Portuguese research—of which the pioneer work by Bensaúde (1884) stands out. Results are partial and usually restricted to the artefacts or raw materials that most attracted the researchers' attention. As a consequence, identified networks of raw material exchange or circulation are not necessarily representative of past systems or of patterned behaviours.

- The former limitation is also true regarding isotopic datasets aiming to detect mobility patterns—in this case, from the actual actors of the phenomena under study. Research projects analysing strontium and oxygen isotopes from human remains have only begun in Portugal in the present decade. Moreover, the results are markedly restricted to local or micro-regional scales; broader, inter-regional perspectives are tentatively proposed by eliminating the more unlikely geological hypotheses rather than by defining past, regional 'isoscapes' that could be used as reference baselines.

2. Early and Middle Neolithic evidence from Estremadura

Lying along the central–southern coast of Portugal, the Estremadura region is dominated by a north–south chain of Jurassic limestone massifs that constitute its backbone, interspersed with Cretaceous sandstones and conglomerates. The elongated riverine plains that border the right banks of the Tagus Valley are dissected by a series of East–flowing streams across Pliocene, Miocene and Pleistocene sandstones, sands, clays and marls. With the exception of the eruptive massif of the Sintra Mountain, on an east–west axis at the southern tip of the region, Estremadura lacks the metamorphic schists and the igneous granites that characterises its confining provinces of Beira Litoral, to the North, and Alentejo, to the interior.

As important as its local geology—and therefore exploitable raw materials—is Estremadura's location along the Atlantic and the number of important rivers that, flowing from the interior regions (even from inner Iberia, in the case of the Tagus River), converge on this coastal region: this is the case, from north to south, of the Mondego, Tagus and Sado rivers (Figure 1). Moreover, along the coast and especially in the Tagus Valley, there were at the time—during the maximum of the Flandrian transgressive phase—large estuaries of fresh- or brackish waters that penetrated deep inland (e.g., Dias *et al.* 2000; Vis *et al.* 2008). Overall, these geomorphologic features provided Estremadura with excellent conditions for early navigation that may have played an important role in human (and goods) mobility.

The above-mentioned geomorphologic features may have well contributed to the role Estremadura seems to have played from the end of the fourth millennium BC onwards (Late Neolithic and Chalcolithic). Indeed, some geologic raw materials recorded in the Early and Middle Neolithic periods—variscite, fibrolite, amphibolite—experienced a boom-effect measurable by the increasing number of artefacts per site. Along with this phenomenon, previously unrecorded raw materials, either geologic or organic, make their first appearance in the region. Apart from the exploitation and propagation of the use of metal—copper and gold—during the third millennium BC, there are now objects made of ivory from elephant and sperm whale (Schuhmacher 2017 and references therein), fluorite (Cardoso *et al.* 2012), cinnabar and amber (Rocha *et al.* 2015) attested throughout the region, or only occasionally represented but of clear exotic origin, as in the case of adornments made with shells of the North African mollusc species *Conus papillionaceous* and *Patella safiana* (Cardoso 2003).

As we will see below—for a previous synthesis on geologic resources use in the Neolithic and Chalcolithic of Portugal, see Cardoso (2003)—, this explosion of items and their general frequency differs greatly from the dominant panorama of the earliest, late-sixth to mid-fourth millennia BC phases in Neolithic Estremadura.

2.1. Flint and other knapped rocks

The definition of the main sedimentary units in the Meso-Cenozoic Border and related depositional environments in western Portugal dates back to the nineteenth century. Flint and other siliceous rocks were soon identified in Estremadura, used as stratigraphic markers, and correlated with the earliest traces of human occupation in the region. A recent synthesis on flint sources by Aubry *et al.* (2014; see especially 172–9, Table 1 and Figure 1), not only confirmed a long-lasting perception of its abundance as a locally available rock—for example, Bensaúde (1884, 691) stated that flint sources '[...] *abondent dans nos assises crétacées presque partout où on les a constatées*'—but also provided a first systematic attempt at mapping sources and describing their lithologic characteristics. In fact, the overall image is that of a ubiquitous raw material at a regional scale but, however, unevenly distributed if more local scales are considered.

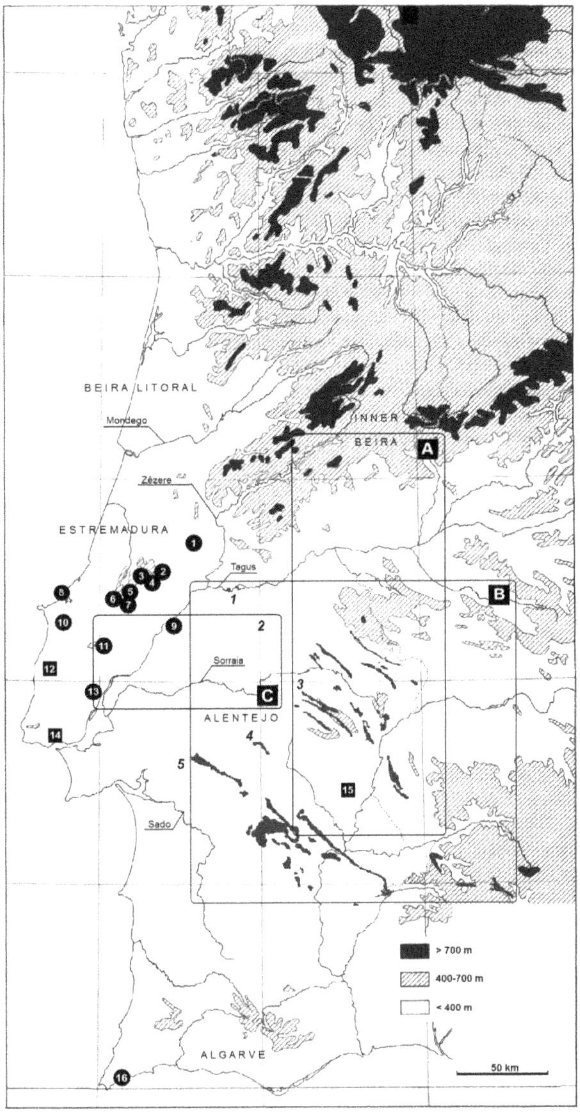

Figure 1. Sites mentioned in text (circles: Early and Middle Neolithic; squares: Chalcolithic): 1 - Caldeirão, 2 - Cerradinho do Ginete, 3 - Laranjal de Cabeço das Pias, 4 - Cisterna Gallery of the Almonda Cave, 5 - Lugar do Canto, 6 - Bocas, 7 - Cabeço de Porto Marinho, 8 - Óbidos Lagoon, 9 - Cortiçóis, 10 - Casa da Moura, 11 - Bom Santo, 12 - Cova da Moura, 13 - Moita da Ladra, 14 - Leceia, 15 - Perdigões, 16 - Padrão.

Box A: Presumable fibrolite source areas (Pinto 1928; Carreira and Cardoso 2000/01).

Box B: Amphibolite sources of the Ossa–Morena Metavulcanic Zone (dark-grey strips): 1 - Abrantes, 2 - Ponte de Sor, 3 - Avis, 4 - Arraiolos, 5 - Montemor-o-Novo (after Read et al. 1997, Figure 1).

Box C: hypothetical territory of the Bom Santo population (after Carvalho 2014, Figure 6.5).

With the exception of the work by Aubry *et al.* (2008) on Early Neolithic contexts from the lower Mondego valley, most provenance studies focused on Palaeolithic or Chalcolithic cases. The mentioned authors recognized, through petrographic analysis, a twofold strategy regarding the acquisition of flint: the dominance of local varieties along with the exploitation of sources located outside the analysed river basin, the latter types being imported under the form of elongated blanks or preformed cores. This petrographically-based model corroborates inferences previously obtained elsewhere in the Aire and Candeeiros limestone mountains, where the predominance of local resources was observed—mainly quartz and quartzite—for expedient flake productions, whereas flint went through more elaborate knapping procedures aiming at a blade/bladelet production. But, more importantly, for the first time in the region—see Soares (1995) for similar research developments on the Alentejo coast—a 'dual' management to respond to local variations in lithic availability was recognized, and deserves to be fully quoted in its essentials (Carvalho 1996, 126–7; Portuguese original):

> 'Pieces in quartzite and quartz generally reveal opportunistic (Nelson 1991) or expedient (Binford 1979) strategies [...]. A concrete example of these strategies may be the use given to quartzite during the occupation of the Laranjal do Cabeço das Pias settlement [Figure 1]. If the functional interpretation that is made about the site is correct [...], the occupation related to the agricultural exploitation of the area may have been planned by the group that settled there foreseeing in advance the presence, at the foot of the Arrife [a local fault escarpment], of quartzite pebbles able to provide blanks (flakes) for unspecific toolkits (retouched or blank flakes to cut, notches and denticulates to repair the sickles' wooden handles, etc.). In contrast, essential tools in the context of the activities carried out during the same occupation that could only be produced in flint (such as blades for "sickle implements") would have to be transported to the site (in one or more distinct modalities: untrimmed or preformed cores, unretouched blanks, or retouched toolkits). This different strategy, though taking place simultaneously, and probably in articulation with the former ones, has been designated as "curation" (Binford 1979).
>
> 'A very limited distribution of flint sources in the region, implying therefore greater access difficulties, may have accentuated this unique role of flint within the strategies of raw materials management, a fact which led, in sum, to the widespread circulation of elongated blanks in flint.'

These very same conclusions were resumed and clarified (Carvalho 1998, 89–90) but it was not until a greater volume of lithic assemblages were studied that inter-site correlations and insights on the circulation of flint could be established. This is, for example, the case of the Early Neolithic sector IIIS at Cabeço de Porto Marinho (Figure 1), in Rio Maior, where there are important sources, in secondary deposition, of a reddish-to-brownish type of flint. According to the lithic analysis of the assemblage, it was possible to verify the '[...] local preparation of flint cores for export, which means a deliberate exploitation of a local abiotic resource by this site's inhabitants aiming at the integration of these products in exchange networks or their provision for future use by themselves' (Carvalho 2008, 90; Portuguese original). Conversely, at the Cortiçóis campsite, located on the opposite banks of the Tagus (Figure 1), the technological characteristics of flint assemblage—which includes the Rio Maior type—indicate '[...] the import of semi-knapped cores and/or finished elongated blanks (mostly of bladelet sizes). This reality provisionally points to the hypothesis according to which this vast archaeological site resulted from successive occupations by groups that would have been in different stages of flint consumption' (Cardoso *et al.* 2013, 58; Portuguese original). The only instance where chemical analyses of Early Neolithic flint assemblages was performed—at the Cardial campsite of Cerradinho do Ginete, in Torres Novas—, it was possible to observe the exploitation of several flint sources located along the eastern rim of the region's limestone massifs, therefore implying the existence of north–south transportation routes of around 30 kilometres length (Carvalho and Pereira 2017).

All the above examples indicate curated strategies in the exploitation and management of flint—visible mainly in the circulation of cores and elongated blanks in geographic sectors of flint sources—and thus testimony to a certain degree of human mobility during the Early and Middle Neolithic. If the whole picture is taken in consideration—the abundant use of local, coarse grained rocks when available; the presence of different pottery types and sizes; the use of polished stone axes and adzes; or the presence of grinding stones—it strongly suggests we are dealing with group mobility rather than that of specialist craftsmen.

2.2. Fibrolite

A first inventory of fibrolite tools from Portuguese prehistoric sites was made by Bensaúde (1884). In the course of the twentieth century, both Pinto (1928) and Ferreira (1953) dedicated a couple of works to these tools, converging in the conclusion that these artefacts are found from north to south across the country, but seldom in well-established stratigraphies (indeed, most are surface collections), and that their geological sources are unknown.

Of particular interest is the Casa da Moura cave site (Figure 1), from where six polished fibrolite tools were exhumed during its excavation in the mid-nineteenth century. However, their specific stratigraphic context is unclear, leading authors like Ferreira (1953) to suggest they must have been brought to the site in 'Eneolithic' times. It was only more recently that a few were recovered under controlled stratigraphic conditions, in Early Neolithic contexts. This is the case of Cerradinho do Ginete (Carvalho 2008), Moita da Ladra (Cardoso and Caninas 2010) and Cortiçóis (Cardoso *et al.* 2013) (Figure 1). As a norm, we are dealing with small-sized artefacts, with intact, sharp edges, thus contrasting with the remaining polished stone tools exhumed from the same sites. Together with their intrinsic beauty, these aspects suggested an inherent ritual character to some authors.

Independently of specific roles, their geographic provenance remains an open question. The first published opinion is the one by Bensaúde (1884, 692); in his own words, '[...] *cette substance se trouve généralement intercalée dans les schistes cristallins si largement développés dans le Portugal, et il ne paraît pas impossible que la fibrolithe se trouve chez nous. En tout cas elle ne devait pas être abondante puisqu'on a même profité des plus petits morceaux* [...]'. Later, Pinto (1928, 193; Portuguese original) would move a step forward claiming that '[i]f searched for in Portugal, deposits of fibrolite are found, for example, in Alentejo, associated with serpentines and amphibolites, in Portel, Monforte and Cabeço de Vide [in the inner areas of the upper and middle sectors of the region] [...]. I thus believe to have located a production centre, which must have had an exceptional importance [...]'. In turn, Ferreira (1953) mentions, as a possible origin, the fibrolite sources known in the Somosierra sector of the Guadarrama Mountains, in the Spanish Meseta, north of Madrid. More recently, Carreira and Cardoso (2001/02, 258; Portuguese original), state that this raw material is '[...] unknown in Portuguese territory, especially in sufficiently important numbers permitting the making of these tools' but, acknowledging a particular concentration of polished fibrolite tools in the Inner Beira province, the authors consider this '[...] a consequence of close proximity to raw material sources' in the region.

In the absence of provenance studies on the Portuguese fibrolite (see Cassen *et al.* [2012, 974–975] for a West-European overview), the hypothetical fibrolite sources closer to Estremadura are the ones Pinto (1928) pointed to in the inner Alentejo (Figure 1: box A). This represents a minimum distance of 200 kilometres, and it is thus admissible that only through exchange would these pieces be acquired by Early Neolithic groups in Estremadura. The absence, to date, of fibrolite tools in clear Middle Neolithic contexts in the region should be noted.

2.3. Amphibolite and other polished stones

Bensaúde (1884) put forward two main conclusions that are still valid today: first, that '*parmi les roches qui ont été le plus souvent appliquées à la fabrication des haches, prédominent de beaucoup les amphibolites*' (p. 683) and, second, that '*quoiqu'il ne soit pas possible, de fixer exactement les localités, il me semble hors de doute que ces matériaux proviennent du pays*' (p. 685). He cites Leceia (Figure 1), a hilltop walled settlement dated to the Late Neolithic and Chalcolithic, as one of the sites where this raw material was found. And this is indeed a site that has been receiving particular attention regarding the exploitation and use of amphibolite in Estremadura, despite the fact that the archaeologist who first studied it, Ribeiro (1878), mistakenly considered its collection of axes and adzes to be made of diorite, rather than of amphibolite.

The first modern provenance study of the Leceia amphibolites was published by Cardoso and Carvalhosa

(1995), who follow the analytical procedures—namely petrographic determinations based on thin sections of sampled artefacts—originally carried out at the Bugio Cave (Cardoso *et al.* 1992). Although all 24 analysed artefacts are attributable to the Late Neolithic and Chalcolithic, the conclusions outlined by the mentioned authors can, to some extent, be transposed to the previous Early and Middle Neolithic periods (see below). These are the following (see also Cardoso 2003):

1. Amphibolite tools, which represent around two thirds of the total pieces, were massively imported under the form of 'lithic ingots' (i.e. preforms), not finished tools. The remaining lithologies are represented by varied types—igneous, metamorphic, sedimentary and meta-sedimentary rocks—obtained elsewhere.

2. A mutually exclusive relation seemed to exist between tool and rock types: amphibolites were used mostly for axes (and the much less common hammers, chisels and gouges) whereas adzes were made mostly with the other, softer raw materials.

3. Exploited amphibolite sources must have been those located in the western border of the Hesperian Massif. The authors selected two possible outcrops due to their proximity to Leceia: the Montemor-o-Novo and the Abrantes areas, respectively *ca.* 90 and 130 kilometres to the east and north-east of the site (Figure 1: box B). The other rocks may have been exploited in the lower sector of the Estremadura region, in the borders of the Meso-Cenozoic limestones.

4. The number of pieces recorded at the site seems to attest the existence of stable and long-lasting circulation routes, despite the low ratio of ingots per year—an average of less than two ingots per year was calculated based on an estimation of the site's occupation length of around one millennium (for data, see Cardoso 2003).

Another research project on polished stone tools was also carried out in Estremadura, by Lillios (1997; see also Read *et al.* [1997] for methodological options). It included petrographic and geochemical (X-ray fluorescence) analyses of both artefacts and rock samples collected in the two areas in Portugal where amphibolite outcrops occur: the Morais–Bragança Ophiolite Zone, in the Trás-os-Montes region, and the Ossa–Morena Metavolcanic Zone, in the inner Alentejo. It attempted not only a lithologic characterisation of artefacts but also to pinpoint their sources. After recognizing that amphibolites from both regions are mineralogically and texturally distinctive—thus allowing provenance to be more easily determined—, it was possible to conclude that the sampled amphibolite artefacts (from Late Neolithic and Chalcolithic sites) were sourced in the latter region. Sampled rocks indicated outcrops in the Montemor-o-Novo and Arronches areas (Figure 1: box B). The other rock types represented between 22 to 45 per cent of all the polished tools.

In addition to the relatively restricted number of well-defined archaeological contexts, the problem with Early and Middle Neolithic polished stone assemblages is their usual scarcity in the former period—where they make up less than half a dozen artefacts per site—and the total absence of petrographic or chemical studies permitting sound provenance inferences to be established. These are the reasons why the two most comprehensively studied sites in this regard are Middle Neolithic cemeteries where larger assemblages were exhumed during excavations: the Lugar do Canto (Cardoso and Carvalho 2008) and Bom Santo (Cardoso 2014) cave sites (Figure 1).

At the former site, it was possible to handle and examine macroscopically 12 axes and 16 adzes, plus one gouge. The first tools were all attributed to amphibolite whereas adzes were made '[...] in most cases, of very thin siliceous schists, of black-greenish colours, being noticeable their macroscopic resemblance with vulcanites in the "green schists" group, whose most likely origin is situated in the structural unit designated as the Portuguese South Zone, that develops through the whole of Lower Alentejo, extending up to Spanish territory' (Cardoso and Carvalho 2008, 274; Portuguese original). A specific origin for amphibolites is not provided. At Bom Santo, the obtained panorama is similar, despite the lower number of analysed tools: seven axes and 14 adzes. Again, whereas all axes and one adze were made with amphibolites, '[...] the remaining rocks present dark, microcrystalline textures, which by alteration became whitened to grey. In the absence of petrographic studies, the origins of these rocks are difficult to establish. We are probably dealing with several sources of supply, some with a regional character—rocks derived from the Meso-Cenozoic western border—while others would come from the Lower Alentejo—volcano-sedimentary rocks. These observations are corroborated by the Lugar do Canto evidence, where only two out of the 16 adzes collected were made in amphibolite; the rest were identical to those in Bom Santo Cave' (Cardoso 2014, 193; see Lillios [2000] for slightly different petrographic classifications).

If the inferences regarding the Late Neolithic and Chalcolithic origin of the amphibolite tools, as outlined above, can be transposed to the previous phases of the Neolithic—and nothing in the archaeological records prevents such inference being made—Early and Middle Neolithic communities had forcibly exploited the very same outcrops on the western borders of the Hesperian Massif. The closest to Lugar do Canto and Bom Santo are distributed along an arc encompassing, from north to south, the Abrantes, Ponte de Sor, Avis and Montemor-o-Novo areas (around 90–100 kilometres distance; see Figure 1: box C). Conversely, the metavolcanic rocks are more widely distributed but can be found in the Lower Alentejo (*ca.* 150 kilometres) and the Alcácer do Sal (*ca.* 40 kilometres) areas south of Estremadura.

Expectably, amphibolites and metavolcanic rocks were, for the greater part, imported to Estremadura via exchange network systems. Direct access to amphibolite sources may have taken place in particular circumstances, when the group's economic territories equally comprised Estremadura and amphibolite-rich geological areas. As will be seen below, the population buried at Bom Santo may be testimony to one of these cases (Carvalho 2014; Carvalho *et al.* 2016).

2.4. Clays, tempers and pottery productions

Until very recently, only a few studies aiming at the characterization and provenance of clays and tempers based on petrographic analyses had been published for Early Neolithic contexts in the Estremadura region. The first dealt with the sites in the lower Mondego basin (Tavares 1988), which was immediately followed by a site-focused project on the Caldeirão Cave (Barnett 1987, 1992) and broader research, more comprehensive in scope—it also included sampling of local clays and rocks—on Neolithic sites in the Rio Maior area (Masucci 1995). Among other conclusions, all these studies seemed to reveal a trend according to which part of the Cardial productions were clearly distinct from some other similarly-decorated pots and, more frequently, from pots decorated with typical Epicardial motives.

In order to verify this trend, research based on the systematic petrographic and chemical characterization of potteries and sediments was carried out. It included sites from the Aire and Candeeiros limestone massif and comparisons were established with results obtained in coeval sites from the Western Algarve. Its main results were published very recently by Masucci and Carvalho (2015), where the protocols used and methodological options are described in detail. In this chapter only a few conclusions are discussed.

This project was based on 33 geological samples—which were collected within a seven-kilometre radius around each of the eight selected sites in the region—and 48 potsherds. From this assemblage, it was possible to define three clay groups and three fabric classes (both with subgroups). However, among the 48 analysed potsherds there are three that were left unassigned because their petrographic and/or chemical traits do not fit any of the clay groups or fabric classes: these are all Cardial potsherds—from the Cisterna Gallery of the Almonda karst system, Bocas Rock-shelter and Cabeço de Porto Marinho (Figure 1)—that represent six per cent of all sampled potsherds and twenty-five per cent of all sampled Cardial sherds in the region. Based on a much larger database, this conclusion reinforces previous suggestions and definitely indicates that Cardial productions clearly played a different role (of what nature?) in Early Neolithic pottery productions.

Only further work will be able to define circulation patterns of Cardial pots in greater detail and clarify the questions pending. However, a very interesting observation may already be taken as proven: the long-distance transport of Cardial pots (Masucci and Carvalho 2016). Indeed, the above-cited Cardial pot from Cisterna (Vessel XXI) was made with clays and tempers identified in the Western Algarve; conversely, a Cardial-decorated pot from Padrão (Vessel 1), in the latter region (Figure 1), was made with clays and tempers from the middle Tagus basin. Although terrestrial transport via exchange should not be excluded, coastal navigation by *cabotage* along the South-West coast of Portugal and across the then wider, inner estuaries seems a more likely possibility to describe such long-distance (*ca.* 350 kilometres) transport of fragile goods. This piece of evidence attests not only the likelihood of the maritime colonization model to explain the spread of the earliest Neolithic in these regions (Zilhão 1993, 2001, 2014), but also the establishment of recurrent—even if only occasional—maritime travel in both directions along the Atlantic coastline of Iberia.

Another site-focused project was carried out to determine production techniques and provenances of pots, in this case from the Middle Neolithic burial-cave of Bom Santo (Figure 1). Only four samples were analysed by thin section petrography. All seem to correspond to locally or regionally available raw materials; one (Sample ABS#1), however, '[...] also utilizes a rare technological recipe with the inclusion of dolerite, possibly a temper, as seen in the later Neolithic sites of the Rio Maior area (Forno da Telha and Bocas [Figure 1]). Even if the dolerite is not due to temper, the potters who produced the Bom Santo vessel utilized a sediment type which has not been located' (Carvalho and Masucci 2014, 170). The possibility is that communities living in the Rio Maior area were depositing their dead and the accompanying grave goods in this more southerly cave, implying a *ca.* 35-kilometre journey. These movements probably occurred in the context of the regular, itinerant lifeways of these Middle Neolithic societies (see Carvalho [2014] and Carvalho *et al.* [2016] for a first interpretative model).

2.5. Variscite and other green minerals

Usually designated as 'green stones', this mineralogical group is abundantly represented among personal adornments from archaeological sites of the Portuguese later Prehistory. Despite the erroneous classification of '*ribeirite*' by Bensaúde (1884, 693) as a '*nouvelle variété de la calaïte*' named after Carlos Ribeiro (one of the founders of the *Commisão Geologica de Portugal* in 1857), the works by Canelhas (1973) and Gonçalves (1979; Gonçalves and Reis 1982) were able to establish on solid analytical foundations that these adornments are made of a variety of mineral types: muscovite, talc, chlorite and, above all, variscite.

To date, there is only one site in Estremadura with variscite and muscovite beads attributed to the Early Neolithic, the Caldeirão Cave (Zilhão 1992) (Figure 1). Other Estremadura sites with Early and Middle Neolithic occupation phases lack stratigraphic references or specific contexts from which sound chronocultural assignments can be retrieved. Moreover, only part of these minerals were characterized by X-ray examination or other analyses (e.g., PIXE), and thus remain classified only macroscopically, either broadly as 'green stones' or more specifically as '*calaíte*'.

At Caldeirão, the mineral classification was based on X-ray diffraction analysis, allowing the identification of one muscovite and three variscite beads. These grave goods were exhumed from the Epicardial occupation, radiocarbon dated to *ca.* 4900–4600 cal BC. Possible sources in Portugal have been tentatively located in Mangualde (Gonçalves and Reis 1982), Ponte de Lima (Ferreira *et al.* 1999) and in several locations in the Trás-os-Montes province (Meireles *et al.* 1987), between 200 and 300 kilometres, respectively, to the north and north-east of the site. However, according to Real (1992, 316; Portuguese original), '[...] it is likely that the raw material used in the making of the variscite beads from Caldeirão Cave had a close origin, probably in the Silurian outcrops of the Zêzere basin [Figure 1], located a little more than twenty kilometres to the north-east of the cave'.

In sum, there are two possibilities to explain the presence of variscite and muscovite beads in Caldeirão in such a precocious moment within the Neolithic period:

1. The existence of variscite sources in Silurian outcrops within the likely mobility range of the human group that used Caldeirão as a burial ground, thus within a radius necessarily shorter than the 200–300 kilometres mentioned above but comprising the geologically more favourable, schistose areas of the surrounding metamorphic formations where still-to-be-found sources may exist—in sum, a possibility that is in line with Real's (1992) initial proposal.

2. They mark the early exploitation stages of the two variscite sources in Western Iberia that are known to have been exploited since Prehistoric times, probably from the fifth millennium BC onwards: Palazuelo de las Cuevas (Zamora) and Pico Centeno (Huelva). The presence of variscite beads in Neolithic Estremadura would be, under this hypothesis, the result of long-distance processes of transportation.

Distribution maps of 'green stone' items—classified either macroscopically or chemically—show an overall scarcity of this raw material in Early and Middle Neolithic times, despite its more or less uniform presence across the country. Indeed, its scarcity before the Late Neolithic and Chalcolithic periods has long been recognized. For example, Leisner and Leisner (1951, 148; Portuguese original) state that '[c]allais beads are very rare in the municipality [of Reguengos de Monsaraz], only two, of medium sizes, having been found in Dolmen 2 of Comenda (Est. XI, 66, 67), besides a small, flat object with a central perforation, in Dolmen 1 of Passo (Est. XIX, 45)'. This panorama may be transposed to Middle Neolithic dolmens from the northern half of the country: at Carapito 1 (Leisner and Ribeiro 1968) and Seixo da Beira (Leisner, 1998), nine and five variscite beads, respectively, were macroscopically identified by the authors; and at Areita (Gomes *et al.* 1998) and Sangrino (Carvalho 2005) 13 variscite plus one fluorite beads and one variscite bead, respectively, were classified by X-ray analysis (P. S. Carvalho, pers. inf.).

The above trend and the generalized lack, not only of provenance analyses that could pinpoint their geologic sources, but even of more rigorous mineralogical classifications, prevent for the time being any of the above hypotheses—exploitation of local Silurian outcrops or the early exploitation of Palazuelo de las Cuevas and/or Pico Centeno—to be chosen as the most likely to explain the observable distribution patterns of variscite finds in Early and Middle Neolithic caves and megalithic monuments.

3. Palaeoisotopic evidence for human mobility

A recently-finished research project focused on the burial-cave of Bom Santo (Figure 1), in the Montejunto Mountain, is the only one so far published for Middle Neolithic sites aiming at systematic provenance determination of raw materials and goods—pottery clay and tempers, shell adornments, and polished stone tools (see previous section)—alongside isotopic analyses of human and animal remains to determine mobility patterns (Carvalho *et al.* 2012, 2016). Fourteen out of 73 individuals were sampled, thus representing around one fifth (19 per cent, to be exact) of the total population deposited in the cave's Rooms A and B. Similar analyses were applied to five herbivore remains (three sheep / goat and two red deer) for the determination of local strontium baselines (Price 2014).

Personal adornments were made from shells that may have been obtained in the Tagus estuary—that reached about a dozen kilometres wide in front of the cave in the Middle Holocene—or in the nearest Atlantic littoral (Dean and Carvalho 2014). One of the four analysed pots may have been made in Rio Maior, 30–35 kilometres to the north (Carvalho and Masucci 2014; see above), and some of the metamorphic rocks can only have been brought, either from the Hesperian Massif (90–100 kilometres to the east) in the case of amphibolites, or from the Alcácer do Sal or Lower Alentejo areas (80–90 and 150 kilometres to the south, respectively) in the case of the metavolcanic rocks (Cardoso 2014). However, the most surprising result was the conclusion that, according to the strontium isotopic results (Price 2014), only three individuals out of 14 (21 per cent) are 'locals'; the remaining 11 (79 per cent) show isotopic patterns pointing to the frequentation, at least during childhood, of regions geologically older than Montejunto Mountain. Equally interesting is the observation that two out of the three caprines revealed isotopic results similar to the 'non-local' humans.

A first interpretative model was built upon these results (Carvalho 2014; Carvalho *et al.* 2016). It proposes the frequentation of a large area, *ca.* 100 kilometres long, encompassing the territory between the Montejunto Mountain and the Mora plain, in the Alentejo, broadly coinciding with the Flandrian valleys of the Ota and Sorraia rivers (Figure 1: box C). These water bodies would then facilitate human mobility between both sides of the Tagus estuary—due to favourable navigation conditions—and would explain the relatively high percentages (average above 20 per cent) of estuarine / riverine food-sources isotopically detected in the Bom Santo population (Petchey 2014; Carvalho *et al.* 2016), with no similar parallel in other Neolithic populations from Estremadura. Human groups would inhabit this territory (accompanied by their livestock) and would acquire raw materials by direct access to their sources, or through exchange networks, in the case of adjacent or more remote sources.

Mobility studies based on strontium analysis were also applied to Late Neolithic and Chalcolithic populations in the Torres Vedras area. The results, however, contrast totally with those from the Bom Santo Cave. Indeed, according to Waterman *et al.* (2014), only five out of 55 individuals were classed as 'migrants', which means nine per cent of the sampled population. If compared with Bom Santo, the logic conclusion is that of a major change in human mobility across the Neolithic–Chalcolithic boundary in the region: from group to individual mobility[1]. This has obvious implications for the modalities according to which goods circulated.

4. Conclusions: the context of human mobility

If confirmed by future research in the region, the aforementioned changes—that may have taken place some time within the last quarter of the fourth millennium BC—seem to give rise to a twofold phenomenon that will characterize human mobility in the following millennium:

1. The people moving across territories are no longer 'segments' (i.e. an aggregation of families) of a larger community—in the sense of a 'Neolithic type of mobility' (see below)—but instead single individuals or small human groups—i.e. a 'Chalcolithic type of mobility'. A drastic reduction in the size of the groups travelling across regions seems to be a plausible hypothesis to be tested as the number of isotopic studies increases in future research.

2. A significant enlargement in the distances being travelled. Indeed, two of the 'migrants' from Torres Vedras showed strontium ratios that can match the older geological formations of the inner Alentejo (Waterman *et al.* 2014); furthermore, a similar study on the burials from Tomb 1 at Perdigões (Boaventura *et al.* 2010), in the Reguengos de Monsaraz area of Alentejo, reinforced this possibility and led to the suggestion that '[...] people, in addition to goods, were also migrating from the Portuguese interior to the coastal Estremadura' (Waterman *et al.* 2014, 125), in this case totalizing a *ca.* 200 kilometres journey.

It should be noted that the strontium and oxygen analyses of human samples from Tomb 1 at Perdigões, mentioned above, also indicated that six out of eight (75 per cent) individuals were 'migrants' (Boaventura *et al.* 2010, 2014), a result that seems to contradict the above model, at least as regards the 'Chalcolithic type of mobility'. Some Chalcolithic funerary contexts in the western part of southern Spain, where larger samples were used, also revealed relatively high numbers of 'migrants' in some cases, although in variable percentages (Díaz-Zorita *et al.* 2014): five out of 17 (29 per cent) at la Pijotilla (Badajoz) and six out of 19 (32 per cent) at Valencina (Seville). However, considering current interpretations of these huge archaeological complexes as 'aggregation sites' may explain the presence of an otherwise abnormal number of 'non-locals'.

Though beyond the scope of this chapter, it is also important to note the correlation of this new type of mobility with two other observations. First, it coincides with the emergence of craft specialization—e.g. in metalworking or knapped stone—along with what may be the emergence of permanent forms of social inequality. Second, it also coincides with a notable increase in the frequency of rare or exotic goods, 'ideotechnic' artefacts that respond to a vast and complex series of structural changes that characterize Chalcolithic societies on several levels, from cosmology and forms of death management (e.g. Valera 2009, 2012) to the ways in which the Sacred was materialized.

In sum, 'before metal', goods would have been acquired by the human groups themselves, either through direct access to the respective geological formations in the context of their regular itinerancy (if these were located within their territories of immediate economic exploitation), or through exchange systems. The latter have been described according to several theoretical models[2] and under distinct

[1] It should be noted that four of the five 'migrants' are from the cave of Cova da Moura, which presents major contextual and stratigraphic limitations. Indeed, there is a sharp contrast between the diversified material culture items (that, corroborated by radiocarbon determinations, span between the Neolithic and the Bronze Age) and the simplicity of the field observations that recognized only a 'bottom layer', or '*fundführende schicht*' in the words of Spindler (1981, add. 4), despite the apparent care with which the screening of the sediments was carried out, allowing the recovery of abundant small-sized items (Belo *et al.* 1961). Direct radiocarbon dating of the four human samples in question would give us the real perception of the change—if gradual or abrupt—from one type of mobility to another in Estremadura.

[2] A mention should be made, in this regard, to the fact that these behaviours do not necessarily and exclusively fall within the sphere of economic behaviour, as commonly acknowledged by most Portuguese scholars, who usually employ terms such as 'trade' or 'commerce' to describe it. Indeed, circulation of goods is an archaeological observable phenomenon that may reflect also a myriad of social and ritual practices.

perspectives but their structuring features are always relying on the relation between spatial distribution of goods and raw material sources, the variable distance ranges comprised in the exchange system under study, and the models that can be built upon the retrieved observations. This is namely the case of the 'central place redistribution models' and the 'symmetrical, homogeneous, reciprocal exchange networks'—to use Renfrew's (1977) terms—that can be best applied, respectively, to the aforementioned Chalcolithic and Neolithic differences.

Terrestrial circulation is implicit in most—if not all—of the examples discussed in the previous sections. With the exception of the Cardial ware, this would be the case of all the other materials: flint, fibrolite, amphibolite and green minerals. Though regular navigation within the Tagus and Sorraia estuaries is foreseen, terrestrial circulation is also explicit in the case of the model put forward to explain the Bom Santo Cave evidence, which was framed and understood according to three successive radii, or 'geographical belts', with the site as epicentre (Carvalho 2014; Carvalho *et al.* 2016; see Figure 1: box C).

However, if the Cardial pots from Cisterna and Padrão can be considered a strong case demonstrating navigation along the South–West coast of Portugal in the second half of the sixth millennium BC (Masucci and Carvalho 2016)—thus in line with interpretations for the early neolithisation of Iberia in the context of Mediterranean navigation, as recently reaffirmed (Zilhão 2014)—another find from Estremadura can also be correlated with Neolithic navigation routes but in this case pointing to the more northerly regions of the Atlantic façade. This is the case of the perforated hand-axe found in the Óbidos Lagoon (Figure 1), which was made with amphibolite presumably imported from the inner areas of central Portugal (Lillios *et al.* 2000). This exceptional artefact was recently reclassified as an Iberian imitation—the so-called 'Cangas type'—of the Carnacean Tumiac prototypes, which were made with Alpine jade and circulated across Western Europe in the second half of the fifth millennium BC. According to Petrequin *et al.* (2012, Figure 3 and 217–9), the distribution of these '*object–signes à très forte valeur rituelle et probablement religieuse*' show '[...] *un épicentre au nord-ouest de l'Espagne et une large diffusion dans la péninsule, au moins jusqu'en Catalogne et au sud du Portugal* [...] *à 1000 km du Morbihan à vol d'oiseau*'. Moreover, these artefacts circulated together with Iberian fibrolite tools and variscite adornments, with Carnac, in the Gulf of Morbihan, acting as the epicentre. Their main (but not exclusive) transportation routes were the Atlantic seaways that connected not only Brittany with Iberia (Domínguez-Bella *et al.* 2016) but also the former region with Britain and Ireland (Cassen *et al.* 2012). Such maritime routes have been receiving renewed attention in recent years in the debate on the transition to farming in these insular territories (e.g. Callaghan and Scarre 2009; Rowley-Conwy 2011) but are also the same providing explanation to the wide distribution of the aforementioned valuables.

Is it in this broader context that the Óbidos axe, as well as the variscite and fibrolite items found in Early and Middle Neolithic sites from Estremadura, can be understood—i.e., as prestige, interchangeable goods (as claimed by Pétrequin *et al.* 2013) in otherwise egalitarian, segmentary and itinerant farming communities (as implicit in the model by Carvalho *et al.* 2016)?

Statements that this circulation in the prehistoric past is confined to economic practices ignore other realms of human behaviour that surely had a role to play in the regular ways of life of these early farming communities.

Acknowledgments

To Pedro Sobral de Carvalho, for personal information on the X-ray analyses (performed by A. Huet Bacelar Gonçalves) on the variscite and fluorite beads from Areita (São João da Pesqueira) and Sangrino (Penedono) dolmens.

References

Aubry, Thierry; Mangado, Javier; Matias, Henrique. "Matérias-primas das ferramentas em pedra lascada da Pré-História do centro e nordeste de Portugal." In *Proveniência de materiais geológicos: abordagens sobre o Quaternário de Portugal*, edited by P. Dinis, A. Gomes and S. Monteiro-Rodrigues, 165–192. Porto: Associação Portuguesa de Estudo do Quaternário, 2014.

Aubry, Thierry; Neves, Maria João; Almeida, Miguel; Mangado, Javier. "Modalidades de aprovisionamento em matérias-primas líticas no Baixo Mondego durante o Holocénico: dados novos e revisão de séries arqueológicas." In *IV Congreso del Neolítico Peninsular*, vol. II, 258–265. Alicante: Museo Arqueológico de Alicante, 2008.

Barnett, William K. "The Early Neolithic impressed pottery from the Gruta do Caldeirão (Tomar, Portugal)." *O Arqueólogo Português* 5 (1987): 67-88.

Barnett, William K. "The physical analysis of Early Neolithic impressed pottery from Gruta do Caldeirão." In *Gruta do Caldeirão. O Neolítico antigo*, edited by J. Zilhão, 297–312. Lisboa: Instituto Português do Património Arquitectónico e Arqueológico, 1992.

Belo, Ricardo; Trindade, Leonel; Ferreira O. da Veiga. "Gruta da Cova da Moura (Torres Vedras)." *Comunicações dos Serviços Geológicos de Portugal* 45 (1961): 391–418.

Bensaúde, Alfredo. "Note sur la nature minéralogique de quelques instruments de pierre trouvés en Portugal." In *Congrès International d'Anthropologie et d'Archéologie Préhistoriques (Neuvième session)*, 682–697. Lisbonne: Académie Royale des Sciences, 1884.

Binford, Lewis. "Organization and formation processes: looking at curated technologies". *Journal of Archaeological Method and Theory* 3 (1979): 57–100.

Boaventura, Rui; Ferreira, Maria Teresa; Neves, Maria João; Silva, Ana Maria. "Funeray practices and anthropology during Middle-Late Neolithic (4th and 3rd millennia BCE) in Portugal: old bones, new insights." *Anthropologie* 52 (2014): 183-205.

Boaventura, Rui; Hillier, Maria; Grimes, Vaughan. "Moving around? Testing mobility with strontium isotopes ($^{87}Sr/^{86}Sr$) in the Late Neolithic of South–Central Portugal" (unpublished poster).

In *8.º* Encontro de Arqueologia do Algarve. *A Arqueologia e as outras ciências*. Silves: Câmara Municipal de Silves, 2010.

Callaghan, Richard; Scarre, Chris. "Simulating the western seaways." *Oxford Journal of Archaeology* 28 (2009): 357–372.

Canêlhas, Maria da Graça Salvado. "Estudo radiográfico de 'calaítes' portuguesas." *Revista de Guimarães* 83 (1973): 125–144.

Cardoso, João Luís. "O comércio de matérias-primas de origem geológica, dos meados do VI milénio a.C. aos finais do III milénio a.C., no Ocidente peninsular: breve ensaio." *Boletim da Sociedade de Geografia de Lisboa* 1 (2003): 91–106.

Cardoso, João Luís. "Polished stone tools." In *Bom Santo Cave (Lisbon) and the Middle Neolithic Societies of Southern Portugal*, edited by A. F. Carvalho, 185–194. Faro: Universidade do Algarve, 2014.

Cardoso, João Luís; Caninas, João Carlos. "Moita da Ladra (Vila Franca de Xira). Resultados preliminares da escavação integral de um povoado calcolítico muralhado." In *Transformação e mudança no centro e sul de Portugal: o 4.º e o 3.º milénios a.n.e. Actas do colóquio internacional*, edited by V. S. Gonçalves and A. C. Sousa, 65–96. Cascais: Câmara Municipal de Cascais, 2010.

Cardoso, João Luís; Carvalhosa, A. Barros e. "Estudos petrográficos de artefactos de pedra polida do povoado pré-histórico de Leceia (Oeiras). Análises de proveniências." *Estudos Arqueológicos de Oeiras* 5 (1995): 123–152.

Cardoso, João Luís; Carvalho, António Faustino. "A gruta do Lugar do Canto (Alcanede) e sua importância no faseamento do Neolítico no território português." In *Octávio da Veiga Ferreira. Homenagem ao Homem, ao Arqueólogo e ao Professor*, edited by J. L. Cardoso, 269–300. Oeiras: Câmara Municipal de Oeiras, 2008.

Cardoso, João Luís; Carvalho, António Faustino; Gibaja, Juan Francisco. "O sítio do Neolítico antigo de Cortiçóis (Almeirim, Santarém)." *Revista Portuguesa de Arqueologia* 16 (2013): 27–61.

Cardoso, João Luís; Domínguez-Bella, Salvador; Martínez-López, J. "Ocorrência de contas de fluorite no Neolítico final e no Calcolítico da Estremadura (Portugal)." In *IX Congresso Ibérico de Arqueometria*, edited by M. I. Dias and J. L. Cardoso, 35–42. Oeiras: Câmara Municipal de Oeiras, 2012.

Cardoso, João Luís; Monteiro, R.; Ferreira, O. da Veiga; Coelho, A. V. Pinto; Guerra, Filomena; Gil, F. Bragança; Pais, João. "A Lapa do Bugio." *Setúbal Arqueológica* 9–10 (1992): 89–226.

Carreira, Júlio Roque; Cardoso, João Luís. "A gruta da Casa da Moura (Cesareda, Óbidos) e a sua ocupação pós-paleolítica." *Estudos Arqueológicos de Oeiras* 10, (2001/02): 249–362.

Carvalho, António Faustino. *O Neolítico antigo do Maciço Calcário Estremenho. Tecnologia e tipologia da indústria de pedra lascada* (unpublished M.A. dissertation). Lisboa: Universidade de Lisboa, 1995.

Carvalho, António Faustino. *Talhe da pedra no Neolítico antigo do Maciço Calcário das Serras d'Aire e Candeeiros (Estremadura Portuguesa). Um primeiro modelo tecnológico e tipológico*. Lisboa: Colibri, 1998.

Carvalho, António Faustino. *A neolitização do Portugal meridional. Os exemplos do Maciço Calcário Estremenho e do Algarve ocidental*. Faro: Universidade do Algarve, 2008.

Carvalho, António Faustino. "Bom Santo Cave in context. A preliminary contribution to the study of the first megalith builders of Southern Portugal." In *Bom Santo Cave (Lisbon) and the Middle Neolithic Societies of Southern Portugal*, edited by A. F. Carvalho, 209–230. Faro: Universidade do Algarve, 2014.

Carvalho, António Faustino. "Antes dos metais: mobilidade humana e circulação de bens no Neolítico do centro de Portugal." In *Tráfego de objetos, tráfego tecnológico. Sintomas das ideologias dominantes na Ibéria*, edited by A. R. Cruz and E. Cerrillo, 33–37. Tomar: Centro de Pré-História do Instituto Politécnico de Tomar, 2015.

Carvalho, António Faustino; Alves-Cardoso, Francisca; Gonçalves, David; Granja, Raquel; Cardoso, João Luís; Dean, Rebecca M.; Gibaja, Juan Francisco; Masucci, Maria A.; Arroyo-Pardo, Eduardo; Fernández, Eva; Petchey, Fiona; Price, T. Douglas; Mateus, José E.; Queiroz, Paula Fernanda; Callapez, Pedro M.; Pimenta, Carlos; Regala, Frederico Tátá. "The Bom Santo Cave (Lisbon, Portugal): catchment, diet and patterns of mobility of a Middle Neolithic population." *European Journal of Archaeology* 19 (2016): 187–214.

Carvalho, António Faustino; Gonçalves, David; Granja, Raquel; Petchey, Fiona. "Algar do Bom Santo: a Middle Neolithic necropolis in Portuguese Estremadura." In *Funerary practices in the Iberian Peninsula from the Mesolithic to the Chalcolithic*, edited by J. F. Gibaja, A. F. Carvalho and P. Chambon, 77–90. Oxford: British Archaeological Reports, 2012.

Carvalho, António Faustino; Masucci, Maria A. "Pottery." In *Bom Santo Cave (Lisbon) and the Middle Neolithic Societies of Southern Portugal*, edited by A. F. Carvalho, 161–172. Faro: Universidade do Algarve, 2014.

Carvalho, António Faustino; Pereira, Telmo. "Flint variability in a Cardial context. A preliminary evaluation by portable X-ray fluorescence of artefacts from Cerradinho do Ginete (Portuguese Estremadura)." In *The exploitation of raw materials in Prehistory: sourcing, processing and distribution*, edited by T. Pereira, X. Terradas and N.F. Bicho, 265–283. Cambridge: Cambridge Scholars Publishing.

Carvalho, Pedro Sobral. *A necrópole megalítica da Senhora do Monte (Penedono, Viseu). Um espaço sagrado pré-histórico na Beira Alta*. Viseu: Centro de Estudos Pré-Históricos da Beira Alta, 2005.

Cassen, Serge; Boujot, Christine; Domínguez-Bella, Salvador; Guiacarc'h, Mikaël; Le Pennec, Christophe; Prieto, María Pilar; Querré, Guirec; Santrot, Marie-Hélène; Vigier, Emmanulle. "Dépôts bretons, tumulus carnacéens et circulations à longue distance." In *Jade. Grandes haches alpines du Néolithique européen. V^e et IVe millénaires av. J.-C.*, vol. 2, edited by P. Pétrequin, S. Cassen, M. Errera, L. Klassen and A. Sheridan, 918–995. Besançon: Presses Universitaires de Franche-Comté, 2012.

Dean, Rebecca M.; Carvalho, António Faustino. "Faunal remains, adornments and bone tools." In *Bom Santo Cave (Lisbon) and the Middle Neolithic Societies of Southern Portugal*, edited by A. F. Carvalho, 195–205. Faro: Universidade do Algarve, 2014.

Dias, João Alvarinho; Boski, Tomasz; Rodrigues, Alexandre; Magalhães, Fernando. "Coast line evolution in Portugal since the Last Glacial Maximum until present: a synthesis." *Marine Geology* 170 (2000): 177–186.

Díaz-Zorita, Marta; Waterman, Anna J.; Peate, David. "La movilidad de las poblaciones de la Edad del Cobre en el Suroeste de España a través de los análisis de isótopos estables de $^{87/86}Sr$ y ^{18}O." In *2.º Congreso de Prehistoria de Andalucía: movilidad, contacto y cambio, 111–120.* Sevilla: Consejería de Educación, Cultura y Deporte, 2014.

Domínguez-Bella, Salvador; Cassen, Serge; Pétrequin, Pierre; Přichystal, Antonín; Martínez, Javier; Ramos, José; Medina, Nieves. "Aroche (Huelva, Andalucía): a new Neolithic axehead of Alpine jade in the southwest of the Iberian Peninsula." *Archaeological and Anthropological Science* 16 (2016): 205–222.

Ferreira, M. D.; Silva, V.; Lima, M. F.; Gomes, C. L. "Anatomia de algumas ocorrências de gemas e seu enquadramento em protocolos de ordenamento territorial. Contributo ara uma reflexão sobre o estatuto dos depósitos gemíferos portugueses." *Cadernos do Laboratório Xeológico de Laxe* 24 (1999): 31–44.

Ferreira, O. da Veiga. "Os instrumentos de fibrolite do Museu dos Serviços Geológicos." *Anais da Faculdade de Ciências do Porto* 37 (1953): 37–44.

Gomes, Luís Filipe Coutinho; Carvalho, Pedro Sobral; Perpétuo, João André; Marrafa, Carmo. "O dólmen de Areita (S. João da Pesqueira, Viseu)." In *A Pré-História na Beira Interior*, 33–94. Viseu: Centro de Estudos Pré-Históricos da Beira Alta, 1998.

Gonçalves, A. A. Huet Bacelar. "Elementos de adorno de cor verde provenientes de estações arqueológicas portuguesas. Importância do seu estudo mineralógico." In *I Mesa-Redonda sobre o Neolítico e o Calcolítico em Portugal*, 209–225. Porto: Grupo de Estudos Arqueológicos do Porto, 1979.

Gonçalves, A. A. Huet Bacelar; Reis, Maria de Lurdes. "Estudo mineralógico de elementos de adorno de cor verde proveniente de estações arqueológicas portuguesas." *Trabalhos do Instituto de Antropologia Dr. Mendes Correia* 40 (1982): 153–166.

Leisner, Georg; Leisner, Vera. *Antas do concelho de Reguengos de Monsaraz. Materiais para o estudo da cultura megalítica em Portugal.* Lisboa: Instituto para a Alta Cultura, 1951.

Leisner, Vera. *Die megalithgräber der Iberischen Halbinsel. Die Westen.* Berlin: Walter de Gruyter, 1998.

Leisner, Vera; Ribeiro, Leonel. "Die dolmen von Carapito." *Madrider Mitteilugen* 9 (1968): 11–62.

Lillios, Katina T. "Amphibolite tools of the Portuguese Copper Age (3000-2000 BC): a geoarchaeological approach to Prehistoric economics and symbolism." *Geoarchaeology* 12 (1997): 137–163.

Lillios, Katina T. "A biographical approach to the ethnogeology of Late Prehistoric Portugal." *Trabajos de Prehistoria* 57 (2000): 19–28.

Lillios, Katina T.; Read, Caroline; Alves, Francisco. "The axe of the Óbidos Lagoon (Portugal): an uncommon find recovered during an underwater archaeological survey (1999)." *Revista Portuguesa de Arqueologia* 1 (2000): 5–14.

Masucci, Maria A. "Early Neolithic pottery production in the Rio Maior valley, Portuguese Estremadura." In *The ceramics cultural heritage. 8th CIMTEC: World ceramics congress and forum on new materials*, edited by P. Vincenzini, 493–503. Faenza: Techna Srl, 1995.

Masucci, Maria A.; Carvalho, António Faustino. "Ceramic technology and resource use during the Neolithic in Central–Southern Portugal." *Archaeometry* 58 (2016): 201–221.

Meireles, Carlos; Ferreira, N.; Reis, Maria de Lurdes. "Variscite occurrence in Silurian formations from Northern Portugal." *Comunicações dos Serviços Geológicos de Portugal* 73 (1987): 21–27.

Nelson, Margaret C. "The study of technological organization." *Journal of Archaeological Method and Theory* 3 (1991), 57–100.

Petchey, Fiona. "Radiocarbon chronology and palaeodiets." In *Bom Santo Cave (Lisbon) and the Middle Neolithic Societies of Southern Portugal*, edited by A. F. Carvalho, 143–150. Faro: Universidade do Algarve, 2014.

Pétrequin, Pierre; Errera, Manuel; Martin, Araceli; Fábregas, Ramón; Vaquer, Jean. "Les haches en jades alpins pendant les Ve et IVe millénaires. L'exemple de l'Espagne et du Portugal dans une perspective européenne." In *Xarxes al Neolític. Circulació i intercanvi de matèries, productes i idees a la Mediterrània occidental (VII-III mil·lenni a.C.)*, edited by M. Borrell, F. Borrell, J. Bosch, X. Clop and M. Molist, 213–222. Barcelona: Museu d'Arqueologia de Catalunya, 2012.

Pétrequin, Pierre; Cassen, Serge; Errera, Manuel; Klassen, Lutz; Pétrequin Anne-Marie; Sheridan, Alison. "The value of things: the production and circulation of Alpine jade axes during the 5th-4th millennia in a European perspective." In *Economic Archaeology: from structure to performance in European Archaeology*, edited by T. Kerig and A. Zimmermann, 65–82. Bonn: Habelt, 2013.

Pinto, Rui de Serpa. "Museu de Martins Sarmento. I - Machados de pedra polida." *Revista de Guimarães* 38 (1928): 192–194.

Price, T. Douglas. "Isotope proveniencing." In *Bom Santo Cave (Lisbon) and the Middle Neolithic Societies of Southern Portugal*, edited by A. F. Carvalho, 151–158. Faro: Universidade do Algarve, 2014.

Read, Caroline; Grapes, Rodney; Lillios, Katina T. *Petrography and chemical analyses of Prehistoric amphibolite artefacts from Portugal and possible source rocks from Western Iberia.* Wellington: Victoria University of Wellington Press, 1997.

Real, Fernando. "Estudo mineralógico de adornos de cor verde do Neolítico antigo da Gruta do Caldeirão." *Gruta do Caldeirão. O Neolítico antigo*, edited by J. Zilhão, 315–319. Lisboa: Instituto Português do Património Arquitectónico e Arqueológico, 1992.

Renfrew, Colin. "Alternative models for exchange and spatial distribution." In *Exchange systems in Prehistory*, edited by T. K. Earle and J. E. Ericson, 71–90. New York: Academic Press, 1977.

Ribeiro, Carlos. *Noticia de algumas estações e monumentos prehistoricos. Noticia da estação humana de Licêa*, vol. I. Lisboa: Typographia da Academia, 1878.

Rocha, Leonor; Oliveira, Jorge; Dias, Cristina Barroca; Mirão, José; Dias, Luís; Manhita, Ana. "Sobre a presença de materiais exóticos em alguns monumentos megalíticos funerários alentejanos: os casos do cinábrio e do âmbar." In *Tráfego de objetos, tráfego tecnológico. Sintomas das ideologias dominantes na Ibéria*, edited by A. R. Cruz and E. Cerrillo, 43–46. Tomar: Centro de Pré-História do Instituto Politécnico de Tomar, 2015.

Rowley-Conwy, Peter. "Westward Ho! The spread of agriculture from Central Europe to the Atlantic." *Current Anthropology* 52: supplement (2011): 431–451.

Schuhmacher, Thomas X. "Ivory exchange networks in the Chalcolithic of the Western Mediterranean." In *Key ressources and sociocultural developments in the Iberian Chalcolithic*, edited by M. Bertelheim, P. Bueno and M. Kunst, 291–312. Tübingen, 2017.

Soares, Joaquina. "Mesolítico-Neolítico na costa sudoeste: transformações e permanências." In *1.º Congresso de Arqueologia*

Peninsular, vol. 6, 27–45. Porto, Sociedade Portuguesa de Antropologia e Etnologia, 1995.

Spindler, Konrad. *Cova da Moura. Die besiedlung des atlantischen küstengebietes Miittelportugals vom Neolithikum bis an das Ende der Bronzezeit.* Madrid: Deutsches Archäologisches Institut, 1981.

Tavares, António. "Estudo petrográfico de algumas cerâmicas de jazidas neolíticas do Baixo Mondego." In *Subsídios para o estudo da Pré-História recente do Baixo Mondego*, edited by R. Vilaça, 66–73. Lisboa: Instituto Português do Património Cultural, 1988.

Valera, António Carlos. "Cosmological bonds and settlement aggregation processes during late Neolithic and Copper Age in South Portugal." In *Reimagining regional analyses: the Archaeology of spatial and social dynamics*, edited by T. L. Thurston and R. B. Salisbury, 234–265. Newcastle: Cambridge Scholars Publishing, 2009.

Valera, António Carlos. "Ditches, pits and hypogea: new data and new problems in south Portugal Late Neolithic and Chalcolithic practices." In *Funerary practices in the Iberian Peninsula from the Mesolithic to the Chalcolithic*, edited by J. F. Gibaja, A. F. Carvalho and P. Chambon, 103–112. Oxford: British Archaeological Reports, 2012.

Vis, Geert-Jan; Kasse, Cornelis; Vandenberghe, Jef. "Late Pleistocene and Holocene palaeogeography of the Lower Tagus Valley (Portugal): effects of relative sea level, valley morphology and sediment supply." *Quaternary Science Reviews* 27 (2008): 1682–1709.

Waterman, Anna J.; Peate, David W.; Silva, Ana Maria; Thomas, Jonathan T. "In search of homelands: using strontium isotopes to identify biological markers of mobility in late prehistoric Portugal." *Journal of Archaeological Science* 42 (2014): 119–127.

Zilhão, João. *Gruta do Caldeirão. O Neolítico antigo.* Lisboa, Instituto Português do Património Arquitectónico e Arqueológico, 1992.

Zilhão, João. "The spread of agro-pastoral economies across Mediterranean Europe: a view from the Far West." *Journal of Mediterranean Archaeology* 6 (1993): 5–63.

Zilhão, João. "Radiocarbon evidence for maritime pioneer colonization at the origins of farming in West Mediterranean Europe." *Proceedings of the National Academy of Sciences* 98 (2001): 14180–14185.

Zilhão, João. "Early Prehistoric navigation in the Western Mediterranean: implications for the Neolithic transition in Iberia and the Maghreb." *European Prehistory* 11 (2014): 185–200.

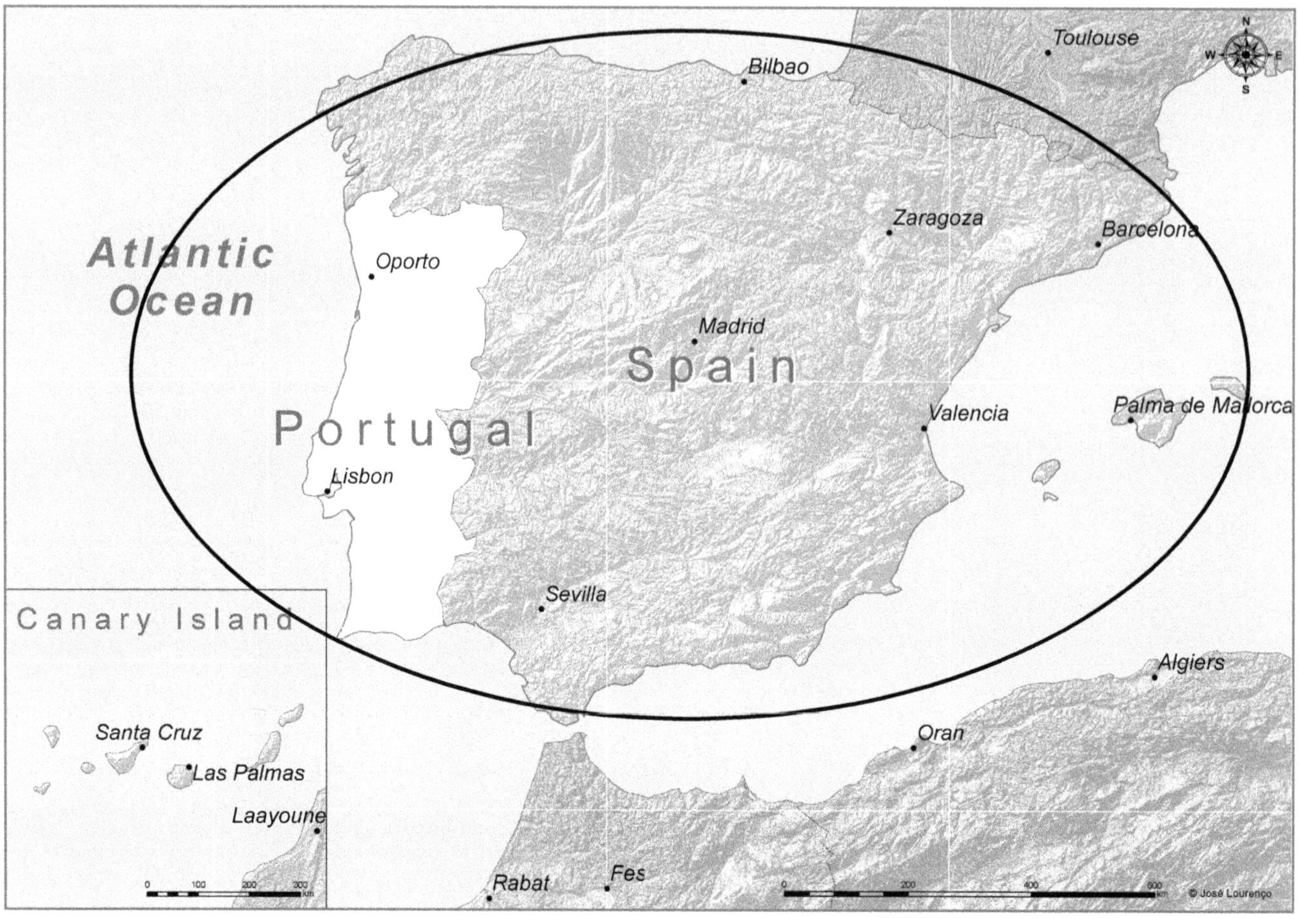

Spain - Iberian Peninsula.
Source: José Martinho Lourenço.

Chapter 5

Green and/or Far Away: The Case of the Alpine Axes in Iberia

Ramón Fábregas Valcarce[1], Arturo de Lombera-Hermida[1,2], Carlos Rodríguez-Rellán[1], Pierre Petrequin[3]

[1]Grupo de Estudos para a Prehistoria do Noroeste Ibérico. Arqueoloxía, Antigüidade e Territorio (GEPN-AAT), Dpto. Historia, Universidade de Santiago de Compostela, 15782, Santiago de Compostela, Spain, ramon.fabregas@usc.es, artulomb@gmail.com, carlos.rellan@usc.es

[2]Institut Català de Paleoecologia Humana i Evolució Social (IPHES), C/ Marcel. lí Domingo s/n - Campus Sescelades URV (Edifici W3), 43007 Tarragona, Spain,

[3]MSHE C.N. Ledoux, CNRS et Université de Franche-Comté, Besançon, France, archeo.petrequin@free.fr

Abstract: Large polished axes of Alpine jades have circulated across Europe during the 5th and 4th Millennia BC. The presence of the Alpine axes in the Iberian Peninsula is further restricted than elsewhere in Western Europe, though still significant. Over 40 alpine axes have been catalogued in Iberia. Along with those Alpine jades, there are long axes made of local stones that can be considered as an imitation of the Alpine examples (ie. Cangas Type). Their distribution over the Iberian Peninsula can be interpreted within the exchange networks of other materials, such as variscite beads or certain varieties of flint. The important concentration identified in Catalonia may be related with the expansion of the Chasséen culture. As for the other Iberian occurrences, a leapfrog model typical of the seafaring is proposed for the coastal distribution that was complemented with the use of major river valleys for their spread into inland areas. Finally, the distribution of the Cangas-type axes on Northwest Iberia may point to an Atlantic coastal connection between the European *finisterrae*. Contextual analysis and a few radiocarbon dates point to a timespan between the second half of the Vth and the beginning of the IVth Millennia BC, however in Southern Spain seem to last into contexts of the IIIrd and even IInd Millennia BC.

Keywords: Neolithic, Chalcolithic, Alpine jades, sillimanite, variscite, Northwest Iberia.

1. Introduction

Throughout the fifth millennium and the first half of the fourth, polished axes in Alpine jades (jadeite, omphacite, eclogite and some amphibolites) circulated in Western Europe over considerable distances, up to 2000 km as the crow flies. From the Italian Alps, where primary deposits of these rocks and Neolithic exploitations have been identified -particularly in the sectors of Mont Viso and the Mont Beigua (Pétrequin *et al.* 2012d)-, the long distance transfers reached the Atlantic seashore and Great Britain in the west, Denmark to the north, the Black Sea shores and the Turkish coast to the east and, finally, Malta to the south (Pétrequin *et al.* 2012b). At the time, the magnitude of this social phenomenon, based on the ideological transformation of a stone tool into a sign-object embedded in religious mythologies (Pétrequin *et al.* 2012a; Pétrequin 2013) has no equivalent other than the huge copper production in South-Eastern Europe, so that –during the fifth millennium– a "Europe of jade" is opposed to a "Europe of copper" (Pétrequin *et al.* 2002, 2012c; Klassen *et al.* 2012).

In the context of marked social inequalities within societies where the handling of polished axes by dominant individuals is based on religious and political concerns (Pétrequin *et al.* 2012a; Pétrequin *et al.* 2013), the choice of Alpine jades is explained by the rarity of these precious raw materials -we barely know a dozen sources on the planet-, the light-catching colour, and their extraordinary tenacity and fine grain allowing bright and sometimes extraordinarily polished surfaces. An added value would reside perhaps on the hardships of quarrying works in the Mont Viso, between 1700 and 2400 m altitude, carried through in the course of summer expeditions (Pétrequin *et al.* 2012d). These jades are now well characterized through spectroradiometric analysis (Errera *et al.* 2012) and their macroscopic features (Pétrequin *et al.* 2012d). They have been set both on spatial and chronological terms, but there is always a certain risk –in the case of isolated objects–

of confusion with polished axes of Mesoamerican origin, brought from there in historic times (Farrujía and Arco 2004).

The craze for the jades and the ideational complex around polished axes –that grew increasingly longer until they became oversized for functional purposes– begins in the earlier centuries of the 5th millennium Northern Italy with the Bégude type, a long narrow adze blade. It spreads further to the southern half of France and arrives in Brittany a little before the mid 5th millennium (Cassen *et al.* 2012; Pétrequin *et al.* 2012b).

From the middle of the 5th millennium, the production passes to the hands of communities at the French side of the Alps, with the Altenstadt-Greenlaw and Durrington models. The expansion then continues to the north-west of Europe, northern France, Germany and Britain while the Gulf of Morbihan functions as a powerful centre of attraction for large blades of Alpine jades, often re-polished to make them inimitable and create specific models for this region: Carnacean axes, whose most emblematic examples –Tumiac type– were butt-perforated. The European distribution of the Carnacean axes (Pétrequin *et al.* 2012b, 2012c) and their imitations in local rocks (Fábregas *et al.* 1992, 2012; Pétrequin *et al.* 2010, 2012b, 2012c) suggest that the Gulf of Morbihan functioned as a sort of attractor, drawing Alpine jade blades and delivering a number of repolished pieces towards the Paris Basin, Switzerland, Germany and the northwest of the Iberian Peninsula. This indisputable influx of Carnacean models from the Morbihan to the rest of Western Europe presumably accompanied the expansion of rituals and mythologies that emerged in this region (Cassen and Vaquero 2000; Cassen *et al.* 2012; Dominguez *et al.* 2015; Pétrequin *et al.* 2012a, 2012b, 2012c).

Around 4300 BC, the growing influence of the Chalcolithic of SE Europe and the introduction of the copper metallurgy in Italy are underlined by the introduction of the Puy type, a polished blade with quadrangular section, while the influence of the Carnacean region decreases rapidly. The distribution of the Puy axes shows that not only the expansion of jades stalled, but begun to decrease, particularly in Britain. Moreover, from 4000 BC the Alpine production plummets and the distribution of the most recent types –Pauilhac, Vihiers and Remedello– hardly surpasses the 400-500 km radius, heralding the utter collapse of the system of beliefs related to Alpine jades in the early third millennium.

2. The Iberian case

For a long time, it was assumed that –with the partial exception of Catalonia– the Iberian Peninsula was barely affected by the jade network (Ricq- de Bouard 1996). Outside the Catalonian lands, the few axes of alleged Alpine origin (Dima, Sádaba, Vilapedre) known in Iberia since the early twentieth century, seemed to endorse such a view. Still, as so often happens in the archaeological endeavours, that impression has changed in the last two decades and, while the number of Alpine axes is more restricted than elsewhere in Western Europe, it is still significant and poses some questions as to their arrival to the Iberian Peninsula and the eventual existence of local imitations of the Alpine models.

A turning point on that subject took place with the extension to the Iberian Peninsula of the research led by P. Pétrequin, incorporating several of us (RFV, C.R.R. and A.L.H.) in 2 projects of pan-European scope (JADE and JADE-2) starting in 2006 and running until the present date. These aimed at cataloguing and studying the axes on jade and other alpine raw materials and their relationship with the circulation of high social value items within the Neolithic communities of Western and Central Europe. As a result of the Spanish participation in that research project, over forty presumably Alpine axes have been catalogued in the Iberian Peninsula. Furthermore, a number of axe-blades whose raw material would be more or less local but whose morphology displays striking similarities with particular Alpine axe types could be added to that census.

In general terms, the geographic distribution of the reputedly Alpine axes has experienced some changes along the 7 years that the JADE scheme has been going on: after the works carried out during the first edition of the project (2006-2009), we were left with the impression of a phenomenon affecting the northern half of the Iberian Peninsula. A view only reinforced by the significant concentration of finds in Catalonia, some sparser discoveries further west and, above all, the marked NW spread of the Cangas butt-perforated axes. After the survey done in the framework of JADE2 (2013-2015), that picture has changed somewhat: although more effectives were reported in northern Iberia, a significant number of axes were documented in locations further south, posing some interesting questions about the spread mechanisms and the chronology of those pieces (Figure 1). As to the raw material, our assessment is hampered by the scarcity of available petrographic analysis, otherwise done with different techniques. That said, the majority of the axes that, exclusively on typological grounds, could be thrown in the Alpine lot would be made on metamorphic rocks such as schist or amphibolite. Sillimanite, an easily recognizable stone under the naked eye, ranges second in the number of identifications and it occurs particularly linked to the butt-perforated axes we shall talk about later. The Alpine-originated rocks (jadeite, eclogite, omphacite) have been identified by means of spectroradiometry in twelve of the Catalonian samples (Vaquer *et al.* 2012: 912-916). Two other pieces have been recently characterized in Galicia and the Meseta as jadeite by using FRX analysis and these same techniques reported omphacitic jadeite and jadeite, respectively, for another two axes from Western.

Andalusia (Domínguez *et al.* 2015). Perhaps it is worth noting that, in almost every case of suspected Alpine

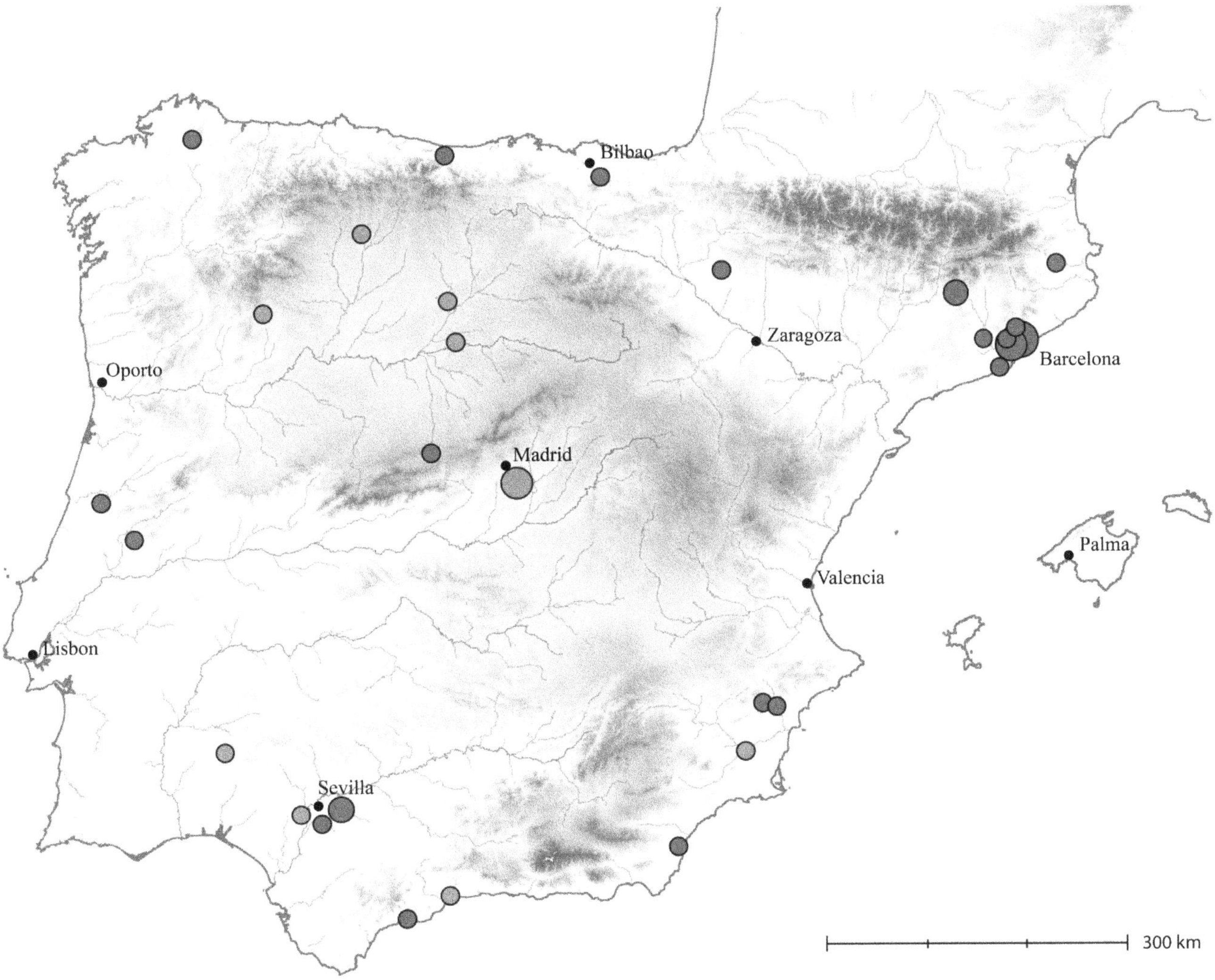

Figure 1. Axes of Alpine origin in the Iberian Peninsula. Dark grey dot, location of the axes with known origin. Light grey dots, probable location of pieces from unsecure context and/or the museums where they are on deposit. | Source: By the Authors.

source, the petrographic analyses corroborated that purported origin.

With respect to their morphology, the Durrington and Puy types (as defined by Pétrequin *et al.* 2012b) are the most frequent in the Iberian Peninsula, although other varieties are known too (Bégude or Pauilhac). Their size may depart widely from the average (15,2 cm long): the largest being the axe of Sádaba (34 cm) while the smallest is that displayed in the Museum of Valencina (9,06 cm). In about 70% of the examples the manufacture is very careful, as many as the 35% of the pieces displaying overpolishing (Figure 2).

A most peculiar kind of axe is the so-called Cangas type: they are finely polished, possess a flat cross-section, a perforation in the butt-end and a roughly triangular shape. They cluster in NW Iberia and nearly always are manufactured on sillimanite, a rock found in several places of Spain, though rich sources are reportedly known in the Meseta (Domínguez-Bella *et al.* 2004) (heavily exploited in prehistoric times judging by the number of sillimanite axes –some quite large– found in that region). Still, the general design strikingly resembles that of the Tumiac axes from Brittany, usually made of Alpine jadeite, which is precisely the material we have just identified in one of the Galician specimens (Figure 3).

The most parsimonious explanation, accounting for the typological similarity and the peculiar geographical distribution, would be the existence of contacts between Iberia and Brittany, through which that particular design and, eventually, raw materials were moving two ways.

As elsewhere in Europe, most Iberian specimens come from insecure contexts, isolated findings, or old private collections. However, a few Alpine items come from funerary contexts and other presumably local reinterpretations do too. That fact, together with their co-occurrence in spatial terms with valuable raw materials such as variscite or certain varieties of flint, may help us to devise an approximate time frame and a pattern of distribution.

Figure 2. Axes of Alpine origin in the Iberian Peninsula. From left to right: Palencia (Palencia, Castilla y León), Diego Álvaro (Ávila, Castilla y León), Bragança (Bragança, Portugal) and Bòbila Padró (Barcelona, Cataluña).

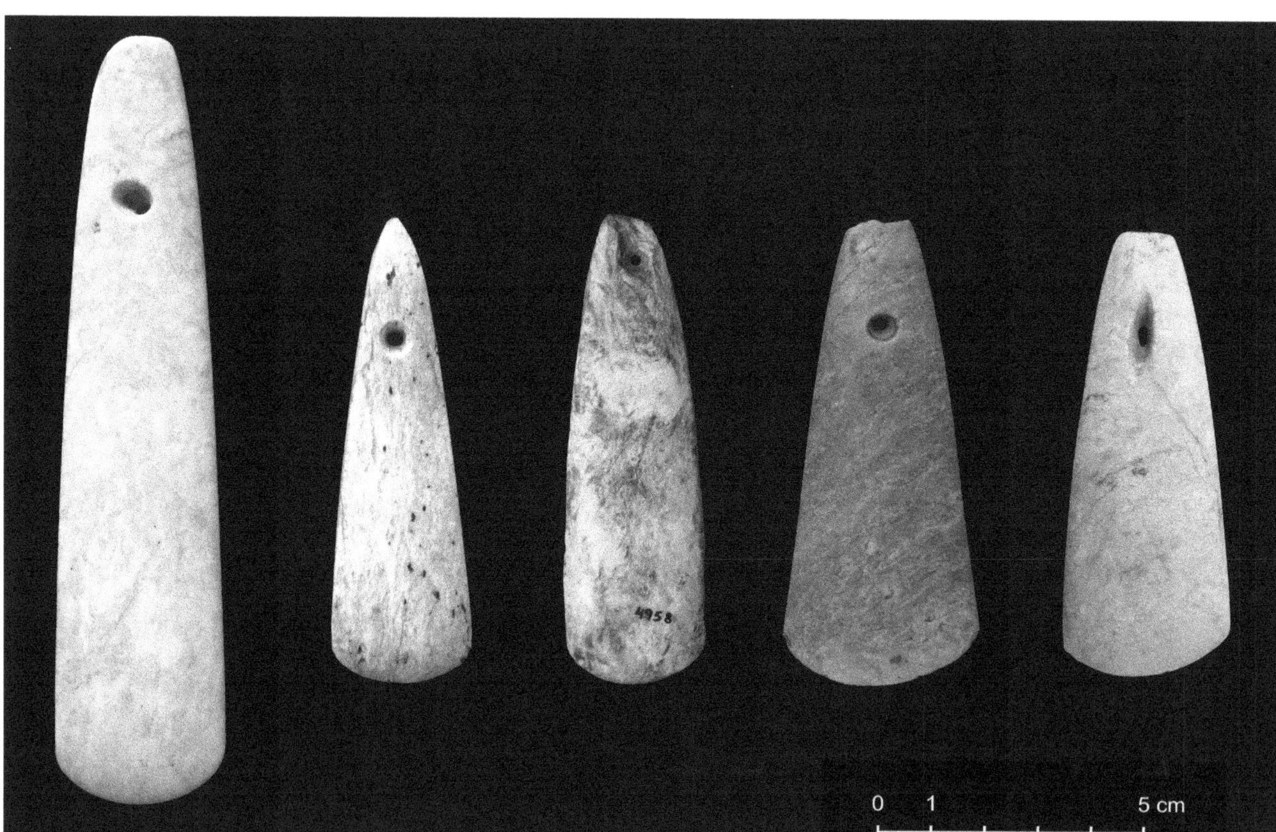

Figure 3. Butt-perforated types. From left to right: Río Fortes (Ávila, Castilla y León), Vilalba (Lugo, Galicia), Monte das Cabras (Pontevedra, Galicia), Vilapedre (Lugo, Galicia), Dolmen de Santa Cruz (Cangas de Onís, Asturias). All are sillimanites, except that from Vilapedre, which is made on jadeite. | Source: By the Authors.

In the Northeast a large concentration of Alpine axes is documented, some of them recovered from burial contexts like –interestingly– the sepulture 83 from the variscite mines of Can Badosa. Other tombs belong to the "Cultura de los Sepulcros de Fosa" while a few, like Caserna de Sant Pau, would be slightly earlier. The chronological range spans from the end of the 5th to the mid 4th millennium BC (Molist *et al.* 2012; Vaquer *et al.* 2012; Pétrequin *et al.* 2012 b). Artifactual associations among the grave-goods suggest, on one hand, the direct relationship of jade axes and variscite (Borrell and Bosch 2012), on the other the involvement with the exchange networks linking the French Southeast and Catalonia, as shown by the exchange of prestige items such as Bedoulien flint, obsidian or red coral. Finally, it is worth noting that the Alpine axes from Catalonia are clearly clustered around two points (Cardona and Gavà) where two much-sought commodities were mined (salt and variscite, respectively) (Weller and Fíguls 2012).

In the rest of the Iberian Peninsula, we observe a sparser distribution of those items and, unlike the aforementioned Catalonian cases, no secure contexts are reported for genuine Alpine axes. It is true, though, that we could muster several threads of evidence pointing out to a chronological framework not dissimilar to that proposed for the Northeast specimens. The piece from Eira Pedrinha (Condeixa-a-Nova, Portugal) constitutes an old find from a place where material culture stretching from the Early Neolithic to the Copper Age was retrieved. If we pay attention to the Cangas type, it is worth noting that two examples come from a passage-grave (Dolmen de Santa Cruz, Asturias) and a third from a mound with a very disturbed stone chamber (Dehesa de Río Fortes, Ávila), the latter with a date in the earlier half of the 4th millennium, although –in both cases– we lack details about the precise location of the axes. Last to mention, but not less significant, the large and finely polished axe-blade from the megalithic tomb of Carapito 1 (Aguiar da Beira, Portugal) that already at the time of its discovery, fortunately through a regular digging, was linked to the Breton counterparts (Figure 4).

The collapse of one of the tomb's uprights sealed the primary level of the chamber, C-14 dated to the early 4th millennium BC. It was precisely at this bottom layer where the (allegedly) *copycat* jadeite axe was found, together with a number of variscite beads and other goods.

No reliable data about any of the South Iberian pieces is available beyond the Alpine sourcing of the axe from Aroche (Huelva). It is somehow enigmatic that two other items were recovered from sites or places (Gatas and Gandul, respectively, also in Andalusia) that might suggest this sort of artefacts were still around by the 3rd millennium BC, certainly a late date if compared with the sequence further north (see above). Could that epigonic character account for the fact that as many as three of those southern pieces are either very diminute (Valencina, Seville), a simple fragment (Gatas) or reused as a pestle (Málaga) (?).

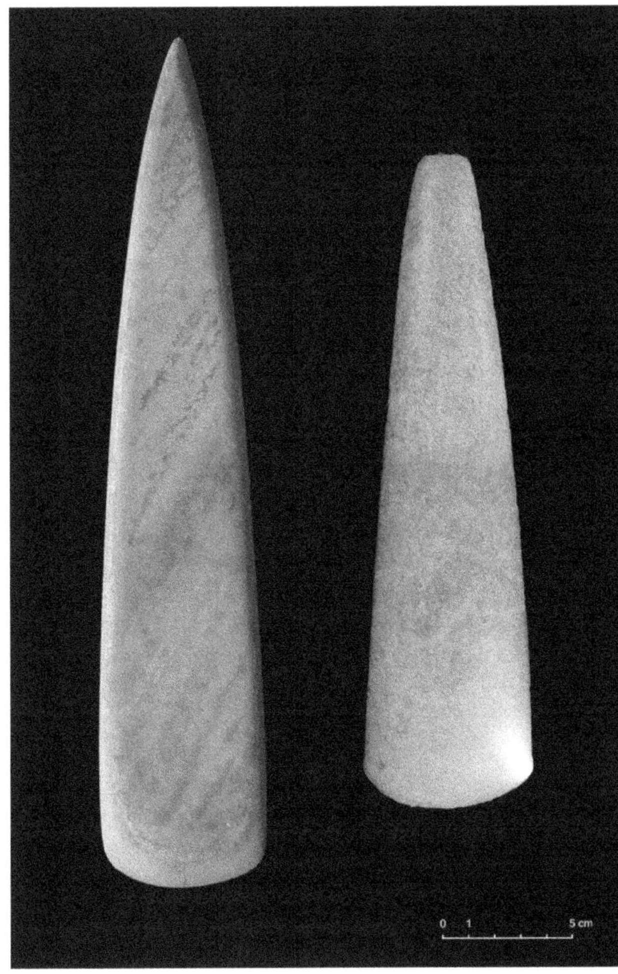

Figure 4. Possible local imitation: Carapito I (Guarda, Portugal) (Left) and an Alpine model: Dima (Bizkaia, Basque Country) (Right). | Source: By the Authors.

Admitting that, at least, a significant part of the catalogued Iberian blades had the Alpine quarries as its ultimate source, it is necessary to evaluate the possible routes that were followed. We might put forward two possible distribution models, not mutually exclusive: a «long-way round», following the Mediterranean coast from the Gavà/Cardona cluster in Catalonia, could account for the finds in Alicante, Murcia and Málaga, up to Western Andalusia. Large river valleys such as Ebro, Guadalquivir or Tagus would have acted as access roads into the inland regions, thus explaining the presence of these artefacts in the Spanish Meseta or the Ebro basin.

A second distribution pattern, more centred along the SW Europe Atlantic coast would be consistent with the findings of the Cantabrian axes (Santander, Asturias) and the already mentioned cluster of Cangas butt-perforated blades in the Iberian Northwest (Pétrequin *et al.* 2012; Fábregas *et al.* 2012). In this case, Brittany would play a redistributive role and the goods reach NW Iberia either by a direct maritime connection across the Biscay gulf or leap-frogging along the coast of Western France and Northern Spain. A land route from the Aquitaine through the Western Pyrenees, spreading then into the Douro basin and along the Cantabrian coast would also be feasible.

Those proposed links between the French and Iberian Finisterres, starting at least from the early 4th Millennium BC, are attested by the presence of variscite from Palazuelo de las Cuevas (Zamora) and Encinasola (Huelva) amidst the grave-goods at several sepultures of Western France (Querré *et al.* 2008). Other evidence for this sort of contacts lies on the presence of Castellic-inspired pottery in the passage-grave of Dombate (A Coruña) or certain motives carved on Galician and Breton megaliths, namely the so-called "The Thing" (Cassen *et al.* 2012; Fábregas *et al.* 2012).

During the second half of the V Millennium and most part of the IV Millennium BC, the circulation of axes on Alpine jades shows the insertion of these elements within networks of exchange of goods between the different territories of Western Europe. Presently, the extension to the Iberian Peninsula of this network is well documented but still much remains to be sought in terms of raw analytical data, precise archaeological contexts and the economic and ideological background of such an exchange endeavour. With the information at our disposal, it seems reasonable that the diffusion of the Alpine axes and typological designs across the Iberian Peninsula may be related to the mechanisms of distribution of variscite from production sites (Palazuelo, Encinasola and Can Tintorer) towards French territory. Other commodities such as salt, certain flint varieties or amber, that were exchanged at medium or long distance within Iberia might be also a part of that wider sphere of interaction in Neolithic times.

Acknowledgments

This study was completed within the framework of the JADE2 Project " Object-Signs and Social Interpretations of Alpine Jades in Neolithic Europe " (ANR-12- BSH3-0005-01) of the French National Research Agency.

Bibliography

Borrell, F. and Bosch, J. "Las minas de Variscita de Gavà (Barcelona) y las redes de circulación en el Neolítico." In *Congrés Internacional Xarxes al Neolític – Neolithic Networks. Rubricatum. Revista del Museu de Gavà*, 5 (2012): 315–322.

Cassen S. and Vaquero J. "La forme d'une chose." In, *Eléments d'architecture. Exploration d'un tertre funéraire à Lannec er Gadouer (Erdeven, Morbihan). Mémoire, XIX*, edited by S. Cassen, 611-656. Chauvigny, Association des Publications Chauvinoises, 2000.

Cassen S., Boujot C., Dominguez Bella S., Guiavarc'h M., LE Pennec C., Prieto Martinez M.P., Querre G., Santrot M.E. and Vigier E. "Dépôts bretons, tumulus carnacéens et circulations à longue distance." In, *Jade. Grandes haches alpines du Néolithique européen. Ve et IVe millénaires av. J.-C.* edited by P. Pétrequin, S. Cassen, M. Errera, L. Klassen, A. Sheridan and A.M. Pétrequin. 918-995. Cahiers de la MSHE C.N. Ledoux. Tome 2. Besançon: Presses Universitaires de Franche-Comté et Centre de Recherche Archéologique de la Vallée de l'Ain, 2012.

Cruz, D.J. and Vilaça, R. "O Dólmen do Carapito (Aguiar da Beira, Guarda): novas datações de Carbono 14." In *Actas do Seminário "O Megalitismo no Centro de Portugal"*, 63-68. Viseu, 1994.

Domínguez-Bella, S.; Calado, D.; Cardoso, J.L.; Clop García, X.; Tarriño Vinagre, A. "Raw materials in the Neolithic-Aeneolithic of the Iberian Peninsula." *Slovak Geological Magazine* 1-2 (2004): 17–42.

Dominguez-Bella S., Cassen S., Petrequin P., Prichystal A., Martinez R., Ramos Muñoz J. and Medina N. "Aroche (Huelva, Andalousie): a new axehead of Alpine jade in the Southwest of Iberian Peninsula." *Archaeological and Anthropological Sciences* (2015), on line, DOI 10.1007/s12520-015-0232-922.

Errera M., Pétrequin P. and Pétrequin A. M. "Spectroradiométrie, référentiel naturel et étude de la diffusion des haches alpines." In *Jade. Grandes haches alpines du Néolithique européen. Ve et IVe millénaires av. J.-C.* edited by P. Pétrequin, S. Cassen, M. Errera, L. Klassen, A. Sheridan and A.M. Pétrequin, 440-533. Cahiers de la MSHE C.N. Ledoux, Tome 1. Besançon: Presses Universitaires de Franche-Comté et Centre de Recherche Archéologique de la Vallée de l'Ain, 2012.

Estremera Portela, Mª. S. and Fabián García, F. "El túmulo de la Dehesa de Río Fortes (Mironcillo, Ávila): Primera manifestación del Horizonte Rechaba en la Meseta Norte." *Boletin del Seminario de Estudios de Arte y Arqueología*, LXVIII (2002): 9-48.

Fábregas Valcarce R. "Nuevos útiles perforados del interior de Galicia: Una reflexión sobre el momento epimegalítico." *Espacio, Tiempo y Forma*, 5 (1992): 227-241.

Fábregas Valcarce R., de Lombera Hermida A. and Rodríguez Rellán C. "Spain and Portugal: long chisels and perforated axes. Their context and distribution." In *Jade. Grandes haches alpines du Néolithique européen. Ve et IVe millénaires av. J.-C.* edited by P. Pétrequin, S. Cassen, M. Errera, L. Klassen, A. Sheridan and A.M. Pétrequin, 1108-1135. Cahiers de la MSHE C.N. Ledoux. Tome 2. Besançon: Presses Universitaires de Franche-Comté et Centre de Recherche Archéologique de la Vallée de l'Ain, 2012.

Farrujia de la Rosa A. and Arco Aguilar M. C. del. "Las hachas de jadeíta de el Museo Canario: historia, contextualización y revisión arqueológica e historiográfica de unos artefactos introducidos en Canarias en la segunda mitad del siglo XIX." In *Arqueología, raza y gestión estudios historiográficos.* edited by A. Farrujia de la Rosa and M. C. del Arco Aguilar, ERES 12, 37-70. Santa Cruz de Tenerife, Museo Arqueológico, 2004.

Klassen L., Cassen S. and Pétrequin P. "Alpine axes and early metallurgy." In *Jade. Grandes haches alpines du Néolithique européen. Ve et IVe millénaires av. J.-C.* edited by P. Pétrequin, S. Cassen, M. Errera, L. Klassen, A. Sheridan and A.M. Pétrequin, 1280-1309. Cahiers de la MSHE C.N. Ledoux, Tome 2. Besançon: Presses Universitaires de Franche-Comté. 2012

Leisner, V. and Ribeiro, L. "Die Dolmen von Carapito", *Madrider Mitteilungen*, 9 (1968): 11-62.

Molist, M., Bofill, M., Borrell, F., Bosch, J., Buxó, R., Chambon, Ph., Clop, X., Gibaja, J.F., Gómez, A., Nadal, J., Oliva, M., Ortiz, A., Saña, M. and Vicente, O. "La Caserna de Sant Pau del Camp (Barcelona): Una aproximación a los modelos de circulación de productos e ideas en un contexto funerario postcardial." *Congrés Internacional Xarxes al Neolític – Neolithic Networks. Rubricatum. Revista del Museu de Gavà*, 5 (2012): 449-458.

Pétrequin P., Cassen S., Croutsch C. and Errera M. "La valorisation sociale des longues haches de l'Europe néolithique" In *Matériaux, productions, circulations du Néolithique à l'Age du Bronze* edited by J. Guilaine, 67-98. Paris: Editions Errance, 2002.

Pétrequin P., Gauthier E. and Pétrequin A.M. "Les haches en silex de type Glis en France, en Suisse et en Allemagne du Sud-Ouest. Des imitations de haches alpines à la la transition V^e-IVe millénaires" In *Vernetzungen. Aspeckte siedlungsarchäologischer Forschung*, edited by I. Matuschik, C. Strahm *et al.*: 237-252: Freiburg-in-B.: Lavori Verlag, 2010.

Pétrequin P., Cassen S., Errera M., Klassen L. and Sheridan A. "Des choses sacrées… fonctions idéelles des jades alpins en Europe occidentale." In *Jade. Grandes haches alpines du Néolithique européen. V^e et IVe millénaires av. J.-C.* edited by P. Pétrequin, S. Cassen, M. Errera, L. Klassen, A. Sheridan and A.M. Pétrequin, 1354-1423. Cahiers de la MSHE C.N. Ledoux, Tome 2. Besançon: Presses Universitaires de Franche-Comté et Centre de Recherche Archéologique de la Vallée de l'Ain, 2012a.

Pétrequin P., Cassen S., Gauthier E., Klassen L., Pailler Y. and Sheridan A., avec la collaboration De Desmeulles J., Gillioz P.A., Le Maux N., Milleville A., Pétrequin A.M., Prodeo F., Samzun A. and Fábregas Valcarce R., "Typologie, chronologie et répartition des grandes haches alpines en Europe occidentale." In *Jade. Grandes haches alpines du Néolithique européen. V^e et IVe millénaires av. J.-C.* edited by P. Pétrequin, S. Cassen, M. Errera, L. Klassen, A. Sheridan and A.M. Pétrequin, 574-727. Cahiers de la MSHE C.N. Ledoux, Tome 1. Besançon: Presses Universitaires de Franche-Comté et Centre de Recherche Archéologique de la Vallée de l'Ain, 2012b.

Pétrequin P., Cassen S., Klassen L. and Fábregas Valcarce R. "La circulation des haches carnacéennes en Europe occidentale." In *Jade. Grandes haches alpines du Néolithique européen. V^e et IVe millénaires av. J.-C.* edited by P. Pétrequin, S. Cassen, M. Errera, L. Klassen, A. Sheridan and A.M. Pétrequin, 1015-1045. Cahiers de la MSHE C.N. Ledoux, Tome 2. Besançon: Presses Universitaires de Franche-Comté et Centre de Recherche Archéologique de la Vallée de l'Ain, 2012c.

Pétrequin P., Errera M. and Rossy M., En Collab. Avec D'amico C. and Ghedini M. "Viso ou Beigua : approche du référentiel des « jades alpins »." In *Jade. Grandes haches alpines du Néolithique européen. V^e et IVe millénaires av. J.-C.* edited by P. Pétrequin, S. Cassen, M. Errera, L. Klassen, A. Sheridan and A.M. Pétrequin, 292-419. Cahiers de la MSHE C.N. Ledoux, Tome 1. Besançon: Presses Universitaires de Franche-Comté et Centre de Recherche Archéologique de la Vallée de l'Ain, 2012d.

Petrequin P., Errera M., Martin A., Fabregas Valcarce R and Vaquer J. "Les haches en jades alpins pendant les Ve et IVe millénaires av. J.-C. L'exemple de l'Espagne et du Portugal dans une perspective européenne." *Congrés Internacional Xarxes al Neolític – Neolithic Networks. Rubricatum. Revista del Museu de Gavà*, 5 (2012e): 213-222.

Petrequin, P., Cassen, S., Errera, M., Klassen, L., Petrequin, A.M. and Sheridan, A. The value of things: the production and circulation of alpine jade axes during the 5th – 4th millenia in a European perspective." In *Economic archaeology: from structure to performance in European archaeology*, edited by T. Kerig and Zimmermann A., 65-82. Bonn: Habelt ed., 2013.

Querré, G.; Herbault, F., and Calligaro, T. "Transport of Neolithic variscites demonstrated by PIXE analysis." *X-Ray Spectrometry* 37 (2008), 116–120.

Ricq -De Bouard M. *Pétrographie et sociétés néolithiques en France méditerranéenne. L'outillage en pierre polie*. Monographies du CRA, 16. Paris: CNRS éditions, 1996.

Vaquer J, Martin A., Pétrequin P., Pétrequin A-M. , and Errera M. "Les haches alpines dans les sépultures du Néolithique moyen pyrénéen : importations et influences." In *Jade. Grandes haches alpines du Néolithique européen. V^e et IVe millénaires av. J.-C.* edited by P. Pétrequin, S. Cassen, M. Errera, L. Klassen, A. Sheridan et A.M. Pétrequin, 872-917. Cahiers de la MSHE C.N. Ledoux, tome 2. Besançon: Presses Universitaires de Franche-Comté et Centre de Recherche Archéologique de la Vallée de l'Ain, 2012.

Weller, O., Fíguls, A. "Los intercambios a media y larga distancia y el rol de la sal en el Neolítico Medio en el Altiplano y el Prepirineo Central Catalán." *Congrés Internacional Xarxes al Neolític – Neolithic Networks. Rubricatum. Revista del Museu de Gavà*, 5 (2012): 201–212.

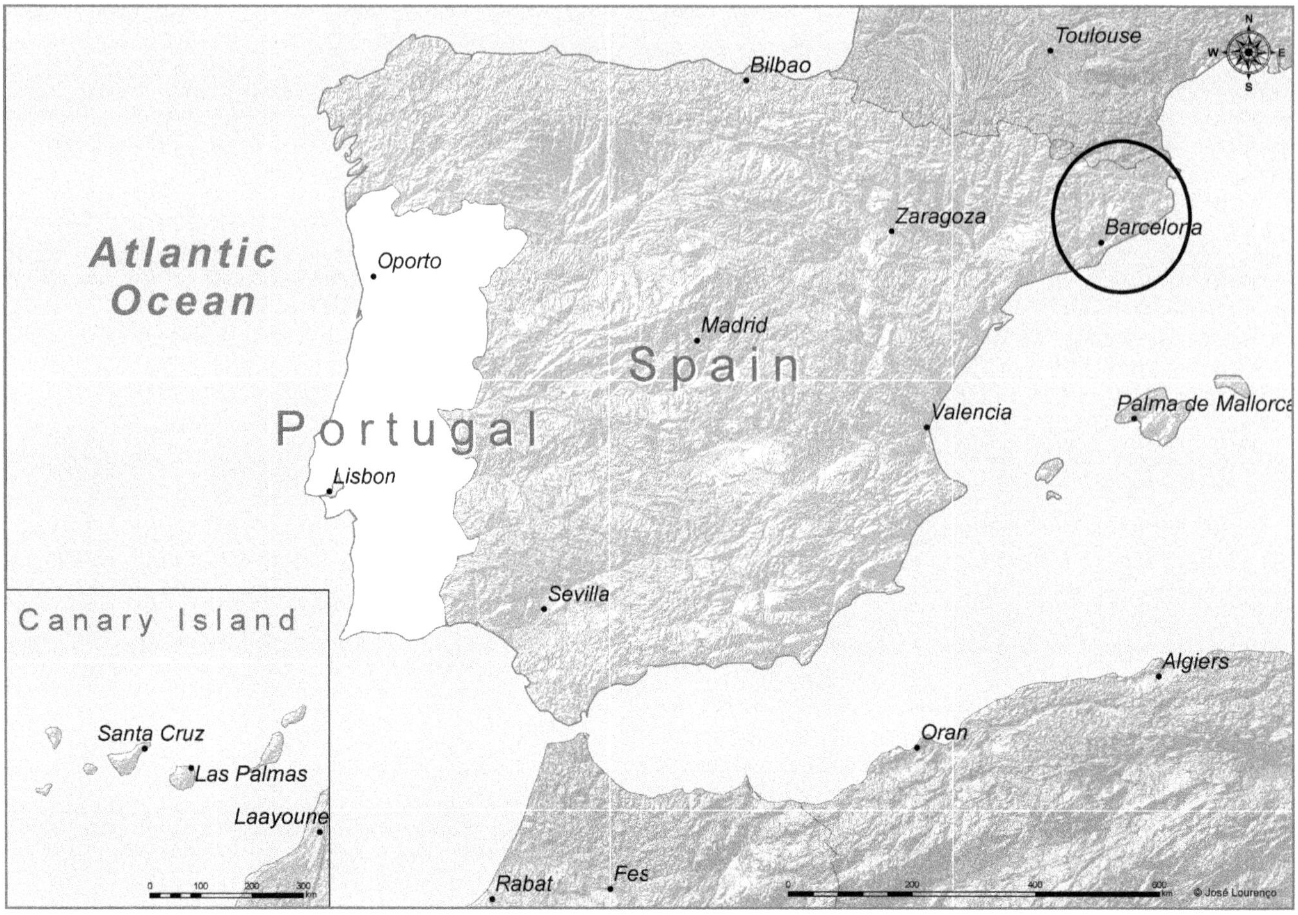

Spain - North-eastern Iberian Peninsula. | Source: José Martinho Lourenço.

Chapter 6

Symbolism, Exchange and Differential Grave Building Efforts during the Neolithic of the North-eastern Iberian Peninsula. The Necropolis of Bòbila Madurell-Can Gambús 1-2: An Example of Unequal Objects and Grave Goods Distribution

Juan F. Gibaja[1], Stephanie Duboscq[2], Berta Morell[2], Alba Masclans[3], Maria Eulàlia Subirà[4], Araceli Martín[5], Jordi Roig[6], Joan Manel Coll[6], Millán Mozota[1], Gerard Remolins[7], Xavier Oms[8], Miriam Cubas[9], Antoni Palomo[2], Javier Plasencia[2], Paloma González[2], Pilar Bravo[10], Emiliano Hinojo[10]

[1]Intitució Milá i Fontanals (IMF-CSIC). Grupo Agrest e ICArHEB, jfgibaja@imf.csic.es, millanmozota@gmail.com

[2]Departament de Prehistòria. Universitat Autònoma de Barcelona, duboscqstephanie@gmail.com, morell.berta@gmail.com, antonipalomo@gmail.com, javiplasencia@hotmail.com, paloma.gonzalez@uab.cat

[3]Departament d'Història i Història de l'Art. Universitat de Girona. Grupo Agrest, alba.masc@gmail.com

[4]Unitat d'Antropologia Biològica. Departament de biologia animal, de biologia vegetal i d'ecologia. U.A.B., eulalia.subira@uab.cat

[5]Generalitat de Catalunya-Departament de Cultura, amcolliga@yahoo.es

[6]Arrago S.L., jordiroig@arragosl.com, info@arragosl.com

[7]Regirarocs, S.L., info@regirarocs.com

[8]Universitat de Barcelona, xavieroms@gmail.com

[9]BioArCh-University of York. Sociedad de Ciencias Aranzadi, mcubas.morera@gmail.com

[10]Codex Arqueologia i Patrimoni, pbravo@codex.cat, ehinojo@codex.cat

Abstract: One of the elements that defines the so-called "Pit Burial Horizon" is the presence within certain burials of a set of tools and ornaments which were made of exogenous materials or which their acquisition and processing required an enormous investment effort. Chronologically, we stand at end of the 5th and beginning of the 4th millennium cal. BC, a period that stands out due to the relevance of its funerary structures, usually burial chambers containing a single individual. In this paper, we will identify the type of raw materials that travelled long distances during this lapse of time, recognise and explain who the receivers of those instruments and ornaments were. The best known archaeological site of this period is Bòbila Madurell-Can Gambús, which will serve as an example to examine this topic. This is a context with a considerable potential, not only due to the number of burials (more than 170 in Bòbila Madrell-Can Gambús), but also because of the substantial number of grave goods and instruments made with exogenous rocks.

Keywords: North-eastern Iberian Peninsula, Neolithic, burial practices, exogenous materials.

1. Introduction: The Neolithic graves of the 5th-4th Millennium cal. BC

The north-eastern Iberian Peninsula Neolithic funerary record is enormously relevant, not only because of the number of documented burials, but also due to the high degree of conservation of many of these funerary contexts. This was, and still is, such that at the beginnings of the 20th century Dr. Bosch Gimpera grouped them as "dug graves" (1913-1914) and later Dr. Maluquer (1950) included them in a new "culture". Dr. Tarradell (1962) defined the inhabitants of this period as "farmers from the plain" while during the sixties Dr. Muñoz (1965) and Ripoll and Llongueras (1963) published the first systematic compilations of the Pit Burial archaeological record. Ever since, the literature written on this subject has grown exponentially (Bosch-Gimpera 1913-1914; Tarradell 1962; Muñoz 1965; Riuró and Fusté 1980; Marti et al. 1997, among many others).

Such a significant number of graves is not observed along all the Neolithic period. Up until now, the quantity of burials discovered between the middle of the 6th and the middle of the 5th millennium cal. BC has been fairly anecdotal (Bosch and Tarrús 1991; Blasco et al. 2005; Gonzalez et al. 2011; Oms et al. in press). This situation changes towards the second half of the 5th millennium cal BC. It is then, when a proliferation of funerary evidence becomes available, either in the form of necropolises or as isolated burials in different areas of the north-eastern Peninsula (Martin 2009). In recent years, the signatories of this work have opened new lines of study on this period's funerary practices, in order to better understand aspects such as the burial systems (Roig et al. 2010; Alliese 2016; Martin et al. in press b), the social organisation (Duboscq 2014; Duboscq and Gibaja 2016), the dietary habits of the buried individuals (Fontanals et al. 2015), the function and distribution of stone and bone artifacts (Gibaja 2003; Millan and Gibaja 2015; Masclans 2017; Masclans et al. 2017), the origin of the grave goods' raw materials (Terradas and Gibaja 2002; Vaquer et al. 2012; Terradas et al. 2014; Masclans et al. 2017), and the ornaments' characteristics (Oliva 2015). This has been possible thanks to the two projects of research funded by the Spanish Ministry of Economy and Competitiveness: *Aproximación a las primeras comunidades neolíticas del NE peninsular a través de sus prácticas funerarias* - HAR2011-23149- and, *Aproximación a las primeras comunidades neolíticas del Mediterráneo nordoccidental: construyendo respuesta desde los análisis paleoantropológicos y genéticos* - HAR2015-67323.

According to the information available, it is possible to affirm that homogeneous trends regarding the complete set of buried population cannot be found, given that the type of burial, the form in which bodies were deposited, and the grave goods' characteristics, among others, show significant variability.

With regards the funerary structures, two large groups can be identified: burial pits dug in the soil, and sepulchres made of stone cists. These two groups equally exhibit certain variations concerning their morphology, size, and the employed constructive elements (Martin et al. in press). At the same time, some of the burials were not made *ex profeso*, but by re-using different kinds of structures; we refer to the re-use of silos in which the wastes included one or several individuals or the re-use of mines as burial places, which is the case of the Prehistoric Mines of Can Tintorer/Gavà (Bosch and Borrell 2009; Villalba 1999).

Usually, these burials contain a single individual: man, woman, or child (Figure 1). Only sporadically, there are structures enclosing three or more individuals. Bodies are usually deposited in *supine decubitus* with folded legs and arms in variable positions. Occasionally bodies are found fully stretched or in *decubitus*. However, certain graves exhibit bodies with no anatomical connection, or displaying only a partial connection, while on particular occasions, individuals have been identified displaced towards the sides of the tomb to make room for those buried later. Recent studies on funeral taphonomy have provided important information about certain aspects that had not been treated so far. Thus, for example, today we know that these individuals were not simply deposited in the bottom of the funerary structure, but occasionally placed in the interior of the tomb within rigid boxes, probably wooden, or in bags (Allièse *et al.* 2014).

One of the elements that define these burials is the common presence of grave goods items deposited next to the buried individuals. The amount of objects and their quality stands out in comparison with other funerary evidence of neighbouring areas with which they probably had contact. We refer to the funerary practices of the French Chassey, the Italian VBQ, or the Swiss Cortaillod. Among the documented lithic instruments, are found cores and various flint instruments, in particular blades, microblades, lamellae, geometric microlites, and

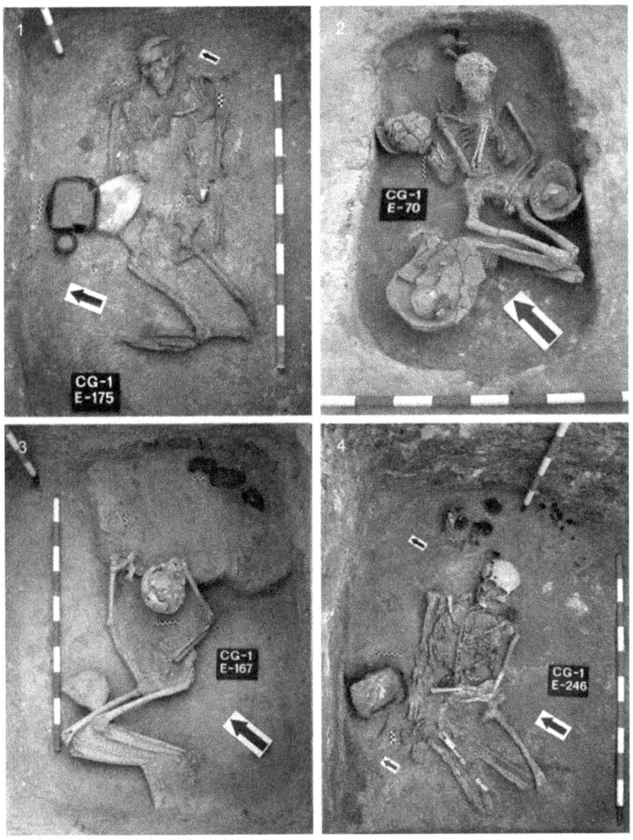

Figure 1. Funerary structures found in Can Gambús 1 sector (photo J. Roig, Arrago, S.L.).

arrowheads (Terradas and Gibaja 2002; Gibaja 2003; Gibaja and Terradas 2012). Occasionally, blades or blade fragments are also found made with other types of rocks, such as obsidian or jasper. Furthermore, it is also common to find macrolithic tools, particularly represented by the presence of polished and bevelled artefacts, such as adzes and axes (Vaquer *et al.* 2012; Masclans 2017; Masclans *et al.* 2017), and, on very few occasions, grinding mills and polished schist punches.

Regarding the bone instruments, punches and spatulas made from metatarsal bones are highlighted, while less common utilities such as needles are a minority (Martí *et al.* 1997; Mozota and Gibaja 2015). For such artifacts, sheep and occasionally deer metatarsal bones were used (Martín *et al.* 2016). As for ceramic vessels, a great variety of forms and sizes are documented being the most common the carinated vessels, both spherical and subespherical, as well as those known as square mouth vessels. Cups, and bitronconic vessels and cups are seldom found in graves. In general, these artifacts are not decorated (Masvidal *et al.* 2003; Roig and Coll 2010).

Another of the common elements deposited in graves are jewellery ornaments. Although one of the most representative are beaded variscite necklaces and bracelets, occasionally beads made with other types of rocks and elements such as teeth, bones or shells. In this context, perforated wild boar tusks were quite common (Oliva 2015). Finally, animal skeletal parts are also found associated with burials, although on specific occasions the complete animal is buried. The latter can be found directly associated with the buried person or located in any part of the grave without a clear relationship with the buried person (Martín *et al.* 2016). The most of the remains are of domestic species, and less frequently, wild species (mostly deer, wild boars, small carnivores).

2. Objectives

In this work we will discuss the raw materials employed in the production of lithic instruments, as well as certain ornaments within the Neolithic burials of Bòbila Madurell-Can Gambús' necropolis. Particular attention will be given to those objects produced with exogenous rocks, as well as those whose elaboration process required an enormous effort. In this way we will begin studying the objects' social and economic interpretations starting from its origins, uses, and connections with the living population.

The second step will be to identify if there is any correlation between these instruments and ornaments and the people buried in the Bòbila Madurell-Can Gambús necropolis, taking into account the gender and age of the individuals. Based on the results obtained, we will build an historical interpretation of the human community living in this site. Such interpretations should be based on solid and accurate information of what we are going to analyse (types of burials, individuals' gender/age, radiocarbon dating, taphonomic studies, and grave goods characteristics) and on a statistical analysis of the data. A study such as the one being presented here is completely unprecedented with regard to the site. In this sense, specific analyses have been performed, but never displaying a global perspective with the aim of proposing an explanatory hypothesis on the basis of the exogenous raw material distribution.

3. The archaeological site of Bòbila Madurell-Can Gambús

Bòbila Madurell-Can Gambús (Sant Quirze del Vallès/Sabadell) is referenced as one of the most important Neolithic contexts known in Western Europe (Figure 2). Dozens of publications and hundreds of references in the literature mentioned this site due to the richness and quality of the archaeological remains. The site is located within the so-called Vallès-Penedès rift valley, which separates the coastal and mountain ranges, and is an ideal place for agricultural practices due to its climate, geology and the numerous water sources.

Bòbila Madurell-Can Gambús has undergone various excavation campaigns carried out intermittently since the beginning of the 20th century (Figure 3). Although the first archaeological evidence was discovered in 1921, it was not until the 1930s and 1940s, that 70 structures, of which more than 50 were Neolithic, were discovered, that this site became important. These works were initially led by V. Renom, followed by J. de Serra-Ràfols in 1944 (Renom

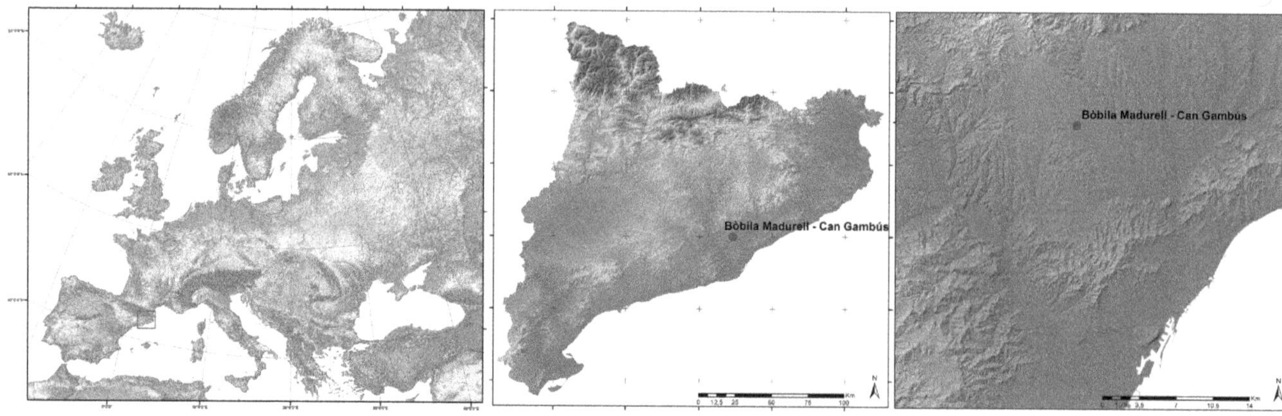

Figure 2. Map showing the location of the site studied in this work (photo G. Remolins).

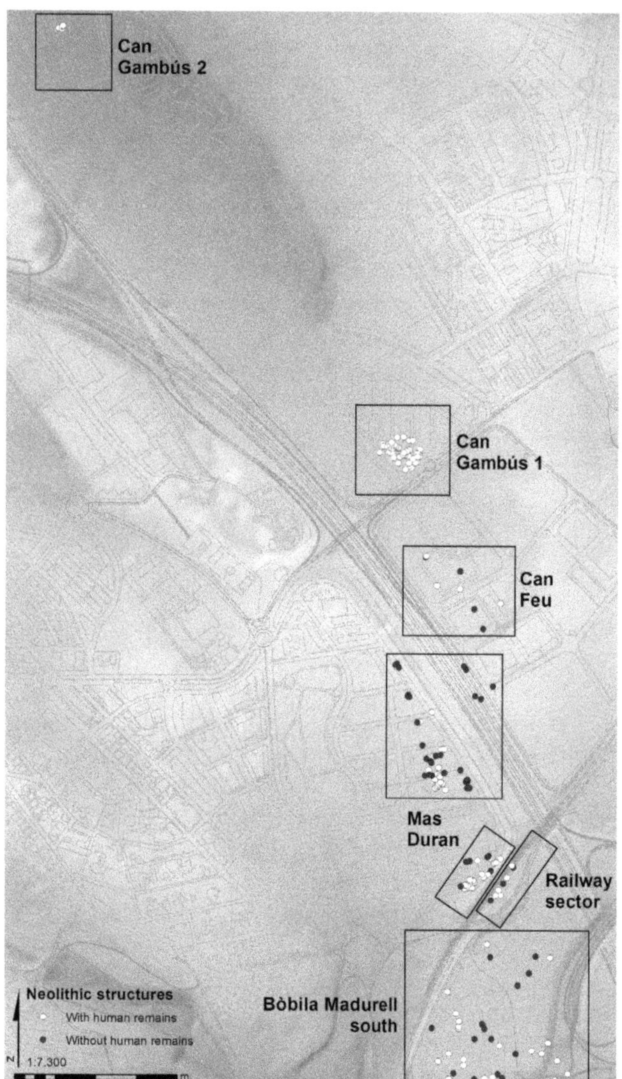

Figure 3. Bòbila Madurell–Can Gambús Pit burial structures, including both domestic and funerary structures (map produced by G. Remolins).

1934 and 1944; Serra Ràfols 1947; Ripoll and Llongueras 1963; Muñoz 1965; Martín *et al.* in press a). Between 1975 and 1984 several structures were excavated, some of which were Neolithic (three silos, two graves and a possible pit known as habitat 1). Such works were carried out under the direction of E. Ripoll and M. Llongueras, who subsequently were joined by R. Marcet and M. A. Petit (Llongueras et al. 1986). In 1987 A. Martin and J. Miret were involved in Bòbila Madurell's Can Feu sector excavation together with A. Martin and Josep Bosch. They found 112 structures, 9 of which were Neolithic. In Can Feu's, 7 silos and 8 graves were found (Martín *et al.* 1988a).

In 1989, two areas were re-excavated: Bòbila Madurell-South (known as "Madurell Sud" or "Alcampo"), and the place near the railway station (which was called "Madurell Ferrocarrils"). Such archaeological works were directed by R.M. Blanch, M.A. Alaminos and P. Lazaro who revealed 63 structures in Madurell-Sud, and 17 in Madurell-Ferrocarrils. From those, 25 and 6, respectively, hosted human remains (Alaminos *et al.* 1991). In 1991-1992 works were developed in the sector of Bòbila Madurell-Mas Duran, in this case coordinated by R. Mora and A. Martin. The directors of the excavations were A. Bordas and J. Diaz, who were joined afterwards by M. Buch, A. Parpal and R. Pou. A total of 103 Neolithic structures, of which 30 were silos and 32 structures with human remains, were documented (Bordas *et al.* 1994). In 1996, a new excavation was directed by J. Diaz in Can Feu-sector, close to the A-18 (today the C-58) motorway of the Can Feu sector. In this site, 4 structures were identified, 3 of them corresponding to the Neolithic period (Diaz 1996).

The last few interventions correspond to the Can Gambús sector, on the other side of the C58 motorway. Although investigations were conducted in different areas, all were named Can Gambús 1, 2 and 3, with only the first two delivering Neolithic structures. Can Gambús 1 was excavated between 2003 and 2006 under the direction of J. Roig and J.M. Coll (ÁRRAGO S.L. *Arqueologia i Patrimoni)*. During these years a total of 625 structures were excavated, of which the 47 Neolithic ones particularly stand out (Roig and Coll 2010; Roig *et al.* 2010). The Can Gambús 2 sector was excavated between 2003 and 2004 under the direction of P. Bravo and E. Hinojo (*Codex Arqueologia i Patrimoni*). Among the various documented structures, 5 Neolithic tombs were found (Bravo *et al.* 2015).

4. The chronology

We have traced the chronology of Bòbila Gambús Madurell-Can Gambús necropolis, based on a total of 49 datings from 49 structures (27 from Bòbila Madurell and 22 from Can Gambús 1–2). All the samples come from human bones with less than 50 ± standard deviation.

The analysis has been based on the sum of probability intervals, taking into account different variables in order to draw their temporal distribution. This statistical technique allows us to calculate the probability of independent events occurring at a particular time. The function combines the set of dates using the averaged sum of probability distributions without using the standard error values (Barceló 2008; Contreras and Meadows, 2014; Steele 2010; Williams 2012). This statistical analysis was performed with CalPal 2016 software (Jöris and Weninger 1998). For calibrations, IntCal 13 calibration curve has been used (Reimer et al. 2013). The statistical analysis here presented is part of the thesis of one of the authors of the article (Berta Morell). As we can see in Figure 5, there are no discontinuities in the chronological distribution of the necropolis, which would be about 4190-3550 cal. BC (2σ). Furthermore, if we group the dates differentiating them by sectors (Figure 6), we can see that, while Bòbila Madurell sector (upper part of the graph) would start between 4210-3670 cal. BC (2σ), Can Gambus sector (bottom part of the graph) would do so between 4100 and 3510 cal. BC (2σ).

Keeping in mind the objective of specifying the chronological distribution of these burials and their relationship with the presence or absence of exogenous materials or items for which their elaboration required a considerable effort, we have also performed a sum of probabilities. As we can see in Figure 4, the burials belonging to the Pit Burial Horizon are distributed chronologically between the 4530-3420 cal. BC (2σ), approximately. However, the presence of exogenous high-valued materials in the funerary structures is distributed in the following manner:

- Those which are associated with honey flint from Provence (13 dates) between the 4270-3510 cal. BC (2σ).
- Those which contain obsidian items (2 dates) between the 4320-3790 cal. BC (2σ).
- Those linked to variscite (5 dates) ornaments between the 4060-3520 cal. BC (2σ).
- Those related to polished axes and adzes of exogenous origin (2 dates) between 4560-3940 cal. BC (2σ).

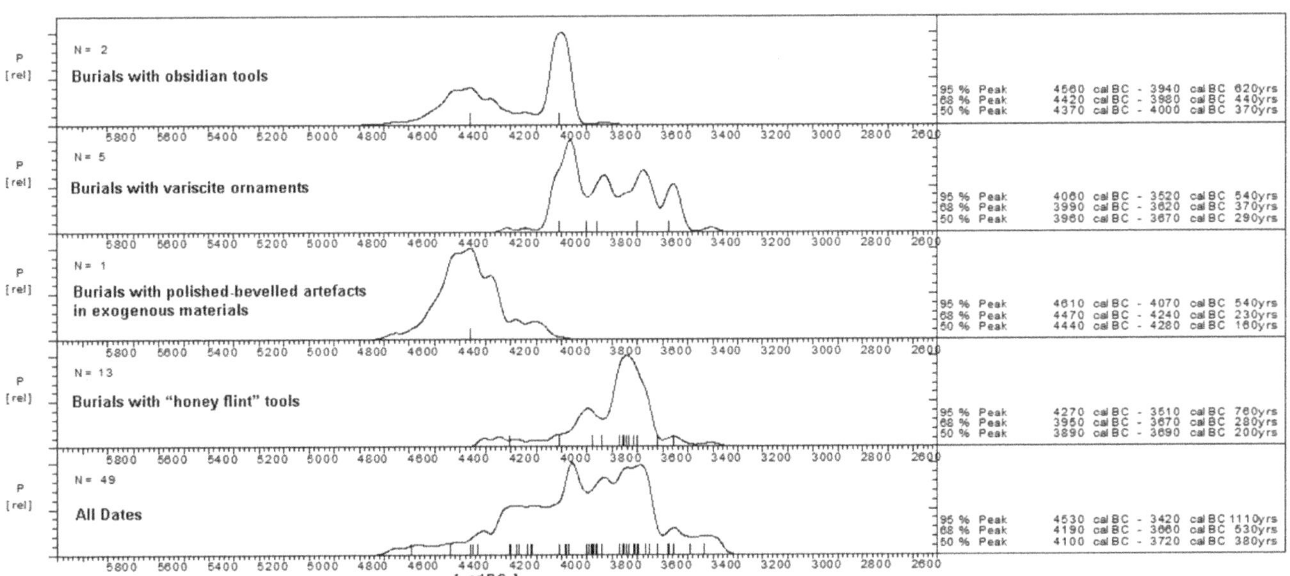

Figure 4. Sum of Probabilities using 49 radiocarbon datings from several Pit burial's graves of the "Sepulcres de Fossa" cultural horizon according to certain variables. From bottom to top of the graph: 1. General Sum of Probabilities of all radiocarbon datings. 2. Radiocarbon datings associated with burials containing honey flint. 3. Radiocarbon datings associated with burials containing exogenous polished and bevelled artefacts. 4. Radiocarbon datings associated with burials containing variscite elements. 5. Radiocarbon datings associated with burials containing obsidian items. | Source: By the Authors.

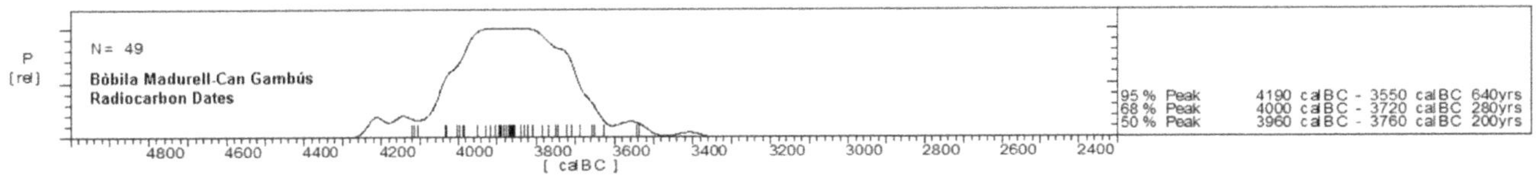

Figure 5. Sum of Probabilities of radiocarbon datings of Bòbila Madurell-Can Gambús. | Source: By the Authors.

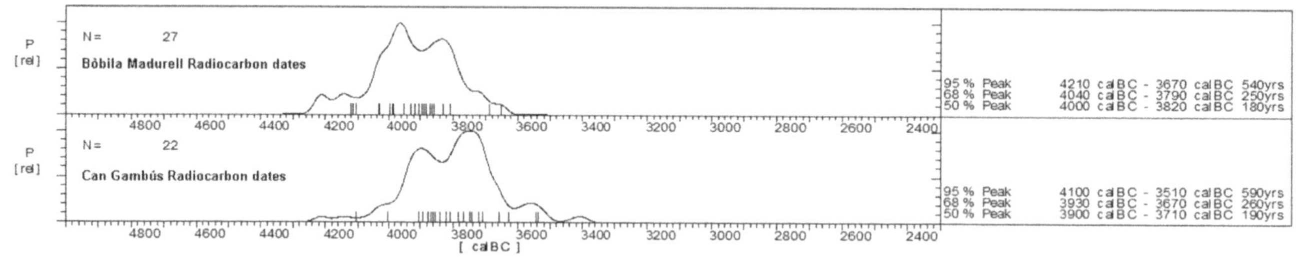

Figure 6. Sum of Probabilities concerning the radiocarbon datings of Bòbila Madurell (upper part of the graph) and Can Gambús (bottom part of the graph) sectors separately. | Source: By the Authors.

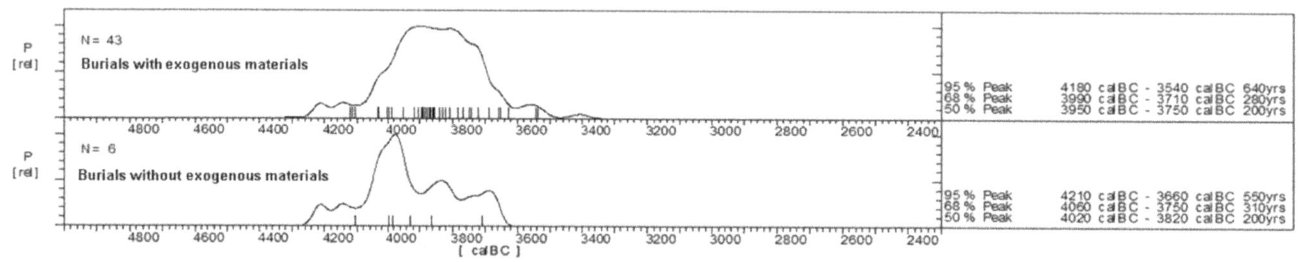

Figure 7. Sum of Probabilities Distribution of radiocarbon datings of Bòbila Madurell-Can Gambús taking into account the structures containing exogenous raw materials or items whose elaboration required high labour investment (upper part of the graph) and structures where those elements are absent (lower part of the graph).

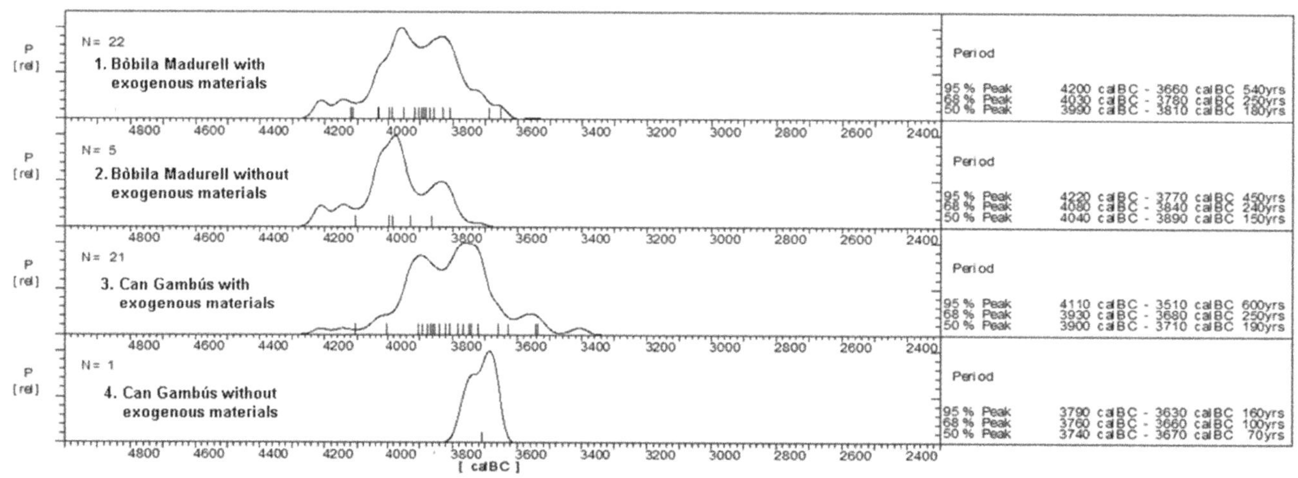

Figure 8. Sum of Probabilities Distribution of radiocarbon datings of Bòbila Madurell-Can Gambús taking into account the presence of exogenous raw materials or items whose elaboration required high labour investment according to the sectors. From the top to the bottom of the graph: 1. Bòbila Madurell (presence), 2. Bòbila Madurell (absence), 3. Can Gambús -1 (presence). 4. Can Gambús-2 (absence). | Source: By the Authors.

We observe that, while the funerary structures containing exogenous raw materials, or those involving items for which significant effort was invested in obtaining them, are concentrated between 4180 and 3540 cal. BC (2σ) (Figure 7), the chronology of the tombs in which such materials are not present is distributed between 4210-3660 cal. BC (2σ). Therefore, it seems that these types of materials appear practically contemporarily to the necropolis first funerary structures.

The sum of probability distributions have also been carried out regarding the presence and absence of those raw materials, differentiating the two sectors of the necropolis in order to prove if there were chronological differences between them. As the graph shows (Figure 8), the appearance of such materials also seems to be later than the beginning of the necropolis, except for the case of a single grave from the Can Gambús sector. However, we have tested the degree of contemporaneity of this radiocarbon dates with the rest of them from this sector using the Chi-squared test (Bronk Ramsey 2009; Long and Rippetau 1974), with a negative outcome. Therefore, the results of this test do not indicate that structures with exogenous raw materials are slightly more recent than the other ones.

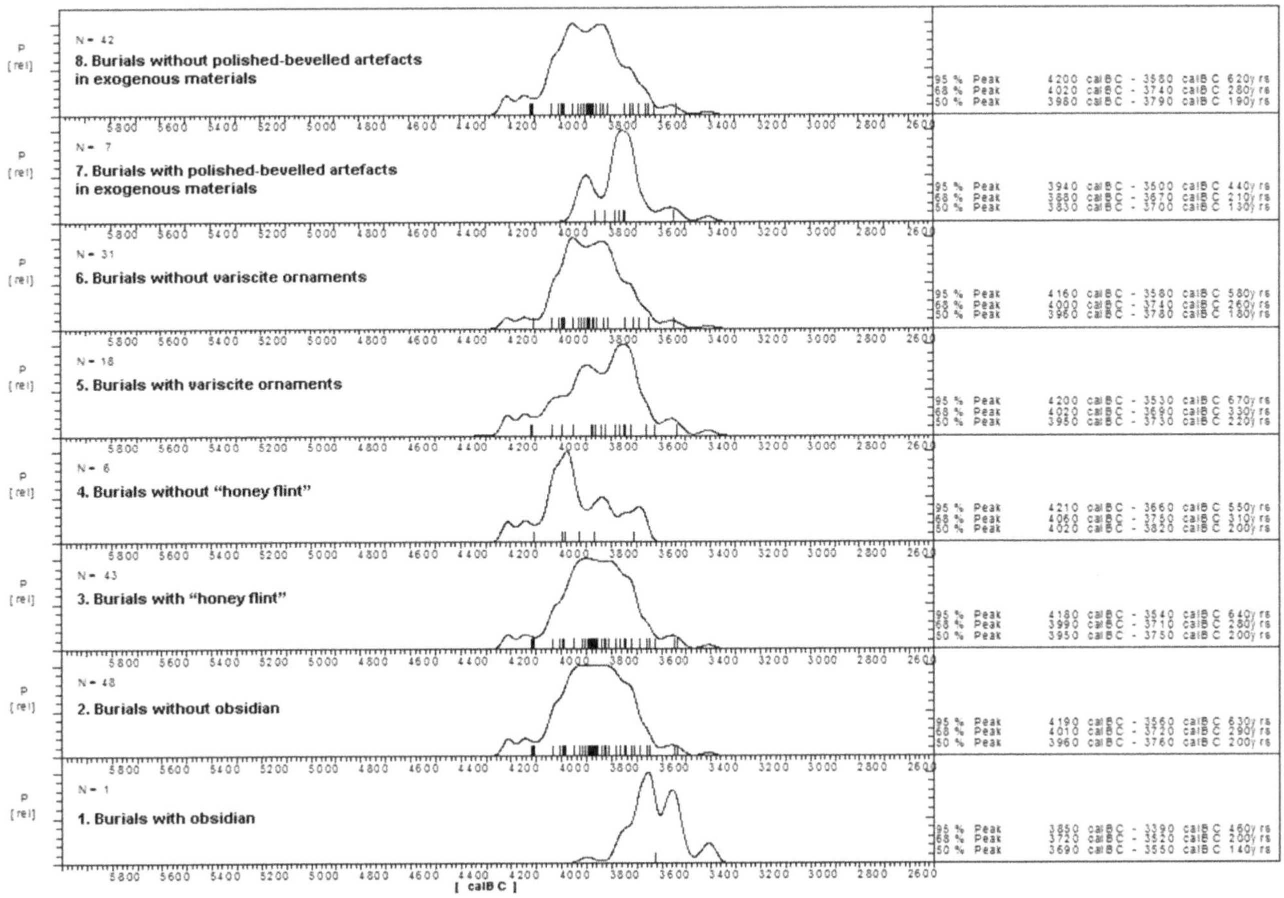

Figure 9. Temporal distribution concerning the presence of each material in Bòbila Madurell-Can Gambús necropolis. From the bottom to the top of the graph: 1. Obsidian presence. 2. Obsidian absence. 3. Honey flint presence. 4. Honey flint absence. 5. Variscite presence. 6. Variscite absence. 7. Exogenous polished and bevelled artefacts presence. 8. Exogenous polished and bevelled artefacts absence. | Source: By the Authors.

If we compare the temporal distributions of the presence and the absence of each of the raw materials in the entire necropolis (these are: honey flint, variscite and foreign axes and adzes), this chronological pattern distribution does not seem to be so clear (Figure 9). Depending on the available data, most of the exogenous raw materials are distributed throughout the chronological occupation of the necropolis.

In any case, before taking these results as absolute, we must pay attention to the data representativeness. In the necropolis of Bòbila Madurell-Can Gambús, we have analysed the chronology of 49 structures, of which 43 (58.90%) had exogenous materials, or that their extraction or processing involved a large investment of effort, and 6 not (27.7%). This means that the results presented are just an approximate explanation of the chronology of the sites. A greater number of radiocarbon datings will give further strength to these proposals.

5. The origin of the raw materials used in the production of items deposited as grave goods

Among the grave goods assemblages, we find some rocks from very remote areas, or which obtaining them required considerable time and effort. We refer to certain types of honey flint, obsidian, jadeite, eclogite, amphibolite, fibrolite, cinerite, and variscite items.

Indeed there are many flint instruments found in the graves made from what is known as "honey flint". This type of flint is represented by different sizes laminar cores, and blades with or without retouching, geometric microlites and arrowheads. In non-funerary contexts the honey flint representativeness is smaller, cores are never documented, geometric microlites and arrowheads are only rarely found, and the most common products are fragments of blades and flakes (Gibaja 2003). For the time being, there are no analysis that confirm the origin of this type of flint, though it was most likely brought from the South-East of France. Their similarity and the technical and morphological parallels are the criteria we have used so far to make this claim (Binder 1998; Léa 2005; Gibaja *et al.* 2013). Obsidian is represented by only a few specimens: a small core and ten blades or blade fragments. An initial analysis of some of the obsidian pieces, whether by LA-ICP-MS *(Laser Ablation Inductively Coupled Plasma Mass Spectrometry*) or X-Ray Fluorescence (XRF), show that they originated from a lava stream from the Monte Arci volcano (Sardinia,

Italy,) about 1200 Km away from the site (Gibaja *et al.* 2014; Terradas *et al.* 2014).

Regarding the polished axes and adzes a dual strategy is followed in their manufacture: the use of local rocks, especially hornfels, schists and slates (Bosch 1984; Masclans 2017; Masclans *et al.* 2017), and the use of rocks of foreign origin, such as jadeite and eclogite probably coming from the Alps, amphibolite from the Pyrenees, or the cinerite and fibrolite originated in the French Massif Central (Pétrequin *et al.* 2012; Vaquer *et al.* 2012; Maillé *et al.* 2016). It is remarkable the fact that the polished and bevelled items documented in domestic contexts are generally broken and fragmented, whereas the ones selected as grave goods are practically always in perfect condition, though showing evidence of having been used (Masclans 2017; Masclans *et al.* 2017).

Finally, the Prehistoric Mines of Can Tintorer/Gava (Barcelona) were exploited during the period of the funerary practices to which we refer in this article, with the objective of obtaining variscite. This mineral was used in the making of necklaces and bracelets and is found, almost exclusively, within burials (Villalba *et al.* 1986; Villalba 1999; Bosch and Borrell 2009). The presence of ornaments made with this material is especially concentrated in areas near the mines, however extending to all of the north-eastern Iberian Peninsula and crossing the Pyrenees to the South of France (Edo *et al.* 1998; Villalba 2002).

6. Instruments and objects, to whom?

The necropolis of the Bòbila Madurell-Can Gambús contains more than 170 structures with human remains. The number is rather inaccurate, because it is likely that some of the structures were destroyed or had gone unnoticed by the clay factory workers and the amateur archaeologist, Mr. Renom, during the initial phases of the site excavation. In addition, there are areas where a complete absence of Neolithic archaeological record can be attested due to the presence of later period's remains. Furthermore, empty spaces could correspond to domestic structures destroyed by the agricultural works.

In this paper, we will consider 125 structures with human remains, without taking into account those excavated by Mr. Renom. A recent taphonomic survey has led us to develop a general classification of these funerary structures (Duboscq 2017, Masclans 2017):

- Group A. Funerary structures made *ex profeso* to accommodate individuals deposited following a precise model: *decubitus supine* or lateral. A total of 98 graves with one or several individuals buried following this pattern have been documented.
- Group B. Structures in which individuals appear in a "non-normative" position, or even as isolated human remains. This fact suggests that they might reflect another type of funerary practices or even non-respectful treatment towards certain individuals (two examples would be MF18 or MS78 structures). They consist of domestic pits, often mixed with pottery fragments, lithic instruments or fractured animal bone remains. Six structures belong to this group.
- Group C. Altered or destroyed structures, as a result of the agricultural or industrial activity. They also contain very altered human remains, but their degree of deterioration does not allow us to define them as funerary structures *per se*. Up to 21 structures have been included in this group.

A total of 69 of the 98 Group A funerary structures possess exogenous materials. In 7 cases exogenous materials are included, which cannot be considered as grave goods because they were found in the filling of the tomb. As for the Group B structures, we cannot consider with certainty the items found in their filling as part of the grave goods set of any of the individuals. From the altered structures in Group C, only in 8 cases exogenous materials have been identified. However, we cannot be sure that they are part of the grave goods ensemble.

As a result, after consideration, the total amount of individuals reliably associated with exogenous materials or variscite ornaments is 69. Once materials are identified and their chronology known, the next step is to cross these data with the age and gender of the deceased. In this point, the first thing that must be said is that from those 69 individuals, 12 are women, 26 are men, 13 are children, and 18 are adults of indeterminate gender. Regarding the age, setting aside the 13 children, there is one juvenile, one young adult, 24 adults, 27 mature, and 3 elderly individuals. These age categories are calculated following the work carried out at anthropological level: child I (1-6 years), children II (7-12 years), youth (13-18/20 years), young adult (20-29 years), mature adult (30-49 years), and older adult (> 50 years) (Villar *et al.* 2006; Duday *et al.* 2010; Bravo *et al.* 2014; Allièse 2016).

6.1. Who is linked to the exogenous raw materials and variscite ornaments?

In the following lines, a very global view will be undertaken in order to check the connection between the variscite ornaments and the exogenous raw materials with the gender and the age of individuals.

The *honey flint*. As discussed above, the comparative studies carried out on this type of flint seem to indicate that it probably came from the South-East of France (*Binder* 1998; *Léa* 2005; Gibaja *et al.* 2013). Cores and honey flint tools have been found alongside all the 69 individuals. Although at first glance it might seem that there is no differential distribution to be valued on the level of presence/absence, a more in-depth analysis reveals important distinctions. Thus, we can say that individuals who have eight or more items made with this type of flint

Figure 10. Burial B6 from Bòbila Madurell: honey flint core (photo J. Ariza, SAP Archive).

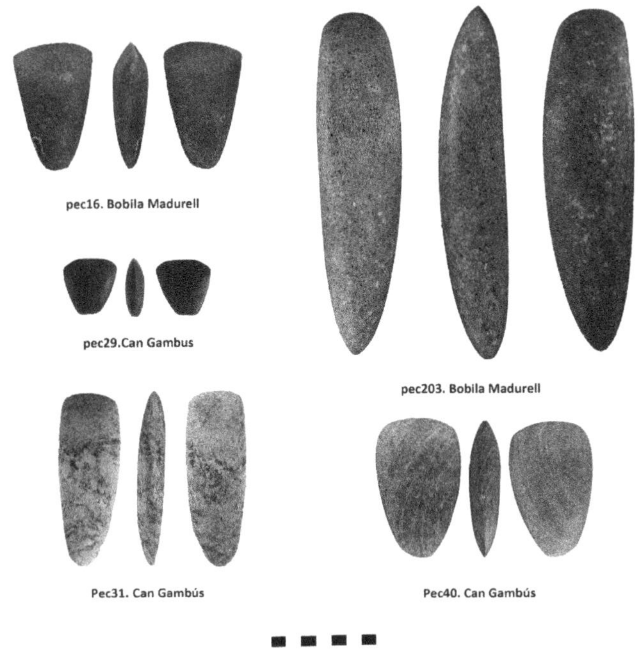

Figure 11. Polished and bevelled artefacts from Bòbila Madurell-Can Gambús (photo A. Masclans).

are exclusively men, 3 of them in adulthood, 4 mature, and 2 elderly (Figure 10).

The obsidian: Obsidian is one of the less represented rocks in the archaeological record from this period. Distributed in funeral and non-funerary contexts, its importance lies more on its rarity and the distance from supply source (Monte Arci, Sardinia, Italy), than on its quantity (Gibaja *et al*., 2014; Terradas *et al*., 2014). In any case, the only piece that we have safely attributed to the gender and age of a buried individual, is a male adult from Can Gambús-1 sector (grave CG1-E110).

Jadeites, amphibolites, eclogites and nephrites: These are the different rocks used for making the polished axes and adzes found in the graves. The ones that we have included in the set of exogenous materials are those that possibly came from the Alps and Pyrenees (Pétrequin *et al.* 2012; Vaquer *et al.* 2012). Such instruments are solely found in 8 burials, but in the case of the 3 axes found in burial M-5, we have not attributed them to a particular individual. Therefore, we count 7 axes that can be related to 7 individuals, three of them are male mature or elderly individuals; two are women (1 adult, 1 mature) and two more are mature individuals of indeterminate gender. Although there seems to be no relationship as regards the gender of the buried individuals and the polished and bevelled artefacts, it is possible to find a connection regarding their age, since they are linked only to adult individuals (Masclans 2017; Masclans *et al.* 2017) (Figure 11).

Variscite: Coming from the Prehistoric mines of Can Tintorer/Gava (Villalba *et al.* 1986; Bosch and Borrell, 2009), ornaments made with this material have been found on 28 of the 69 individuals. Variscite ornaments are associated with 9 men, 4 women, 7 children and 8 adult or mature individuals of indeterminate gender (Table 1). If we look solely at the age, it is linked with 9 adults, 12 mature or elderly individuals, and, as previously mentioned, 7 infants. Making comparisons regarding this type of item is a difficult topic since the collars and bracelets are composed of a different number of beads with varying sizes, and because in some burials it seems that lootings occurred that led to the disappearance of much of those beads (Roig *et al.* 2010). Nonetheless, even although there are individuals with one or two beads, others have over 100 (Figure 12).

7. Conclusions

With this article we have presented an overview of the material found in the Neolithic burials in the north-east of the Iberian Peninsula that had a high objective value, if we take into account the efforts invested in obtaining, preparing, and transporting them. We refer to the honey flint from the South- East of France, Sardinian obsidian, the different materials used to make polished and bevelled axes and adzes from the Alps and the Pyrenees, and the variscite ornaments coming from the Prehistoric Mines of Can Tintorer/Gavà.

To exemplify the representativeness of these materials, we have gone to the largest of the necropolis known to date: Bòbila Madurell-Can Gambús, which concentrates most of the exogenous materials known in the north-east of the Iberian Peninsula. This led us to consider that perhaps this settlement was a preferential place of arrival and redistribution of such materials to other neighbouring communities (Martín *et al.* 1996; Gibaja 2003). This hypothesis, which had already been raised by other French authors like F. Briois et al (1998) to explain the presence of the honey flint at certain sites in the southeast of France, it has been recently been taken up again by V. Lea (2012) to

Table 1. Total number of beads and variscite "plaquetas" found together with the buried individuals in Bòbila Madurell- Can Gambús. | Source: By the Authors.

Burial	Sex	Age	Number of Beads	Number of "plaquetas"
E122	Femenine	Adult	106	
E246	Femenine	Mature	74	
E162	Femenine	Mature	4	
E175	Femenine	Mature	25	
E70	Masculine	Mature	13	
E110	Masculine	Adult	170	
E167	Masculine	Mature	157	
E176	Masculine	Adult	3	
E184	Masculine	Senile	4	
E130	Masculine	Senile	31	
E668	Masculine	Adult	30	
H10	Masculine	Mature	4	
B6	Masculine	Mature	5	
11.3	indet.	Infantile	6	
M9	indet.	Infantile	4	2
M15	Indet	Infantile	62	
B11	Indet	Infantile		3
MS61	Indet	Infantile	109	
MF12a	Indet	Infantile		17
MF17	Indet	Infantile		1
MS62	Indet	Adult	5	
G10	Indet	Mature	23	
G12	Indet	Mature	3	
M11	Indet	Adult	1	
E166	Indet	Mature	8	
E442	Indet	Adult	2	
E170	Indet	Adult	9	
E112	Indet	Adult	1	

explain the amount of obsidian from Sardinia at the site of Terres Longues (French Midi).

In the case of Bòbila Madurell-Can Gambús, we have observed that, while these types of rocks are common in certain graves, their presence is not homogeneous, which means that there was an unequal distribution of such materials among different buried individuals. The fact that not all individuals are associated with such instruments and ornaments shows that not everyone in the group had equal access to those goods.

Those differences were initially detected in the type of burial structure and the diet of the buried individuals. In the case of the graves, we have observed that while some individuals are deposited in complex tombs, requiring a high investment in construction work, others were left in simple graves, or even deposited in structures with waste that initially did not function as graves. As far as diet is concerned, the first

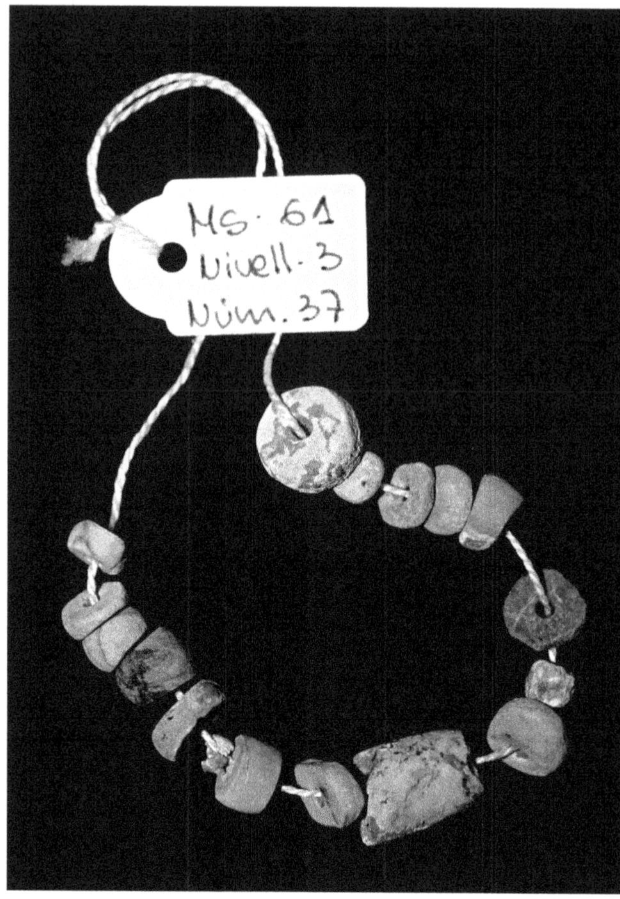

Figure 12. MS-61 Sepulchre from Bòbila Madurell: variscite beads (SAP Archive, 1991 and 2011).

data also shows evidence of a different intake by certain individuals. Indeed, although Bòbila Madurell-Can Gambús population had a diet mainly from agriculture and animal resources, only some men ate animal protein (Fontanals *et al.* 2015).

In short, we believe that we are on the right track towards explaining social issues leading the organisation of the Neolithic Iberian North-eastern communities. However, it is essential to continue studying more sites with similar characteristics located in different areas of the Western Mediterranean.

Acknowledgements

Part of the developed analyses presented in this study was conducted within the framework of the projects: "Approach to the first Neolithic communities of the peninsular NE through their funerary practices" (HAR2011-23149) and "Approach to the first Neolithic communities of the Mediterranean Northwest: building response from paleo-anthropological and genetic analysis "(HAR2015-67323-C2-1-P and HAR2015-67323-C2-2-P), financed by the Spanish Ministry of economy and competitiveness. We also would like to acknowledge the collaboration of the Departament d'Arqueologia de la Generalitat de Catalunya and the various museums that we have visited to study the deposited materials of the Bòbila Madurell-Can Gambus: Museu d' Història de Sabadell, Museu Arqueològic of Barcelona and Museu d' Història de Catalunya.

References

Alaminos, A., Blanch, R. M. and Lázaro, P. "Bóbila Madurell. Su contribución al Neolítico Medio en Catalunya". *Revista de Arqueologia* 128, (1991): 14-23.

Allièse, F. *Les sépultures de la Bòbila Madurell-Can Gambús (Vallès occidental). Éclairages sur les pratiques funéraires du nord-est de la péninsule Ibérique à la fin du Ve et au début du IVe millénaire.* Unpublished PhD dissertation, Université de Paris 1 Panthéon-Sorbonne, Universitat Autònoma de Barcelona, 529 p, 2016.

Allièse, F., Roig, J., Coll, J.M., Subirà, M.E., Ruíz, J., Chambon, Ph. and Gibaja, J.F. "Les pratiques funéraires dans la nécropole du Néolithique moyen de Can Gambús-1 (Sabadell, Espagne). De la préparation du corps à la fermeture de la tombe". *Bulletin de la Société préhistorique française* 111/3, (2014): 453-468.

Barceló, J.A. "La incertesa de les cronologíes absolutes en Arqueología.Probabilitat I estadística". *Cypsela* 17, (2008): 23-33.

Binder, D. "Silex blond et complexité des assemblages lithiques dans le Néolithique liguro-provençal". In *Production et identité culturelle. Actualité de la recherche*, edited by André D'Anna and Didier Binder, 111-128. Antibes, Éditions APDCA, 1998.

Blasco, A., Edo, M. and Villalba M.J. "Cardial, epicardial y postcardial en Can Sadurní (Begues, Baix Llobregat). El largo fin del Neolítico Antiguo en Cataluña". *Actas III Congreso del Neolítico en la Península Ibérica*: 867-878, 2005.

Bordas, A., Díaz, J., Pou, R., Parpal, A. and Martín, A. "Excavacions arqueològiques 1991-92 a la Bòbila Madurell-Mas Duran (Sant Quirze del Vallès, Vallès Occidental)". *Tribuna d'Arqueologia*, 1992-1993, (1994): 31-47.

Bosch, A. "Les destrals polides del nord de Catalunya: tipologia i petrología". *Fonaments* 4, (1984): 221-245.

Bosch, J. and Borrell, F. *Intervencions arqueològiques a les mines de Gavà (sector serra de les Ferreres). Anys 1998–2009. De la variscita al ferro: neolític i antiguitat.* Museu de Gavà. Rubricatum 4, 2009.

Bosch Gimpera, P. "Necròpolis a Sant Genís de Vilassar, a Secció arqueològica, excavacions i troballes". *Anuari de l'Institut d'Estudis Catalans* V, part II (1913-1914): 806-810.

Bosch, A. and Tarrús, J. *La cova sepulcral del Neolític antic de l'Avellaner, Cogolls, Les Planes d'Hostoles (La Garrotxa).* Girona, Sèrie Monogràfica 11, Centre d'Investigacions Arqueològiques, 142 p, 1991.

Bravo, P., Hinojo, E., Subirà, M.E., Allièse, F., Masclans, A., Santana, J., Santos, F.J., Agulló, L., Gómez-Martínez, I., Remolins, G. and Gibaja, J.F. "Les sépultures néolithiques de Can Gambús-2 (Sabadell, Espagne): nouvelles données sur les pratiques funéraires de la culture des Sepulcros de fosa". *L'Anthropologie* 119, (2014): 38-57.

Briois, F., Brossier, S., Gernigon, K. and Vaquer, J. "Polymorphisme des industries chasséennes en silex entre le Rhône et l'Aquitaine". In *Production et identité culturelle. Actualité de la recherche*, edited by André A. D'Anna and D. Binder, 129-144. Antibes, Éditions APDCA, 1998.

Bronk Ramsey, C. "Bayesian analysis of radiocarbon dates". *Radiocarbon* 51/1, (2009): 337–60.

Contreras, D.A. and Meadows, J. "Summed radiocarbon calibrations as a population proxy: a critical evaluation using a realistic simulation approach". *Journal of Archaeological Science* 52, (2014): 591-608.

Diaz, J., *Memòria de l'actuació arqueològica al sector Bòbila Madurell/Can Feu (vial Centre de Moda).* Arxiu del Servei d'Arqueologia i Paleontologia. Memoria número 6540 (inédita), 1996.

Duboscq, S. "Marco teórico y primeros datos acerca de la división social del trabajo y la desigualdad de género durante el Neolítico (VI-IV milenio a.C.) en el noreste de la Península Ibérica". *Arqueogazte* 4, (2014): 63-82.

Duboscq, S. and Gibaja, J.F. "Evidence of violence in the Neolithic period in the north east of the Iberian Peninsula". In *Beyond war: archaeological approaches to violence*, edited by Albert García and Assumpció Vila, 115-140. Cambridge Scholars Publishing, 2016.

Duboscq, S. *Caracterización de las relaciones sociales de las comunidades del Nord-este de la Península Ibérica entre la segunda mitad del V y la segunda mitad del IV milenio cal BC a partir del estudio de las prácticas funerarias.* PhD Thesis Universitat Autònoma de Barcelona, 2017.

Duday, H., Depierre, G. and Janin Th. "Validation des paramètres de quantification, protocoles et stratégies dans l'étude anthropologique des sépultures secondaires à incinération. L'exemple des nécropoles protohistoriques du Midi de la France". *Archéologie de la Mort, Archéologie de la Tombe au Premier Age du Fer.* Actes du XXIe Colloque International de l'AFEAF, MAM 5, (2000): 7-29.

Edo, M., Blasco, A., Villalba, M.J., Gimeno, D., Fernández-Turiel, J.L. and Plana, F. "La caracterización de la variscita del complejo minero de Can Tintorer. Una experiencia aplicada al conocimiento del sistema de bienes de prestigio durante el Neolítico". In *Los recursos abióticos en la Prehistoria. Caracterización, aprovisionamiento e intercambio,* edited by Teresa Orozco, Joan Bernabeu and Xavier Terradas, 83-109. Universitat de València, 1998.

Fontanals, M., Subirá, M.E., Díaz-Zorita, M., Duboscq, S., and Gibaja, J.F. "Investigating paleodietary and social differences between two differentiated sectors of a Neolithic community, La Bòbila Madurell-Can Gambús (NE-Iberian Peninsula)". *Journal of Archaeological Science: Reports* 3, (2015): 160-170.

Gibaja, J.F. *Comunidades Neolíticas del Noreste de la Península ibérica. Una aproximación socio-económica a partir del estudio de la función de los útiles líticos*, BAR International Series, S1140. BAR Publishing, Oxford, 318, 2003.

Gibaja, J.F. and Terradas, X. "Tools for Production, Goods for Reproduction. The Function of Knapped Stone Tools at the Neolithic Necropolis of Can Gambus-1 (Sabadell, Spain)". *Comptes Rendus Palevol* 11, (2012): 463-472.

Gibaja, J.F., Léa, V., Luglié, C., Bosch, J., Gassin, B. and Terradas, X. "Between Sardinia and Catalonia: contacts and relationships during the Neolithic". In *Iberia e Sardegna. Legami linguistici, archeologici e genetici sul Mesolitico all'Età del Bronzo*, edited by Eduardo Blasco, Francalacci Paolo, Nocentini Alberto, Tanda Giuseppa, 214-233. Le Monnier Università, 2013.

Gibaja, J.F., González, P., Martín, A., Palomo, A., Petit, M.A., Plasencia, X., Remolins, G. and Terradas, X. "New finds of obsidian blades at Neolithic sites in north-eastern Iberia" *Antiquity Project Gallery*, (2014): 340.

Gibaja, J., Duboscq S., Esteve, X., Coll, J.M., Martí, M., Martín, A., Mestres, J., Oms, X., Pou, R., Roig, J., Subirá, M.E. Restes humains dans des structures néolithiques du nord-est de la péninsule Ibérique : dépôts ou sépultures ?. In *Qu'est-ce qu'une sépulture ? Humanités et systèmes funéraires de la Préhistoire à nos jours. XXXVIè rencontres internationales d'archéologie et d'histoire d'Antibes.* Edited by Michel Lauwers and Aurélie Zemour, 179-195. Éditions APDCA, 2016.

González, J., Harzbecher, K. and Molist, M. "Un nou assentament del V mil.leni a la costa de Barcelona". *Quarhis* 7, (2011): 86-100.

Jöris, O. and Weninger, B. *CalPal. Computer software. CalPal. Vers. 2016.* N.p., n.d. Web. http://www.calpal-online.de/, 2016.

Léa, V. "Raw, pre-heated or ready to use: discovering specialist supply systems for flint industries in mid-Neolithic (Chassey culture) communities in southern France". *Antiquity* 79, (2005): 51-65.

Léa, V. "The Diffusion of Obsidian in the North-West Mediterranean: toward a New Model of the Chassey Culture?". *Journal of Mediterranean Archaeology* 25/2 (2012): 147-173.

Llongueras, M., Marcer, R. and Petit, M.A. "Darrers treballs a la Bòbila Madurell (Sant Quirze del Vallès, Vallès Occidental)". *Tribuna d'Arqueologia* 1984-1985, (1986): 25-34.

Long, A. and Rippeteau, B. "Testing Contemporaneity and Averaging Radiocarbon Dates". *American Antiquity* 39/2, (1974): 205-15.

Maillé, M., Vaquer, J., Rodrigue, A., Recoules, A and Defranould, E. *La cinérite de Réquista. Productions et diffusion.* Archives d'Écologie Préhistorique. Toulouse, 2016.

Maluquer De Motes, J. "La cultura neolítica del Vallès en el marco de la Prehistoria del Occidente mediterráneo". *Arrahona* 1-2, (1950): 61-75.

Martín, A. "Les sociétés du Néolithique moyen en Catalogne et leur gestion funeraire". In *Séplutures et sociétés. Du Néolithique à l'Histoire*, edited by Jean Guilaine, 45-67. Séminaire du Collège de France. Collection des Hesperides. Paris, Editions Errance, 2009.

Martí, M., Pou R. and Carlús, X. *Excavacions a la Ronda Sud de Granollers, 1994. La necròpolis del neolític mitjà i les restes romanes del Camí de Can Grau (la Roca del Vallès, Vallès Oriental). Els jaciments de Cal Jardiner (Granollers, Vallès Oriental).* Excavacions Arqueològiques a Catalunya 14, Generalitat de Catalunya. Departament de Cultura, Barcelona, 1997.

Martín, A., Miret, J., Blanch, R.M., Aliaga, S., Enrich, R., Colomer, S., Albizuri, S. and Bosch, J. "Campanya d'excavacions arqueologiques 1987-1988 al jaciment de la Bòbila Madurell-Can Feu (Sant Quirze del Valles, Valles Occidental)". *Arrahona* 3, (1988a.): 9-23.

Martin, A., Miret, J., Bosch, J., Blanch, R.M., Aliaga, S., Enrich, R., Colomer, S., Albizuri, S., Folch, J., Martinez, J. and Casas, T. "Les excavacions al paratge de la Bòbila Madurell i de Can Feu (Sant Quirze del Vallès, Vallès Occidental)". *Tribuna d'Arqueologia* 1987-1988, (1988b.): 77-92.

Martín, A., Bordas, A. and Martí, M. "Bòbila Madurell (Sant Quirze del Vallès, Barcelona). Estrategia económica y organización social en el neolítico medio". I Congrés del Neolític a la Península Ibèrica. *Rubricatum* 1/1, (1996): 423- 428.

Martín, A., Pou, R., Oms, X., Mestres, J., Martí, M., Esteve, X., Duboscq, S., Gibaja, J.F., Subirà, M.E. "La question de l'homogénéité des pratiques funéraires dans la « Culture des Sepulcres de Fossa » du Néolithique moyen. Révision des typologies à la lumière des dernières découvertes". In *Le Chasséen, des Chasséens: Retour sur une culture nationale et ses parallèles, Sepulcres de Fossa, Cortaillod, Lagozza,* edited by Philippe Chambon, Juan F. Gibaja, Gwenaelle Goude and Thomas Perrin. AEP Archives d'Ecologie Préhistorique, in press a.

Martín, A., Blanch, R.M., Albizuri, S., Alaminos, A., Mercadal, O., Vives, E., Lázaro P., Bosch, J. Colomer, S. Miret, J., Enrich, R. and Aliaga S. "El paraje de Bòbila Madurell (Sant Quirze del Vallès, Vallès Occidental, Barcelona)". In *Mirando a la Muerte: Las prácticas funerarias durante el neolítico en el noreste peninsular*, edited by Juan F Gibaja, Maria Eulàlia Subirà, Araceli Martín, Millán Mozota, and Jordi Roig. E-ditArx - Publicaciones Digitales, in press b.

Martín, P., Albizuri, S., Nadal, J., Mozota, M. and Gibaja, J.F. Les dépôts d'origine animale dans les espaces funéraires de la culture des "Sepulcros de Fossa" (Catalogne). In *11e Rencontres Méridionales de Préhistoire Récente: De la Tombe au Territoire,* edited by Jessie Cauliez, Ingrid Sénépart, Luc Jallot, Pierre Arnaud de Labriffe, Christophe Gilabert and Xavier Gutherz, 167-173. Archives d'Écologie Préhistorique. Toulouse, 2016.

Masclans, A. *Aproximació a les comunitats pertanyents a l'Horitzó c.4.000- 3.400 cal ANE al NE de la Península Ibèrica a partir dels estudis tecno-funcionals dels artefactes polits i bisellats situats en contextos funeraris i d'hàbitat.* PhD Thesis Universitat Autònoma de Barcelona, 2017.

Masclans, A., Gibaja, J.F., Oliva, M., Palomo, A., Terradas, X., Oms, X., Mozota, M., Clemente, I. and Mazzuco, N. "Que laissait-on dans les tombes néolithiques du nord-est de la péninsule ibérique ?". In *11e Rencontres Méridionales de Préhistoire Récente: De la Tombe au Territoire,* edited by Jessie Cauliez, Ingrid Sénépart, Luc Jallot, Pierre Arnaud de Labriffe, Christophe Gilabert and Xavier Gutherz, 175-183. Archives d'Écologie Préhistorique. Toulouse, 2016.

Masclans, A., Palomo, A., Gibaja, J.F., Remolins, G. and Gómez, D. "Use-wear analysis of Neolithic polished axes and adzes: the site of "Bòbila Madurell- Can Gambús 1-2" (North East of the Iberian Peninsula). *Quaternary International*, 427, (2017): 158-174.

Masvidal, C., González, P. and Mora, R. "El conjunto cerámico de Bóbila Madurell (Sant Quirze del Vallès, Barcelona): bases para su estudio funcional y contextual". In *III Congreso de Neolítico de la Península Ibérica,* edited by Roberto Ontañón, Cristina García and Pablo Arias, 305-316. Universidad de Cantabria, 2003.

Mozota, M. and Gibaja, J.F. "For a few awls more. Bone tools in Northeastern Iberia Neolithic Burials (4th-5th millennia calBC). A morpho-technical and functional approach". *Journal of Archaeological Science: Reports* 4, (2015): 65-77.

Muñoz, A.M. *La cultura neolítica catalana de los Sepulcros de Fosa.* Publicaciones eventuales 9. Instituto de Arqueología y Prehistoria. Universitat de Barcelona, 1965.

Oliva, M. *Aprofitament i transformació de matèries primeres per a l'elaboració d'ornaments durant la prehistòria recent (5600-3400 cal. ane) al nord-est de la península Ibèrica.* Unpublished PhD dissertation. Departament de Prehistòria, Universitat Autònoma de Barcelona, Bellaterra, 2015.

Oms, F.X., Daura, J., Sanz, J., Mendiela, S., Pedro, M. and Martínez, P. "First evidence of a collective human inhumation from the Cardial groups (Cova Bonica, Barcelona, NE Iberian Peninsula)". *Journal of Field Archaeology*, in press.

Pétrequin, P., Errera, M., Martín, A., Fabregas, R., and Vaquer, J. "Les haches en jades alpins pendant les Ve e IVe millénaires. L'exemple de l'Espagne et du Portugal dans une perspective européenne". In *Networks in the Neolithic. Exchange of raw materials, products and ideas in the Western Mediterranean (VII-III millennium BC),* edited by Mónica Borrell, Ferrán Borell, Josep Bosch, Xavoer Clop and Miquel Molist, 213-222. Gavà, Museu de Gavà, Rubricatum 5, 2012.

Reimer,P.J., Bard, E., Bayliss, A., Beck, J.W., Blackwell, P.G., Bronk Ramsey, C., Buck, C.E., Cheng, H., Edwards, R.L., Friedrich, M., Grootes, P.M., Guilderson, T.P., Haflidason, H., Hajdas, I., Hatte, C., Heaton, T.J., Hoffmann, D.L., Hogg, A.G., Hughen, K.A., Kaiser, K.F., Kromer, B., Manning, S.W., Niu, M., Reimer, R.W., Richards, D.A., Scott, E.M., Southon, J.R., Staff, R.A., Turnery, C.S., and Van der Plich, J. "IntCal13 and Marine13 radiocarbon age calibration curves 0–50,000 years cal BP". *Radiocarbon* 55, (2013): 1869–1887. Available from: http://dx.doi.org/10.2458/azu_js_rc.55.16947

Renom, V. "La secció de Prehistòria". *Anuari del Museu de Sabadell*, (1934): 18-21.

Renom, V. "Prehistòria". *Anuari del Museu de Sabadell*, (1944): 25-37.

Ripoll, E. and Llongueras, M. "La Cultura Neolítica de los Sepulcros de Fosa en Cataluña". *Ampurias* XXV, (1963): 1-90.

Riuró, F. and Fusté, M. *Les estacions prehistòriques del Puig d'en Roca.* Associació Arqueològica de Girona. Girona, 81 p., 1980.

Roig, J. and Coll, J. M. "La necròpolis del neolític mitjà de Can Gambús-1 (Sabadell, Vallès Occ.): Nova tipologia dels sepulcres de fossa i pràctiques funeràries durant el IV mil·lenni Cal BC a Catalunya". *Cypsela* 18, (2010): 93-122.

Roig, J., Coll, J.M., Gibaja, J.F., Chambon, P., Villar, V., Ruíz, J., Terradas, X. and Subirà, M.E. "La necrópolis de Can Gambús 1 (Sabadell, Barcelona). Nuevos conocimientos sobre las prácticas funerarias durante el neolítico medio en el noreste de la Península Ibérica". *Trabajos de Prehistoria* 67, (2010): 59-84.

Serra-Ráfols, J. "La exploración de la necrópolis neolítica de la Bòbila Madurell en Sant Quirze de Galliners". *Anuario del Museo de la Ciudad de Sabadell* III, (1947): 57-75.

Steele, J. "Radiocarbon dates as data quantitative strategies for estimating colonization front speeds and event densisite". *Journal of Archaeological Science* 37/8, (2010): 2017-30.

Tarradell, M. *Les arrels de Catalunya.* Barcelona, 322 p., 1962.

Terradas, X. and Gibaja, J.F. "La gestión social del sílex melado durante el neolítico medio en el nordeste de la Península Ibérica". *Trabajos de Prehistoria* 59/1, (2002): 29-48.

Terradas, X., Gratuze, B., Bosch, J., Enrich, R., Esteve, X., Oms, X. and Ribé, G. "Neolithic diffusion of obsidian in the western Mediterranean: new data from Iberia". *Journal of Archaeological Science* 41, (2014): 69-78.

Terradas, X., Gibaja, J.F., Borrell, F., Bosch, J. and Palomo, A. "Des réseaux d'échanges entre les vallées du Rhône et de l'Ebre: Un point de vue du Nord-est de la Péninsule ibérique". In *Le Chasséen, des Chasséens: Retour sur une culture nationale et ses parallèles, Sepulcres de Fossa, Cortaillod, Lagozza,* edited by Philippe Chambon, Juan F. Gibaja, Gwenaelle Goude and Thomas Perrin. AEP Archives d'Ecologie Préhistorique, in press.

Vaquer, J., Martín, A., Pétrequin, P., Pétrequin, A.M. and Errera, M. "Les haches alpines dans les sépultures du Néolithique moyen pyrénéen: importations et influences". In *JADE. Grandes haches alpines du Néolithique européen. Ve et IVe millénaires av JC, edited by* Pierre Pétrequin, Serge Cassen, Lutz Klassen, Alison Sheridan and Anne-Marie Pétrequin, 872-917. Gray, Presses Universitaires de Franche-Comté, 2012.

Villalba, M.J. "Las sepulturas neolíticas del complejo de Can Tintorer y el modelo social de la población minera". *Revista d'Arqueologia de Ponent* 9, (1999): 41-73.

Villalba, M.J. "Le gîte de variscite de Can Tintorer: production, transformation et circulation du minéral vert". In *Matériaux, productions, circulations de Néolithique à l'Age du Bronze*, edited by Jean Guilaine, 115–127. Paris, Errance, 2002.

Villalba M.J., Bañolas L., Arenas, J. and Alonso, M. *Les mines neolítiques de Can Tintorer (Gavà). Excavacions 1978–1980*, Barcelona, Generalitat de Catalunya. Excavacions arqueològiques a Catalunya 6, 1986.

Villar, V., Ruiz, J. and Subirà, M.E. *Estudi antropològic de les restes neolítiques del jaciment de Can Gambús I (Sabadell, Vallès Occidental). Universitat Autònoma de Barcelona, Departament de Biologia Animal, de Biologia Vegetal i d'Ecologia.* unpublished, 2006.

Williams, A.N. "The use of summed radiocarbon probability distributions in Archaeology: A review of methods". *Journal of Archaelogical Science* 39/3, (2012): 578-89.

Amber sites - 1: Mamoa Vila Chã Orcas; 2: Orca de Seixas; 3: Senhora da Guia; 4: Anta Pinheiro Abraços; 5: Moreirinha; 6: Ana Vale d`Antas; 7: Cabeço da Amoreira; 8: Anta dos Pombais; 9: Bela Vista; 10: Gruta Correio Mor; 11: Anta Grande; 12: Atalaião; 13: Alcarapinha; 14: Anta Grande Zambujeiro; 15: Coroa do Frade; 16: Barranco Nora Velha; 17: Alcalar3; 18: Alcalar 4

Cinnabar sites - 1: Anta da Cabeçuda; 2: Anta Bola da Cêra; 3: Anta Horta; 4: Anta Grande Zambujeiro; 5: Sobreira de Cima

Portugal - Funerary megalithic monuments in Alentejo.
Source: José Martinho Lourenço and the authors.

Chapter 7

About the Presence of Exotic Materials in Some Funerary Megalithic Monuments in Alentejo (Portugal): The Cases of Cinnabar and Amber

Leonor Rocha[1], Jorge de Oliveira[1], Cristina Barrocas Dias[2], José Mirão[2], Luís Dias[2], Ana Manhita[2]

[1]CHAIA - Centre for Art History and Artistic Investigation, University of Évora/ECS, Portugal, lrocha@uevora.pt, joli@uevora.pt

[2]HERCULES Laboratory, University of Évora, Portugal, cmbd@uevora.pt, jmirao@uevora.pt, luisdias1234@gmail.com, anaccm@uevora.pt

Abstract: In the Iberian Peninsula, the Alentejo region is of particular importance for the number, of both funerary and non funerary, number of Megalithic monuments. The majority of these monuments were excavated during the last century, however methodologies used were not always the most appropriate, allowing for new studies using modern technology. From the excavated sites a large numbers of archaeological artefacts are stored in various National Museums. During the last couple of years a project was developed to study some exotic materials recovered from the Megalithic monuments of Alentejo region and, in this communication, the results on the presence of red pigments (cinnabar, ochre) and amber in some of these monuments is analysed.

Keywords: Funerary megalithic monument, Alentejo, cinnabar, amber.

1. Megalithism in Alentejo

Alentejo region (Portugal) internationally known for the number and monumentality of its megalithic monuments, mainly as a result of the work carried by Virgil Correia (Correia 1921) and Georg and Vera Leisner (Leisner 1944, 1949, Leisner and Leisner 1959) whom inventoried, excavated and published hundreds of burial megalithic monuments of this region.

A global analysis of the Alentejo Megalithism allows us to understand the great diversity of monuments existing in this region, some with clear morphological similarities between them (passage graves), and others completely dissimilar. In fact, from more than 1,200 existing monuments, we can consider that there are four main groups: 1) small graves, open or closed, for individual or single-family burials; 2) the passage grave, with the variable length corridor, for collective burials; 3) the tholoi for collective burials; 4) the hypogea and other negative structures, apparently also for collective burials.

Naturally, this diversity of architectures represents different chronologies, especially if analyzed from a regional perspective, so the monuments and spoils, may or not, be very consistent between them.

Regardless of the anomalies that may exist in this relationship, certain presences and absences are quite significant, since they indicate different behaviors of the magical - religious communities who built and used them.

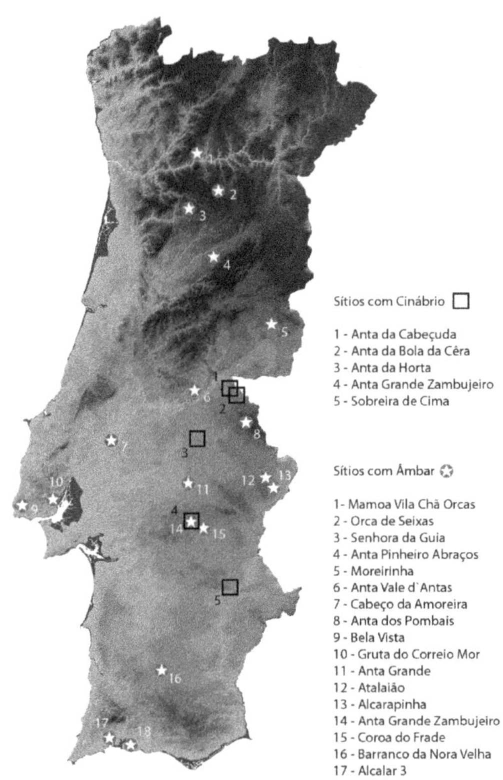

Figure 1. Archaeological sites with presence of cinnabar (black squares) and amber (white stars) in Portugal. Source: By the Authors.

The appreciation, although preliminary of the available data allows us to identify some monuments, in the Alentejo region, that stand out by the nature of their spoils.

1.1. Dolmen of Zambujeiro

Despite the extensive inventory of the megalithic monuments by numerous researchers who have worked in this area, Anta Grande do Zambujeiro (AGZ) remained unpublished until the 1960s. In fact, only in March 1964,did Henrique Leonor Pina, who was in the municipality of Évora, working in the Barrocal dolmen, receive an oral report from Mr. António Rebocho, allowing him to identify the monument, in the place known as "o cabeço da anta" the AGZ, completely preserved by the tumulus (Alegria and Dias 2007). This late identification could have been a good sign, but it was not. In fact, the crown jewel of Portuguese megalithism was pawned and lost. From the various archaeological interventions there is only one published article (Soares and Silva 2010), and the overwhelming majority of the recovered material has no stratigraphic context.

The studies of materials that we have been conducting in Évora Museum, focus on a vast variety of materials without a defined stratigraphy.

The AGZ is located in the municipality of Évora, in the parish of Nossa Senhora da Tourega. It is within its typology, the biggest European monument, if not of the world. It features polygonal chamber, with seven orthostatsand long corridor centered in a surrounding tumulus that was intact at the time of its identification in the 1960s.

1.2. Dolmen of Bola da Cera

Located in the Marvão municipality, this dolmen of short corridor and regular polygonal chamber is formed by seven orthostats of granite. The excavation in 1981 revealed a funerary deposit dated to the Bronze Age under a thin layer of soil. Below this layer, a large fragment of an orthostat was found sealing the Neolithic burial deposits. In the Neolithic level there were two skeletons in lateral decubitus facing each other and showing partial cremation signs, possibly carried out inside the monument. They were accompanied by several votive materials including two plate idols.

One of the plaques with anthropomorphic decoration has recently been analyzed. Inside the decor negative reliefs a reddish pigment was found. Its identification in the course of this study has allowed its identification as cinnabar.

The radiocarbon dating of a burned bone sample collected in the same level was dated as 3258 - 2900 cal AC.

1.3. Dolmen of Cabeçuda

The Dolmen of Cabeçuda located on the banks of the Sever river in the municipality of Marvão was excavated in the late 1980s. It is a monument with a short corridor and a regular polygonal chamber formed by seven orthostats. At the base of the chamber was opened a small pit (silo) where a polished ax, a significant amount of red pigment and coal were found.

A sample of these coals was subjected to radiocarbon dating providing the date 2274 - 1971 cal BC.

The red pigment has now been examined and was proved to be cinnabar.

1.4. Dolmen of Horta

The Dolmen of Horta is located in Alter do Chão municipality, an agricultural area of Coudelaria de Alter do Chão. This monument, with a short corridor and a regular polygonal chamber of seven orthostats, was excavated and rehabilitated in 2001.

The monument revealed a rich collection from which stands out a rare set of idols-plaque, mostly anthropomorphic. One of these idols was recently under study and the presence of cinnabar was found on its surface. Human bones collected near this idol-plate were subjected to radiocarbon dating and provided the following date: 3350 - 3020 cal BC.

2. Materials and Methods

2.1. Samples

The samples that were studied and the archaeological site from which they were recovered can be found in Table 1. These samples, comprised of red powder material mixed with soil and red powder dust, were recovered from stone artefacts and resin beads.

Table 1. Analyzed samples. | Source: By the Authors.

Archaeological site	Sample i.d.	Sample description
Bola da Cera Dolmen	BCD1	Red pigment on a schist plaque
Cabeçuda Dolmen	CD1	Lumps of red pigment
Horta Dolmen	HD1	Red pigment on a schist plaque
Zambujeiro Dolmen	ZD1	Red pigment on a schist crozier
	ZD2	Red pigment on a schist plaque
	ZD3	Red pigment on amber beads
	ZD4	Lumps of red pigment
	ME13687	Fragment of resin bead

2.2. Stereomicroscopy

Macroscopic observations and corresponding photographic documentation were obtained using a stereomicroscope Leitz-Wetzeler with x65, and x110 magnifications and equipped with a Leica DC500-2002 photo camera.

2.3. Scanning electron microscopy with energy-dispersive X-ray spectroscopy (SEM-EDX)

Scanning electron microscopy coupled with energy dispersive X-ray spectrometry analysis were carried out using a Hitachi™ 3700N scanning electron microscope coupled with a Bruker™XFlash 5010 SDD Detector®. The analyses were done at high vacuum using an accelarating voltage of 20 kV, allowing both microstructural characterization of the pigment particles and elemental composition (point analysis and 2D mapping) of the individual particles.

2.4. X-ray Diffraction (XRD)

X-ray diffraction was performed in a Bruker D8 Discovery diffractometer with using Cu Kα radiation and a GADDS detector. Integration of the 2D diffraction image enabled its conversion into a conventional diffractogram from 12-80° 2θ and 0.02°/s steps.

2.5. Micro-Raman spectroscopy

Spectra were collected with anHoriba Xplora confocal spectrometer, using 1% of the power coming from a 25mW laser diode operating at a wavelength of 637.1 nm was used for this analysis. This low power was used to avoid sample degradation. To improve the signal-to-noise ratio, several spectra are accumulated for an exposure time of 120s for each sample.

2.6. Fourier Transformed Infrared Spectroscopy with Attenuated Total Reflectance (FTIR-ATR)

Spectra were obtained using a Bruker ALPHA FTIR spectrometer equipped with a diamond crystal ATR module. All spectra were acquired between 4000 and 500 cm^{-1}, with 128 accumulations and a spectral resolution of 4 cm^{-1}.

3. Results and discussion

3.1. Cinnabar

The importance of the funerary rituals during the Neolithic period is evident from the numerous megalithic monuments disperse throughout the Western Europe, suggesting that large resources were spent in the veneration of their deceased. Red pigments are often found in archaeological contexts, where they are used to cover the bodies, however their ritual significance is not consensual among archaeologists. The red pigments recovered from the dolmens has been mainly identified as red ochers, based solely on visual inspection and its wide availability.

Chemical analysis performed on red pigments recovered in Neolithic and Chalcolithic sites from the south of Spain, surprisingly, identified cinnabar alone or together with ocher in Zueros (Cordoba) (Rogerio-Candelera *et al.* 2013, Dolmens la Vellila (Palencia) (Martín-Gil 1995), Alberite (Cadiz) (Domínguez Bella *et al.* 1995), Montelirio (Sevilla (Rogerio-Candelera *et al.* 2013), the graves of Paraje of Monte Bajo (Cadiz) (Lazarich González *et al.* 2009), and the site of Cova de l'Or (Alicante) (Rogerio-Candelera *et al.* 2013) and Casa Montero (Madrid) (Hunt Ortiz *et al.* 2011).

Unlike what happens with the ocher, cinnabar (HgS) is not common in nature, and there are only four places for its mining the Iberian Peninsula (Rogerio-Candelera *et al.* 2013): Las Alpujarras (Granada), Sierra de los Filabres (Almeria), Usagre (Ossa Morena, Badajoz) and the most important of them all, Almadena (Ciudad Real).

Apart from the Iberian Peninsula, there are a few other European sites were the presence of cinnabar has been reported. In the Italian pensinsula, the use of cinnabar was reported in a few sites from the Neolithic and Chalcolithic periods (end of the 7th to mid 4th millenium BC) in northern and central Italy (Volante 2016a, b). In southwestern and central Europe, the use of cinnabar was reported by the Vinca culture (5700-4500 BC) (Gajic-Kvascev *et al.* 2012). In the eastern Mediterranean (mid 8th century and 6th millenium BC) the presence of cinnabar was found in archaeological contexts in the Levant (Nigel Goring-Moris 2015), and in Anatolia (Anderson *et al.* 2014; Zararsiz *et al.* 2018).

Despite the fact that they look alike, ochre and cinnabar are very different in chemical terms. The red colour in ochers is mainly due to the presence of the mineral hematite (Fe_2O_3), while goethite (FeOOH) provides a yellowish color. Ochers are also usually rich in alumino-silicates, such as kaolinite or illite, quartz, and carbonates, such as, calcite or dolomite, which ultimately contribute for the pigment final hue.

The red pigment samples were studied by stereomicroscopy, SEM-EDX, μ-XRD and μ-Raman spectroscopy. SEM-EDX is an elemental technique that allows point and mapping analysis. The difference in composition allowed the distinction and identification of cinnabar and ocher red pigments.2D mapping allowed the elemental analysis of a selected area of the sample (various particles) and provided information about the purity of the sample.

X-Ray diffraction allowed the identification of the crystalline phases present in a mixture; apart cinnabar or ochre, other minerals present in the sample couldal could be identified (data not shown).

Raman spectroscopy is a molecular technique, and allows unequivocal identification of the molecules of cinnabar and ochre, by comparison of the sample spectra with spectra from a database of pigments.

As an example of the analysis performed, some of the spectra obtained for samples CD1 and ZD2 are presented in Figures 2 and 3. Table 2 summarizes the information about the nature of the red pigments studied.

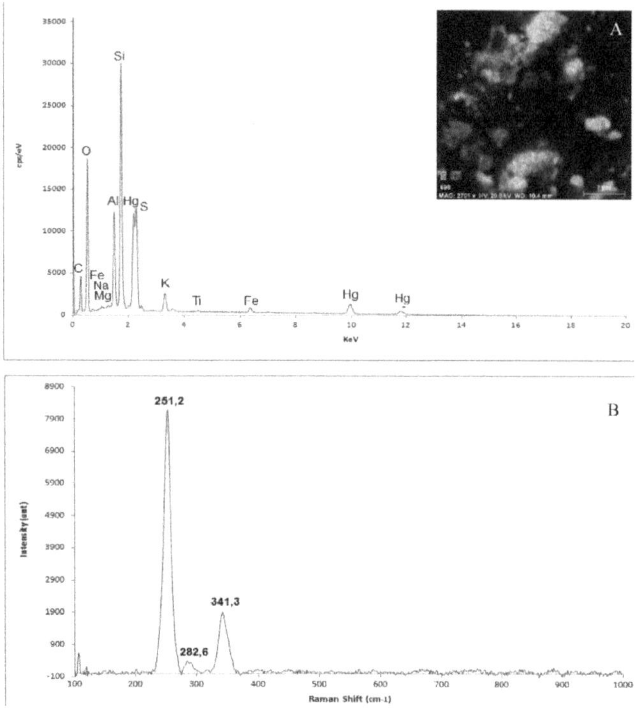

Figure 2. SEM-EDX (A) and Raman spectra (B) of sample CD1 from Domen of Cabeçuda. SEM- EDX spectra indicate the presence of cinnabar with silicates (phyllosilicates?) and a small amount of iron oxide. The bands in the Raman spectra are due to stretching modes of the cinnabar (HgS). Source: By the Authors.

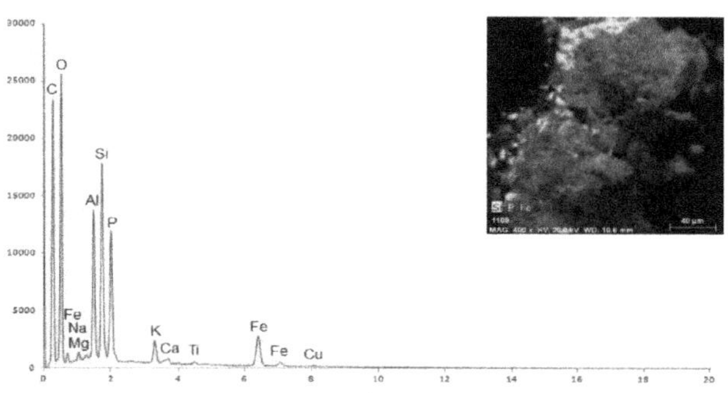

Figure 3. SEM-EDX analysis of sample ZD2 from Zambujeiro Dolmen. Spectra show the presence of iron oxide and silicates (phyllosilicate?). | Source: By the Authors.

Table 2. Identification of the red pigments analyzed. Source: By the Authors.

Archaeological site	Sample i.d.	Sample description	Pigment identification
Bola da Cera Dolmen	BCD1	Red pigment on a schist plaque	Cinnabar with small amounts of iron oxide
Cabeçuda Dolmen	CD1	Lumps of red pigment	Cinnabar with small amounts of iron oxide
Horta Dolmen	HD1	Red pigment on a schist plaque	Cinnabar with small amounts of iron oxide
Zambujeiro Dolmen	ZD1	Red pigment on a schist crozier	Cinnabar with small amounts of iron oxide
	ZD2	Red pigment on a schist plaque	Iron oxide
	ZD3	Red pigment on amber beads	Cinnabar
	ZD4	Lumps of red pigment	Cinnabar

In the majority of studied samples cinnabar was found together with small amounts of ochre, but the presence of the iron pigment might be due to soil contamination (evidence of phyllosilicates are also present). Due to the small amount of red pigment available in the majority of the samples, we cannot ascertain if the mixture of ochre was deliberate or just due to contamination with the local soil. In Sobreira de Cima hypogeum some sepulchres yielded cinnabar samples that seem to have been mixed with ochre, while in others only cinnabar or ochre was used (Dias and Mirão 2013).

The reasons why these pre-historic communities used the rare red pigment (cinnabar) when they had a local widely available and visually undistinguishable red pigment (ochre) will always be a mystery. Some archaeologists suggest a ritual and magical significance for the use of the red pigments, while others, like Martin Gil (1995), one of the first researchers to identify large amounts of cinnabar in a Neolithic funerary context, propose a pragmatic reason for the choice of cinnabar which is related to the preservative properties of this pigment. In any case, the distance between the cinnabar mining places and the studied dolmens suggests the existence of commercial trading routes for this pigment in the Iberian Peninsula. The likely high cost of cinnabar raises the hypothesis that the nature of the red pigments used in funerary contexts depended on the social status of the individual.

3.2. Amber

Amber is a soft, fossil, vegetable resin, typically exhibiting pale red and orange colours. Amber forms from residual vegetal resins originating chiefly from conifers and some angiosperms, which have overtime undergone a process of fossilization and polymerization until the volatile compounds are lost. The non-volatile compounds, diterpenes and triterpenes, are those that generally fossilize forming extensive and irregular masses of amber (Guiliano 2007; Murillo-Barroso 2012).

Amber deposits are relatively abundant across the world, with the most famous being in the Baltic Sea. There are, however, other deposits in Romania, Sicilia and even in the Iberian Peninsula – the Cretaceous deposits in the Cantabrian coast, and smaller deposits in Central Norwest and South Spain (Murillo-Barroso 2012).

The determination of the geologic origin of the ambers has attracted much attention from researchers since the 19th century. Fourier Transform Infrared Spectroscopy (FTIR) has been widely used in the analysis of these resins, with the Baltic amber being identified by the presence of the "Baltic shoulder", an intense absorption peak in the 1160-1150 cm^{-1} region invariably proceeded by a flat band between 1250 and 1180 cm^{-1}. No other European amber shows this feature (Murillo-Barroso 2012).

The collection of Zambujeiro amber beads are not all very well preserved and some of them are broken into smaller pieces. As it can be seen in Figure 4 A and B, the beads exterior layer presents a different structure and colour from that of the inner core. A red pigment can also be seen in the surface of some of the beads (Figure 4 C).

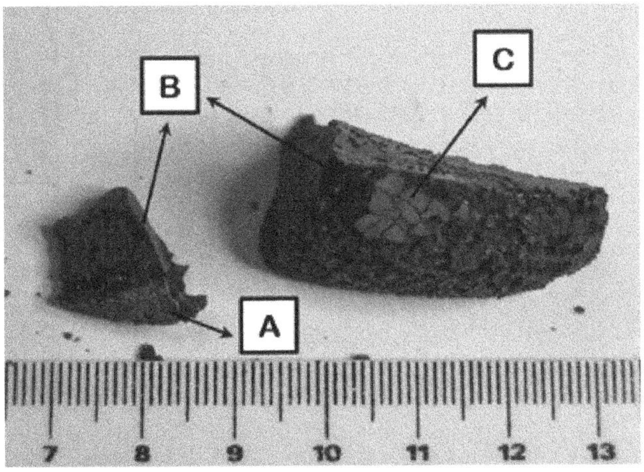

Figure 4. One of the amber beads collected in Great Dolmen of Zambujeiro (Évora Museum collection, inventory nr. ME13687). It is possible to distinguish an outer layer (A), an inner core (B) and also a red pigment on the upper layer (C).

The FTIR-ATR spectra of the samples indicate that the analyzed beads are all made from a similar amber material which is not Baltic amber (Figure 5 A and B).

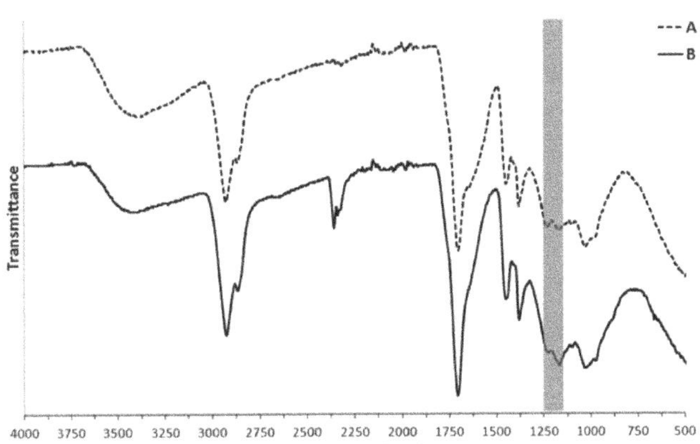

Figure 5. FTIR-ATR spectra of the outer layer (A) and inner core of the amber beads (B). | Source: By the Authors.

FTIR-ATR spectra of the two layers can be observed in Figure 5 A and B and the main differences are in the regions of the OH stretching (3400 cm^{-1}), the carbonyl region (1700-1650 cm^{-1}) and the fingerprinting region (977-1275 cm^{-1}). The intensity of carbonyl acidic band (1705 cm^{-1}) diminishes in the outer layer, appearing a new shoulder at 1651 cm-1 likely due to the C=C stretch, indicating a likely diminish of the total number of organic acids. This is also come in agreement with the reduced intensity of the band at 1170 cm-1, due to the C=O stretch, in the outer layer when compared to the inner core spectra.

Concerning the origin of the Zambujeiro amber the most likely provenance is the Cantabria region, because of the similarities between their FTIR-ATR spectra. The Cantabrian amber spectra presents two absorption bands in the 1250-1150 cm^{-1} region, with a maximum peak at about 1160-1150 cm^{-1} and a second peak at about 1250-1180 cm^{-1}; it also shows two absorption peaks at 1020 and 960 cm-1 (Fernandez 2005).However, one cannot discard simetite as the raw material of the Zambujeiro amber beads. The simetite, Sicilian amber, can be distinguished by the absorption in the 1300-1000 cm^{-1} region of the FTIR spectra with a maximum peak at about 1241 cm^{-1}and a second peak, usually less intense, at about 1181 cm^{-1} (Murillo-Barroso 2012). In the Iberian Peninsula there are a few analyzed amber artefacts from the Neolithic period and those few are said to be made from simetite, although sometimes, a local origin is not discarded (Murillo-Barroso 2012).

Figure 4 shows the presence of a red pigment attached to the amber bead. Raman analysis of the red pigment indicates that it is cinnabar (Figure 6).

Amber is always a rare archaeological find, reflecting its high value, and the fifty amber beads recovered in the Zambujeiro Dolmen, confirms the exceptional value of this National Monument. Cinnabar could also be identified as being present in some of the beads surface.

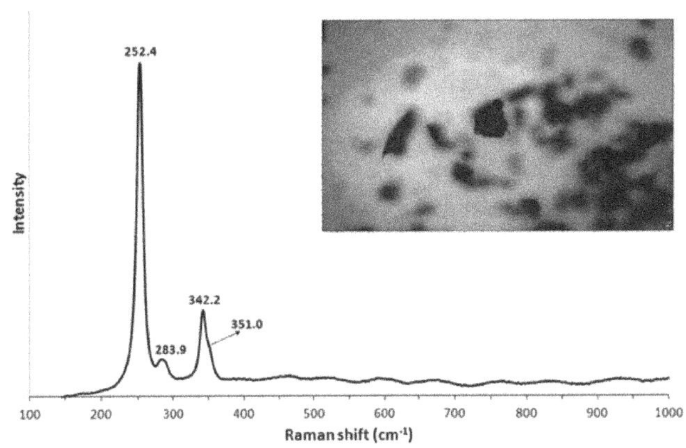

Figure 6. Raman spectra of the red pigment found in the surface of the amber beads. The identified bands are due to stretching modes of the cinnabar (HgS). | Source: By the Authors.

4. Conclusions

The presence of exotic materials in several Dolmen of the Alentejo region suggests the existence of commercial trading routes for these materials in the Iberian Peninsula. Cinnabar and amber travelled hundreds of kilometres to be found in these funerary monuments, which can only be explained by the high symbolic value attributed by our ancestors to cinnabar and amber.

Apart from the Iberian Peninsula, there are a few other European sites were the presence of cinnabar has been reported. In the Italian pensinsula, the use of cinnabar was reported in a few sites from the Neolithic and Chalcolithic periods (end of the 7th to mid 4th millenium BC) in northern and central Italy (Volante 2016a, b). In southwestern and central Europe, the use of cinnabar was reported by the Vinca culture (5700-4500 BC) (Gajic-Kvascev *et al.* 2012). In the eastern Mediterranean (mid 8th century and 6th millenium BC) the presence of cinnabar was found in archaeological contexts in the Levant (Nigel Goring-Moris 2015), and in Anatolia (Anderson *et al.* 2014; Zararsiz *et al.* 2018).

Acknowledgments

The authors acknowledge the financial support of IMAGOS programme (Innovative Methodologies in Archaeology, Archaeometry and Geophysics - Optimizing Strategies) and project LARES – Laboratorial Archaeometric and Archaeological Research – Engaging Sciences, operation n.º ALENT-07-0224-FEDER-001761, INALENTEJO, QREN.

References

Alvarez Fernandez, Esteban; Penalver Molla, Enrique; Delclòs, Xavier, "La presencia de ámbar en los yacimientos prehistóricos (del Paleolítico Superior a la Edad del Bronce) de la Cornisa Cantábrica y sus fuentes de aprovisionamiento". Zephyrus. LVIII. Ediciones Universidad de Salamanca (2005): 159-182.

Anderson, E.; Almond, M. J.; Matthews, W.; Cinque, G.; Frogley, M.D. 2014: Analysis of Red Pigments from the Neolithic sites of Çatalhöyük in Turkey and Sheikh-e Abad in Iran. Spectrochimica Acta Part A:Molecular and Biomolecular Spectroscopy, 131:373–383.

Arnaud, José Eduardo Morais, "Corôa de Frade. Fortificação do Bronze Final dos arredores de Évora. Escavações de 1971-72". *Madrider Mitteilungen.* Heidelberg, 20 (1979): 56-100.

Borja, Pablo García, *Saguntum.* 38. Valencia (2006): 49-60,

Dias, L; Oliveira, J.; Rocha, L.; Rosado, L.; Dias, C; Ferreira, T; Candeias, A; Mirão, J. "Sobre a presença de Cinábrio em rituais funerários no Megalitismo do Alentejo, Portugal", Poster, *IX Congresso Ibérico de Arqueometria*, Lisboa, 2011.

Dias, C; Mirão, J. "Identificação de pigmentos vermelhos recolhidos no hipogeu da Sobreira de Cima por microscopia de raman e microscopia electrónica de varrimento acoplada com espectroscopia de dispersão de energias de raios-x (MEV-EDX)". In: Sobreira de Cima. Necrópole de hipogeus do Neolítico (Vidigueira, Beja). Coord. António Carlos Valera. *Era Monográfica 1.* Lisboa: Núcleo de Investigação Arqueológica – NIA (2013): 101-108

Domingo, I.; García-borja, P; Roldán, C. "Identification, Processing and Use of Red Pigments (Hematite and Cinnabar) in the Valencian Early Neolithic (Spain)". *Archaeometry*, 54 (2012): 868–892.

Domínguez Bella, S.; Morata Céspedes, D. "Aplicación de las técnicas mineralógicas y petrológicas a la arqueometría. Estudio de materiales del dolmen de Alberite (Villamartín, Cádiz)". *Zephyrus*, XLVIII (1995): 129-142.

Fernandéz, Martínez, *Sanguntum Extra*, 2 (1999): 111-116.

Gajic-Kvascev, M; Maric Stojanovic, M.; Smit, Z.; Kantarelou, V.; Germanos Karydas, A.; Sljivar, D.; Milovanovic, D.; Andric V. 2012: New evidence for the use of cinnabar as a colouring pigment in the Vinca culture. *Journal of Archaeological Science*, 39: 1025-1033

García Borja, P; Domingo Sanz, I; Roldán García, C., "Nuevos Datos Sobre el Uso de Materia Colorante Durante el Neolítico Antiguo en las Comarcas Centrales Valencianas". *Saguntum*, 38 (2006): 49-60.

Guiliano, Michel; Asia, Laurence; Onoratini, Gerard, Mille, Gilbert, "Applications of diamond crystal ATR FTIR spectroscopyto the characterization of ambers". *Spectrochimica Acta Part A*. 67, (2007): 1407–1411

Hunt-Ortiz, M. A; Consuegra-Rodríguez, S; Del Río-Español, P. D; Hurtado-Pérez, V; Monteroruiz, I. "Neolithic and Calcolithic – VI to II Millennia BC – Use of Cinnabar (HgS) in the Iberian Peninsula: Analytical Identification and Lead Isotope Data for an Early Mineral Exploitation of the Almadén (Ciudad Real, Spain) Mining District". *Instituto Geológico y Minero de España* (2011): 3-13.

Hunt Ortiz, M. A; Hurtado Pérez, V.M. "Pigmentos de sulfuro de mercurio e cinabrio e en contextos funerarios de época calcolítica en el sur de la Península Ibérica: investigaciones sobre el uso, depósitos minerales explotados y redes de distribución a través de la caracterización composicional e isotópica". *Seminario de Arqueología y Etnología Turolense*. Teruel (2010): 123-131.

Hunt Ortiz, M. A; Consuegra-Rodrígues, S; Díaz Del Rio-Español, P; Hurtado Pérez, V, Montero-Ruiz, I., "Neolithic and Chalcolithic – VI to III millenia BC – use of cinnabar (HgS) in the Iberian Peninsula: Analytical identification and lead isotope data for an early mineral exploitation of the Almadén (Ciudad Real, Spain) mining district", in: Ortiz, J.E., Puche, O., Rábano, I., Mazadiego, L.F., (Eds.), History of research on mineral resources. *Cuadernos del Museo Geominero*. 13. IGME, Madrid (2011): 3-13.

Lazarich González, M; Fernández de la Gala, J. V; Jenkins, V; Peralta, P; Briceño, E., Ramos, A; Richarte, M. J; Carreras, A. M; Núñez, M; Versaci, M; Stratton, S; Sánchez, M; Grillé, J. M., "Paraje de Monte Bajo (Alcalá de los Gazules). Una nueva necrópolis de cuevas artificiales en el Sur de la provincia de Cádiz". *Almoraima*. 39 (2009):67-83.

Martín Gil, J; Martín Gil, F.; Delibes de Castro, G; Zapatero Magadaleno, P; Sarabia, F. J. "The First Known Use of Vermilion". *Experientia*, 51. Basel (1995): 759-761.

Martínez Fernández, M. J; Gavilán Ceballos, B.; Barrios Neira, J; Montealegre Contreras, M. "Materias primas colorantes en Murciélagos de Zueros (Córdoba), caracterización y procedencia". *Sanguntum Extra*, 2 (1999): 111-116.

Morán, Elena; Parreira, Rui, *Alcalar 7. Estudo e reabilitação de um monumento megalítico*. Lisboa: IPPAR, 2004.

Murillo-Barroso, M; Martínon-Torres, M. "Amber Sources and Trade in the Prehistory of the Iberian Peninsula". *European J. Archaeology.* 15: 2, (2012): 187-216.

Nigel Goring-Morris, A., 2005: Life, death and the emergence of differential status in the near eastern Neolithic: evidence from Kfar HaHoresh, lower Galilee, Israel. Clark, J. (Ed.), *Archaeological Perspectives on the Transmission and Transformation of Culture in the Eastern Mediterranean Levant Supplementary Series,* vol. 2. Oxbow Books and The Council for British Research in the Levant: 90-105.

Oliveira, Jorge, *Monumentos Megalíticos da Bacia Hidrográfica do Rio Sever*. Lisboa: Colibri, 1997.

Rogerio-Candelera, M. A; Herrera, L. K; Miller, A. Z; Sanjuán, L. G; Molina, C. M.; Wheatley, D. W; Justo A; Saiz-Jimenez, C. "Allochthonous red pigments used in burial practices at the Copper Age site of Valencina de la Concepción (Sevilla, Spain): characterisation and social dimension". *Journal of Archaeological Science*. 40 (2013): 279-290.

Valera, A. C. Coord. Sobreira de Cima. Necrópole de Hipogeus do Neolítico (Vidigueira, Beja). *Era Monográfica*. 1. Lisboa: NIA, 2013.

Vilaça, Raquel, "Hierarquização e conflito no Bronze Final da Beira Interior. In Existe uma Idade do Bronze Atlântico?" Lisboa: Instituto Português de Arqueologia. *Trabalhos de Arqueologia*. 10. (1998): 203-217.

Vilaça, Raquel, "Todos os caminhos vão dar ao Ocidente: Trocas e contactos no Bronze Final". Oeiras: Câmara Municipal de Oeiras. *Estudos Arqueológicos de Oeiras*. 15 (2007): 135-154

Vilaça, R.; Beck, C; Stout, E. "Provenience analysis of prehistoric amber artefacts in Portugal". 43. Madrid. *Madrider Mitteilungen*. (2002): 61-78.

Volant, N., 2016a: Spaccasasso cave: a complex copper age funerary contest on the Uccellina mountains (Alberese e Grosseto). In: Rickards, O., Sarti, L. (Eds.), *Biological and Cultural Heritage of Central-southern Italian Population through 30 Thousand Years*, EPIC, Proceeding of the PRIN 2010-11 Meeting, Villa Mondragone, Monte Porzio Catone Roma, 6 novembre 2015: 93-104.

Volant, N., 2016b. Notizia preliminare sulla cava neolitica di Cinabro sul Poggio di Spaccasasso nel Parco Regionale della Maremma (Alberese - GR). *Notiziario della Soprintendenza per i Beni Archeologici della Toscana*. All'Insegna del Giglio, Firenze: 429-440.

Zararsiz, A., Özen, L., Kalayci, Y., Bostanci, O., Elyildirim, I., Toker, A., Karydas, A.G., 2008: Characterization of Neolithic wall-painting pigments (Çatalhoyuk 7000e8000 B.C.) by means of a hand-HELD XRF spectrometer. In: Tiano, P., Pardini, C. (Eds.), In Situ Monitoring of Monumental Surfaces, Book of Proceedings of the International Workshop SMW08, Firenze, 27-29 October 2008. Edifir e Edizioni, Firenze: P97-P102.

Portugal – Upper Morgado Shelter. | Source: José Martinho Lourenço.

Chapter 8

Upper Morgado Shelter, Still a Peripheral Funeral Context, or Perhaps Not? (Tomar, Central Portugal)

Ana Cruz[1], João Carlos de Senna-Martinez[2], Luis Santos[3], Cláudia Relvado[4], Cheila Ribeiro[5], Teresa Fernandes[6], Ana Curto[7]

[1]Transdisciplinary Center of Archeologies of the Polytechnic Institute of Tomar, Tomar, Portugal and the Archaeology Unit, Geology Department of Life Sciences and Environment – UTAD (Portugal), anacruz@ipt.pt

[2]Centre of Archaeology (Uniarq), University of Lisbon, Lisbon, Portugal, smartinez@fl.ul.pt

[3]Geosciences Quaternary Group and Natural Hazards Research Center, Polytechnic Institute of Tomar, Tomar, Portugal, lsantos@ipt.pt

[4]Research Centre for Anthropology and Health, Department of Life Sciences, University of Coimbra, Coimbra, Portugal, claudia.relvado@gmail.com

[5]Department of Life Sciences, University of Coimbra, Coimbra, Portugal,cheilamribeiro.94@gmail.com

[6]Department of Biology, University of Évora, Évora, Portugal Research Centre for Anthropology and Health, Department of Life Sciences, University of Coimbra, Coimbra, Portugal, tmf@uevora.pt

[7]Human Osteology Lab, Skeletal Biological Research Centre, School of Anthropology and Conservation, University of Kent, Canterbury, UK Research Centre for Anthropology and Health, Department of Life Sciences, University of Coimbra, Coimbra, Portugal, arqc3@kent.ac.uk

Abstract: The Upper Morgado shelter is a karst cavity located in the Nabão river valley whose material culture is in many aspects associated to the dolmen world. This shelter was used and reused in a long diachrony (since Neolithic times until the Early Bronze Age). Exchange and /or Interchange is confirmed through the occurrence of some metal artefacts that observed a complete set of relationships with items found travelling through the Portuguese Estremadura and Alentejo, across borders to Almeria and as far France.

The upper Morgado shelter fits the purpose of a long-term study where the thesis that the funerary features themselves travelled across borders as ideological exchange. Recent research found several ritual actions regarding the systematic burial of individuals of both sexes and of all ages. Since the primary burial, in an unstructured pit, that with time transforms itself into a Chalcolithic ossuary; further complemented with vestigial nuclei of human bones from the Neolithic. Those ossuaries were posteriorly displaced and containerised in a circular rock structure, with small rock niche-ossuary structures containing a limited number of unstructured bones. All this material culture behaviour results in the complex nature of this site.

Keywords: Shelter, Ossuary, Primary burial, Neolithic, Chalcolithic.

1. Outline of a geomorphological picture of the karst cavities in the Nabão valley

Situated within the carbonated units of the Middle Jurassic, along with those of the Lower Jurassic, enclosed in a meridian outcropping formation between Condeixa and Tomar, defining a specific Morpho-structural unit: the limestone Massif of Sicó-Alvaiázere (Cruz 1988; Galopim de Carvalho 1996).

The Meridian Jurassic carbonated stretch initiates in Condeixa and finishes in Tomar, individualizing the Morpho-structural unit of the Massif of Sicó-Alvaiázere-Tomar which belongs to the larger Meso-cenozoic western rim. This geomorphological terminus is located to the South-southeast of the Nabão river watershed exhibiting a wavy orography, typical of a karst landscape, with altitudes that do not exceed the 150 meters (Hypsometric Chart of Portugal 1984; Military Charts of Portugal 1969).

The Upper Morgado shelter is in a karst area (Geological survey maps 1992), defined as belonging to the Middle Jurassic (limestones of Sicó and Oolithic limestones of Santo António das Lapas). This site is characterized by fissured compressed formations of variable permeability, framed in the Orogenic Alpine cycle. The site is in the proximity of a sedimentary nature geologic flaw. The cavity is associated to the Ribeira do Fetal, a tributary of the Nabão River, in an extremely accentuated meander that the locals nicknamed Canteirões (Portuguese Military Survey Charts 1969) (Figure 1).

Archaeological interventions initiated on 1979 and are currently (2017), evaluated as primary sources that allow us to interpret the burial practices in Diachrony along with various funerary environments (Anastácio and Cruz 2015; Arsénio and Batata 1992; Batata 1997; Cruz 1997, 2000, 2011; Cruz and Oosterbeek 1985a; 1985b, 1998; Zilhão 1992; Oosterbeek 1994; Oosterbeek and Cruz 1990, 1991, 1998; Nobre 2002; Figueiredo 2007). (Figure 2).

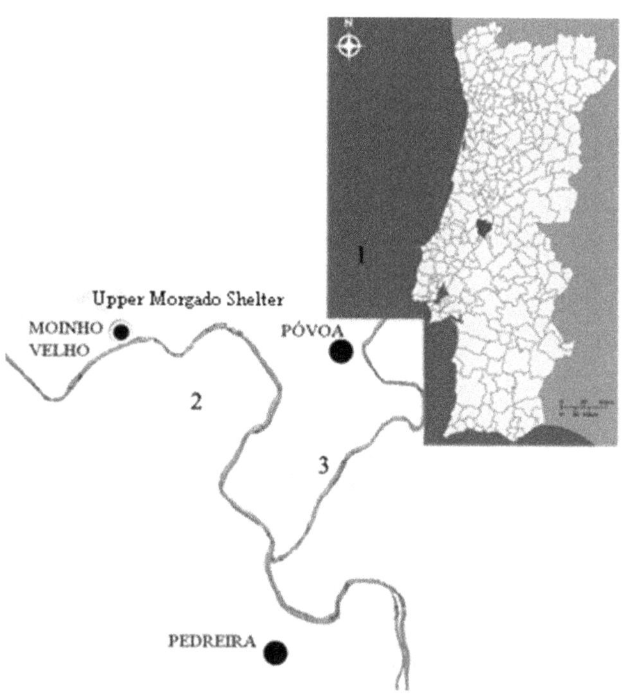

Figure 1. 1: Geographic position of the municipality of Tomar in Portugal; 2: Nabão river; 3: Milheira Stream.

2. Local Raw Material Issue

This intertwined relationship between the Middle Tagus communities (the region located in the centre of Portugal, geographical hinge between the Mid-Tagus and lower-Tagus), and the neighbouring regions are of a dual nature. Primarily, evidences in the transition from the Epi-Palaeolithic — to the Neolithic-Chalcolithic inheriting the legacy from prior communities, ancient inter-community relationships, with the massive limestone Estremadura and the Atlantic coastline; giving rise to a secondary progressively new contact relationship with Estremadura and the South, mainly with the aim of obtaining raw materials such as flint, shells, quartz crystals, amphibolite, shale and items devoted to the symbolic scope. During the Bronze age new relationships would have been created to obtain amber, copper and later tin.

As yet, no chemical or physical material analysis was performed on material provenance, however, several studies on flint artefacts allow us to draw generic associations based on the various studies developed in the region (Almeida *et al.* 2003; Almeida 2005; Aubry 1988, 2002, 2009; Aubry *et al.* 2001, 2003a, 2003b, 2007; Aubry and Igreja 2008; Aubry and Walter 2003; Bicho 2001; Geneste and Rigaud 1989; Shokler 2002, 2007; Zilhão 1997; Aubry *et al.* 2009, 147, Figure 5.1.1-8,148, Figure 5.1.1-9, 153, Figure 5.1.1-10, 1).

Sites comprising contemporaneous flint sources:

1. In the westernmost range of the middle Tagus, in the municipality of Ourém, deep in the Nabão river basin lies the so-called "Sílex de Azenha-Agroal", situated only 10 kilometres from the city of Tomar. The flint nodules appear in secondary deposits in the alluvial plains of the Nabão (Aubry, Mangado Llach and Sampaio 2009, 151, 155);

2. Near Ribeira da Sabacheira, last tributary on the right margin of the Nabão River, immediately before the resurgence of Agroal, there are large flint nodules (Aubry, Mangado Llach and Sampaio 2009, 152).

3. In the municipality of Ferreira do Zêzere, at a distance of about 3 km from the Avecasta Cave we will find Ribeira da Murta' flint, in this case the flint nodules result from the accumulation in the debritic deposits (Aubry, Mangado Llach and Sampaio 2009, 153).

4. In the limestone outcrops, within the municipality of Alcanena and Rio Maior (the latter already outside the Middle Tagus territory), flint nodules were located in

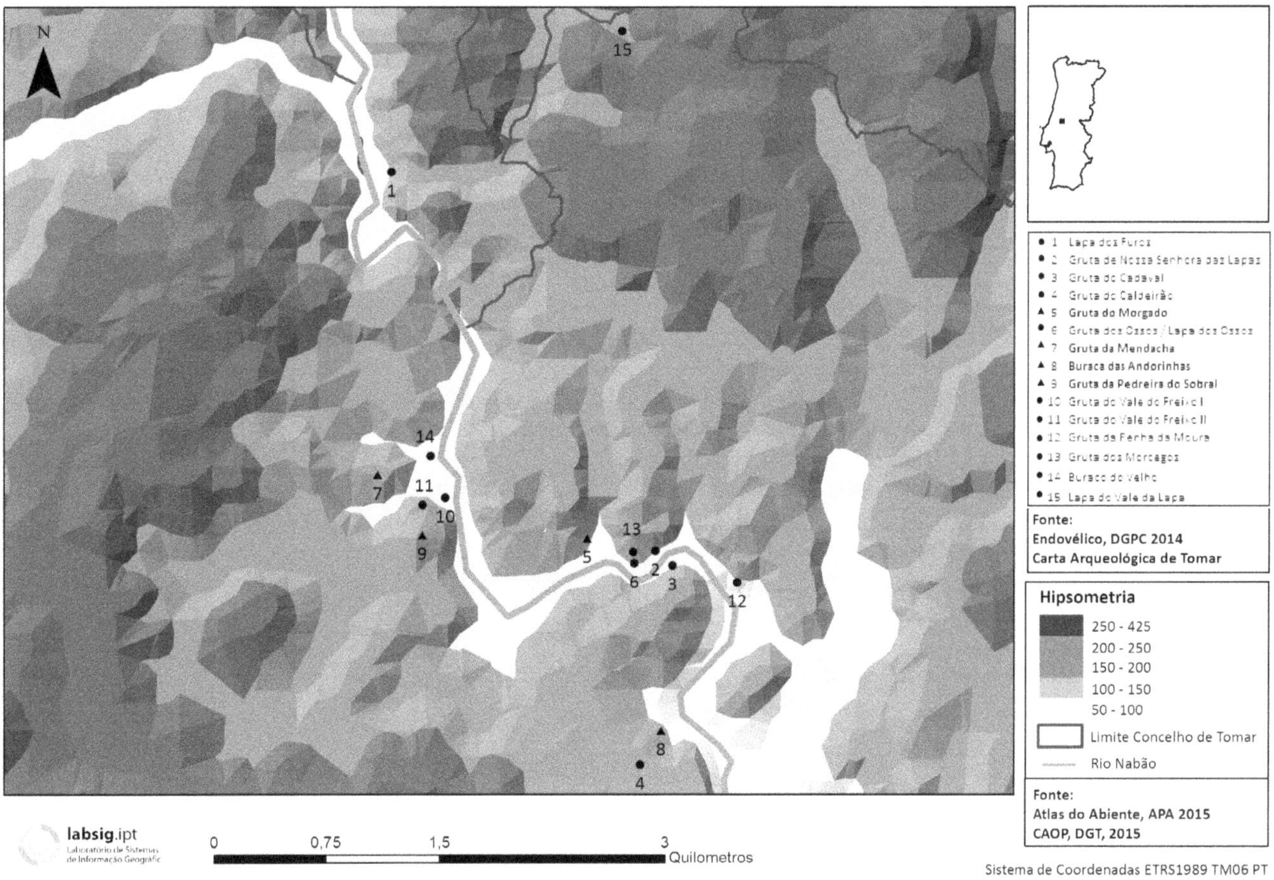

Figure 2. Digital terrain model comprising the meander and the karst cavities of archaeological interest: 1: Lapa dos Furos; 2: Gruta de Nª Sª das Lapas; 3: Gruta do Cadaval: 4: Gruta do Morgado; 5: Gruta do Morgado Superior; 6: Gruta dos Ossos; 7: Gruta da Mendacha, 8: Buraca das Andorinhas; 9: Gruta da Pedreira do Sobral; 10: Gruta do vale do Freixo I; 11: Gruta do vale do Freixo II; 12: Gruta da Penha Moura; 13: Gruta dos Morcegos; 14: Buraco do Velho; 15: Lapa do vale da Lapa. | Source: Endovélico - Rita Anastácio.

secondary deposition (Marks, Shokler and Zilhão 1991; Bicho 1992; Zilhão 1997; Thacker 2000; Shokler 2002).

The conclusions drawn from this geographic scenario lead us to conclude the existence of exchange networks with a reasonable amplitude (100km), spanning the entire Middle Tagus and beyond, through the continuous chronological periods.

From the point of view of access this raw material we believe there were two different supply routes. One the archaeological sites located or set up in the vicinity of the deposits would have secured direct access to flint nodules, practicing local supply trading. As an example, we refer some from the Neolithic, the Chalcolithic and the Bell Beaker periods [Laranjal de Cabeço das Pias (Torres Novas) (Carvalho 1996, Carvalho and Gibaja 2005); Cerradinho do Ginete (Torres Novas) (Carvalho 1996, Carvalho and Gibaja 2005); Cadeirão Cave (Tomar) (Zilhão 1992); Cadaval Cave (Tomar) (Oosterbeek 1994; Cruz 1997, 2011); Ossos Cave (Tomar) (Oosterbeek 1994; Cruz 1997, 2011); Nossa Senhora das Lapas Cave (Tomar) (Oosterbeek 1994; Cruz 1997, 2011); Upper Morgado shelter (Tomar) (Oosterbeek 1994; Cruz, 1997, 2011, 2016; Cruz *et al.* 2013, 2014, 2015); Settlement of Fonte Quente (Tomar) (Oosterbeek 1994; Cruz 1997, 2011); Settlement of Fonte Quente II (Tomar) (Batata and Borges 2011); Covão da Arrascada (Tomar) (Oosterbeek 1994); Algar do Barrão (Alcanena) (Carvalho 1996, Carvalho and Gibaja 2005); Marmota Cave (Alcanena) (Gonçalves 1972); Carrascos Cave (Alcanena) (Gonçalves and Pereira 1979), Colos Hypogeum (Cruz *et al.* 2015)].

The second, the distant communities that would have access to the materials produced or the raw material itself as a result of trade.

3. The Upper Morgado shelter

The upper Morgado shelter is one of several karst cavities of the meander which were used and re-utilized successively with funeral purposes during the Holocene, and underlining the refuge nature assumed in some historical periods of Discontinuity, for example, during the troubled period of the restoration of independence in XVII century (oral information by Mário Monteiro).

This cavity was excavated in 1988 (Oosterbeek and Cruz 1998) and subsequently excavated in 2012 (Cruz 2012, 2013; Cruz *et al.* 2013), in 2015 (Cruz and Berruti

2015) and in 2016 (Cruz 2016). The intervention of 1988 did not provide sufficient material culture to financially justify the continuity of the work, hence the discontinuity of research.

This site is dated, through the absolute dates, as between the initial Neolithic and the end of the Chalcolithic, through the relative chronology, also in the Early Bronze Age (Graphic 1).

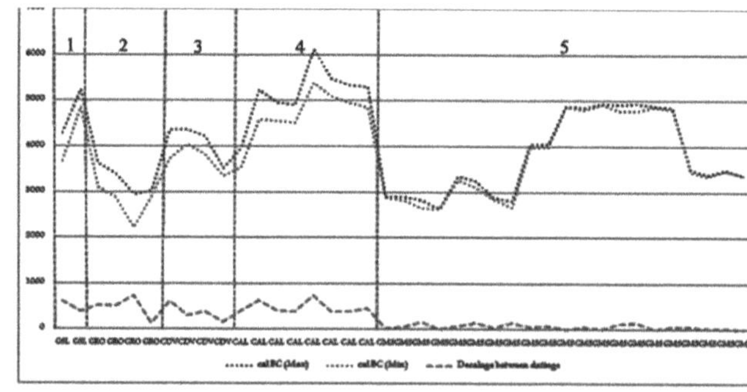

Graphic 1. Absolute datings, diachronic evolution of the meander cavities: 1: Nª Srª das Lapas Cave; 2: Bones Cave; 4: Cadaval Cave; 5: Upper Morgado Shelter. Source: Cruz and Berruti 2015, Oosterbeek 1994, Zilhão 1992.

The funerary archaeology in the Canteirões is not a novelty *tout court*, however, Upper Morgado Shelter, when compared with the caves of Caldeirão, Ossos and Nossa Senhora das Lapas, either at the human osteological level, or at the material culture level, is the most abundant site, considering the material excavated up to date. Its "Collection Package" proved to be the most important consisting of 4 distinct categories:

1. Lithic Industry (nucleus, trapeze, arrowheads, blades, lamellae, firing pins, hammerstones, splinters and spicules in flint, hyaline quartz, quartzite, amphibolite and shale).

2. Bone industry (spatulas, punches).

3. Open and closed ceramic containers. Found hemispheric containers with both flat and convex basis; The shape of the edges varies between the round, flat and pointed and the direction varies between the straight and the protruding. Absence of any decorative motif.

4. The adornments are represented by shells (elliptical perforation and quadruple perforated, one of them possesses double perforation), rings, polished bone pendants, wild boar tusks and carnivore canines, green stone pendants also with incisions, and discoid bone, schist beads. Hair pins (body and false head, with corrugated and incised decoration) (Figure 3).

5. The Ideotechnical artifacts are represented on Figure 4:

Figure 3. Bone hair pins (body and false head, with corrugated and incised decoration, and plain. | Source: Ana Cruz.

This adornments and Ideo-technical elements are evidences of the circulation of goods to fairly large distances, not only demonstrate connections to the ancient massif that is within a 40 kilometres buffer range, but also as connections to the Megalithic universe (*circa* 400km to South and *circa* 250km to North) and with Portuguese Extremadura (about 50 kilometers) (Carreira and Cardoso 2001-2002, 277-278). These materials demonstrate the existence of a network of cultural influences in the Portuguese Estremadura, Alentejo and Algarve, and most likely by interchange, Almeria (*circa* 800km).

According to J. L. Cardoso the small zoomorphic statuette with about 2 cm long, 1.5 cm wide and 65 mm thick belongs to the final Neolithic amulets category (Cardoso 2000, 182). However, as mentioned in archaeological publications, they had a continuity until the final Chalcolithic times. They could be correlated with the consolidation of the agropastoralism system, representing fertility symbols. It is possible to reference through O. da Veiga Ferreira (1970, 68-70) the existence of other zoomorphic parallels in Portuguese Estremadura, originating from the collection of Manuel Heleno. According to the same author, other figurines emerge in the Gruta da Galinha, Lapa do Suão, Cova da Moura, Cabeço da Arruda, Gruta da Carrasca, Quinta das Lapas, Castro da Ota, Portalegre, Vila Franca de Xira, Elvas, Monumento de Casainhos, Gruta de Carenque, Monumento das Conchadas, Grutas de Cascais, Montemor-o-Novo, Lapa do Bugio (Ferreira, Monteiro and Zbyszewski 1971), Anta da Comenda da Igreja (Ferreira 1970, 168-170) and Anta do Olival da Pega (Gonçalves 1992).

Figure 4. 1: A fragment of an Almeriense idol; 2: Small fragment of shale idol anthropomorphic with impregnation of what looks like ochre; 3: Small fragment of shale idol anthropomorphic with impregnation of what looks like ochre; 4: A tiny zoomorfic statuette, considered by João Luis Cardoso (2000, 182-183) as "statuette of a lagomorph"; 5: small fragment of "Schist plates". | Source: Ana Cruz.

Figure 5. Early Bronze Age metals. | Source: Ana Cruz.

Which geographically means a larger territory from Estremadura to Alentejo.

It is still important to highlight the existence of three polished bone anthropomorphic idols, where curiously one of them is decorated with what we identified as ochre. We find parallels for these artefacts regarded as objects of magical-symbolic character (Cardoso 1992, 112, 115) in the Almeriense idol of Lapa do Bugio, in Anta Grande do Olival da Pega, Reguengos de Monsaraz (Cardoso 1992, 115; Gonçalves 2004, 170), Perdigões (Valera 2003), geographically located in Spain.

The two metallic artefacts addressed in Figure 5 are probably made of Cu or Cu+As and are two typical examples from the Portuguese Estremadura's Early Bronze Age metal productions (Senna-Martinez, 1994, 172).

The barbed arrowhead (GMS-K51-392), completes the presently know distribution of the type in Portuguese Estremadura (Senna-Martinez 1994), that goes together in Iberia with its presence in the "Argaric World" (Lull 1983, 218), the Central Mesetas (Hernando Grande 1992, 122-124) and the Galician Roufeiro's hoard (Harbinson 1968, 50-1, Figure 2).

The double awl (GMS-I51-1175) can be considered a variant from the "furadores lozângicos" (Senna-Martinez 1994, 172), known in Portuguese Estremadura from Vila Nova de S. Pedro (Paço and Jalhay 1945, Lams. XVII, 9-10 and XVIII, 18-19) and Abrigo Grande das Bocas (Carreira 1994), as well as being present in Alentejo at a Southwest Bronze Age cist burial at Monte Novo dos Albardeiros (Gonçalves 1988/89). The type is current in Southern France's Early/Middle Bronze Age – Provence (Courtin 1976, 448, Figure l), Languedoc (Roudil and Guilaine 1976, 461, Figure l) and Pyrenees (Guilaine 1976, 524, Figure l) – as well as in Catalonia (Rovira and

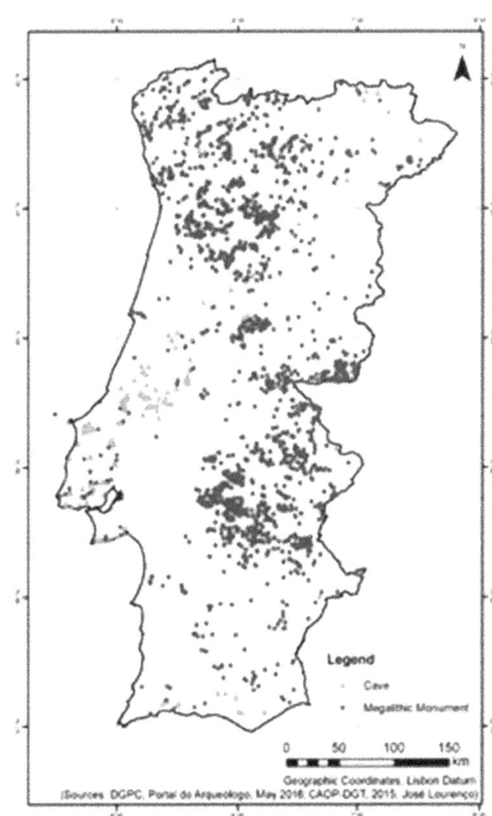

Figure 6. Comparative distribution between the karst cavities with burials and the Dolmen monuments. | Source: The Archaeologist Portal Endovelicus, 2016.

Petit 1983, 75) where the typology is comparable with the double awls excavated in this site.

Establishing parallels with the settlement contexts that mediate the Chalcolithic and the end of the Earlier Bronze Age, extending the scope of interregional trading networks between the cave communities and those of dolmens' (Figure 6).

Promoting the comparison with some of the contexts already studied and previously analysed in the Portuguese Estremadura, for example, Lugar do Canto (Ferreira and Leitão 1981), Lapa da Galinha and Lapa dos Carrascos (Gonçalves 1978), Abrigo Grande das Bocas (Rio Maior), (Cardoso 2000, 335-6), Lapa do Suão, Cova da Moura, Cabeço da Arruda (Ferreira 1970, 168-70), Carrasca Cave (Carreira, Cardoso 2001-2002, 261-262), Lapa do Bugio (Cardoso 1992, 111), Cascais Caves (Ferreira 1970, 168-170; Cardoso 1992, 112, 115), Monumento da Praia das Maçãs (Cardoso 2004, 59). As to correlate them with megalithic sites, Anta 1 de Val da Laje (Oosterbeek 1994); Antas I e II do Rego da Murta (Figueiredo 2007), Anta Grande do Olival da Pega, Reguengos de Monsaraz (Cardoso 1992, 115; Gonçalves 2004, 170), promotes a colossal, but necessary task to better understand the differences, if there are any, between burial in caves and dolmen monuments.

When looking at Figure 6 it is obvious that this map comprising the 2 types of funerary monuments, one with 94% of built monuments against 6% of natural caves, we observe many different behaviours towards death as an all, and yet very similar. We believe that if more karst cavities were available the number of burials inside them would have been larger. One should underline an opportunistic behaviour, which reused natural cavities over millennia, most probably in situations of political instability, such as is the case of Roman burials in caves (Lapa Rasteira do Castelejo) or Visigoth (Caldeirão Cave).

It appears that, the Megalithic dolmens arise to bridge the scarcity of sedimentary rocks in Portugal and not because there was a predisposed preference to take over the 'megalithic package', since it has already been understood by the material culture of the Upper Morgado Shelter where there are no special differences between both funerary types regarding material culture. On the other hand, we do not think that the social organisation of these communities is different since the geographical distances and the information conveyance existed and were contemporary. What really arises as diverse is in the ritual mortuary gestures that may differ from those of megalithic cults.

Another aspect to be emphasized in relation to the structural and architectural composition of the burials comprises a technique/manner of structuring limestone blocks aimed at corpse demarcation by implementing a structure that contained the deceased. The explanation for not finding the continuation of the rock structures is the "carelessness" of posterior burials which have distorted the objectives of the first burials. With time and the subsequent reuse of this site, other subsidence blocks were used in the composition of the initial graves or removed from their original locations and emerged, today, only as subsidence blocks randomly placed "by chance".

Forasmuch as the material culture we also have a question that is worth discussing. The exhumation of artefacts is too poor considering the number of buried individuals. At this point we can draw three hypotheses for this evidence:

1. The community is too poor and therefore carefully selects the items that are devoted to the deceased.

2. In certain burials there are no items and such practice is reserved to the most important elements of the community.

3. Each deceased was buried with artefacts and other items; however, this would have been recycled and subsequently withdrawn from the burials as a result of reuse.

4. Biological anthropology

Here we present preliminary results from the human remains recovered from Upper Morgado's shelter and the presented data should be regarded with caution. All the data analysed was registered during the excavation and already described at the excavation anthropological reports (Tomé 2013; Tomé and Cunha 2015; Curto 2015; Relvado and Anselmo 2016; Ribeiro 2017).

4.1. Funerary anthropology

Among the taphonomic factors taking action on Upper Morgado shelter the human disturbance is the most important. Humans have been disturbing this shelter from at least the Chalcolithic period and there were also indications of human occupation during the Early Bronze Age, Restoration of Independence from Spain (XVII century), the French Invasions and more recently by the local population. There were no signs of animal scavenging on the human remains; however, the activity of small mammals dispersed small bones through their burrows. The action of plants roots especially problematic in the outer areas of the shelter, led to the destruction and displacement of some bones. While the dynamics of the shelter had a higher impact on the inner areas, covering some teeth and bones on the surface with calcite.

Overall, the human remains recovered indicate a poor bone preservation level and a high degree of fragmentation (Table 1).

All skeletal parts are represented but with very different levels of preservation. There is a predominance of teeth and small bones, such as hand and foot bones, while other bones, particularly the ones from the cranium, scapula, ribs and *os coxa*, are not frequent and are very fragmented (Table 1). Poor preservation of human remains had been frequently described not only in other caves in the regions of Tomar (Tomé and Oosterbeek 2011), but also in other Portuguese burial caves (e.g. Tomé 2013; Silva *et al.* 2014). The higher number of teeth and small bones, as well as their better state of preservation, suggest that the individuals would be buried in the Upper Morgado's shelter before the bodies skeletonization (Silva 1996, 2000; Duday 2005), since bones of small dimensions would easily be forgotten or lost in case of skeletons relocation. The funerary area

Table 1. Preservation of anatomical regions at Morgado's shelter. | Source: Ana Curto, 2017.

	Preservation (%)
Cranium	0 - 25
Teeth	75 - 100
Vertebrae	25 - 50
Scapulae	0 - 25
Ribs	0 - 25
Long bones	25 - 50
Hand bones	75 - 100
Os coxae	0 - 25
Patella	75 -100
Feet bones	75 - 100

would be frequently disturbed, since bones with a larger area are more susceptible to mechanical forces (Nielsen-Marsh and Hedges 2000). Upper Morgado's shelter was a primary collective burial place with consecutive reductions, similarly to other cave burials (e.g. Tomé and Oosterbeek 2011; Tomé 2013; Boaventura *et al.* 2014).

To date only 2 anatomical connexions were registered, at the lower stratigraphic units excavated near the South wall, suggesting funerary processes leading to a complete disarticulation of the human remains. The first anatomical connection was excavated at square J52 and represents the 3rd, 4th and 5th left metatarsals, a left 1st metatarsal, navicular and cuboid were found near the anatomical connection and may be part of the same foot. The second anatomical connection was found at square K51, a medial hand phalange, from a non adult, and its epiphysis.

During the last 5 years, 9,866 human bone fragments and 2,551 human teeth were collected and coordinated in three-dimensional space from the approximately $4m^2$ that comprise the ossuaries from Upper Morgado's shelter.

The higher density of human remains close to the South wall of the shelter (Figure 7) indicate a clear preference for this area as a burial place.

This area was delimited by stones (Figure 8), arranged in a way that suggest an individual nature with possible reduction. Since Morgado's shelter seems to be a place of primary inhumations, it is possible that the delimited area with stones would be used as a primary individual burial followed by reduction in a cyclic manner.

A collectivisation process was also suggested at other Neolithic burial caves in Tomar's region (Tomé and Oosterbeek 2011) and is a phenomenon widely spread throughout Western Europe (Cawe 1999). This preference for the South wall may have been intentional or caused by limitations accessing other areas, possibly

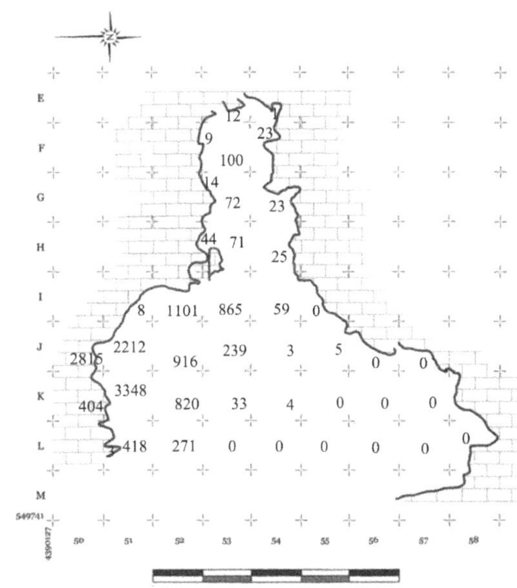

Figure 7. Number of human bone fragments and teeth recovered between 2012 and 2017 at Morgado's shelter. Source: Ana Curto, 2017.

Figure 8. Areas delimited by stones near to the South wall of the Morgado's shelter. | Source: Ana Cruz, 2013.

due to the abatement of some roof blocks. The high density of human remains in less than $4m^2$ confirms that Upper Morgado's shelter was frequently re-used as a burial place, apparently without an organization pattern identifiable during the excavation. Upper Morgado's shelter had different occupations during at least the last 5,000 years. Carbon dating from human bone fragments from the inner part of the shelter (squares G54 and F53, Figure 2) fall within 4,930 to 3,435 cal. B.C. (Table 2), while the human bone fragments close to the South wall (squares J50 and J51, Figure 2) were dated between 3,344 to 2,830 cal. B.C.

Table 2. Sex estimated by calcaneus and talus and stature estimated by calcaneus, talus, 1st metatarsal and 2nd metatarsal. Source: Ana Curto, 2017.

	F	M	F	M	Undetermined	Undetermined
	Calcaneus		Talus		1st metatarsal	2nd metatarsal
N	14	7	17	39	11	14
Mean	1.53	1.68	1.56	1.65	1.54	1.59
sd	0.08	0.01	0.01	0.04	0.04	0.05
Minimum	1.28	1.67	1.52	1.59	1.49	1.50
Maximum	1.61	1.70	1.56	1.72	1.61	1.67

4.2. Non adults

Age at death was estimated through analysis of the fusion of epiphyses and diaphysis (Scheuer and Black 2004) and dental maturation and eruption (AlQahtani *et al.* 2010). It was possible to estimate age from 80 bone or teeth elements, however, some of these elements might belong to the same individual. From the 80 non-adults 19 (24%) would have between 1 and 4 years of age, 29 (36%) individuals between 5 and 9 years old, 20 (25%) individuals between 10 and 14 years old and 12 (15%) individuals between 15 and 19 years old.

According with Ledermann (1969) the number of individuals aged between 1 and 4 years old are at the lower limit of what would be expected for Upper Morgado's chronology while the ones aged between 5 and 9 years old and between 10 and 14 years old are overrepresented. The percentage of individuals with estimated age between 15 and 19 years old fall within the expected values for Upper Morgado's chronology. The different mortality observed for the non adults at Upper Morgado's shelter might represent this particular community, slightly different maturation rates or be biased by the methodology applied, particularly considering the preliminary nature of the data presented and possible inter-observer errors. A more detailed analysis is necessary to study the non adults from Upper Morgado's shelter. The need to raise this issue lays in the intention to comparatively analyse the typology of burials in this site with others in distinct geographical locations in order to establish parallels between age, sex and material culture elements used in those burials.

4.3. Adults

Due to the poor preservation of the bones recovered from Upper Morgado's shelter, particularly the *os coxae*, age at death estimation was only possible for 1 individual, estimated based on the pubic symphysis (Brooks and Suchey 1990). This individual would have between 26 and 49 years old and it was not possible to define the sex.

The poor preservation of the human bones also limited sex estimation. Sex was mostly estimated by metric analysis of the talus and calcaneus (Silva 1995). While the calcaneus suggests a sex ratio in favour of females, the talus indicates a sex ratio in favour of males (Table 2).

During Middle-Late Neolithic, in Portugal, there seems to be a sex ratio in favour of females which can be related to different funerary practices between sexes or a sex ratio biased by the methodology applied, particularly the absence of more sexually dimorphic bones such as the pelvis and cranium (Boaventura *et al.* 2014). The ambiguity of the sex ratio recorded at Upper Morgado's shelter suggests that sex estimation might be biased by metric methods but the possibility of different funerary practices for males and females cannot be excluded.

Stature was estimated by the talus (Holland 1995), calcaneus (Holland 1995), 1st metatarsal (Cordeiro 2009) and 2nd metatarsal (Santos 2002). Female mean stature varies between 1.53m and 1.56m, while male stature varies between 1.65m and 1.68m depending on the bone analysed (Table 2). For humans, a 7% difference between male and female mean stature is expected for sex differences in body composition (Kirchengast 2010), but at Upper Morgado's shelter a higher sexual dimorphism in stature was observed. A high sexual dimorphism in stature has also been observed in other samples (e.g. Silva 1996, 2002) particularly at Gruta dos Ossos and Gruta do Cadaval (Tomé and Oosterbeek 2011), both near Upper Morgado's shelter. At Gruta dos Ossos the mean stature calculated is approximately 1.70m for the males and 1.58 for the females, while at Gruta do Cadaval the mean stature for the males is 1.70m and approximately 1.50 for the females (Tomé and Oosterbeek 2011). Since the same bone (calcaneus or talus) was used for sex and stature estimation, the difference between male and female stature might be biased by redundancy in methodology. The results presented are preliminary and researchers have been using different methodologies to estimate stature, which hinders comparisons between the different osteological collections. Additionally, stature estimation was not possible for most individuals.

4.4. Minimum number of individuals (MNI)

The minimum number of individuals (MNI) was calculated (Herrmann *et al.* 1990) for the total number of human remains recovered from Upper Morgado's shelter and not by stratigraphic unit. During the last five years of excavation the MNI was estimated in 80 non-adults: 19 individuals between 1 and 4 years of age, 29 individuals between 5 and 9 years old, 20 individuals between 10 and 14 years old and 12 individuals between 15 and 19 years old. So far 154 right first superior incisors were recovered from Upper Morgado's shelter, since these teeth are completely formed at approximately 12 years old (AlQahtani *et al.* 2010), only the individuals estimated as having less than 10 years old (NMI=48) were considered for the total NMI. A minimum number of 202 individuals were buried at Upper Morgado's shelter; this number may increase in the future as the excavation is still ongoing.

Comparing with Gruta de Nossa Senhora das Lapas (NMI=26), Gruta do Cadaval (NMI=25) and Gruta dos Ossos (NMI=9), other burial caves at the region of Tomar (Tomé and Oosterbeek 2011), Upper Morgado's shelter has the largest MNI (NMI=202).

4.5. Health

Concerning paleopathology and other health indicators, the data analysed are based on macroscopic observations considering the lesions as present or absent.

Degenerative joint disease is not common in the individuals collected so far, which may suggest low intense physical activities or young age at death (Waldron 2009). Entheseal changes were particularly common at the hand phalanges, suggesting constant handling of objects. However, hand phalanges were also the most common bones recovered from Upper Morgado's shelter and it is possible that other bones would also have entheseal changes. A detailed analysis of both degenerative joint disease and entheseal changes would help to better understand these individuals' activities and if low frequency of degenerative joint disease represents low physical activity or young adults. Signs of possible infectious diseases were registered in at least 23 bone fragments, most of them long bones fragments. Healed bone fractures were observed at 18 bones, most of them in metatarsals and metacarpals. Additionally, 13 ankylosis of at least two feet phalanges were registered. The high fragmentation of skeletal remains observed at Morgado's shelter might in fact be masking the real frequencies of traumatic injuries and infectious diseases on the communities who used this burial site.

Dental caries recorded are of small dimensions and have a low frequency, being present in less than 6% (N=2,029) of permanent teeth and about 2% (N=522) in deciduous teeth, suggesting a diet poor in cariogenic foods (Hillson 1996). Dental calculus was present at about 30% (N=2,029) of permanent teeth, being more common at the upper dentition. There is a predominance of low to moderate degrees of dental wear, as well as low teeth loss, suggests that these individuals had a low abrasive diet and/or were young (Cruwys 1989; Holst and Coughlan 2000). Oral pathology at Morgado's shelter is not common, similarly to other burial places from these chronologies (e.g. Duarte 1993; Araújo 1996; Silva 1999b, 2002; Silva and Cunha 2002; Gama 2003), when compared to other caves in Tomar's region (Tomé and Oosterbeek 2011).

Dental hypoplasias were registered in approximately 12% (N=2,029) of the permanent teeth recovered so far, while only 0.2% of the deciduous teeth (N=522) presented dental hypoplasias. Usually, the frequency of dental hypoplasias registered in Portugal during the late Neolithic and Calcolithic is less than 6% (e.g. Silva 1996, 1999a, 1999b, 2002; Cardoso and Cunha 1995; Umbelino 1998; Antunes-Ferreira 2003) with only the teeth from Algar Covão do Poço having similar frequency of dental hypoplasias (13%; Silva and Cunha 2002). These values might group the presence of hypoplasias in both permanent and deciduous teeth and therefore have lower frequencies. However, even grouping all the analysed teeth from Morgado's shelter the frequency (9.5%, N=2,551) of dental hypoplasias is higher than it would be expected. Dental hypoplasias are frequently used as signs of physiological stress (Cunha 2004, Lewis 2007); the low presence of dental hypoplasias suggests that these individuals did not pass through periods of physiological stress or did not survive the physiological stress long enough for it to be registered in the skeleton (Wood *et al.* 1992).

4.6. Partial conclusions

Upper Morgados's shelter is a probable primary collective burial place with recurrent reductions and a minimum number of 202 individuals in about 4m^2. The presence of individuals of all ages and both sexes suggest that there were no biological factors limiting who could be buried at Upper Morgado's shelter. The data presented here is preliminary, deriving from field-based interpretations during the excavation, it is necessary to study the human remains with more detail and using different methodologies, taking into consideration the different stratigraphic units. It is imperative to standardize methodologies not only to study Upper Morgado's shelter but also the other surrounding caves to better understand these groups living close together.

5. Interchange periphery or the Geography of Death: a theoretical approach.

To undertake ideological understanding, in "Nabantinas" Diachrony, within the mortuary practices of the recent pre-history communities that used and reuse karst cavities, is an aim that still incorporates the understanding of established dynamics Interaction between the world of the living and the world of the dead by identifying and analysing their potential cultural signs, recorded in the material culture, whether they have traditionally been indigenous, or whether they have been imported, i.e. promoting other readings Diffusionists and Evolutionists, proposing the transregional funerary imaginary.

While it is obvious for modern civilization to perceive current practices as having its origins in past behaviours, Archaeologists are expected to exert an uninfluenced approach to scientific interpretations, however historically they were often biased by such influences.

One of the views adapted from modern Economistic views confer centralization of craft production or import substitution as a natural aggregational process that enhances efficiency of production and distribution. Centralization is encouraged by political elite who offer protection and the use of territory, and provide benefits such as land, water, access to raw materials, and middlemen trading groups, which is easily perceived as a possible interpretation to past practices (Goody 1982). The past political integration serving as a regulatory forum in which political/control hierarchies, interacted controlling the exchange channels is a possibility (Kusimba 2005; Sinopoli 2003; Trigger 2003).

The understanding of the archaeological concept of trade evidences the erratic history within archaeological thought. Evidence from early works worldwide revealed the evidence of trading behaviour in the past, though archaeological similarities in styles and function of material culture were attributed to diffusion (Kidder 1962), whereas diffusion concepts, and related concepts of culture areas and migrations helped define archaeological approaches to interactions for most of the 1920s and 1930s (Schortman and Urban 1992).

The growing evidence of interactions between prehistoric and historic societies and the critiques of diffusion as a passive process, led some diffusionists to create a methodology by which diffusion could be seen in the archaeological record and the underlying mechanisms as a driving diffusion (Davis 1983; Schortman and Urban 1987). Ideas, such as propinquity in which intensity and rate of diffusion depended on cultural differences between societies, and others where different rates of development created cultural diversity flourish through the 1940's (Schortman and Urban 1992). The 1950's, gave rise to a prolific debate where ideas and goods flowing between societies led to the development of concepts such as "interaction spheres" (Caldwell 1964; Seeman 1979).

The 1970's gave rise to new currents such as World System Theorists, continuing through the 1980's, which excluded any deviation from Wallerstein's original model and insisted on the core-periphery dichotomy and relationships in prehistoric economies (Frank 1993). The argument that such relations did exist in the past, outlined a supra-regional system of rise and decline of civilizations based on intercultural trade and contact/takeover between large dominant cores and subordinate peripheries.

The single word system, though supported by premodern archaeologists, underwent criticism from pre Iron Age archaeologists (Stein 1999), who advocated cautious in the use of regionally focused core-periphery ideas to understand prehistoric political economies, giving the examples of Neolithic and Early Bronze Age societies of the Iberian Peninsula (Algaze 1989).

Since the 1990's ideological interpretations did not deviate from the concepts of mainstream regions and periphery, though some scholars still regard prehistoric trade as the socially mandated exchange of goods and favors between elites in a stratified society and limited to luxury items (Earle 1994).

In general, exchange of material goods between mainstream and periphery villages took place as gift exchange to cement social, marital, and political alliances; under duress as tribute, tax, or plunder; and for mobilizing resources, thus minimizing risk during marginal/critical conditions (Braun and Plog 1982; Damon 1980; Renfrew 1975).

Ancient Civilizations and trade suggest that increasing complexity demanded increasing efficiency of distribution, and in most societies, this was seen in the tendency toward centralization of distribution, whether for primary or secondary production this might have not been such a linear practice (Sabloff and Lamberg-Karlovsky 1975). Various papers centred on trade, and specifically individual trading activities, consider the general concept as significant for the development of social complexity, as for third millennium B.C. Mesopotamia, where the effect of trade on political decisions is widely discussed (Adams 1975; Webb 1975).

The Portuguese reality can be reviewed as a miscellanea of theoretical approaches depending on evolutionary trade routes with divergence in terms of geographical span. The evidence from various historical moments, explicitly exposes the contrast between semi-peripheral during the Calcholitic and the evolution to core region during bronze (discussed as Bronze Atlantico) (Briard 1965; Briard 1998; Brun 1990).

The main question remains, as if Portugal was a periphery or a core region? To which we theorise that before Bronze age, Portugal was in fact a periphery, whereas during the Bronze age Portugal was a core region. The facts supporting this theory, rely on the provenance of raw materials and the need to establish core regions in the proximity of resources (i.e. Tin and Copper mines) (Kristiansen 1994; Kristiansen and Larsson 2005; Sherratt 1993, 2001).

References

Adams, Robert McC "The emerging place of trade in civilizational studies." Sabloff, Jeremy and Lamberg-Karlovsky, Carl (eds.) *Ancient Civilization and Trade*. Albuquerque: University of New Mexico Press. (1975): 451–466.

Algaze, Guillermo "The uruk expansion, cross-cultural exchange as a factor in early Mesopotamian civilization" *Current Anthropology* 30 (1989): 571–608.

Almeida, Miguel. *Première approche à l'interprétation palethnologique du groupe solutréen des Maitreaux, perspective sur la technologie et répartition spatiale des vestiges lithiques et ses implications pour l'interprétation du registre archéologique*. Dissertation presented to University of Paris I for D.E.A. degree, 2005.

AlQahtani, Sakher Jaber, Hector, Mark and Liversidge, Helen "Brief communication: The London atlas of human tooth development and eruption" *American Journal of Physical Anthropology* 142 (2010): 481-490.

Anastácio, Rita and Cruz, Ana "Carta de Interesse Cultural para a região do Médio Tejo / Portugal: Modelação em sistemas de Informação Geográfica" *SÉMATA, Ciencias Sociais e Humanidades* 27 (2015): 221-238.

Arnaud, José Morais and Alves Bento, José "Caracterização da ocupação pré-histórica da Gruta do Casal Papagaio (Fátima, Vila Nova de Ourém)" *Algar* 2 (1988): 27-34.

Arsénio, Paulo and Batata, Carlos "O desenvolvimento da Espeleologia na Região de Tomar" *Boletim Cultural da Câmara Municipal de Tomar* 16 (1992): 11-29.

Aubry, Thierry "Étude de l_approvisionament en matieres preimieres siliceuses, l'exemple du Solutreen du centre de la France" *Trabalhos de Antropologia e Etnologia - 2° volume das Actas do Colóquio de Arqueologia do Nordeste Peninsular* (1988): 18-23.

Aubry, Thierry, Figueiral, Isabel, Moura, Helena and Plisson, Hugues "Modalités d'occupations au Paléolithique supérieur dans la grotte de Buraca Escura (Redinha, Pombal, Portugal)" *Revista Portuguesa de Arqueologia* 4, nº 2 (2001): 19-46.

Aubry, Thierry "Modalités d'exploitation des ressources lithiques régionales et des sílex d'origines lointaines sur les sites du Paléolithique supérieur de la Vallée du Côa (Portugal) - quels indices de productions spécialisées?" *Cahiers des thèmes transversaux ArScAn. Thème 3 - Systèmes de production et de circulation* 3 (2002): 63-68.

Aubry, Thierry and Mangalo Llach, Xavier "Interprétation de l'approvisionnement en matières premières siliceuses sur les sites du Paléolithique supérieur de la vallée du Côa (Portugal)" *Les matières premières lithiques en Préhistoire (table ronde internationale organisée à Aurillac, Cantal, du 20 au 22 juin 2002)* (2003a): 27-40.

Aubry, Thierry and Mangalo Llach, Xavier. "Matérias-primas líticas nos sítios do Paleolítico Superior do Vale do Côa: dos dados à interpretação". In *Paleoecologia humana e arqueociências. Um programa multidisciplinar para a arqueologia sob a tutela da cultura*, edited by Marta Moreno-García, and José Mateus. 340-343. Lisboa: Instituto Português de Arqueologia. 29, 2003b.

Aubry, Thierry and Walter, Bertrand, *Reconstitution des modalités d' approvisionnement et de diffusion des matières premières lithiques pendant le Paléolithique Supérieur - L'apport du site solutréen et badegoulien des Maîtreaux (Indre-et-Loire, France)*, 2003, 41-49.

Aubry, Thierry, Almeida, Miguel, Neves, Maria João, Peyrouse, Jean-Baptiste and Walter, Bertrand "Mythes et réalités préhistoriques: apport du site des Maîtreaux à la définition de la variabilité des productions lithiques au Solutréen" *Congrès du Centenaire: Un siècle de construction du discours scientifique en Préhistoire (Avignon)* 3 (2007): 105-124.

Aubry, Thierry and Igreja, Marina "Economy of lithic raw material during the Upper Paleolithic of the Côa Valley and the Sicó Massif (Portugal): technological and functional perspectives". In *Estudos funcionais recentes em matérias-primas alternativas ao sílex: avanços metodológicos e inferências arqueológicas*, edited by Marina Igreja and Ignacio Clemente-Conte. 1-25. Lisboa: IGESPAR, 2008.

Aubry, Thierry, Mangado Llach, Xavier and Sampaio, Jorge Davide, "Estudo do aprovisionamento em matérias-primas". In *200 séculos da história do Vale do Côa: incursões na vida quotidiana dos caçadores-artistas do Paleolítico*, edited by Thierry Aubry, 52, 147-169. Lisboa: IGESPAR, 2009.

Aubry, Thierry, Mangado Llach, Xavier and Matias, Henrique "Matérias-primas das ferramentas em pedra lascada da Pré-história do Centro e Nordeste de Portugal", edited by Pedro Dinis, António Alberto Gomes and *Sérgio Monteiro-Rodrigues Proveniências de Materiais Geológicos*. 165-192. Braga: Associação Portuguesa para o Estudo do Quaternário, 2014.

Aubry, Thierry, Mangado, Javier and Matias, Henrique, "Matérias-primas das ferramentas em pedra lascada da Pré-História do centro e nordeste de Portugal". *Proveniência de materiais geológicos: abordagens sobre o Quaternário de Portugal*, edited by Pedro Dinis, António Alberto Gomes and *Sérgio Monteiro-Rodrigues*, 165-192. Porto: Associação Portuguesa de Estudo do Quaternário, 2014.

Atlas do Ambiente *Carta de grandes grupos de utilização do solo*. Agência Portuguesa do Ambiente. Lisboa: Direcção Geral dos Recursos Naturais. escala 1:1.000.000, 1979-80.

Atlas do Ambiente *Carta de capacidade de uso do solo*. Agência Portuguesa do Ambiente. Lisboa: Direcção Geral dos Recursos Naturais. escala 1:1.000.000, 1980.

Atlas do Ambiente *Carta Litológica*. Agência Portuguesa do Ambiente. Lisboa: Direcção Geral dos Recursos Naturais 1:1.000.000, 1982.

Atlas do Ambiente *Carta ecológica fito-edafo-climática*. Agência Portuguesa do Ambiente. Lisboa: Direcção Geral dos Recursos Naturais. escala 1:1.000.000, 1984.

Atlas do Ambiente *Carta de acidez e alcalinidade dos solos*. Agência Portuguesa do Ambiente. Lisboa: Direcção Geral dos Recursos Naturais. escala 1:1.000.000, 1987.

Atlas do Ambiente *Carta de declives*. Agência Portuguesa do Ambiente. Lisboa: Direcção Geral dos Recursos Naturais. escala 1:1.000.000, 1987.

Antunes-Ferreira, Nathalie. *Paleobiologia e paleopatologia de grupos populacionais do Neolítico Final/Calcolítico do Poço Velho (Cascais)*. Dissertação para obtenção do grau de Mestre em Arqueologia. Braga: Instituto de Ciências Sociais da Universidade do Minho, 2003.

Araújo, Maria *Os dentes humanos das grutas artificiais de São Pedro do Estoril. Incidência de algumas lesões patológicas e estudo do desgaste numa amostra de dentes do Neolítico final/Calcolítico*. Dissertação para obtenção do grau de Mestre em Arqueologia. Braga: Instituto de Ciências Sociais da Universidade do Minho, 1996.

Boaventura, Rui, Ferreira, Maria Teresa, Neves, Maria João and Silva, Ana Maria "Funerary practices and anthropology during Middle-Late Neolithic (4th and 3rd millennia BCE) in Portugal: old bones, new insights" *Anthropologie* 52, (2), (2014): 183.

Batata, Carlos, *As Origens de Tomar - Carta Arqueológica do Concelho*. Tomar: Centro de Estudos e Protecção do Património da Região de Tomar, 1997.

Batata, Carlos and Borges, Nelson *A Importância da Fonte Quente enquanto "Lugar Central" no contexto do povoamento pré-histórico do Alto Ribatejo, durante a Pré-História recente*. Lisboa: Estradas de Portugal, SA., 2011.

Bicho, Nuno Ferreira "Sistemas de povoamento, mobilidade e aproveitamento dos recursos naturais no território português durante a transição Plistocénico-Holocénico" *Arqueologia, História da Arte e Património* 1 (2001): 31-58.

Bordo, Michael and Flandreau, Marc "Core, Periphery, Exchange Rate Regimes, and Globalization". In Michael Bordo, Alan Taylor and Jeffrey Williamson (eds.) *Globalization in Historical Perspective*. University of Chicago Press (2003): 417-472.

Braun, David, and Plog, Stephen "Evolution of "tribal" social networks: Theory and prehistoric North American evidence" *American Antiquity* 47, (1982): 504–525.

Briard, Jacques "Les Dépôts Bretons et l'Age du Bronze Atlantique" Travaux du laboratoire 'Anthropologie– Préhistoire – Protohistoire – Quaternaire Armoricains. Rennes: Université de Rennes, 1965.

Briard, Jacques "Flux et Reflux du Bronze Atlantique vus d' Armorique. Le Bronze Ancien". *Existe uma Idade do Bronze Atlântico? Trabalhos de Arqueologia.* Lisboa: IGESPAR 10 (1998): 114-124.

Brooks, Steven, Suchey, Judy Myers " Skeletal age determination based on the os pubis: a comparison of the Acsádi-Nemeskéri and Suchey-Brooks methods" *Human Evolution* 5. 3 (1990): 227-238.

Brun, Patrice "Le Bronze Atlantique et ses Subdivisions Culturelles: Essai de Définition". In Chevillot, Christian and Coffyn, André (dir.), *L'Age du Bronze Atlantique. Ses Faciès, de L'Écosse a L'Andalousie et Leurs Relations avec Le Bronze Contonental et La Méditerranée.* 11-24. Beynac-et-Cazenac: Actes do 1° Colloque du Parc Archéologique de Beynac, 1990.

Caldwell, Joseph, "Interaction spheres in prehistory". In Caldwell, Joseph, and Hall, Robert (eds.) *Hopewellian Studies, Scientific Papers*. Springfield: Illinois State Museum. No 12 (1964): 133–143.

Cardoso, João Luis, Santinho Cunha, Armando, *A lapa da Furada (Sesimbra). Resultados das escavações arqueológicas realizadas em Setembro de 1992 e 1994.* Sesimbra: Câmara Municipal de Sesimbra, 1995.

Carreira, Júlio Roque "A Pré-História Recente do Abrigo Grande das Bocas (Rio Maior)." *Trabalhos de Arqueologia da EAM. 2.* Lisboa. Colibrí, 1994.

Cauwe, Nicolas "Àpropos des sépultures collectives dans le Groupe de Montbolo" *Sagvntvm, Extra-2.* (*Actes del II Congrés del Neolitic a la Peninsula Ibérica*). *Valencia, Espanha, 7-9 de Abril.* Valencia: Departament de Prehistòria i d'Arqueologia, Universidade de Valencia. (1999): 453-459.

Cardoso, João Luis "A Lapa do Bugio" *Setúbal Arqueológica* IX-X. Setúbal: Assembleia Distrital de Setúbal, (1992): 289-225.

Cardoso, João Luis, *Pré-História de Portugal.* Lisboa: Editorial Verbo, 2000.

Cardoso, João Luis "A Baixa Estremadura dos finais do IV milénio a.C. até à chegada dos Romanos: Um ensaio de História Regional" *Estudos Arqueológicos de Oeiras* 12. Oeiras: Centro de Estudos Arqueológicos do Concelho de Oeiras, 2004.

Carvalho, António and Cardoso, João Luis "A Cronologia Absoluta das Ocupações Funerárias da Gruta da Casa da Moura (Óbidos)". *Estudos Arqueológicos de Oeiras* 18. Oeiras: Câmara Municipal, (2010-2011): 393-405.

Carreira, Júlio Roque and Cardoso, João Luis "A Gruta da Casa da Moura (Cesareda, Óbidos) e a sua Ocupação Pós-Paleolítica" *Estudos Arqueológicos de Oeiras* 10. Oeiras: Câmara Municipal, (2001-2002): 249-361.

Carta Geológica de Portugal. Lisboa: Serviços geológicos de Portugal, escala 1: 500.000, 1992.

Carta Hipsométrica de Portugal. Lisboa: Instituto Geográfico e Cadastral, escala 1: 600.000), 1984.

Carta Militar de Portugal. Lisboa: Instituto Geográfico do Exército, nº 310, escala 1: 25.000, 1969.

Carvalho, António Faustino *O Neolítico Antigo do Maciço Calcário Estremenho: tecnologia e tipologia da indústria de pedra lascada.* Lisboa: Colibri. 1996.

Carvalho, António Faustino and Gibaja, Juan Francisco "Talhe da pedra no Neolítico Antigo do Maciço Calcário Estremenho (Portugal): matérias-primas, tecnologia e análise funcional" *Museu d'Arqueologia de Catalunya*, (2005): 373-381.

Cruz, Ana, *Vale do Nabão: do Neolítico à Idade do Bronze.* Arkeos - Perspectivas em Diálogo, 3. 209-210. Tomar: Centro Europeu de Investigação da Pré-História do Alto Ribatejo, 1997.

Cruz, António João "Geoquímica dos preenchimentos sedimentares de grutas: a matéria orgânica na gruta do Caldeirão" *Algar* 2 (1988): 17-26.

Cruz, Ana and Oosterbeek, Luiz "A Pré-História Recente do Alto Ribatejo: ponto da situação em Janeiro de 1998". *Arkeos* 4, 11-20. Tomar: Centro Europeu de Investigação da Pré-História do Alto Ribatejo,1998.

Cruz, Ana "Necrópoles de Gruta no Contexto da Neolitização do Alto Ribatejo". In *Neolitização e Megalitismo da Península Ibérica*, coordenated by Maria de Jesus Sanches and Pablo Arias. III. 61-79. Porto: ADECAP, 2000.

Cruz, Ana, *A Pré-História Recente do vale do baixo Zêzere – Um Olhar Diacrónico.* Tomar: Centro Europeu de Investigação da Pré-História do Alto Ribatejo, 30, 2011.

Cruz, Ana, *Relatório Técnico da campanha de escavação de emergência na Gruta do Morgado Superior.* Lisboa: DGPC, 2012.

Cruz, Ana, Graça, Ana, Oosterbeek, Luiz, Almeida, Fátima and Delfino, Davide "Gruta do Morgado Superior – Um Estudo de Caso Funerário no Alto Ribatejo (Tomar, Portugal)" *Las crisis en la historia: noción y realidades* 2, (2013): 143-168.

Cruz, Ana, Graça, Ana, Delfino, Davide and Oosterbeek, Luiz "A Integridade da Paisagem Antropizada do Alto Ribatejo". In edited by Juliano Bittencourt Campos, Jairo José Zocche, Jedson Francisco Cerezer and Luiz Oosterbeek *Arqueologia Ibero-Americana e Transatlântica. Arqueologia, Sociedade e Território*, 17-39. Criciúma: UNESC- ITM, 2014.

Cruz, Ana, Graça, Ana and Oosterbeek, Luiz, "Caves, Megalithism and Tumuli – Three diachronic realities in funerary archaeology from Alto Ribatejo". In edited by Ana Cruz, Enrique Cerrillo-Cuenca, Primitiva Bueno Ramirez, João Caninas and Carlos Batata *Rendering Death: Ideological and Archaeological Narratives from Recent Prehistory (Iberia)*, 61-75. (BAR 2648). Oxford: British International Series, 2014.

Cruz, Ana and Berruti, Gabriele "A use-wear analysis of the knapped lithic grave goods from Gruta do Morgado Superior (Tomar, Portugal)". In edited by Pascual Izquierdo-Egea *Arqueología Iberoamericana* 28 (2015): 81-94.

Cruz, Ana "Reciprocity ↔ Mutuality: Funerary Behaviour in Middle Tagus Region (Central Portugal) ". In edited by Primitiva Bueno Ramirez *ARPI. Arqueología y Prehistoria del Interior peninsular. 04 Extra. Homenaje a Rodrigo Balbín Behrmann,* 191-204. Madrid: Area de Prehistoria, Universidad de Alcalá de Henares, 2016.

Cordeiro, Cristina, Muñoz-Barús, José, Wasterlain, Sofia, Cunha, Eugénia, and Vieira, Duarte "Predicting adult stature from metatarsal length in a Portuguese population" *Forensic Science International* 193, (2009): 131.e1-131.e 4.

Cruwys, Elizabeth "Tooth wear and the archaeologist: the role of the human tooth wear in archaeological research". In Roberts Charlotte, Lee Francis and Bintliff, John (eds.) *Burial archaeology current research, methods and developments*. Oxford: Bar Series 211, 1989.

Cunha, Eugénia "Paleobiologia, história e quotidiano: critérios de transdisciplinaridade possível". In Andrade A.; Silva, J. (ed.) *Estudos Medievais*. 117-141. Lisboa: Livros, Horizonte, 2004.

Curto, A. *Gruta do Morgado Superior: Relatório Antropológico da Campanha de escavação de 2015*. Unpublished excavation report, 2015.

Courtin, Jean « Les civilizations de l'Age du Bronze en Provence. Le Bronze Ancien et le Bronze Moyen ». In Jean Guilaine (ed.) *La Préhistoire Française*. 445-451. Paris. CNRS. Vol. II, 1976.

Davis, Dave "Investigating the diffusion of stylistic innovation". *Advances in Archaeological Method and Theory* 6, (1983): 53–89.

Damon, Frederick "The Kula and generalised exchange: Considering some unconsidered aspects of 'the elementary structures of kinship.'" *Man n.s.* 15 (1980): 267–292.

Duday, Henri « L'archéothanatologie ou l'archéologie de la mort » *Objets et méthodes en paléoanthropologie*. Paris: CTHS, (2005): 153-215.

Duarte, Cidália *Analysis of wear and pathological conditions in human teeth from the Neolithic site of grutas de Tojal de Vila Chã*. Thesis of the degree of Master of Arts. University of Alberta, Edmonton, 1993.

Earle, Timothy "Positioning exchange in the evolution of human society". In Baugh, Timothy, Ericson, Jonathon (eds.) *Baugh Prehistoric Exchange Systems in North America*, 419–438. New York: Plenum Press, 1994.

Economist HOMO ECONOMICUS? Sound economics may lie at the heart of humanity's evolutionary success. *The Economist*, April 7 (2005): 67.

Ferreira, Octávio da Veiga, Monteiro, Rafael and Zbyszewski, Georges "Nota preliminar sobre a lapa pré-histórica do Bugio (Azoia Sesimbra)" *Actas do 2º Congresso Nacional de Arqueologia, Coimbra, 1970*. Coimbra: Junta Nacional de Educação, vol. 1, (1971): 107-120.

Ferreira, Octávio Da Veiga *O Arqueólogo Português*. Série III, vol. 4, (1970): 165-173.

Ferreira, Octávio Da Veiga and Leitão, Manuel *Portugal Pré-Histórico; seu enquadramento no Mediterrâneo*. Mem Martins: Publicações Europa-América, 1981.

Frank, Andre Gunder "The Bronze Age world system and its cycles" *Current Anthropology* 34 (1993): 383–413.

Gama, Rui Pedro "Necrópole neolítica do Algar do Bom Santo: contexto cronológico e espaço funerário" *Revista Portuguesa de Arqueologia* 1, 2 (2003): 107-118.

Galopim de Carvalho and António Marcos *Geologia-Morfogénese e Sedimentogénese*. Lisboa: Universidade Aberta, 1996.

Geneste, Jean-Michel and Rigaud, Jean-Philippe *Matières premières lithiques et occupations de l'espace*. 205-218. Paris: CNRS, 1989.

Gonçalves, Vítor dos Santos "Uma nova necrópole da Idade do Bronze: a Gruta da Marmota" *O Arqueólogo Português*, III, VI, (1972): 213-218.

Gonçalves, Vítor dos Santos "Para um programa de Estudo do Neolítico em Portugal. (Salamanca)" *Zephyrus* XXVIII-XXVXIX, (1978): 147-162.

Gonçalves, dos Santos and Pereira, Ana Ramos *Considerações sobre o espólio neolítico da gruta dos Carrascos, Monsanto, Alcanena*. Lisboa: Direcção-Geral do Património Cultural, 1979.

Gonçalves, Vítor dos Santos "Manifestações do sagrado na Pré-História do Ocidente peninsular 5. O explícito e o implícito. Breve dissertação, invocando os limites fluidos do figurativo, a propósito do significado das placas de xisto gravadas do terceiro milénio a.n.e" *Revista Portuguesa de Arqueologia* 7, nº 1 (2004): 165-183.

Gonçalves, Vítor dos Santos "A ocupação pré-histórica do Monte Novo dos Albardeiros (Reguengos de Monsaraz)" *Portugalia (NS)* IX-X, (1988/89): 49-6l.

Gonçalves, Victor Manuel dos Santos "Revendo as antas de Reguengos de Monsaraz" *Cadernos da UNIARQ*. Lisboa: Instituto Nacional de Investigação Científica, 2 (1992): 264.

Goody, Esther *From Craft to Industry: The Ethnography of Proto-Industrial Cloth Production*. Cambridge: Cambridge University Press, 1982.

Guilaine, Jean « Les civilisations de l'Age du Bronze dans les Pyrénées ». In Jean Guilaine (ed.) *La Préhistoire Française*. 522-531. Paris: CNRS. Vol. II, 1976.

Herrmann, Bernd, Grupe, Gisela, Hummel, Susanne, Piepenbrink, Hermann and Schutkowski, Holger, *Prähistorische Anthropologie: Leitfaden der Feld-und Labormethoden*. Springer-Verlag, 2013.

Harbinson, Peter "Três tipos de machados de bronze do norte de Portugal e suas prováveis origens" *Revista de Guimardes* 78, (1968): 49-54.

Hernando Grande, Amparo *Materiales metálicos de la Edad del Bronce en la Meseta: Armas*. Madrid: UNED, 1992.

Hillson, Simon, *Dental Anthropology. Cambridge*. Cambridge University Press, 1996.

Holland, Thomas Dean "Estimation of adult stature from the calcaneus and talus" *American Journal of Physical Anthropology* 96, nº3, (1995): 315-320.

Holst, Malin and Coughlan, Jennifer "Dental health and disease. Blood Red Roses: the archaeology of a mass grave from the battle of Towton AD 1461". In Fiorato Veronica, Boylston Anthea, Knusel, Christopher (eds). Oxford: Oxford Books, 2000.

Horan, Richard, Bulte, Erwin, and Shogren, Jason "How trade saved humanity from biological exclusion: An economic theory of Neanderthal extinction" *Journal of Economic Behavior and Organization* 58 (2005): 1–29.

Isaac, Barry "Retrospective on the formalist-substantivist debate". In Isaac, B. L. (ed.), *Research in Economic Anthropology*. Greenwich, CT: JAI Press 14 (1993): 213–233.

Kidder, Alfred Vincent *An Introduction to the Study of Southwestern Archaeology*. New Haven, CT: Yale University Press, 1962.

Kirchengast, Sylvia "Gender Differences in Body Composition from Childhood to Old Age: An Evolutionary Point of View" *Journal of Life Science* 2, nº 1 (2010): 1-10.

Kristiansen, Kristian "The Emergence of the European World System in the Bronze Age: Divergence, Convergence and Social Evolution during the First and Second Millennia BC in Europe". In Kristiansen, Kristian and Jensen, Jørgen (eds.) *Europe in the First Millennium B.C.* 7–30. Sheffield: Sheffield Archaeological Monographs. Sheffield: J.R. Collis Publications. 6, 1994.

Kristiansen, Kristian and Larsson, Thomas B., *The Rise of Bronze Age Society. Travels, Transmissions and Transformations.* Cambridge: Cambridge University Press, 2005.

Kusimba, Chapurukha "African cities and their hinterlands". *Paper presented at the Arthur M. Sackler Conference on Early Cities at the National Academy of Sciences*. Washington, DC, 2005.

Ledermann, Sully "Nouvelles tables types de mortalité. INED" *Travaux et documents* 53. Paris: Presses Universitaires de France, 1969.

Lewis, Mary, *The bioarchaeology of children: Perspectives from biological and forensic anthropology.* Cambridge: Cambridge University Press, 2007.

Lull, Vicente, *La «Cultura» de El Argar.* Madrid: Akal, 1983.

Manuppella, Giuseppe and Balacó Moreira, José Carlos "*Panorama dos Calcários Jurássicos Portugueses*" *Comunicação apresentada ao II Congresso Ibero-Americano de Geologia Económica. Buenos Aires. Argentina. 15 a 19 de Dezembro de 1975*, 1975.

Marks, Anthony, Shokler, Jeff and Zilhão, João "Raw Material Usage in the Paleolithic: the effect of local availability on Selection and Economy". In edited by Anta Montet-White and Steven Holen, *Raw material economies among Prehistoric Hunter-Gatherers,* 127-139. Lawrence, KA: University of Kansas, 1991.

Nielsen-Marsh, Christina and Hedges, Robert "Patterns of diagenesis in bone I: the effects of site environments" *Journal of Archaeological Science* 27, nº12 (2000): 1139-1150.

Nobre, Cláudia *Relatório Técnico de Trabalhos de limpeza na Gruta da Mendacha*. Lisboa: IGESPAR, 2002.

Oka Æ, Rahul, Chapurukha M. Kusimba "The Archaeology of Trading Systems, Part 1: Towards a New Trade Synthesis" *Journal of Archaeology Res* 16 (2008): 339–395. DOI 10.1007/s10814-008-9023-5.

Oosterbeek, Luiz, *Echoes from the East: the western network. An insight to unequal and combined development, 7000-2000 BC*. Dissertation presented to University of London for PhD degree, 1994.

Oosterbeek, Luiz and Cruz, Ana "Gruta do Morgado Superior" *Techne* 4 (1998): 201-209.

Oosterbeek, Luiz and Cruz, Ana "Gruta do Cadaval – Gruta dos Ossos – Anta 1 de Val da Laje". In edited by Carlos Veloso and Maria de la Salete da Ponte, *Imagens de Tomar – Roteiro histórico*, 15-20. Tomar: Secretariado do VIII Encontro de professores de história da Zona Centro, 1990.

Oosterbeek, Luiz and Cruz, Ana "A Arqueologia da Morte: considerações a propósito da interpretação dos contextos sepulcrais na região de Tomar" *Boletim Cultural da Câmara Municipal de Tomar* 15 (1991): 267-291.

Paço, Afonso do and Jalhay, Padre Eugénio "El Castro de Vila Nova de San Pedro" *Actas e Memorias Sociedad Española de Antropología, Etnografía y Prehistoria*" XX. Vol. II (1945):183-265. Reprinted In *Trabalhos de Arqueologia de Afonso do Paço.* Lisboa. Associação dos Arqueólogos Portugueses, 1970.

Plog, Stanley "Changing perspectives on north and middle American exchange systems". Ericson, Jonathan and Baugh, Timothy (eds.), *The American Southwest and Mesoamerica: Systems of Prehistoric Exchange* 285–292. New York: Plenum Press, 1993.

Relvado, Cláudia and Anselmo, Daniela *Gruta do Morgado Superior: Relatório Antropológico da Campanha de escavação de 2016*. Unpublished excavation report, 2017.

Renfrew, Colin "Trade as action at a distance, questions of integration and communication". In Sabloff, Jeremy and Lamberg-Karlovsky, Clifford Charles (eds.), *Ancient Civilization and Trade*. Albuquerque: University of New Mexico Press, (1975): 3–59.

Ribeiro, Cheila *Gruta do Morgado Superior: Relatório Antropológico da Campanha de escavação de 2017*. Unpublished excavation report, 2018.

Roudil, Jean-Louis and Guilaine, Jean "Les civilizations de l'Age du Bronze en Languedoc". In Jean Guilaine (ed.), *La Préhistoire Française.* 459-469. Paris: CNRS. Vol. II, 1976.

Rovira Port, Jordi and Petit, Mendlzábal "El Bronce Antiguo-Medio" *Arqueología en Catalunya.* 74-75. Barcelona: Departement de Cultura de la Generelitat de Catalunya, 1983.

Sabloff, Jeremy and Lamberg-Karlovsky, Clifford Charles (eds.) *Ancient Civilization and Trade*. Albuquerque: University of New Mexico Press, 1975.

Santos, Cristina Maria Gomes Cordeiro, *Estimativa da estatura a partir dos metatársicos*. Unpublished MA thesis, University of Coimbra. 2002.

Scheuer, Louise and Black, Sue. *Developmental Juvenile Osteology*. Elsevier: Academic Press, 2004.

Schortman, Edward Mark and Urban, Patricia "Modeling interregional interactions in prehistory". In Schiffer, Michael Brian (ed.) *Advances in Archaeological Method and Theory*. Orlando, FL: Academic Press, Vol. 11 (1987): 37–95.

Schortman, Edward Mark and Urban, Patricia "The place of interregional studies in archaeological thought". In Schortman, Edward Mark and Urban, Patricia (eds.) *Resources, Power, and Interregional Interaction*. New York: Plenum Press, (1992): 3–15.

Seeman, Mark, *The Hopewell Interaction Sphere: The Evidence for Interregional Trade and Structural Complexity*. Indianapolis: Indiana Historical Society, 1979.

Senna-Martinez, João Carlos "Subsídios para o estudo do Bronze Pleno na Estremadura Atlântica: (1) A alabarda de tipo «Atlântico do Habitat das Baútas" (Amadora)" *Zephyrus* XLVI (1994): 161-182.

Sherratt, Andrew George "What would a Bronze-Age World System look like. Relations between temperate Europe and the Mediterranean in Later Prehistory" *Journal of European Archaeolog* 1, nº 2 (1993): 1-57.

Sherratt, Andrew George "The Emergence of Elites: Earlier Bronze Age Europe, 2500-1300 BC". In Cunliffe, Barry (ed.)

The Oxford Illustrated History of Prehistoric Europe. 244-276. Oxford: Oxford University Press, 2001.

Shokler, Jeff "Approaches to the Sourcing of Flint in Archaeological Contexts: Results of Research from Portuguese Estremadura". In edited by John Herrmann Jr, Norman Herz and Richard Newman, *Asmosia 5: Interdisciplinary Studies on Ancient Stone*, 176-187. London: Archetype Publications, 2002.

Shokler, Jeff "Hunter-Gatherer Movement in the Portuguese Upper Paleolithic: Archaeological Results of a Regional Lithic Sourcing Project". In edited by Nuno Bicho, *From the Mediterranean basin to the Portuguese Atlantic shore: Papers in Honor of Anthony Marks - Actas do IV Congresso de Arqueologia Peninsular*, 141-161. Faro: Universidade do Algarve, 2007.

Silva, Ana Maria "Sex assessment using the calcaneus and talus" *Antropologia Portuguesa* 13, (1995): 107-119.

Silva, Ana Maria "O Hipogeu de Monte Canelas I (IV-III milénios a.C.): Estudo paleobiológico da população humana exumada" *Trabalho de síntese. Provas de Aptidão Pedagógica e Capacidade Científica*. Coimbra: Departamento de Antropologia, Faculdade de Ciências e Tecnologia da Universidade de Coimbra (policopiado), 1996.

Silva, Ana Maria "A Necrópole Neolítica do Cabeço da Arruda (Torres Vedras, Portugal): os dados paleobiológicos" *Sagvntvm – Plav* II, Extra 2 (1999a): 355-360.

Silva Ana Maria "Human remais from the artificial cave of São Pedro do Estoril II (Cascais, Portugal)" *Human Evolution* 14, 3 (1999b): 199-206.

Silva, Ana Maria "Inumações colectivas: Algumas considerações sobre a respectiva análise paleobiológica". In Abreu, Mila Simões de, Alonso Mathias, Fernán, Badal Garcia, Ernestina, Cunha, Eugénia, Etxeberria, Francisco; Figueiral, Isabel.; Tresseras, Jordi Juan I; Rivero, Pilar; Rubinos Pérez, Antonio (coords.), Actas do 3° Congresso de Arqueologia Peninsular, Vol. IX. "Terrenos da Arqueologia da Península Ibérica". Porto: ADECAP, (2000): 321-329.

Silva, Ana Maria *Antropologia funerária e paleobiologia das populações Portuguesas (litorais) do Neolítico final/Calcolítico.* PhD thesis. Departamento de Antropologia, Universidade de Coimbra, Coimbra, 2002.

Silva, Ana Maria and Cunha, Eugénia "O algar do Covão do Poço: Nota antropológica sobre os ossos humanos recuperados". *Actas da "I Jornadas de Património e Arqueologia do Litoral Centro. Resultados e perspectivas. Porto de Mós, 31 Maio – 1 Junho.* 2002.

Silva, Ana Maria, Leandro, Inês; Pereira, Daniela; Valera, António Carlos "Collective secondary cremation in a Pit Grave: a unique funerary context in Portuguese Chalcolithic burial practices" *Journal of Comparative Human Biology* 66, n° 1 (2014): 1-14.

Sinopoli, Carla, *The Political Economy of Craft Production: Crafting Empire in South India, c. 1350–1650.* Cambridge: Cambridge University Press, 2003.

Stein, Gil, *Rethinking World-Systems: Diasporas, Colonies, and Interaction in Uruk Mesopotamia*. Tucson: University of Arizona Press, 1999.

Thacker, Paul "The relevance of regional analysis for Upper Paleolithic archaeology: A case study from Portugal". In edited by Peterkin, Gail Larsen and Heather Price, Regional Approaches to Adaptation in Late Pleistocene Western Europe, 25-45. Oxford: BAR Publishing, 2000.

Trigger, Bruce, *Understanding Early Civilizations*. Cambridge: Cambridge University Press, 2003.

Tomé, Tiago and Oosterbeek, Luiz "One region, two systems? A paleobiological reading of cultural continuity over the agro-pastoralist transition in the North Ribatejo". In edited by Primitiva Bueno Ramirez, Enrique Cerrillo Cuenca, Antonio Gonzalez Cordero, *From the origins: the prehistory of the Inner Tagus Region.* BAR International Series 2219 (2011): 43-54.

Tomé, Tiago *Gruta do Morgado Superior: Relatório Antropológico da Campanha de escavação de 2012*. Unpublished excavation report, 2013.

Tomé, Tiago and Cunha, Cláudia *Gruta do Morgado Superior: Relatório Antropológico da Campanha de escavação de 2013*. Unpublished excavation report. 2015.

Umbelino, Cláudia *Paleodietary Reconstruction of two Iberian Neolithic Populations: Sant Pau Del Camp (Spain) and Alqueves (Portugal). Trace elements and dental microwear as a pathway and paleobiocultural inferences.* European Master in Anthropology and Human Biology. Coimbra: Departamento de Antropologia da Faculdade de Ciências e Tecnologia da Universidade de Coimbra, 1998.

Valera, António Carlos "Mobilidade estratégica e prolongamento simbólico: problemáticas do abandono no povoamento calcolítico do Ocidente peninsular". *(Era) Arqueologia*. Lisboa. 5 (2003): 126-148.

Waldron, Tony *Paleopathology*. Cambridge, Cambridge University Press, 2009.

Webb, Malcolm "The flag follows trade: An essay on the necessary interaction of military and commercial factors in state formation". Sabloff, Jeremy and Lamberg-Karlovsky, Clifford Charles (eds.) *Ancient Civilization and Trade*. Albuquerque: University of New Mexico Press, (1975): 155–210.

Wood, James, Milner, George, Harpending, Henry and Weiss, Kenneth The osteological paradox: problems of inferring prehistoric health from skeletal samples. *Current Anthropology*. 33. 4 (1992): 343-370.

Zilhão, João *Gruta do Caldeirão*. Lisboa: IPA, 6, 1992.

Zilhão, João *O Paleolítico Superior da Estremadura Portuguesa*. Lisboa: Colibri, 1997.

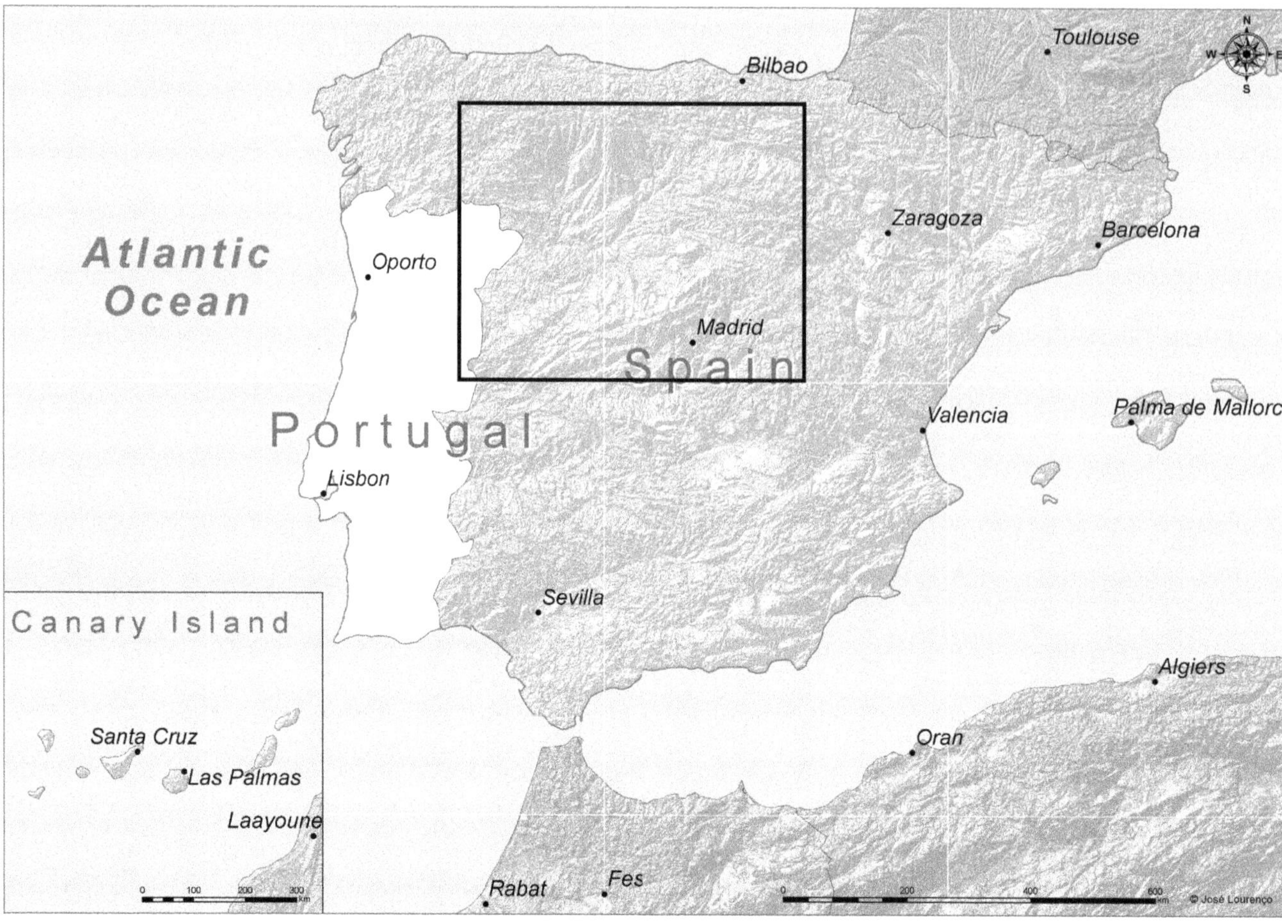

Spain - Spanish Northern Meseta. | Source: José Martinho Lourenço.

Chapter 9

Evolution of the Systems of Socio-technic Artefacts Used during the Neolithic and the Copper Age of the Spanish Northern Meseta

Rodrigo Villalobos García

Departamento de Prehistoria, Arqueología, Antropología Social y CC. y TT. Historiográficas de la Universidad de Valladolid
Facultad Filosofía y Letras. Pz/ del Campus s/n 47011 Valladolid, España,
rodrigovillalobosgarcia@gmail.com

Abstract: The archaeological record of the Late Prehistory of the Spanish Northern Meseta offers a wide variety of socio-technic artefacts such as different types of ornaments, spatula-idols, or copper goods. From the beginning of the Early Neolithic and through the Late Neolithic and the Copper Age these sets of objects were severely transformed. This paper focuses on an analysis based on quantifying variables such as 1) the amount of energy or labour used on their production, 2) the number of colours employed, and 3) the proportion of the people who used them. It also focuses on identifying the dynamics of these variables along the time. After applying the analysis it can be said that between the Early Neolithic and the Copper Age the labour applied on the crafting and the number of colours employed grew while the proportion of people who used them decreased. At the same time, the size and density of the networks in which these artefacts were exchanged also grew. These dynamics could be interpreted as a process in which socio-technic artefacts changed from being used for showing different aspects of the social person – sex, age-grade, associations, etc.– to being used for showing, in the most cases, rank inequalities.

Keywords: Socio-technic artefacts, Social inequalities, Neolithic, Copper Age, Spanish Northern Meseta.

1. Introduction[1]

The Spanish Northern Meseta is an inner region of the Iberian Peninsula which comprises the sedimentary lands of the Douro valley and the surrounding mountains of the Cantabric, Iberic, and Central Systems. On the late 6th millennium BCE this place was colonized by Neolithic farmers and herders, on the late 5th millennium BCE these people started to monumentalize the territory by building megaliths and from the late 4th millennium BCE at least some of them began to live in ditched enclosures or stone walled settlements. These three periods of time are usually called Early Neolithic (*c.* 5300-4200 BCE), Late Neolithic or Megalithic Neolithic (*c.* 4200-3100 BCE) and Copper Age (*c.* 3100-2200 BCE) (Delibes de Castro and Fernández Manzano 2000; Villalobos García 2014a). Along these periods there were several changes in aspects such as settlement pattern (Delibes de Castro *et al.* 1997; 2014), subsistence economy (Delibes de Castro 2011), craft production systems (Val Recio and Herrán Martínez 1995; Fábregas Valcarce and Rodríguez Rellán 2008; Abarquero Moras *et al.* 2012; Villalobos García and Odriozola 2016) and, probably as a consequence of all of them, there were also transformations in the expression of social inequalities (Delibes de Castro 1995; Guerra Doce *et al.* 2009; Villalobos García 2014b).

One way of approaching the analysis of prehistoric social organization is through the study of socio-technic artefacts, those who serve as the symbolic or 'extra-somatic means of articulating individuals one with another' (Binford 1962, 219). One kind of socio-technic artefacts are the personal ornaments, such as beads, pendants, rings, bracelets, etc. These objects, known in almost all cultures, are appropriate to send encoded information about issues such as sex, age, ethnicity, etc. and, also, about social rank or class (Vanhaeren 2005).

[1] This text is an English abridged version of one more exhaustive wrote in Spanish, published in the journal BSAA Arqueología, 82 (https://uvadoc.uva.es/handle/10324/25149).

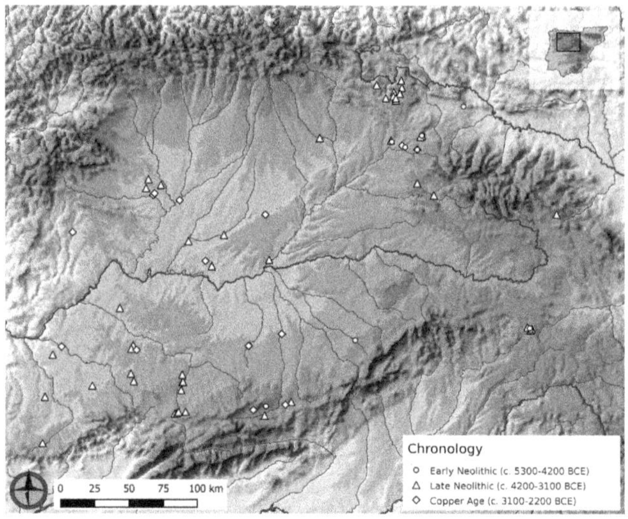

Figure 1. Location of the Spanish Northern Meseta in the Iberian Peninsula and distribution of the sites that have offered personal ornaments. | Source: By the Author.

The Neolithic and Copper Age sites of the Spanish Northern Meseta have offered different kinds of personal ornaments and other objects, such as spatula-idols or copper goods, which –probably– served as sociotechnic artefacts (Figure 1). During the Early Neolithic, slate and limestone bracelets, perforated river shells, bone rings and pendants and slate and limestone beads were used (Uribarri Angulo and Martínez González 1987; Estremera Portela 2003; Rojo Guerra *et al.* 2008; 2016; Ortega Martínez *et al.* 2008; Alameda Cuenca-Romero *et al.* 2011; Guerra Doce *et al.* 2012; Alonso Fernández and Jiménez Echevarría 2015). During the Late Neolithic the bone and slate ornaments were still in use, but new materials appeared for ornament crafting such as greenstone (variscite, muscovite, talc, etc.), jet, amber, seashells or clear quartz prisms (Delibes de Castro and Santonja Gómez 1986; Delibes de Castro *et al.* 1987; 1993; 1997; Palomino Lázaro 1990; Rojo Guerra *et al.* 1996; 2005; Fabián García 1997; Villalobos García 2012). Some other possible Late Neolithic socio-technic artefacts could have been the San Martín-El Miradero spatula-idols (Mújika Alustiza 1998; Delibes de Castro *et al.* 2012) and some exotic axeheads (Villalobos García 2015a). The Northern Meseta Copper Age could be divided in two moments, the Early Copper Age or pre-Bell Beaker Copper Age, and the Bell Beaker Copper Age. During the former, greenstone beads (López Plaza 1974; Delibes de Castro 1988; Fabián García 1995; 2006; Blanco Majado *et al.* 1996), copper awls and daggers (Delibes de Castro *et al.* 1996; Carmona *et al.* 2010) and exotic objects (Villalobos García 2013) were used as socio-technic artefacts, and during the latter this function was probably fulfilled by the bell beaker set, specifically by copper daggers and spearheads and different types of gold ornaments (Maluquer de Motes 1960; Martín Valls and Delibes de Castro 1989; Rojo Guerra *et al.* 2005; Fitzpatrick *et al.* 2016).

How modern archaeologist could approach the significance of prehistoric artefacts is a question still open to debate (*e.g.* Clarke 1976; Hodder 1982; Renfrew 1994; LaMotta and Schiffer 2001) but I think that we are able to decipher at least one part of the original coded message. Different aspects of the crafting, distribution and consumption of socio-technic artefacts could be quantified, for example the total amount of energy or labour wasted in their production, the number of colours employed or the proportion of people that used them. Looking at these variables one by one is little more than useless, but analyzing them as a set inside their social context and also during the long-term, could provide a wider and more comprehensive perspective.

2. The energy or labour wasted in the production of socio-technic artefacts

In economics there are different ways of estimate the value of some objects –dependent to the relation of supply and demand, related with non quantifiable and subjective criteria, etc.– but one of the most important is the so called *labour theory of value*, which argues that the value of every object is determined by the quantity of labour wasted on it. This approach has been widely used in archaeology since it was in the very first time employed by David Clarke (1976), and even if it can be admitted that there could be other non measurable variables, it can also be said that the energy or labour wasted in socio-technic artefacts is a good indicative of the rank that the wearers desired to express.

The total amount of energy or labour wasted in a socio-technic artefact could be estimated as follows: The labour required to obtain the raw material plus the labour required to craft the object together with the effort needed to acquire the skill and knowledge required to fulfil all of these activities, so $E = (Krm + Lrm) + (Kc + Lc)$, being "E" the total amount of energy wasted in the object, "Krm" the knowledge required to obtain the raw material, "Lrm" the labour required to obtain the raw material, "Kc" the knowledge required for the artisan to craft the object, and "Lc" the labour required for the artisan to craft the object. If we know the provenance of the raw materials used to craft the prehistoric ornaments of the Northern Meseta and, via experimental archaeology, the skill and labour required for its transformation, it is possible to estimate the quantity of "E", at least in a semi-quantitative dimension.

2.1. Early Neolithic

During this period there were only two main categories of raw materials used for crafting personal ornaments, which are bone and common widespread rocks such as slate or limestone. In both cases the raw material could be easily obtained. Crafting bone objects does not require so much skill or effort (Mújika Alustiza 2008) and, in the case of the limestone bracelets, some research show that, on the one hand, they require a small amount of time but, on the other hand, that in the production loci a lot of broken pieces are found (Martínez Sevilla and Salmerón Juan 2014). This last evidence suggests that stone bracelets are easy to craft but maybe also that some kind of specialized knowledge is required.

For that reason it can be said that the knowledge required for gathering the raw materials was *null* and the labour for this activity was *low*. In the case of the crafting, the bone artefacts required *low* knowledge and *low* amount of labour, and the stone bracelets required *medium* knowledge and *low* amount of labour.

2.2. Late Neolithic

The new artefacts that appeared in the 4th millennium BCE includes beads and pendants made on materials, such as variscite, jet, amber, etc. that require mining activities (Villalobos García and Odriozola 2016) and perhaps, due to the number of broken pieces obtained in crafting experiments (Noain Maura 1996), a more skilled crafting. Other item was the spatula-idols, an object that requires also a somehow skilled crafting (Mújika Alustiza 1998; 2008). Experiments on mining with prehistoric technology suggest that it is an affordable activity (Shepherd 1980, 30; Pickin and Timberlake 1988; Jeudy *et al.* 1995, 270; Capote Fernández 2011, 236), but because mining is more complex than surface gathering and also because variscite, jet and amber are rare materials, it would probably require higher specialized knowledge. So, in the case of spatula-idols, obtaining the raw material would have required *null* knowledge and *null* labour but for crafting the objects *medium* knowledge and *medium* labour. In the case of ornaments made on rare materials obtaining the raw material would have required *medium* knowledge and labour and the crafting *medium* knowledge and *low* labour.

2.3. Copper Age

During the Copper Age some new socio-technic artefacts appeared, mainly copper tools and weapons and also bell beaker pottery. The labour devoted to mining copper minerals should not be, considering the technology and size of the mines (Blas Cortina 1998; Hunt Ortiz 2003; Blas Cortina and Suárez Fernández 2010), different as mining variscite, jet or amber, but the copper metallurgy it is a more complex issue. It requires ore reduction, casting, forging, etc. (Montero Ruiz 2010), although the total amount of labour required is not very high (Rovira Llorens 2012). In the case of the beaker pottery it must be said that all the analysed vases known in the Northern Meseta suggest that the clay used was from local origin (Carmona Ballestero 2010; 2013, 257-67; Odriozola and Martínez-Blanes 2012) and it is generally admitted that the amount of labour wasted on each vase was low (Clarke 1976).

For that reasons, the knowledge and labour expended on obtaining copper minerals would have been *medium*, and the crafting of copper artefacts would have required *high* knowledge and *medium* labour. The Bell Beaker pottery would have required *low* knowledge and *null* labour for obtaining raw material and *low* knowledge and *low* labour for the crafting.

2.4. Diachronic evolution

By putting the entire results together (Table 1) an interesting trend is shown. In the Early Neolithic there were low skill and labour involved in the socio-technic production, but in the Late Neolithic a new effort on obtaining rare and exotic raw materials emerged. Finally, in the Copper Age a new kind of skilled crafting appeared. So, from the Early Neolithic to the Copper Age the knowledge and labour wasted on the socio-technic artefacts did increase in a sustained way.

Table 1. Amount of total energy (knowledge, labour) spent in each type of socio-technic artefact. | Source: By the Author.

Period	Socio-technic artefacts	Krm	Lrm	Kc	Lc	Total energy wasted
Early Neolithic	Bone ornaments and river shells	null	null	low	low	() + () + (X) + (X)
	Schist and limestone bracelets	low	null	medium	low	(X) + () + (XX) + (X)
Late Neolithic	Bone ornaments, quartz prisms	null	null	low	low	() + () + (X) + (X)
	Schist and limestone beads	low	null	medium	low	(X) + () + (XX) + (X)
	Spatula-idols	null	null	medium	medium	() + () + (XX) + (XX)
	Greenstone, jet and amber ornaments	medium	medium	medium	low	(XX) + (XX) + (XX) + (X)
Copper Age	Beaker pottery, stone wrist-guards	low	null	medium	low	(X) + () + (XX) + (X)
	Greenstone ornaments	medium	medium	medium	low	(XX) + (XX) + (XX) + (X)
	Copper and gold artefacts	medium	medium	high	medium	(XX) + (XX) + (XXX) + (XX)

3. The use of colours in the socio-technic artefacts sets

Colour is one of the physical attributes of objects that is more easily and quickly perceived. Probably for that reason, colour codes are widely employed along cultures of different parts and times (Hovers *et al.* 2003). A cross-cultural survey concerned on colour naming shows that middle range societies use at most six terms, which are black, white, red, green, blue and yellow. For that reason these are called the Basic Colour Terms (Kay *et al.* 1991, Figure. 1). The ornaments found in the Neolithic and Copper Age of the Northern Meseta are white (limestone, bone, shells), black (slate, jet), green (variscite, muscovite) and red (amber, red muscovite, kaolinite), four of these six. There are not blue ornaments, but yellow can be found in gold and, probably, copper artefacts.

During the Early Neolithic beads, pendants and bracelets were made on bone, shells, limestone and slate, so the colours used were only *black* and *white*. In the Late Neolithic *white* ornaments were in bone, shells and limestone, *black* were in slate and jet and two new colours, *red* and *green*, appeared. The former is present in amber and kaolinite and the latter in variscite, muscovite, talc, etc. Red can also be found in the ochre and cinnabar employed in some megalithic funerary rituals (Delibes de Castro 2000) and megalithic art (Bueno Ramírez *et al.* 2015). At last, the Copper Age has some cases of *white* (bone and white muscovite), *black* (slate and black muscovite) and *red* (red muscovite) ornaments and a lot of *green* (mainly variscite), together with the *yellow* of the copper and the gold (Figure 2).

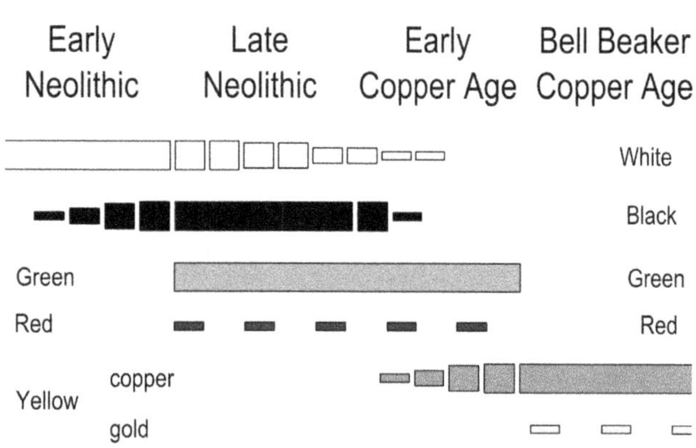

Figure 2. Scheme representing the use of colours along the Late Prehistory in the Northern Meseta. | Source: By the Author.

The aforementioned cross-cultural surveys also suggest that the process of adoption colour terms follows an order predetermined by bio-psychological constraints. There are cultures with only two terms, which are black and white. The cultures with three colour terms use black, white and red. In the cases of cultures with four, these are black, white, red and green or yellow. The cultures with five colour terms use black, white, red, green and yellow. At last, in the cases with six colour terms they are the six Basic Colour Terms. These ethnographic observations have lead to suggest that our bio-psychological condition sets us for this cultural expression, and that the process of colour terms adoption follows the order black/white → red → green → yellow → blue (Kay *et al.* 1991; 1997; Cook *et al.* 2005). This is also the order identified in the diachronic use of ornaments in the Northern Meseta: black and white in the Early Neolithic, black, white, red and green in the Late Neolithic and all of these plus yellow in the Copper Age.

4. The proportion of people that used the socio-technic artefacts[2]

One part of the ornaments of the Neolithic and Copper Age of the Spanish Northern Meseta were recovered in domestic sites from the Early Neolithic (Estremera Portela 2003; Rojo Guerra *et al.* 2012) and the Copper Age (López Plaza and Arias González 1988; Delibes de Castro and Val Recio 1990; Domínguez Bolaños 1991; Fabián García 1995; 2006), which proves that these socio-technic artefacts were used in different activities of the everyday life. But the objects found as grave goods offer the possibility to inquire if some of them could be related to the expression of sex, age-grades or social rank.

4.1. Early Neolithic

There are a small amount of burials dated in the Early Neolithic. Some of these people were buried without socio-technich artefacts, such as the old woman of La Lámpara (Rojo Guerra *et al.* 2008, 377-94) or the two women of El Prado (Alonso Fernández and Jiménez Echevarría 2014). Others, instead, did have socio-technic artefacts as grave goods. The old man of Fuente Celada wore some bone rings around his neck (Alameda Cuenca-Romero *et al.* 2011). The adults of Molino de Arriba and El Hoyo had bone beads and a pair of river shell ornaments (Alonso Fernández and Jiménez Echevarría 2015; Rojo Guerra *et al.* 2016). The child of Alto de Rodilla had one quartz prism (Alonso Fernández and Jiménez Echevarría 2015).

This small sample (n=7) shows that it does not seem to have existed any kind of age-restriction for wearing socio-technic artefacts, but in all the known cases of women, they were buried without this kind of objects. Nevertheless, the sex of the buried people of Molino de Arriba, El Hoyo or Alto de Rodilla is still unknown. All that can be said is that there are three people (all of them women) who were buried without socio-technic artefacts, and that these represents the 43% of all the Early Neolithic known buried individuals.

[2] In a previous version of this paper, published as the pre-proceedings of the Mesa-redonda hold in Abrantes (Villalobos García 2015b), the proportion of population that used socio-technic artefacts was slightly different. The reason of these changes is that since then, new publications have offered new data about these question.

4.2. Late Neolithic

There are a lot of megalithic collective burials in the Northern Meseta, most of them hosting a mixed ossuary with grave goods such as flint blades and arrowheads, axeheads and different kinds of ornaments and idols. But there are a small amount of them with well preserved bodies and their grave goods associated, such as the phase II of El Túmulo de la Sima (Rojo Guerra *et al.* 2005, 161-72), La Tarayuela (Rojo Guerra *et al.* 2005, 215-24), La Velilla (Zapatero Magdaleno 2012, 2015), La Peña de la Abuela (Rojo Guerra *et al.* 2005, 58-65), El Miradero (Guerra Doce *et al.* 2009), La Cabaña or La Cista de Nava Alta (Delibes de Castro *et al.* 1993; Etxeberría Gabilondo and Rojo Guerra 1994).

The number and groups of artefacts and the MNI of buried people in these sites show that not everybody were buried with socio-technic artefacts and that there are people with greater accumulations of them than the others. It can also be observed that there seem to be no remarkable differences between men and women and between adults and children: examples of all of these categories have been found with socio-technic artefacts and also without socio-technic artefacts. The two best preserved sites, La Velilla and the phase II of La Sima, suggest that less than the 50% of the buried people of the Late Neolithic wore socio-technic artefacts.

4.3. Copper Age

During the 3rd millennium BCE the individual or double burials re-emerged. In El Ollar (Delibes de Castro 1988), El Picón del Rey (Fabián García 1995, 111-12), Colmenares (Herrán Martínez and Rojo Guerra 1999), El Hornazo (Carmona Ballestero 2013), Casla (Municio González 1981) and El Portalón (Pérez-Romero *et al.* 2015) some of the buried people were accompanied with socio-technic artefacts such as copper awls and daggers and ornaments such as green, red, white and black beads. In other sites there are burials with technomic grave goods such as pottery vessels, flint sickles and arrowheads or stone axeheads but without socio-technic artefacts, and there are also Copper Age burials without any kind of grave goods. These are the cases of La Serna-Cantazorras, Camino de Ciguñuela, El Tomillar, Los Cardos, La Cascajera, Las Peñas de Villardondiego, El Soto de Tovilla, Santa Cruz, Piedra Alta, El Cerro de la Cabeza, Fuente Celada or El Hornazo (Delibes de Castro 1987; Fabián García 1995; Arnáiz Alonso *et al.* 1997; García Barrios 2007, 213-18; Esparza Arroyo *et al.* 2008; Delibes de Castro *et al.* 2012; Fabián García and Blanco González 2012; Carmona Ballestero 2013).

To sum up, there are between 44 and 54 people without ornaments or copper objects out of a total of 59 buried people, which means that between the 75% and the 92% of the people did not use socio-technic artefacts.

4.4. Diachronic evolution

The Early Neolithic sample is still low and the amount of people using grave goods in Late Neolithic collective burials is difficult to quantify but, instead of this, there seems to be an interesting trend. During the Early Neolithic, more than the half of the people were buried with bone, river shell or stone ornaments. During the Late Neolithic, probably less than the half of the people were buried with ornaments such as bone, jet, greenstone, amber, etc. beads and pendants, and these objects were used by men, women and children. At last, during the Copper Age, less than the fourth part of the people were buried with socio-technic artefacts.

5. Socio-technic artefacts and exchange networks

These data demonstrate that during the Early Neolithic more than the half of the buried people wore socio-technic artefacts, that these objects were made on black and white materials, and that these materials could be easily obtained in the surroundings of the places where those people lived. Passing the time, this situation changed, because in the Copper Age the socio-technic artefacts were used by a smaller proportion of the buried people, show more colours and their crafting were considerably harder (Figure 3).

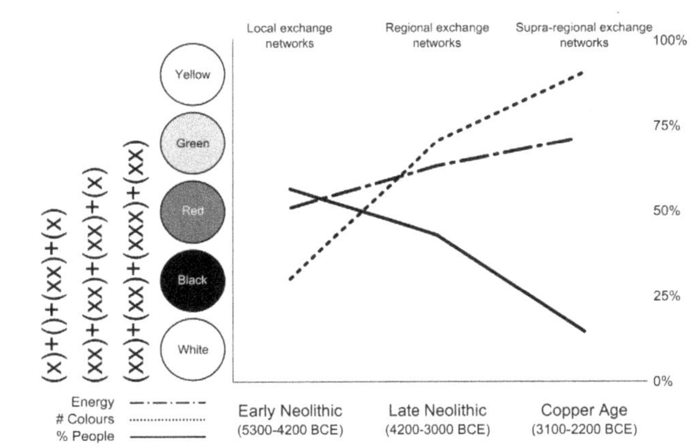

Figure 3. Graph representing the evolution of the different variables described along the text. | Source: By the Author.

During this period of time the socio-technic artefacts exchange networks grew in size and density. In the Early Neolithic all of them were made over local materials. During the Late Neolithic some regional exchange networks appeared and slate, jet, variscite. etc. started to be widely used far away from their origins (Guerra Doce *et al.* 2009; Villalobos García 2012). There are also some cases of seashells and jadeitite axeheads that suggest some kind of supra-regional network exchange (Delibes de Castro and Rojo Guerra 1988; Rojo Guerra *et al.* 1996; Fábregas Valcarce *et al.* 2012). At last, during the Copper Age the regional exchange networks continued its functioning by distributing copper artefacts (Delibes de Castro *et al.* 2006) and variscite ornaments (Villalobos García 2012), but the supra-regional exchange networks grew, distributing idols, limestone artefacts and ivory from the southern part of Iberia into the Northern Meseta (Villalobos García 2013) and, also, variscite from the Northern Meseta into the southern part of Iberia (Villalobos García and Odriozola 2016).

The aforementioned trend of growing colour numbers and labour wasted in socio-technic artefacts run in parallel with the growing of the exchange networks that were used to distribute them, but when this happened, there were less people using them. This process could be interpreted as a shift in a socio-technic system based on representing categories such as sex, age-grades, etc. of an *egalitarian society* (Early Neolithic) to a system based on representing categories such as sex, age-grades, etc. and, also, social rank, of a *ranked society* (Late Neolithic and Copper Age).

Bibliography

Abarquero Moras, F. J., Guerra Doce, E., Delibes de Castro, G., Palomino Lázaro, Á. L., and Val Recio, J. *Arqueología de la Sal en las Lagunas de Villafáfila (Zamora): investigaciones sobre los cocederos prehistóricos*. Valladolid: Junta de Castilla y León: 2012.

Alameda Cuenca-Romero, M. C., Carmona Ballestero, E., Pascual Blanco, S., Martínez Díez, G., and Díez Pastor, C. "El "campo de hoyos" calcolítico de Fuente Celada (Burgos): datos preliminares y perspectivas" *Complutum* 22, no. 1 (2011): 47–69.

Alonso Fernández, C., and Jiménez Echevarría, J. "Contribución al estudio del poblamiento, modos de vida y ritual funerario del Neolítico Antiguo: el asentamiento al aire libre de El Prado (Pancorbo, Burgos)" *Zephyrus* 74 (2014): 41–64.

Arnáiz Alonso, M. Á., Pascual, S., and Rojo, A. V. "Los semejantes y los otros: La sepultura múltiple simultánea de Villayerno-Morquillas, Burgos. Nota preliminar". *Boletín del Seminario de Estudios de Arte y Arqueología* 63 (1997): 49–69.

Binford, L. R. "Archaeology as Anthropology". *American Antiquity* 28, no. 2 (1962): 217–225.

Blanco Majado, J., López Alonso, M. A., Edo i Benaiges, M., and Fernández Turiel, J. L. "Estudio analítico de determinación mineralógica y de composición química de las cuentas de collar de calaíta y otras materias del yacimiento de Las Peñas (Quiruelas de Vidriales, Zamora)". In *I Congrés del Neolític a la Península Ibérica. Formació i implantació de les comunitats agrícolas. Vol. 1*, 222–237. Barcelona: Museu de Gavà, 1996.

Blas Cortina, M. Á. de. "Producción e intercambio de metal: la singularidad de las minas de cobre prehistóricas de El Aramo y El Milagro (Asturias)". In *Minerales y metales en la Prehistoria Reciente. Algunos testimonios de su explotación y laboreo en la península ibérica* edited by G. Delibes de Castro, 71-103. Valladolid: Universidad de Valladolid, 1998.

Blas Cortina, M. Á. de, and Suárez Fernández, M. "La minería subterránea del cobre en Asturias: un capítulo esencial en la Prehistoria reciente del norte de España". In *Cobre y Oro. Minería y metalurgia en la Asturias prehistórica y antigua* edited by J. Fernández Tresguerres, 43-82. Oviedo: Real Instituto de Estudios Asturianos Principado de Asturias, 2010.

Bueno Ramírez, P., Balbín Behrmann, R., Laporte, L., Gouézin, P., Cousseau, F., Barroso Bermejo, R., Hernanz Gismero, A., Iriarte Cela, M., and Quesnel, L. "Natural and artificial colours: the megalithic monuments of Brittanny". *Antiquity* 89, no. 343 (2015): 55–71.

Campillo Cueva, J. "Memoria de las excavaciones realizadas en el término de Tablada de Rudrón (Burgos). «El Túmulo Campaniforme de Tablada del Rudrón (Burgos)»". *Noticiario Arqueológico Hispánico* 26 (1985): 7–86.

Campillo Cueva, J. 2004. "Dos sortijas cubrededos de oro halladas en el túmulo campaniforme de Tablada del Rudrón (Burgos)". In *Homenaje al Profesor Dr. Juan Ma. Apellániz. Vol 1*, 257-267. Bilbao: Diputación Foral de Bizkaia, 2004.

Capote, M. "Working in the flint mine: Percussion tools and labour organisation at Casa Montero (Spain)". In *Proceedings of the 2nd International Conference of the UISPP Commission on Flint Mining in Pre- and Protohistoric Times* edited by M. Capote, S. Consuegra Rodríguez, P. Díaz-del-Río, and X. Terradas, 231-242. Oxford: BAR Publishing, 2011.

Carmona Ballestero, E. *Prestigio y emulación en espacios marginales: la cerámica campaniforme de Paulejas (Quintanilla del Agua, Burgos)*. Burgos, Universidad de Burgos, 2010.

Carmona Ballestero, E. *El Calcolítico en la Cuenca Media del Arlanzón (Burgos, España). Comunidades campesinas, procesos históricos y transformaciones,* BAR International Series 2559. Oxford: BAR Publishing, 2013.

Carmona Ballestero, E., Arnaiz Alonso, M. Á., and Montero Gutiérrez, J. "Consumo de metal durante la Prehistoria Reciente en el centro de la Península Ibérica. Una aproximación a través del análisis de los contextos funerarios en fosa". *Trabajos de Prehistoria* 67, no. 2 (2010): 373–387.

Clarke, D. L. "The Beaker Network - Social and Economic Models". In *Glockenbecher Sympoision Oberried 1974* edited by J. N. Lanting and J. D. Van der Waals, 459–477. Bussum: Fibula-Van Dishoeck, 1976.

Cook, R. S., Kay, P., and Regier, T. "The World Color Survey database". In *Handbook of Categorization in Cognitive Science* edited by H. Cohen and C. Lefebvre, 223-241. Amsterdam: Elsevier, 2005.

Delibes de Castro, G. "Sobre los enterramientos del grupo campaniforme de Ciempozuelos. Diversidad y tradición". In *El Origen de la Metalurgia en la Península Ibérica. Vol. 2* edited by M. Fernández Miranda, 37–51. Madrid: Universidad Complutense de Madrid, 1987.

Delibes de Castro, G. "Enterramiento calcolítico en fosa de «El Ollar», Donhierro (Segovia)". *Espacio, Tiempo y Forma. Prehistoria y Arqueología* 1 (1988): 227–238.

Delibes de Castro, G. "Ritos funerarios, demografía y estructura social entre las comunidades neolíticas de la Submeseta Norte". In *Arqueoloxía da Morte na Península Ibérica desde as Orixes ata o Medievo* edited by R. Fábregas Valcarce, F. Pérez Losada, and C. Fernández Ibáñez, 61–94. Xinzo de Limiá: Exmo. Concello de Xinzo de Limiá, 1995.

Delibes de Castro, G. "Cinabrio, huesos pintados en rojo y tumbas de ocre: ¿Prácticas de embalsamamiento en la Prehistoria?" In *Scripta in honorem. Enrique A. Llobregat Conesa* edited by M. Olcina Domènech and J. A. Soler Díaz, 223-236. Valencia: Generalitat Valenciana, 2000.

Delibes de Castro, G. *El Pan y la Sal. La vida campesina en el Valle Medio del Duero hace cinco mil años*. Valladolid: Real Academia de Bellas Artes de la Purísima Concepción, 2011.

Delibes de Castro, G., Alonso Díez, M., and Rojo Guerra, M. Á. "Los sepulcros colectivos del Duero Medio y las Loras y su conexión con el foco dolménico riojano". In *El Megalitismo en la Península Ibérica*, 181–198. Madrid: Ministerio de Cultura, 1987.

Delibes de Castro, G., Benet Jordana, N., Pérez Martín, R., and Zapatero Magdaleno, P. 1997. "De la tumba dolménica como referente territorial, al poblado estable: Notas sobre el hábitat y las formas de vida de las comunidades megalíticas de la Submeseta Norte". In *O neolitico atlántico e as orixes do megalitismo* edited by A. A. Rodríguez Casal, 779–808. Santiago de Compostela: Universidad de Santiago de Compostela, 1997.

Delibes de Castro, G., Fabián García, J. F., Fernández Manzano, J., Herrán Martínez, J. I., Santiago Pardo, J., and Val Recio, J. 1996. "Los más antiguos testimonios del uso y producción de metal en el suroeste de la Submeseta Norte: Consideraciones tipológicas, tecnológicas y contextuales". In *Humanitas. Estudos en homenaxe ó Prof. Dr. Carlos Alonso del Real. Vol. 1* edited by A. A. Rodríguez Casal, 163–201. Santiago de Compostela: Universidade de Santiago de Compostela, 1996.

Delibes de Castro, G., and Fernández Manzano, J. "La trayectoria cultural de la Prehistoria Reciente (6400-2500 BP) en la Submeseta Norte: principales hitos de un proceso". In *Actas do 3o Congresso de Arqueología Peninsular. Pré-Historia Recente da Península Ibérica* edited by V. O. Jorge, 95–112. Porto: Adecap, 2000.

Delibes de Castro, G., Fernández Manzano, J., and Herrán Martínez, J. I. "La metalurgia del inicio de la Edad del Cobre en la Submeseta Norte Española: Los desafíos del aprovisionamiento". *Sautuola* 12 (2006): 127–134.

Delibes de Castro, G., García García, M., Olmo Martín, J., and Santiago Pardo, J. *Los recintos de fosos calcolíticos del valle medio del Duero: Arqueología Aérea y Espacial*, Studia Archaeologica 100. Valladolid: Universidad de Valladolid, 2014.

Delibes de Castro, G., Guerra Doce, E., Zapatero Magdaleno, P., and Villalobos García, R. "Les spatules-idoles de type San Martín-El Miradero: Identité, symbolisme, liturgie et prestige dans les mobiliers des tombes mégalithiques de la Vielle Castille (Espagne)". In *Sépultures collectives et mobiliers funéraires de la fin du Néolitique en Europe occidentale* edited by M. Sohn and J. Vaquer, 305–331. Toulouse: Archives d'écologie préhistorique, 2012.

Delibes de Castro, G., Moreno Gallo, M. Á., Villalobos García, R., and Basconcillos Arce, J. *Piedra Alta. El guardián del tiempo. San Pedro Samuel (Burgos)*. Burgos: Diputación de Burgos, 2012.

Delibes de Castro, G., and Rojo Guerra, M. Á. "En torno al origen del foco megalítico del oriente de la Meseta: de nuevo el sepulcro de Cubillejo de Lara". *Boletín del Seminario de Estudios de Arte y Arqueología* 54 (1988): 5–21.

Delibes de Castro, G., Rojo Guerra, M. Á., and Represa Bermejo, J. I. *Dólmenes de La Lora. Burgos*. Valladolid: Junta de Castilla y León, 1993.

Delibes de Castro, G., and Santonja Gómez, M. *El fenómeno megalítico en la provincia de Salamanca*. Salamanca: Ediciones de la Diputación de Salamanca, 1986.

Delibes de Castro, G., and Val Recio, J. "Prehistoria reciente zamorana: del Megalitismo al Bronce". In *I Congreso de Historia de Zamora. Vol. 2.*, 53–99. Zamora: Instituto de Estudios Zamoranos Florián de Ocampo, 1990.

Domínguez Bolaños, A. "Los Paradores de Castrogonzalo. Un yacimiento Calcolítico y Romano". *Anuario del Instituto de Estudios Zamoranos Florián de Ocampo* 1991 (1991): 191–207.

Esparza Arroyo, Á., Delibes de Castro, G., Velasco Vázquez, J., and Cruz Sánchez, P. J. "Historia de un golpe en la cabeza: Sobre el enterramiento calcolítico del hoyo 197 de "El Soto de Tovilla" (Tudela de Duero, Valladolid)". *BSAA Arqueología* 74 (2008): 9–48.

Estremera Portela, M. S. *Primeros agricultores y ganaderos en la Meseta Norte: el Neolítico de la Cueva de la Vaquera (Torreiglesias, Segovia)*. Valladolid: Junta de Castilla y León, 2003.

Etxeberría Gabilondo, F., and Rojo Guerra, M. Á. "Diente humano perforado procedente del megalito de La Cabaña (Sargentes de La Lora, Burgos): Un ejemplo de tafonomía". *Munibe (Antropologia-Arkeologia)* 46 (1994): 117–122.

Fabián García, J. F. *El aspecto funerario durante el Calcolítico y los inicios de la Edad del Bronce en la Meseta Norte*. Salamanca: Ediciones de la Universidad de Salamanca, 1995.

Fabián García, J. F. *El dolmen del Prado de las Cruces (Bernuy-Salinero, Ávila)*. Valladolid: Junta de Castilla y León, 1997.

Fabián García, J. F. El *IV y III milenio AC en el Valle Amblés (Ávila)*. Valladolid: Junta de Castilla y León, 2006

Fabián García, J. F., and Blanco González, A. (2012). "Cuatro enterramientos calcolíticos en hoyo del Cerro de la Cabeza (Ávila)". *Complutum* 23, no. 1 (2012): 99–120.

Fábregas Valcarce, R., and Rodríguez Rellán, C. "Gestión del cuarzo y la pizarra en el Calcolítico peninsular: El "santuario" de El Pedroso (Trabazos de Aliste, Zamora)". *Trabajos de Prehistoria* 65, no. 1 (2008): 125–142.

Fábregas Valcarce, R., Lombera Hermida, A., and Rodríguez Rellán, C. "Spain and Portugal: long chisels and perforated axes. Their context and distribution". In *JADE. Grandes haches alpines du Néolithique européen. Ve et IVe millénaires av. J.-C. Vol. 2* edited by P. Pétrequin, S. Cassen, M. Errera, L. Klassen, A. Sheridan, and A.-M. Pétrequin, 1108–1135. Besançon: Presses Universitaires de Franche-Comté, 2012.

García Barrios, Á. S. *Los inicios de la Edad del Cobre en el Valle Medio del Duero: Una aproximación a los modos de vida en el centro de la Meseta en los albores de la Metalurgia*, Unpublished PhD Dissertation, Valladolid: University of Valladolid, 2007.

Guerra Doce, E., Cruz, P. J., Fabián, J. F., Zapatero Magdaleno, P., and López Plaza, S. "Una referencia en el paisaje. Canchales graníticos y procesos de neolitización en el Valle Amblés (Ávila)". In *Actes Xarxes al Neolític* edited by M. Borrell, F. Borrell, J. Bosch, X. Clop, and M. Molist, 507–515. Gavà (Barcelona): Museu de Gavà, 2012.

Guerra Doce, E., Delibes de Castro, G., Zapatero Magdaleno, P., and Villalobos García, R. "Primus Inter Pares: estrategias de diferenciación social en los sepulcros megalíticos de la Meseta Norte Española". *BSAA Arqueología* 75 (2009): 41–65.

Herrán Martínez, J. I., and Rojo Guerra, M. Á. "¿Una nueva tumba en fosa calcolítica?: el hallazgo de Colmenares (Portillo, Valladolid, España) y su contexto arqueológico". *Estudos Pré-Históricos* 7 (1999): 111–124.

Hodder, I. *Symbols in action. Ethnoarchaeological studies of material culture*. Cambridge: Cambridge University Press, 1982.

Hovers, E., Ilani, S., Bar-Yosef, O., and Vandermeersch, B. "An Early Case of Color Symbolism: Ochre Use by Modern Humans in Qafzeh Cave". *Current Anthropology* 44, no. 4 (2003): 491–522.

Hunt Ortiz, M. A. *Prehistoric mining and Metallurgy in South West Iberian Peninsula*, BAR International Series 418. Oxford: BAR Publishing, 2003.

Jeudy, F., Jeunesse, C., Monnier, J.-L., Pelegrin, J., Pétrequin, A.-M., Pétrequin, P., and Praud, I. "Les carrières néolithiques de Plancher-les-mines (Haute-Saône). Exemples d'une approche intégrée". In *Les mines de silex au Néolithique en Europe: avancées récentes* edited by J. Pelegrin and A. Richard Paris, 241–280. Paris: Comité des travaux historiques et scientifiques, 1995.

Jiménez Echevarría, J., and Alonso Fernández, C. "El Neolítico en el corredor Alto Ebro-Alto Duero: dos hallazgos funerarios del Neolítico Antiguo y Reciente en Monasterio de Rodilla (Burgos)". In *5o Congresso do Neolítico Peninsular* edited by V. Gonçalves, M. Diniz and A. C. Sousa, 540–546. Lisboa: Universidade de Lisboa, 2015.

Kay, P., Berlin, B., Maffi, L., and Merrified, W. "Color naming across languages". In *Color categories in thought and language* edited by C. L. Hardin and L. Maffi, 21–58. Cambridge: Cambridge University Press, 1997.

Kay, P., Berlin, B., and Merrified, W. "Biocultural Implications of Systems of Color Naming". *Journal of Linguistic Anthropology* 1, no. 1 (1991): 12–25.

LaMotta, V. M., and Schiffer, M. "Behavioral Archaeology. Towards a New Synthesis". In *Archaeological Theory Today* edited by I. Hodder, 14–64. Cambridge: Polity Press, 2001.

López Plaza, S. "Materiales de la Edad del Bronce hallados en Muñogalindo (Ávila)". *Zephyrus* 25 (1974): 121–143.

López Plaza, S., and Arias González, L. "Aproximación al poblado Calcolítico de "Tierras Lineras", La Mata de Ledesma, Salamanca". *Zephyrus* 41 (1988): 171–198.

Maluquer de Motes, J. "Nuevos hallazgos de la cultura del vaso campaniforme en la meseta". *Zephyrus* 11 (1960): 119–130.

Martínez Sevilla, F., and Salmerón Juan, J. "La artesanía de los brazaletes líticos de la cueva-sima de La Serreta (Cieza, Murcia): Tecnología, útiles y funcionalidad del sitio". *Zephyrus* 74 (2014): 65–87.

Martín Valls, R., and Delibes de Castro, G. *La cultura del vaso campaniforme en las campiñas meridionales del Duero. El enterramiento de Fuente-Olmedo (Valladolid)*, 2nd edition. Valladolid: Junta de Castilla y León, 1989.

Montero Ruiz, I. "Tecnología de la metalurgia de la base cobre". In *Manual de Arqueometalurgia* edited by I. Montero Ruiz, 159–188. Alcalá de Henares (Madrid): Museo Arqueológico Regional de Madrid, 2010.

Mújika Alustiza, J. A. "Ídolos-espátulas del País Vasco: Fabricación, cronología y paralelos". *Veleia* 15 (1998): 121–144.

Mújika Alustiza, J. A. "La gestión de la materia prima ósea en la fabricación de objetos durante la Prehistoria". *Veleia* 24-25 (2008): 531–568.

Municio González, L. "Materiales de la cueva sepulcral calcolítica de Casla (Segovia)". *Nvmantia* 1 (1981): 171–179.

Noain Maura, M. J. "Las cuentas de collar en variscita de las minas prehistóricas de Gavà (Can Tintorer). Bases para un estudio experimental". *Cuadernos de Prehistoria y Arqueología Universidad Autónoma de Madrid* 23 (1996): 37–86.

Odriozola, C. P., and Martínez-Blanes, J. M. "Cerámica para la producción de sal en Villafáfila: estudio tecnofuncional a la luz de los análisis de pasta". In *Arqueología de la Sal en las Lagunas de Villafáfila (Zamora): investigaciones sobre los cocederos prehistóricos* authored by F. J. Abarquero Moras, E. Guerra Doce, G. Delibes de Castro, Á. L. Palomino Lázaro, and J. Val Recio, 436–465. Valladolid: Junta de Castilla y León, 2012.

Ortega, A. I., Juez, L., Carretero Díaz, J. M., Ortega, M. C., Arsuaga, J. L., and Pérez-González, A. "El Neolítico en la nueva secuencia estratigráfica del yacimiento del Portalón de la Cueva Mayor (Sierra de Atapuerca, Burgos)". In *IV Congreso del Neolítico Peninsular. Vol. 1* edited by M. S. Hernández Pérez, J. A. Soler Díaz, and J. A. López Padilla, 221–229. Alicante: Museo Arqueológico de Alicante, 2008.

Palomino Lázaro, Á. L. "Nuevas aportaciones al conocimiento del fenómeno megalítico de la provincia de Zamora". In *I Congreso de Historia de Zamora. Vol. 2*, 173–200. Zamora: Instituto de Estudios Zamoranos Florián de Ocampo, 1990.

Palomino Lázaro, Á. L., Rojo Guerra, M. A., García Martínez de Lagrán, Í., Garrido Pena, R., Alday Ruiz, A., García Gazólaz, J., and Sesma Sesma, J. (2011). El Molino de Arriba (Buniel, Burgos). In *Las primeras producciones cerámicas: el VI milenio cal AC en la península Ibérica* edited by J. Bernabeu, M. A. Rojo, and L. Molina, 113–115. Valencia: Universitat de València, 2011.

Pérez-Romero, A., Iriarte, E., Galindo-Pellicena, M. Á., García-González, R., Rodríguez, L., Castilla, M., Francés-Negro, M., Santos, E., Valdiosera, C., Arsuaga, J. L., Alday, A., and Carretero Díaz, J. M. "An unusual Pre-bell beaker Copper Age cave burial context from El Portalón de Cueva Mayor site (Sierra de Atapuerca, Burgos)". *Quaternary International* 433, no. Part A (2017): 142–155.

Pickin, J., and Timberlake, S. "Stone hammers and fire-setting: a preliminary experiment at Cwmystwyth mine, Dyfed". *Bulletin of the Peak District Mines Historical Society* 10, no. 3 (1988): 165–167.

Renfrew, C. "Towards a cognitive archaeology". In *The ancient mind. Elements of cognitive archaeology* edited by C. Renfrew and E. B. W. Zubrow, 3–12. Cambridge: Cambridge University Press, 1994.

Rojo Guerra, M. Á., Delibes de Castro, G., Edo i Benaiges, M., and Fernández Turiel, J. L. "Adornos de calaíta en los ajuares dolménicos de la provincia de Burgos: Apuntes sobre su composición y procedencia". In *I Congrés del Neolític a la Península Ibérica. Formació i implantació de les comunitats agrícolas. Vol. 1*, 239–250. Barcelona: Museu de Gavà, 1996.

Rojo Guerra, M. Á., Kunst, M., Garrido Pena, R., García Martínez de Lagrán, Í., and Morán Dauchez, G. *Un desafío a la eternidad: Tumbas monumentales del Valle de Ambrona*. Valladolid: Junta de Castilla y León, 2005.

Rojo Guerra, M. Á., Kunst, M., Garrido Pena, R., García Martínez de Lagrán, Í., and Morán Dauchez, G. *Paisajes de la Memoria: Asentamientos del Neolítico Antiguo en el Valle de Ambrona (Soria, España)*. Valladolid: Universidad de Valladolid, 2008.

Rovira Llorens, S. "Arqueometalurgia experimental en el departamento de Prehistoria y Arqueología de la U.A.M". *Cuadernos de Prehistoria y Arqueología Universidad Autónoma de Madrid* 37-38 (2012): 105–120.

Schuhmacher, T. X. "El marfil en España desde el Calcolítico al Bronce Antiguo". In *Elfenbeinstudien faszikel 1. Marfiles y elefantes en la península Ibérica y el Mediterráneo Occidental* edited by A. Banerjee, J. A. López Padilla, and T. X. Schuhmacher, 45–68. Mainz: Verlag Philipp von Zabern, 2012.

Shepherd, R. *Prehistoric Mining and Allied industries*. London: Academic Press, 1980.

Uribarri Angulo, J. L., and Martínez González, J. M. "Primeros asentamientos humanos en el término municipal de la ciudad de Burgos". *Caesaraugusta* 64 (1987): 135–156.

Val Recio, J., and Herrán Martínez, J. I. 1995. "El calcolítico precampaniforme en el Duero Medio". In *Origens, Estruturas e Relações das Culturas Calcolíticas da Península Ibérica* edited by M. Kunst, 293–303. Torres Vedras: Instituto Português de Património Arquitectónico e Arqueológico, 1995.

Vanhaeren, M. 2005. "Speaking with beads: The evolutionary significance of personal ornaments". In *From Tools to Symbols: from Early Hominids to Modern Humans* edited by F. d'Errico and L. Backwell, 525–553. Johannesburg: Wits University Press, 2005.

Villalobos García, R. "Adornos exóticos en los sepulcros tardoneolíticos de la Submeseta Norte Española. El ejemplo de Las Tuerces como nodo de una red descentralizada de intercambios". In *Actes Xarxes al Neolític* edited by M. Borrell, F. Borrell, J. Bosch, X. Clop, and M. Molist, 265–271. Gavà (Barcelona): Museu de Gavà, 2012.

Villalobos García, R. "Artefactos singulares de filiación meridional en el Calcolítico de la Meseta Norte Española: un vaso calcáreo procedente de El Fonsario (Villafáfila, Zamora)". *Zephyrus* 71 (2013): 131–148.

Villalobos García, R. "La trayectoria historiográfica de los inicios de la Prehistoria Reciente (VI a III milenios cal AC) en la Meseta Norte Española". In *II Jornadas de Jóvenes Investigadores del Valle del Duero. Del Neolítico a la Antigüedad Tardía* edited by J. Honrado Castro, M. Á. Brezmes Escribano, A. Tejeiro Pizarro, and Ó. Rodríguez Monterrubio, 17–31. Valladolid: Glyphos Publicaciones, 2014.

Villalobos García, R. "The megalithic tombs of the Spanish Northern Meseta. Material, political and ideological ties between the Neolithic people and their territory". *Préhistoires Méditerranéennes* Colloque 2014 (2014).

Villalobos García, R. "El simbolismo de las hachas pulimentadas neolíticas a través de los documentos arqueológicos de la Submeseta Norte Española. Entre el colectivismo y la individualización". In *5º Congresso do Neolítico Peninsular* edited by V. Gonçalves, M. Diniz and A. C. Sousa, 578–584. Lisboa: Universidade de Lisboa, 2015.

Villalobos García, R. "Evolución de los sistemas de artefactos socioténicos empleados en la Meseta Norte Española durante el Neolítico y Calcolítico". In *2ª Mesa-redonda Peninsular Tráfego de Objetos Tráfego Tecnológico: síntomas das ideologias dominantes na Ibéria. Para-Actas* edited by A. Cruz and E. Cerrillo Cuenca, 25–32. Tomar: Centro de Pré-História do Instituto Politécnico de Tomar, 2015.

Villalobos García, R. and Odriozola, C. P. "Organizing the Production of Variscite Personal Ornaments in Later Prehistoric Iberia: The Mines of Aliste and the Production Sites of Quiruelas de Vidriales (Zamora, Spain)". *European Journal of Archaeology* 19, no. 4 (2016): 631–651.

Zapatero Magdaleno, P. "El sepulcro de La Velilla, en Osorno (Palencia), dentro del marco del fenómeno megalítico en la Meseta Norte". *Patrimonio Histórico de Castilla y León* 46 (2012): 51–58.

Zapatero Magdaleno, P. *El Neolítico en el noreste de la Cuenca del Duero: el yacimiento de La Velilla en el Valle de Valdavia (Palencia)*, Unpublished PhD Dissertation, Valladolid: University of Valladolid, 2015.

Spain - Interior of the Iberian Peninsula.
Source: José Martinho Lourenço.

Chapter 10

The Swansong of Knapping. Chalcolithic and Bronze Age Lithic Industries in the Interior of the Iberian Peninsula

Nuria Castañeda

UMR 8215 Trajectoires. Université Paris I Panthéon Sorbonne
nuriacastanyeda@gmail.com

Abstract: This work highlights the technological changes that took place in knapping industries from the Chalcolithic to the Late Bronze Age, taking the upper Tagus basin as a case study. As a preliminary reflection, it focuses on the reasons for the end of lithic production. Lithic studies in this geographical area are scarce and diverse in character and content. The collapse of blade production is the most important element of this technological change. The hypothesis proposed here combine several factors: the collapse of the blade circulation network, the loss of the social significance of lithic items and changes in cereal processing techniques.

Keywords: Chalcolithic; Bronze Age; Lithic Technology.

1. Introduction and objectives

After reaching the highest level of technical complexity and mastery during the Chalcolithic, lithic technology subsequently seems to undergo a widespread decline in Europe and Asia (i.e. Eriksen 2010; Greenfield 2000; Rosen 1996; van Gijn 2010, 199-232). There are many reasons why the phenomenon and its causes have not been properly treated in research (Rosen 1997). Firstly, research has tended to be dominated by the social and material complexity of the Chalcolithic and Bronze Age. Secondly, there is a tacit assumption inherent in cultural evolutionist interpretation that flint technology clearly became obsolete and was replaced by metal tools which, from an a priori and functionalist point of view, were more efficient than stone (van Gijn 2010, 199). And thirdly, the lack of aesthetic qualities and evidence of technical development, have meant that this later industry has only attracted the attention of a small number of technologists, earning it the title of 'the Cinderella of lithic studies' (Van Gijn and Niekus 2001).

Knapped stone tools continued to be used for agricultural tasks (threshing) until the second half of 20th century in Spain (Álvarez and de Andrés 2011) and other countries (p. ex. Whittaker, Kamp and Yilmaz 2009). The use of flint pieces specifically for threshing purposes occurred within living memory. Consequently, flint remained useful for an extended period, however limited to tasks, such as butchering, hunting, woodwork, and thus lost much of its cultural and symbolic meaning. Therefore, the lithic record post-dating the Middle Bronze age is scant or non-existent and lithics often remain unrecorded even if present on Proto-historic and historic sites because they are unexpected.

Tracking the replacement of stone tools by metal in the archaeological record is difficult, as is the detection of metallurgy on small sites. Metal implements were often recycled or kept and therefore are rarely found on sites even if their widespread use is well attested. Thus, the absence of metal on a site does not mean that it was not being used. Taking this two-way reasoning a step further, the absence of lithic items in a domestic context does not necessarily mean the absence of lithic manufacture and use, a fact confirmed by ethnographical evidence. There are several factors to consider when attempting to explain and understand the complex issue of the replacement of lithic industries by metal industries. This subject remains poorly addressed in general, and especially in research within the Iberian Peninsula.

Two of the questions that need to be answered are whether the change was sudden or progressive and when exactly this change took place. The Chalcolithic lithic industry was healthy even following the appearance of copper elements. We can assume that metal use was not generalized and therefore, flint tools did not have metal equivalents.

The study of cut marks on faunal remains in the Balkans and Near East has demonstrated that this type of analysis can track the substitution of stone by metal in butchering in the Middle Bronze age with the introduction of better and more resistant copper alloys (Greenfield 2010). Thus, systematic taphonomic analysis is needed in order to throw light on this important change in Iberian Prehistory.

This study tackles this phenomenon and proposes an hypothesis involving a complex model that includes several factors: firstly, the collapse of the raw materials, knowledge and certain stone implement exchange networks due to significant social, political and economic changes; secondly, the loss of the social meaning pertaining to flint and flint working; and finally, the change and development of cereal processing with the emergence of threshing and the displacement of flint working to distant areas from habitation sites.

In order to throw light on this issue, I have chosen to focus on the upper Tagus Basin in the central part of the Iberian Peninsula (Spain) (Figure 1) where the archaeological record is quite complex for the Chalcolithic and Bronze Age periods. This area is far from the classic reference sites of South-eastern Spain for the research on emergence of social complexity (Bernabeu *et al.* 2006, 97-98). Recent studies (Díaz-del-Río 2004; 2006) show that the upper Tagus basin is a good example of the diversity in socio-political complexity development that occurs in the Iberian Peninsula. Metal work and use are not so clear in this area when compared to others (Díaz-del-Río 2006, 75). Therefore, it is the perfect framework to support that the introduction of metal did not determine the end of flint knapping.

The technological transformation will be described and supported using several case studies and the chronological moment at which this technological transformation took place will be discussed. In general, it must be noted that there is a lack of specific data in order to address this last issue.

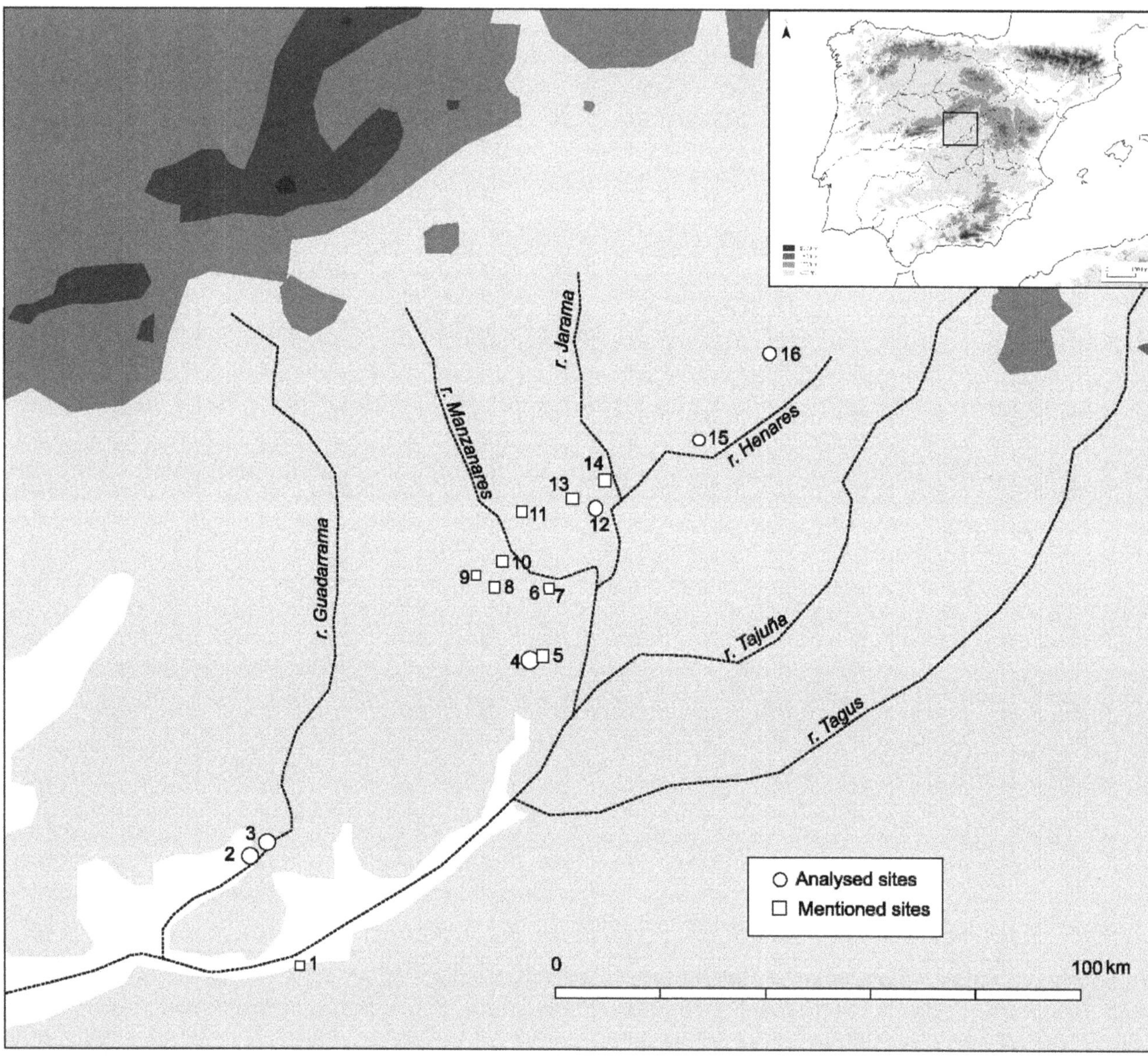

Figure 1. Study area and sites mentioned in this study. 1 - Cero del Bu (TO); 2 - Mejorada I (TO); 3 - Cerro de Marialvares (TO); 4 - Parque Acuático Warner (MAD); 5 - Gózquez de Arriba (MAD); 6 - Fábrica de Ladrillos (MAD); 7 - Cámpo de Fútbol (MAD); 8 - El Ventorro (MAD); 9 - El Juncal (MAD); 10 - El Espinillo (MAD); 11 - El Capricho (MAD); 12 - Casa Montero (MAD); 13 - Camino de las Yeseras (MAD); 14 - Las Matillas (MAD); 15 - KM 34 Barcelona road (MAD); 16 - Ampliación Aguas Vivas (GU). | Source: By the Author.

2. Case studies and methodology

During the past 15 years, the author had the opportunity to analyse several lithic assemblages from the later prehistoric period in the upper Tagus basin. These assemblages were sometimes quite limited in size (29 pieces in some cases). Comparisons between these sites are difficult but they can illustrate some aspects of the general problem. Deficiencies in the meaningfulness of the sample have been addressed by reference to published sources. Some of the studies were conducted as part of research projects and others were part of archaeological interventions in collaboration with other colleagues. Although all of the assemblages were studied using the same methodology, the depth of study is not the same in all cases because of time availability.

All of the assemblages have been studied using a technological approach following the *Operative Sequence* framework (e.g. Bar Yosef and Van Peer 2009) and the author's own adaptation of same (Castañeda 2014, 49-124; forth.).

The sample studied in this work comes from the following sites: Ampliación Aguas Vivas (Guadalajara), Km 34 Barcelona Road-Avón (Alcalá de Henares, Madrid), Casa Montero (Madrid), Parque Acuático Warner (San Martín de la Vega, Madrid), Cerro de Marialvares and Mejorada I (Bargas, Toledo) (Figure 1).

Aguas Vivas (Castañeda and Fernández 2010; Cantalapiedra and Ísmodes 2010) is a complex site covering 58 ha which yielded 286 features and 8566 lithic items. In terms of dating, it spans from the Late Neolithic to the Late Bronze Age (Table 1). It underwent its greatest development during the Chalcolithic phase. While no actual houses were identified for this period, there are plentiful traces of domestic activities, as well as several possible enclosures, mud wall remains, storage pits reused as rubbish dumps, and a lithic workshop which yielded a possible oven for heat treatment and an antler tool for pressure retouch. In addition, there were several votive animal deposits, including the remains of a dog and a deer. These features show interesting parallels with Camino de las Yeseras (San Fernando de Henares, Madrid) (Blasco *et al.* 2007; Liesau *et al.* 2008; 2013) and El Juncal (Getafe, Madrid) (Martínez, López and Moreno 2014). A total of 822 lithic items from 10 features on this site can be related to the site chronology and are included in this analysis (Table 1).

The site of Km. 34 Barcelona Road-Avón is unpublished. It is composed of at least 34 storage/rubbish pit structures that could be a part of a larger site although this remains unproven to date (Víctor Cantalapiedra *pers. comm.*). The relative chronology, constructed on the basis of pottery remains, places the site in the Late Bronze Age (LBA). Both the pottery and lithic finds relate to domestic activities. The lithic assemblage includes 34 items (Table 1).

Casa Montero is a well-known site because of its Early Neolithic phase in which flint outcrops were mined (cf. Díaz-del-Río *et al.* 2010). However, there is no evidence for mining or quarrying on the site during the Middle Bronze Age. Forty-seven structures have been attributed to this phase: apart from two burials, most of the structures are interpreted as storage pits (Castañeda and Criado 2006, 231-32; Consuegra, Gallego and Castañeda 2004, 131). This site has special characteristics that have been considered in this study. As the Bronze Age structures cut the ancient mining shafts, some lithic remains are mixed and often reused. The raw material selection is different in both periods: Neolithic miners searched for a special quality of recrystallized flint from silicification episodes II to IV, while in the Bronze Age chert from episode I was preferred (Castañeda and Criado 2006, 231-32; Bustillo *et al.* 2009). Six structures, yielding 1178 lithic items, are included in this study (Table 1).

Parque Warner (Cantalapiedra *et al.* 2016) includes four storage structures that may be part of Gózquez de Arriba, a Chalcolithic settlement with enclosures (Díaz-del-Río 2001; 2004). In the case of Parque Warner, the pottery found belongs to the Middle Bronze Age. Only one of the structures contained lithic remains (29) (Table 1).

Cerro de Marialvares and Mejorada I are two sites that were included in a research project on Bronze Age communities in Bargas (Toledo) (Uriarte *et al.* 2011). Thanks to an archaeological survey, these two sites were excavated, but no lithic analyses have been published.

Cerro de Marialvares is located on the summit of a small hill that includes an outcrop of heterogeneous flint. It has been interpreted as an Early to Middle Bronze Age (EMBA) lithic workshop (Ignacio Montero *pers. comm.*). The 331 lithic remains included in this study are from three horizontal levels (Table 1).

In contrast, Mejorada I has been interpreted as an habitation site. One radiocarbon date (Ignacio Montero *pers. comm.*; IDEArq 2016) allows us to situate the occupation between the Chalcolithic and Early Bronze age. A total of 238 items, from several horizontal levels and one Chalcolithic negative feature, are included in this study.

All of these sites, except Marialvares, are composed of negative structures the functions of which have been inconsistently interpreted, i.e., storage and rubbish pits, habitations, burials, ovens, etc. Because the structures do not overlap, it is impossible to build a stratigraphy, a common problem on Late Prehistoric sites in this study area (e.g. Díaz-del-Río 2001, 131-42). In addition, lithic items often occur without pottery or any other remains that might allow for relative or absolute dating.

Aguas Vivas, Casa Montero and Mejorada I have been dated by radiocarbon dating and the other assemblages are dated relative to the pottery chronology. This study only uses material from structures with a chronological attribution (Table 1).

Although this is an heterogeneous and problematic sample it can contribute to research on Chalcolithic and Bronze Age lithic technology in this area. Therefore, the results must be completed and contrasted in the future with more and better data.

Table 1. Distribution of the analysed material. Number of lithic items by sites and chronological phases. AV: Aguas Vivas; K34: Km. 34 Barcelona Road; CM: Casa Montero; MV: Cerro Marialvares; MJ: Mejorada I; PW: Parque Acuático Warner. CHAL: Chalcolithic; EMBA: Early and Middle Bronze Age; LBA: Late Bronze Age. | Source: By the Authors.

Chronological phase	AV	KM34	CM	MV	MJ	PW	Total*
CHAL	720	0	0	0	225	0	945
EMBA	51	0	1178	331	13	29	1602
LBA	51	34	0	0	0	0	85
TOTAL**	822	34	1178	331	238	29	2632

*χ^2 value: 1332.95. A normal distribution for the sample is rejected.

** χ^2 value: 2450.27. A normal distribution for the sample is rejected.

3. Features of lithic technology during the Chalcolithic and Bronze Age

Research on Chalcolithic lithic technology in the Iberian Peninsula is very uneven and focuses mainly on long blade and arrowhead production outside the area selected for this study (i.e. Clop *et al.* 2001; 2010; Gibaja *et al.* 2006; 2012; Pelegrin 2006, Morgado and Pelegrin 2012). Only a handful of works provides detailed information for central Iberia (i.e. Baquedano *et al.* 2000; Blasco *et al.* 2007, 156-58; Luque y Baena 1994; Priego and Quero 1992).

Regarding the Bronze Age, the situation is even less satisfactory and detailed lithic analysis is rare (i.e. Carrion *et al.* 2005-07; Gibaja 2003).

Therefore, it is difficult to synthetize the general features of the lithic material for these periods. However, there are often tacit references to the marked contrast between high specialization and skill levels in Chalcolithic lithics and 'poor' or *'regressive, old-fashioned'* Bronze Age lithics. In fact, the knapped lithic industry disappears from discussions in textbooks dealing with the Bronze Age. This fact, together with the small number of lithic technologists that work on the Holocene record, means that the published data is often useless from a technological point of view.

The technological changes that occur in lithic technologies between the Chalcolithic and the Late Bronze age can be summarised as follows:

- gradual disappearance of the blade industry
- disappearance of leaf-shaped pieces and long blade production
- disappearance of heat treatment
- change in raw material selection criteria
- dramatic decrease in the number of lithic remains on sites
- disappearance of lithic material in funerary deposits
- duality between blade and flake production reduction sequences

All of these changes result in a marked contrast between Chalcolithic and Late Bronze Age lithic industries.

Blade technology in the Chalcolithic was of high quality and is characterised by its complex execution. Raw materials were carefully selected and heat treatment was often used to improve and homogenise rocks of lower quality and to facilitate pressure flaking and retouch. Blades usually occur in smaller quantities than flakes and are found in broken or used condition. Selected, visually attractive blades are found in burials (i.e. Bueno *et al.* 1999, 148-49). Cores, rejuvenation flakes and crests are only found on sites with workshops. Occasionally, structures interpreted as having been used for heat treatment are also found on these sites (Cantalapiedra and Ísmodes 2010; Luque and Baena 1994, 179-80).

Chalcolithic settlements usually show evidence of blade production. Researchers agree with the fact that pressure-flaked blade production was a specialised activity during the Chalcolithic and the Bronze Age, where blade products were circulated via complex trade or exchange networks.

Aguas Vivas was a pressure-flaked blade production centre during the Chalcolithic. The blades were eight to 10 cm in length. The presence of conjoined blades and cores, together with rejuvenation tablets and crests and a structure for heat treatment (structure 2050; Cantalapiedra and Ísmodes 2010: Figure 23) indicate a specialized manufacturing process on site. Other Chalcolithic blade production centres, such as El Espinillo (Baquedano *et al.* 2000: 87), El Ventorro (Madrid) (Priego and Quero 1992), Las Matillas (Díaz-del-Río *et al.* 1997) and Campo de Fútbol (Luque and Baena 1994), occur within the current study area. In Camino de las Yeseras, where another type of lithic workshop has been recorded, there is little evidence for blade production in the Chalcolithic to date (Ríos 2010: 503; Liesau *et al.* 2013, 143-44).

For the remaining studied sites, the presence of blade production is not so clear, because the presence of blades on a site does not necessarily mean that they were manufactured on site. Blades usually occur in a small number of cases and tend to appear fractured and retouched, with significant use wear. There is no production or maintenance waste or cores. Due to this lack of information, it is difficult to create a model for the circulation of blades from the production centres.

Since the beginning of the Bronze Age, it seems that these products were progressively disappearing and by the Late Bronze Age the regression is clearly evident (Table 2) (i.e. Baquedano *et al.* 2000, 87; Carrión *et al.* 2005-07, 151, 162). Perhaps the know-how involved in these productions was only possessed by a few specialized people, and access to this knowledge was limited to few selected individuals. The rest of the group may have been supplied by these specialists through a mechanism of exchange. It is important to determine, through more detailed and systematic analysis, if there was a knapper in each settlement during each period or not. When there are fewer specialists in an area, a higher level of specialization is reached, the knowledge and the goods become more difficult to acquire and the interchange networks become longer and more fragile. Therefore, based on the data available at the moment, we can say that the demand for and significance of these blades were strong enough to maintain a fragile network that depended on a few highly skilled individuals.

Table 2. Percentages of blade production remains in the studied sample. RT: rejuvenation tablet; BPI: blade production items; CHAL: Chalcolithic; EMBA: Early and Middle Bronze Age; LBA: Late Bronze Age. | Source: By the Author.

	Core	RT	Crest	Tool	Blade[1]	BPI[2]
CHAL n:156/945	3.21	1.92	8.33	33.97	52.56	16.51
EMBA n:62/1602	1.61	0	6.45	16.13	75.81	3.87
LBA n:18/85	0	0	5.56	38.89	55.56	21.18

[1]Blades and fragments of blades.

[2]Percentage of the items from blade production in the lithic assemblage considered.

Although there is considerable variation in the size and type of sites considered in this study, absolute numbers indicate that there is a reduction in the number of cores, crests and rejuvenation tablets between the Chalcolithic and the Late Bronze Age (Table 2). In the absence of additional data, three scenarios can be proposed. The first one, scenario A, includes the consideration of blade knappers as specialists for the hole period. Therefore, a decreasing number of blade production remains, would means the decreasing number of blade knappers, and that the production centres were far from the area. This case could indicate that blade circulation networks were getting weaker during Early and Middle Bronze age and perhaps they collapsed in Late Bronze age. An in-depth analyses of raw material circulation is needed to define these networks in the area.

The second case, scenario B, considers that blade production was quotidian and the access to knowledge of knapping was open and unlimited to every member of the group. Following this hypothesis, the disappearance of blade production remains from the sites can be explained by the movement of blade production away from the domestic sites if the need of blades continued. In this case, the tools should have been made in blade blanks even in LBA.

The third, scenario C, is the substitution of the demand of blades, independently of the level of specialisation needed to produce blades.

The sample analysed shows that the need for blade fragments continued during all the considered period (Table 3). The tools were made both on flakes and blade blanks, but there is a special preference for blades to make the sickle or threshing elements. In LBA the cereal processing tools seem to maintain the production of blades.

Table 3. Percentages of the preference of flake or blade blanks on tool manufacture and on specifically sickle and/or threshing board elements. | Source: By the Author.

	Tool Blank			Sickle/Treshing Elements	
	Flake	Blade	Frag.	Flake	Blade
CHAL (n: 107/72)	47.66	49.53	2.80	36.11	63.89
EMBA (n: 29/16)	62.07	34.48	3.45	50	50
LBA (n: 16/7)	46.15	53.85	0	28.57	71.43
Total (n: 149/95)	50.34	46.98	2.68	37.89	62.11

Available data for LBA lithics from other sites are scarce. Fábrica de Ladrillos assemblage, however, reflects the absolute preference for flakes in the EMBA (89.3 per cent) and LBA (100 per cent) manufacture of sickle elements, but also the residual presence of some blades (four), together with the dramatic general reduction of the number of lithic elements at the end of this period (Carrión *et al.* 2005-07).

As a consequence, blades continued being useful in LBA, though very scarce. For the moment, we only can affirm that both scenarios A and B are possible.

The case of **long blade production** (more than 15 cm long and fragments more than 20 mm wide) has been studied in several areas of the Iberian Peninsula such as Portugal, and southern and north-eastern Spain (i.e. Clop *et al.* 2001; Gibaja *et al.* 2010; Morgado and Pelegrin 2012; Pelegrin 2006). It is a lithic marker of craft specialisation and long distance exchange. These types of product are usually present in burials in these regions and they often show signs of use (Gibaja *et al.* 2010, 445). They were produced by means of reinforced pressure technique that implies a complex preparation of the core.

Within the study area these long blades are very scarce, considering the low reliability of the lithic descriptions in the literature. Only four fragments, including one crest blade, have been documented in Aguas Vivas, perhaps seven additional fragments from the Chalcolithic structures at El Espinillo (Baquedano *et al.* 2000, Figures 25.2, 25.4, 25.15, 26.14, 33.19 and 39.12), one from Las

Matillas (Díaz-del-Río *et al.* 1997, 101) and two from Cerro de Juan Barbero (Martínez-Navarrete 1984, 21). It is not clear how many and which type of items are present in Camino de las Yeseras (Ríos 2010, 503).

Even though the sample under consideration here is limited, it seems that long blade production centres were located far from this area. In other parts of Iberian Peninsula and Europe. This kind of production has been interpreted in terms of its social meaning, social differentiation and prestige (i.e. van Gijn 2010, 140; Manolakakis 1996, 122-23). This level of complexity was not present in the interior of the peninsula (i.e. Díaz-del-Río 2004, 117; 2006; Díaz-Andreu 1995, 28), or maybe these items lacked a social significance in the area covered by this study. In any case, more detailed analysis is needed. Keeping in mind the scarcity of data regarding long blades in the upper Tagus basin, all known finds occur in Chalcolithic contexts and none are from burials (Aliaga 2010).

The high level of complexity of both blade and long blade techniques required very careful selection of **raw materials** to suit pressure knapping. Blade production depends critically on two factors: high skill in core shaping and raw material reliability. Where this need for quality raw material could not be satisfied**, heat treatment** was often used to improve the quality of rocks (Terradas and Gibaja 2001). Heat treatment appeared in the Late Palaeolithic but its incidence is higher on Neolithic and Chalcolithic sites (Table 3). It is difficult to recognize heat treatment, so it is possible that this factor has been under represented in publications by non-technologists, taking into account that this area presents abundant outcrops of opaline which gloss is often very similar to heat treated flint.

The geographical framework chosen for this work is characterized by, and well-known for, the abundance of siliceous outcrops of continental genesis. The use of controlled heat treatment in areas of abundance indicates that the quality of the outcrops exploited was probably lower than required. A notable exception is the high quality opaline flint from episodes II to IV of the Casa Montero silica formation (Bustillo *et al.* 2009). The pieces manufactured from this type of flint were usually not heat treated, as for example the Early Neolithic blade production from the flint mine (Castañeda *et al.* 2015, 481), the leaf-shape sickle from El Capricho (Díaz-del-Río, Gibaja and Castañeda 2014) and some leaf shaped elements and arrowheads from Camino de las Yeseras (Liesau *et al.* 2013, 144). However, there is no enough data about the raw material used for blade production from Chalcolithic to Late Bronze Age (LBA) in the area.

The sample examined in the current study shows a dramatic change in the use of heat treatment between Chalcolithic sites (76.68 per cent) and sites from the beginning of the Bronze Age (24.63 per cent) (Figure 2), although blade production seems to have progressively receded (Table 2). In explaining this, several factors need to be considered such as the gradual decrease in lithic items and the quality of the flint used. The same factors are responsible for the proportion of heat-treated pieces in the Late Bronze Age (LBA) sample (90.91 per cent). On the one hand, the size of the sample is quite small to consider the results (66 pieces), and, on the other hand, the absence of knapping waste in LBA sites can hinder the comparison of data.

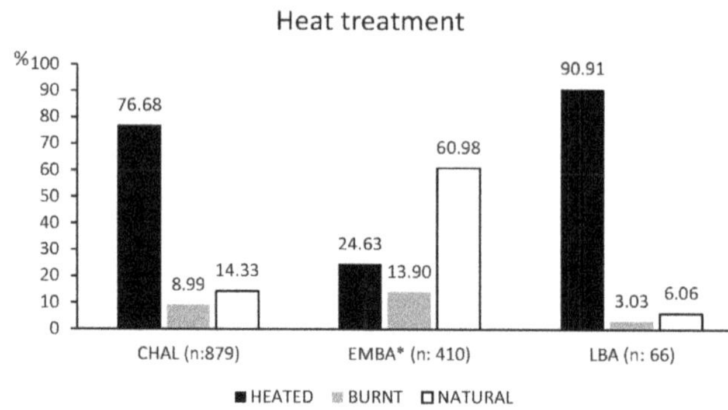

Figure 2. percentages of flint pieces with heated, burnt and natural surfaces for each period considered. CHAL: Chalcolithic; EBA-MBA: Early-Middle Bronze Age (*Casa Montero 1178 pieces are not included); LBA: Late Bronze Age Source: By the Author.

In any case, together with the other elements analysed in this study, the general tendency shows that something had changed in lithic production at the beginning of the Bronze Age in this area. The disappearance of long blade technology and its quality requirements are directly related to the end of heat treatment and the use of new raw material selection criteria oriented towards new needs.

Leaf-shaped implements and arrowheads were both produced from flake blanks by means of pressure retouch, and they are characteristic Chalcolithic products. Based on data provided by the literature, **leaf-shaped implements** are scarce in this area, and some of them were used as sickles (Díaz-del-Río, Gibaja and Castañeda 2014). Although these pieces have evident aesthetic qualities, their use and rejuvenation allows us to interpret them as tools in daily use (Díaz-del-Rio, Gibaja and Castañeda 2014, 368), but their scarcity suggests that they represent a specialized tool type. There is a significant difference between blade sickles like the specimens found in Aguas Vivas (Castañeda and Fernández 2010, 103) and leaf-shaped sickles such as those from El Capricho (Figure 3.3) and Camino de las Yeseras (Figure 3.5). This fact probably illustrates the complexity of a form of cereal working that disappeared in the Early Bronze Age rather than a prestige element which served to differentiate people. Despite the limited presence of knapped material in funerary contexts in this area (Aliaga 2010), these pieces do not appear in burials and therefore are likely to have lacked any special social meaning.

The examples of leaf-shaped elements from the study area come exclusively from Chalcolithic domestic contexts.

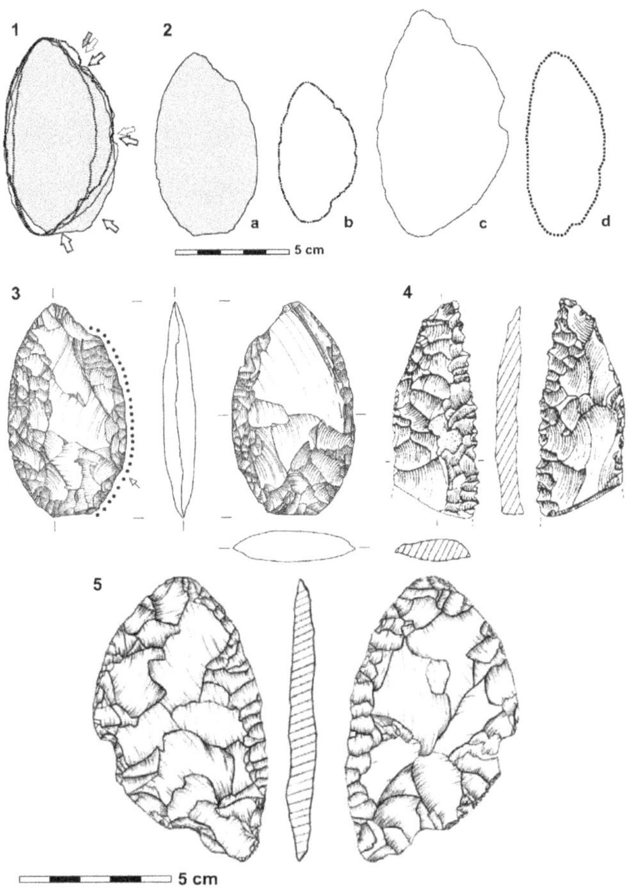

Figure 3. Leaf-shaped implements mentioned in this study. 1 - comparison of silhouettes and position of notches (probably resulting from use). 2 - silhouettes of the pieces in relation to scale: a - El Capricho sickle (based on Díaz-del-Río, Gibaja and Castañeda 2014: 369, Figure 2); b - Yeseras (based on Ríos 2013: 389, Figure 268); c - Yeseras (based on Liesau et al. 2013: 144, Figure 4.c); d - Yeseras (based on Ríos 2013: 399; Figure 269). 3- El Capricho (Díaz-del-Rio, Gibaja and Castañeda 2014: 369, drawing by Paco Fernández-Dibujantes de Arqueología); 4 - El Espinillo (Baquedano et al. 2000: 105, Figure 25.11, without data of the author of drawing); 5 - Camino de las Yeseras (version by Irene Ortiz published in Liesau et al. 2013:144, Figure 4.c)

The example from El Capricho has been studied in detail (Díaz-del-Río, Gibaja and Castañeda 2014) (Figure 3.3). There are at least eight pieces from Camino de las Yeseras (Ríos 2010, 396) (Figure 3.2 b-d) found in the context of a pressure retouch workshop. One of them exhibits macroscopic traces of cereal polish (Ríos 2010, 399). At least one is recorded from El Espinillo (Baquedano *et al.* 2000, 105, Figure 25.11; 162, lam X.C) (Figure 3.4) and at least one published from El Juncal (Getafe, Madrid) (Martínez *et al.* 2014: 155, Figure 6). These two pieces are different in shape: they are denticulated and narrow. The descriptions and drawings available from El Ventorro (Madrid) are not sufficiently clear to affirm the presence of these types of artefact (Priego and Quero 1992, 162, 180).

Macroscopic analysis suggests that the specimens from El Capricho, Yeseras and El Espinillo (Figure 3.3-5) were made of the same Casa Montero recrystallized type 1 flint (Bustillo *et al.* 2009; Díaz-del-Río, Gibaja and Castañeda 2014, 367; Ríos 2010, 409). The proximity to the outcrop (approx. five km) and the existence of a pressure retouch workshop, support the hypothesis that Camino de las Yeseras could be the origin of these pieces. This important feature, and the great similarity in shape between artefacts from El Capricho and Yeseras (approx. 10 km apart) (Figure 3.1-2) suggest that the leaf-shaped implements on the three sites could have been made by the same knapper. A more detailed analysis is needed to confirm this hypothesis and to determine the relationship networks in the area.

In conclusion, the disappearance of these elements may reflect a dramatic change in cereal working instead of a loss of social meaning, in contrast to other areas of Europe where daggers and other elements of more technical complexity were made and used (i.e. van Gijn 2010, 199-232).

Arrowhead production and use could also be considered in the domestic sphere. As they were needed for hunting, the people who hunted must have controlled the arrowhead making knowledge. Arrowhead workshops, or at least the presence of unfinished products or preforms, are relatively frequent in the sample studied and also in published literature: most of them occur in Chalcolithic contexts but they also occur in the Early and Middle Bronze Age (i.e. Marialvares). An arrowhead workshop existed at Aguas Vivas (Castañeda and Fernández 2010) where 58 arrowheads have been documented for various phases of fabrication. To date, the workshop of Camino de las Yeseras is probably the best studied and published, with several preforms and arrowheads in different stages of fabrication, and knapping tools (Liesau *et al.* 2013). El Ventorro (Madrid) clearly possesses another arrowhead workshop in the context of a wider lithic production (Priego and Quero 1992, 112) and El Espinillo also yielded arrowheads in different manufacture stages (Baquedano *et al.* 2000, 65, 103, Figure 23).

In contrast to other lithic remains, arrowheads tend to be highlighted, drawn and photographed in publications. Arrowheads occur more frequently than blades and leaf-shaped implements, even at small sites such as Marialvares or Mejorada I. The variability in their shape could reflect different levels of skill, less quality exigence or could mean that they are the by-products of a workshop. During the analysed period, projectile points from the same site often present different qualities of raw material, and even the use of stone other than flint, e.g. quartzite, in the Bronze Age (Fernández 2014, 118, pers. comm.) or bone (López 2001, 253) and, even in the LBA, they are often heat treated. These features reinforce the idea that they were products of the domestic sphere which utilised different available raw material, because the need for arrowheads was permanent and perhaps it was the availability of good flint or heated preforms that was interrupted or difficult. A comparative analysis between arrowhead raw materials and chronology would help our understanding of the moment when the availability of good flint went into decline.

Together with these specialized and *high* quality productions, coexisted domestic **production of small standardized flakes** made of local raw materials. These flakes were produced by means of bifacial centripetal cores or parallel series cores. Data from the studied sample in Table 4 shows that, centripetal cores decrease and parallel series cores increase between Chalcolithic and Early-Middle Bronze Age. This fact suggests increasing pragmatism and standardization in flake production.

Table 4. percentages of flake core reduction types in the studied sample. H: hierarchical; NH: non-hierarchical; CHAL: Chalcolithic; EMBA: Early-Middle Bronze Age; LBA: Late Bronze Age. | Source: By the Author.

		Centripetal		
	Parallel series	H	NH	Total Centripetal
CHAL (n:18)	22.22	33.33	44.44	77.78
EMBA (n:12)	58.33	16.67	25	41.67
LBA (n:1)	0	100	0	100

This production was present on every site, except burials, and may not have depended on only a few highly skilled craftsman. Moderate skill is required to carry out this type of production, the outputs of which tend to be small and of standardised size.

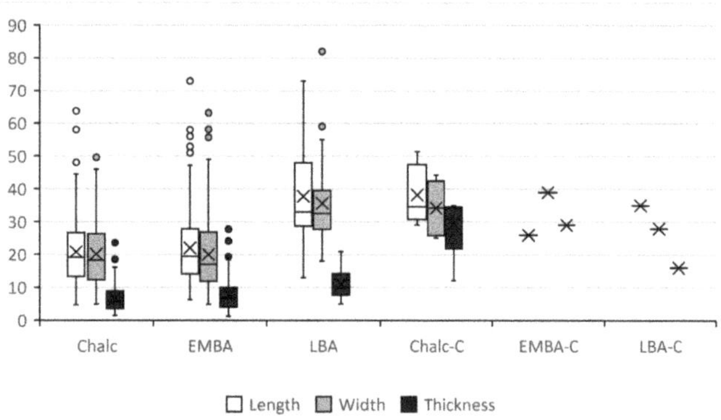

Figure 4. size of flakes and cores for the analysed sample. Chalc: Chalcolithic flakes; EMBA: Early Middle Bronze Age flakes; LBA: Late Bronze Age flakes; Chalc-C: Chalcolithic cores; EMBA-C: Early-Middle Bronze Age cores; LBA-C: Late Bronze Age cores. | Source: By the Author.

Unfortunately, these products are usually not represented, well described or interpreted in published sources. They are described as being of '*poor*' manufacture. However, this type of production can be defined as standardized, *specialized* and pragmatic. As a consequence of this pragmatism, core blanks were selected according to size from the beginning (Luque and Baena 1994, 202). The initial volume of cores allows the serial production of small flakes of predetermined dimensions (Figure 4). This is the reason why flake cores of the Chalcolithic and Bronze Age are described in the literature as being exhausted (Baquedano *et al.* 2000; Liesau *et al.* 2014). Regardless of the site or its date, the cores are always of a similar small size and are consistent with the size of the products and local acquisition of raw materials.

In contrast to the flint required for blade production, the upper Tagus valley outcrops are suitable for the production of small flakes. Therefore, raw material supply for this industry was usually local. These cores and flakes were not usually heat treated to improve the quality of the raw material as it was unnecessary. The requirements for this kind of production are likely to have been high resistance to wear and fracture. This assumption is supported by the preference for better silicified materials, larger grain size as well as the increasing use of quartzite (i. e. 28 per cent in Km. 34 Barcelona Road). In the Casa Montero Middle Bronze Age lithic sample, the selection of raw material used was different to that produced by the Neolithic mine. While Neolithic miners chose the most opaline and micro-cryptocrystalline varieties from silica episodes II to IV, Bronze Age knappers preferred the best silicificate chert from episode I (Bustillo *et al.* 2009, 178-80; Castañeda and Criado 2006, 231).

In any case, it is clear that aesthetic qualities were not instrumental in raw material selection. This may be one of the reasons why this type of production is described as being '*poor*' in appearance.

Small flake products do not occur as funerary goods in burials or maybe they are not recorded or remarked in publications. In the Chalcolithic, only blades and sometimes cores are found in such contexts (Aliaga 2010). This could mean that the operative sequences of blades on the one hand, and of small flakes, on the other hand, did not only differ radically in terms of raw material selection criteria and the level of skill needed, but also in terms of their social significance for the groups that used them. The characteristic lack of goods in Bronze Age burials makes it difficult to evaluate any change in social meaning attached to knapped lithics.

5. Timing of the change

In the absence of a wider geographical analysis for the Iberian Peninsula, the selected study area has inherent difficulties due to the nature of its archaeological record.

One of the most important features of Chalcolithic and Bronze Age sites in this area is the absence of stratigraphic sequences as most of the sites are composed of assemblages of negative structures which vary in nature and which do not intersect (Díaz-del-Río 2001). For this reason, discussions regarding the construction of a regional series are difficult (Blasco 1997; Díaz-del-Río 2001). Moreover, relative chronologies have been built based on the ceramic and metal productions and significant problems arise regarding overlapping.

The dated sites generally lack lithic studies that relate the chronology. The most serious ones analyze the lithic assemblages globally divided in chronological phases (i.e. Baquedano *et al.* 2000; Carrión *et al.* 2005-07). As a result, it is very difficult to use data from published sources. Moreover, there is an assumption that associates the presence of blades or blade technology with the Chalcolithic. In the absence of pottery or dating, it may be, that some Early Bronze Age material have been classified as Chalcolithic.

In this study, which will hopefully lead to more detailed research in the future, there are insufficient data to state precisely when the change in lithic production took place. There are clear differences with the Late Bronze Age but for the moment it is impossible to affirm whether the change was gradual or abrupt. Regression in blade production might support the first model, while other features suggest the second.

The data obtained for the sample suggest that there was an initial moment of change at the beginning of the Bronze Age that included the radical cessation of the manufacture of long blades and leaf-shaped implements.

During the Early and Middle Bronze Age, blade production became uncommon in this area, as part of a general phenomenon, and the blade circulation network was probably declining and fragile.

During a second period of change, in the Late Bronze Age, knapped lithic items practically disappeared from domestic sites and the only knapped production that survived was standardized small flake production. Arrowheads are occasionally found.

In addition, the arid episode documented in Europe and southeastern Spain at 4.2 ky BP (i.e. López *et al.* 2014), may well have impacted on cereal processing or may have played a role in transforming circulation networks in the Upper Tagus basin, for example.

6. Discussion

The demise of blades and leaf-shaped implements, points to an important change in the social perception of knapped flint: aesthetic qualities and special value were abandoned in favour of pragmatism. More detailed analysis is needed to properly understand the implications of this fact, but it is important to note that at the onset of metal use, at least blade production still had a special social value. Therefore, the search for greater efficiency in butchering or cutting was not the reason for the demise of knapping.

The work of researchers in other European regions suggests that the substitution of lithic tools by metal ones for butchering indicates that the efficiency of the new metal tools was the reason for the end of flint knapping (i.e. Greenfield 2000). But due to the lack of more systematic and detailed use wear research, it is difficult to define which lithic tools were used for butchering before this change occurred. It seems that the lithic items that disappeared in the Upper Tagus basin were not those used for butchering. The question, therefore, becomes more complex and interesting.

Therefore, the disappearance of good quality products meant the end of craftsmen, the collapse of flint interchange networks, and the demise of the transmission of that knowledge. The sparse evidence for metalworking in this area, in contrast with other parts of Iberia (Díaz-del-Río 2006, 75), may support the hypothesis that the replacement of flint by metal was a separate phenomenon from the collapse of knapping production.

Interestingly, cereal processing continued to be an activity where stone dominated the toolkit. Leaf-shaped sickles were never abundant, but they disappear in favour of the so called 'sickle elements' which are often denticulate. It is important to define why we consider leaf-shaped sickles as special items: is it because of their scarcity, their aesthetic appearance or both? Are they really harder to make than a blade sickle? Are they made of exogenous or special raw materials? If they coexisted with blade sickles, we must ask why two tool types existed for a similar purpose.

On the other hand, the 'sickle elements' are not always blade fragments (Table 3). Unfortunately, this modest tool has not attracted enough interest of researchers, however as an alternative hypothesis, I suggest that these small pieces could be interpreted as threshing board elements. However, for the moment there is a lack of systematic use wear analysis. This hypothesis is consistent with standardized production of small flakes, with a particular desire for hard-wearing raw materials, pragmatism in the reduction sequence and extremely eroded edges of some pieces.

The development of threshing might also explain the lack of stone implements on domestic sites. They would have been made at outcrops and only repaired in the domestic areas. Threshing requires the existence of surplus cereal production. Certain studies indicate that threshing originated in the Chalcolithic (Gibaja *et al.* 2012; Clemente-Comte *et al.* 2014) or earlier in the case of the Levant (Whittaker, Kamp and Tilmaz 2009). We can suggest that in the upper Tagus basin its generalization can coincide with the Middle Bronze Age.

7. Concluding Remarks

Changes in knapped lithic technology between the Chalcolithic and Late Bronze age seems to be more complex than the straightforward replacement by metal tools and they reveal the concurrence of several different factors.

This paper proposes that increasing craft specialisation lead to the fragility of the blade production network. High quality raw materials and the high levels of skill needed became accessible to few people. Under these conditions, any change could destroy the fragile system.

The loss of social meaning pertaining to flint, socioeconomic, palaeoclimatic and demographic changes, together with the emergence of new techniques for cereal processing, create a complex and interesting framework for research.

The Bronze Age lithic industry should not be considered as 'poor' or 'primitive', but rather as pragmatic and standardized, well adapted to a specialized need. While in-depth analysis is still in demand, the emergence of threshing, can be proposed as one of the causes for this transformation.

The sites presented here are only a sample that bring to light the problems associated with addressing this topic due to traditional indifference on the part of researchers towards the Bronze Age lithic industry. Systematic and multidisciplinary research is needed, especially in the upper Tagus basin where the archaeological record for Late Prehistory is abundant and complex.

Acknowledgements

This research was undertaken while the author held a Post-Doctoral Fellowship for Foreign Researchers funded by the Paris Council at the Unité Mixte de Recherche (UMR) 8215 *Trajectoires de la sedentarisation à l'etat* and the University Paris I-Panthéon Sorbonne.

I would like to thank Pedro Díaz-del-Río and Susana Consuegra for their help and for facilitating access to the material and data for the Bronze Age phase at Casa Montero that was studied at the Institute of History of the Spanish National Research Council (CSIC) as part of an agreement between the *Consejería de Cultura y Deportes de la Comunidad de Madrid*, the CSIC, and *Autopistas Madrid Sur Concesionaria Española, S.A.* for the research, preservation and diffusion of the Casa Montero archaeological site. I have been permitted to publish data from Marialvares and Mejorada thanks to Ignacio Montero and Antonio Uriarte under agreement with the Diputación de Toledo and Bargas council for the study of Bronze Age communities in the municipality of Bargas (Toledo). The data from Km 34 Barcelona Road has been included thanks to Víctor Cantalapiedra (GEA Arqueólogos S.L.).

I would like to thank to Juan Manuel Vicent for his help and access to the IDEArq Radiocarbon Database (http://www.idearqueologia.org/). Finally, I wish to express my gratitude to Jacobo Fernández and Patricia Ríos for their availability to answer questions regarding Cerro del Bu and Camino de las Yeseras respectively.

Bibliography

Aliaga, Raquel. "Sociedad y mundo funerario en el III y II milenio A.C. en la región del Jarama." PhD diss., Universidad Autónoma de Madrid, 2010.

Álvarez, David and Herrero, María de Andrés. "El impacto de los conjuntos de trilleros en el registro paleolítico de la Meseta. Una aproximación etnoarqueológica." *Complutum,* 22, 1 (2011): 177-191.

Baquedano, Mª. Isabel, Blanco, Francisco, Alonso, Pablo and Álvarez, Dolores. "El Espinillo: un yacimiento calcolítico y de la Edad del Bronce en las terrazas del Manzanares." *Arqueología, Paleontología y Etnografía* 8 (2000): 58-136.

Bar Yosef, Ofer. and Van Peer, Philip. "The '*Chaîne Opératoire'* Approach in Middle Paleolithic Archaeology." *Current Anthropology.* 50, 1 (2009): 103-131.

Bernabeu, Joan, Molina, Lluis, Díez, Agustín and Orozco, Teresa. "Inequalities and power. Three millennia of prehistory in Mediterranean Spain (5600–2000 cal BC)." In *Social Inequality in Iberian Late Prehistory,* BAR IS1525, edited by Pedro Díaz-del-Río and Leonardo García-Sanjuán, 97-116. Oxford. British Archaeological Reports, 2006.

Blasco, Mª. Concepción. "La Edad del Bronce en el interior peninsular. Una aproximación al II Milenio AC en las cuencas de los ríos Duero y Tajo." *Cuadernos de prehistoria y arqueología de la Universidad Autónoma de Madrid* 24 (1997): 59-100.

Blasco, Mª. Concepción, Delibes, Germán, Baena, Javier, Liesau, Mª del Coro and Ríos, Patricia. "El poblado calcolítico de Camino de las Yeseras un escenario favorable para el estudio de la incidencia campaniforme en el Interior Peninsular." *Trabajos de Prehistoria,* 64,1, (2007): 151-153.

Bueno, Primitiva, de Balbín, Rodrigo, Barroso, Rosa, Rojas, J.M., Villa, R., Félix, R. and Rovira, Salvador. "Neolítico y Calcolítico en Huecas (Toledo): el túmulo de Castillejo: campaña de 1998." *Trabajos de Prehistoria* 56, 2 (1999): 141-160.

Bustillo, Mª. Ángeles, Castañeda, Nuria, Capote, Marta, Consuegra, Susana, Criado, Cristina, Díaz-Del-Río, Pedro, Orozco, Teresa, Pérez-Jiménez, José Luis and Terradas, Xavier. "Is the Macroscopic Classification of Flint Useful? A Petroarchaeological Analysis and Characterization of Flint Raw Materials from the Iberian Neolithic Mine of Casa Montero." *Archaeometry* 51, 2 (2009): 175-196.

Cantalapiedra, Víctor and Ísmodes, Alicia, eds. *El yacimiento arqueológico de Aguas Vivas: Prehistoria reciente en el valle del río Henares (Guadalajara),* Arqueología y Patrimonio 1. Madrid: Ediciones La Ergástula, 2010.

Cantalapiedra, Víctor, Fernández, Francisco Javier, Castañeda, Nuria and Ísmodes, Alicia. "Intervención arqueológica en el yacimiento 'Parque Warner': problemática y resultados." In *Actas de la I Reunión de Arqueología Madrileña. Alcalá de Henares 2014,* 179-90. Madrid: Dirección General de Patrimonio Cultural de la Comunidad de Madrid, 2016.

Carrión, Elena, Baena, Javier, Blanco, J.F. and Blasco, Mª. Concepción. "La industria lítica." *Estudios de prehistoria y arqueología madrileñas,* 14-15 (2005-2007):125-166.

Castañeda, Nuria. "Metodología de análisis del material lítico de la mina de sílex neolítica de Casa Montero." In *Casa Montero (Madrid). Una mina de sílex del Neolítico Antiguo,* edited by Susana Consuegra and Pedro Díaz-del-Río. Madrid: Consejo Superior de Investigaciones Científicas, forthcomming.

Castañeda, Nuria. "El trabajo del sílex. La mina del Neolítico antiguo de Casa Montero y su sistema técnico." PhD diss., Universidad Autónoma de Madrid, 2014.

Castañeda, Nuria and Criado, Cristina. "La industria Lítica de Casa Montero (Vicálvaro, Madrid); resultados preliminares." In *Do Epipaleolítico ao Calcolítico na Península Ibérica.* Actas do *IV Congresso de Arqueologia Peninsular. Faro, 14 a 19 setembro de 2004,* edited by Nuno Bicho and Hugo Verísssimo, 229-234. Faro: Universidade do Algarve, 2006.

Castañeda, Nuria and Fernández, Francisco Javier. "El conjunto lítico de Aguas Vivas". In *El yacimiento arqueológico de Aguas Vivas: Prehistoria reciente en el valle del río Henares (Guadalajara),* Arqueología y Patrimonio 1, edited by Víctor Cantalapiedra and Alicia Ísmodes, 87-108. Madrid: Ediciones La Ergástula. 2010.

Clemente-Conte, Ignacio, Mazzucco, Niccolò and Soares, Joaquina. "Instrumentos para siega y procesado de plantas desde el Calcolítico al Bronce antiguo de Chibanes (Palmela, Portugal)." *Trabajos de Prehistoria* 71, 2 (2014): 330-342.

Clop, Xavier, Gibaja, Juan Francisco, Palomo, Antoni and Terradas, Xavier. "Un utillaje lítico especializado: las grandes láminas de sílex del noroeste de la Península Ibérica." *Bolskan* 18 (2001): 311-322.

Consuegra, Susana, Gallego, Mª. Mar and Castañeda, Nuria. "Minería neolítica de sílex de Casa Montero (Vicálvaro, Madrid)." *Trabajos de Prehistoria* 61, 2 (2004): 127-140.

Díaz-Andreu, Margarita. "Complex societies in Copper and Bronze Age Iberia: a reappraisal." *Oxford Journal of Archaeology* 14, 1 (1995): 23-39.

Díaz-del-Río, Pedro. *La formación del paisaje agrario: Madrid en el III y II milenios BC.*, Arqueología, Paleontología y Etnografía 9. Madrid: Consejería de Bellas Artes, 2001.

Díaz-del-Río, Pedro. "Copper Age ditched enclosures in central Iberia." *Oxford Journal of Archaeology* 23, 2 (2004): 107-121.

Díaz-del-Río, Pedro. "An appraisal of social inequalities in Central Iberia (c. 5300-1600 cal BC)." In *Social Inequality in Iberian Late Prehistory,* BAR Int. S1525, edited by Pedro Díaz-del-Río and Leonardo García-Sanjuán, 67-79. Oxford: BAR Publishing, 2006.

Díaz-del-Río, Pedro, Consuegra, Susana, Capdevila, Enrique, Capote, Marta, Casas, Cristina, Castañeda, Nuria, Criado, Cristina and Nieto, Aurora. "The Casa Montero Flint Mine and the Making of Neolithic Societies in Iberia." In *Mining in European History and its Impact on Environment and Human Societies. Proceedings for the 1st Mining in European History-Conference of the SFB-HIMAT* (Innsbruck 2009), edited by Peter Anreiter, Gert Goldenberg, Klaus Hanke, Rüdiger Krause, Walter Leitner, Franz Mathis, Kurt Nicolussi, Klaus Oeggl, Ernst Pernicka, Mario Prast, Jörg Schibler, Ingo Schneider, Harals Stadler, Thomas Stöllner, Gerhard Tomedi and Peter Tropper, 351-55. Innsbruck: Innsbruck University Press, 2010.

Díaz-Del-Río, Pedro, Consuegra, Susana, Peña Chocarro, Leonor, Márquez, Belén, Sampedro, Cristina, Moreno, Ruth, Albertini, Daniele and Pino, Beatriz. "Paisajes agrarios prehistóricos en la Meseta Peninsular: el caso de 'Las Matillas' (Alcalá de Henares, Madrid)." *Trabajos de Prehistoria* 54, 2 (1997): 93-111.

Díaz-del-Río, Pedro, Gibaja, Juan Francisco and Castañeda, Nuria. "Análisis tecnológico y funcional del cuchillo calcolítico de la cabaña de 'El Capricho' (Barajas, Madrid)." In *Actas de las IX Jornadas de Patrimonio Arqueológico en la Comunidad de Madrid, 2012,* 367-371. Alcalá de Henares: Dirección General de Patrimonio Histórico y Museo Arqueológico Regional, 2014.

Eriksen, Berit Valentin, ed. "*Lithic Technology in Metal Using Societies: Proceedings of a UISPP Workshop, Lisbon, September 2006.*" Højbjerg: Jutland Archaeological Society Publications, 2010.

Fernández, Jacobo. "*Aproximación al conocimiento de la Edad del Bronce en la Cuenca Media del Tajo: el Cerro del Bu (Toledo)*". Madrid: Audema ediciones, 2014.

Gibaja, Juan Francisco. "Hoces líticas argáricas del sudeste peninsular," *Rampa* 6 (2003): 115-136.

Gibaja, Juan Francisco, Crespo, Manuel, Delibes, Germán, Fernández, Julio, Fraile, Cristina, Herrán, José Ignacio, Palomo, Antoni and Rodríguez, José Antonio. "El uso de trillos durante la Edad del Cobre en la Meseta española. Análisis traceológico de una colección de denticulados de sílex procedentes del 'recinto de fosos' de El Casetón de la Era (Villalba de los Alcores, Valladolid)." *Trabajos de Prehistoria* 69, 1 (2012): 133-148.

Gibaja, Juan Francisco, Palomo, Antoni, Francès, Joan and Majó, Tona. "Les puntes de sageta de l'hipogeu calcolític del carrer Paris (Cerdanyola): caracterització tecnomorfològica i funcional." *Cypsela* 16 (2006): 127-133.

Gibaja, Juan Francisco, Terradas, Xavier, Palomo, Antoni and Clop, Xavier. "La industria lítica del IV/primera mitad II milenio cal BC en el Noreste de la península Ibérica: contextos funerarios versus contextos domésticos." *Munibe* 32 (2010): 440-451.

Greenfield, Haskel J. "Animal bone fragmentation and the origins of metallurgy in the central Balkans." In *Technology, Style and Society: Contributions to Innovations between the Alps and the Black Sea in Prehistory*, BAR Int. S854 edited by Lolita Nikolova, 93-96. Oxford: British Archaeological Reports, 2000.

CSIC. "IDEArq." Accessed November, 9, 2016. http://www.idearqueologia.org/.

Liesau, Corina, Blasco, Concepción, Ríos, Patricia, Vega, Jorge, Menduiña, Roberto, Blanco, J. Francisco, Baena, Javier, Herrera, Teresa, Petri, Aldo and Gómez, José Luis. "Un espacio compartido por vivos y muertos: El poblado calcolítico de fosos de Camino de las Yeseras (San Fernando de Henares, Madrid)." *Complutum* 19, 1 (2008): 97-120.

Liesau, Corina, Rios, Patricia, Aliaga, Raquel, Daza, Aránzazu, Llorente, Laura and Blasco, Concepción. "Hut structures from the bell beaker horizon: housing, communal or funerary use in the Camino de las Yeseras site (Madrid)." In *Current researches on Bell Beakers. Proceedings of the 15th International Bell Beaker Conference: From Atlantic to Ural. 5th - 9th May 2011-Poio (Pontevedra, Galicia, Spain),* 139-152, edited by Mª Pilar Prieto and Laure Salanova. Santiago de Compostela: Copynino-Centro de Impresión Digital, 2013

López, Juan Antonio. "El trabajo del hueso, asta y marfil." In *Y acumularon tesoros: mil años de historia en nuestras tierras: Valencia, Murcia, Castellón, Alicante, Barcelona, 2001-2002,* 247-58. Valencia: Caja de Ahorros del Mediterráneo, 2001.

López-Sáez, José Antonio, Sánchez, Francisca Alba, Nájera, Trinidad, Molina, Fernando, Pérez, Sebastián, and Sabariego, Silvia. "Paleoambiente y sociedad en la Edad del Bronce de La Mancha: la Motilla del Azuer." *Cuadernos de Prehistoria y Arqueología de la Universidad de Granada* 24 (2014): 391-422.

Luque, Manuel and Baena, Javier. "La industria lítica." In *El horizonte campaniforme de la región de Madrid en el centenario de Ciempozuelos*, edited by Concepción Blasco, 173-226. Madrid: Universidad Autónoma de Madrid, 1994.

Manolakakis, Laucence. "Production lithique et émergence de la hiérarchie sociale: l'industrie lithique de l'Enéolithique en Bulgarie (Première moitié du IVe millénaire)." *Bulletin de la Société préhistorique française* 93, 1 (1996): 119-23.

Martínez-Navarrete, Mª. Isabel. "El comienzo de la metalurgia en la provincia de Madrid: la cueva y el cerro de Juan Barbero (Tielmes, Madrid)." *Trabajos de Prehistoria* 41, 2 (1984): 17-127.

Martínez, Victoria, López, Óscar and Moreno, Ester. "El poblado calcolítico de *El Juncal* (Getafe, Madrid)." In *Actas de las IX Jornadas de Patrimonio Arqueológico en la Comunidad de Madrid, 2012,* 149-158. Alcalá de Henares: Dirección General de Patrimonio Histórico y Museo Arqueológico Regional, 2014.

Morgado, Antonio and Pelegrin, Jacques. "Origin and Development of Pressure Blade Production in the Southern Iberian Peninsula (6th–3rd Millennia B.C.)" In *The Emergence of Pressure Blade Making: From Origin to Modern Experimentation* edited by. Pierre M. Desrosiers, 219-35. New York: Springer, 2012.

Pelegrin, Jacques. "Long blade technology in the Old World: an experimental approach and some archaeological results." In *Skilled production and social reproduction*, edited by Jan Apel and Kjel Knutsson, 39-68. Uppsala: Societas Archaeologica Upsaliensis, 2006.

Priego, Carmen and Quero, Salvador. *El Ventorro, un poblado prehistórico de los albores de la metalurgia,* Estudios de Prehistoria y Arqueología Madrileñas 8. Madrid: Museos Municipales del Ayuntamiento de Madrid, 1992.

Ríos, Patricia. *"Territorio y sociedad en la Región de Madrid durante el III milenio AC: el referente del yacimiento de Camino de las Yeseras."* PhD diss., Universidad Autónoma de Madrid, 2010.

Rosen, Steven A. "The decline and fall of flint." In *Stone Tools: Theoretical Insights Into Human Prehistory*, edited by George H. Odell, 129-58. New York: Springer Science & Business Media, 1996.

Rosen, Steven. A. *Lithics after the Stone Age: a handbook of stone tools from the Levant.* Walnut Creek: Rowman Altamira, 1997.

Terradas, Xavier and Gibaja, Juan Francisco. "El tratamiento térmico en la producción lítica: el ejemplo del Neolítico medio catalán." *Cypsela* 13 (2001): 31-58.

Uriarte, Antonio, Pereira, Juan, Montero, Ignacio, Martínez-Navarrete, Mª. Isabel and Carrobles, Jesús. "La Edad del Bronce en el bajo Guadarrama (Bargas, Toledo): Trabajos de Prospección Arqueológica 2005-2007." In *Tecnologías de información geográfica y análisis arqueológico del territorio. Actas del V Simposio Internacional de Arqueología de Mérida*, Anejos de Archivo Español de Arqueología 59, edited by Vitorino Mayoral and Sebastián Celestino, 69-77. Madrid: Consejo Superior de Investigaciones Científicas, 2011

Van Gijn, Annelou. *Flint in focus. Lithic Biographies in the Neolithic and Bronze Age*. Leiden: Sidestone Press, 2010.

Van Gijn, Annelou and Niekus, Marcel J. L. Th. "Bronze Age settlement flint from Netherlands. The Cinderella of lithic research." In *Patina: essays presented to Jay Jordan Butler on the occasion of his 80th birthday*, edited by Willy Hendrike Metz; Bernhard Leopold van Beek and Hannie Steegstra, 305-20. Amsterdam: Groningen, 2001.

Whittaker, John, Kamp, Kathryn and Yilmaz, Emek. "Çakmak Revisited: Turkish Flintknappers Today." *Lithic Technology* 34, 2 (2009): 93-110.

Portugal - The Tagus Estuary region.
Source: José Martinho Lourenço.

Chapter 11

The Tagus Estuary Region in a Transitional Period: An Outsider's Reflection on Regional Late Bronze Age

Rodrigo Banha da Silva

FSCH-Universidade Nova de Lisboa / CHAM- Portuguese Centre for Global History, rodrigobanhadasilva@gmail.com

Abstract: Recent years provided scarce data on Late Bronze Age occupations in the Tagus Estuary Region, despite the revitalizing interest in this subject. Past data was therefore addressed, however present perspectives still rely heavily on well established readings from the 1990's, where pottery evidence allowed the distinction between two evolutionary stages in the regional Late Bronze Age, with correspondence with two different territorial settlement patterns. The author focused his reflection on the empirical basis of these interpretations, and argues on the pertinence of including this former aspect in the historical evaluation, highlighting effective Phoenician presence in the Tagus Estuary as the main factor for societal change.

Keywords: Tagus Estuary; Late Bronze Age; "ornatos brunidos" pottery; settlement patterns.

1. Opening remarks

In recent years, the transitional periods of the Late Bronze Age (henceforth LBA) and the first moments of the Iron Age in the Tagus River estuary and its adjacent areas saw an increase in attention by Portuguese investigators, which provided fresh readings on the scarce available data. Regional synthesis concerning the various issues at stake for the last centuries of the 2nd millennium (henceforth M.) BCE and the early 1st M. BCE have been published, mainly by João Luís Cardoso (Cardoso 2004, 2015), with important contributions by Ana Margarida Arruda (1994, 2015; Vilaça and Arruda 2004; Arruda and Sousa 2014) and others (Sousa 2016), to quote only the most significant ones.

The region, taken as a whole, has a long tradition in Portuguese studies on LBA and the early Iron Age, since the discoveries of the so-called "*Urn field Culture*" of Alpiarça by Mendes Correia in the 1910's, defined only later in the 1930's, when new finds occurred (Vilaça, Gonçalves and Cruz 1999). This *culture* was later reconfigured by Gustavo Marques under the designation of "*Alpiarça Culture*" (Marques 1972, 1994; Marques and Andrade 1974).

Simultaneously, Bronze Age finds were made in several earlier Chalcolithic settlements explored in those central decades of the 20th century, such as Pragança (Cadaval), Ota or Pedra do Ouro (Alenquer) (Kunst, 1995), enlarging our knowledge of the effective territorial occupation during the period. Also the relevant work of Eduardo da Cunha Serrão on the categorization of a significant pottery group designated as "ornatos brunidos" (geometric burnished decoration) found at Lapa do Fumo (Sesimbra) cave, a ceramic type that, since identified, became a useful tool in attributing contexts to LBA (Serrão 1958, 1959, 1970; for further bibliography Cardoso 1995a and Almeida 2014).

Wider and thorough knowledge of the Bronze Age in the Alpiarça area was later achieved in the 1970's and early 1980's by a group of investigators from the German Archaeological Institute, which studied previous material and made new excavations on settlements and their correspondent necropolis, refining the available data (Kalb 1980; Kalb and Höck 1981-1982, 1982, 1985, 1988; Kunst 1995).

When in 1982 the discovery of Tapada da Ajuda (Lisbon) was haphazardly made, after earthworks. Remaining parts of the site were archaeologically excavated until 1987, and sadly destroyed soon after (Cardoso *et al.* 1980/1981; Cardoso 1987; Cardoso and Silva 2004: 227-229). Nevertheless, it became a key site, since it allowed Cardoso to understand the diachronic evolution of LBA material culture in the region (Cardoso and Carreira 1993, 199; Cardoso 1995c, 2004, 2010-2011, 2014; 2015; Cardoso and Silva 2004). The series of C14 dates from the site pointed out to a period of occupation from the 14th to early 10th c. BCE, most likely between the 13-12th c. BCE (Cardoso and Silva 2004: 233; Cardoso 2010-2011, 70), or 13th-11th c. BCE (Cardoso 2015, 151; for criticism on chronological inferences about C14 series from Tapada da Ajuda see Félix 1999, 716, note 4). The type of pottery and other associated material culture, together with the domestic architecture and settlement pattern, turned out to be the defining model for an earlier stage of the region's LBA: a phase I, corresponding to some specific features in clear opposition to the characteristics of the later stage, defined as phase II (Cardoso and Carreira 1993, 199; Gomes 1998; Cardoso 1999/2000, 2004, 2010-2011, 2014, 2015; Cardoso and Silva 2004, and others- see bibliography).

The last two to three decades saw several other relevant developments on readings of the LBA in the region.

On the one hand, empirical data grew slightly, mainly thanks to the outcome of a new archaeological *praxis* in Portugal, implying regular and frequent preventive or rescue excavations and surveys, accompanied by a more solid organizational and legal structure than before. On the other hand, both old and new information was approached again.

The numerous publications from João Luís Cardoso, alone or in collaboration (see bibliography list), and the ones performed by Ana Margarida Arruda, alone or in collaboration (idem) are simply the highlights of a much broader interest on the subject which also has to include other names, such as Raquel Vilaça (Vilaça *et al.* 1999; Vilaça and Arruda 2004; Vilaça 2007), João de Senna-Martinez (1990, 1994a, 1994b, 2002, 2007, 2013; Melo and Senna-Martinez 2001) or António Monge Soares, for assorted reasons but mainly because of new C14 dating work (see regional table in Cardoso 2015).

In any case, it is of the utmost justice to state that Lisbon University's various professors, and its archaeological investigation centre, Uniarq, are directly responsible for the advent of a younger generation of proficient researchers (one can quote as examples, from a much broader list, Elisa de Sousa, João Pimenta or Rui Boaventura). This academy is, as well, responsible for the state of the art of readings on LBA and early Iron Age in the Portuguese Lower Tagus and Estuary region, including the adjacent areas of Ribatejo and Estremadura.

2. Some remarks on landscape conditions

The Tagus Estuary's intimate relationship with the Ocean, and the importance in the past of navigation through the *circa* 90 km long section of the river connecting its mouth to the Ribatejo area near Santarém, are the primary issues to take into account in the moment of addressing the geography of the region. Those are aspects of obligatory mention, patent in all the studies concerning regional relationships occurring in the Bronze and Iron Ages, and are in fact the major factors for explaining the region's specificities at that time (Arruda 1994, 1999-2000, 2005, 2015; Gomes 1998; Vilaça and Arruda 2004; Cardoso 2004, 2015; Senna-Martinez 2013; Sousa 2016 - picked from a much longer list).

Taking in account the geography of the south and central zones in the western façade of the Iberian Peninsula, the coast's morphology doesn't provide many areas for inland penetration. From the extreme south to the centre, only three points provide it, south to north: the Mira river and the large estuaries of the Sado and Tagus rivers.

Emphasis has to be given to the fact that from the bulk of penetration points in the whole western façade of Iberia, the Tagus is the most navigable river and, along with the Galician "rias" on the extreme NW, the most profound and wide penetration point on the coast (Daveau 1994, 24).

Looking slightly north of Lisbon, the coast displays abrupt cliffs until Peniche, when sandy smooth beaches show up, and ancient Holocene lagoons make their appearance until Nazaré, shortly after (Idem; Ramos-Pereira, Trindade and Neves, 2005). This coastal configuration conditioned all external influxes coming by sea, from the 2nd to 1st M. BCE.

Other elements of major landscape importance are the areas adjacent to the Tagus river.

The north corresponds to the Lisbon Peninsula, limited south and east by the river, west by the Atlantic Ocean, and north by an artificial parallel linking Peniche (still an island at the time), the southern limit of the Mira de Aire-Candeeiros mountain ridge and Santarém.

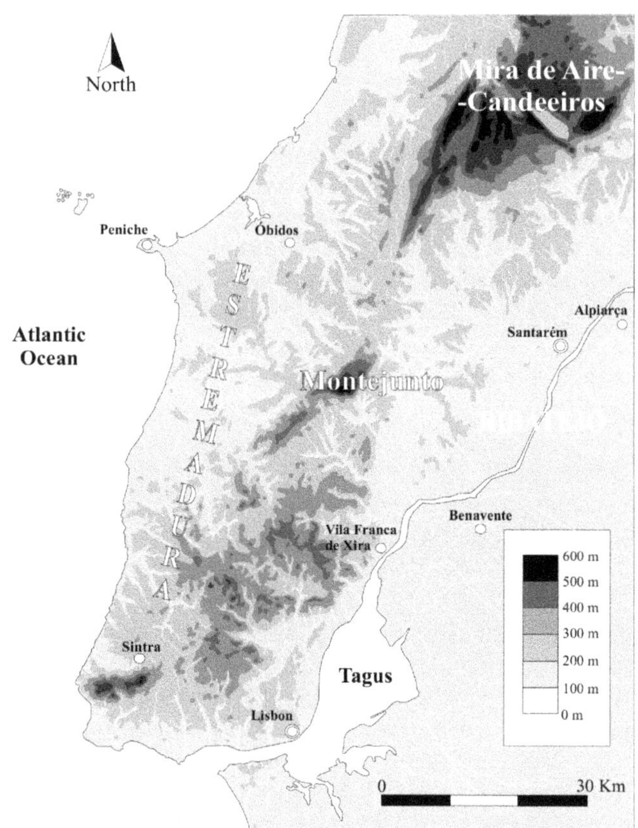

Figure 1. Geography of the Tagus Estuary and its adjacent areas. Source: By the Author.

The mountain range of Mira de Aire-Candeeiros, with its Montejunto prolongation, constitutes a neat central ridge across this peninsula, establishing a sharp natural division between the parts nearer to the Tagus and the ones closer to the Atlantic. Most of the inland landscape is of carsick origin, with sandstone and limestone, the soils being generally poor. The exceptions are the southern parts of Monsanto's basaltic mantle and Sintra's small mountainous area, both integrating Lisbon's volcanic complex, and the majority of alluvial fillings of small river and brook valleys, especially fit for agriculture.

On the other hand, the whole inland territory is a succession of small hills and plains. This, along with the Mira de Aire-Candeeiros and Montejunto mountain ranges, made circulation by land difficult, especially north to south and east to west, between the Tagus riverside area to the Atlantic shore.

For the reasons aforementioned, the importance of small rivers and major streams for human settlement was enormous, particularly for proto-historical communities, since they provided various essential resources, but also because their valleys facilitated itineraries for communication and circulation. That is the case of the Colares brook and of the Sizandro river on the west Atlantic coast, Trancão and Alenquer-Rio Grande da Pipa river systems connected from the east to the Tagus, or the Alcântara river system and almost all the small rivers and major brooks of the southern part of the Lisbon Peninsula (Jamor, Oeiras, amongst others).

The left bank of the Tagus Estuary displays a different landscape from the northern riverside. Being part of the Setúbal Peninsula, Arrábida's mountain range marks to the south the visual limit of an alluvial Tertiary plain area, with an indented rivershore facing the Tagus, providing various important bays. Further upriver, starting in the Benavente area, already in Ribatejo, Tagus quaternary alluvial plains and a continuous line of terraces dominate the river valley landscape until Alpiarça. Water-logged areas are quite frequent and of vast proportions on the Estuary's left bank. Soils are, again, poor, but only until Benavente. The valleys of the Coina river and Muge brook allowed penetration to the south, but it was the hydrological system of the Sorraia river that apparently assumed first role in communications further south, since it directly connected the area to the heart of Upper Alentejo.

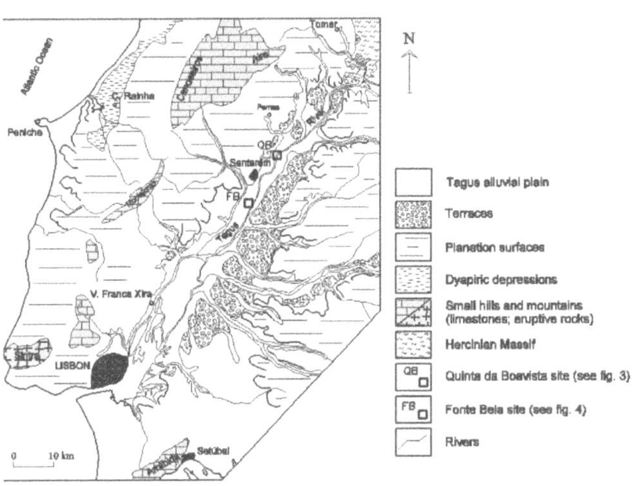

Figure 2. Geomorphology of the Tagus Estuary and adjacent areas of Lisbon's and Setubal's peninsulas and Portuguese Lower Tagus, (according to Ramos *et al.*, 2002).

Despite the lack of paleo-environmental studies for the Tagus Estuary, relevant differences in regard to the past certainly occurred, especially referring to the period between the 2nd to 1st M. BCE. A global idea of the situation circa 1000 BCE was graphically essayed, among others, by João de Senna-Martinez (1998, 220, Figure 1, see under, extract), reflecting work on landscape evolution performed by geographers from Lisbon University (Daveau 1994). Considering their large dimensions, the relevance of the ancient lagoons becomes obvious, specially north to Peniche in the West Atlantic coast, and, for the same reason, the Trancão and Alenquer-Rio Grande da Pipa hydrological systems, inside the Tagus Valley.

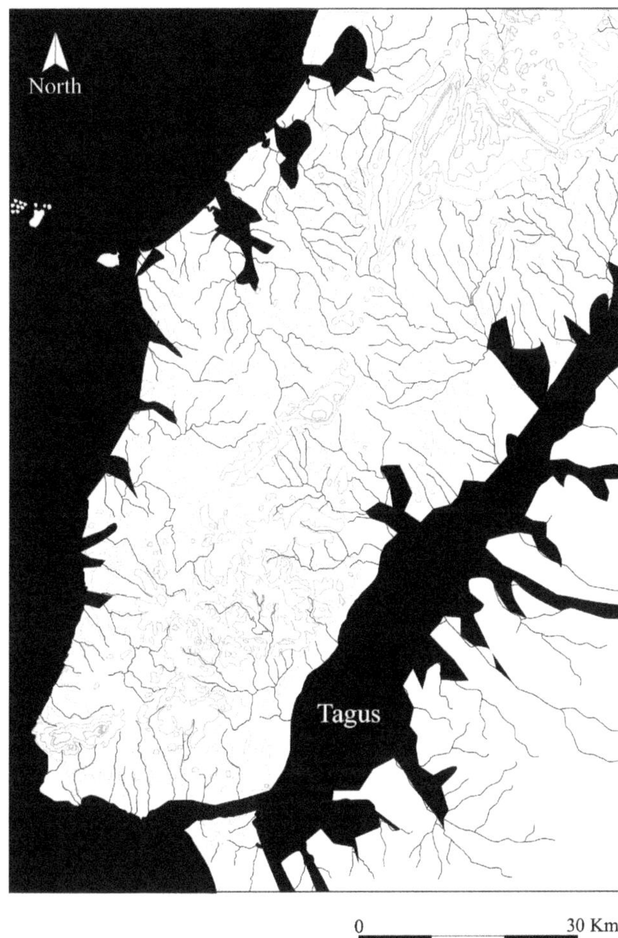

Figure 3. The Tagus Estuary circa 1000 BCE (ac. Senna-Martinez, 1998, 220, Figure 1, reelaborated).

Nevertheless, this kind of essay on paleo-geography, although appealing, was no more than a cunningly built approach, for it simply considers all values under 10 or 5 meters as water-logged or even underwater. Consequently, its value is only to provide an impressionistic look at the whole picture. As an example, if we zoom it in downtown parts of Lisbon, the site of Praça da Figueira becames underwater, as here LBA occupational levels were established on the shore of an ancient water line at absolute height values of +2,50/2,60-2,90/3.04 m (Silva 2013, 47, Figure 7, 53, Figure 14).

Appart from the urgent need for real paleo-environmental studies, the crucial geographical position of the Tagus Estuary is the key factor, as mentioned by various authors (Arruda, Cardoso, Félix, Senna-Martinez, Vilaça and others - see bibliography). It was this condition that allowed a region without raw materials for bronze metallurgy to become one of the main production areas of artifacts and ingots, as it became also the main gateway for interchange and trade, favoured by fluxes from the southern copper zone in Alentejo, tin from Beiras and the contacts established through maritime navigation both with the European North Atlantic coastal areas and (slightly later) the Mediterranean (Vilaça 2007; Arruda 2015; Cardoso 2015).

On top of those issues, salt (Cardoso 1999-2000) and alluvial gold were also present in several spots on the region: Quinta do Marcelo finds and analysis demonstrated it thoroughly (Barros 1998; Cardoso 1999-2000, 385-287), as eventually Penha Verde also did (Cardoso 2010-2011b; Cardoso and Sousa 2014). The same happened with gold explored in High Ribatejo and Beira, which followed the same path of circulation through the Tagus Estuary.

3. Before LBA in the Tagus Estuary

The gap between the first and middle centuries of the 2nd M. BCE, which is to say the Middle Bronze Age (henceforth MBA), possesses what might be designated as a degree of archaeological invisibility that makes interpretation somewhat risky (Jorge 1991, 387; Cardoso 1999/2000, 2004, 2005). The whole Bronze Age data for most stages is known almost exclusively with basis on old excavations, survey recollections of decontextualized material and, finally, isolated finds, especially those of metallic artifacts, where conditions of deposition are, for most cases, completely unknown (Vilaça and Arruda 2004: 25; Vilaça 2006; Arruda and Sousa 2015; Sousa 2016, 388).

One has to stress also that MBA occupations were in various cases detected in settlements already being used for a very long time, sometimes covering a continuous sequence from the Late Neolithic or Early Chalcolithic to the Bronze Age (Kunst 1995, 125-126). But, if the previous stages are well characterized through a structural panoply of different functional profiles, the occupations that matter here aren't, and the more detailed cases of LBA occupation referred after Penha Verde (Sintra) (Cardoso 2010-2011b; Cardoso and Sousa, 2014; Cardoso 2015) and Penedo do Lexim (Mafra) (Sousa 2000; Sousa *et al.* 2004; Cardoso and Sousa 2014; Cardoso 2015; Sousa 2016) advocate for caution when reading the significance of some of those presences.

In spite of those problematics, investigators dedicated to the study of this stage in the region's history point out that the data is consistent with a progressive phase covering the Early and Middle Bronze Age stages, where Chalcolithic territorial strategies progressively loose their relevance, as happened too with their respective "religious-ideological structure", a time when previous hill-top fortified settlements as Zambujal (Torres Vedras), Vila Nova de São Pedro (Azambuja), Pragança (Cadaval), Ota or Pedra do Ouro (Alenquer), among others, become definitely abandoned (Jorge 1981, 386-387; Cardoso 2004; Cardoso 2015).

The causes for this disarticulation of previous territorial patterns, at use for such a long time, are complex, and Michael Kunst and João Luis Cardoso linked them to a possible demographical crisis (Kunst 1995; Cardoso 1999-2000, 367-369; 2004, 2005). The origins of this crisis were eventually attributed to an ecological degradation occurring during the first half of the 2nd M.BCE, in parallel with one attested in the Guadalquivir Valley (Cardoso 1999-2000, 367-369; 2005, 8). As the last author also points out, no record of that kind is available for the Tagus case due to the lack of paleo-environmental studies (idem). Nevertheless, and as Cardoso emphasizes, it becomes quite evident that regional settlement density was decreasing strongly from the Chalcolithic to the Bronze Age. Thus, demographical issues arise as one of the probable key explanations for space occupation changes produced during the 2nd M. BCE (Cardoso 1999-2005, 2004, 2015).

Apparently, other settlements made their appearance then, located instead in smooth hill slopes or lower areas, and the fact that no fortification work of any kind is known so far from MBA sites (Idem) shows that strategies involved in defining settlement at that time were not concerned with visual control of landscape or some sort of status statement through the erection of monumental architectures (Jorge 1991).

The fact is that, as Susana Oliveira Jorge pointed out long ago, MBA societies, in this case the ones from the Tagus Estuary region, are more strongly involved in inter-regional relations of exchange than before, and the perception is that the geographical scale of those interactions between large regions becomes noticeably enlarged, prestige goods produced in gold, silver, copper and bronze being an archaeological expression of the phenomenon (Jorge 1991). On the other hand, and still following Jorge's reflection path, an improved social hierarchy or complexification within societies during the 2nd M. BCE can still be defended on the basis of a shift in the means of its manifestation, from Chalcolithic funerary and monumentalized settlement expressions to the so called "metal deposits" or "hiding places" (Idem; Vilaça 2006; Sousa 2016, 398).

In any case, the lack of available data for the region is evident, and the best way to demonstrate it is the fact that only one settlement, Catujal (Loures), has so far been fully published (Cardoso and Carreira 1993; Cardoso 1994; Carreira 1997).

This site cares for further reflection, with an impact on current perspectives on MBA settlement patterns, for it is located in a high ground position with a very good defensive condition and vast visual control over the surrounding landscape, namely over the Tagus delta (Cardoso 1999-2000, 360; 2005).

Destroyed by "urban development" in 1982, the site provided a C14 date, ICEN - 843 - 2028-1752 BCE, with an intersection in 1892 BCE (Cardoso 1999-2000, 369; 2005, 8-9). As Cardoso stresses, bell-beaker pottery is already absent here (Idem). Also of strong significance is the presence of Alentejo's "SW Bronze Age" pottery or ceramic type models, namely "Santa Victória" cups and strangled neck bottles (idem). This feature was put forward by the author in relation with other similar published occurrences of SW Iberia ceramic artifacts on the Lower Tagus and/or Estremadura, as the one of a vase used as grave good in Pedra do Ouro (Alenquer), a SW style cup from Lapa do Suão (Bombarral) cave, another of "Santa Victória" type from Cova da Moura (Torres Vedras) cave, and a three nipple appendix vase from a cave-like shelter located under the hill-top Chalcolithic settlement of Rotura (Setúbal), similar to another found in a grave in Monte Novo dos Albardeiros (Reguengos de Monsaraz) (Cardoso 1999-2000, 369; 2005, 9). These evidences, along with alien imported metallurgical type models (idem: 369-371; Carreira 1994; Vilaça 2006), clearly demonstrate the vigor of connections of the interregional exchange at place between the Tagus Estuary and SW Iberia, and the influence of the former in the region during the MBA (Carreira 1997; Cardoso 2005).

Similar arguments, in this case metallurgical, prove the great vitality of relationships with the Portuguese Beiras (Vilaça and Arruda 2004; Cardoso 2004, 2015; Arruda 2015; Sousa 2016).

4. LBA in the Tagus Estuary region

As with the MBA, the beginning of the LBA is only attested in the whole region through one study case, the already mentioned site of Tapada da Ajuda. This brings again the question of how to explain such scarcity of data for the period between the 13th-11th c. BCE.

As referred already, Ajuda served to define a model for LBA evolution, where the strategy applied in settlement location would have been made following earlier Bronze Age preoccupations, that is to say, in pursuit of a low ground location, on a smooth slope, mainly concerned with agricultural exploitation. This would be emphatically demonstrated through Ajuda's case, with its local conditions of high quality soil and water presence. Malacological remains documenting nearby gathering, mamalogical bones of *bos, ovis* and *sus domesticus* as testimony of cattle breeding, and a high quantity of flint sickle elements proving extensive cereal crop, were the economical basis of the local LBA community (Cardoso 2004, 177; Cardoso and Silva 2004; Cardoso 2010-2011, 71; Cardoso 2015, 150-151; criticism- Sousa 2016, 389-390).

This kind of site implied an intensive agricultural exploitation, all year round, therefore generating a surplus of cereal (Cardoso 2004, 177; Cardoso 2015, 150-151). Criticism on the significance of the high concentration of flint sickle elements in Ajuda, and consequently on the aforementioned agricultural surplus, is simply misplaced, because the juggling one can practice with numbers doesn't mask the obvious archaeological importance infered by the presence of hundreds of those elements on site, and its implications. The existence of silos for storage in some other regional settlements is another strong argument in favour, invoked by Cardoso to reaffirm the existence of this surplus (Cardoso 2015, 150).

This economic specialization suggested by the former author is, consequently, plausible, and, according to him, implies the existence in the area of a central-place elite location, managing and controlling exchange and trade (Cardoso 2004, 2015).

This reading on LBA territorial patterns has been well synthetized by Elisa de Sousa (2006, 388), and her approach still marks the overall regional interpretations (Cardoso 2010-2011; 2015): on one side, high ground settlements with a visual control over the landscape, where elite-groups reside or perform their activities - in a regular or seasonal manner - and some specific artifacts occur, namely metal objects (gold, silver, bronze) and geometrical burnished decorated pottery ("ornatos brunidos"), a type of settlement thoroughly present in the region's archaeological record; on the other, lower ground settlements, sometimes designated as "farms" or "small farms" in the tradition of Gustavo Marques (Marques and Andrade 1974), in which we include the wider and more complex Tapada da Ajuda. This last model would have emerged during LBA I, and survived until LBA II as documented by numerous sites such as Praça da Figueira-Encosta de Sant'Ana (Lisbon), Moinho da Atalaia (Amadora), Abrunheiro, Alto das Cabeças, Quinta Nova de Santo António (Oeiras), Quinta do Percevejo (Almada) (Sousa 2016, 389), Anços and Funchal (Sintra) (Cardoso and Carreira 1996: 340) Adenaia (Vila Franca de Xira - a LBA I site?) (Pimenta and Mendes 2015) and Quinta da Aramenha (Cartaxo) (Tereso and Ferreira 2007), places devoted to activities such as agriculture, animal breeding and seafood recollection, in any case intended to supply centers of power located on high ground (Sousa 2016, 389).

To be fair, apparently the territorial patterns of settlement between LBA I and II are hard to distinguish for an outsider. In fact, if the existence of the only known "low ground" LBA I site, Tapada da Ajuda, already implies its dependency on a contemporary "high ground" LBA I, and, as observed, known LBA II "low ground" places were dependent on "high ground" contemporary ones, doesn't that mean that LBA I territorial strategy is no different from LBA II?

The need to readdress Tapada da Ajuda is therefore necessary, for it is the only place surely dated from LBA I, and in particular because of the question of the whereabouts of the "central-place" from which it was supposedly dependent: as far as we know, no such place has been found on the right bank of the Tagus Estuary, to which to relate Tapada da Ajuda with.

Regardless of these questions, it becomes clear through information given by Cardoso, that it is hard to look at Ajuda as a "farm" or "small farm" (Vilaça and Arruda 2004, 27; Félix 1999, 2006), the term "small village", or something of the sort, being more appropriate (in this sense Cardoso 2015). The fact is that, despite the extensive destruction observed in the 1980's, previous survey work had already identified a wide area of findings covering circa 20000 square meters (Cardoso and Silva 2004), too large for just one or two closely linked "small farms", and better suited to several more. This is still visible today on the spot for anyone who visits the place. Since spatial organization wasn't for sure concentrated, it consequently admits the theory of a multi-familiar community of wide, albeit unknown, proportions.

A closer look at Tapada da Ajuda provides other kind of data. The recognized LBA I occupation area is, in fact, located on a smooth hill slope, covering the tiny "valley" of a small water line, especially suited for agriculture. From here, part of the Tagus valley can be seen, as well as part of the Alcântara valley and the small paleo-bay that survived at the brook's end until the 18th c. AD. All these features can be observed in spite of the settlement's discretion in the landscape. Tapada da Ajuda might have had a quite different configuration at the late 2nd M. BCE.

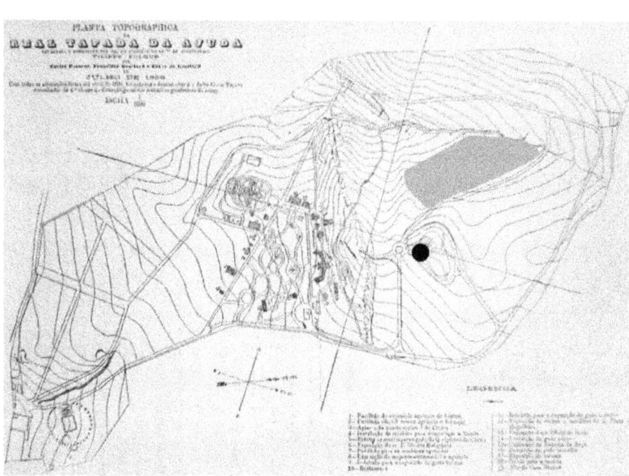

Figure 4. Topographic plan from Tapada da Ajuda (1859) prior to 1987 destruction. In dark grey Tapada da Ajuda LBA I settlement recognized and excavated in 1983-1987 (Cardoso, 1987) and in black the 1996 finds of LBA ceramic near the belevedere.

During survey works performed by the author in the 1990's on behalf of the City Council for the Museum of Lisbon, other occupations were detected on the same hill-top in which slope the site excavated and surveyed in the 1980's lays. Some material dating from the Iron Age and the Roman Republican Period, along with very scarse LBA ceramic shards were detected on the hill-top, an area unfortunately deeply dismantled by an ancient stone quarry and a belvedere built by Lisbon University in the 1950's. The visual reach of this small hill-top place where the Tapada da Ajuda belvedere was installed is remarkable: towards the Tagus valley it dominates a good portion of the upriver section and the already mentioned Alcântara brook valley; southwards, the horizon is only interrupted by the Arrábida mountain range, allowing a 50 km wide view. This issue is, in all rigor, no more than suggestive of a highly complex composition for the Tapada da Ajuda site, but it might also imply that what we are dealing with here is a small "high ground" site with its own agricultural dependent areas, as in later LBA II site Cabeço do Mouro (Cascais), C14 dated from the 10th-9th c. BCE (Cardoso 1991; Cardoso 2006a, 45-46; in this sense, see the clarifications by Elisa de Sousa- 2016, 390).

The previous remarks about territorial pattern distinctions between LBA I and II forces us to turn back to other criteria in order to distinguish them, bearing in mind the already mentioned scarcity of data for 13th-11 th c. BCE. Cardoso stresses the significant absence from Tapada da Ajuda of geometrical burnished decorated ceramics ("ornatos brunidos"), a symptom of its antiquity in relation to other sites were those appeared, C14 dating being an almost thorough confirmation of this understanding (Cardoso 2004, 2014, 2015; Cardoso and Siva 2004). "Ornatos brunidos" consequentely turn out to be a useful tool for chronological definition within the LBA in the Tagus Estuary.

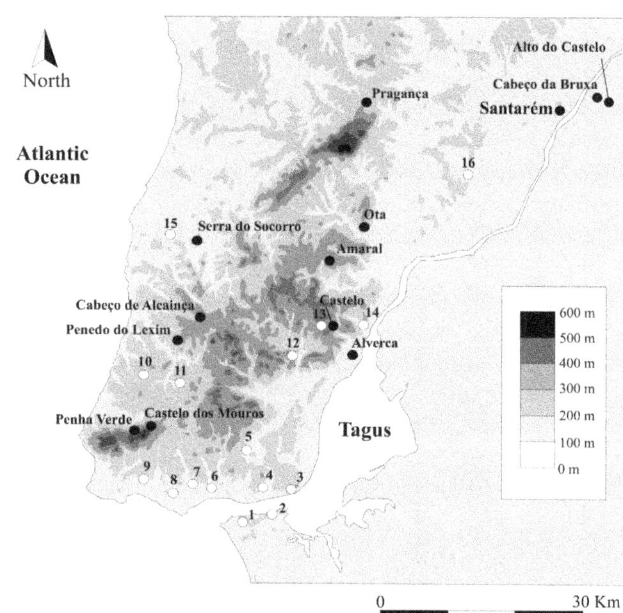

Figure 5. Late Bronze Age sites (mentioned on text) on Tagus Estuary region. | Source: By the Author.

At the same time, one can ask if we aren't overestimating it in our readings. Is it possible that its significant presence in one site is masking other early LBA human presences in the same place, only documented through other kind of pottery productions? Are functional context definitions available in the region enough to answer this sort of question? Is there any other chronological information available suggesting it?

If we look at the overall regional ceramic LBA II typologies, and contrast them with what's knows for LBA I, as Arruda and Sousa did, the conclusion is that they are, in fact, quite the same (Arruda and Sousa 2015, esp.181 Table 1). This means that, theoretically, if we address LBA pottery from sites with "ornatos brunidos", we are compelled to attribute all the ceramic bulk to the 10th-9th c. BCE, despite the fact that some might be previous to this chronological gap. The issue is that we remain incapable of demonstrating it for the lack of both fine stratigraphic sequences and C14 dates. But one has to say that, if verified, this hypothesis would partially solve the lack of data for LBA I, among other aspects.

Chronological issues arise, crucial for readings of the 13th-9th c. BCE evolution, and therefore to addressing the overall question of "ornatos brunidos" dating.

In this respect, regional LBA C14 dates reunited by Cardoso (2015, 163, Figure 2) are quite consistent with the conventional chronological interpretation, perfectly justifying the assumption of an *ante quem* at 9th/early 8th c. BCE in C14 dates provided by overlapping LBA layers from earlier Iron Age deposits in Santarém (Arruda 1999-2000; espec. Arruda and Sousa 2015, 185). Only one slight discrepancy was spotted in Quinta do Percevejo (Almada) (Barros 1998, 32; Cardoso 2015, 163, Figure 2), almost certainly dated from before 1000 BCE, being worth noting that this is a site where "ornatos brunidos" pottery is present (Barros 1998, 32).

Looking the other way, the question here is exactly until when did "ornatos brunidos" survive. The latest regional contexts in which they appear are scarce but strongly suggestive. In Castelo de São Jorge (Lisbon), a still unpublished pit (Silva 2013, 59-60; Sousa 2016) provided "ornatos brunidos" along with some LBA tradition handmade pottery, orientalised wheel made ceramics, including amphorae, and even a shard bearing a Phoenician graffito inscription, attributed through palaeographical criteria to the 1st half of the 7th c. BCE, although admitting the possibility of being slightly earlier (Arruda 2013; Zamora López 2013, 308-309; Sousa 2016; Sousa and Pinto 2016, 65). On Castelo de São Jorge's southern slope, another Early Iron Age context ascribed to the same chronology provided one very small shard with burnished geometric decoration (Pimenta, Calado and Silva 2013, 730, Figure 7, n.° 17). Finally, from Casa dos Bicos (Lisbon), on the shore of the Tagus, three other shards were published together with manual pottery produced in the LBA tradition, unfortunately collected without stratigraphical preoccupation in 1982, probably corresponding to Early Iron Age moments (Pimenta, Sousa and Amaro 2015, 164-165, Figures 3-7). One might ask if it would be suitable to add to this list the finds in Moinho da Atalaia (Amadora), considering that the lower levels identified were already from the Iron Age (Pinto and Parreira 1978; Fontes 2004).

Altogether, available C14 dates and other finds indicate a clear possibility that "ornatos brunidos" pottery might be present in the region from the 2nd half of the 11th c. BCE onwards, having survived until the 8th c. BCE, for the most. The transition from LBA to EIA seems, consequently, to have incorporated relevant elements from previous local Bronze Age traditions, although strongly subjected to a severe Phoenician impact that deeply altered material culture traces in the region, especially in the areas more exposed to maritime influence. The most evocative archaeological benchmark is the recently discovered epitaph from Casa Sommer (Lisbon), bearing the Phoenician funerary inscription read as *mṣbt* (stela of) *Wadbar* (a non NW Phoenician name) *bn* (son of) *[--] Ibadar* (other non-Semitic name ?) (Neto *et al.* 2015, 126).

The impact of effective Phoenician presence in the Tagus estuary on LBA communities is, nevertheless, hard to perceive due to the the lack of information available. One has to underline the continuity of LBA-EIA in the "high ground" settlement of Alcáçova de Santarém as an example of "collaboration", since archaeological data displays no gaps (Arruda and Sousa 2015).

Regional "high ground" settlements, founded during the LBA in the majority of cases, are numerous. Variations of importance among them are worth a mention, according to their strategic implantation and landscape control that, by the way, are common to "lower ground" places, that sometimes visually dominate vast areas and/or itineraries.

Considered to be in a higher status, of political elite-type locations (Cardoso 2004, 178), most of the "high ground" sites share multi-visibility with other(s) of the "same rank", thus composing territorial networks. Despite probable differences in status among them, one could include in this position a numerous list of sites: Penha Verde (Cardoso 2010-2011b; Cardoso and Sousa 2014), Castelo dos Mouros (Sintra) (Carreira 1994; Cardoso 1997-1998a; Cardoso and Sousa 2014), Cabeço de Alcainça ou dos Moinhos (Vicente and Andrade 1971; Ponce 2013), Serra do Socorro (Matias 2003), Penedo do Lexim (Mafra) (Sousa 2000; Sousa *et al.* 2004), Castelo da Amoreira (Odivelas) (Marques 1987; Boaventura and Pimenta 2013), Castelo-Adenaia (Pimenta and Mendes 2015), Castelo de Alverca (Vila Franca de Xira) (Pimenta and Mendes 2007), Castro do Amaral (Pimenta and Mendes 2011), Ota (Alenquer) (Barbosa 1956), Pragança (Cadaval) (Senna-Martinez 2002), Alto do Castelo (Alpiarça) (Kalb and Höck 1982, 1988) and Santarém (Arruda and Sousa 2015).

Some of these were very specific places, for they are seen as corresponding to very confined spatial occupations, limited in time, with metallurgical production and/or control of commercial connections, used by a small group of people, as Quinta do Marcelo, Penha Verde, Penedo do Lexim and, likely, Pragança and Ota (Cardoso 2010-2011b; Cardoso and Sousa 2014; Sousa 2016).

Others are not the case. They correspond to a wider spatial occupation, with a more permanent character during the LBA. Among them, the short list of the ones that surely had occupation during the Iron Age: Castelo dos Mouros (Silva and Sousa 2016), Castelo de Alverca (Pimenta and Mendes 2007), Santarém (Arruda and Sousa 2015; Arruda 1999-2000) and Alto do Castelo (Arruda *et al.* 2014). But, if the strata sequence for Santarém shows effective continuity, the remaining data is, until the moment, clearly insufficient to support such a statement and, at least in the case of Alto do Castelo, the scarcity of Iron Age vestiges is in strong contrast to the exuberance of LBA ones, making it, by far, the biggest settlement in the whole region during the late 2nd - early 1st c. M. BCE.

The apparent counterpart to the abandonment of most "high ground" LBA settlements during the EIA was the appearance of new and bigger settlements, among which the highlight goes to both Almaraz (Almada) and Lisbon, closer to the mouth of the Tagus Estuary. Here, natural harbour facilities seemed to have been the decisive factor. The strongly orientalised character of both sites is out of the question, and thoroughly supports the statement made by Ana Arruda and Elisa de Sousa: "*resistance and/or collaboration with the Phoenician groups that arrived in the Tagus estuary is clear, unlike what occurred at most sites in the region*" (Arruda and Sousa 2015, 185-186).

5. Bibliography

Almeida, Sara. "Estilos e tendências na cerâmica de ornatos brunidos do sudoeste peninsular". In *Idade do Bronze do Sudoeste: novas perspectivas sobre uma velha problemática,* ed. Raquel Vilaça and Miguel Serra, 127-147. Coimbra: Instituto de Arqueologia, Palimpsesto- Estudo e Preservação do Património Cultural, Centro de Estudos em Arqueologia, Artes e Ciências do Património, 2014.

Arruda, Ana Margarida. "A Península de Lisboa entre o Norte atlântico e o Oriente mediterrânico". In *Lisboa Subterrânea (Catalog),* ed. Ana Margarida Arruda, 52-57. Lisbon: Museu Nacional de Arqueologia, 1994.

Arruda, Ana Margarida. *Los Fenicios en Portugal. Fenicios y mundo indígena en el centro y sur de Portugal (siglos VIII-VI a.C.).* Barcelona: Laboratorio de Arqueología de la Universidad Pompeu Fabra, 1999-2000.

Arruda, Ana Margarida. "O 1° milénio a.n.e. no Centro e no Sul de Portugal: leituras possíveis no início de um novo século". *O Arqueólogo Português* 4, no. 3 (2005): 9-156.

Arruda, Ana Margarida. "Do que falamos quando falamos de Tartesso". In *Tarteso. El emporio del metal,* ed. Juan M. Campos and Jaime Alvar, 211-222. Espanha: Almuzara, 2013.

Arruda, Ana Margarida, Sousa, Elisa de, Pimenta, João, Mendes, Henrique Calé, and Soares, Raquel. "Alto do Castelo's Iron Age occupation (Alpiarça, Portugal)". *Zephyrus,* no. 74 (2014): 9-14.

Arruda, Ana Margarida And Sousa, Elisa. "Late Bronze Age in Alcáçova de Santarém (Portugal)". *Trabajos de Prehistoria* 72, no.1 (2015): 176-187.

Barbosa, Ernesto. "O castro da Ota (Alenquer)". *O Arqueólogo Português* 2, no.3 (1956): 75-85.

Barros, Luís and Espírito-Santo. "Quinta do Percevejo - Almada. Uma intervenção de emergência". In *Actas das IV Jornadas Arqueológicas da Associação dos Arqueólogos Portugueses (Lisboa, 1990)*, 333-342. Lisbon: Associação dos Arqueólogos Portugueses, 1991.

Barros, Luís. *Introdução à Pré e Proto-História de Almada.* Almada: Câmara Municipal de Almada, 1998.

Barros, Luís. *O fim do Bronze e a Idade do Ferro no território de Almada.* Lisbon: Faculdade de Letras da Universidade de Lisboa (*MBA thesis*), 2000.

Cardoso, Guilherme. *Carta Arqueológica de Cascais.* Cascais: Câmara Municipal de Cascais, 1991.

Cardoso, João Luís, Carreira, Júlio Roque. "Le Bronze Final et le début de l'Âge du Fer dans la région riveraine de restuaire du Tage". *Mediterrâneo* no. 2 (1993): 193-206.

Cardoso, João Luís (1995a)- "As cerâmicas de ornatos brunidos da Lapa do Fumo". In *A Idade do Bronze em Portugal. Discursos de Poder (Catálog)*, 1995(a), ed. Susana Oliveira Jorge, 88-89. Lisbon: Museu Nacional de Arqueologia, 1995 (a).

Cardoso, João Luís . "Os povoados do Bronze Final a norte do Estuário do Tejo". In *A Idade do Bronze em Portugal. Discursos de Poder (Catalog)*, ed. Susana Oliveira Jorge, 126-127. Lisbon: Museu Nacional de Arqueologia, 1995 (b).

Cardoso, João Luís. "O Bronze Final da Baixa Estremadura e as cerâmicas de ornatos brunidos da Lapa do Fumo (Sesimbra)". *Sesimbra Cultural* no. 5 (1996): 6-14.

Cardoso, João Luís, Cardoso, Guilherme. "O povoado do Bronze Final do Alto das Cabeças (Leião, Oeiras)". *Estudos Arqueológicos de Oeiras* no. 5 (1996): 351-359.

Cardoso, João Luís, Carreira, Júlio Roque. "Materiais Campaniformes e da Idade do Bronze do concelho de Sintra". *Estudos Arqueológicos de Oeiras* no. 6 (1996): 317-340.

Cardoso, João Luís. "O povoado do Bronze Final do Castelo dos Mouros (Sintra)". *Estudos Arqueológicos de Oeiras* no. 7 (1997/1998a): 169-187.

Cardoso, João Luís . "O povoado do Bronze Final do Castelo dos Mouros". *Estudos Arqueológicos de Oeiras* no. 7 (1997-1998b): 169-177.

Cardoso, João Luís, Leitão, Manuel, Ferreira, Octávio da Veiga, North, Carlos T., North, José. "As cerâmicas de ornatos brunidos da gruta do Correio-Mor (Loures)". *Estudos Arqueológicos de Oeiras* no. 7 (1997/1998): 155-167.

Cardoso, João Luís. "Aspectos do povoamento da Baixa Estremadura no decurso da Idade do Bronze". *Estudos Arqueológicos de Oeiras* no. 8 (1999/2000): 355-413.

Cardoso, João Luís (2000)- "A sepultura da Roça do Casal do Meio (Sesimbra) no quadro dos rituais funerários da Idade do

Bronze da Baixa Estremadura". *Discursos. Língua, Cultura e Sociedade* 3, no.2 (2000): 243-251.

Cardoso, João Luís. "A gruta do Correio-Mór (Loures)". *Estudos Arqueológicos de Oeiras* no. 11 (2003): 229-321.

Cardoso, João Luís. *A Baixa Estremadura dos Finais do IV milénio a.C. até à chegada dos Romanos: um ensaio de História regional* (*Estudos Arqueológicos de Oeiras* no. 12). Oeiras: Câmara Municipal de Oeiras), 2004.

Cardoso, João Luís, Silva, Inês Mendes da. "O povoado do Bronze Final da Tapada da Ajuda (Lisboa): estudo do espólio cerâmico". *Revista Portuguesa de Arqueologia* no.7-1 (2004): 227-271.

Cardoso, João Luís . "Visibilidade e invisibilidade do património arqueológico: o caso do Bronze Pleno da estremadura". *Discursos. Língua, Cultura e Sociedade* 3, no. 6 (2005): 7–27.

Cardoso, João Luís. "A estação do Bronze Final do Cabeço do Mouro (Cascais): resultados das escavações realizadas". *Revista Portuguesa de Arqueologia no.* 9- 1 (2006): 21-46.

Cardoso, João Luís. "Dos depósitos da Idade do Bronze e das intenções que estiveram na sua origem (comentário a um estudo de Raquel Vilaça)". *O Arqueólogo Português* 4, no. 24 (2006b): 115-123.

Cardoso, João Luís. "O casal agrícola do Bronze Final de Abrunheiro (Oeiras)". *Estudos Arqueológicos de Oeiras* no. 18 (2010/2011a): 33-74.

Cardoso, João Luís. "A ocupação do Bronze Final do povoado pré-histórico da Penha Verde (Sintra)". *Estudos Arqueológicos de Oeiras* no. 18 (2010/2011b): 579-590.

Cardoso, João Luís. *Arqueologia do concelho de Oeiras*. Oeiras: Câmara Municipal de Oeiras, 2011.

Cardoso, João Luís. "Moita da Ladra 2 (Vila Franca de Xira), um sítio ritual do Bronze Final da região de Lisboa". *Revista da Faculdade de Letras (Homenagem a Armando Coelho Ferreira da Silva)* no. 12 (2013): 49-67.

Cardoso, João Luís, Sousa, Maria João. "O Bronze Final na Serra de Sintra". *Estudos Arqueológicos de Oeiras* no. 21 (2014): 361-374.

Cardoso, João Luís. "Between the Atlantic and the Mediterranean: the Late Bronze Age around the Tagus estuary (Portugal). Economic, social and cultural aspects". *Rivista di Scienze Preistoriche* no. 65 (2015): 149-170.

Carreira, Júlio Roque. "A jazida da Idade do Bronze Final da Tapada da Ajuda". *Lisboa-Revista Municipal* 2, no.15 (1986): 3-18.

Carreira, Júlio Roque. "A Pré-História Recente do Abrigo Grande das Bocas (Rio Maior)". *Trabalhos de Arqueologia da EAM* no.2 (1994): 47-144.

Carreira, Júlio Roque. "As ocupações das Idades do Cobre e do Bronze da Lapa da Bugalheira (Torres Novas)". *Nova Augusta,* no.10 (1996 a): 91-112.

Carreira, Júlio Roque. "Materiais da Idade do Bronze da gruta da nascente do Almonda (Torres Novas)". *Nova Augusta,* no.10 (1996 b): 113- 123.

Carreira, Júlio Roque. "Catujal: um povoado da Idade do Bronze (Médio) à entrada da "ria de Loures". Contribuição para o estudo das influências do Bronze do Sudoeste na formação do Bronze estremenho". *Vipasca no.*6 (1997): 119-140.

Carvalho, António Faustino, Bragança, Filipa, Neto, Filipa, Justino, Lígia. "O sítio da Idade do Bronze "pleno" do Casal da Torre (Assentiz, Torres Novas)". *Trabalhos de Arqueologia da EAM* no.5 (1999): 63-81.

Daveau, Susane. "A foz do Tejo, palco da história de Lisboa". In *Lisboa Subterrânea (Catalog),* ed. Ana Margarida Arruda, 24-31. Lisbon: Museu Nacional de Arqueologia, 1994.

Delfino, Davide, Cruz, Ana Rosa, Graça, Ana, Gaspar, Filomena, Batista, Álvaro. "A problemática das continuidades e descontinuidades na Idade do Bronze do Médio Tejo Português". In *A Idade do Bronze em Portugal: os dados e os problemas,* ed. S Lopes, 147-202. Tomar: Centro de Pré-História, 2014.

Félix, Paulo Jorge Soares. "O Final da Idade do Bronze no Centro-Oeste Peninsular: a Contribuição do Ribatejo Norte". *Revista de Guimarães,* special volume no.2 (1999): 715-740.

Félix, Paulo. "Serra de Alvaiázere: um povoado fortificado do Bronze Final no centro de Portugal". *Almadan* 2, no. 8 (1999): 63-71.

Félix, Paulo. "Os finais da Idade do Bronze e inícios da Idade do Ferro no Ribatejo norte (Centro de Portugal). Uma breve síntese dos dados arqueográficos". *Conímbriga* no.45 (2006): 65-92.

Figueiredo, E., Melo, A. A.; Araújo, Maria de Fátima. "Artefactos metálicos do Castro de Pragança: um estudo preliminar de algumas ligas de cobre por Espectrometria de Fluorescência de Raios X". *O Arqueólogo Português* 4, no.25 (2007): 195-215.

Fontes, T. "Estudo de 145 artefactos cerâmicos da Idade do Bronze do Moinho de Atalaia Oeste (Reboleira) e a problemática das ocupações da Idade do Bronze na área circundante". *ARQA Património em revista* no.1(2004): 52-61.

Gomes, Mário Varela. "2ª Parte – Proto-História do Sul de Portugal". In *Proto-História de Portugal,* ed. Armando Coelho Ferreira da Silva and Mário Varela Gomes, 99-185. Lisbon: Universidade Aberta, 1998

Jorge, Susana Oliveira. "Idade do Bronze: apontamento sobre a natureza dos dados arqueológicos". *Revista da Faculdade de Letras* 2 no. 8 (1991): 385-391.

Kalb, Philinne. "Zur Atlantischen Bronzezeit in Portugal". *Germania- Anzeiger der Römisch-Germanischen Komission des Deutschen Archäologischen Institute,* no. 58 (1980): 25-59.

Kalb, Philinne, Höck, Martin. "Cabeço da Bruxa, Alpiarça (distrito de Santarém). Relatório preliminar da escavação de Janeiro e Fevereiro de 1979". *Portugália* 2, no. 3 (1981-1982): 61–69.

Kalb, Philinne, Höck, Martin. "Alto do Castelo, Alpiarça, Distrikt Santarém. Vorbericht über die grabung 1981". *Madrider Mitteilunge* no. 23 (1982): 145-151.

Kalb, Philinne, Höck, Martin. *Cerâmica de Alpiarça. Catálogo.* Alpiarça: Câmara Municipal, 1985.

Kalb, Philinne, Höck, Martin. "O povoamento pré-histórico de Alpiarça". *Arqueologia* no. 17 (1988): 193-200.

Kunst, Michael. "A Idade do Bronze na Estremadura". In ed. Jorge de Alarcão, *A Idade do Bronze em Portugal. Discursos de Poder (Catálogo),* ed. Susana Oliveira Jorge, 124-125. Lisbon: Museu Nacional de Arqueologia, 1995.

Madeira, João, Gonçalves, João Ludgero, Raposo, Luís, Parreira, Rui. "Achados da Idade do Bronze no Monte da Pena (Barro – Torres Vedras) – notícia prévia". *O Arqueólogo Português* 3, no.6 (1972): 207-218.

Marques, Gustavo. "Arqueologia de Alpiarça. As Estações representadas no Museu do Instituto de Arqueologia do Porto". *Trabalhos de Antropologia do Instituto Doutor Mendes Corrêa* (1972).

Marques, Gustavo, Andrade, Gil Miguéis de.- "Aspectos da proto-história do território português I- definição e distribuição geográfica da cultura de Alpiarça (Idade do Ferro)", in *Actas do III Congresso Nacional de Arqueologia,* 125-148. Lisbon: Ministério da Educação, 1974.

Marques, Gustavo. "Aspectos da Proto-História do território português. III-Castelo da Amoreira (Odivelas, Loures)". *Boletim Cultural Loures* no.1 (1987): 51-58.

Marques, Gustavo. "A Cultura de Alpiarça". In, *Idade do Ferro (Catalogue),* ed. Isabel Pereira, 63-69. Figueira da Foz: Museu Municipal de Santos Rocha, 1994.

Matias, Carla. "Serra do Socorro: Uma aproximação à sua caracterização arqueológica no contexto da Estremadura Atlântica". *Boletim Cultural (Mafra)* no.3 (2003): 308-358.

Melo, Ana Ávila de, Senna-Martinez, João Carlos de. "Agricultores e Metalurgistas, da Troca ao "Mercado: Alguns aspectos e problemas do Bronze Final e Primeira Idade do Ferro na Península de Lisboa". *Turres Veteras,* no.4 (2001): 95-118.

Neto, Nuno, González, C., Rebelo, Paulo, Santos, Raquel, Rocha, Miguel. "Trabalhos arqueológicos na Quinta Nova de Santo António ou dos Ingleses – Carcavelos. A ocupação do Bronze Final". *Cira – Arqueologia,* no. 2 (2013): 19-39.

Neto, Nuno, Rebelo, Paulo, Ribeiro, Raquel Augusto, Rocha, Miguel, Zamora López, Josep Ánton. "Uma inscrição lapidar fenícia em Lisboa". *Revista Portuguesa de Arqueologia,* no.18 (2015): 123-128.

Pimenta, João, Mendes, Henrique. A intervenção arqueológica na Casa da Câmara de Alverca do Ribatejo (Vila Franca de Xira)". In *Alverca- Da terra às gentes (Catalog),* 53-70. Vila Franca de Xira: Museu Municipal de Vila Franca de Xira, 2013.

Pimenta, João, Mendes, Henrique - "Novos dados sobre a presença fenícia no vale do Tejo. As recentes descobertas na área de Vila Franca de Xira", in *Estudos Arqueológicos de Oeiras* no.18 (2010-2011): 591-618.

Pimenta, João, Silva, Rodrigo Banha da, Calado, Marco. "Sobre a ocupação pré-romana de *Olisipo*: a intervenção arqueológica urbana da Rua de São Mamede ao Caldas n.º 15 (Lisboa)". In *Fenícios e Púnicos por terra e por mar- Actas do VI Congresso Internacional de Estudos Fenícios e Púnicos* (col. *Estudos e Memórias,* 6), ed. Ana margarida Arruda, 724-735. Lisbon: Uniarq, 2013.

Pimenta, João, Soares, António Monge, Mendes, Henrique. "Cronologia absoluta para o povoado pré-romano de Santa Sofia (Vila Franca de Xira)". *Cira-Arqueologia* no. 2 (2013): 181–195.

Pimenta, João, Mendes, Henrique. "Casal dos Pegos I e o Povoamento Orientalizante do Rio da Silveira (Vila Franca de Xira)". *Cira-Arqueologia* no.4 (2015): 19-54.

Pimenta, João, Sousa, Elisa de, Amaro, Clementino. "Sobre as mais antigas ocupações da Casa dos Bicos, Lisboa: da *Olisipo* pré-romana aos primeiros contactos com o mundo itálico". *Revista Portuguesa de Arqueologia* no.18 (2015): 161-180.

Pinto, Clara Vaz, Parreira, Rui. "Contribuição para o estudo do Bronze Final e do Ferro Inicial a norte do Estuário do Tejo". In *Actas das III Jornadas da Associação dos Arqueólogos Portugueses (Lisboa 1977*), I, 147-163. Lisbon: Associação dos Arqueólogos Portugueses, 1978.

Ponce, Mónica Alves. *O Bronze Final na Península de Lisboa: o caso o Cabeço de Alcainça na transição entre o 2º e o 1º milénio A.C. (Dissertação de Mestrado em Arqueologia).* Lisbon: Faculdade de Letras da Universidade de Lisboa, 2013. (http://hdl.handle.net/10451/9936)

Ramos-Pereira, Ana, Trindade, Jorge, Neves, Mário. "Portugal Coastal Dynamics. Field Trip Guide- A1". In *Sixth International Conference on Geomorphology (Zaragoza, 2005).* Lisbon: Centro de Estudos Geográficos, 2005. (http://www.geomorfologia.es/sites/default/files/A1%20Portugal.pdf)

Ramos, Carlos, Reis, E., Ramos-Pereira, A., Freitas, M.C., Andrade, C. "Late Holocene evolution of the Lower Tagus alluvial plain and heavy metals content: preliminary results", in *Environmental Change and Water Sustainability*, ed. José María García-Ruiz, J.A.A.Jones, José Arnáez, 267-182. Zaragoza: Instituto Pirenaico de Ecología, Consejo Superior de Investigaciones Científicas, 2002.

Senna-Martinez, João Carlos de. *Idade do Bronze na Estremadura Atlântica. Subsídios para um programa de estudo (Prova complementar de Doutoramento em Pré-História e Arqueologia).* Lisbon: Faculdade de Letras da Universidade de Lisboa, 1990.

Senna-Martinez, João Carlos de. "Entre Atlântico e Mediterrâneo: algumas reflexões sobre o Grupo Baiões/Santa Luzia e o desenvolvimento do Bronze Final peninsular". *Trabalhos de Arqueologia da EAM* no. 2 (1994a): 215-232.

Senna-Martinez, João Carlos de. "Subsídios para o estudo do Bronze Pleno na Estremadura atlântica: (1) A alabarda de tipo "atlântico" do habitat das Baútas (Amadora)". *Zephyrvs* no. 46 (1994b):161-182.

Senna-Martinez, João Carlos de. "Desestruturação e Complexização: Aspectos e Problemas da 1º Idade do Bronze na «Península de Lisboa»". *Turres Veteras* no. 4 (2002): 75-93.

Senna-Martinez, João Carlos de. "Aspectos e problemas das origens e desenvolvimento da metalurgia do bronze na fachada atlânctica peninsular". *Estudos Arqueológicos de Oeiras* no.15 (2007): 119-134.

Senna-Martinez, João Carlos de. "Um rio na(s) rota(s) do estanho: O Tejo entre a Idade do Bronze e a Idade do Ferro". *Cira-Arqueologia* no. 2 (2013): 7-18.

Serrão, Eduardo da Cunha. "Cerâmica proto-histórica da Lapa do Fumo (Sesimbra) com ornatos brunidos e coloridos". in *Zephyrus* no. 9 (1958): 177-186.

Serrão, Eduardo da Cunha "Cerâmica com ornatos a cores da Lapa do Fumo (Sesimbra)" In *Actas e Memórias do I Congresso Nacional de Arqueologia,* 337-359. Lisbon: Instituto de Alta Cultura, 1959.

Serrão, Eduardo da Cunha "As cerâmicas de «retícula bruñida» das estações arqueológicas espanholas e com «ornatos brunidos» da Lapa do Fumo", in *Actas das I Jornadas Arqueológicas (Lisboa, 1969)*, 2, 271-308. Lisbon: Associação dos Arqueólogos Portugueses, 1970.

Silva, Rodrigo Banha da. "A ocupação da Idade do Bronze Final da Praça da Figueira (Lisboa). Novos e velhos dados sobre os antecedentes da cidade de Lisboa". *Cira- Arqueologia* no.2 (2013): 40-62.

Silva, Rodrigo Banha da, Sousa, Maria João. "O Castelo dos Mouros nos Primeiros Séculos do I Milénio a.C.". *Almadan* 2, no. 20 (2016): 22-26.

Sousa, Ana Catarina, Valério, Pedro, Araújo, Maria de Fátima. "Metalurgia antiga do Penedo do Lexim (Mafra): Calcolítico e Idade do Bronze". *Revista Portuguesa de Arqueologia* no. 7-2 (2004): 97-117.

Sousa, Ana Catarina. *O povoado pré-histórico do Penedo do Lexim: resultados preliminares da campanha de 1999.* (*Cadernos de Arqueologia de Mafra*, 1) Mafra: Câmara Municipal de Mafra, 2000.

Sousa, Elisa de. "Algumas considerações sobre a ocupação do final da Idade do Bronze na península de Lisboa". In *Terra e Água. Escolher sementes, invocar a deusa- Estudos em homenagem a Victor S.Gonçalves* (col. *Estudos & Memórias*, no. 9), ed. Ana Catarina Sousa, António Carvalho and catarina Viegas, 387-401. Lisbon: Uniarq, 2016.

Sousa, Elisa de, Pinto, Marina. "A ocupação da Idade do Ferro na colina do Castelo de São Jorge (Lisboa, Portugal): novos dados das escavações realizadas na Rua do Recolhimento /Beco do Leão". *Apontamentos de Arqueologia e Património* n.º 11 (2016): 59-67.

Tereso, Sofia Gabriel, Ferreira, Sónia Duarte. "O povoado proto-histórico da Quinta da Aramenha (Santana, Cartaxo)". *Revista Portuguesa de Arqueologia* no.10-1 (2007): 179-208.

Vicente, Eduaro Prescott, Andrade, Gil Miguéis de. "A estação arqueológica do Cabeço de Moinhos. Breve notícia". In *Actas do II Congresso Nacional de Arqueologia*, I, Coimbra: Universidade de Coimbra, 1971.

Vilaça, Raquel, Cruz, Domingos de Jesus, Gonçalvez, Antóni Huet Bacelar. "A necrópole de Tanchoal dos Patudos (Alpiarça, Santarém)", in *Conimbriga*, no. 38 (1999): 5-29.

Vilaça, Raquel, Arruda, Ana Margarida. "Ao longo do Tejo, do Bronze ao Ferro". *Conimbriga* no. 43 (2004): 11-45.

Vilaça, Raquel. "Todos os caminhos vão dar ao ocidente: trocas e contactos no Bronze Final". *Estudos Arqueológicos de Oeiras* no. 15 (2007): 135-157.

Zamora López, Josep Ánton. "Novedades de Epigrafía Fenicio-Púnica en la Península Ibérica y sus aledaños". *Paleohispanica no.* 13 (2013): 359-384.

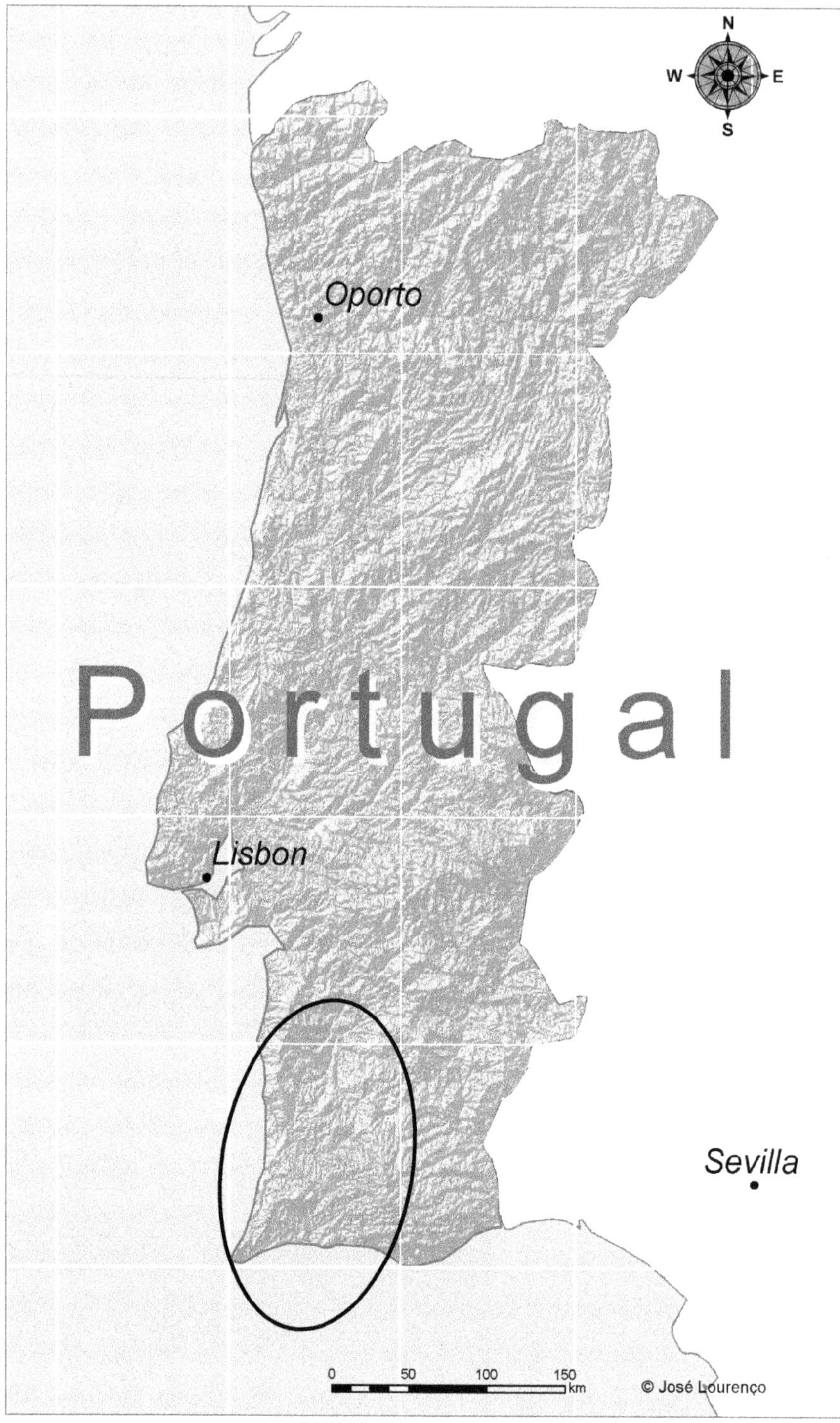

Portugal - Baixo Alentejo.
Source: José Martinho Lourenço.

Chapter 12

It's Right Over There! Trans-regional Contacts in Bronze Age Baixo Alentejo? Brief Reflections from the Hypogea Necropolis of Torre Velha 3 (Serpa, Portugal)

Eduardo Porfírio, Miguel Serra

Palimpsesto - Estudo e Preservação do Património Cultural, Lda.
eduardoporfirio@palimpsesto.pt, miguelserra@palimpsesto.pt

"Let's only care about the place where we are.
There's beauty enough in being here and not anywhere else.
If there's someone beyond the curve in the road,
Let them worry about what's past the curve in the road,
That's what the road is to them.
If we have to get there, when we get there we'll know.
For the time being all we know is we're not there.
Here there's only the road before the curve, and before the curve
There's only the road without any curve whatsoever."

Alberto Caeiro – *"Beyond the curve in the road"*. Translation based on the critical edition by Teresa Sobral Cunha in http://alberto-caeiro.blogspot.pt/

Abstract: Some of the funerary contexts from the hypogea of Torre Velha 3 (Serpa/Beja), dated from the Middle Bronze Age, show elements that can attest interactions with other contemporary peninsular societies. Among these we find the faunal remains associated with feasting rituals, but also the pedestalled cups whose typology resembles the argaric forms, or even the metallic artefacts made in bronze, when in this region the arsenic copper artefacts were still predominant. These elements matched with other from some archaeological contexts identified in Baixo Alentejo result from the exchange of ideas and materials related to interaction processes. In this context we considered, among others, the funerary artefacts found in the Belmeque burial (Serpa/ Beja), the sword of Horta do Folgão (Serpa/Beja), and the stelae group called Alentejo slabs. Even if the archaeological record doesn't show any intensification in regional and extra-regional contacts, similar to those documented in previous and especially posteriors times, the reality is that these communities, despite knowing processes of social transformation in whose dynamics are defined by different regional rhythms, are still related to other contemporary societies. At this point it's hard to evaluate, based only on the current southwest Bronze age available data, the real importance that these inter-relationships had on the sociocultural framework of these communities.

Keywords: Inter-regional Contacts; Bartering; Funerary Architectures; Middle Bronze Age; Southwest of the Iberian Peninsula.

Introduction

The phenomenon of objects and raw materials' circulation, sometimes over long distances, is well known and frequently debated by the archaeological community. The reasons and mechanisms behind such movements, or the mentalities, social behaviours and ideologies of the societies involved in the interaction processes are also discussed and perhaps even more enthusiastically.

Identifying this phenomenon in the archaeological record has been essentially rooted in the evaluation of the foreign nature of artefact types and raw materials. In the last case archaeometric analysis has played an important role, mainly contributing to the definition of resource catchment areas used for artefact production.

In southern Portugal's recent Prehistory there are many well documented cases of objects and raw materials circulation between different regions, sometimes encompassing distant geographical areas. Some examples are ornaments made in green stones and in rare rocks (Odriozola *et al.* 2016), in amber (Vilaça *et al.* 2002), or the instruments made in amphibolites and other lithologies (Gonçalves and Sousa 2012), also ivory objects (Schumacher *et al.* 2009) found in sites with occupations attributed to the end of the Neolithic and Chalcolithic period. Latter the geographic spreading of the Beaker phenomenon consistently signals the intensity of long distance interaction systems. In addition to the European dimension, which is clearly the most studied, some materials associated with the "Beaker package" have also been identified in North Africa (Bokbot 2005), arising from previous contacts, many dating back to the Neolithic (Cortés Sánchez *et al.* 2012) or to previous periods (Souville 1998).

Concerning the Bronze Age and particularly its final stage, trade activities arising from the Mediterranean stand out and have a great impact. Its consequences are characterized by deep material and world view changes within coeval Iberian peninsula's societies. In parallel, contacts with the Atlantic world, already initiated in previous times, experience a higher intensity mainly expressed by metallurgical productions.

During the time interval between the beginning and end of the Bronze Age – here considered as corresponding to the time period that elapsed between the second century of the 2nd millennium BC and the middle of its last quarter (Mataloto *et al.* 2013, 330) - the archaeological record of the Portuguese Southwest is characterized by some poverty and scarcity in materials circulation, particularly when compared to the elements available in the adjacent periods mentioned. Such perspectives integrate some syntheses about the Bronze Age in this region. As an example, at the end of the last century Manuel Calado (1995, 332) wrote that: *"The large interregional movement of luxury artefacts, particularly metals, which was developing since the Chalcolithic reveals long-distance relationships. It is thought that such materials would encourage the development of elites that were partly materially established by the control of raw materials and commercial channels. Nevertheless, in the territory that is now Portuguese it seems that this process may have halted during the 2nd millennium...* ".

After considering recent data, collected in intense and extensive archaeological research in Alentejo (namely those developed during numerous irrigation projects promoted by EDIA S.A.), António Carlos Valera (2014, 311) notes that: "... *what the empirical data seems to be saying is that from the end of the 3rd millennium there is an abrupt and significant contraction in social complexity, trans-regional interactions and probably in regional demography, combined with a profound change of cosmological and ontological patterns...* "

The truth is that, although the empirical and material data shows a very significant decrease of inter-regional interactions during the span between the end of the 3rd millennium and the beginning/middle of the 2nd millennium BC, it does not support their absence. In fact, there are metallic and pottery evidences (despite being faint and archaeologically poorly represented as already mentioned) allowing to presume that there were interactions between different geographical areas during the mid 2nd millennium BC. Some of these evidences will be briefly presented here.

Before data presentation, however, it is important to give some attention to the geomorphological context provided by this region. Although regional determinism should not be overly emphasized, regional characteristics are important features in this analysis, reflecting the easiness or hardness in people's, goods' and ideas' of mobility.

Geographically, the area under study comprises part of Alentejo, roughly matching Beja and Serpa municipalities, although other sites in the Portuguese Southwest are referred because of their relevance to the subject in discussion.

Besides having very fertile soils this region is also characterized by two types of relief. In some areas it shows an immense succession of small and smooth rounded hills created by the quaternary rejuvenation of the Guadiana valley. In others it is flat or nearly flattened, corresponding to the best preserved areas of the tertiary plain, named peneplain of Alentejo in the wake of a classic work by Mariano Feio (1952). In the North this last unit is limited by the cliff of the fault of Vidigueira, which establishes a well demarcated landscape boundary between the Lower and Higher Alentejo. The geomorphological features that counterbalance the extensive plains are rare. Besides the embedded valley of Guadiana and of some of its tributary rivers, there are also some tectonic origin reliefs like the hills of Grândola, Cercal, Barrancos and Caldeirão (Rebelo and Cunha 1991). The first two are the western limits of Alentejo's peneplain, while the eastern limit is set by the Serra de Barrancos hills and the Spanish border. The southern boundary is more difficult to define, it is somewhat located in the parallel of Castro Verde, because from this point southwards the relief gains altitude up to the peaks of Monchique and Serra do Caldeirão (Feio 1952). There are also some elevations due to the hardness of marble (Serra de Ficalho) and quartzite (Serra de Alcaria Ruiva). Lower than all these, but also worth to mention, are the hills where the cities of Beja and Serpa emerged (Oliveira 1992).

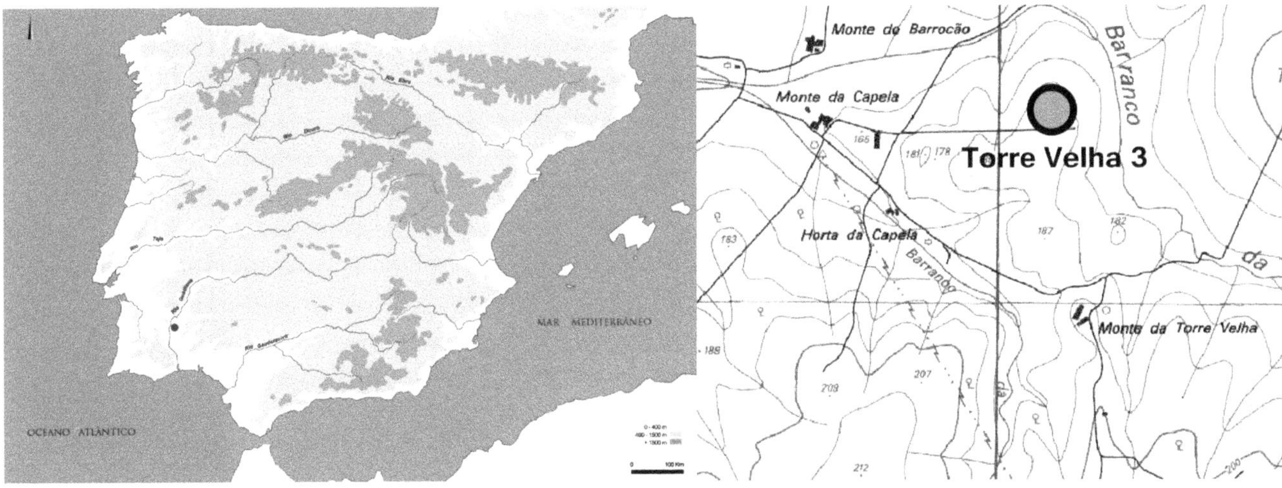

Figure 1. TV3 location in the Iberian Peninsula and in the Ordinance Survey Map, Sheet n.º 523.

Archaeological contexts from Torre Velha 3

The archaeological site of Torre Velha 3 is located in Serpa Municipality in a valley area that currently belongs to the Parish Union of São Salvador and Santa Maria, where the Laje dam was built over the stream with the same name. The building process of this infrastructure involved holding several archaeological interventions comprised by an impact minimization plan on cultural heritage. In fact all this area belongs to the Torre Velha Estate, known, for long time, in Portuguese archaeological historiography by its Roman remains (Lopes *et al.* 1997, with references). Archaeological excavations were performed in several sites located on both banks of the Laje stream, allowing not only to confirm the importance of Roman occupation in this territory but also its human occupation back to Prehistorical times. This was particularly clear at Torre Velha 3, where many underground structures where found dug in the soil, some showing funerary use and reuse and whose archaeological materials support Chalcolithic chronologies (Alves *et al.* 2012, 2014a) and may even go back to Late Neolithic. In the opposite chronological extreme an Islamic period burial ground, which should also be mentioned, as well as various funerary contexts dated into Late Antiquity. From this last period some domestic contexts were also found, providing the only positive archaeological structures found in the area intervened at this site, which comprised *circa* fourteen thousand square meters (Alves *et al.* 2012, 2013, 2014 and Vaqueira 2015). An Iron Age occupation was also found, limited to a single structure which provided, amongst others, several fragments of a *pithos* and a double spring's fibula. These are the oldest 1st Iron Age materials identified in the inner of the Baixo Alentejo (Estrela *et al.* 2012).

Besides the aforementioned periods there is also a Bronze Age intensive occupation. It is mainly observed as underground negative structures, like a 25 hypogea necropolis and various pits, some of them where reused with funerary purposes. The hypogea are tombs excavated in the soft bedrock of that region having a burial chamber, where inhumations and funerary gifts were deposited, and an antechamber. The chambers show concave walls and circular plans while the antechambers are more variable. Some antechambers where based in a rectangular or squared plan (however, the side where the burial chamber is placed may vary), others show an oval or circular morphology model, although this last two solutions are clearly minoritary. The burial chamber always presented a deeper position than the antechamber and was usually accessed through a ramp. Nevertheless, there are three hypogea where that solution was replaced by steps. Subsequently, the burial chamber was sealed by large stony blocks and wedged with small slabs (Alves *et al.* 2010, 2012 and 2014a). In nearly 13 hypogea, it was found that the spaces between the stones from the closing structure were filled with a mixture of clay, propolis and beeswax (Frade *et al.* 2014).

The overwhelming majority of burials found within Torre Velha 3's hypogea were individual. In fact, besides two inconclusive cases there were only three more where the primary inhumation was associated to remains resulting from a reduction process and a single case of a funerary chamber having three skeletons, belonging to a double burial and remains resulting from a reduction process. Another singular case was identified where the inhumation was placed in the antechamber, which will be analysed in better detail latter in this text. All the inhumations were placed in lateral decubitus, either over the left side either over the right side, having the anterior and posterior members flexed in a position usually named as flexed position. The information gathered by the anthropological study of these burials allowed verifying that the majority of the population inhumated in hypogea is adult (11 males and 9 females), while only five cases are non-adult individuals and a single one didn't allow the evaluation of that parameter (Fidalgo 2014 and Fidalgo *et al.* 2016).

Most burials were accompanied by funerary gifts, usually a pottery container, a metal artefact or a meat offering. The most common pottery displays simple hemispherical shapes and oval profiles. The rims are mostly rounded, sometimes with a slight inwards inflexion. The less common shapes are vessels with straight rims and oval or spherical bodies with convex bases. Besides these morphologies, which recall regional older pre-history periods, there are also carinated profiles, such as bowls with high and low carinations and vessels matching the bowl types "Atalaia" and "Odivelas". Other "Bronze of the Southwest" classical shapes are also present like the small jugs with vertical ribs and a bottle with incised decoration (Alves *et al.* 2010, 142).

On the other hand there are two vessels from a different type, the pedestalled cup, completely unknown in "Bronze of the Southwest" assemblages, either from cists or hypogea necropolises. These type of vessel may testify for supra-regional contacts, namely with the so called argaric world where this type of vessels, very similar to shape 7 (Schubart 2004), are more common (Alves *et al.* 2010, 150).

Concerning pedestalled cups, it is interesting to notice that both specimens recovered at Torre Velha 3 came from hypogea whose funerary contexts show distinctive features, standing out from the remaining burials. These peculiarities are the choice of the antechamber to perform the burial, in hypogeum [1662]-[1664], and the post-mortem handling of the human bone remains buried inside hypogeum [2471]-[2472].

Hypogeum [1662]-[1664] is composed of a chamber and a sub-circular antechamber, classified as a pit tomb antechamber. This is clearly a less common architectural solution – counting only two cases – when compared to the remaining antechamber hypogea typologies at Torre Velha 3 (Alves *et al.* 2010, 139).

Inside the chamber, near the western wall, human bones resulting from a reduction process [1532] and an inhumation [1534] were found. The inhumation was a non-adult individual (11 to 14 years of age at death) whose body was deposited in the flexed position (left lateral decubitus), oriented NE-SW[1], having the skull placed over the right cheek. The anthropological study also found that the deposition process is likely to have occurred in open space. As to the remains resulting from a reduction process [1532], the anthropological characteristics indicate that it is an adult (> 25 years) female (Fidalgo 2014 and Fidalgo *et al.* 2016). The grave goods collected nearby the human bones are composed of a pedestalled cup and a meat offering comprising the left radius of a sheep (Alves *et al.* 2010).

Nevertheless, as mentioned before, it is worth noticing that this grave's antechamber was used to bury an individual

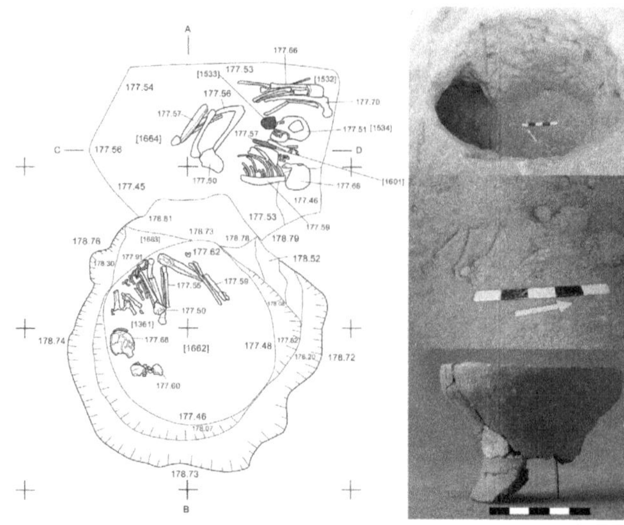

Figure 2. Hypogeum [1662] – [1664], burial context and pedestalled cup. | Source: By the Authors.

[1361], being the only case as such identified at Torre Velha 3. In fact, if one excludes hypogea 46, 52 and 63 from Outeiro Alto 2 (Alves *et al.* 2010 and Filipe *et al.* 2013), it turns out that this practice is absent from the remaining hypogea necropolis already published. Burial [1361] belonging to an adult (> 25 years) male, deposited in the flexed position (left lateral decubitus), oriented SE-NW, having the skull placed over the left cheek (Fidalgo 2014 and Fidalgo *et al.* 2016). There were no funerary gifts associated to this burial, although layer [1278] provided two bowl rim fragments (Alves *et al.* 2009). Contrary to burial [1534] the decomposition process took place in a closed space, which could explain the presence of the pottery sherds (Fidalgo 2014 and Fidalgo et al 2016.).

The full understanding of the stratigraphic sequence from this funerary structure, however, is hindered by the scarcity of data. That is, there are doubts in confirming if the deposition of burial [1361], followed by the filling of the antechamber [1662], was a simultaneous act which definitely closed the tomb or if, on the other hand, inhumation [1361] had already been covered by another layer when the remains of individual [1534] where overlaid with sediment (Alves *et al.* 2010, 140).

An assemblage of human remains was found inside tomb [2471]-[2472]. It relates to the double burial of individuals [2367] and [2368], placed in the centre of the funerary chamber, and also the remains of a reduction process [2365] + [2458][2], placed near the NE chamber wall. The reduction remains where probably moved at the time of the simultaneous burial of individuals [2367] and [2368] in order to make space inside the chamber. Nevertheless, it

[1] Burial orientation is always mentioned regarding the sequence skull-feet.

[2] This counting of anthropological contexts differs from other published texts, which only mentioned data from field analysis. In the meanwhile, a deeper anthropological study was performed (Fidalgo 2014) constituting the latest reference in this subject.

should be noted that the right foot bones [2458] where in the normal anatomical order. The analysis of these human bones showed that they belong to an adult (> 30 years old) male (Fidalgo 2014 and Fidalgo *et al.* 2016).

Burial [2367] was placed in the left lateral decubitus and oriented E-W. The anthropological study revealed that it is a non-adult individual that died aged 5 to 9 years old. Individual [2368] also belongs to the same age group. It was buried near the Northern wall of the funerary chamber, in the left lateral decubitus and oriented SE-NW. It is noteworthy that none of these inhumations had the skull in the normal anatomical position. Part of the skull from individual [2368] was found near the northern chamber wall, while the corresponding jaw was found near burial [2367]. As to the skull of this last burial it was found close to skull [2368], near the northern wall of this tomb (Fidalgo 2014 and Fidalgo *et al.* 2016).

The grave goods recovered from this hypogeum are a pedestalled cup, placed near the reduction remains [2365]+[2358], and a tale vertebrae[3], found in the space where individuals [2367] e [2368] were placed (Alves *et al.* 2010).

of the osteological remains, because the skulls of non-adult individuals [2367] and [2368] were found adjacent to the Northeast wall of the chamber, displaced from their anatomical position. This circumstance recalls the situation documented in Belmeque, but also other funerary contexts of the Bronze Age of the Southwest where the skull was subjected to diverse practices of manipulation (Fidalgo *et al.* 2016, Porfírio and Serra 2010, with bibliography). In hypogeum [1662] – [1664] the antechamber was chosen to bury an adult individual, while in the chamber was deposited the body of a non-adult next to the osteological remains of an adult woman, whose bones, as part of a reduction process, had to be relocated inside the funerary chamber. The funerary goods recovered in this last space consisted in one pedestalled cup (as mentioned above) and in the only meat offering of ovine among the whole identified in Torre Velha 3 hipogea's (Alves *et al.* 2010, Fidalgo *et al.* 2016).

Besides pottery, metal artefacts from Torre Velha 3 also provide some relevant data in the scope of this discussion. Metallography and chemical analysis were made on a total of 40 artefacts from Torre Velha 3. They came not only from Bronze Age hypogea but also from negative structures

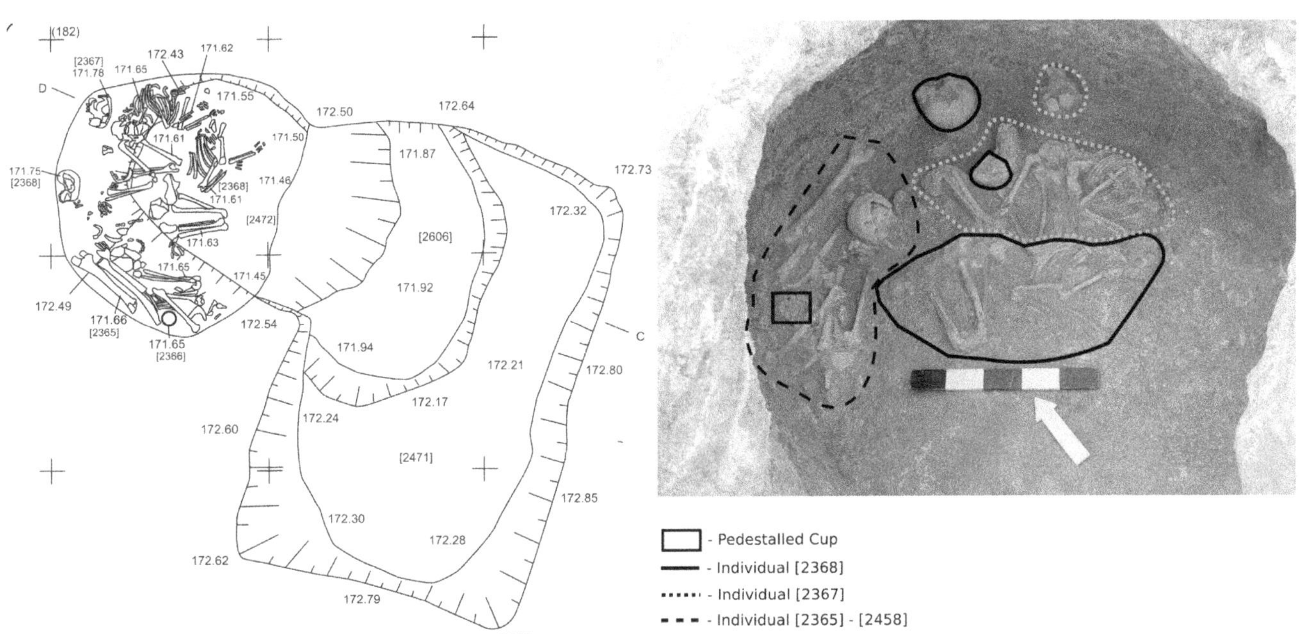

Figure 3. Funerary context of Hypogeum [2471] – [2472] (Adapted from Alves et al. 2009 and Fidalgo et al. 2016).

The two funerary contexts we finished to present stand out by the characteristics of burial rituals that, somehow, disregard the funerary patterns of Torre Velha 3 hipogea's. The hypogeum [2471] – [2472] presents the largest number of individuals (n=three) inhumated in the funerary chamber of a single hypogeum. In addition, their burials exhibits elements that may evidence the post mortem manipulation

related to several human occupations identified at this archaeological site. Concerning Bronze Age metallurgy, it turns out that the majority of artefacts are produced with arsenical copper through a long *chaine opératoire*, having several hammering and annealing stages. Such productions, which at first sight seem archaic, are different from Chalcolithic ones, due to their high arsenical contents.

[3] Verbal information from Dr. Cleia Detry (UNIARQ), whom we acknowledge and thank.

According to the data already known (Valério 2012) this last fact may be characteristic of the Middle Bronze Age in this region. Within this assemblage four awls (no. 393[4], 395, 418, 422) and a dagger (no. 714) stand out. They were produced in a binary alloy having standardized tin contents, 8-12 per cent, which is a technological solution characteristic of a more refined bronze metallurgy, like that of the Late Bronze Age (Valério *et al.* 2013 and Porfírio *et al.* 2013).

Object no. 393 is the only one that came from a non funerary context. It was found in structure [1139], a depression having an irregular plan and a maximum depth of around 35cm. The stratigraphic sequence therein identified consisted of three loose and sandy-clayey layers. The last layer [577] included many charcoal pieces. The archaeological materials identified where mainly Bronze Age pottery fragments. Within this assemblage the finding of a carinated bowl having a single knob with two perforations, stood out.

Awl no. 395 was found in the layers filling a pit from Late Antiquity. This pit cut and almost entirely destroyed a Bronze Age hypogeum, of which only part of the antechamber remained. After chemical analysis it was found that the awl's alloy composition wasn't compatible with Late Antiquity metallurgy. On the contrary, it had all the characteristics of Bronze Age productions. Given this fact it seems likely that it belonged to the grave goods from the destroyed hypogeum destroyed (Valério *et al.* 2013, 75).

Hypogeum [2356]-[2357] was also partly affected by the construction of Late Antiquity structures. Nevertheless, burial [2051] and its grave goods, deposited in the southern and western wall of the chamber, were preserved. Burial [2051] was placed in the flexed position, having both members flexed and the skull placed over the right cheek, oriented NO-SE. The anthropological analysis indicates that the inhumated remains belonged to an adult (> 25 years old) woman. The study of this woman's teeth showed that the superior second right molar had atypical and severe wearing, inclined towards the tongue. Such wearing probably resulted from friction between the teeth and an object, or material, during a systematic and repetitive activity, implying the use of teeth as tools (Fidalgo 2014 and Fidalgo *et al.* 2016). The funerary gifts associated were: a vessel with a carination at mid-body and a slightly everted rim, awl no. 418 and a meat offering (Alves *et al.* 2009). The meat offering was composed by the diaphysis and proximal radius fragment, the ulna diaphysis and four carpal bones still placed in the normal anatomical order. Faunal analysis showed that these bone fragments belong to a bovine left distal extremity (Alves *et al.* 2010, 145).

Awl no. 422 belonged to the grave goods of individual [2241] buried in hypogeum [2417]-[2418]. Late Antiquity's negative structures also partially destroyed this hypogeum, by piercing part of the chamber and antechamber, although not affecting the burial and associated funerary gifts. Inhumation [2241] was placed in the flexed position, having the anterior and posterior members flexed and the skull placed over the right cheek. This body belonged to an adult (> 30 years old) female, was oriented SE-NO, and presented ochre[5] traces in the right clavicle (Fidalgo 2014 and Fidalgo *et al.* 2016). Besides the awl, the other goods from this grave were an Odivelas-type bowl and a copper dagger (Alves *et al.* 2010, 144 and Valério *et al.* 2014, 72).

In turn, dagger n. ° 714 was part of the grave goods related to individual [1714], buried in hypogeum [1267] - [1792] near its NE wall. The body was placed in the flexed position, oriented NE-SO, having the skull placed over the left cheek. Burial [1714] belongs to an adult (> 25 years old) female. Similarly to individual [2051] it showed dental wearing resulting from the use of teeth as tools (Fidalgo 2014 and Fidalgo *et al.* 2016). All funerary gifts related to this individual where deposited nearby the skull. They were a quadrangular section awl and a pottery vessel with an oval profile and a vertical rim that contained dagger no. 714 on the inside. Dagger no. 714 was made in arsenical copper having two silver rivets (Alves *et al.* 2010, 144 and Valério *et al.* 2014, 72). Related to these goods there was also a meat offering made up of the proximal fragment and the left radius dyaphisis of an adult bovine (Alves *et al.* 2010, 145).

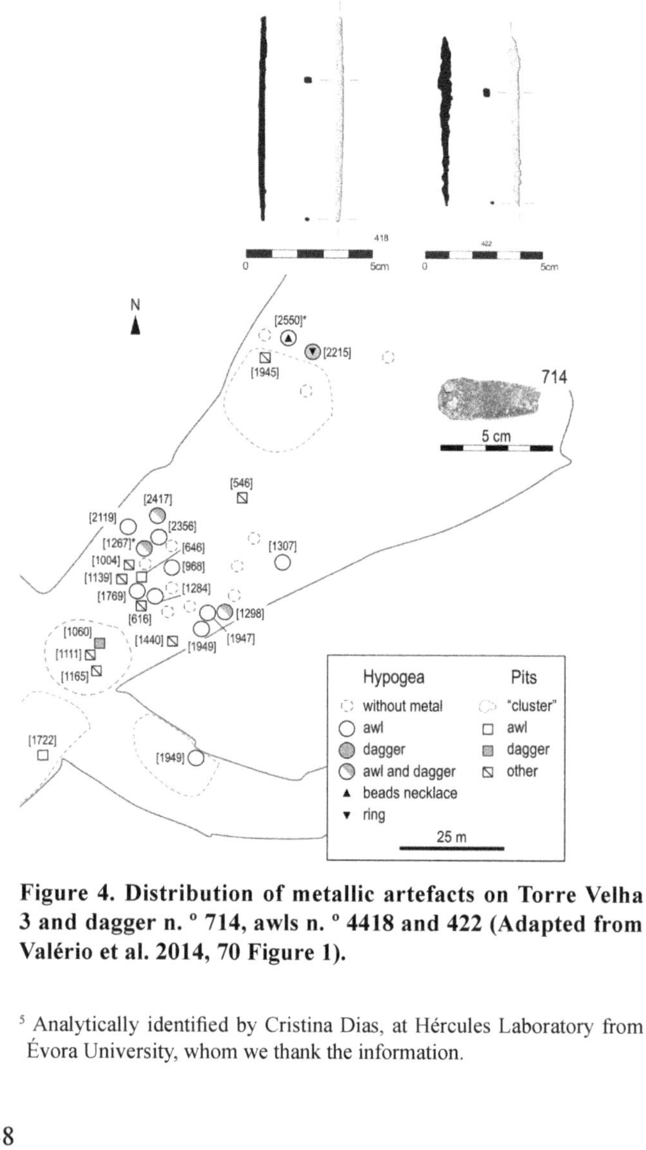

Figure 4. Distribution of metallic artefacts on Torre Velha 3 and dagger n. ° 714, awls n. ° 4418 and 422 (Adapted from Valério et al. 2014, 70 Figure 1).

[4] The classification of this object as an awl is not completely clear. In fact it is a fragment of a small bronze rod whose morphological characteristics suggest it should be typologically classified as an awl.

[5] Analytically identified by Cristina Dias, at Hércules Laboratory from Évora University, whom we thank the information.

Apart from the rivets of dagger n.º 714, the silver was used in two beads that were part of a necklace with which the female individual [2069] was inhumed. The osteological remains of this female show that she died at about the age of 35 years (Fidalgo 2014 and Fidalgo *et al.* 2016). In addition to the afore mentioned silver beads, the necklace was made up with more six beads: two in bone material, other two in an unidentified shell (*Dentalium*?), and a third pair in arsenical copper (Alves *et al.* 2010 and Valério *et al.* 2014). Unfortunately this hypogeum [2550] – [2551], was extensively affected by post-depositional phenomena, which was reflected in the poor conservation of the osteological remains and in the difficulty of classifying a left bovine radius [2016] as a meat offering, because it was removed from its original position. Nevertheless, it was possible to determine that burial [2069] was performed in flexed position (right lateral decubitus), oriented SE-NW, having the skull placed over the right cheek (Fidalgo 2014 and Fidalgo *et al.* 2016). The grave goods directly associated with inhumation [2069] consisted in a vessel decorated with vertical ribs and an arsenical copper awl (Alves *et al.* 2010 and Valério *et al.* 2014). Near the western wall of the funerary chamber was recovered the osteological remains of an adult male [2068], poorly preserved. The position of these bones were clearly the result of a reduction process whose primary position is unknown (Fidalgo 2014 and Fidalgo *et al.*, 2016).

In addition to the female [2069] necklace, the remaining personal ornaments found in Torre Velha 3 hipogea's are a spiral-shaped ring in arsenical copper and a necklace made of 31 whelks (species to be identified) belonging to individual [604]. In the first case it was the burial of a non-adult individual whose age of death has been estimated between 5 and 9 years old. It was buried near the western wall of the chamber of hypogeum [2215] – [2231], in flexed position (right lateral decubitus), having the skull placed over the left cheek, oriented SE-NW (Fidalgo 2014 and Fidalgo *et al.* 2016). The grave goods were deposited between the burial and the eastern wall of the funerary chamber, and are composed by an arsenical copper dagger and a pottery vessel (Alves *et al.* 2010 and Valério *et al.* 2014).

In the second case, individual [604] was recovered inside the hypogeum [697] – [710]. The corpse was placed in flexed position, with the higher and the lowers members flexed, having the skull placed over the trunk. An isolated skull from a different body was recovered near the lower members of burial [604]. Following the first anthropological study, done in the field, the age of death of individual [604] has been estimated between 4 and 5 years old, despite the bad conservation of the osteological remains (Ferreira 2009).

Finally, a few words about the meat offerings, because this issue has already been analyzed in other papers (Porfírio e Serra 2010 and 2016). In Torre Velha 3 the meat offerings show a selection of certain osteological elements, usually the left distal extremities of mostly sub-adult sheep/goats (there's only one single case of bovine). This situation constitutes a defining characteristic of the funerary ritual (or at least part of it) that built and used the hypogea of Torre Velha 3, since this type of offering is present in 10 of the 25 tombs of this necropolis. It should be noted that the identification of faunal remains as part of the grave goods is a phenomenon present in numerous cultural systems of different geographies and chronologies. However, the standardization or the tendency towards a pattern of the meat offerings from Torre Velha 3 (it is true that this pattern does not find an exact correspondence with the other hipogea necropolises, the data from these ones does not contradict the identified tendency) echoes similar trends observed in the argaric world (Alves *et al.* 2010, 145 and Porfirio e Serra 2016, 69).

Discussion

In addition to the data gathered in Torre Velha 3, there are other elements that are commonly pointed has a material testimony to the existence of interaction processes between the Bronze Age communities of Baixo Alentejo with other contemporaneous groups. We refer, first and foremost, to the Belmeque burial (Serpa/Beja). This monument is dated by radiocarbon to the middle of the 2nd millennium BC, and its exceptional character is highlighted by his pottery and metallic artefacts. About the latter, it was already mentioned that the knife and one of the daggers were produced using a bronze alloy that included a high concentration of tin. Metallographic analysis also revealed that the rivets of the knife were produced from a natural gold alloy (*electrum*) whose percentage of silver and copper aren't equivalent to those found in the regional metallurgy from this period, still mostly dominated by arsenical copper. Facing this data, it's possible to advance with the hypothesis that we stand before exogenous objects that came from foreign geographical areas. However at this moment it's still too early to classify such artefacts has importations *stricto sensu*, it seems safer to infer that such occurrences lead us to believe in possible regional or inter-regional interactions, whatever the characteristics they may have assumed (Schubart 1974, Soares 1994 and Mederos Martín 2009). However, a portion of the accounted silver in the knife's gold alloy rivets of the Belmeque burial is yet different from the ones present in other artefacts of the Bronze Age of Baixo Alentejo, for these were made using gold, silver and native gold alloys, for example the torcs of Vila Nova de São Bento (Serpa/Beja) or the gold spiral chain of Vale Viegas (Serpa/Beja). The percentage of silver present in the latter is above the 20 per cent, while the copper is less than one per cent, clearly assuming a vestigial role. One of the best parallels for the alloy used on the knife's rivet of Belmeque can be found in a golden artefact of Antas (Almeria), with an alloy of gold around 25 per cent and copper values between 0,32 and 0,35 per cent, and without any traces of tin (Soares 1994, 183, Soares et al 2004, 131).

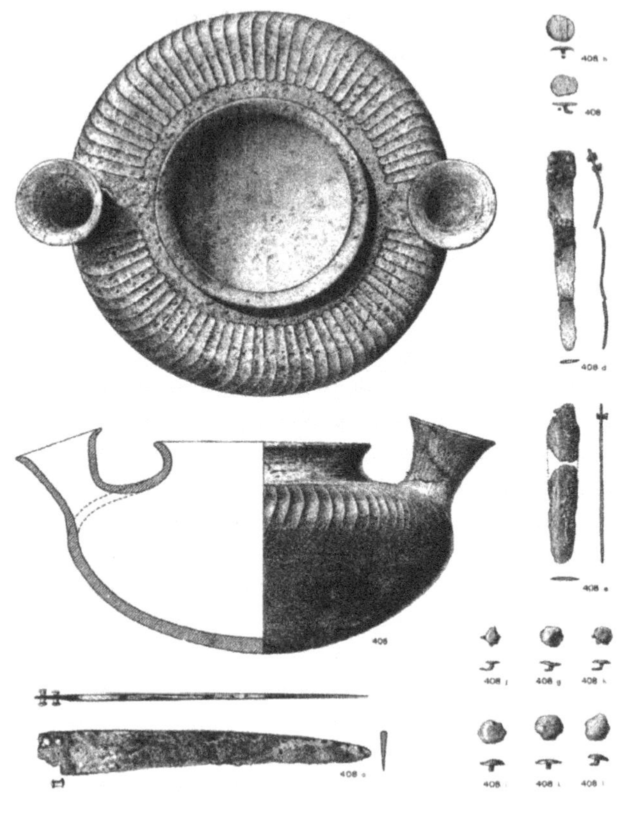

Figure 5. Funerary gifts from the grave of Belmeque (adapted from Schubart 1975, lam 59).

While the metal and pottery artefacts from Belmeque still maintain most of its exceptionality that characterized them when first discovered in the beginning of the 70s from the past century, on the other hand the architecture and some aspects of the funerary rituals have now parallels in other necropolises, somehow synchronous, in the region of Serpa in Baixo Alentejo. Henceforth, both the burials made underground and the funerary meat offerings are now practices that can be found in other hypogea necropolises. We now have the examples of Outeiro Alto 2/Monte do Gato de Cima 3 (Valera and Filipe 2010 and Filipe *et al.* 2013), Montinhos 6 (Baptista *et al.* 2012), Horta do Folgão (Ponte *et al.* 2013) and Torre Velha 3 and 12 (Gomes *et al.* 2013).

Although there are some peculiarities in the necropolis referred, it's possible to identify some common elements between them, including Belmeque monument. They all exhibit the same funerary architecture, consisting in a rock-cut tomb, resembling the argaric burials known as *covachas* (Soares 1994), like the tomb 95 of Fuente Álamo (Alves *et al.* 2010 and Schubart *et al.* 1989). We can also infer the parallelism between the tombs with the four hypogea built in the *tholos* of Las Canteras (Alcala de la Guadaira, Sevilla), even if the stone wrist-guard found in one of the burial puts this contexts in a previous moment, the ceramic vessels fits perfectly with the typologies of the Bronze Age of the Southwest (Alves *et al.* 2010 and Hurtado and Amores 1984). The hypogea 1 and 2 from this site are also mentioned has parallels for the structures Type B from Outeiro Alto 2, along with three others identified in Huerta de San Francisco and with the tomb T.1 from Plazuela de Santiago (Carmona). Are also referred the similarities between the hypogea Type A from Outeiro Alto 2 and the tomb from Vejer de la Frontera (Cádis) (Filipe *et al.* 2013 with bibliography).

Similarities as well in the way that most of the inhumations were made, in flexed position (body deposited in lateral decubitus with both inferior and superior members flexed), there is a clear tendency for the individualization of the burial, even if maintaining some familiar ties, or the presence of faunal remains has funerary offerings, which leads to assume that commensality played an important role in the funerary rituals.

In general, considering the pottery and metallic typologies of the funerary assemblages recovered at the hypogea necropolises, we verified that, as in the case of Torre Velha 3, they are consonant with the grave gods identified at the typical cists of the Bronze Age of the Southwest. Although, there are some elements that clearly stand out from the referred assemblages, like the already mentioned pedestalled cups of Torre Velha 3 or the sword recovered from Horta do Folgão (Serpa/Beja), of which we will speak next.

The sword were recovered in the hypogeum 3 over the inferior members of an adult, possibly male, who was buried in left lateral decubitus, with both the inferior and superior members flexed. Like in the cases above mentioned about Torre Velha 3, this burial also stands out, mainly because of the funerary architecture, but also because of the deposition of the inhumation. With regard to the first subject, hypogeum 3 stands out by the using of large blocks of limestone lithology, roughly sculpted, which was intentionally placed in an oblique position, along with smaller stones and a black "greasy" clay sediment mixed with propolis and beeswax (Frade *et al.* 2014). On the other hand, the interior of the funerary chamber was divided through an alignment of stone blocks. Parallel to these and in the area destined to the inhumation of the body were disposed two blocks of gabbro to outline the inhumation (Ponte *et al.* 2013). The sword of Horta do Folgão has 46,6cm of length and has a triangular blade with a hexagonal section. Two of the rivets were found *in loco*, while the remaining four were recovered already loose. The analysis revealed that both the sword and one of the rivets were manufactured in an alloy of arsenical cooper, and according to a process that led to the manufacture of a clearly functional artefact, but without losing its quality of prestige good. The best typological and chronological parallel for this sword can be found in a burial from La Mesa de Setefilla (Lora del Rio, Sevilla), this one differs from the previous because it has a slightly superior length (50,2 cm) and has a blade with an angled section (Ponte *et al.* 2013 and Valério *et al.* 2012).

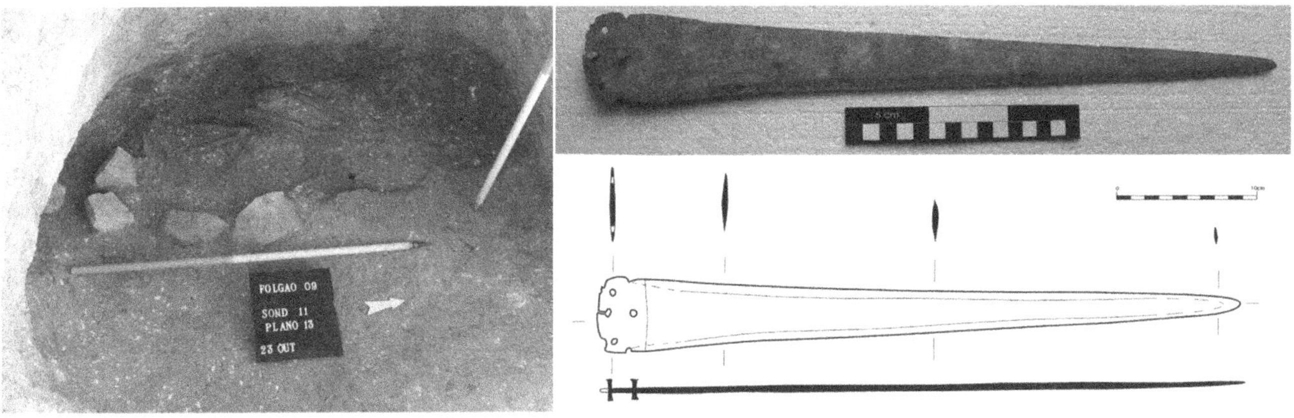

Figure 6. Burial level of Hypougeum 3 of Horta do Folgão and the sword associated with the inhumation (adapted from Ponte et al. 2013, 280-281, Figure n.º 17 and 18).

Still related to the metallurgical domain, it deserves reference, while it wasn't recovered in a hypogeum, a lead ring with a flattened circular section from the archaeological site known as Horta do João Lopes (Vidigueira/Beja). The ring was recovered along with the bones of a left hand from the burial of an adult female, deposited in flexed position (lateral left decubitus) in the interior of a pit. The radiocarbon dating from the bone material points to the middle of the first half of the 2nd millennium BC With the exception of another finding from the necropolis of Las Palomas (Badajoz), the ring of Horta do João Lopes is the only evidence of lead in the metallic assemblages of the Bronze Age of the Southwest (Valério *et al.* 2016).

The existence of objects manufactured in bronze and in lead alloys in a context defined by the extremely conservative character of the metallurgical practices, which still be dominated by productions of arsenical copper, is of great importance to the regional and extra-regional interactions, since it is one of the hypothesis to justify the presence of such objects in this geographical areas. However, this hypothesis should be viewed with caution because of the data supplied by the archaeological site Malhada do Vale da Água (Ferreira do Alentejo/ Beja) which revealed numerous elements related to metallurgical activities (copper and bronze alloys), such has casting crucibles, metallic nodules, fragments of ores and slags with traces of copper and tin. All the radiocarbon dates for these contexts fall in the interval between 1535 and 1294 BC for 2 sigma (Valério *et al.* 2016).

Another element usually associated with this problematic is the type I stelae or "Alentejo" slabs, so called because the main concentration of that kind of stelae is located in that region. Lots of aspects related to this matter are still in discussion, starting by its functionality, and going through its association with graves because sometimes they were used to cover cists, or because they could also be used for other purposes, such as territorial markers, which is justified by the fact that some stelae don't show any iconography in their inferior part, opening the possibility of their vertical positioning. Their chronology is also being intensely discussed, which makes it impossible for us to explain in the current text extent, however we can mention two recent proposals, one from Mário Varela Gomes (2006) and another from Marta Díaz-Guardamino Uribe (2010). The first author divides the stelae in three subtypes, whose chronological extremes range from 1600-1400 BC to the subtype A, from 1500-1300 BC to the subtype B and 1300-1200/1100 BC to the subtype C. (Gomes 2006, 57 and 2015, 122). The second author presents another chronological hypothesis that goes back to 2000 BC for the stelae of the type 1 which displays representations of swords, and for the type 2 (anchor-shaped object) the oldest ones goes back to 1400/1200 BC, from here forward the more recent stelae show other iconographic patterns such has the triad composed by the sword, anchor-shaped object and halberd, but also other representations such has axes, chisels/awls and bows (Díaz-Guardamino 2010, 314).

Therefore and following the opinion of Marta Díaz--Guardamino (2010; 319), one may assume that the representations of swords and halberds in the "Alentejo" slabs are an indicator of interactions between the Bronze Age of the Southwest and other peninsular regions. This also seems to be attested, either by the typology of the elements represented on the stelae or by their arrangement in the iconographic space, which recalls representations and figurative structures of other Iberian Peninsula regions and even extra-peninsular. From these figurative parallels we can infer inter-relationships between the Bronze Age of the Southwest, with the North of Portugal, the Northwest of the Iberian Peninsula, and the Central Cantabria region. The most intense connections appear to be with the Northern region of the Meseta, more precisely with its Southwestern sector, for these are the only two areas where we can see the iconographic association between the wide leafed blade sword and the halberd (Díaz-Guardamino 2010, 319). Moreover, there are three pottery fragments of a carinated vessel

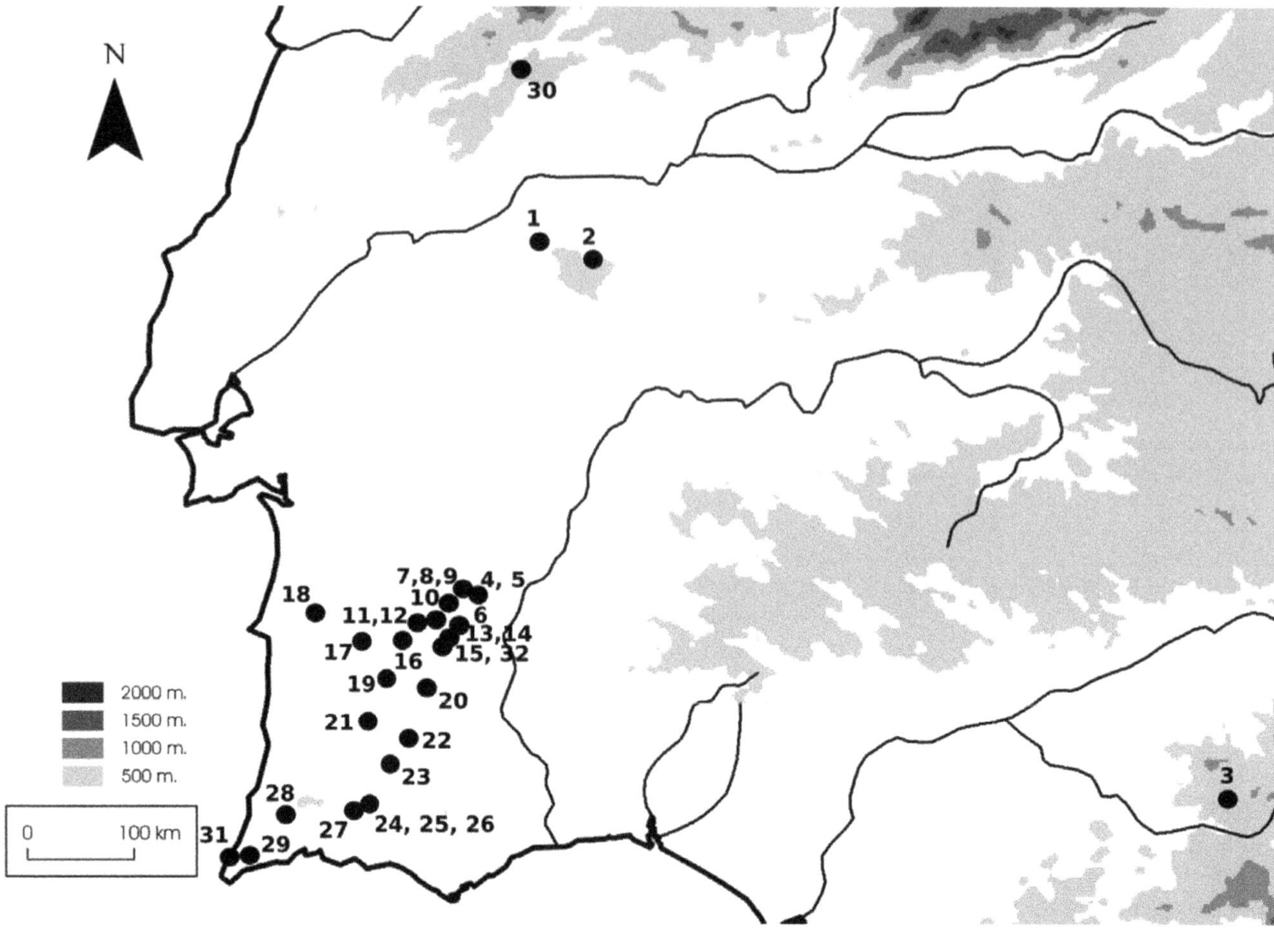

Figure 7. Map from the Iberian Peninsula showing the geographical distribution of type I stelae or "Alentejo" slabs (adapted from Serra et al. 2015, Figure 7; Díaz-Guardamino, 2010, 170 and Gomes, 2015, 122). 1 - Tapada da Moita, 2 - Valência de Alcântara, 3 - El Torcal, 4 - Trigaches I, 5 - Trigaches II, 6 - Monte de Abaixo, 7 - Mombeja I, 8 - Mombeja II, 9 - Mombeja III, 10 - Ervidel, 11 - São João de Negrilhos, 12 - Monte da Carniceira, 13 - Santa Vitória, 14 - Pedreirinha, 15 - Assento, 16 - São Salvador, 17 - Defesa, 18 - Abela, 19 - Panóias, 20 - Castro Verde, 21 - Atalaia, 22 - Mouriços, 23 - Gomes Aires, 24 - Passadeiras I, 25 - Passadeiras II, 26 - Passadeiras III, 27 - Alfarrobeira, 28 - Marmelete, 29 - Bensafrim, 30 - Donas, 31 - Milrei 1, 32 - Monte do Ulmo. | Source: By the Authors.

recovered from a pit from Casarão da Mesquita 3 (S. Manços, Évora), whose decoration consists of impressed circles and broken incised lines that may be associated with the Proto-Cogotas tradition (Santos *et al.* 2008, 73).

These interactions also seem to be attested by the stelae of Tapada da Moita (Castelo de Vide (Portalegre), of Valdefuentes de Sangusín (Salamanca) and Corgas (Fundão/Castelo Branco) (Banha *et al.* 2009), but also by some representations of weapons in the rock art of the Tejo valley wich shows parallels with the iconography of the "Alentejo" slabs. This allows us to foresee the importance played by the Tejo river and some of it main tributaries, such as the Zêzere, in the interrelationships between different cultural areas of the Peninsular Bronze Age. A similar role could be played by the Guadalquivir river, in this case with regard to interactions with the Southeast, as could be suggested by the stela of El Torcal near the spanish city of Córdoba (Díaz-Guardamino 2010).

Although we don't pretend to discuss here the complex issues associated with the diffusion of bronze metallurgy in the Peninsular territory, it must be said that these stelae, like the one recovered near Corgas, have been considered has territory markers of the probable networks through which circulated the materials, objects, techniques and people involved in that process (Senna Martinez 2007 and 2013).

Another discussed subject regarding the stelae is related to one of the most represented iconographic elements, the anchor-shaped object, about which remains to clarify almost everything that concerns it. We cannot list here all the interpretations presented, since the past century, by the archaeological bibliography about that issue (see for example Serra *et al.* 2014 with bibliography), but it's worth to note, has a brief appointment and with the reservations that this kind of approach deserves, the similarities that some authors have identified between the anchor-shaped object represented on the stelae and other representations from the North African rock art (Gomes 1994). This similarities, according to Anati (1968 *apud* Gomes 1994) are registered in both representations as in compositional structures between certain elements featured in the "Alentejo" slabs and in the rock art from the Moroccan Atlas, especially considering the anchor-shaped object. Later, Martín Almagro (1971) found new parallels for the anchor-shaped object in other rock art sites located near the Ocidental Saara. However, besides the anchor-shaped object, some authors that have studied the rock art from these geographical regions point to other figurative parallels between the two sides of the Strait of Gibraltar, such has the representation of halberds, axes and daggers (Souville 1986). These iconographic "echoes" are not so far-fetched if we take into account that beyond these representations, there are other elements which resemble typologies from the Peninsular Bronze Age, such has metallic objects like axes, halberds and the sword found in the Ria de Larache. There are also references to some similarities in the funerary structures, with burials being made in ceramic vessels, or even the existence of inhumations deposited in pits, resembling funerary features of the argaric world (Souville 1986).

Some practices of the 4th and 3rd millennium BC, continues in the Southwest Bronze Age, however, the scale of coverage is very different from the one previously reached These pratices include, for example, the usage of greenstone, among other rare rocks, for the production of ornaments like necklace beads. Without being exhaustive, we can mention some cases such as the ones found in the cist 12 from Provença (Sines/Setúbal) where two green beads were recovered along with a gold spiral-shaped bead (Silva and Soares 1981), or in the cist 1 from the monument II from Pessegueiro (Sines/Setúbal) that contained three silver spirals and 23 beads, from which 20 are discoid and green, two are made from a raw material of beige color and the last one has a sub-cylindrical shape made from a dark brown raw matter (Silva and Soares 2009). More to the South we can find the tomb 5 from Vale da Telha (Aljezur/Faro) which contained two beads (Gomes 2015). Another spherical-shaped bead in talc can be found in the tomb of Santa Vitória (Beja), without any additional information except for the fact that it was deposited in the National Museum of Archaeology before 1906, along with a bowl of type "Atalaia" (Gonçalves *et al.* 2005). The cist 2 from the necropolis of Carapinhais (Serpa/Beja) revelead 17 beads, from which 12 were connected, some aligned, and the remaining were collected outside their original context. All of them were produced from a brown-gray stone, integrated in the chlorite group, according to the analysis made from one of the beads (Soares *et al.* 2009 and Gonçalves 2007). To the South, in a cist (tomb U) from Maudinheiro (Castro Marim/Faro), Estácio da Veiga mentions three beads made from what was commonly called *calaíte*, a term frequently used and widely discussed in the archaeological bibliography at the time (Veiga 1891, 120 and Schubart 1975).

However, it seems that the exotic raw materials, especially greenstones, don't assume the same symbolic role to the Bronze Age communities as they once did during the Chalcolithic. The hypothesis proposed by Ignacio Montero Ruiz and Mercedes Murillo-Barroso (2016) is based on the premise that a bigger weight was given to the individual component in the funerary world since the Bell-Beaker culture, leading to the reduction of the communal ideologies that dominated the previous funerary conceptions. In the middle of that process the metal artefacts will assume a new status and new symbolic role. However a possible *terminus* in the contacts with the Mediterranean, which was the source of exotic raw materials to the Iberian Peninsula, it is not well explicited. A similar situation seems to occur with gold and probably silver, which starts being used for personal ornaments (absent of any decoration) since the beginning of the Bronze Age (Murillo-Barroso *et al.* 2014).

Another interpretative hypothesis implies a change in our scale of analysis to a macro level, and consider that the

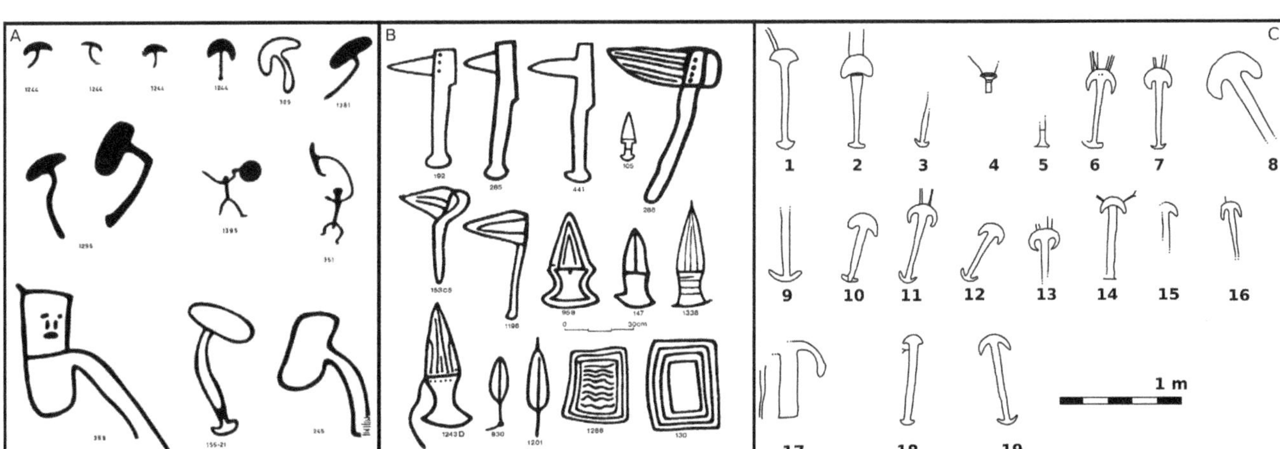

Figure 8. A - Some representations of anchor-shaped objects from the rock art of the Great Atlas. Scale: number 1.242 at 1/12, all the others at 1/8 relative to natural size (adapted from Malhome 1959 and Almagro Basch 1971, 27). B - Representations of Bronze Age weapons from the rock art of the Great Atlas (adapted from Malhome 1959 and Souville 1986, 110). C - Some representations of anchor-shaped objects from the "Alentejo" slabs (adapted from Serra et al. 2014, Figure 6).

less expressive dispersion of exotic raw materials in the 2nd millennium BC, such as the personal ornaments, is related with a higher centralization of its distribution networks, assuming a relationship of dependency of the Southwest in favor of the Southeast of the Iberia Peninsula, entailing the "... *impoverishment of the rural communities...*" (Silva 2016, 369). Being so, the elites of this period, concentrated on the El Argar region, and the basis of their power is in the stewardship and management of their medium and long-range exchange networks, mainly regarding metallic elements and the already mentioned exotic raw materials. This situation could justify the importance that the horse assumed in the faunal accounts of the argaric territory, while its presence in the Southwest is, up until now, extremely low (Soares and Silva 2016). Even if the use of this animal seems at first glance more adequate to the amplitude of the plains that characterize some areas of the Southwest than to the argaric geography. Following this hypothesis, the dynamism of the plains of Santa Vitória (Beja/Serpa), as showed by the greatest concentration of stelae (Díaz-Guardamino 2010), by the metallurgy of Malhada do Vale da Água (Valério *et al.* 2016) and by the value of the funerary gifts of some burials, one may argue that it might correspond to a relatively powerful regional center which could arise during the process that led to the desegregation of the argaric socio-political structure (Soares and Silva 2016). From a certain point of view this premise was already advanced by Mário Valera Gomes (1995, 135): "*It is possible that an important focus of social-economic growth occurred in the Beja region, directly related to the exploration of the existent mineral resources, but also, with the good fields for agriculture which could be reflected in the construction of a great number of stelae, [...]making possible the exogenous contacts and cultural complexity that originated the II Bronze Age of the Southwest and its development*".

The materialization of such relationships and their repercussion in the elites of these societies could be reflected in the exceptional auriferous artefacts from Herdade do Sardoninho (Aljustrel/Beja), composed by a diadem, by a guard and a pommel of a gold dagger (Armbruster and Parreira 1993), that if we accept the chronology of the first second half of the 2nd millennium BC (Soares and Silva 2016, 370), which is surrounded by great uncertainty, since B. Armbruster and R. Parreira (1993) propose a timeline near the passing from the 2nd to the 1st millennium BC However, it will have to be taken in consideration the fact that the guard and the pommel of the dagger from Herdade do Sardoninho have been produced using the lost-wax casting technique, making it comparable (up to a certain point) to the dagger from Alange (Badajoz), thus suggesting that the first assemblage may come from a Southwest Bronze Age context (Correia 2013).

Other authors question the existence of such socio-political structure in the Southwest Bronze Age, assuming the development of different socio-political centers opened to exogenous influences (for example those with origin in the argaric or in the proto-cogotas world), characterized by a high level of regionalism, given the potential of the resources available locally (Pavón Soldevila and Duque Espino 2014).

Anyway, the region of Santa Vitória-Beja-Serpa joins, in the same geography, natural resources and archaeological contexts that document the dynamism of the communities that inhabited these peneplains during the 2nd millennium BC As we approach the ending of the 2nd millennium BC there is a gradual increase of material elements that corroborate the relationships with foreign areas outside de Iberian Peninsula, for example the glass paste beads dated to the middle of the 2nd millennium BC from the necropolis of Atalaia (Ourique/Beja) (Schubart 1975 and Cardoso 2007), or even the gold technology used in some objects from Villena-Estremoz typology (Armsbruster and Perea 1994).

Concluding Remarks

We are aware that many elements presented above are still coming from a research position that we would classify has "classic", mainly based on formal typologies, taking into account the way that, actually, archaeology deals with interactions issues. This last term is itself a more neutral way to approach the subject, thus avoiding to put the emphasis in the commercial approach, which when considered in a purely capitalist manner, is hardly comparable with the Bronze Age societies, even with those of its final steps that maintained more contacts with other cultural realities from the Atlantic and the Mediterranean. However, these are the elements available at the moment and we are perfectly aware that future investigations have to explore this thematic in a more profound way, according to the later analytical developments that archaeology has experiencing.

Having this in mind, we would like to leave some final remarks on the subject. During the Chalcolithic and the Bell-Beaker period the material culture of these societies can be found spread along the region of Baixo Alentejo, which reflects the existence of large-scale networks of interaction. However, the Initial and Middle Bronze Age periods would be marked to this, as at other levels, by a stagnation that would only be reverted during the Late Bronze Age. Considering the material evidences, it seems to us that this difference it's more a question of scale rather than a stagnation, although this difference still had its repercussions at several levels in these societies. Firstly, in the way in which the communities of the Southwest Bronze Age treated their deceased, despite the multiplicities patented in the funerary architecture and in the burial rituals (Soares *et al.* 2009), some of them made burials in monuments of the 4th/3rd millennium BC (Mataloto 2005), there are certain elements that recall very directly some aspects of the argaric funerary rituals. Among these there are comparable features between the hypogea and the so called argaric "covachas", the presence of faunal remains that document the practice of commensality during burial rites, as well as the presence in Torre Velha 3 of two pedestalled cups whose typology is uncommon in the ceramic assemblages of the Southwest Bronze Age.

Also, the stela of El Torcal could be an argument in favor of these relationships, despite being relatively atypical and geographically isolated in the Guadalquivir basin. When considered in this context this stela's framework becomes more meaningful.

On the other hand, it also seems evident the relations between the Meseta region and the North Iberian Peninsula, given the geographical distribution of some of the "Alentejo" slabs more eccentric relative to the central core, or even by the existent parallels between some metallic objects present in this stelae, in the statues-menhirs of Alto Douro, or in some engravings from the Tejo valley. The circulation of goods in this networks would involve other elements such has ornaments and beads made in rare rocks, and also probably seashells, if such confirmation is given to the necklace made of 31 whelks found in the burial [604] from Torre Velha 3, or for the two beads made in shell that integrated the necklace of the skeleton [2069] from the same necropolis.

Comparing the archaeological elements pointed in our frame of reference it is clear the importance of the interrelationships in the Iberian Peninsula, especially because foreign elements out of this geographic region are scarce, although there are the already mentioned similarities between weapon representations such has the anchor-shaped object in the stelae and parietal art from the North of Africa. It is yet to be evaluated the impact of the elements adducted by G. Souville (1998) who speak in favor of a relationship between the Bronze Age from both sides of the Strait of Gibraltar. In fact, there is nothing new given the relative ancestry of these interactions. The interactions with the Mediterranean, especially those related with the "Mycenaean vector", as proposed by some authors to explain some of the materials associated with the Belmeque burial, especially the knife (Schubart 1975, 91, Torres Ortiz 2008 and Mederos Martín 2009), but also the socketed axes represented in some of the stelae (Monte Abaixo, Ervidel I, Santa Vitória e Assento/Beja), the glass paste beads found in the Atalaia necropolis, or the technology used in the jewellery of Villena-Estremoz (Días-Guardamino 2010; 324 with bibliography).

Most of these manifestations, for example the Mycenaean pottery from Llanete de los Moros (Córdova), or the ceramic fragments made using a potter's wheel recovered on La Cuesta del Negro (Granada), are chronologically placed in a period a little bit posterior to the 2nd millennium BC, more precisely between 1400-1200/1100 BC (Torres Ortiz 2008). The truth is that we have yet to evaluate the impact of such contacts between the Mediterranean and the Iberian socio-political structures, especially in the Southwest, since these artefacts represent only a very small sample and they don't suggest the establishment of foreign communities or either the influence of these groups as far as technological aspects (Arruda 2015). However, has we approach the 1st millennium BC are concern, the influence and impact of the contacts with exogenous cultural structures from both the Atlantic and the Mediterranean will increase, gradually and profoundly, on the communities that inhabited the Alentejo's peneplains.

References

Almagro Basch, Martín. "A propósito de unos objetos hachiformes representados en el arte rupestre del Sahara Ocidental." *Munibe* año XXIII, n.° 1 (1971): 25-35.

Alves, Catarina, Costeira, Catarina, Estrela, Susana, Porfírio, Eduardo. and Serra, Miguel *Torre Velha 3. Relatório Final (2ª fase). Minimização de Impactes sobre o Património Cultural decorrentes da Construção da Barragem da Laje (Serpa)*, Unprinted report: Palimpsesto Lda., 2009.

Alves, Catarina, Costeira, Costeira, Estrela, Susana, Porfírio, Eduardo and Serra, Miguel. "Torre Velha 3 (Serpa): Dados preliminares." *Al-madan adenda electrónica* II série, n.° 17-1 (2012): 31-38.

Alves, Catarina, Costeira, Catarina, Estrela, Susana, Porfírio, Eduardo and Serra, Miguel. "Necrópole Tardo-Antiga da Torre Velha 3, Serpa (Baixo Alentejo/Portugal)." In *VI Encuentro de Arqueología del Suroeste Peninsular, Villafranca de los Barros, 4 a 6 de Octobre de 2012*, edited by Javier Jiménez Ávila, Macarena Bustamante, Miriam García Cabezas, 1929-1966. Villafranca de los Barros: Ayuntamiento de Villafranca de los Barros, 2013.

Alves, Catarina, Costeira, Costeira, Estrela, Susana, Porfírio, Eduardo and Serra, Miguel. "Análise preliminar dos contextos da Antiguidade Tardia do sítio Torre Velha 3 (Barragem da Laje – Serpa)." In *Actas do IV Colóquio de Arqueologia de Alqueva, O Plano de Rega (2002-2010)*, 203-211. Évora: EDIA/Direcção Regional de Cultura do Alentejo, 2014.

Alves, Catarina, Costeira, Catarina, Estrela, Susana, Porfírio, Eduardo, Serra, Miguel, Soares, António M. and Moreno-García, Marta. "Hipogeus funerários do Bronze Pleno da Torre Velha 3 (Serpa, Portugal). O Sudeste no Sudoeste ?!" *Zephyrus* LXVI (2010): 133 -153.

Alves, Catarina, Costeira, Costeira, Estrela, Susana, Porfírio, Eduardo and Serra, Miguel, Soares, António M. and Moreno-García, Marta. "Caracterização preliminar da ocupação pré-histórica da Torre Velha 3 (Barragem da Laje – Serpa)." In *Actas do IV Colóquio de Arqueologia de Alqueva, O Plano de Rega (2002-2010)*, 103-111. Évora: EDIA/Direcção Regional de Cultura do Alentejo, 2014.

Anati, Emmanuel. *Arte rupestre nelle regioni Occidentalli della Penisola Iberica*. Capo di Ponte: Edizioni del Centro Camuno di Studi Preistorici, 1968.

Armbruster, Barbara and Parreira, Rui. *Inventário do Museu Nacional de Arqueologia, Colecção de Ourivesaria, 1.° volume - Do Calcolítico à Idade do Bronze*. Lisboa: Instituto Português de Museus, 1993.

Arruda, Ana Margarida. "Intercultural contacts in the far West at the beginning of the 1st millenium BC: through the looking-glass." In *The mediterranean mirror. Cultural contacts in the mediterranean sea between 1200 and 750 BC*, edited by Andrea Babbi, Friederike Bubenheimer-Erhart, Beatriz Marín-Aguilera, and Simone Mühl, 269-283. Main: Verlag des Römisch-Germanischen Zentralmuseums, 2015

Banha, Carlos, Veiga, André M., Ferro, Sara. "A estátua-menir de Corgas (Donas, Fundão). Contributo para o estudo da Idade do Bronze na Beira Interior." *Açafa online* 2 (2009): 1-16.

Bokbot, Youssef. "La civilizacion del Vaso Campaniforme en Marruecos y la cuestion del sustrato Calcolítico precampaniforme."

In *El campaniforme en la Península Ibérica y su contexto europeo*, edited by Manuel A. Rojo-Guerra, Rafael Garrido-Pena, and Iñigo García-Martínez de Lagran, 137-149. Valladolid: Universidad de Valladolid/Junta de Castilla y León, 2005.

Burillo-Barroso, Mercedes, Costa Caramé, Manuel E., Díaz-Guardamino Uribe, Marta, García Sanjuán, Leonardo and Mora Molina, Coronada. "A Reappraisal of Iberian Copper Age Goldwork: Craftmanship, Symbolism and Art in a Non-funerary Gold Sheet from Valencina de la Concepción." *Cambridge Archaeological Journal* 25, n.º 3 (2015): 565-596.

Calado, Manuel. "A Idade do Bronze." In *História de Portugal, dos tempos pré-históricos aos nossos dias*, edited by João Medina, 327-353. Lisboa: Amigos do Livro, 1995.

Correia, Virgílio H. "A ourivesaria arcaica no ocidente peninsular. Estado da questão, problemáticas arqueológicas e perspetivas de desenvolvimento do campo de estudo." *O Arqueólogo Português* Série V n.º 3 (2013): 15–114.

Costa Caramé, Manuel E., García Sanjuán, Leonardo, Murillo-Barroso, Mercedes, Parrilla Giráldez, Rubén and Wheatley, David W. "Artefactos elaborados en rocas raras en los contextos funerários del IV-II milénios cal ANE en el Sur de España: una revisión." In *Exploring time and matter in prehistoric monuments: absolute chronology and rare rocks in European megaliths. Proceedings of the 2nd European Megalithic Studies Group Meeting, Sevilla, Spain, November 2008*, edited by Leonardo García Sanjuán, Chris Scarre and David H. Wheatley. *Menga, Revista de Prehistoria de Andalucía Série Monográfica, n.º* 1 (2011): 253-293.

Estrela, Susana, Costeira, Catarina, Alves, Catarina, Porfírio, Eduardo, and Serra, Miguel. "Torre Velha 3 (Serpa): um novo ponto no mapa da Idade do Ferro do Sudoeste." In *V Encontro de Arqueologia do Sudoeste Peninsular - Almodôvar - 18 a 20 de Novembro de 2010*, edited by Manuela de Deus, 235-268. Almodôvar: Município de Almodôvar, 2012.

Feio, Mariano. *A evolução do relevo do Baixo Alentejo e Algarve. Estudos de Geomorfologia*. Lisboa: Instituto para a Alta Cultura/ Centro de Estudos Geográficos, 1952.

Ferreira, Maria T. *Torre Velha 3 (Barragem da Laje, Serpa), Relatório dos trabalhos de Antropologia Biológica desenvolvidos no âmbito da minimização de impactes no sítio da Torre Velha 3*, Unprinted report, 2009.

Fidalgo, Daniel. *Contextos funerários e estudo antropológico dos restos ósseos humanos dos hipogeus de Torre Velha 3 (São Salvador, Serpa): Uma aproximação ao estudo das comunidades humanas do Bronze do Sudoeste*, Master Thesis. Universidade de Coimbra, 2014

Fidalgo, Daniel, Porfírio, Eduardo. and Silva, Ana Maria. "Novos dados sobre os hipogeus do Bronze Pleno de Torre Velha 3 (Serpa): contextos sepulcrais e estudo do espólio osteológico humano." *Estudos do Quaternário* 15 (2016): 1-25.

Filipe, Victor, Godinho, Ricardo, Granja, Raquel, Ribeiro, Artur and Valera, António C. "Bronze Age funerary spaces in Outeiro Alto 2 (Brinches, Serpa, Portugal): the hypogea cemitery." *Zephyrus* LXXI (2013): 107-129.

Gomes, Mário.V. "A necrópole de Alfarrobeira (S. Bartolomeu de Messines) e a Idade do Bronze no concelho de Silves." *Xelb* 2 (1994).

Gomes, Mário V. "Estelas funerárias da Idade do Bronze Médio do Sudoeste Peninsular – a iconografia do poder." In *Actas do VIII Congresso Internacional de Estelas Funerárias (O Arqueólogo Português – Suplemento 3)*, 47-62. Lisboa: Museu Nacional de Arqueologia, 2006.

Gomes, Mário V. "Representações de armas na arte rupestre do Vale do Tejo – importância sócio-económica, cronológica e cognitiva." In *From the origins: the prehistory of the inner Tagus region*, edited by Primitiva Bueno Ramirez, Eduardo Cerrillo Cuenca, and Antonio Gonzalez Cordero, 177-198. Oxford: British Archaeological Reports International Series, 2011.

Gomes, Mário V. *The Vale da Telha Necropolis (Aljezur) in the context of the Southwest Iberian Bronze Age*. Lisboa: Instituto de Arqueologia e Paleociências, Universidade Nova de Lisboa, 2015.

Gonçalves, António A. "Identificação mineralógica de uma conta da Necrópole dos Carapinhais (Sobral da Adiça, Moura)." *Vipasca – Arqueologia e História* 2ª série, n.º 2 (2007): 191-193.

Gonçalves, António P., Valério, Pedro, Soares, António. M. and Araújo, Maria de F. "A stone bead from a SW Bronze Age burial: analysis by EDXRF and X-Ray diffraction." *O Arqueólogo Português* série IV, n.º 23 (2005): 257-264.

Gonçalves, Victor .S. and Sousa, Ana C. "In and out. Tecnologias, símbolos e cultura material. Interacções e identidades regionais no centro e sul de Portugal no 3.º milénio a.n.e." In *Congrés Internacional Xarxes al Neolític – Networks in neolithic. Exchange of raw materials, products and ideas in the Western Mediterranean (VII-III millenium BC), Gavá, Bellaterra, 2011*, edited by Mónica Borrell, Ferran Borrell, Josep Bosch, Xavier Clop and Miquel Molist. *Rubricatum* 5 (2012): 383-392.

Hurtado, Victor and Amores, Fernando. "El Tholos de Las Canteras y los enterramientos del Bronce en la necrópolis de El Gandul (Alcalá de Guadaira, Sevilla)." *Cuadernos de Prehistoria de la Universidad de Granada* 9 (1984): 147-174.

Lopes, Maria C., Carvalho, Pedro C. and Gomes, Sofia M. *Arqueologia do concelho de Serpa*. Serpa: Câmara Municipal de Serpa, 1997

Malhome, Jean. *Corpus des gravures rupestres du Gran Atlas*. Rabat: Service des Antiquités du Maroc, 1959.

Mataloto, Rui. "As ocupações Proto-históricas do Castelo do Giraldo (Évora)." *Revista de Guimarães* Volume Especial, n.º I (1999): 333-362.

Mataloto, Rui. "A propósito de um achado na Herdade das Casas (Redondo): Megalitismo e Idade do Bronze no Alto Alentejo." *Revista Portuguesa de Arqueologia* Vol. 8, n.º 2 (2005): 115-128.

Mataloto, Rui., Martins, José. M. and Soares, António. M. "Cronologia absoluta para o Bronze do Sudoeste. Periodização, base de dados, tratamento estatístico." *Estudos Arqueológicos de Oeiras* 20 (2013): 303-338.

Mederos Martín, Alfredo. "La sepultura de Belmeque (Beja, Bajo Alentejo). Contactos com el Egeo durante el Bronce Final I del Suroeste de la Península Ibérica (1625-1425 AC)." *Veleia* 26 (2009): 235-264.

Montero Ruiz, Ignacio and Burillo-Barroso, Mercedes. "Los inicios de la metalurgia y el valor del metal." *Menga* 7 (2016): 15-29.

Odriozola, Carlos P., Villalobos García, Rodrigo, Burbidge, Cristopher I., Boaventura, Rui, Sousa, Ana C., Rodríguez-Ariza, Olica, Parrilla-Giraldez, Rubén, Prudêncio, Maria I. and Dias, Maria I. "Distribution and chronological framework for Iberian variscite mining and consumption at Pico Centeno, Encinasola, Spain." *Quaternary Research* 85 (2016): 159-176.

Oliveira, J.T. (1992). *Carta Geológica de Portugal – escala 1:200 000, Notícia explicativa da folha 8*. Lisboa: Serviços Geológicos de Portugal.

Pavon Soldevila, Ignacio and Duque Espino, David. "40 años de Bronce del Suroeste: aportaciones desde su perifieria extremeña." *Revista de Estudios Extremeños* Tomo LXX, n.º I (2014): 35-66.

Ponte, Teresa N. da, Soares, António M., Araújo, Maria de F., Frade, José C., Ribeiro, Isabel, Rodrigues, Zélia, Silva, Rui J. and Valério, Pedro. "O Bronze Pleno do Sudoeste da Horta do Folgão (Serpa, Portugal). Os Hipogeus Funerários." *O Arqueólogo Português* Série V, n.º 2 (2012): 263–293.

Porfírio, Eduardo and Serra, Miguel. "Rituais funerários e de comensalidade no Bronze do Sudoeste da Península Ibérica: novos dados a partir de uma intervenção arqueológica no sítio da Torre Velha 3 (Serpa)." *Estudos do Quaternário* 6 (2010): 49-66.

Porfírio, Eduardo and Serra, Miguel. "Bronze Age funerary commensality in the southwest of the Iberian Peninsula. A perspective from Torre Velha 3 and other hipogea sites found in the portuguese left bank of the Guadiana river." In *To feed the body, to nourish the soul, to create sociability. Food and commensality in pre and protohistoric societies* edited by Raquel Vilaça and Miguel Serra, 55-83. Coimbra: Instituto de Arqueologia-FLUC/Centro de Estudos Pré-históricos da Beira Alta/Palimpsesto - Estudo e Preservação do Património Cultural Lda.

Porfírio, Eduardo, Serra, Miguel, Valério, Pedro, Soares, António M., Araújo, Maria de F. and Silva, Rui J. "Os metais da Idade do Bronze de Torre Velha 3 (Serpa) e os seus contextos arqueológicos." *In Arqueologia em Portugal 150 anos. Actas do I Congresso da Associação dos Arqueólogos Portugueses*, 563-571. Lisboa: Associação dos Arqueólogos Portugueses, 2013.

Rebelo, Fernando and Cunha, Lúcio. "Relevo de Portugal." In *Enciclopédia Temática – Portugal Moderno – Geografia*, 13-27. Lisboa: POMO/Edições Portugal Moderno, 1991.

Cortés Sánchez, Miguel, Jiménez Espejo, Francisco J., Simón Vallejo, Maria D., Gibaja Bao, Juan F., Carvalho, António F., Martinez-Ruiz, Francisca, Rodrigo Gamiz, Marta, Flores, José A., Paytan, Adina, López Sáez, José A., Peña-Chocarro, Leonor, Carrión, José S., Morales Muñiz, Arturo, Roselló Izquierdo, Eufrasia, Riquelme Cantal, José A., Dean, Rebecca M., Salgueiro, Emília, Martínez Sánchez, Rafael M., De la Rubia de Gracia, Juan J., Lozano Francisco, María C., Vera Peláez, José L., Llorente Rodríguez, Laura and Bicho, Nuno F. "The Mesolithic-Neolithic transition in southern Iberia." *Quaternary Research* 77 (2012): 221-234.

Santos, Filipe J., Arez, Luis, Soares, António M., Deus, Manuela de, Queiroz, Paula F., Valério, Pedro, Rodrigues, Zélia, Antunes, Ana S. and Araújo, Maria de F. "O Casarão da Mesquita 3 (S . Manços, Évora): um sítio de fossas " silo " do Bronze Pleno/Final na Encosta do Albardão." *Revista Portuguesa de Arqueologia* Vol. 11, n.º 2 (2008): 55-86.

Schubart, Hermanfrid. "Novos achados sepulcrais do Bronze do Sudoeste II." In *Actas das II Jornadas Arqueológicas*, Vol. II, 65-86. Lisboa: Associação dos Arqueólogos Portugueses, 1974.

Schubart, Hermanfrid. *Die Kultur der Bronzezeit in Südwesten der Iberischen Halbinsel*, Berlim:Walter de Gruyter & Co, 1975.

Schubart, Hermanfrid. "La cerámica argárica en la estratigrafía de Fuente Álamo. Campañas de 1977-1982." *SPAL* 13 (2004): 35-82.

Schubart, Hermanfrid, Arteaga, Oswaldo M. and Pingel, Volker. "Fuente Álamo. Vorbericht über die Grabung 1988 in der bronzezeitlichen Höhensiedlung." *Madrider Mitteilungen* 30 (1989): 85-90.

Schuhmaker, Thomas X., Cardoso, João L. and Banerjee, Arun. "Sourcing African ivory in Chalcholithic Portugal." *Antiquity* 83 (2009): 983-997.

Senna-Martinez, João C. "Aspectos e problemas das origens e desenvolvimento da metalurgia do bronze na fachada atlântica peninsular." *Estudos Arqueológicos de Oeiras* 15 (2007): 119-134.

Senna-Martinez, João C. "Metals, techniques and society. The Iberian Peninsula between the first peasant societies with metallurgy and the «Urban revolution»." In *A ourivesaria pré-histórica do Ocidente Peninsular Atlântico. Compreender para preservar*, edited by Maria F. Guerra and Isabel Tissot, 11-20. Lisboa: Projecto AuCorre, 2013.

Serra, Miguel, Porfirio, Eduardo and Soares, Sofia. "A estela da Idade do Bronze do Monte do Ulmo (Santa Vitória, Beja)." *Conimbriga*, 53 (2016): 5-30.

Silva, Carlos T. da and Soares, Joaquina. *Pré-história da área de Sines*. Lisboa: Gabinete da Área de Sines, 1981.

Silva, Carlos T. da and Soares, Joaquina. "Práticas funerárias no Bronze Pleno do Litoral Alentejano: o Monumento II do Pessegueiro." *Estudos Arqueológicos de Oeiras* 17 (2009): 389-420.

Soares, António M. "O Bronze do Sudoeste na margem esquerda do Guadiana. As necrópoles do concelho de Serpa." In *Actas das V Jornadas Arqueológicas (Lisboa, 1993)*, Vol. 2, 179-197. Lisboa, Associação dos Arqueólogos Portugueses, 1994.

Soares, António, Araújo, Maria. de F. and Alves Luís C. "Análise química não-destrutiva de artefactos em ouro pré e proto-históricos: alguns exemplos." *Revista Portuguesa de Arqueologia* 7, n.º 2 (2004): 125-138.

Soares, António M, Deus, Manuela de and Correia, José. "Necrópole dos Carapinhais, (Sobral da Adiça, Moura)." *Vipasca – Arqueologia e História* 2ª série, n.º 2 (2007): 180-190.

Soares, Joaquina and Silva, Carlos T. da "Bronze Médio do Sudoeste. Indicadores de complexidade social." In *Terra e água. Escolher sementes, invocar a deusa. Estudos em homenagem a Victor S. Gonçalves* edited by Ana C. Sousa, António Carvalho, and Catarina Viegas, 359-384. Lisboa: Centro de Arqueologia da Universidade de Lisboa/Faculdade de Letras da Universidade de Lisboa, 2016.

Souville, George. "Témoignages sur l'âge du bronze au Maghreb ocidental." *Comptes-rendus des séances de l'Académie des inscriptions et Belles-Lettres* 130e année n.º 1 (1986): 97-114.

Souville, George. "Contacts et échanges entre la péninsule Ibérique et le Nord-Ouest de l'Afrique durant les temps préhistoriques et protohistoriques." *Comptes rendus des séances de l'Académie des Inscriptions et Belles-Lettres* 142e année n.º 1 (1988): 163-177.

Torres Ortiz, Mariano. "Los «tempos» de la precolonización." In *Contacto cultural entre el Mediterráneo y el Atlántico (siglos XII-VIII ane). La precolonización a debate*, edited by Sebástian Celestino Pérez, Nuria Rafel i Fontanals, Xosé Lois Armada, 59-91. Madrid: Consejo Superior de Investigaciones Científicas/ Escuela Española de Historia y Arqueologia en Roma, 2008.

Valera, António C. "Continuidades e descontinuidades entre o 3.º e a primeira metade do 2.º milénio a.n.e. no Sul de Portugal: alguns apontamentos em tempos de acelerada mudança." In *A Idade do Bronze em Portugal: os dados e os problemas (Antrope - Série*

Monográfica 1), 298-316. Tomar: Centro de Pré-história/Instituto Politécnico de Tomar, 2014

Valério, Pedro, Baptista, Lídia, Gomes, Sérgio, Pinheiro, Rui, Fernandes, Sandrine, Soares, António M. and Araújo, Maria de F. "Malhada do Vale da Água – novos dados sobre a metalurgia do Bronze Pleno do Sudoeste." In *Actas do VII Encontro de Arqueologia do Sudoeste* Peninsular, Aroche-Serpa, Novembro-Dezembro 2013, 575-586. (in press).

Valério, Pedro, Silva, Rui J. Ponte, Teresa N. da, Araújo, Maria de F. and Soares, António M. "Estudo arqueometalúrgico das dádivas funerárias dos hipogeus do Bronze Pleno do Sudoeste da Horta do Folgão (Serpa, Portugal)." *Estudos Arqueológicos de Oeiras* 19 (2012): 203-208.

Valério, Pedro, Soares, António M., Araújo, Maria de F., Silva, Rui J., Porfírio, Eduardo. and Serra, Miguel. "Arsenical copper and bronze in Middle Bronze Age burial sites of Southern Portugal: the first bronzes in Southwestern Iberia." *Journal of Archaeological Science* 42 (2014): 68-80.

Vaqueira, Lívia. *O sítio de Torre Velha 3 entre a Antiguidade Tardia e a Alta Idade Média: contextos materiais do "Ambiente II"*. Master Thesis. Universidade de Coimbra, 2015.

Veiga, Sebastião P. *Paleoetnologia – Antiguidades Monumentaes do Algarve – Tempos pré-históricos, Vol. 4*. Lisboa, Imprensa Nacional, 1891.

Vilaça, Raquel, Beck, Curt W. and Stout Edith C. "Provenience analysis of prehistoric amber artifacts in Portugal." *Madrider Mitteilungen* 43 (2002): 61-79.

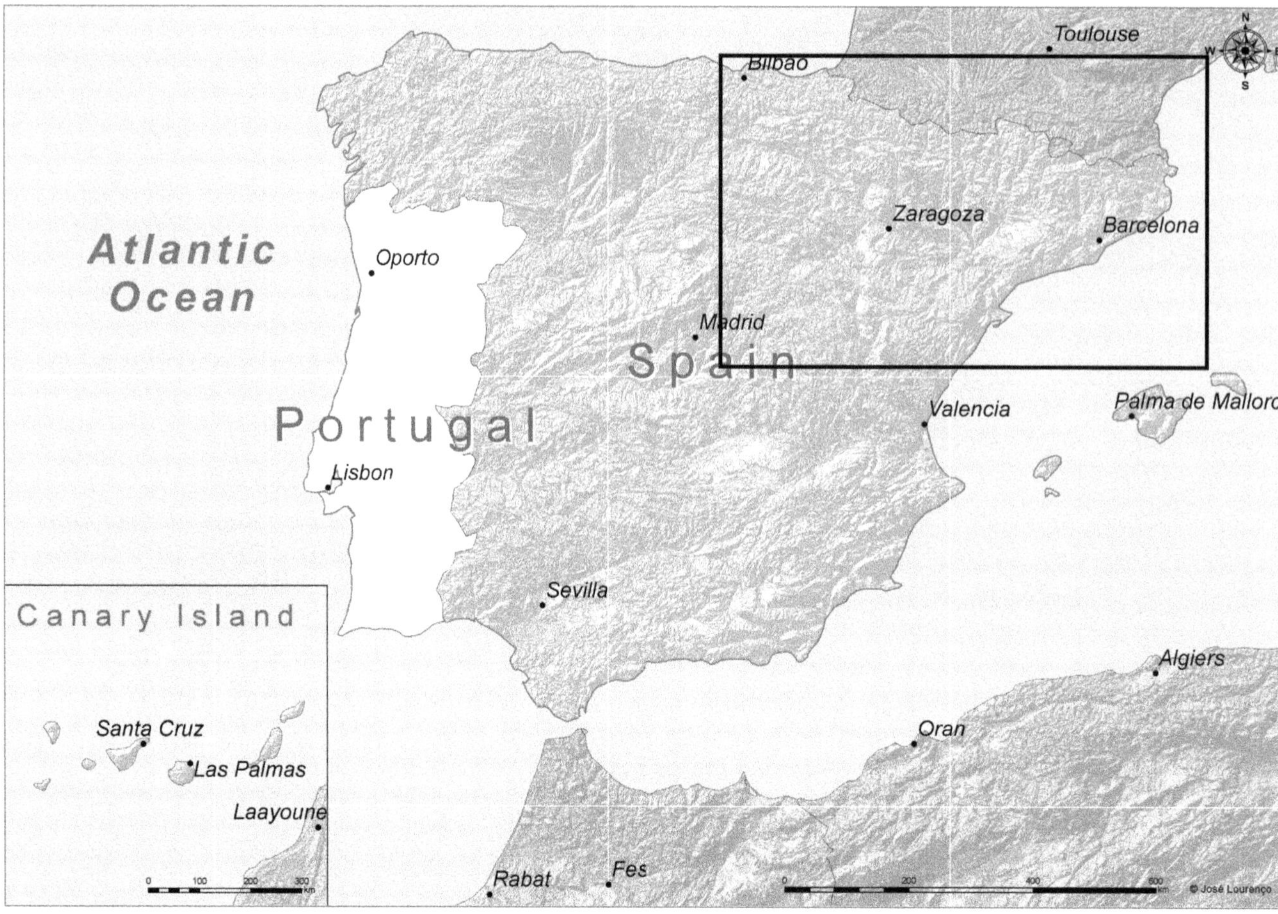

Spain - Middle Ebro Valley.
Source: José Martinho Lourenço.

Chapter 13

Interaction and Interchange. The Genesis of the Late Bronze and Early Iron Age in the Middle Ebro Valley

José Mª Rodanés Vicente, Jesús V. Picazo Millán

Departamento de Ciencias de la Antigüedad, Universidad de Zaragoza
jrodanes@unizar.es, jpicazo@unizar.es

Abstract: This article deals with the genesis of Late Bronze Age and Early Iron Age groups in Ebro valley. After a historiographical review, the archaeological features of the different territories are analysed, assessing the substrate and the incidence of influx or external contacts. These are manifested in three ways: (1) those derived from vessels related to Urnfield, (2) pre-colonial and colonial influences from the Mediterranean and (3) Western contacts related to Cogotas and the Atlantic Bronze. The impact of these factors is uneven across regions, but they all affect in a greater or lesser extent in the formation of Early Iron Age societies. This is evidenced in the so-called Middle Ebro group, one of whose main exponents is Cabezo de la Cruz (La Muela, Zaragoza).

Keywords: Late Bronze Age, Early Iron Age, Urnfield, Atlantic Bronze, Cogotas, Mediterranean influences, Ebro valley, Iberian peninsula.

Two basic premises must be explained before studying exchange processes, object circulation, technology transfer, or simple interactions between prehistoric communities: namely, the relevant spatial scale and time frame.

Permeability, accessibility, optimal routes, and the resulting communication routes are geographical factors that must be considered when assessing potential relationships. A regional exploration of the processes that we will identify in the middle Ebro valley must take into account the dynamic role of the valley in integrating the northeast quadrant of the Iberian Peninsula and neighbouring territories (Figure 1). The extent and permeability of the Ebro basin makes it an excellent means for east-west communication between the Mediterranean, the peninsular interior, and the Atlantic. The apparent barriers posed by the Pyrenees mountains to the north and the Iberian System to the south did not prevent relations between communities because the basins of the Ebro tributaries present a series of natural openings for north-south contact. This fact is especially important in the north given that the Pyrenean passes have historically functioned as the sole points of land contact with the rest of Europe – and so these passes have focussed external communications.

The time period we are evaluating stretches from the Late Bronze to the Early Iron Age, between 1300 and 500 cal BC. During this period, a series of processes affected the configuration of various cultural groups. There is no agreed definition nor unanimously accepted nomenclature for these groups; and attempts to explain their genesis and evolution have been reflected in various syntheses, periodisation schemes, and proposals. This may be the area where the most hypotheses have been proposed in the study of the peninsular Bronze Age – but also where the fewest number of fieldwork studies have been made. Theory has usually been imposed over the archaeological records because studies have not been supported by continued field research. Most of the proposed solutions have been made by authors using arguments valid for north Pyrenean regions (sometimes importing terms, chronologies, and foreign cultural paradigms). As Pellicer remarked: "The forced transfer of a European system that was applied as a patent to the Iberian Peninsula, has undoubtedly caused stagnation in our research," (Pellicer 1984a, 401).

In this article we discuss some of these questions. Much of our contribution comes from our experience in various sectors of the Ebro valley and mainly from excavations in 2004 at the Cabezo de la Cruz site (La Muela, Zaragoza). This site can serve as a reference for the documentation and, where applicable, an explanation of the interaction and exchange that occurred at that time.

1. Historiography

The genesis and development of societies in the Late Bronze and Early Iron Age in the NE peninsular has been studied by numerous researchers throughout the 20th century. The Urnfields of the northeast peninsular and their evolution have been one of the recurring themes of research

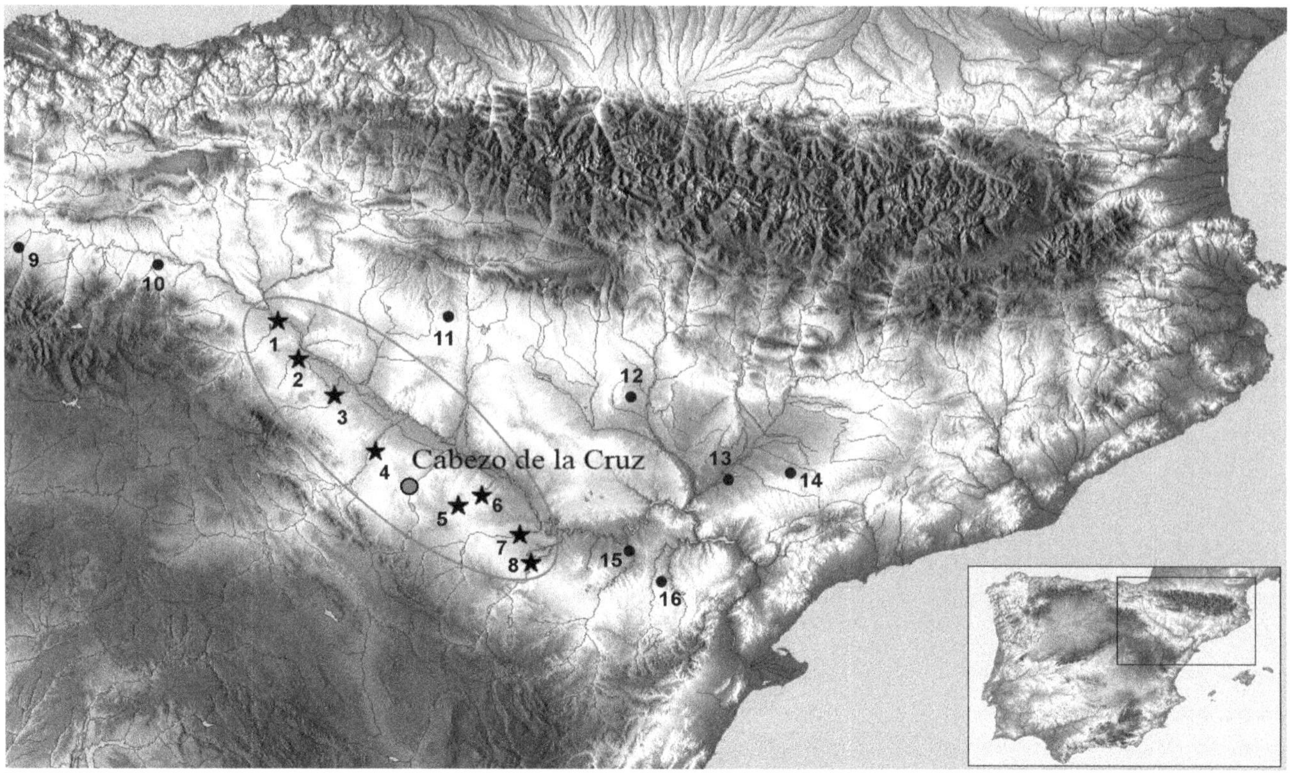

Figure 1. Map showing the location of Cabezo de la Cruz and main sites of the Middle Ebro group of the Early Iron Age: 1 - Necrópolis del Castillo, 2 - Alto de la Cruz, 3 - El Morredón, 4 - Cabezo de Ballesteros, 5 - Los Castellazos, 6 - Cabezo Morrudo, 7 - Cabezo de Alcalá-Azaila, 8 - Pompeya. Other sites of the Late Bronze Age and Early Iron Age cited in the text: 9 - Los Cascajos, 10 - Sequero, 11 - Estela de Luna, 12 -Tozal de Macarullo, 13 - Genó, 14 - Vilars, 15 - Cabezo de Monleón, 16 - Les Ferreres. Source: By the Authors.

and the subject of numerous proposals for historiographical periodisation and repeated revisions. A useful summary for the NE is found in the thesis of López Cachero (2005) which is supplemented with recent references for Bajo Aragón and Matarraña (Fatás 2007) and the rest of Aragón (Aranda and Rodanés 2014). Whatever the nature of the research, P. Bosch Gimpera (1921, 1932, 1945) is the author of reference and the fountain for all subsequent work. Throughout his extensive career he added overlaying schemes with varying characteristics but always with a common denominator: population movements caused cultural change. The same paradigm underlies the work of authors such as J. Martínez Santa Olalla (1946; 1950), M. Almagro Basch (1952), J. Maluquer (1954; 1971) or A. Beltrán (1956; 1960) despite differences in timing, phases, and expansion processes.

S. Vilaseca (1947; 1973) published a study based on internal evolution from an analysis of cultural material – mostly ceramics. His scheme influenced later works, especially after the 70s and 80s with the decline of the traditional 'invasion model'. In those years, a new generation of archaeologists continued relating trends in current European research. Catalan prehistorians adopted French schemes (Maya 1977; 1990; 1992-1993) that drew on the work of Guilaine (1972) and Roudil (1972), and which were based, in turn, on earlier work by Hatt. Meanwhile, the approach of M. Almagro Gorbea (1977) and subsequent more complete works by G. Ruiz Zapatero (1985) revealed a Germanic inspiration – accepting small-scale population movements rather than the mass arrivals proposed by earlier researchers (Ruiz Zapatero 2014a, Figure 2). These two models are still used and have an easy correlation; moreover, they have tended to converge in recent systematisations (Maya 1998; Ruiz Zapatero 2014a, 2014b). However, there are differences given that the French model is more instrumental as its periods may include Urnfields and other cultural manifestations, whereas the contrasting German proposals give predominance to the idea of homogeneity, even if nominal, and the entire cultural framework revolves around this phenomenon (something that does not necessarily coincide with reality).

Faced with the preponderance of these two models, M. Pellicer (1982; 1984a; 1984b) discussed the importance of the substrate and introduced a critical perspective on many of these approaches. He highlighted orientalising influences, as well as elements that are Hallstattian or from beyond the Pyrenees. "We might critically ask what is the value of these periodisations, where is the firm chronological basis of so much theory, and what is the origin and formation of cultures of the late Bronze and Early Iron Age in northeast Spain," (Pellicer 1984a, 402). An evaluation of the different aspects and origins present in the genesis and evolution of Late Bronze and Early Iron Age societies is something we wish to emphasis in this work, despite excessively low chronologies (now dismissed) that are answered in the work of Neumaier (1995).

In this debate, the still rare C14 series has been decisive and was the basis of further testing in the late 20th and early 21st centuries (Castro 1994; Castro, Lull and Micó 1996). These tests underlined the importance of the Bronze Age population substrate and lessened the importance of Urnfields (whose significance is limited to the presence of ceramics with grooved motifs). These arguments are implicitly recognised in many investigations and taken to an extreme by a group of researchers from the Universidad de Lérida who argue for local development and a 'continuum' during the Bronze Age: thereby adopting a clearly indigenous position that is theoretically near to the processual archaeology arguments (Junyent 2002).

2. The research process: new and old proposals

Pellicer noted in the 1980s that to advance it is necessary to change certain century-old research dynamics and his observation remains true. First, we must overcome and alleviate the sharp decline in the production of scientific fieldwork focussed on these epochs in comparison with the rise of studies dedicated to other periods of prehistory. We offer a series of reflections with the aim of contributing to a reversal of this decline.

2.1. Excavations. The same information has been used for a long time. It is time to start building schemes with the data provided by new excavations, and if possible from large-scale excavations as they offer the only way to gain a complete and structured vision of a settlement or necropolis. Complete and interdisciplinary descriptions are essential and should create primary and lasting documentation. The current trend for producing numerous short and specialised articles sometimes frustrates obtaining a broad and lasting vision that goes beyond fads or trends. One example is the paradigmatic case of the Cortes de Navarra site – which is still an important reference over half a century later.

2.2. Stratigraphic criteria should prevail and with absolute dates whenever possible. This does not imply any form of disdain for typologies. Given the scepticism about the possible impact of the 'Hallstatt plateau' in radiocarbon dating and the a priori denial of such impacts, it is necessary to push for a radically different research policy. We must intensify efforts, compare them, and analyse them statistically. We should not accept only a few datings that mark the beginning of a process until its confluence with historical dates. It is incomprehensible how few dating have been made of the remains contained in urns when compared to other periods, including in the various spaces and levels of the settlements themselves. The radiocarbon dating of a necropolis should be quantitatively significant, and individually specific where conditions permit.

2.3. It is necessary to provide fieldwork with a series of archaeometric and interdisciplinary approaches that are increasingly common in other areas of prehistory. Without wishing to underestimate the importance of theory, the greatest advances and changes in interpretation are produced by applying new techniques. It is a determining factor that must be taken into account in the synthesis of economic and societal factors and the interaction processes we are examining. Provenance, exchange, or commercial networks can be identified with the application of analytical techniques that support typological arguments.

2.4. The periodisations previously discussed in the historiography remain valid as hypotheses to be tested – while remembering that a confluence has been reached among the French instrumental models and the more culturalist Germanic models (Maya 1998; Ruiz Zapatero 2014). These models remain highly useful references but they must be permeable and accept variations. Otherwise, an academic reality may be created that ignores the archaeological evidence and this would take a long time to be corrected.

2.5. Continuity and change always appear in a study of historical processes in any region – regardless of the periodisation systems used. Not everything must be explained by the continuous arrival of people or influences; and not everything is a product that can be interpreted as an immovable or scarcely permeable reality. It is clear that Neolithic culture, ironworking, button-handled ceramics, and the elements of Urnfields did not originate in our region. However, these manifestations appear with greater or lesser frequency without implying that populations are constantly changing or moving. We must take into account the dynamic factors among the unchanging factors, the reluctance to change alongside the acceptance of new forms and cultural traits (sometimes only material, but sometimes economic, social, and even ideological) when interpreting the archaeological record and reconstructing historical processes.

2.6. Cultural events are the result of complex processes. Rarely can we simply and lineally describe the paradigm of different flows of usually exogenous peoples. This automatically makes us participants in a large-scale 'hyper-reality' that endows an identity such as 'Hallstattic', 'Indo-European', 'Celtic', or other historicist labels adapted from ethnic, linguistic, or archaeological fields. Perhaps for this reason, little attention has been paid to explaining changes associated with the Early Iron Age, a period that usually appears diluted within the framework of the Urnfields as a secondary phenomenon linked to the evolution of that period.

2.7. Studies on ethnogenesis or identity have recently expanded (Fernández Götz 2008; Fernández Götz and Ruiz Zapatero 2011). These studies bring new perspectives – providing they do not involve a return to theoretical positions from the first half of the 20th century with a mere change of terminology. But given the difficulties such studies must overcome because of a lack of written sources or oral traditions, they should at least be built on archaeological features and not simply based on loosely instrumental constructions – as has been the case in the last decade (Ruiz Zapatero 2009).

2.8. We must remember the diverse nature of the study territory. The middle Ebro valley appears as a cultural conglomerate in which, starting from a substrate, various influences can be perceived over various centuries according to the neighbouring territories and potential avenues of contact, etc. This can be seen when describing the peculiarities of each area and external interactions.

2.9. Therefore, the substrate must be understood and some progress has been made for the centuries before the Late Bronze Age. The situation is complex and there is no dominant culture (Picazo 2005). The diversity observed in materials and other system components, especially in the settlements, prevents us discussing a horizon that is archaeologically defined and easily identifiable. The inevitable failure to describe coherent and cohesive circles leads to a certain pessimism – and in response various periods are unified because of an archaeological homogeneity and an alleged lack of uniqueness. This is the case of the dual divisions of Early and Late Bronze Ages (Maya and Mestres 1996) or the establishment of very generic definitions such as the Northeast Group (Maya and Petit 1986) that encompass very heterogeneous realities. Research since the late 80s shows a mosaic with fuzzy boundaries that we can describe, date, and interrelate – without needing for the moment to define as a homogenous group (Picazo 2005; Picazo and Rodanés 1997, 2002). We are constantly discovering more about the Bronze Age in the Iberian mountainous south of the Ebro (Picazo 1993; Burillo and Picazo 1991-1992), and in upper Aragon – especially the Valle del Cinca (Rodanés and Sopena 1998), Ribera Navarra (Sesma and García 1994), or the upper Ebro (Rodanés 1995; Llanos 2009).

3. The Cinca-Segre. The first Urnfields. N-S continental influences

3.1. There is a tendency for an equivalence to be given between Late Bronze and Early Urnfield. However, it seems increasingly clear that the structure and definition of this horizon is an archaeological construction of the late 20th century based on schemes by S. Vilaseca that were mostly developed by M. Almagro Gorbea (1977) and G. Ruiz Zapatero (1985) and in which not all the configured elements have the same origin and dynamic. Many of the components were previously present in many of the territories, and this justifies the criticisms made about this strongly expansive and homogenising model (Pellicer 1984a; Castro 1994; Castro, Lull and Micó 1996). Nevertheless, we should not fall into the opposite extreme and propose a totally autonomous evolution of the local substrate in all its manifestations (Junyent 2002). In any case, in the northeast, and therefore in the middle Ebro valley, there are a number of features that can be described within the term of Urnfield and regardless of nuances. This conglomerate, whose meaning is chronological rather than cultural (López Cachero 2007, 104), is nourished by contributions from north of the Pyrenees and substrate elements from the interior and the Mediterranean area that prevent simplifications. Explaining these events is a different question. The migrationist thesis has long been discounted and increasing credibility is given to mixed hypotheses that describe small population movements with social interactions among the inhabitants.

3.2. Without excluding contacts with Europe through the passes of the western Pyrenees, a hypothesis that has been maintained thanks to the presence of certain materials in the Basque Country and beyond (Llanos 2009), the eastern passes and even the central passes are currently described as the communications routes to the Ebro valley. Thus, in the NE peninsular, specifically in the Segre-Cinca valleys, the end of the Late Bronze Age is marked by the appearance of ceramics with grooved motifs: something that has become synonymous with the early Urnfield elements in these territories (Rodanés and Sopena 1998; Rodanés and Picazo 1997; 2002; Picazo 2005; Picazo and Rodanés 2009). The appearance of these ceramics and other associated features was gradual from an origin north of the Pyrenees – while the use of resources, location of habitats, and stone constructions scarcely changed. The process of incorporating various cultural traits is more similar to acculturation or percolation than a rapid imposition and replacement. The way of life of the population changed little and the same population continued to occupy the zone: the economic system and possibly the social system being established in a previous period – Late Bronze Age. This process has been explored with several excavations in the Cinca valley by teams from the University of Zaragoza and in Segre by researchers linked to the University of Lérida and Barcelona (Rodanés and Picazo 1997; 2002; Rodanés and Sopena 1998; Ferreruela 1993; Maya 1998; Maya *et al.* 1998; López Melcion 2000; Moya *et al.* 2005).

3.3. The beginning of the process, as we have said, cannot be tied to a set moment in time. No clear confirmation can be found for the dates of 1100 bc or 1300 cal BC. The problems behind some of the reference dating for the beginning of this process have already been discussed in other publications. It is clear that in the cave at Moro Olvena the earliest date GrN-12116 3040 ± 35 bp corresponds to the Late Bronze Age without Urnfield elements (Rodanés and Ramón 1996). The earliest date for the necropolis of Castellets II in Mequinenza (GrN-13977 3040 ± 140 bp) disagrees significantly with others in the same cemetery and shows a high level of deviation and an imprecise context: coals in a tumulus (Royo 1994-1996). The oldest dating at Genó (GrN-18061 2970 ± 54 bp) is 110-150 years older than the other two from the same occupation and attempts have been made to explain this discrepancy through the peculiarities of the sample itself (Maya, Cuesta and López Cachero 1998.155). The same could happen in the case of Carretela (Maya *et al.* 2001-2002) with two datings (I-12448 3020 ± 90 bp and I-12449 3040 ± 90 bp) obtained from long-lived samples in a complex sequence.

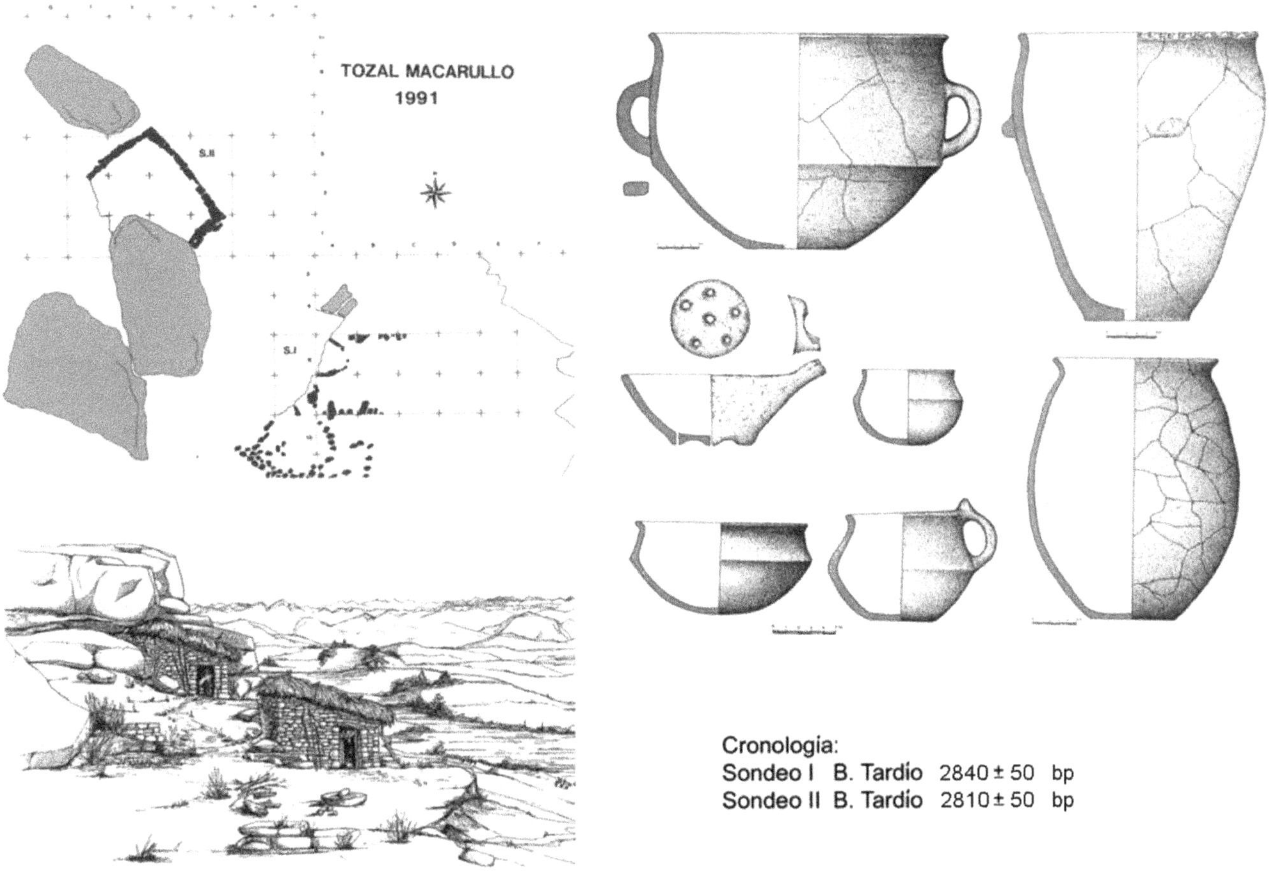

Figure 2. Tozal de Macarullo (Estiche, Huesca). Settlement dated ca. 1000 cal BC, with typical ceramic features of the Bronze Age but no evidence of Urnfield. | Source: By the Authors.

Two other datings have subsequently been added (Ua-19333 3035 ± 50 bp and Ua-19332 2935 ±50 bp) for these initial moments. These datings were taken from very flattened Bronze Age levels without structures and located under an Iberian wall in the *oppidum* of Mongrós (López Mullor and Riera 2004, López Mullor 2011, 144). The sample contained Urnfield ceramics with an advanced typology (which does not fit well with the high chronology of the datings).

The argument for a clear and precise start for an Urnfield period or phase does not seem to have an archaeological base. To this it must be added that in the valley of the River Cinca and along the left bank of the Ebro, numerous settlements have been documented (Macarullo, La Torraza, Pialfort, Tozal de Andrés, Masada de Ratón, and Macerado de Leciñena) that show an identical chronology and are good examples of the final moments of the Middle Bronze Age, or what we have called the Late Bronze Age as the grooved motif ceramics associated with the Urnfield are absent (Figure 2). A well-documented example that could be paradigmatic was found in the settlement of Vincamet – with absolute datings that confirm the process. The lower level provides a characteristic ceramic assemblage from the Late Bronze Age with the presence of carenated vessel, button handles, and a minimal percentage of grooved motif ceramics (0.88%) that gradually increases in the following phase (Moya et al. 2005). And the same occurs outside the Ebro valley on the eastern edge of Catalonia in sites such as Can Vinyalets II (Barcelona) or Can Barraca (Besalú, Girona) where the remains of hut structures incorporate materials that are typical of the Late Bronze without Urnfield elements, yet with chronologies near the key dates of 1100 bc / 1300 cal BC.

3.4. Another element that has been identified with the presence of Urnfields is the type of settlement included in the European 'pull' focused on the Segre (extending in specific cases through to Monegros) and also found extensively in Bajo Aragón. These are closed villages or '*villages clos*' with a central street or space – and whose compact and elevated construction can be explained as the recurring solution to the problem of defence. Such villages do not seem to be generalised throughout the NE and are not found in regions such as the Catalan coast (López Cachero 2007, 101). The only comparable examples are located in the lower Ebro from the 7th century BC in settlements such as Barranc de Gafols (Sanmartí *et al.* 2000). Some authors attribute these types of sites to Phoenician influences (Asensio *et al.* 2001, 257) but a possible origin from the interior has also been suggested and this is supported by a prior presence in Bajo Aragón.

3.5. The change or implementation stage coincides, in our opinion, with the Late Urnfield or Late Bronze Age III – during the 11th and 10th century cal BC. It is during this period that the incineration necropolis becomes generalised and while some settlements continued uninterruptedly others arose to reoccupy old sites. New territories on alluvial soils were colonised and this phenomenon spread into the central and western Ebro valley.

3.6. The First Iron Age, from 800 cal BC, is a period of continuity that develops on a substrate with a significant Urnfield presence. This is reflected in overlapping worksites in several excavations and the continued presence of certain elements (such as funeral rituals and dwelling structures). But there is also evidence of important technological, economic, and social innovation with changing land use, more complex settlements, and a frequent presence of elements and influences from the Mediterranean world. As an example the site of Vilars, with its impressive defenses and several hearts in the form of ingot ox-hide type (Grup d' Investigació Prehistòrica 2005).

4. Bajo Aragón. N-S dynamic in the Late Bronze Age. E-W dynamic in the Early Iron Age.

4.1. The historiography of Bajo Aragón converted it into to a paradigmatic zone and the base area for several of the schemes proposed for the development of the Late Bronze and Early Iron Age in the NE peninsular (Fatás 2007). Currently the lack of continuity in research and the non-publication of investigations from the 1980s and early 90s has converted a region that is archeologically rich into a mystery with more gaps than certainties. A review and an interdisciplinary study regarding new initiatives is necessary.

4.2. In addition to the traditional schemes produced in the first half of the last century and previously commented – use is still made of the schemes produced by Ruiz Zapatero (1985) and A. Álvarez (1990) with contributions from F. Pellicer (1984b) or J. Eiroa (1982).

4.3. The substrate supporting the population of the Late Bronze Age is unknown. The phase that follows the Middle Bronze Age settlements with an Ibero-Levantine character (similar to Cabezo del Cuervo) and whose end occurred around 1600-1500 cal BC is poorly defined, although there have been attempts to identify a local Middle-Late Bronze Age site (Sancharancón horizon) (Álvarez 1990, 102).

4.4. If a horizon is identified that incorporates ceramics with incision-print and excision design (Cogotas-type) as found along the valley with dates around 1400 cal BC (Picazo 2005, 108) then these ceramics could be the basis for subsequent excision ceramic findings at sites such as Palermo, Záforas, or Monleón (Álvarez 1990, 108). This phenomenon is yet to be explained and could be parallel to that found in the upper Ebro with the 'Redal style' and precedents found at Cogotas I.

4.5. There is some consensus in indicating an origin or direct relationship with the Segre-Cinca Group. The few datings of significant findings (such as Monleón, Záforas, or Palermo) could be coincident with this group (López Cachero 2007, 102-103).

4.6. Urban plans show coincidences in the layout of some settlements. This is a question that has an extensive bibliography with a wide range of views about origin and development (Burillo and Picazo 1992-1993; 1994).

4.7. By the Late Bronze Age it is possible to see the early Mediterranean influences that would help shape the Early Iron Age. The Phoenician and then Greek presence are reflected in many elements found in tombs and settlements with varying frequencies. These influences spread upwards along Ebro valley and helped trigger the Early Iron Age.

5. Mediterranean influences. E-W exchanges

5.1. Pre-colonial or colonial oriental influences in the Ebro valley (first Phoenician and later Etruscan and Greek) have been highlighted by several authors, especially E. Sanmartí Grego (1975), as well as M. Pellicer (1982, 218) or M. Almagro Gorbea (1992). Numerous articles have been presented on specific objects (Lucas Pellicer 1989, Neumaier 1996, Rafel 2002, Armada and Rovira 2011).

Figure 3. Estela de Luna (Luna, Zaragoza). Anthropomorphic stela 1,30 m high representing typical Mediterranean features. Central figure: notched scutum (shield with a V-shaped indentation). Bottom figure: Lyre-like musical instrument. | Source: By the Authors.

Figure 4. Bronze support with horse from warrior tomb of Les Ferreres (Calaceite, Teruel). Photo: Arantxa Boyero Lirón http://ceres.mcu.es

5.2. The objects that testify to the beginning of relations are elements of prestige owned by the social elites and associated with 'pre-colonial' trade. Socio-ideological innovations in customs or concepts are difficult to explain without accepting a Mediterranean influence reflected through objects such as the musical instrument on the 'estela de Luna' funeral monument (Figure 3), the tripod found on La Clota (Rafel 2002, 79), or the support found at the Les Ferreres (Armada and Rovira 2011) (Figure 4). These objects are considered to have been made in the peninsular but inspired by articles from across the Mediterranean (mainly Cyprus) whose prototypes go back to the tenth and eighth centuries BC and reveal contacts reaching the Iberian Peninsula through Sardinia (Rafel et al. 2008, 251-252).

5.3. The colonial tradition became generalised from the 8th century BC (Almagro Gorbea 1990, 655-657). In addition to ironwork attributed to a Phoenician influence in Bajo Aragón, a number of objects (again the Les Ferreres tomb of the warrior) and prestige goods were circulating that had previously been restricted to coastal regions. These goods spread throughout the Ebro valley, as evidenced by several findings in Navarre – such as at the necropolis at El Castillo in Castejón (Navarra) (Faro and Unzu 2006; Faro 2015).

5.4. Commercial interactions with indigenous elites operated regularly. Contacts are increasingly evident in settlements and necropoli along the Ebro in an E-W direction. A greater intensity is noticeable in regions near to the river delta, and these may have functioned as intermediate distribution points. The phenomenon is global and rapid with the local aristocracy in the middle Ebro Valley playing a prominent role in contacting directly (or through products) with eastern traders. This had consequences for the economic expansion and consolidation of the emerging aristocracy, and is a factor to consider in the shaping of territorial groups, the formation of more complex settlements, and ultimately, in the construction of new defensive systems in the valley centre.

6. The Middle Ebro Valley Group. Urnfield consolidation during the Late Bronze Age and beginning of the Early Iron Age

To explain the process at the centre of the Ebro basin we will take as a reference the Cabezo de la Cruz site (La Muela, Zaragoza) (Picazo and Rodanés 2009). A Late Bronze settlement was identified in the base with three overlapping Early Iron Age settlements that reflect continuity in certain traditions but also reveal significant developments in the elements of material culture (and other areas) that clearly distinguish both horizons (Figure 5).

6.1. Late Bronze Age

6.1.1. Occupancy dated from the 10th century BC in what would be the Late Bronze III using traditional periodisation. This chronology is consistent with the ceramics recovered in excavations that showed cup types with grooved motif decorations. The settlement ended in a non-catastrophic manner in the second half of the 9th century cal BC. The floors of the dwellings were found virtually empty and with no significant destruction.

6.1.2. The wide dispersal of the remains indicates a relatively large site extending along a low slope and, perhaps, the summit. Although only two houses about 44 m apart were identified, other intermediate indications would seem to show that the slope was occupied almost continuously. The design does not match the typical central street model that was generalised at this time in nearby regions such as the lower Segre or Bajo Aragón. The houses are rectangular with a minimum area of 30 m2 and made from adobe walls with holes for external supports. This coincides with the models found in other settlements of the era such as the Cabezo de Monleón (Caspe, Zaragoza) (Beltrán 1989) or Genó (Lérida) (Maya, Cuesta and López 1998). However, the dwellings are somewhat simpler than in Cabezo de Monleón (which featured rear compartments and benches) and the dwelling style at Monleón was subsequently reproduced in the Early Iron Age settlements.

Figure 5. Stratigraphy of the settlements of Cabezo de la Cruz. Phase I: Late Bronze Age. Phases II, III and IV: Early Iron Age. Source: By the Authors.

6.1.3. From the territorial point of view, the position of the settlement by the River Huerva reflects a major change in the pattern of settlement and a movement towards riverbeds: a tendency linked to colonisation and farming alluvial soils (Picazo, 2005, 113; Pérez-Lambán 2013).

The process can also be seen in other settlements of similar chronology alongside the River Huerva, such as Lugar Viejo de María de Huerva (Burillo 1981, 67), and in neighbouring regions such as the Ginel river valley (Ferreruela, Mínguez and Picazo 2003, 387).

6.1.4. The economy was based on cereal farming. Barley (*Hordeum vulgare L.)* and millet (*Panicum miliaceum*) were the most common species with a clear predominance of millet. Most of the wheat varieties are *Triticum aestivum-durum* rather than *Triticum monococum / dicoccum* (Pérez Jordá 2009, 174). The most striking aspect is the importance of millet. It appeared in large quantities from 1250 BC in some Central European regions (Jacomet 2014, 89) but was rare until the Iron Age in the Iberian Peninsula (Buxó 1997, 100). It appears in Late Bronze levels –Urnfield- at Cabezo de la Cruz, and this points to a significant change in crops.

6.2. Early Iron Age

After the occupation of the Late Bronze Age and a brief period of neglect that caused the erosion of the old settlement, an Early Iron Age settlement (800-525 cal BC) was established. Several consecutive episodes of construction and destruction occurred over the 250 years, and three general construction phases have been identified as well as numerous partial reconstructions (Figure 5). These settlements incorporate a significant number of changes at an urban, economic, and social level – as well in the elements of material culture (with the cylindrical necked vessels appearing in fairly standardised shapes and sizes). Such vessels (Figure 6) constitute a index fossil for the middle Ebro (Pérez-Lambán *et al.* 2014). Towards the end of settlement (phase IV, *ca* 520 cal BC), *wheel-made pottery is present* -including imitation of Phoenician amphorae (Perales 2009, 384).

6.2.1. The first settlements developed in a climate that was only slightly different from today's climate – with a favourable and humid Mediterranean weather (around 700 mm of annual rainfall compared to 400 mm today) (Espinar and Voltas 2009) and better vegetation and soil cover than today. By the end of the period some soil deterioration can be perceived – noticeable by an increase in the pollen spectra of the goosefoot plant family (*Chenopodiaceae*) relative to grasses (Iriarte 2009). This phenomenon is also observed in phase III at Vilot de Montagut (Alonso *et al.* 2002, 174).

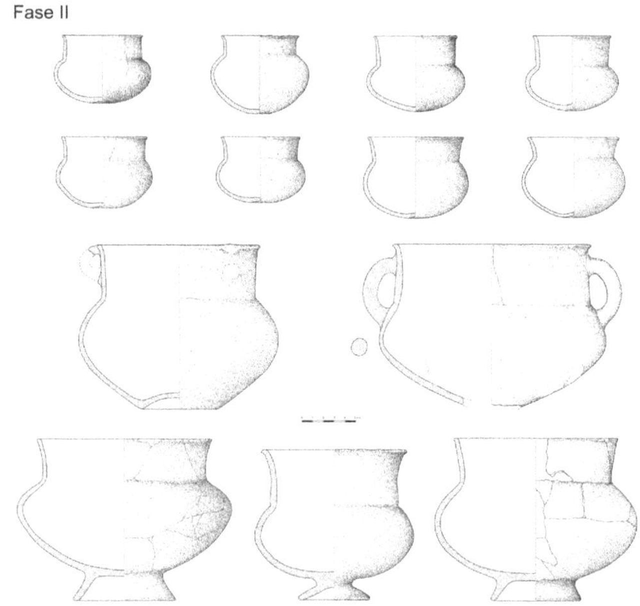

Figure 6. Characteristic ceramics of the Cabezo de la Cruz. Phase I: Late Bronze Age (Urnfield), vessels with grooved decorations. Phase II: Early Iron Age, vessels of different sizes with cylindrical neck. | Source: By the Authors.

Figure 7. Cabezo de la Cruz, phase II, Early Iron Age. Plan and cross section of the sector SW of settlement. Highlights the defensive system composed by moat and wall reinforced by square and massive towers. | Source: By the Authors.

6.2.2. Extensive farming featured barley, wheat, and millet as the main crops with fruits such as figs (Pérez Jordá 2009). The most important innovation was grapevines (*Vitis vinifera*) which were absent from Late Bronze Age but frequent in the Early Iron Age settlements from around 800 BC, thus confirming its early presence in the Ebro valley following a rapid spread inward after introduction from Phoenician-influenced Mediterranean coastal communities. Sheep, goats, cows, and pigs were raised and deer hunted (Pérez Ripoll and López Gila 2009). Horses have a special importance and provide 11% of the remains, much more than is usual in other contexts (Altuna 1980, Iborra 2003, Liesau 2005). Horses were used as pack animals and for traction (Pérez Ripoll and López Gila 2009, 194) and in addition to their economic importance, we must not lose sight of their prestige value and possible impact on the battlefield. Craft activities, some of a specialised nature, completed the economic activities and reflected significant innovations. The most important was the early introduction of iron, whose production, probably in small quantities, is found in settlements from the first moments. Other activities such as textile production, ceramic manufacture, or medium and long-distance trade were favoured by locations in the lower Huerva region and in the central area of the Ebro basin (Picazo and Rodanés 2009, 459-463).

6.2.3. These circumstances, and others that have surely escaped our attention, enabled the development of a settlement whose extension is estimated at between 11,000 to 13,000 square metres. The minimum population was about 400 inhabitants in phase II, with a likely increase in phase III. These figures evidence the existence of large villages. The population almost doubles estimates for contemporary sites in Cortes de Navarra and differ clearly from the model established by some authors for the Early Iron Age in the NE peninsular.

6.2.4. From the first settlement after 800 cal BC we find a complex and expensive defensive system (Figure 7) consisting of a moat and palisade, a reinforced escarpment, and a wall with massive square bastions facing the outside (Rodanés, Picazo and Peña 2011). This seems to reflect an effort to more effectively control the territory and can also be seen in a regular distribution of villages along the valley (Pérez-Lambán, Fanlo and Picazo 2010, 305). This is only possible in settlements with sufficient resources and demographic diversity to assume the needed tasks and functions, and a social structure that supports complex organisation (Picazo and Rodanés 2009, 459). The construction of fortifications reflects the socioeconomic needs of each area, the geographical constraints of the settlement, and the greater or lesser colonial impact (a factor that influences the type of fortifications). In many cases, the genesis of the construction and management of the works could be indigenous – but the concepts may well have come from the east. In short, we can say that the settlement does not respond to the traditional view of a community based on small units with low population density, but is an example of Early Iron Age settlements arranged in a regular form along the right bank of the Ebro.

6.2.5. During the Early Iron Age a group of settlements existed in the middle Ebro with very similar characteristics to those described above and these settlements extended along the right bank of the valley – at least from the River Martín to La Huecha – with continuity in southern Navarra and La Rioja. From E to W we can mention: Cabezo de Alcalá (Azaila), Cabezo Morrudo (Rodén-Fuentes de Ebro), Los Castellazos (Mediana de Aragón), Cabezo de la Cruz (La Muela), Morredón (Fréscano), Burrén and Burrena (Fréscano), Alto de la Cruz (Cortes de Navarra) or Las Eretas (Berbinzana). The roots of these settlements are found in the Urnfield tradition but they had a personality that differed from peers in eastern Catalonia, the lower Ebro, Bajo Aragón, and Segre-Cinca (Pérez Lambán *et al.* 2014).

7. La Rioja. Cogotas I. Atlantic Bronze Age. The W-E dynamic.

7.1. On the Middle/Late Bronze Age substrate were superimposed a series of horizons that gradually and without drastic breaks became the genesis of the stages we are examining (Rodanés 1995). With varying frequencies and origins, we can see the presence of elements with a central-western origin linked to Cogotas I and Atlantic Bronze and on which typical Urnfield features are added.

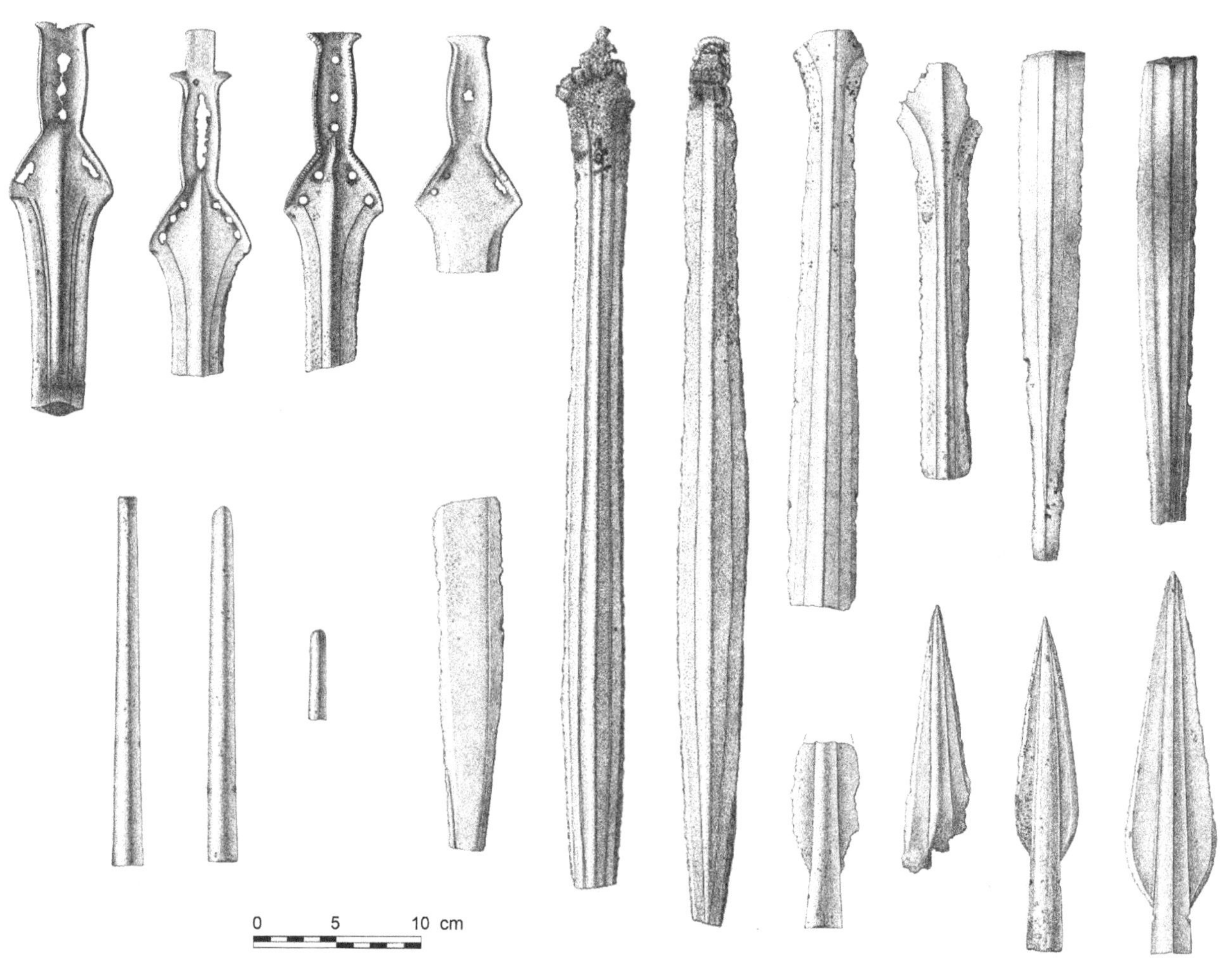

Figure 8. Los Cascajos (Grañón, La Rioja). Hoard with bronze weapons (swords, spearheads, and ferrules) of Atlantic Bronze Age (Alonso and Jiménez 2009).

7.2. An understanding of the final stages of the Bronze Age at La Rioja, as in much of the Ebro valley, requires an examination of Cogotas I. The identification of a nuclear area in the Meseta Norte and the corresponding expansion towards other territories (Fernández Posse 1986; Abarquero 2005, 15) leaves its mark on the numerous settlements found around Alava and the right bank of the Ebro – both on the plains and in the foothills of the Iberian System.

7.3. A new complexity in configuring the Late Bronze Age in the peninsula was added with the spectacular arms discovery at 'Los Cascajos' in Grañón. This hoard dates from the Late Bronze I-II and is characteristic of Atlantic Bronze with clear parallels in parts of northern France and the English Thames valley (Alonso and Jiménez 2009). The finding is characteristic and fully comparable with concealments that were common around the Atlantic coast and are part of the identity of the Atlantic Bronze Age. It is among the most important finds made in Iberia because of the typology of the swords, spearheads, and ferrules, as well as the number of pieces (18). Ten swords are significant and include an Erbenheim-type hilt that is identical to one found near the River Lea in Stratford (London) and dated between 1200 and 1000. Ferrules with parallel designs (Alonso and Jiménez 2009, 35) are also noteworthy. Like most of these findings in Western Europe we lack an archaeological context. These are not the typical tools of a habitat or burial regalia, and so various explanations have emerged. Such finding are sometimes described as stocks of goods on the way to market, or material stored for melting down – and these ideas cannot be ruled out – but greater credence is given to explanations of a ritual character that highlight their symbolic importance (Delibes and Herrán 2007, 251) and the strategic importance of the locations (Alonso and Jiménez 2009, 36).

7.4. Another important factor in shaping the Late Bronze Age is the influence of Urnfields, whose characteristic grooved motif ceramics are frequently found in the zone. They are associated with a significant cultural, economic, and social change that is reflected in patterns of habitat and land use – and with a clear connection to neighbouring regions of the central sections of the Ebro valley. These developments converge in various findings and give the territory a certain personality which has led to names such as the 'Redal-Cortes Culture' (Almagro Gorbea 1986-87, 33). Such names, in our opinion, are based more on the impact of the works and the long bibliographic tradition of the sites rather than any affinities between the sites. It is the sites at La Rioja that present greater affinities, such as El Sequero, Santa Ana, El Redal, Sorbán, La Torre or Las Caracolas. These sites blend the tradition of Cogotas – especially in pottery with the enduring designs, grooved motif decorations, and Urnfield shapes. All of these sites are strategically located on excellent alluvial farmlands beside the Ebro and are clear examples of the phenomenon we have documented downstream.

7.5. The Late Bronze Age develops from a rich substrate containing a notable presence of Cogotas I in traditional ceramics and Atlantic Bronze in metal objects. Absolute datings and metal types place this phenomenon between the late 12th century and tenth centuries cal BC. To this we must add, from the 10th and eleventh centuries BC, the influence of the Urnfield horizon along the Ebro valley. During the Late Bronze Age there were changes in the settlements, patterns of land use, and ceramic materials. Certain metal elements or pottery decorations (excised patterns are the most representative) were maintained, while new styles were incorporated (such as the grooved motif patterns of the Urnfields).

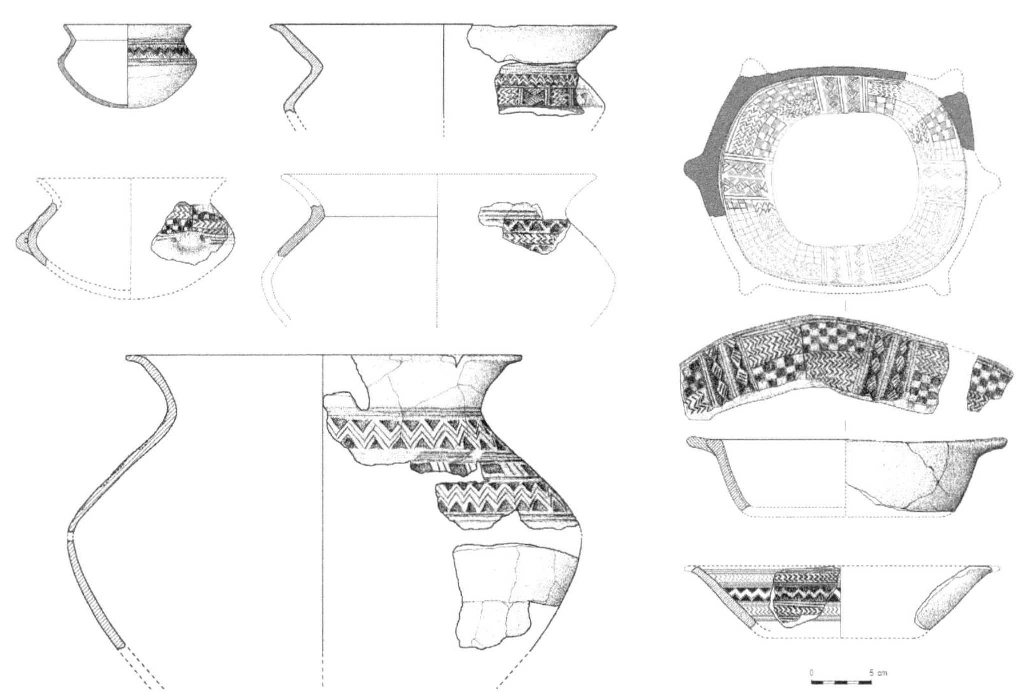

Figure 9. Ceramics with excised decoration of El Sequero (Arrubal, La Rioja). | Source: By the Authors.

7.6. In some of these sites – such as El Redal or Cerro de Sorban – the horizons of the Early Iron Age appear. The evolution is particularly marked in the types of ceramic forms: with a strong presence of cylindrical neck profiles, plates, or bowls, and the absence of incised and excised decorations. Grooved motifs continued in some cases. This horizon extends from the late 9th century and early 8th century BC until the appearance of the first ceramics thrown on wheels.

8. Final considerations

Starting from a substrate that is extremely heterogeneous in its archaeological manifestations and perhaps rather less so in economic and social aspects, the 'game of influences' or interaction with other territories is clear throughout the half-millennium. The influence of continental cultures (stretching north-south from beyond the Pyrenees) is shown in the various elements that travelled through the Pyrenean passes to the Ebro valley in the Late Bronze Age. It seems likely that the Segre-Cinca axis is now accepted as the transit route – or at least the place where some of the features coexisting with well-defined Late Bronze Age characteristics were first documented. Many of these features quickly appeared in Bajo Aragón and the middle Ebro valley and spread west.

The nuances differ in some areas, especially when they come into play with other substrates or influences (in this case, the W-E or interior – whose greatest exponent is Cogotas I and which is distributed in much of the valley and especially along the right bank as a result of its 'expansion' from the *meseta*). Interaction with previous horizons shows some peculiarities – especially in pottery with the continuance of decorations based on incisions-impresions and excisions. These peculiarities were determinant in settlements in lower Aragon and the upper Ebro valley, although this is less certain in La Huecha and the Ribera Navarra. The presence of metallic elements of the Atlantic Bronze Age is evident in the upper Ebro, perhaps linked in some cases to the presence of Cogotas, and a dispersed group of findings throughout the basin. For the moment, it is difficult to determine the effects on the economy and society given the particular context of the finds.

Although elements from different backgrounds (not all which have a corresponding parallel in Central Europe) appeared in the Late Bronze Age we cannot deny that, for at least two centuries, the whole territory acquired a certain uniformity that did not previously exist. Therefore, the development of a cultural horizon with strong Urnfield features cannot be denied and this is supported in many aforementioned works and references.

The reality that we have documented (with nuances in various areas) during the Late Bronze Age became the substrate necessary for explaining, along with Mediterranean influence, the genesis of the Early Iron Age and its almost immediate expansion from small areas in the eastern peninsular and westward spread along the Ebro valley. This led to the genesis of groups in the middle Ebro with a complex social and economic order and settlements configured similarly to Cabezo de la Cruz. These settlements then led to the emergence of the Iberian/Celtiberian societies of the Second Iron Age.

Acknowledgement

Project HAR2015-65620-P: Paisaje y Sociedad: el valle medio del Ebro entre el 6000 y el 500 cal ANE (MINECO/FEDER)

Bibliography

Abarquero, F.J. *Cogotas I. La difusión de un tipo cerámico durante la Edad del Bronce*, Arqueología en Castilla y León. Monografías 4. Junta de Castilla y León, 2005.

Almagro Basch, M. "La España de las invasiones célticas y el mundo de las colonizaciones". In Historia de España, T. I, vol. II, edited by R. Menéndez Pidal, 141-240, Madrid: Espasa Calpe, 1952.

Almagro Gorbea, M. "El Pic del Corbs, de Sagunto y los Campos de Urnas del NE de la Península Ibérica". *Saguntum* 12 (1977): 89-144.

Almagro Gorbea, M. "Los Campos de Urnas en la meseta". *Zephyrus* XXXIX-XL (1986-1987): 31-43.

Almagro Gorbea, M. "Los intercambios culturales entre Aragón y el Litoral Mediterráneo durante el Bronce Final". In *Aragón-litoral Mediterráneo: intercambios culturales durante la prehistoria*, edited by M.P. Utrilla Miranda, 633-658, Zaragoza: Institución Fernando el Católico, 1992.

Alonso, C. and Jiménez, J. "El depósito de armas del Bronce Final de "Los Cascajos", Grañón (La Rioja)". *Gladius* 29 (2009): 7-38.

Alonso, N. *et alii. L'assentament protohistòric, medieval i d'època moderna de El Vilot de Montagut (Alcarràs, Lleida)*, GIF-Generalitat de Catalunya, 2002.

Altuna, J. "Historia de la domesticación animal en el País Vasco desde sus orígenes hasta la romanización". *Munibe* 32 (1980): 1-163.

Álvarez Gracia, A. "El Bronce Final y el Hierro Inicial en la región aragonesa". In *Estado actual de la arqueología en Aragón*. vol I, 97-131. Zaragoza: Institución Fernando el Católico.

Aranda-Contamina, P. and Rodanés Vicente, J.M. "El Bronce Final y la Primera Edad del Hierro en Aragón. Una revisión crítica". In *Actas del IV Congreso Internacional de Historia de la Arqueología (Madrid, 11- 13 de diciembre de 2014)*, Madrid (en prensa), 2014.

Armada, X.L. and Rovira, S. "El soporte de Les Ferreres de Calaceite (Teruel): una revisión desde su tecnología y contexto". *Archivo Español de Arqueología* 84 (2011): 9-41.

Asensio Vilaró, D., Morer de Llorens, J., Rigo Jovells, A., Sanmartí Greco, J. "Les formes d'organització social i econòmica a la cossetània ibèrica. Novesdades sobre l' evolució i tipologia dels assentaments entre els segles VII-I a.c." In *Territori polític i territori rural durant l' edat del Ferro a la Mediterrània occidental*, edited by A. Martín and R. Plana, 253-272. Museu d' Arqueologia de Catalunya, 2001.

Beltrán Martínez, A. "El Bronce Final y la Edad del Hierro en el Bajo Aragón". In *Prehistoria del Bajo Aragón*, edited by M. Almagro, A. Beltrán and E. Ripoll, 109-159. Teruel: Instituto de Estudios Turolenses, 1956.

Beltrán Martínez, A. "La indoeuropeización del Valle del Ebro". En *Primer Simposium de Prehistoria Peninsular* (Pamplona, 1959), 103-124. Pamplona: Institución Príncipe de Viana, 1960.

Bosch Gimpera, P. "Los celtas y la civilización céltica en la Península Ibérica". *Boletín de la Sociedad Española Excursionista* XXIX (1921): 248-301.

Bosch Gimpera, P. *Etnología de la Península Ibérica*, Barcelona: Editorial Alpha, 1932

Bosch Gimpera, P. *El poblamiento antiguo y la formación de los pueblos de España*, México: Imprenta Universitaria, 1945.

Burillo Mozota, F. "Hallazgos de la I Edad del Hierro en el curso final de la Huerva", *Bajo Aragón Prehistoria* III (1981): 63-82.

Burillo Mozota, F. and Picazo Millán, J.V. "Cronología y periodización de la Edad del Bronce en la provincia de Teruel". *Kalathos* 11-12 (1991-92): 43-89.

Burillo Mozota, F. and Picazo Millán, J.V. "Contribución al origen del poblamiento con estructuras estables en el valle medio del Ebro". *Bajo Aragón Prehistoria* IX-X (1992-1993): 203-214

Burillo Mozota, F. and Picazo Millán, J.V. "L' urbanisme protohistòric a la vall mitjana de l' Ebre". *Cota Zero* 10 (1994): 102-114.

Buxó, R. *Arqueología de las plantas. La explotación económica de las semillas and los frutos en el marco mediterráneo de la Península Ibérica*. Barcelona: Crítica, 1997.

Castro Martínez, P.V. *La sociedad de los Campos de Urnas en el Nordeste de la Península Ibérica. La necrópolis de El Calvari (El Molar, Priorat, Tarragona)*, BAR IS592. Oxford: British Archaeological Reports, 1994.

Castro Martínez, P.V., Lull Santiago, V. and Micó Pérez, R. *Cronología de la prehistoria reciente de la Península Ibérica and Baleares (c. 2800-900)*, BAR IS652. Oxford: British Archaeological Reports, 1996.

Delibes, G. and Herrán, J.I. *Prehistoria del Valle Medio del Duero*, Colección Biblioteca Vallisoletana 2. Valladolid: Diputación Provincial, 2007.

Eiroa, J.J. *La Loma de los Brunos y los Campos de Urnas del Bajo Aragón*. Zaragoza: Institución Fernando El Católico, 1982.

Espinar, C. and Voltas, J. "El marco paleoclimático. Aproximación a partir del análisis de isótopos estables en carbones de especies forestales". In *Los poblados del Bronce Final y Primera Edad del Hierro. Cabezo de la Cruz. La Muela. Zaragoza*, edited by J.V. Picazo and J.Mª. Rodanés, 100-107. Zaragoza: Gobierno de Aragón, 2009.

Faro Carballa, J.A. "La necrópolis de El Castillo (Castejón, Navarra). Vajilla e instrumental metálico de sacrificio y banquete en el valle medio del Ebro (S. VI – III a. C.)". *Lucentum* XXXIV (2015): 31-118

Faro Carballa, J.A. and Unzu Urmeneta, M. "La necrópolis de la Edad del Hierro de El Castillo (Castejón, Navarra). Primeras valoraciones: campañas 2000-2002". *Complutum* 17 (2006): 145-166.

Fatás Fernández, L. "La Edad del Hierro en el Valle del Matarraña (Teruel). Las investigaciones del Institut d' Estudis Catalans en el Bajo Aragón". PhD diss., Universidad de Zaragoza, 2007.

Fernández Götz, M.A. *La construcción arqueológica de la etnicidad*. Noia (A Coruña): Toxosoutos, 2008.

Fernández Götz, M.A. and Ruiz Zapatero, G. "Hacia una Arqueología de la Etnicidad". *Trabajos de Prehistoria* 68, no. 2 (2011): 219-236.

Fernández Posse M.D. "La cultura de Cogotas I". In *Actas del congreso 'Homenaje a Luis Siret (1934-1984). Cuevas del Almanzora, 1984*, 475-487. Sevilla: Junta de Andalucía-Consejería de Cultura, 1986.

Ferreruela Gonzalvo, A. "Aproximación a la carta arqueológica de la provincia de Zaragoza: término municipal de Leciñena". *Boletín del Museo de Zaragoza* 12 (1993): 7-274.

Ferreruela, A., Mínguez, J.A. and Picazo, J.V. "Prospecciones arqueológicas en los términos municipales de Fuentes de Ebro y El Burgo de Ebro. Campañas de 2001 y 2002". *Salduie* 3 (2003): 373-393.

Guilaine, J. *L'âge du Bronze en Languedoc occidental, Roussillon, Ariège*, Mémoires de la SSPF, IX. Paris: Société Préhistorique Française, 1972

Grup d' Investigació Prehistòrica. "Dos hogares orientalizantes de la fortaleza de Els Vilars (Arbeca, Lleida)". *Anejos de Archivo Español de Arqueología* XXV (2005): 651-667.

Iborra, P. "Équidos y restos faunísticos de la Calle San José de Alcalá de Xivert (Castellón)". In *El caballo en la antigua Iberia*, edited by F. Quesada and M. Zamora, 201-208. Madrid: Real Academia de la Historia, 2003.

Iriarte Chiapusso, M.J. "Los inicios del Holoceno reciente en el valle del río Huerva: La secuencia palinológica protohistórica del Cabezo de la Cruz". In *Los poblados del Bronce Final y Primera Edad del Hierro. Cabezo de la Cruz. La Muela. Zaragoza*, edited by J.V. Picazo and J.Mª. Rodanés, 108-131. Zaragoza: Gobierno de Aragón, 2009.

Jacomet, S. "Crop Diversity in Southwest Central Europe from the Neolithic onwards". In, *Plants and People. Choices and Diversity through Time*, edited by A. Chevalier, E. Marinova and L. Peña-Chocarro, 82-95. Oxford: Oxbow Books, 2014.

Junyent, E. "Els segles de formació: el bronze final i la primera edat del ferro a la depressió de l'Ebre". *Ilercavònia* 3 (2002): 17-35.

Liesau von Lettow-Vorbeck, C. "Arqueozoología del caballo en la Antigua Iberia". *Gladius* XXV (2005): 187-206.

Llanos, A. "El complejo paso de la Edad del Bronce Final a la Edad del Hierro en el Cantábrico Oriental". *Estudios de Arqueología Alavesa* 24 (2009): 297-354.

López Melcion, J. "L' Evolució del poblament protohistòric a la plana occidental catalana: models d' ocupació del territori i urbanisme", PhD diss., Universitat de Lleida, 2000.

López-Cachero, F.J. "La necrópolis de Can Piteu-Can Roqueta (Sabadell) en el contexto del Bronce Final y la Primera Edad del Hierro en el Vallès: estudio de los materiales cerámicos". PhD diss., Universitat de Barcelona, 2005.

López Cachero, F.J. "Sociedad y economía durante el Bronce Final y la Primera Edad del Hierro en el Noreste peninsular: Una aproximación a partir de las evidencias arqueológicas". *Trabajos de Prehistoria* 64, no. 1 (2007): 99-120.

López Mullor, A. "La muralla principal de l' *oppidum* ibèric del Montgròs (el Brull) i les seves defensas perifèriques". *Revista d' Arqueologia de Ponent* 21 (2011): 141-156.

López Mullor, A. and Riera, M. "Intervencions recents (1997-2001) a l' oppidum del Turó del Montgròs (El Brull, Osona)". *Tribuna d'Arqueologia 2000-2001* (2004): 135-185.

Lucas Pellicer, R. "El vaso teromorfo del poblado grande del Tossal Redó (Calaceite, Teruel) y su contexto arqueológico". *Cuadernos de prehistoria y arqueología* 16 (1989): 169-210.

Maluquer de Motes, J. *El yacimiento halsttático de Cortes de Navarra. Estudio crítico I.* Pamplona: Diputación Foral de Navarra, Institución Príncipe de Viana, 1954.

Maluquer de Motes, J. "Late Bronze and Early Iron in the Valley of the Ebro". In *The European Community in Later Prehistory. Studies in honour of C.F.C. Hawkes*, edited by J. Boardman, T.G.E. Powell and M.A. Brown, 107-120. London: Routledge and Kegan Paul, 1971.

Martínez Santaolalla, J. *Esquema paletnológico de la Península Hispánica.* Madrid: Diana, 1946.

Martínez Santaolalla, J. "La indoeuropeización de España". *Homenaje a Luis de Hoyos Sáinz*, vol. II, 378-387. Madrid, 1950.

Maya González, J.L. *Lérida Prehistórica.* Lérida: Dilagro, 1977.

Maya González, J.L. "El Bronce Final y los inicios de la Edad del Hierro". In *Prehistoria de la Península Ibérica*, edited by I. Barandiarán *et al.*, 317-415. Barcelona: Ariel Prehistoria, 1998.

Maya González, J.L. "La Edad del Bronce y la Primera Edad del Hierro en Huesca". *Bolskan* 7 (1990): 159-196.

Maya González, J.L. "El Bronce Final-Hierro Inicial en la zona norte del valle del Ebro". *Segundos Encuentros de Prehistoria Aragonesa (Caspe-Zaragoza 1986)*, 7-50. Zaragoza: Centro de Estudios Comarcales del Bajo Aragón-IFC, 1992-1993.

Maya Gónzalez, J.L., Cuesta, F. and López, J. (eds.). *Genó: un poblado del Bronce Final en el Bajo Segre (Lleida).* Barcelona: Publicacions de l' Univesitat de Barcelona, 1998.

Maya González, J.L. López, F.J., González, J.R., Junyent, E. and Rodríguez, J.I. "Excavaciones 1981-1983) en el poblado de Carretelà (Aitona, Segrià, Lleida)", *Revista d' Arqueologia de Ponent* 11-12 (2001-2002): 151-233.

Maya González, J.L. and Mestres, J.S. "Approche a la chronologie de l' Âge du Bronze et le Premier Âge du Fer dans la Péninsule Ibérique". In *Absolute Chronology. Archaeological Europe 2500-500 BC* (Verona 1995), edited by K. Randsborg, 251-269. Kobenhavn: Munksgaard, 1996.

Maya González, J.L. and Petit, M.A. "El Grupo del Nordeste. Un nuevo conjunto de cerámicas con boquique en la Península Ibérica". *Anales de Arqueología y Prehistoria de la Universidad de Murcia* 2 (1986): 49-72.

Moya, A., López. J.B., Lafuente, A., Rey, J., Tartera, E., Vidal, A. and Equip Vincamet. "El Grup del Segre-Cinca II (1250-950 cal. A.N.E.) a les terres del Baix Cinca: el poblat clos de Vincamet (Fraga, Osca)". *Revista d'Arqueología de Ponent* 15 (2005): 13-58.

Neumaier, J. "Los Campos de Urnas del sudoeste europeo desde el punto de vista centroeuropeo". *Revista d' Arqueologia de Ponent* 5 (1995): 53-80.

Neumaier, J. "Colgantes zoomorfos de las costas valenciana y catalana". *Quaderns de prehistòria i arqueologia de Castelló* 17 (1996): 255-261.

Pellicer, M. "La influencia orientalizante en el Bronce Final-Hierro del Nordeste hispano". *Habis* 13 (1982): 211-238.

Pellicer, M. "La problemática del bronce final-hierro del nordeste hispano: elementos del sustrato". In *Scripta praehistorica, Francisco Jordá Oblata*, edited by F.J. Fortea Pérez, 399-430. Salamanca: Universidad de Salamanca, 1984a.

Pellicer, M. "Elementos ultrapirenaicos y hallstattizantes en el horizonte del Bronce Final del Noreste hispano". *Habis* 15 (1984b): 309-344.

Perales García, Mª.P. "La cerámica a torno ibérica". In *Los poblados del Bronce Final y Primera Edad del Hierro. Cabezo de la Cruz. La Muela. Zaragoza*, edited by J.V. Picazo and J.Mª. Rodanés, 383-408. Zaragoza: Gobierno de Aragón, 2009.

Pérez Jordá, G. 2009. Estudio paleocarpológico. In *Los poblados del Bronce Final y Primera Edad del Hierro. Cabezo de la Cruz. La Muela. Zaragoza*, edited by J.V. Picazo and J.Mª. Rodanés, 170-187. Zaragoza: Gobierno de Aragón, 2009.

Pérez-Lambán, F. "La Edad del Bronce en los cursos bajos de los ríos Huerva y Jalón. Geoarqueología y análisis espacial de los asentamientos". PhD diss., Universidad de Zaragoza, 2013.

Pérez-Lambán, F., Fanlo Loras, J. and Picazo Millán, J.V. "El poblamiento antiguo en el valle del río Huerva. Resultados de las campañas de prospección de 2007-2009". *Salduie* 10 (2010): 285-315.

Pérez-Lambán, F., Fanlo Loras, J., Picazo Millán, J.V. and Rodanés Vicente, J.M. "Ceramic variability and social organization in the Early Iron Age settlement of Cabezo de la Cruz (Zaragoza, northeast Spain)". In *Understandings Standardization and Variation in Mediterranean Ceramics. Mid 2nd to Late 1^{st}millennium BC*, edited by A. Kotsonas, 97-113. Babesch Supplements 25, Leuven: Peeters, 2014.

Pérez Ripoll, M. and López Gila, M.D. "Análisis de los restos faunísticos". In *Los poblados del Bronce Final y Primera Edad del Hierro. Cabezo de la Cruz. La Muela. Zaragoza*, edited by J.V. Picazo and J.Mª. Rodanés, 188-218. Zaragoza: Gobierno de Aragón, 2009.

Picazo Millán, J.V. *La Edad del Bronce en el Sur del Sistema Ibérico Turolense. I: Los Materiales Cerámicos.* Monografías Arqueológicas del S.A.E.T 7, Teruel: Seminario de Arqueología y Etnología Turolense, 1993.

Picazo Millán, J.V. "El poblamiento en el Valle Medio del Ebro durante la Prehistoria Reciente: zonas y procesos". *Revista d'Arqueologia de Ponent* 15 (2005): 97-118.

Picazo Millán, J.V. and Rodanés Vicente, J.M. "El Bronce Antiguo y Medio en Aragón", *Caesaraugusta* 72.I (1997): 155-215.

Picazo Millán, J.V. and Rodanés Vicente, J.M. "El Bronce Antiguo y Medio en Aragón", *Caesaraugusta* 75.I (2002): 217-272.

Picazo Millán, J.V. and Rodanés Vicente, J.M. *Los poblados del Bronce Final y Primera Edad del Hierro. Cabezo de la Cruz. La Muela. Zaragoza.* Zaragoza: Gobierno de Aragón-Departamento de Educación, Cultura y Deporte, 2009.

Rafel Fontanals, N. "Un trípode de tipo chipriota procedente de La Clota (Calaceite, Teruel)". *Complutum* 13 (2002): 77-83.

Rafel Fontanals, N., Vives-Ferrándiz, J., Armada, X.L. and Graells, R. "Las comunidades de la Edad del Bronce entre el Empordà y el Segura: Espacio y tiempo de los intercambios". In *Contacto cultural entre el Mediterráneo y el Atlántico (siglos XII-VIII ane). La precolonización a debate*, edited by C. Pérez, N. Rafel and X.L. Armada, 239-271. Madrid: CSIC, Escuela Española de Historia y Arqueología en Roma, 2008

Rodanés Vicente, J.M. "El Bronce Medio y Tardío en La Rioja". *Cuadernos de Prehistoria y Arqueología* 22 (1995): 37-82.

Rodanés Vicente, J.M. and Picazo Millán, J.V. "Bronce Final y Primera Edad del Hierro". *Caesaraugusta* 72.1 (1997): 155-216.

Rodanés Vicente, J.M. and Picazo Millán, J.V. "Bronce Final y Primera Edad del Hierro en Aragón". *Caesaraugusta* 75.1 (2002): 273-312.

Rodanés Vicente, J.M. and Ramón, N. "Cerámica de la Edad del Bronce de la cueva del Moro de Olvena". *Bolskan* 13 (1996): 39-131.

Rodanés Vicente, J.M. and Sopena, Mª.C. *El Tozal de Macarullo (Estiche, Huesca): el bronce reciente en el Valle del Cinca.* Monzón: Centro de Estudios de Monzón y Cinca Medio, 1998.

Rodanés Vicente, J.M., Picazo Millán, J.V. and Peña Monné, J.L. "El foso defensivo de la Primera Edad del Hierro del Cabezo de la Cruz (La Muela, Zaragoza)". *Revista d'Arqueologìa de Ponent* 21 (2011): 211-220.

Roudil, J.-L. *L'Âge du Bronze en Languedoc Oriental.* Mémoires de la SPF 10, Paris: Société Préhistorique Française, 1972.

Royo Guillén, J.I. "Ritual funerario y cultura material en las necrópolis tumulares de Los Castellets de Mequinenza (Zaragoza): una aportación al estudio del Bronce Final/Hierro I en el N. E. Peninsular". *Gala* 3-5 (1994-1996.): 93-108.

Ruiz Zapatero, G. *Los Campos de Urnas del Noreste de la Península Ibérica.* 2 vols. Madrid: Universidad Complutense, 1985.

Ruiz Zapatero, G. "Etnicidad protohistórica y arqueología: límites y posibilidades". *Arqueología espacial* 27 (2009): 13-27.

Ruiz Zapatero, G. "Bronce Final-Hierro: La naturaleza de los Campos de Urnas", In *La transició Broze Final-1ª Edat del Ferro en els Pirineus i territoris veïns*, XV Col.loqui Internacional d' Arqueologia de Puigcerdà, 635-658. Puigcerdà: Institutd'Estudis Ceretans, 2014a.

Ruiz Zapatero, G. "Los Campos de Urnas". In *Protohistoria de la Península Ibérica: Del Neolítico a la Romanización*, edited by M. Almagro- Gorbea, 195-215. Burgos: Universidad de Burgos-Fundación Atapuerca, 2014b.

Sanmartí Grego, E. "Las cerámicas finas de importación de los poblados preromanos del Bajo Aragón (comarca de Matarrananda)". *Cuadernos de Prehistoria y Arqueología Castellonense* 2 (1975): 87-127.

Sanmartí, J., Belarte, M.C., Santacana, J., Asensio, D. and Noguera, J. *L' assentament del bronze final i primera edat del ferro del Barranc de Gàfols (Ginestar, Ribera d'Ebre).* Arqueomediterrània 5, Barcelona: Universitat de Barcelona, 2000.

Sesma, J. and García, M.L. "Ocupación desde el Bronce Antiguo a la Edad Media en las Bardenas Reales de Navarra". *Cuadernos de Arqueología de la Universidad de Navarra* 2 (1994): 89-218.

Vilaseca, S. "El Campo de Urnas de Les Obagues de Montsant y la evolución de la cultura de las Urnas en el SW de Cataluña". *Archivo Español de Arqueología* XX (1947): 28-45.

Vilaseca, S. *Reus y su entorno en la Prehistoria.* vol. I. Reus: Edicions Rosa de Reus, 1973.

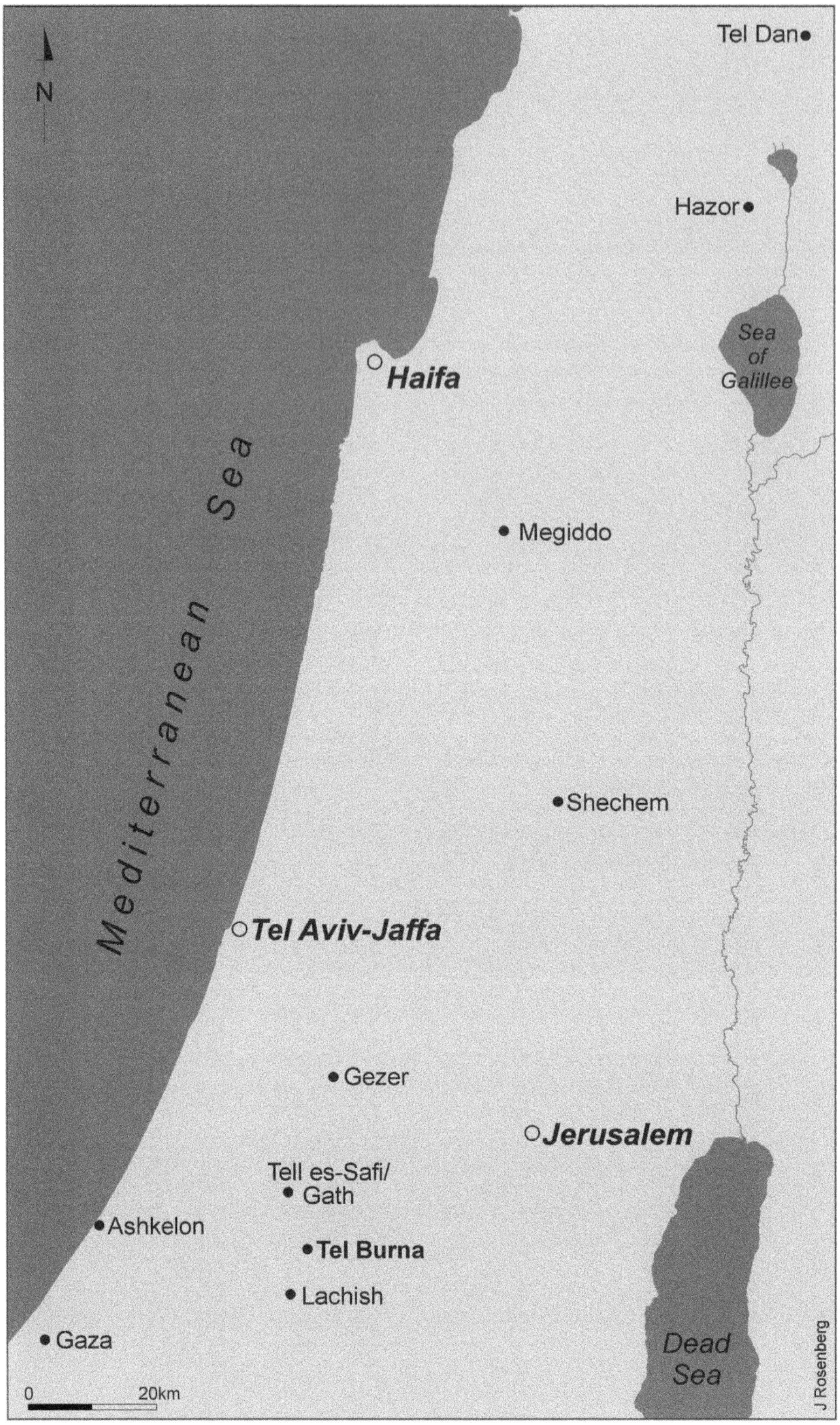

Israel. Sites in the Southern Levant with evidence of trade.
Source: By the Authors.

Chapter 14

Trade and Exchange in the Southern Levant in the 13th Century BCE: A View from Tel Burna, a Town in the Shephelah, Israel

Itzhaq Shai[1], Casey Sharp[2], Antonio de Freitas[3], Deborah Cassuto[4], Chris McKinny[5]

[1]The Department of Land of Israel Studies and Archaeology, Ariel University, Israel, shai.itzick@gmail.com

[2] Haifa University, Israel, caseyasharp@gmail.com

[3] CEHUM, Universidade do Minho, antonio.defreitas@gmail.com

[4] Bar Ilan University, Ramat Gan, Israel, W.F. Albright Institute of Archaeological Research, Jerusalem, debicass@gmail.com

[5] Texas A&M University Corpus Christi, Texas, chrismckinny@gmail.com

Abstract: The excavations at Tel Burna (southern Israel) have exposed a large public building where cultic activity took place. The finds that were recovered in this complex include imported artifcats from the eastern Mediterranean. In this paper, we will present these finds and discuss how they reflect trade and foreign connections with the eastern Mediterranean to the Southern Levant in the 13th century BCE, as well as their importance for understanding the local material culture and ritual activity.

Keywords: Late Bronze Age, Southern Levant, Israel, Cyprus, Cult, Figurines.

1. Introduction

For the Late Bronze in general, and the eastern Mediterranean in particular, the southern Levant was an integral part of the wider eastern Mediterranean economic system (e.g., A. G. Sherratt and Sherratt 1991; A. Sherratt 1993; E. S. Sherratt 2003). As such, items produced in this region can often be discovered as exports the Late Bronze Age contexts of Egypt, Cyprus, and the western Mediterranean. Likewise, imported artifacts have been found in almost every Late Bronze Age stratum that has been exposed in the southern Levant. These imported artifacts well reflect the trade relationships of the eastern Mediterranean in the second half of the second millennium BCE. The cargo discovered on the Ulu-Burun shipwreck is an excellent example of this as it included raw materials, prestige items, and botanical commodities, side by side with artifacts that were used on a daily basis, intended for interregional trade (e.g., Bass 1991; Pulak 2001).

In this brief paper, we would like to present a case study demonstrating the foreign trade relations of the southern Levant with other parts of the Mediterranean as attested by the character and diversity of finds discovered at Tel Burna. Moreover, since the building under discussion was identified as a public building in which cultic activity seems to have taken place (Shai, McKinny, and Uziel 2015), these imported finds mirror not only the economic-system in the southern Levant, but also their role in the ritual and cultic activities of the local inhabitants.

2. Tel Burna

Tel Burna is located in the Judaean Shephelah, along the northern banks of Nahal Guvrin (Figure 1).

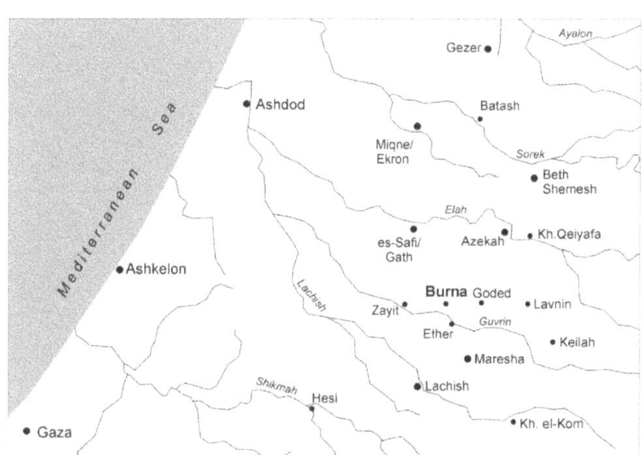

Figure 1. Map of Tel Burna and vicinity. | Source: By the Authors.

In order to gain a better understanding of the trade and exchange in this period, one should emphasize the location of Tel Burna within the hinterland of southern Canaan, as it was not a port settlement nor was it even a significant first or second order site (as is the nearby site of Lachish - Uziel, Shai, and Cassuto 2014, 300). During the Late Bronze Age the settlement at the site was ca. 6 ha, and seems to have been part of the local Canaanite hierarchical town system (Uziel and Shai 2010; Shai and Uziel 2014). Thus far, our excavation of the Late Bronze Age stratum has verified our earlier survey results, illuminating the importance of the settlement in the Late Bronze Age, reflecting primarily the 13th century BCE (Shai, McKinny, and Uziel 2015).

3. Earlier Late Bronze Age Imported Finds

As part of our extensive pre-excavation survey, 1 m diameter by 20 cm deep pits were excavated throughout the tell (Shai and Uziel 2014). In one of these pits, an Egyptian plaque (No. 211111) incised on both sides was found dating to the reign of Amenhotep III (Cassuto, Koch, and Shai 2015). While this is a solitary find and this plaque does little to indicate direct trade, it clearly points to some measure of contact between Tel Burna and Egypt in the 14th century BCE.

A second artifact dating also to the 14th century BCE is a LHIIIA bowl found on the eastern spur of the tell in debris at the mouth of a burial cave left by looters.[1] Imported from the Aegean, this finely crafted vessel was probably part of an assemblage of burial objects buried alongside the deceased.

4. Archaeological Context of Area B1

From a topographical perspective, Area B1 is defined by a flat plateau below and to the west of the Iron II fortifications which mark the summit of the tell. Area B1 is almost completely comprised of a single archaeological strata dating to the Late Bronze IIB Age (i.e., the 13th century BCE). The archaeological deposits here are very shallow ranging in depth from 1.30 m to 0.20 m from topsoil to bedrock. Despite the shallowness, the preservation level of the architecture and in situ remains is extremely high. Broadly construed, Area B1 can be defined as a large 13th century BCE public structure on the western edge of the settlement where cultic activity took place (Shai, McKinny, and Uziel 2015; Sharp, McKinny, and Shai 2015).

A large 1.30 m wide wall (W29305) defines the western side of the large building (Building 29305; Figure 2). Thus far, 15 m of the western wall have been exposed (including W29305 and W41305), and at this stage we have not yet located either the northern or the southern corner of the western wall of the building. Wall 53201, which is poorly preserved, seems to mark the northern edge of the building complex. Also exposed are several walls on the eastern edge of the plateau very near the rising slope of the tell.

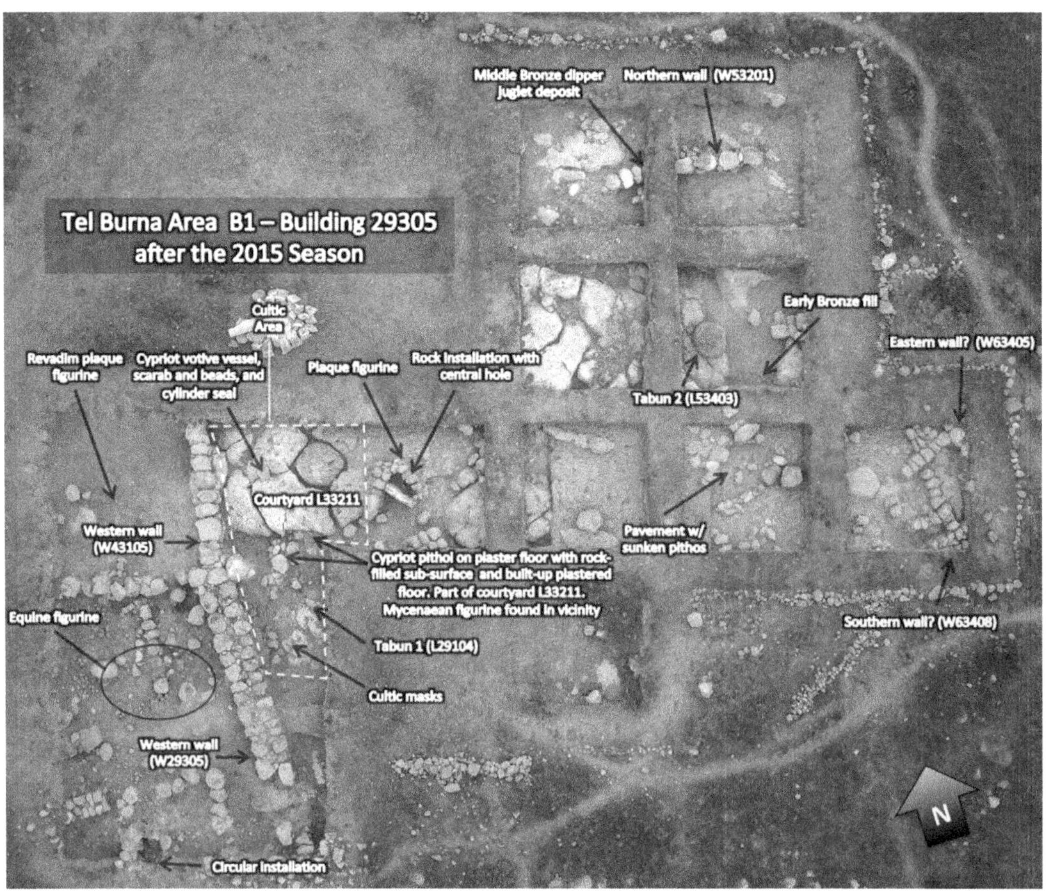

Figure 2. Aerial of Building 29305. | Source: By the Authors.

[1] We would like to thank to Dr. Philip Stockhammer for identifying this bowl.

While it is too early to speak with any certainty, it is possible that these walls (W63405 and W63408) represent the southeastern corner of Building 29305. If this analysis is correct, then Building 29305 measures c. 23 m from east to west and at least 20 m from north to south. At this point, it is not clear if the building or part of the building would have been roofed, and there is some evidence that suggests that at least part, if not the entire construction was used as a large open-air courtyard (see for example two tabuns - L29104 and L53403). Within the building there is evidence of several different types of living surfaces including stone pavements, beaten earth floors with crushed limestone (usually over a rock subfloor), and bedrock. This last type of floor is the most significant for our discussion, as a large number of cultic and imported finds were located on a flat bedrock surface (L33211) just inside the western wall of Building 29305 opposite W41305. A single flat stone was laid in the crevices of the bedrock, and a three-cupped votive vessel from Cyprus was placed directly on this stone. In close proximity to this stone, we found numerous locally made goblets and chalices (alongside other examples of domestic wares), fragments of two locally-made and human-sized ceramic masks, local and imported figurines, a scarab with beads, a cylinder seal in the Mittani glyptic style, different types of small imported vessels from Cyprus (e.g., base ring "bilbil" juglets), and two very large Cypriot wavy-band pithoi.

4.1. The finds

The two Cypriot pithoi (Figure 3:1-2) are of particular importance as they would have had to have been imported by ship from Cyprus to a southern Levantine port (e.g., Jaffa), and then transported c. 35 km overland from a coastal port to the inland site of Tel Burna. Petrographic[2] and Neutron Activation[3] Analyses indicate a strong tendency towards Cyprus as their origin, however the precise provenance of these pithoi has not been pinpointed. The pithoi measure c. 100-120 cm in height and 70-80 cm in diameter and it has been calculated that they would have held between 190-230 liters in volume[4] The exact purpose of these pithoi within Building 29305 is unclear, but their close proximity to finds associated with both cultic (e.g., masks) and prestigious elements (e.g., seal) imply that they were used to store such items. The Ulu-Burun shipwreck, which also dates to the 13th century BCE, provides a primary contextual parallel to the pithoi from Building 29305, as numerous Cypriot wavy-band pithoi were found filled with smaller Cypriot vessels meant to be distributed somewhere along the Mediterranean trade route. In light of the finds from the Ulu-Burun shipwreck, it is interesting to note that the two pithoi from Tel Burna were found next to a high concentration of typical Cypriot imports including base ring, white slip, white shaved, and monochrome wares. These finds might indicate a similar purpose to the wavy-band pithoi found in the Ulu-Burun shipwreck and elsewhere constituting the objects stored within. Notably, it is also possible that they were used to store liquid (e.g., wine) or grain, an analysis of the residues from the pithoi (completed by D. Namdar) was unable to find any residue, likely due to the fact that the vessels were fired at a very high temperature and were not porous enough to retain residue.

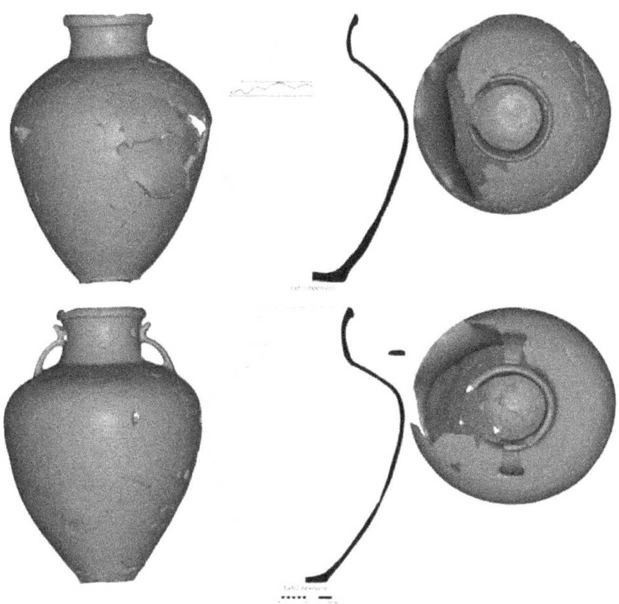

Figure 3. Cypriot pithoi from Tel Burna. | Source: By the Authors.

4.1.1. Cylinder-Seal

Cylinder-seals were omnipresent in all Near-Eastern cultures, from Mesopotamia to the Levant and Anatolia. The first seals appear as early as the 4th millennium BCE and were used as pendants representing feminine and masculine sexual organs as amulet fertility (Porada 1993). Later on, they were engraved with figures and writing symbols and used for other purposes, very often to print on clay tablets. Cylinder-seal production increased parallel with the writing-in-clay culture. They were used to mark ownership, and probably for this reason they were also used as amulets, as protectors of the property (Collon 2005, 5–7).

During the Ur III period, cylinder-seals played a significant role as part of the administrative notarial system used by notaries to seal documents as confirmation of their contents, the participants of a contract would have sealed documents to authorize the acceptance of the conditions, or simply demonstrating ownership of an inventory, and in some cases, the seals were also used to identify envelopes (Collon 2005, 35–39).

The relevance of cylinder seals in ancient Near-Eastern cultures was of such magnitude that a prolific industry of production was developed. During the Late Bronze Age, the Mitannian Empire became a significant producer of

[2] By D. Ben-Shlomo.
[3] By M. Spigelman.
[4] Scanned and measured by A. Karasik.

such objects, with some cities continuing to produce seals even after they fell to the Hittite Kingdom. The trade of seals from Mitanni to the southern Levant during the Late Bronze Age was extensive (Matthews 1990, 4–5).

During the 2012 season at Tel Burna, a cylinder-seal was found in Area B1. The seal is made of steatite, measuring 20 mm height by 7 mm diameter (Figure 4).

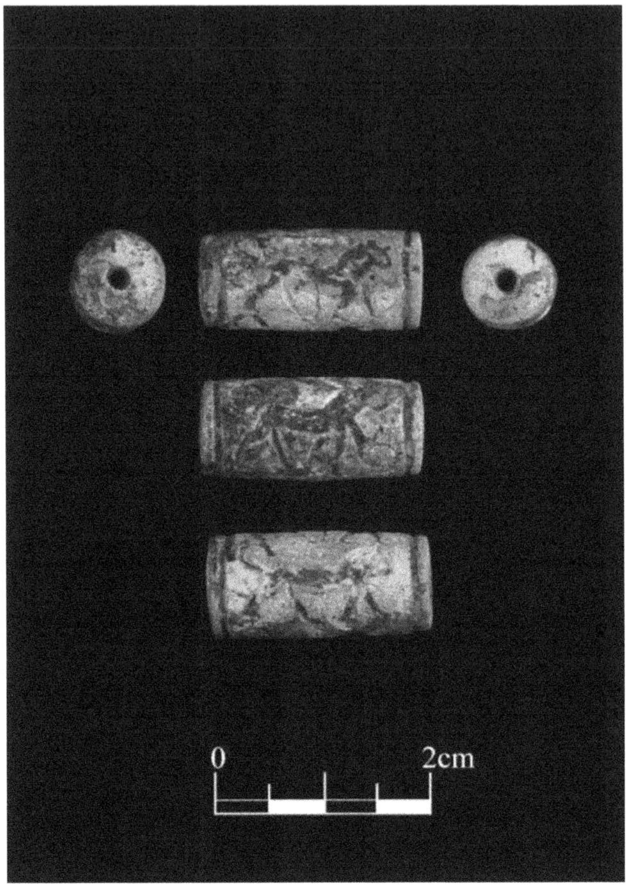

Figure 4. Cylinder seal. | Source: By the Authors.

It shows a procession of running lions moving to the right. The procession of animals was a common motif in seals from Kamid el-Lóz. Even though there are no examples of seals with such a procession of lions, the use of the steatite and the elongated figures of lions has clear parallels with some of the cylinder seals found in Kamid el-Lóz. The presence of two circle border lines on the top and bottom of the seal point towards a Mitannian influence (Kühne and Salje 1996, 55–69). Infra Red (IR) analysis shows that the seal had been submitted to high temperatures, whereas, microscopic analysis, has found traces of bright elements that have been yet to be classified conclusively. Mitannian seals were sometimes glazed when adorned as an ornament. These facts together, lead us to the hypothesis that this particular seal was probably included in a necklace or bracelet and that it was most likely produced outside the land of Canaan, adding an additional element to tracing the commercial activities in this region during the Late Bronze Age.

4.1.2. Mycenaean Zoomorphic Figurine

The head of a relatively rare Mycenaean style zoomorphic figurine depicting either a bull or an ox was found in the vicinity of the greatest concentration of cultic finds in Building 29305 on the bedrock surface.

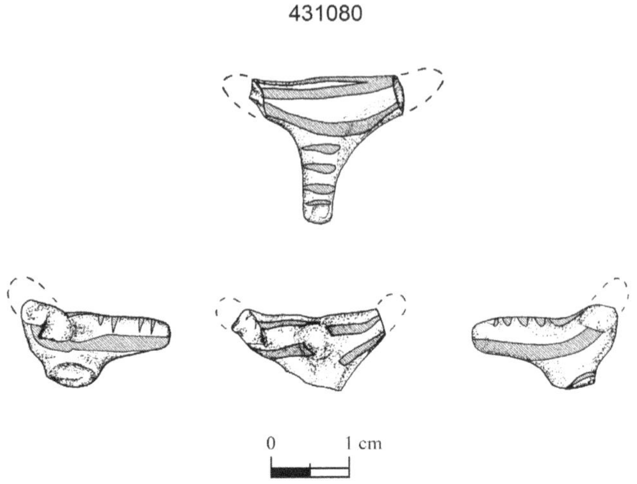

Figure 5. A Mycenaean zoomorphic figurine from Tel Burna. Source: By the Authors.

The figurine (Figure 5) is decorated with a white slip background and painted with stylized black rib lines which would have extended out from the back of the animal's torso to where they are presently visible, on what remains of the head. The tips of the horns are broken, but would have measured about 3 cm from the tip of one horn to the other. The head is molded without any incised or painted features such as eyes or nostrils, which are likewise absent in parallel examples of these stylized Mycenaean zoomorphic figurines (French 1971).

To our knowledge, only two mostly-complete examples of this figurine type have been found in Israel. The first was found in the Late Bronze Age II occupation of Tell Abu Hawam within the confines of modern day Haifa (Hamilton 1935, 54, 318). The LBIIB anchorage at Tel Abu Hawam revealed several other Mycenaean style imports, for which Neutron Activation Analysis has revealed that some were in fact manufactured on Cyprus (Artzy 2013, 14). In French's corpus of Mycenaean figurines, the example from Tell Abu Hawam is listed under the 'Spine 2' type, which dates to the Late Helladic IIIA-B (French 1971). Comparative examples come from Cyprus, Mycenae, and Minet El Beida (French 1971, 157; Tzonou-Herbst 2012, 213). A recent example was recovered by the 2014 Swedish excavation to Hala Sultan Tekke on the eastern coast of Cyprus (Fischer and Burge 2015). A refined classification of Mycenaean figurines by Tzonou-Herbst (2002, 37) dates the Spine 2 zoomorphic figurines to the middle to late LHIIIB, which matches our own LBIIB date for Area B1. The function of these Mycenaean figurines remains a matter of debate, and theories about their use range from children's toys to cultic worship (Tozonou-Herbst 2012). Indeed, some of these debates may be somewhat arbitrary, as the usage and significance of the figurines may have varied by context and individual owner(s). These zoomorphic figurines have been found among a broad cross-section of Mycenaean, Cypriot, and Levantine cultures, and they may have had more than one meaning or function.

The second known example of this zoomorphic figurine type from the same period was found at Tel Dan in a paved courtyard (Biran 1994, 119). Biran suggested some sort of ritual setting for the paved courtyard where the figurine was found (1994, 120). This is the same courtyard where the unique 'Dancer from Dan' plaque figurine was recovered (Biran 2003, 128). The presence of a paved courtyard with a cultic function recalls the paved portion of Area B1at Tel Burna which is where our figurine was found. We await the final publication of Tel Dan's Late Bronze Age excavation to allow for a better comparison of the imported, local, and cultic assemblages of Tel Dan with those of Area B1 at Tel Burna. Though nearby examples in Israel are few, this figurine type nonetheless exhibits the widest geographic distribution of any figurine thus far recovered. Indeed, the Spine 2 zoomorphic figurine has the widest distribution of any figurine from the region in this period and hints at the internationalism of the site. It is interesting that the three largest assemblages of Late Bronze Age Mycenaean imports in Israel come from the north at Tell Abu Hawam, Hazor, and Tel Dan (Zuckerman et al. 2010, 410). The presence of such a relatively rare figurine type at Tel Burna is intriguing and may suggest far-reaching connections for the site, whether direct, intermittent, or residual.

4.1.3. Three Small Cypriot Votive Cups

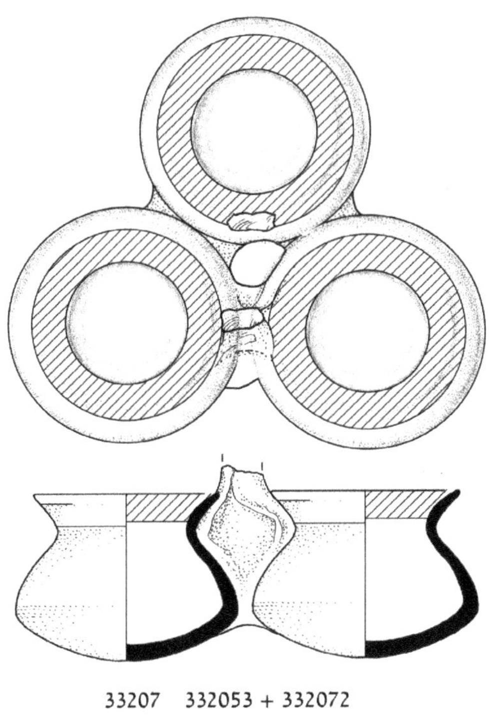

Figure 6. A Cypriot votive vessel from Tel Burna. Source: By the Authors.

Three very small votive Cypriot cups (Figure 6) were found together on a large protruding section of the bedrock surface in the middle of the courtyard's concentration of cultic finds (Shai, McKinny, and Uziel 2015, 127). The cups appear to have been intentionally placed atop a flat nondescript pottery sherd on the bedrock surface. Finds in the very immediate vicinity included a cylinder seal (see discussion above), fragments of two cultic masks, a New Kingdom scarab with beads, and a number of chalices. The three small cups are rounded and closed vessels with everted rims and necks. They are joined at the edges of their outer walls, but without holes so that the contents of each cup could not be mixed with that of the others. Indeed, initial residue analysis reveals that each of the three cups contained different mixtures of oils and possible other substances.[5] There are no known parallels for this set of small votive vessels, but the fabric, technique, and quality of their manufacture all indicate a Cypriot origin. As we have shown above, the two very large Cypriot pithoi were also recovered in this same area along with many other more common wares imported to the southern Levant from Cyprus, as well as possible local imitations of these wares. Common Cypriot wares from B1 include an abundance of 'Bilbil' Base Ring I and II juglets and White Slip II 'milk bowls.'

5. Discussion and Conclusions

The above mentioned artifacts discovered at Tel Burna clearly reflect the far-reaching international economic interconnections that reached the southern Levant in the Late Bronze Age. This vast network was the direct result of Egyptian control over this region at that time. The vassalage of Canaan to the Egyptian Pharaoh can be deduced from some of the Amarna letters[6] (for example, EA 141, EA 292 and 369) as demonstrated by Izre'el (1995). The finds present a wide range of influences and connections in several spheres: elite, quotidian, as well as cultic/ritual activities. In light of this, the location of Tel Burna, about 30-35 km east of the coast, and the size of the site in conjunction with its implicit significance based on the material culture during this period (Uziel, Shai, and Cassuto 2014) contribute greatly to our understanding of the region's geo-political and economic significance during the 13th century BCE.

Daily used imported ceramic vessels were very common in the southern Levant, and thus, it is not surprising to find a significant quantity such vessels at Tel Burna. Most of the Late Bronze Age imported assemblage emanated from Cyprus (e.g., Base Ring, White Slip), but Aegean imported vessels point to connections with this region as well (perhaps imported via Cyprus). The presence of two Cypriot pithoi is very interesting, as their great volumes indicate that even if they were transported while empty they would have been extremely heavy to transport. Therefore, their discovery at an inner site (third-tier in

[5] Personal communication D. Namdar.

[6] We refer to the new edition of the Amarna Letters written by Rainey and edited by Schniedewind and Cochavi-Rainey (2014).

terms of geo-political classification) away from the main trade network along the coastal plain is surprising.

Status symbols were also discovered. While Egyptian scarabs are quite common in Late Bronze Age Canaan, the cylinder seal with its Mittanian tradition may reflect trade connections from earlier phases of the Late Bronze Age (as the LH IIIA bowl and the Egyptian plaque), and also one may wonder if it was used as a status symbol. The shiny metal traces on the seal might indicate that it was glazed with metal further supporting this interpretation. The Cypriot zoomorphic vessels (Shai, McKinny, and Uziel 2015, 126–127, Figures 8:1–2), the Aegean figurine, and the three attached votive cups (Shai, McKinny, and Uziel 2015, 127, Figure 10) clearly indicate not only the economic relationship with the west, but also the influence of the western cult on the local ritual practice at Tel Burna. The fact that these artifacts were discovered alongside local Canaanite cultic objects (ceramic masks, goblets and chalices, cup and saucers and local figurines) probably represents a kind of hybridization of the local cultic activities.

In summary, the Late Bronze Age remains that were discovered at Tel Burna reflect the economic system of this settlement within the 13th century BCE. As a Canaanite town in the southern Levant, a region that was under the control of the Egyptian Empire, imported materials were able to make their ways to this hinterland site. The finds demonstrate economic connections with other regions in the eastern Mediterranean including Cyprus, northern Syria and the Aegean. Yet, the ritual and cult activity that was identified in Building 29305 shows mixed traditions. On the one hand, clear local Canaanite practice and items, such as plaque figurines (for an example of one of the Syrian tradition see Sharp, McKinny, and Shai 2015), goblets and chalices (Shai, McKinny, and Uziel 2015, Figure. 7:1–7), but, on the other hand, the presence of Cypriot zoomorphic vessels (idem, Figure 8:1-2) probably used for libation, an Aegean figurine and three votive Cypriot cups (in which each one contained a different kind of oil), may reflect the influence or even the presence of foreign elements.

References

Artzy, M. 2013. "The Importance of the Anchorages of the Carmel Coast in the Trade Networks During the Late Bronze Period." *Michmanim* 24: 7–24.

Bass, G. 1991. "Evidence of Trade from Bronze Age Shipwrecks." In *Bronze Age Trade in the Mediterranean: Papers Presented at the Conference Held at Rewley House, Oxford, in December 1989*, edited by N.H. Gale, 90:69–82. Studies in Mediterranean Archaeology. Jonsered: P. Åströms Förlag.

Biran, A. 1994. *Biblical Dan*. Jerusalem: Israel Exploration Society, Hebrew Union College-Jewish Institute of Religion.

Biran, A. 2003. "The Dancer from Dan." *Near Eastern Archaeology* 66 (3): 128–32. doi:10.2307/3210917.

Cassuto, D.R., I. Koch, and I. Shai. 2015. "A Note on an Amenhotep III Plaque from Tel Burna." *Journal of Ancient Egyptian Interconnections* 7 (4): 21–26. doi:10.2458/jaei.v7i4.18735.

Collon, D. 2005. *First Impressions: Cylinder Seals in the Ancient Near East*. 2nd Edition. London: British Museum Press.

Fischer, P., and T. Burge. 2015. "The New Swedish Cyprus Expedition 2014: Excavations at Hala Sultan Tekke. Preliminary Results." *Opuscula Atheniensia* 8: 27–29. http://www.gu.se/english/research/publication/?publicationId=225773.

French, F. 1971. "The Development of Mycenaean Terracotta Figurines." *The Annual of the British School at Athens* 66: 101–87. http://journals.cambridge.org/abstract_S0068245400019146.

Hamilton, R.W. 1935. "Excavations at Tell Abu Hawam." *Quarterly of the Department of Antiquities of Palestine* 4: 1–69.

Izre'el, S. 1995. "The Amarna Letters from Canaan." In *Civilizations of the Ancient Near East*, edited by J.M. Sasson, 2411–19. New York: Scribner.

Kühne, H., and B. Salje. 1996. *Kamid El-Loz 15: Die Glyptik*. Saarbrücker Beiträge Zur Altertumskunde 56. Bonn.

Matthews, D.M. 1990. *Principles of Composition in Near Eastern Glyptic of the Later Second Millennium B.C.* Universitätsverlag.

Porada, E. 1993. "Why Cylinder Seals? Engraved Cylindrical Seal Stones of the Ancient Near East, Fourth to First Millennium BC." *The Art Bulletin* 75 (4): 563–82. http://www.tandfonline.com/doi/abs/10.1080/00043079.1993.10786560.

Pulak, C. 2001. "The Cargo of the Uluburun Ship and Evidence for Trade with the Aegean and Beyond." In *Italy and Cyprus in Antiquity: 1500-450 BC: Proceedings of an International Symposium Held at the Italin Academy for Advanced Studies in America at Columbia University, November 16-18, 2000*, edited by L. Bonfante and V. Karagiorgis, 13–60. Nicosia: Costakis and Leto Severis Found.

Rainey, A.F. 2014. *The El-Amarna Correspondence: A New Edition of the Cuneiform Letters from the Site of El-Amarna Based on Collations of All Extant Tablets*. Edited by W.M. Schniedewind and Z. Cochavi-Rainey. 2 vols. Leiden: Brill.

Shai, I., C. McKinny, and J. Uziel. 2015. "Late Bronze Age Cultic Activity in Ancient Canaan: A View from Tel Burna." *Bulletin of the American Schools of Oriental Research*, no. 374: 115–33.

Shai, I., and J. Uziel. 2014. "Addressing Survey Methodology in the Southern Levant: Applying Different Methods for the Survey of Tel Burna, Israel." *Israel Exploration Journal* 64 (2): 172–90.

Sharp, C., C. McKinny, and I. Shai. 2015. "Late Bronze Age Figurines from Tel Burna." *Strata* 33: 61–76. https://www.academia.edu/23289849/Late_Bronze_Age_Figurines_from_Tel_Burna.

Sherratt, A. 1993. "The Growth of the Mediterranean Economy in the Early First Millennium BC." *World Archaeology (Ancient Trade: New Perspectives)* 24 (3): 361–78.

Sherratt, A.G., and E.S. Sherratt. 1991. "From Luxuries to Commodities: The Nature of Mediterranean Bronze Age Trading System." In *Bronze Age Trade in the Mediterranean: Papers Presented at the Conference Held at Rewley House, Oxford, in December 1989*, edited by N.H. Gale, 90:351–86. Studies in Mediterranean Archaeology. P. Åströms Förlag.

Sherratt, E.S. 2003. "The Mediterranean Economy: 'Globalisation' at the End of the Second Millennium BCE." In *Symbiosis, Symbolism, and the Power of the Past: Canaan, Ancient Israel, and Their Neighbors from the Late Bronze Age Through Roman Palaestina*, edited by W.G. Dever and S. Gitin, 37–62. Winona Lake: Eisenbrauns.

Tzonou-Herbst, I. 2002. "A Contextual Analysis of Mycenaean Terracotta Figurines." Ph.D. Dissertation, Cincinnati: University of Cincinnati. http://rave.ohiolink.edu/etdc/view?acc_num=ucin 1015883060.

Tzonou-Herbst, I. 2012. "Figurines." In *The Oxford Handbook of the Bronze Age Aegean*, edited by E.H. Cline, 210–22. Oxford: Oxford University Press.

Uziel, J., and I. Shai. 2010. "The Settlement History of Tel Burna: Results of the Surface Survey." *Tel Aviv* 37 (2): 227–45. http://www.ingentaconnect.com/content/maney/tav/2010/00000037/00000002/art00008.

Uziel, J., I. Shai, and D. Cassuto. 2014. "The Ups and Downs of Settlement Patterns: Why Sites Fluctuate." In *Material Culture Matters Essays on the Archaeology of the Southern Levant in Honor of Seymour Gitin*, edited by J.R. Spencer, R.A. Mullins, and A. Brody, 295–308. Winona Lake: Eisenbrauns.

Zuckerman, S., D. Ben-Shlomo, P.A. Mountjoy, and H. Mommsen. 2010. "A Provenance Study of Mycenaean Pottery from Northern Israel." *Journal of Archaeological Science* 37 (2): 409–16. http://www.sciencedirect.com/science/article/pii/S0305440309003720.

Israel - Philistine pottery production.
Source: José Martinho Lourenço.

Chapter 15

Foreign Techniques and Technology in Philistine Pottery Production

David Ben-Shlomo

Ariel University; 40700, Israel Ariel,
davben187@yahoo.com

Abstract: The Philistines were a group of people, probably immigrants, arriving in the southern coastal plains of Israel (denoted also 'Philistia') during the beginning of the Iron Age. The material culture of the Philistines illustrates several foreign elements that could be traced west of the Levant, in particular appearing during the earlier part of the Iron Age. This article will deal with possible technological innovations or differences in another aspect of the material culture: pottery production. Various aspects of pottery production in Iron Age Philistia will be discussed according to the updated archaeological record, as workshops, kilns and other evidence for production. In particular, the well-preserved and sophisticated early Iron Age kiln from the site of Tell Jemmeh in Philistia will be examined. In addition, the technological aspects of the Philistine decorated pottery and cooking ware will be discussed and it will be examined whether any of these aspects can represent foreign or 'western' influence on this technology.

Keywords: Philistine, pottery, technology, kilns, Iron Age.

1. Introduction

The Philistines were a group of people, probably immigrants, arriving in the southern coastal plains of Israel (denoted also 'Philistia') during the beginning of the Iron Age (ca. 1200 BCE). The origin of this people was from the Aegean region and/or Cyprus and they settled mostly in the five major Philistine cities of Ashkelon, Ashdod, Gaza, Ekron (Tel Miqne) and Gath (Tell es-Safi). The material culture of the Philistines illustrates several foreign elements that could be traced west of the Levant, in particular appearing during the early part of the Iron Age (ca. 1200-1000 BCE). These include for example decorated Philistine style pottery, cooking ware, dietary customs, figurines, and specific types of metal objects and jewellery. The Philistine culture was also mentioned by some scholars as a more technologically sophisticated culture, or a culture introducing technological innovations. In particular, this notion was raised in regarding to metallurgy in general and the development of Iron technology in particular (see e.g., Sherratt 1998:299–300). While this idea was probably largely influenced by a verse in the book of Samuel (1Sam 13:19), there is no actual archaeological evidence so far for a more developed metallurgical technology appearing in the Iron Age Philistine sites. Therefore, this article will deal with possible technological innovations of differences in another field of the material culture: pottery production. Various aspects of pottery production in Iron Age Philistia will be discussed according to updated archaeological record as workshops, kilns and other evidence for production. In addition, the technological aspects of the Philistine decorated pottery and cooking ware will be discussed and it will be examined whether any of these aspects can represent foreign or 'western' influence on this technology.

2. Philistine Pottery

Decorated Philistine pottery is the most well-known and common element of the Philistine material culture (e.g., Dothan 1982; Ben-Shlomo 2006). It is also one of the better examples showing the 'alien' nature of this culture and its connections with the west (Killebrew 2000). It is rather commonly agreed today that this pottery tradition illustrates several typo-chronological stages (see e.g., Dothan and Zukerman 2004; Ben-Shlomo 2006). The earliest stage shows the highest affinities to its Aegean proto-types in form, decoration and fabric appearance. In the next stage, the pottery retains its basic Aegean affinities but combines local tradition influence as well. In the latest stage this pottery shows its foreign affinities only in rather limited, gradually declining way. Recently, the different wares were conveniently denoted as Philistine 1, 2 and 3.

The Philistine 1 pottery represents mostly open forms of table-ware and appears in significant quantities in the earliest Iron I strata in the Philistine- cities. The common forms are bell-shaped bowl (skyphoi), carinated bowls and bell-shaped kraters. A distinctive detail is the use of horizontal handles. Closed forms include stirrup jars, spouted jars, 'feeding bottles', globular jugs with wide necks, and strainer-spouted jugs; other forms appear rarely.

The motifs of decoration, appearing in one color (red or brown), include mostly geometric designs but also rare human depictions, birds, fish and vegetative motifs. There is a distinctive appearance of motifs that may be seen as relating to the sea as fish, and 'tongues', spirals, and wavy patterns that may depicts waves in the sea (see Dothan 1982; Ben-Shlomo 2010). Stylistically, the Philistine 1 assemblage illustrates strong similarities to locally-produced Aegeanizing pottery on LCIIIA Cyprus, especially to Enkomi, yet many parallels come from the Argolid, the Cyclades, the Dodecanese and even Crete (see Dothan and Zuckerman 2004); this is especially true concerning the decorative motifs, which show a certain blend of regional styles.

Beyond forms and decoration motifs this pottery often shows strong resemblances to Mycenaean pottery in terms of fabric appearance and finishing qualities; for example, some vessels have a distinctive light brown clay color and well-executed brown paint on a self wash. In certain cases, although not always, the vessels show a different choice of raw materials and are made of finer clay. The pottery may have been also fired in a more oxidizing environment. In many examples, however, the vessels are made in a similar way as the local-Canaanite type vessels were and from the same clays.

Nevertheless, chemical and petrographic analysis has shown several times that virtually all this pottery was locally made in the Levant, most likely mainly in the different Philistine city sites (Perlman *et al.* 1971; Gunneweg *et al.* 1986; Killebrew 1998; Ben-Shlomo 2006). Moreover, several Iron Age I pottery kilns were excavated in Philistia and are associated with Philistine pottery as at Ekron and Tell Jemmeh (see below; Killebrew 1998; Ben-Shlomo 2006; Ben-Shlomo and Van Beek 2014, 337–349). As this pottery was locally made, it is clearly it is not evidence of trade connections with the Aegean region or Cyprus, but of either a population from these regions moving to the Levant and procuring pottery, or of a strong cultural influence. It is likely that this population also included potters, which some may have produced the Philistine pottery. However, it cannot be ruled out that this pottery, or at least some of it, was produced by the traditional local potters that rather suddenly started to produce it in light of a regional demand for it from the new-coming immigrant communities within Philistia. These may have been the same potters making the Canaanite pottery, which remained unchanged.

The Philistine 2 or Philistine Bichrome ware illustrates a number of changes in relation to the former one. The relative quantities of this ware increase and become up to 50% of the pottery in the main Philistine city sites. The appearance of expands to other sites in Philistia and on its borders as Tel Qasile, Tel Batash, Beth Shemesh, Gezer, Azor, Tell Jemmeh and QuburWalaydeh, as well as to Levantine sites outside Philistia such as Megiddo, Dan and Dor (see Dothan 1982; Ben-Shlomo 2006). Whether this ware outside Philistia was locally produced or imported from Philistia or elsewhere is outside the scope on this paper.

This pottery combines the basic Aegean-related forms (although in less variety than the earlier ware) and decoration motifs, but also illustrates Canaanite, Cypriote and Egyptian influences. The vessels are usually coated by a thick chalky white slip and decorated in red and black paint. Common forms are the bell-shapes bowls and kraters and strainer spouted jugs, as well as other types of bowls and closed vessels (Dothan 1982, 96–150). The repertoire of decorative motifs is rich and diversified, and includes many geometric and linear designs as well as birds, fish, rare human depictions, and other motifs. The finishing and appearance of the clay are more like local Canaanite pottery. Distinct Egyptian motifs include depiction of the lotus plant (Dothan 1982, 198–218). The decoration technique changes in this phase, and most vessels are decorated by a chalky thick white slip and red and black painted designs on it. This technique can be considered in principal a Levantine decoration tradition, attested in the previous periods as the Late Bronze and Middle Bronze Age. The clay choice and treatment and the forming and finishing of the vessels also are similar in most cases to those seen in contemporary Canaanite-style vessels from the same sites.

The final Philistine ware of the Iron Age I is the Philistine 3 pottery. This pottery appears in much smaller quantities than the Bichrome ware both in the Philistine cities and the Yarkon valley (see Dothan 1982, 197; Ben-Shlomo 2006, 35–44). It shows only slight resemblance in forms to the Aegean proto-types; for example, the horizontal handles of the bell-shaped bowls and kraters are attached to the body. The decoration is comprised of either linear designs in red or of red slip, in similarity of local tradition pottery in this period. Possibly, this ware fills the gap between the Iron I and Iron Age II 'Late Philistine' decorated pottery (the 'Ashdod ware), decorated by red slip and black and white paint (Ben-Shlomo *et al.* 2004).

In addition to the decorated pottery appearing during the 12th century BCE a new type of cooking vessel was also introduced in Philistia, the cooking jug (Killebrew 1999; Dothan and Zuckerman 2004; Ben-Shlomo *et al.* 2008). This is a jug with a globular-to-ovoid body, about 20 cm in height, about 2–3 liters in volume. It is made on a fast wheel, as opposed to the Canaanite cooking pots. The cooking jugs can be paralleled to many examples from Cyprus and the Aegean. The cooking jugs commonly have soot marks on the exterior, usually on one side, attesting to their use as cooking vessels. While traditional cooking pots in the Levant are made of a clay tempered with crushed calcareous inclusions, cooking jugs were made usually of a quartz-tempered or non-tempered clay. Cooking jugs were probably not used in strong open fires and thus not exposed to very sudden heat shocks; they were probably placed on heaths common in Philistine sites.

3. Evidence of Pottery Production in Iron Age Philistia

3.1. Ekron

The excavations at Tel Miqne-Ekron yielded several early Iron Age kilns and artifacts related to pottery production. The kilns were excavated in the higher mound, in Field INE and were described by Ann Killebrew (1996; 1998).

This area was especially rich in fine Philistine 1 pottery. The most well-preserved installation interpreted as a kiln is Kiln 4104, found in Stratum VIIA of Field INE (Figure 1; Ben-Shlomo 2006, 106–7, Figure 2.14; Killebrew 1996, 146–147, Figures. 13–15); this is also the earliest feature of its kind in the site.

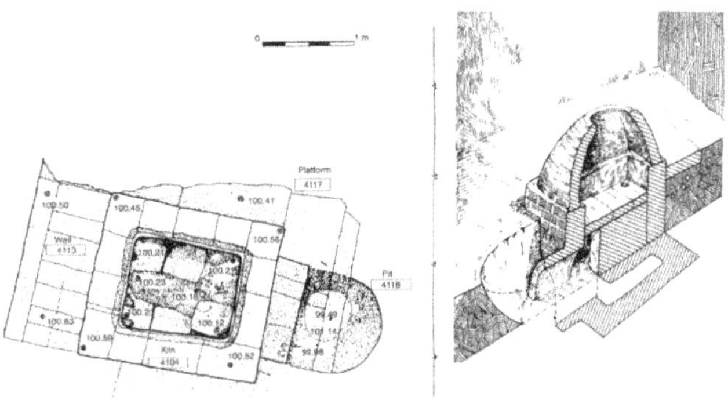

Figure 1. The square kiln from Tel Miqne-Ekron, plan and reconstruction (after Killebrew 1996).

The kiln is roughly square (1.4 × 1.1 m) constructed of irregularly shaped bricks. A brick platform was found below a debris layer and interpreted as the vessel floor; it had several holes in it and stood on a 50 cm thick brick pillar. The subterranean combustion chamber was 50 cm deep. An arched opening and a pit in the eastern part could have been the stoking pit of the kiln (the superstructure is reconstructed as a vaulted one). While hardly any signs of high temperatures or vitrification were observed on the walls of the kiln Killebrew accounts for this by the low temperature, possibly as low as 600°C. If this is a kiln, which seems probable according to its design, it would be a vertical updraft kiln, though of an unusual shape. This shape may have parallels in rectangular horizontal kilns from the potter's quarter at Miletus and from sites in Late Minoan Crete (Niemeier 1997, Type 3, Pls. CXLIV- CXLV; Niemeier 1998, 31, Figure 10).

Four additional kilns of a different shape were discovered in Ekron (Killebrew 1996, 148–149, Figures 16-19, Kilns 36069, 36024, 36054 and 37015). Two oval kilns were built on top of each other in various phases of Stratum VI (Kiln 36069 and 36024 above it); only the lower parts of their combustion chamber were preserved. Kiln 36069 has an inner diameter of 1 m with a central supporting brick pillar; a stoking hole/pit was preserved to the west. Kiln 36024 measuring 1.2×0.8 m indicated several phases of modifications. The combustion chamber was divided by a wall into two sub-chambers, each had a supporting brick pillar. This is an unusual feature, maybe showing a certain adjustment to Philistine pottery manufacture (Killebrew 1996, 149). The other kilns were smaller and more poorly preserved. Other finds from Tel Miqne-Ekron relating to pottery production are potter's tools, such as semicircular ceramic objects with a thumb-hole (Ben-Shlomo 2006, Figure 2.12: center) or oval or polygonal smoothed sherds (Ben-Shlomo 2006, Figure 2.12: right). These could have been used for burnishing and smoothing pottery vessels.

3.2. Tell Jemmeh

Figure 2. The kiln from Tell Jemmeh (during excavation) (Ben-Shlomo and Van Beek 2014, Figure 7.15).

While Tell Jemmeh, a large Bronze and Iron Age site 10 km south of Gaza, is not one of the five main Philistine cities, it lies within the 'Philistine' territory, and has yielded Philistine decorated pottery in its early Iron Age levels. More important, the site yielded the most well-preserved pottery kiln from this period in Philistia (Figure 2; Ben-Shlomo and Van Beek 2014, 341–359). The kiln at Tell Jemmeh Field I FUR is one of the best preserved kilns in the Levant during the Bronze and Iron Ages (Figures. 2–8).

While it was not preserved to its full height, it is preserved at places to a height of over 1 m reflecting several functional levels or stages within the kiln and a sophisticated technological design.

The final ground plan of the inner space of the pottery kiln indicates a symmetrical oval shape, with the western part rounded and the eastern part pointed (Figure 3); it is 3.9 m long and 2.4 m at its widest. This space is created by a brick construction of wall of thickness varying from

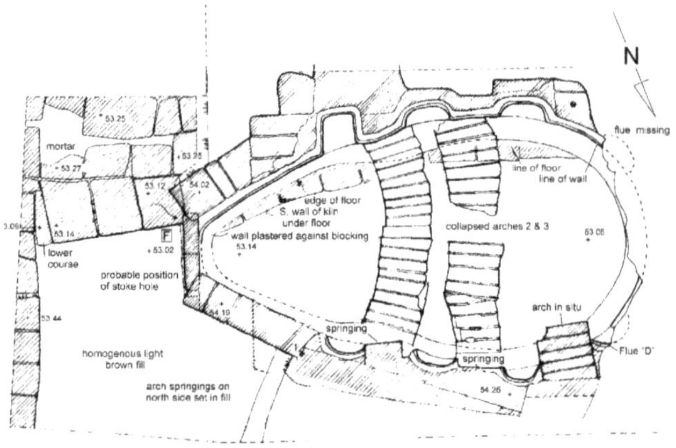

Figure 3. Plan of the Tell Jemmeh kiln (upper part) (Ben-Shlomo and Van Beek 2014, Figure 7.18).

0.3–0.7 m, with the eastern narrower end built of thinner walls. The walls are plastered from the interior, at least as seen on the better preserved southern side (Ben-Shlomo and Van Beek 2014, Figures 7.15–7.17). Elements from the inner construction of the kiln were built of special small narrow flat bricks. Most of the outer walls were built of regular larger bricks or from mud without discerned bricks. Several arches built of narrow bricks were found *in situ* (on the northwest side) while others were found fallen inside the space of the kiln (Figure 2; Ben-Shlomo and Van Beek 2014, Arches 2 and 3; Figures 7.23–7.26). The 'vessel floor' of the kiln (where the vessels were laid for firing) was not found intact during the excavation. However, fragments of perforated fired bricks (Figure 4) showing its substantial thickness, with holes about 8 cm in diameter,were found inside the kiln in various locations at the level of the fallen brick arches, and are probably parts of this floor.

Figure 4. A brick from the vessel's floor, Tell Jemmeh kiln (Ben-Shlomo and Van Beek 2014, Figure 7.27).

Thus, it is assumed that most of these arches represent the supporting construction of the 'vessel floor' of the kiln (Figure 5).

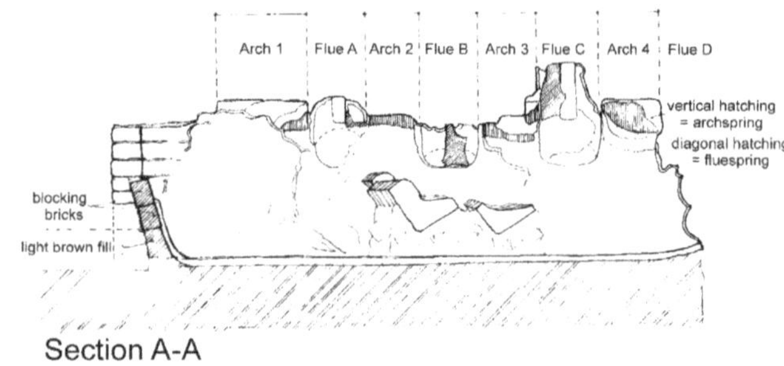

Figure 5. Section through Tell Jemmeh kiln (Ben-Shlomo and Van Beek 2014, Figure 7.35).

Nevertheless, according to the shape of the edges of the side walls, it is probable that such arches supported the roof of the kiln as well. An element from the Jemmeh kiln, which is very rarely found in other Bronze and Iron Age kilns, are the ventilation flues (Figure 6; see below).

Figure 6. Close-up of flues from the Tell Jemmeh kiln (Ben-Shlomo and Van Beek 2014, Figure 7.31).

These are tubes evident by built-in plastered recesses or cavities (sized about 0.4 × 0.2 m each) built in the side walls of the kiln (Figure 7); the southeastern flue ('Flue A') was built deeper inside the wall than the others. Three flues were identified on each side of the kiln; they were symmetrically and equally spaced on both sides. Two additional unpreserved flues may have been located on the western side. In each cavity, there are two tubes with a roughly square section, each about 10–15 cm in width; they are separated by mud lining (a 'flue dividing brick') and covered by small thin bricks, bulging into the inner part of the kiln, thus, protected from the inner space of the kiln.

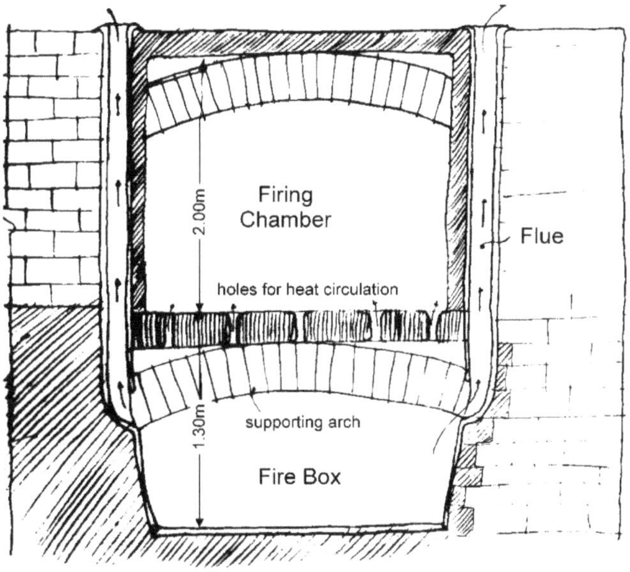

Figure 7. Section of the Tell Jemmeh kiln (Ben-Shlomo and Van Beek 2014, Figure 7.38).

These tubes ran along the outer walls of the kilns as clearly seen in the southern wall the kiln (Figures 6–8), as well as on other fallen fragments of the kiln firing chamber walls and from the inside in the northern balk. They functioned as heat convectors, distributing and circulating the heat to the sides of the kiln, thus achieving better firing (in comparison to heat coming only from below). An additional function of these elements is creating a better air circulation for the burning, as vents or chimneys (assuming they connect the fire box with outer air in the top of the kiln), thus, achieving higher temperature and more oxidized firing. A technological question that should be considered is why the flues are divided into double tubes (Figure 6). This was possibly done in order to enable regulating the air flow in the kiln, reducing it if one of the tubes was blocked. This partial blocking could have been done for a specific firing session or for part of it. The use of flues in pottery kilns during the Bronze and Iron Ages in the Near East was reported on several occasions (Tell en-Naṣbeh, Badè 1928, 28, pl. XII; Rhodes 1968, 20; Swan 1984, 34–5; Wood 1990, 29, 31. For Late Bronze Age Syria, see Tell SabiAbyad, (Duistermaat 2008, 352, 490) and Alalakh, Phase 1b (Yener and BĭkeYazicioğlu, 2010, 17, Figure 2.12:2, Installation 2).

The area including the firing chamber, in between and under the arches, was probably at least 0.8 m deeper than the floor. The lower part of this area was relatively flat (Figures 7, 8), but it is possible that a more rounded bottom pit was used in the original kiln design. In the area of the pointed eastern side of the structure, the kiln wall is represented by upright standing bricks, while several horizontal lying bricks were piled up, blocking a narrow opening (about 0.5 m wide). This is interpreted as the stoking hole or pit of the kiln (Figure 7, the place from which the firing and fuelling was attended), probably blocked in the last phase of the kiln's usage.

According to the excavation in its various stages and according to other known kilns, a complete reconstruction of this relatively large and sophisticated updraft kiln may be suggested (Figure 8).

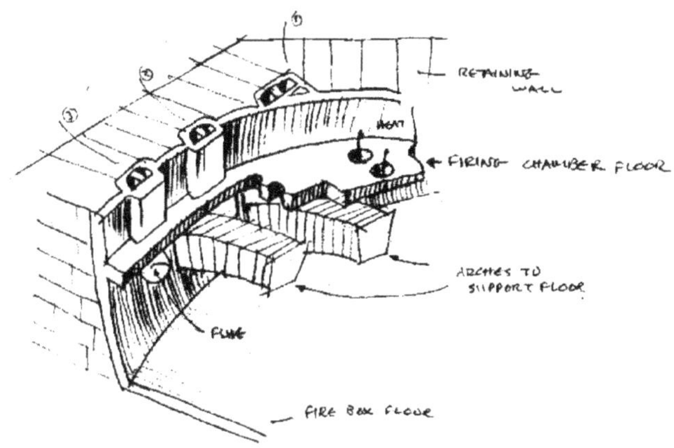

Figure 8. Reconstruction of the Tell Jemmeh kiln (Ben-Shlomo and Van Beek 2014, Figure 7.39).

The floor was supported by two brick arches, with the fire box located under the arches, totaling a depth of 1.3 m. Thus, this is clearly an updraft or 'vertical' kiln (e.g., Swan 1984, 29–34). The fire box floor is also flat with its entrance and stoking hole along the east side. This orientation was probably deliberate as it accords with the direction of the winds, running into the fire box, in the lower part of the kiln. The firing chamber above the floor is reconstructed to a height of 2 m (inner height 1.6 m); the brick roofing and outer walls of the chamber were supported by two additional brick arches. Note, that the height of the kiln is somewhat speculative, since the roof of the kiln was not preserved. The inner maximal width is about 1.9 m. The eight double-tube flues (six were found) run along the outer lining of the upper fire box and firing chamber, ventilating the top of the kiln. Altogether, the height of the kiln structure is reconstructed at about 3.3 m, about 2 of which were above ground. The method of loading the kiln is not completely clear; it might have been from above, opening the kiln's roof or alternatively, an opening may have existed along the lesser preserved northern side of the kiln. Interestingly, while slag was collected from all over the site (sometimes in large quantities), no substantial amounts of slag were found in the kiln or its vicinity, and no wasters were found either. This area was probably carefully cleaned at the time the kiln functioned.

The finds from inside the kiln and its surroundings include pottery as well as gold foil found in the inner fill of the kiln and a scarab (see Ben-Shlomo and Van Beek 2014, Figure 7.43), and some animal bones. Pottery from inside the kiln (Ben-Shlomo and Van Beek 2014, Figure 7.43) probably do not include wasters, and thus was possibly deposited when the kiln went out of use, or, come from an adjacent level, and was mixed with the debris of the kiln structure when it started to collapse. The fills to the east and just above the kiln were very rich in pottery, including Philistine Bichrome and other Iron I forms. Therefore, the date of the construction of the kiln at Tell Jemmeh may be towards the late 12th or early 11th centuries BCE.

The position of the kiln in relation to the rest of the site remains unclear, as the horizontal exposure of contemporary Iron I levels around it were very minimal. It is doubtful that this kiln was part of a large pottery workshop, due both to its location in the center of the site in Field I, and the lack of associated surface finds, such as remains of other kilns, large quantities of wasters, tournettes, piles of clay, potter's tools etc. This sparse evidence may indicate that this was an isolated kiln serving a separated neighbourhood or a specific function.

Other than the almost unique state of preservation of this kiln, this installation is also rather distinctive in the Levantine Bronze and Iron Age record in its construction: the support of the floor and roof by brick arches and especially the existence of divided flues; the size of this kiln is also comparatively quite large. Square installations from Phases 1a-1b at Alalakh (Late Bronze Age, Yener and BĭkeYazicioğlu 2010, 18–19,31–32), which are probably pottery kilns, also seem to have rounded flues in their external walls (Yener and BĭkeYazicioğlu 2010, Figures 2.11:1,2, 2.12:1–3, Installations 1–3). These flues are wider in size and are not divided into two sections as at Tell Jemmeh. Parallels for perforated kiln brick floors come from various periods (see e.g., Wood 1990, 27–29, Figure 6), as at SabiAbyad (LBII-Iron I, Duistermaat 2008, 368–369,489–493, Figures. B.1–B.5, B.21–B.27, Kilns Q, J, K) and Sarepta (LBII, Pritchard 1975, Figure 14). This was a common element in the architecture of ancient pottery kilns.

3.3. Ashdod

Tel Ashdod yielded several pottery kilns, and a potters' workshop (Ben-Shlomo 2006, 98–102), yet most of these dates to the late Iron Age (ca. 800–600 BCE), postdating the period of the decorated philistine pottery. Two Iron I kilns or workshops were reported from Area G at Ashdod but their identification as such is questionable. In Stratum XII, within a building or courtyard, a rectangular installation was reported as a kiln (Dothan and Porath 1993, 72, Pl. 22:1-2). The location of this installation within a structure, its shape and the absence of vitrification signs or wasters, seems to indicate the possibility this was a hearth or other type of installation.

Much clearer evidence of pottery production, dated to the late Iron Age, was discovered mainly in Areas D (Figure 9; Dothan 1971, 89–92, 178, Plans 8,10,12, Pl. XXXVI), M (Dothan and Porath 1982, 7–8, Pls. I:2, II:3, VIII:3) and K (Dothan and Ben-Shlomo 2005, Plan 2.14, Figures 2.68,2.69). In Area D, a more substantial group of kilns and a workshop was uncovered, while the finds from Areas M and K include more isolated kilns. Especially important to this study is the discovery of LPDW vessels inside kilns in Areas D and M.

The group of kilns located in the northern part of Area D can be understood as a pottery workshop or even a potter's quarter that was located on the southwestern edges of the city (Figure 9).

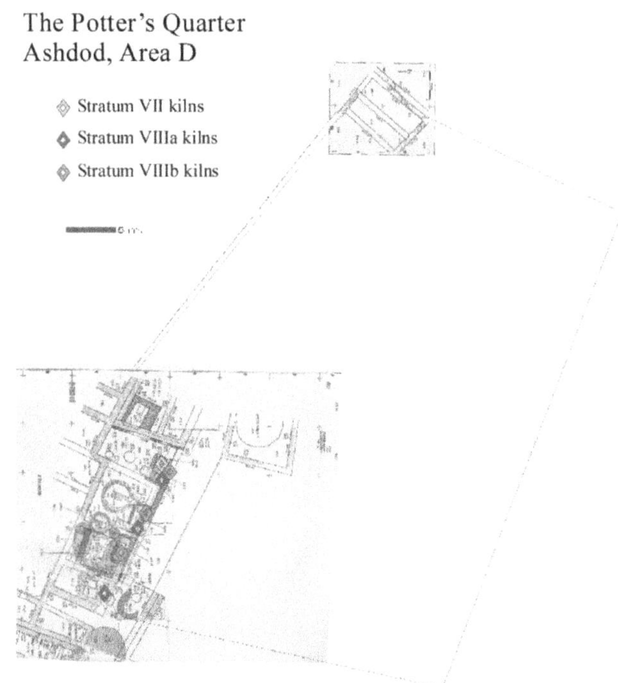

Figure 9. A reconstruction of the pottery workshop of Area D at Ashdod (after Dothan 1971).

Reconstruction of this quarter according to additional rooms with wasters and vitrified clay (Dothan 1971, Pl. XXXVI:2, Plan 10), reveal a very large complex with and area of about 1500 sq. m. (Figure 9; Wood 1990, Figure 15). To the north, portions of domestic structures uncovered may have been the living quarters of the potters (Dothan 1971, 92). Most of the features date to Stratum VIII, the 8th century BCE, with at least two phases of construction (Stratum VIIIa and VIIIb). The preservation of most kilns included an elongated—'bottle-shaped'—pit, which was the firing chamber: Altogether seven kilns were uncovered in Area D; they date to several phases and illustrate changes in orientation. The earlier three kilns dating to Stratum VIIIb were not well preserved and only the lower part of the pit of the firing chamber was recovered. The kilns were located in a series of at least four spaces built of brick walls and oriented north-south. Three kilns were built on top of each other (Dothan 1971, Pl. XXXVI:1), indicating three phases of the workshop. The three kilns dating to Stratum VIIIa were built into and under the eastern wall of the structure. One is an elongated pit adjoining to a rectangular brick structure around; a clay lining, several cm thick, surrounds the kiln. A rounded stoking pit lined with stones was located in the entrance, which was to the east. Inside, several complete holemouth jars were found, located in the rear part of the kiln. It seems that this load was left inside the kiln as the roof of the kiln may have collapsed upon it. The vaulted roof of the kiln was not preserved in most cases. Traces of the roof were preserved above Kiln 1088 (Dothan 1971, 92) and were made of mud and a brick arch.

At least some of the Ashdod kilns were probably single chambered as no signs of a vessel floor were found and the vessels were found together with wasters, vitrified clay and clay lumps, in the bottom of the pit. Thus, the pottery together with the fuel, were put into the pit and fired. From this aspect, the Ashdod kilns were less sophisticated than other contemporary kilns. Another option is that the vessel floor collapsed and was not preserved in all these cases, while Wood defines some of these as horizontal kilns (1990, 32). In addition to the accumulations of wasters in the kilns, ashes, vitrified clay, and crushed kurkar mixed with sherds, were found in this area (Dothan 1971, 90, Pl. XXXVII:2). The waste from the kilns was probably concentrated in pits, which were located at some distance. All of the ash pits excavated in Area D date to Stratum VII (but they could have been in use for a longer time). Perhaps, because the production in Stratum VIII was more extensive, most of the waste was removed to a more distant area beyond the city wall. In Stratum VII (the early 7th c. BCE) it seems that pottery production continued, but was on a smaller scale. Only one kiln dates to this stage; it faces the south and has a similar character as the earlier ones. As most of the potter's quarter at Area D was not excavated, only a few related objects, such as wheels, installations, tools, etc., were unearthed. However, several shallow clay basins (Dothan 1971, Figures 44:23, 51:9, 58:15-16) and burnishing tools are probably related to the pottery production. The production of pottery in the Iron Age IIA-B potter's quarter of Area D at Ashdod continued for about 150–200 years. The changes of orientation of the kilns from stage to stage may be result of constructional constraints relating to other structures (domestic?) that were built nearby. Later, during the Hellenistic period, this area was used again for pottery production with two rounded kilns (Dothan 1971, 115, Plan 13).

Additional evidence for pottery production during the late Iron Age at Ashdod come from Area M at Ashdod, near the fortifications in the southeastern part of the lower city. These remains include only three or four isolated kilns. The kilns seem to be similar to the bottle shaped kilns from Area D, in which vessels and fuel were probably located in the same chamber. These fragmentary kilns are possibly remnants of another potter's quarter that predates the monumental fortifications, as these were dug into virgin soil (Dothan and Porath 1982, 7–8). The building of the gate and the wall in Stratum Xa destroyed them almost completely. If we combine all the kiln fragments, an extensive area of 300–500 sq.m. may be reconstructed. Moreover, vitrified clay, ash layers and wasters were discovered here in large quantities and over large areas. The excavators also suggested that hamra soil was quarried here for bricks and pottery making (Dothan and Porath 1982, 8). Hence, this raw material could justify the relatively distant location of the workshop. Finds related to the workshop include clay basins (Dothan and Porath 1982, Figure 6:6, Pl. XI:6–12). In Area K, one kiln was found in Stratum VI, dating to the end of the 7th c. BCE (Dothan and Ben-Shlomo 2005, Plan 2.14). This was a rounded pit filled with vitrified clay and burnt material. The reconstructed outer diameter of the kiln is c. 2.10 m, the inner diameter 1.50 m and its opening was from the northwest. This kiln, a vertical updraft kiln, differs from the rectangular pit kilns of Area D in its small rounded size, which is more similar to later Persian or Hellenistic kilns at Ashdod (Dothan and Ben-Shlomo 2005, Plan 2.15, see more references therein).

3.4. Other sites

Other sites in Philistia yielded some remains of late Iron Age kilns. At Kfar Menachem, a site adjacent to Tell-Safi/Gath, a series of rectangular installations may be interpreted as pottery kilns (see, e.g., Ben-Shlomo 2006, 103–106). They date to the Iron Age IIB, but may have had other industrial use, not related to pottery production. Possible kilns were found in early Iron Age Beth Shemesh (see Ben-Shlomo 2006, 107), but these are not clearly identified as well. A late Iron Age pit-style pottery kiln was found at Yad Mordechai (Ben-Shlomo 2006, 113); it resembles some of the Ashdod Area D kilns.

4. Discussion

A survey of remains attesting to Philistine pottery production has shown that there is a possibility of evidence for the employment of new or foreign techniques or technologies by the new comers to the Levant. In particular, the well-preserved kiln from Tell Jemmeh and the square kiln from Ekron may testify for this. Nevertheless, while the structure of the Jemmeh kiln shows relatively high technological levels and sophistication, it does not differ in its general oval shape and size than other contemporary kilns (similar to Kiln 23 from Megiddo, Guy and Engberg 1938, Figure 89, although the Jemmeh kiln is somewhat larger). The square Iron I, Stratum VIIA kiln at Tel Miqne-Ekron, 4104 (see above, Killebrew 1989, Ills. 177–179) may also have flues in the corners. The Iron I kilns from Ekron (Ben-Shlomo 2006, 106–107, Figure 2.14), somewhat resembling Bronze Age kilns from the Aegean, such as at Gouves, Crete and Miletus (see, e.g., Shaw *et al.* 1997; Vallianou 1997; Niemeier 1998, 31–32; Ben-Shlomo 2006, 116–117), are also quite sophisticated, yet, are different in their shape and structure details. The most detailed reports come from Late Minoan (LMIA) Crete (Shaw *et al.* 2001; Vallianou 1997 and references therein). At LMII Gouves, two horseshoe shaped kilns were reported along with various installations (water tanks?) and several potter's wheels in situ were found throughout the workshop, which was located on the edge of the settlement (Vallianou 1997, 338–341, Figs. CXXIV–CXXIX). The kilns have internal walls in the firing chamber and a stoking hole. Similar kilns were found at Knossos, Phaistos and Kommos among other places in Crete (Vallianou 1997, 337).

On mainland Turkey, in Miletus a LHIIIA:1-2 pottery workshop including at least seven kilns was unearthed (Niemeier 1997; Niemeier 1998, 31–32, Figures 7,10, Photos 2–4). The kilns are either circular or rectangular. The rounded kilns are common in mainland Mycenaean potters workshops, e.g. in the large workshop at Berbati (Mastos) near Mycenae (see Niemeier 1997, Pl. CXLVI:b). The rectangular kilns (Niemeier 1997, Pls. CXLIV- CXLV; Niemeier 1998, Figure 10, and references therein) are larger, about 3 × 2 m and have 3–6 flues under the vessel floor created by interspaced channels (possibly similar to the example from Tell Jemmeh).

These western or foreign parallels may indicate that this kiln may indicate certain technological innovations brought by the Philistine during the early Iron Age. On the other hand, the very well preserved and possibly dated somewhat earlier (late 2st Millennium, Middle Assyrian) pottery kilns at Tell Sabi Abyad in Syria (Duistermaat 2008, 489–503, Figures B.3, B28–B.31) also have brick arches supporting the vessel floors and flues, showing similar sophistication to the Tell Jemmeh kiln of roughly the same date, and thus the structure of the Tell Jemmeh kiln may not be necessarily related to Aegean influences. During the late Iron Age (ca. 1000–600 BCE) pottery kilns and workshops found in Philistia (mostly at Ashdod) conform with technologies and forms of kilns from other part of the Levant during this period (see, Ben-Shlomo 2006, 116–7).

Petrographic and chemical analysis of the Philistine pottery itself has indicated that in most cases standard and traditional local methods were used to select the clay source, prepare the clay, form and decorate the vessels and fire them. Nevertheless, some of the vessels were made of a more calcareous, finer clay, and may have been fired as a different firing temperature or atmosphere. However, such measures do not necessitate an influence of a foreign technological tradition.

All in all, certain evidence regarding the pottery production in Iron Age Philistia still seems to justify further research and comparison between pottery production techniques in Philistia and in the Aegean region and Cyprus. These may aid to trace or better define further cultural-technological similarities between the regions during the end of the second millennium BCE.

Abbreviations

AJA= American Journal of Archaeology

BASOR= Bulletin of the American Schools for Oriental Research

IAA= Israel Antiquities Authority

IES= Israel Exploration Society

References

Badè, Wiliam F, *Excavations at Tell en-Našbeh, 1926 and 1927, a Preliminary Report,* Berkeley: Palestine Institute, 1928.

Ben-Shlomo, David, *Decorated Philistine Pottery: An Archaeological and Archaeometric Study*, Oxford: B.A.R. International Series No. 1541, 2006.

Ben-Shlomo, David, *Philistine Iconography: A Wealth of Style and Symbolism*, OrbisBiblicus et Orientalis 241. Göttingen: Vandenhoeck & Ruprecht, 2010.

Ben-Shlomo, David and Van Beek, Gus W, *Excavation at Tell Jemmeh, Israel 1970–1990*. Smithsonian Contributions to Anthropology, No. 50. Washington DC: Smithsonian Institution, 2014.

Ben-Shlomo, David, Shai, Izhak and Maeir, Aren M, "Late Philistine Decorated Ware ("Ashdod Ware"): Typology, Chronology, and Production Centers", *BASOR*, 335 (2004): 1–35.

Ben-Shlomo, David, Shai, Izhak, Zukerman, Alexander and Maeir, Aren M, "Cooking Identities: Aegean-Style Cooking Jugs and Cultural Interaction in Iron Age Philistia and Neighboring Regions", *AJA*, 112.2 (2008): 225–246.

Dothan, Moshe, *Ashdod II-III*. 'Atiqot 10–11. Jerusalem: Department of Antiquities, 1971.

Dothan, Moshe, and Ben-Shlomo, David, *Ashdod VI. Excavations of Areas H and K (1968-1969)*, IAA Reports No. 24. Jerusalem: IAA, 2005.

Dothan, Moshe, and Porath, Yosef, *Ashdod IV: Excavation of Area M*. 'Atiqot 15. Jerusalem: Department of Antiquities, 1982.

Dothan, Moshe, and Porath, Yosef, *Ashdod V*, 'Atiqot 23. Jerusalem: IAA, 1993.

Dothan, Trude, *The Philistines and Their Material Culture*, Jerusalem: IES, 1982.

Dothan, Trude, and Zukerman, Alexander, A Preliminary Study of the Mycenaean IIIC:1 Pottery Assemblage from Tel Miqne-Ekron and Ashdod. BASOR, 333 (2004): 1–54.

Duistermaat, Kim, *The Pots and Potters of Assyria. Technology and Organization of Production, Ceramic Sequence and Vessel Function at Late Bronze Age Tell SabiAbyad, Syria*. Papers on Archaeology from the Leiden Museum of Antiquities (PALMA 4), Turhout: Brepols, 2008.

Gunneweg, Jan, Perlman, Isodore, Dothan, Trude, and Gitin, Seymour, "On the Origin of Pottery from Tel Miqne-Ekron", *BASOR*, 264 (1986): 3–16.

Guy, Philip L.O. and Engberg, Romert M, *Megiddo Tombs*. Chicago: Oriental Institute, 1938.

Killebrew, Ann E, "Aegean-Style Early Philistine Pottery in Canaan During the Iron I Age: A Stylistic Analysis of Mycenaean IIIC:1b Pottery and Its Associated Wares. In *The Sea Peoples and their World: A Reassessment*, edited by Eliezer D Oren, 233–253, Philadelphia: University Museum, 2000.

Killebrew, Ann E. "Ceramic Typology and Technology of Late Bronze II and Iron I Assemblages from Tel Miqne-Ekron: The Transition from Canaanite to Philistine Culture" *In Mediterranean Peoples in Transition. Thirteenth to Early Tenth Centuries BCE*, edited by Symour Gitin, Amihai Mazar and Ephraim Stern, 379–405, Jerusalem: IES, 1998.

Killebrew, Ann E, "Late Bronze and Iron I Cooking Pots in Canaan: A Typological, Technological and Functional Study", In *Archaeology, History and Culture in Palestine and the Near East. Essays in Memory of Albert E. Glock* (ASOR Books Volume 3), edited by Tomis Kapitan, 83–126, Atlanta: Scholars Press, 1999.

Killebrew, Ann E, "Pottery Kilns from Deir el-Balah and Tel Miqne-Ekron" In *Retrieving the Past. Essays on Archaeological Research and Methodology in Honor of Gus W. Van Beek*, edited by Joe D. Seger, 135–162, Winona Lake In: Eisenbrauns, 1996.

Killebrew, Ann E, *The Potters' Craft During the Late Bronze and Iron Ages in Eretz Israel. A Description of the Ancient Pottery Manufacturing Process and its Implications for Archaeological Research in Israel.* Unpublished M.A. Thesis, The Hebrew University, Jerusalem, 1989.

Niemeier, Wolfgang, D, "The Mycenaean Potters' Quarter at Miletus", In *TEXNH: Craftsmen, Craftswomen and Craftsmenship in the Aegean Bronze Age*, Aegeum 16, edited by Robert Laffiineur and Philip P Betancourt, 347–352, Liège: Université de Liège, 1997.

Niemeier, Wofgang D, "The Mycenaean in Western Anatolia and the Problem of the Origins of the Sea Peoples", *In Mediterranean Peoples in Transition. Thirteenth to Early Tenth Centuries BCE*, edited by Symour Gitin, Amihai Mazar and Ephraim Stern, 1-765, Jerusalem: IES, 1998.

Perlman, Isodore, Asaro, Frank, and Friedman, David, "Provenience Studies of Tel Ashdod Pottery Employing Neutron Activation Analysis", In *Ashdod II-II*, 'Atiqot 10–11, edited by Moshe Dothan, 215–219. Jerusalem: Department of Antiquities, 1971.

Pritchard, James B, *Sarepta Preliminary Report, the Iron Age*, Philadelphia: University Museum, 1975.

Rhodes, Daniel, *Kilns: Design, Construction and Operation.* Philadelphia: Chilton, 1968.

Sherratt, Sussan, E, "Sea Peoples" and the Economic Structure of the Late Second Millennium in the Eastern Mediterranean", *In Mediterranean Peoples in Transition: Thirteenth to Early Tenth Centuries BCE*, edited by Seymour Gitin, AmihaiMazar and Ephraim Stern, 292–313, Jerusalem: IES, 1998.

Shaw, Joseph, van de Moortel, Aleydis, Day, Peter M, and Kilikoglou, Vassili, "A LM IA Ceramic Kiln in *South-Central Crete: Function and Pottery Production*, Hesperia Supplement 30, Princeton: American Institute of Archaeology, 2001.

Swan, Vivien G, *The Pottery Kilns of Roman Britain.* London: Royal Commission on Historical Monuments, 1984.
Vallianou, Despoina, "The Potters' Quarter in LM III Gouves", In *TEXNH: Craftsmen, Craftswomen and Craftsmenship in the Aegean Bronze Age*, Aegeum 16, edited by Robert Laffiineur and Philip P Betancourt, 333–343, Liège: Université de Liège, 1997.

Wood, Bryant G, *The Sociology of Pottery in Ancient Palestine. The Ceramic Industry and the Diffusion of Ceramic Style in the Bronze and Iron Ages.* JSOT/ASOR Monographs 4. Worcester:Sheffield Academic Press, 1990.

Yener, KutluAslihan, and BīkeYazicioğlu, Gökçe "Excavation Results" In *Tell Atchana, Ancient Alalackh. Volume 1. The 2003-2004 Excavation Seasons*, edited by Kutlu Aslihan Yener, 11–50, Istanbul: Koç University Press, 2010.

Also of interest

Análisis Funcional
Su aplicación al estudio de sociedades prehistóricas
Edited by Ignacio Clemente, Roberto Risch and Juan F. Gibaja

Oxford, BAR Publishing, 2002 BAR International Series **S1073**

Comunidades Neolíticas del Noreste de la Península Ibérica
Una aproximación socio-económica a partir del estudio de la función de los útiles líticos
By Juan Francisco Gibaja Bao

Oxford, BAR Publishing, 2003 BAR International Series **S1140**

Funerary Practices in the Iberian Peninsula from the Mesolithic to the Chalcolithic
Edited by Juan F. Gibaja, António F. Carvalho and Philippe Chambon

Oxford, BAR Publishing, 2012 BAR International Series **S2417**

www.ingramcontent.com/pod-product-compliance
Ingram Content Group UK Ltd.
Pitfield, Milton Keynes, MK11 3LW, UK
UKHW061848041026
15591UKWH00015B/967

9 781407 316369